LEARNING
TO TEACH

LEARNING TO TEACH

Third Edition

RICHARD I. ARENDS
Dean, College of Education
Central Connecticut State University

McGraw-Hill, Inc.
New York   St. Louis   San Francisco   Auckland   Bogotá   Caracas
Lisbon   London   Madrid   Mexico City   Milan   Montreal   New Delhi
San Juan   Singapore   Sydney   Tokyo   Toronto

This book was developed by Lane Akers, Inc.

Acknowledgments appear on page 535 and on this page by reference.

This book is printed on acid-free paper.

3 4 5 6 7 8 9 0 VNH VNH 9 0 9 8 7 6 5

ISBN 0-07-002599-1

This book was set in Palatino by Progressive Typographers, Inc.
The editors were Lane Akers and Sheila H. Gillams;
the production supervisor was Paula Keller.
The cover was designed by Joseph A. Piliero.
The photo researcher was Debra P. Herschkowitz.
Von Hoffmann Press, Inc., was printer and binder.

Cover credit: Abstract # 10 by Diana Ong. Private Collection/Superstock, Inc.

Chapter-Opening Photo Credits

Chapters 1, 4, 5, 12, and 15: Elizabeth Crews; Chapter 2: Russ Kinne/Comstock; Chapter 3: Robert Houser/Comstock; Chapter 6: Spencer Grant/Picture Cube; Chapter 7: Michael Kagan/Monkmeyer; Chapter 8: Joel Gordon; Chapter 9: David Strickler/Picture Cube; Chapter 10: Barrera/TexaStock; Chapter 11: Paul Conklin/Monkmeyer; Chapter 13: Spencer Grant/Stock, Boston; and Chapter 14: Mimi Forsyth/Monkmeyer.

Library of Congress Cataloging-in-Publication Data

Arends, Richard.
    Learning to teach/Richard I. Arends.—3rd ed.
       p.   cm.
    Includes index.
    ISBN 0-07-002599-1
    1. Teaching.   I. Title.
LB1025.3.A74   1994
371.1′02—dc20   93-11851

About the Author

Richard I. Arends is currently Professor of Education and Dean of the School of Education and Professional Studies at Central Connecticut State University. Prior to his coming to Connecticut, Professor Arends was on the faculty and chair of the department of Curriculum and Instruction at the University of Maryland, College Park. He received his Ph.D. in education from the University of Oregon where he was on the faculty from 1975 to 1984. A former elementary, junior high, and high school teacher, his special interests are the social psychology of education, teacher education, and organizational development and school improvement.

Professor Arends has authored or contributed to over a dozen books on education and has worked widely with schools and universities throughout North America and the Pacific Rim, including Australia, Samoa, Palau, and Saipan.

The recipient of numerous awards, he was selected in 1989 as the outstanding teacher educator in the state of Maryland and in 1990 received the Judith Ruskin award for outstanding research in education given by the Association for Supervision and Curriculum Development (ASCD).

In Memory of Mary Crum Arends

Contents in Brief

Contents

Preface

Learning to be a teacher is a long and complex journey full of excitement and challenge. It begins with the many experiences we have with our parents and siblings; it continues as we observe teacher after teacher through sixteen to twenty years of schooling. It culminates, formally, with professional training but continues through a lifetime of teaching experiences.

Learning to Teach is intended for students taking courses in teacher education, commonly labeled General Methods of Teaching. A variety of other course titles, Analysis of Teaching, The Study of Teaching, Principles and Practices of Teaching, or Strategies of Teaching, are sometimes used. Whatever its title, the course's content normally focuses on general models, strategies, and skills that apply to teaching in all subject areas and at all grade levels. Such courses are routinely offered in secondary education programs and are increasingly offered in elementary programs.

Although these courses vary somewhat among institutions, most of them seem to share the following general goals. Most instructors want their students to

1. Begin developing a repertoire of basic teaching models, strategies, and skills.
2. Understand the dynamics of teaching, both inside and outside the classroom.
3. Begin developing an awareness and appreciation of the research base that supports current practices in teaching.
4. Begin developing skills with which to observe, record, and analyse teaching roles and behavior.

In order to help achieve these general course goals, I have tried to produce a text with the following characteristics.

CONTENT COVERAGE

First of all, I have tried to provide a comprehensive and balanced view of teaching. To accomplish this I have organized the book into an initial chapter and three parts. The first chapter, ''The Scientific Basis for the Art of Teaching,'' introduces the book, explores the meaning of effective teaching, and considers the processes and stages beginning teachers go through on the way to becoming expert teachers. This initial chapter also lays out the major themes of the book.

Parts One, Two, and Three, which constitute the heart of the book, are organized around concepts of what teachers do. These sections assume that all teachers are asked to perform three important functions. They are asked to lead a group of students, the *executive or leadership functions of teaching;* they are asked to provide direct, face-to-face instruction to students, the *interactive functions of teaching;* and they are expected to work with colleagues and others to perform the *organizational functions of teaching.* Readers will soon find that these functions are not always discrete; the teacher does not always perform one independently of the others. These functions, however, are convenient organizers for helping teacher candidates make sense out of the bewildering array of events associated with teaching in a complex society.

THEORY-PRACTICE CONNECTIONS

Learning to Teach tries to provide readers with the theory and rationale that underlie and support the specific principles and practices being discussed. Readers are also shown why a recommended principle or procedure works the way it does, not just how to execute it effectively. Because models, principles, and procedures of teaching were not invented yesterday, sometimes a short history lesson is provided. A good example of this can be found in the discussion of cooperative learning. Even though significant developments have helped refine cooperative learning during the past decade, readers will find that the basic model, including its theory and rationale, is lodged firmly in the mainstream of democratic thought and reaches back to Thomas Jefferson and John Dewey.

RESEARCH FOCUS

Because *Learning to Teach* strives to develop the point of view that there is a scientific knowledge base that can and should guide teaching practice, I have included a section entitled "Sampling the Knowledge Base" in each chapter. This section provides a broad sampling of the research base that underlies and supports the recommended teaching practices found in the latter part of each chapter. In addition, each chapter contains a boxed summary of a classic research study pertaining to the chapter topic. Although highly compressed, these summaries are truthful to the investigators' methods and conclusions and, collectively, they reflect the variety and richness of methods used by educational researchers over time and around the world.

Finally, the Resource Handbook found at the end of the text contains two research-oriented units. The first of these offers a succinct guide to reading and understanding the research literature that is available through professional journals. Anyone planning to be a serious student of teaching must learn to consume this literature, and this handbook unit provides a good beginning. The second unit of the handbook provides a succinct guide to action research, a practice that will become increasingly common as the professionalization of teaching continues its long evolution.

BUILT-IN ACTIVITY MANUAL

Some aspects of teaching cannot be learned by merely studying theory-based or research-based knowledge. To truly understand what effective teaching is all about, students must actively observe

others teach, must engage in dialogues about teaching, and must reflect on both their own teaching experiences and those of others. To help promote such active learning experiences, I have included over 100 pages of structured observation, interview, and reflection guides at the end of chapters. Together with the general observation guidelines found in Unit 3 of the Resource Handbook, they constitute a helpful field guide that assists teacher candidates in gathering and interpreting data and in examining their own related experiences.

RESOURCE HANDBOOK

An easily referenced handbook at the end of the book brings together previously scattered reference material dealing with (1) reading and understanding research, (2) conducting action research, (3) guidelines for observing, reflecting, and microteaching. While not central to most courses of this type, the inclusion of such information makes the book more responsive to the needs of more advanced courses and students.

CHAPTER PEDAGOGY

To increase learning efficiency, chapter outlines appear at the beginning of each chapter and lengthy point-by-point summaries conclude each chapter. In addition, lists of key terms appear at the end of chapters and a glossary is at the end of the book.

TEACHING AND LEARNING RESOURCES

This edition of *Learning to Teach* is accompanied by an extensive package of teaching and learning aids that includes an instructor's manual/test bank, a student study guide, a casebook, and access to an award winning video series entitled *The Effective Teacher*.

NEW FEATURES OF THIS EDITION

As with previous editions, revisions were based on my own experience in teaching the text as well as systematically gathered feedback from users across the country. Although the general goals, themes, and features of the previous editions have remained constant, the following changes have been made in the third edition.

- New chapter on inquiry teaching. Feedback from users indicated that the text needed a thorough explication of inquiry teaching and discovery learning. Consequently, I have gathered materials previously tucked under other topics and expanded them into a separate chapter entitled *Inquiry Teaching*.
- Expanded and updated coverage. In addition to a general updating throughout the text, the following changes are worth noting. Much new material has been added to the chapter on teaching in multicultural and mainstreamed classrooms and to the assessment chapter, which includes new discussions of alternative assessment, authentic assessment, and portfolio development. Also, new material on cognitive/constructivist views of teaching and learning have been integrated throughout the text.
- New student study aids. Two new supplements, a student study guide and a casebook, have been added to this edition. The study guide provides students with a variety of study aids such as chapter highlights, practice test items, and independent learning activities. The casebook provides fifteen cases chosen from McGraw-Hill's database of cases in teacher education entitled Primis. Chosen for their relevance to the general methods course, each case documents a particular event or series of related events, and most end with a dilemma that the teacher must resolve.

ACKNOWLEDGMENTS

Because the field of teaching and learning is becoming so comprehensive and so complex, I have relied on colleagues to assist in writing about topics outside my own area of expertise. Outstanding contri-

butions were made by chapter authors Dr. Richard Jantz, University of Maryland, Dr. Virginia Richardson, University of Arizona, and Dr. Nancy Winitzky, University of Utah.

I also want to acknowledge and extend my thanks to the many students in my principles of teaching classes at the University of Maryland, and particularly those in the Master's Certification Program, for their willingness to ask questions and provide reactions to every aspect of the book. Similarly my co-teachers and colleagues over the years, Drs. Hilda Borko, Shelley Clemson, Lenore Cohen, Pat Christensen, Neil Davidson, Margaret Ferrara, Jim Henkelman, Frank Lyman, Joe McCaleb, and Linda Mauro, have not only been a source of support, but each has provided important input on early versions of the manuscript as well as the revision. My graduate assistant, Arlene Burek, and my administrative assistant, Lisa Ingriselli, have provided helpful assistance throughout the revision process and they too have been a constant source of support.

Many reviewers and users have also contributed very useful reactions and critiques that have resulted in a much improved text. They include: Mary Crisp, Western Kentucky University; Carmen Dumas, Nova University; Susan Geis and Jean Shaw, University of Mississippi; John Hoffman, Northeast Missouri State University; Harriet Johnson, Augsburg College; Larry Kortering, University of Delaware; W. C. Martin, University of West Florida; Rita Moretti, Niagara University; Karna Nelson and Sam Perez, Western Washington University; Steve Penn, Vincennes University; George Rawlins, Austin Peay State University; and Kinnard White, University of North Carolina. I also thank Dr. Joyce Murphy who was so helpful in supplying information about the research laboratories and centers found in the Resource Handbook. Finally, a very special thanks to my editor, Lane Akers, who had faith in the book from the beginning and who has provided so much valuable assistance, advice, and support over the years of our relationship.

Richard I. Arends

Skill Locator Guide

CHAPTER 1

The Scientific Basis for the Art of Teaching

Teaching offers a bright and rewarding career for those who can meet the intellectual and social challenges of the job. Despite the recent spate of reports critical of schools and teachers, most citizens continue to support our schools and express their faith in education. The task of teaching the young is simply too important and complex to be handled entirely by parents or through the informal structures of earlier eras. Modern society needs schools staffed with expert teachers to provide instruction and to care for children while adults work.

In our society teachers are given professional status. As experts and professionals, they are expected to use **best practice** to help students learn essential skills and attitudes. It is no longer sufficient for teachers to be warm and loving toward children, nor is it sufficient for them to employ teaching practices based solely on intuition, personal preference, or conventional wisdom. Contemporary teachers are held accountable for using teaching practices that have been shown to be effective, just as members of other professions, such as medicine, law, and architecture, are held to acceptable standards of practice. This book is about how to learn and to use best practice—practice that has a **scientific basis.** It is aimed at helping beginning teachers master the knowledge base and the skills required of a professional.

This book also explores another side of teaching: the **art of teaching.** Like most human endeavors, teaching has aspects that cannot be codified or guided by scientific knowledge alone but instead depend on a complex set of individual judgments based on personal experiences. Nathaniel Gage (1984) of Stanford University, one of the United States' foremost educational researchers, describes the art of teaching as:

> an instrumental or practical art, not a fine art aimed at creating beauty for its own sake. As an instrumental art, teaching is something that departs from recipes, formulas, or algorithms. It requires improvisation, spontaneity, the handling of hosts of considerations of form, style, pace, rhythm, and appropriateness in ways so complex that even computers must, in principle, fall behind, just as they cannot achieve what a mother does with her five-year-old or what a lover says at any given moment to his or her beloved. (p. 6)

Notice some of the words chosen by Gage to describe the art of teaching—*spontaneity, pace, rhythm.* These words describe aspects of teaching that research cannot measure very well but that are nonetheless important characteristics of best practice and are contained in the wisdom of experienced and expert teachers. This book strives to show the complexity of teaching—the dilemmas faced by teachers and the artistic choices that effective teachers make as they perform their daily work. It also presents an integrated view of teaching as a science and as an art.

This chapter begins with a brief historical sketch of teaching, because the basic patterns of teaching today are intertwined in the web of history and culture, which impact the processes of learning to teach. This introduction is followed by the perspective about effective teaching which has guided the design and writing of this book. The final section of the chapter describes a portion of what is known about the processes of learning to teach. It tells how beginners can start the process of becoming effective teachers by learning to access the knowledge base on teaching and reflecting on their experiences. At the end of the chapter several learning aids are provided to assist you with your planning, observation, and reflection.

HISTORICAL PERSPECTIVE ON TEACHING

Teaching has always been a complex role, and it has become more so as schools have taken on increased social responsibility. To understand the role of the teacher as it exists today requires a brief historical review of some of the more important changes that have taken place in teaching and schooling over the past two centuries.

Nineteenth-Century Role Expectations

During most of the nineteenth century the purposes of schooling were rather straightforward, and a teacher's role rather simple compared to later eras. Basic literacy and number skills were the primary goals of nineteenth-century education, with the curriculum dominated by what later came to be called the three Rs: reading, writing, and arithmetic. Most young people were not required (or expected) to attend school, and those who did so remained for relatively brief periods of time. Other institutions in society—family, church, and work organizations—held the major responsibility for child rearing and helping youth make the transition from family to work.

Teachers were recruited mostly from their local communities. Professional training of teachers was not deemed important, nor was teaching necessarily considered a career. Teachers during this era were likely to be young men or women who had obtained a measure of literacy themselves and were willing to "keep" school until something else came along. Standards governing teaching practice were nonexistent, although rules and regulations governing teachers' personal lives and moral conduct could, in some communities, be quite strict. Take, for example, this set of promises women teachers were required to sign in one community in North Carolina even as late as the 1920s:

> I promise to take a vital interest in all phases of Sunday-school work, donating of my time, service and money without stint for the benefit and uplift of the community.
>
> I promise to abstain from dancing, immodest dressing, and any other conduct unbecoming a teacher and a lady.
>
> I promise not to go out with any young man except as it may be necessary to stimulate Sunday-school work.
>
> I promise not to fall in love, to become engaged or secretly married.
>
> I promise to remain in the dormitory or on the school grounds when not actively engaged in school or church work elsewhere.
>
> I promise not to encourage or tolerate the least familiarity on the part of any of my boy pupils.
>
> I promise to sleep eight hours a night, eat carefully. . . . (Brenton, 1970, p. 74)

This list of promises may be more stringent than many others in use at the time, but it gives a clear indication of nineteenth-century concern for teachers' moral character and conduct and apparent lack of concern for teachers' pedagogical abilities.

Twentieth-Century Role Expectations

By the late nineteenth and early twentieth centuries the purposes of education were expanding rapidly, and teachers' roles took on added dimensions. Comprehensive high schools were created, most states passed compulsory attendance laws that required all students to be in school until age 16, and the goals of education moved beyond the narrow purposes of basic literacy. Vast economic changes during these years outmoded the apprentice system that had formerly existed in the workplace, and much of the responsibility for helping youth to make the transition from family to work fell to the schools. Also, the arrival of immigrants from other countries, plus new migration patterns from rural areas into the cities, created large, diverse student populations with more extensive needs than simple literacy instruction. Look, for example, at the seven goals* for high school education issued by the National Education Association in 1918, and notice how much these goals exceed the focus on the three Rs of earlier eras:

1. Health
2. Command of fundamental processes
3. Worthy home membership
4. Vocational preparation
5. Citizenship
6. Worthy use of leisure time
7. Ethical character

Such broad and diverse goals made twentieth-century schools much more comprehensive institutions and also places for addressing some of the societal reforms that have characterized this century. Schools increasingly became instruments of opportunity, first for immigrants and later for African Americans, Hispanics, and other minority groups who had been denied equal access to education. Expanding their functions beyond academic learning, schools provided such services as health care, transportation, extended day care, and breakfasts and lunches. Schools also took on various counseling and mental health functions—duties that in earlier eras belonged to the family or the church—to help ensure the psychological and emotional well-being of youth.

Obviously, expanded purposes for schooling had an impact on the role expectations for teachers. Most states and localities began setting standards for teachers that later became requirements for certification. Special schools were created to train teachers in the subject matters they were expected

to teach and to ensure that they knew something about **pedagogy.** By the early twentieth century teachers were expected to have 2 years of college preparation; by the middle of the century most would hold bachelor's degrees. Teaching gradually came to be viewed as a career, and professional organizations for teachers, such as the National Educational Association and the American Federation of Teachers, took on growing importance both for defining the profession and for influencing educational policy. Teaching practices during this era, however, were rarely supported by research, and teachers, although expected to teach well, were judged by such global criteria as "knows subject matter," "acts in a professional manner," "has good rapport," "dresses appropriately." However, progress was made during this era, particularly in curriculum development for all the major subject areas, such as reading, mathematics, social studies, and science; also, major work was accomplished in helping to understand human intelligence and potential.

Twenty-First-Century Role Expectations

No crystal ball can let us look into the next century, only a few years away. Certain trends, however, are likely to continue, and some aspects of education and teaching will remain the same, while others may change rather dramatically. On the one hand, society will continue to require young people to go to school. Education will remain committed to a variety of goals and some new ones may be added, but **academic learning** will remain the most important. It is not likely that the physical space called school will change drastically, and perhaps the ways of organizing and accounting for instruction will also remain the same, at least in the immediate future. Schools will likely remain based in communities, and teachers will continue to provide instruction to groups of children in rectangular rooms.

On the other hand, contemporary reform efforts show the potential of bringing new and radical perspectives about what academic learning means and how it can best be achieved. New perspectives also are emerging as to what constitutes community and its relationship to the common school. The nature of the student population and the expectations for

---

* These goals were named the Seven Cardinal Principles. Some historians believe that they were symbolic statements of hope that reveal what schools in the new industrial society aspired to do rather than descriptions of reality.

teachers will also be elements that likely will change drastically in the decades ahead.

CONSTRUCTIVIST PERSPECTIVE OF KNOWLEDGE

The schools you attended were, for the most part, very similar to the schools attended by your parents and perhaps even your grandparents because the schools which evolved in the late nineteenth century were built around a set of assumptions about the nature of knowledge and how knowledge is acquired. Also, they were built around a corresponding set of beliefs about how best to ensure that all young citizens acquire this knowledge and in turn become productive adult citizens and workers.

The traditional western view about the nature of knowledge, on which contemporary educational systems have been built, is **objectivist,** a view which regards "knowledge as truths to which humans have access" (Tobin, 1992, p. 2). The objectivist assumption is that the "categories of the mind fit the categories of the world [and that] there is only one correct way to describe experience" (p. 2) and to know. Science and many aspects of inquiry are viewed by objectivists as means to discover this objective reality. Teachers, from the objectivist perspective, are individuals who have acquired a sufficient "chuck" of important knowledge in particular disciplines. Their role is to transmit their knowledge (facts, concepts, principles) to students. Since knowledge is known and fixed (relatively speaking), formal schooling governed by this perspective aims at organizing what is known into formal and standard curricula for all students to learn; in turn, they can demonstrate mastery through performance on standardized tests.

An alternative to the objectivist perspective and one that has gained respectability in some educational circles over the past two decades is known as **constructivism.** Rather than viewing knowledge as fully known, fixed, and transmittable, the constructivist perspective holds that knowledge is somewhat personal and meaning is constructed by the learner through experience. Learning is a social process in which learners construct meaning, which is influenced by the interaction of prior knowledge and new learning events. Tobin (1992) emphasizes that "learning should focus . . . not only on the manner in which an individual attempts to make sense of phenomena, but also on the role of the social in the mediation of learning" (p. 3).

Teaching, from a constructivist perspective, is not viewed as telling or transmitting fixed truths to students but rather as providing students with relevant experiences and subsequent opportunities for dialogue so meaning can evolve and be constructed. The school's curriculum, from this perspective, is no longer viewed as a document of important information, but instead as a set of learning events and activities through which students and teachers, in Doyle's (1990) words, "jointly negotiate content and meaning." We will come back to this idea repeatedly in *Learning to Teach* and you will come to see that a constructivist perspective will require drastic changes in teacher behavior.

PRIVATIZATION OF EDUCATION

Once we move away from notions of fixed curriculum and fixed ways of knowing, we can also start questioning the efficacy of the standardized school. For example, do all students need to be exposed to the same ideas in particular subjects, at the same time and in the same manner? Should all students be required to go to the same type of schools with the same curriculum and for the same lengths of time? An increasing number of policy makers and educators are saying no to these types of questions, and alternatives are being sought to the standard public school.

Alternatives to the standard school are found in many suburban areas of the country today. Normally these alternatives consist of magnet or special-focus schools, where curriculum is designed around the performing arts or science and technology. This type of alternative is financed by public funds, but students and their parents can choose the alternative over other more traditional schools in the community.

A trend more pronounced in schools situated in the larger cities in the United States, where student populations are most diverse and where resources to support public education are most scarce, is privatization. For instance, several large city school systems such as Dade County, Florida, and Baltimore, Maryland, have contracted with a Minnesota-based firm to run some of their schools on a contractual basis and with the intent of making a profit. In the spring of 1992, the president of Yale University resigned to head up Whittle Industries' Edison Project, an effort aimed at creating over 1,000 private, for-profit schools by 1996.

The last decade of the twentieth century has also witnessed attempts to make private use of communication and computer technologies to enhance the education of students. The Tennessee-based Whittle Industries has created and introduced Channel One, a television channel that broadcasts current events programs for high school students. Whittle provides participating schools with free television sets and free access to cable channel broadcasts under an agreement that students will be required to watch the programs and the advertisements that accompany them for 10 minutes a day.

The privatization of schooling and the use of private technology has its critics as well as its advocates. Advocates maintain that private, profit-driven schools will introduce an element of competition into the educational system and that schools, once freed from the bureaucratic structures and political processes that have come to characterize many large city schools, can provide superior education for students for the same or lower cost through innovative programming and more effective use of human resources. Many people are willing to allow these experiments to proceed because of beliefs that the public schools simply are not functioning as they should.

On the other hand, many educators and concerned citizens worry that private schools will not accept the more difficult-to-teach students, thus making the public schools more and more the home for the most helpless and hopeless young people in our society. Others are concerned about the values and moral system reflected, either formally or informally, in for-profit schools. Still others are afraid that the best teachers in the country will be drawn to for-profit schools, leaving the less capable to teach those students who need good teachers the most.

Regardless of the current aspirations or criticisms, it seems that alternatives to public schooling will expand rather than recede as we move into the twenty-first century. These trends seem to be supported by strong political currents as well as shifting perspectives about the nature of knowledge, learning, and the role for teaching and schooling in

our society. It is too early to know exactly what this may mean for teaching, but it is likely that for-profit schools will hold teachers more accountable than do public schools at the present time. It is also likely that more differentiation of roles will be observed as alternatives are developed and new technologies are used. However, several questions have been posed for which predictions at the present time cannot be made. For instance, will for-profit schools hire only teachers who have been duly licensed by the state where the school exists? Will for-profit schools enter into collective bargaining agreements with teachers as most public schools currently do? If they don't, what impact will this have on teacher's organizations such as the National Educational Association and the American Federation of Teachers? Will for-profit schools honor traditions of academic freedom for teachers? These are questions you will probably be confronted with as you launch your teaching career over the next decade.

THE DEMOGRAPHY OF SCHOOLING

Harold Hodgkinson (1983) has written that "every society is constructed on a foundation of **demographic assumptions.** When these assumptions shift, as they do from time to time, the result is a major shock throughout the society" (p. 281).

Schools are experiencing such a demographic shock at the present time; this shock will continue, and it will cause a significant impact on teaching. The most important demographic shift involves the increasing number of students who have ethnic or racial heritages that are non-European or for whom English is a second language. Nationwide the percentage of these young people in schools has increased from a little over 20 percent in 1970 to over 30 percent in 1990. In some states, such as California, over 50 percent of the students in public schools come from backgrounds traditionally defined as minority. Although this demographic shift is most pronounced in the large urban areas, it is not confined to the inner cities alone. Look, for instance, at the enrollment data for Prince George's Public Schools, a large surburban area adjacent to Washington, D.C. (see Figure 1-1). The enrollment patterns changed significantly over the last two decades. In 1972, slightly less than 25 percent of the students were African American. By 1990, this fig-

Figure 1-1 Percent of African-American student enrollment: Prince George's County Public Schools, 1972 to 1990

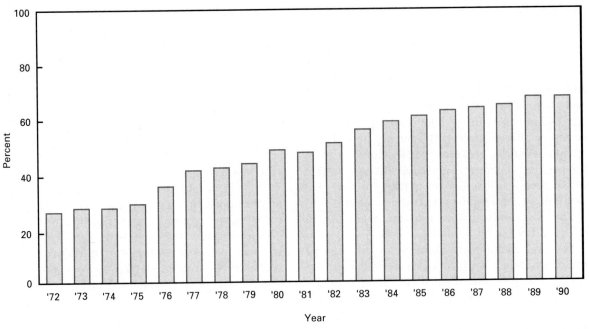

SOURCE: Prince George's County Public Schools.

ure had changed to over 60 percent African American. Indeed, in this school system, and elsewhere, students from non-European heritages and non-English-speaking homes are now a majority.

A trend throughout the history of schools has been to extend educational opportunities to more and more students. Compulsory attendance laws early in the century opened up the doors to poor white children; the now-famous Supreme Court decision, *Brown v. Board of Education of Topeka* (1954), extended educational opportunities to African-American children. The Education for All Handicapped Children Act of 1975 brought an end to policies which prevented handicapped children from getting an education and also changed the enrollment patterns in schools. Figure 1-2 shows the changes in the number of persons served by special education in the 10-year period between 1977 and 1987.

These enrollment trends have significance for teaching and for those preparing to teach in at least two important ways.

First, for both social and economic reasons, society will remain committed to providing educa-tional opportunities to all children. Society will also demand that minority and handicapped students do well in school. Some of these students will come from homes of poverty; others will come from homes in which parents do not speak English; some will be emotionally or physically different from their classmates. These students will experience school differently from those whose parents were themselves educated in our schools and who have prepared their children for them. Working with youth from diverse cultural backgrounds and with various handicapping conditions will necessitate that beginning teachers have a repertoire of effective strategies and methods far beyond those required previously. Beginning teachers will also have to be able to adapt curriculum to make it more suitable for those students who may find school devastatingly difficult or irrelevant to their lives.

Second, it is likely that schools will continue to be scrutinized for racial and ethnic balance in their student and teacher populations. This will mean that during the next several decades teachers can expect to experience complex social and organizational arrangements in which school enrollment

Figure 1-2 Children 3 to 21 served by special education programs, 1977 to 1987

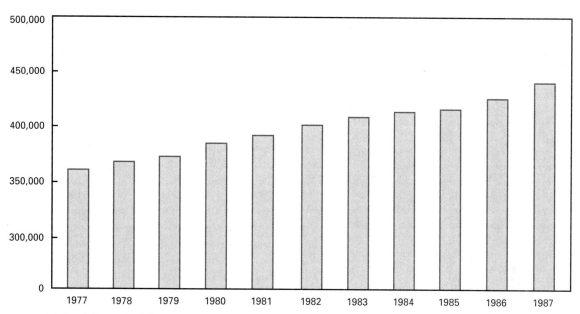

SOURCE: National Center for Education Statistics (1988), *Digest of education statistics.* Washington, D.C.: U.S. Printing Office.

boundaries will be changed often, efforts will be made to diversify student populations through open enrollment and magnet school programs, and teachers themselves may be moved from school to school more often than in the past.

TEACHER DIFFERENTIATION AND ACCOUNTABILITY

Until very recently, teachers were subjected to minimal preparation and few expectations as to performance. However, standards for teachers introduced during this century began to emphasize liberal arts preparation and some exposure to pedagogy. During the next few decades this trend will accelerate rather dramatically. Beginning teachers will increasingly be required to demonstrate their knowledge of pedagogy and subject matter prior to certification, and they will be held **accountable** for using best practice throughout their careers. For instance, as of 1990, 39 states require some type of testing before issuing an initial certificate to teach; plans are under way to institute the same requirements in the remaining states. Most states are using the National Teacher's Examination (NTE),

but alternative and more difficult tests are being considered in a number of states.

Current trends in teacher testing are likely to continue and to lead to extended training programs for teachers. Many of you using this book may be in extended programs now. Most extended programs are characterized by the teacher candidate's obtaining a bachelor's degree with a subject matter major, followed by a master's degree in pedagogy.

Before getting a license to teach you may be required to demonstrate through examination your knowledge and skill in teaching. Competency in academic subject matter will no longer be sufficient, particularly for teaching in classrooms that are culturally diverse and contain students with various handicapping conditions. Neither will liking children, in and of itself, be enough for tomorrow's teachers. Twenty-first-century teachers will be required to have a command of various knowledge bases (academic, pedagogical, social, and cultural) and to be reflective, problem-solving professionals. The following description of teachers appeared in *A Nation Prepared: Teachers for the Twenty-First Century,* sponsored by The Carnegie Forum on Education and the Economy (1986):

Teachers should have a good grasp of the ways in which all kinds of physical and social systems work; a feeling for what data are and the uses to which they can be put; an ability to help students see patterns of meaning where others see only confusion; an ability to foster genuine creativity in students; and the ability to work with other people in work groups that decide for themselves how to get the job done. They must be able to learn all the time, as the knowledge required to do their work twists and turns with new challenges and the progress of science and technology. Teachers will not come to the school knowing all they have to know, but knowing how to figure out what they need to know, where to get it, and how to help others make meaning out of it.

Teachers must think for themselves if they are to help others think for themselves, be able to act independently and collaborate with others, and render critical judgment. They must be people whose knowledge is wide ranging and whose understanding runs deep. (p. 25)

The Carnegie Forum on Education and the Economy has helped organize the National Board for Professional Teaching Standards. This board, formally created in May 1987, has the support of many important education groups, including the two major teachers' unions, the American Federation of Teachers and the National Educational Association. The board's aim is to set standards for the teaching profession and to issue a national teaching certificate. Although the board will not begin its formal assessment until 1994 or 1995, the following proposals are currently being considered as requirements for the national professional certificate: (1) an undergraduate degree in one of the arts or sciences, (2) successful teaching or internship experiences, and (3) a passing score in a set of oral, written, and performance exams. These exams are currently in the process of being field-tested.

A PERSPECTIVE ON EFFECTIVE TEACHING

Central to the process of learning to teach are concepts and definitions of the "good" and the "effective" teacher. Trying to define an effective teacher has long occupied the thoughts of many citizens, teachers, and professional researchers. For example, Gary Griffin (1986) summarizes some of the concepts of teaching that come from literature and the media as: "the strict but kindly teacher (remember Miss Dove?) . . . the bumbling but eventually effective academician (Mr. Chips?) . . . the slightly acerbic and mishap-prone post-teenager (Miss Brooks?)" (p. 5).

Within the educational community there has been a remarkable diversity in the definition of effective teaching. Some have argued that an effective teacher is one who can establish rapport with students and a nurturing, caring environment for personal development. Others have defined an effective teacher as a person who has a love for learning and a superior command of a particular academic subject. Still others argue that an effective teacher is one who can activate student energy to work toward a more just and humane social order.

The content of a teacher education curriculum is itself a statement about what effective teachers need to know. Clinical experiences and tests for certification, such as the National Teacher's Examination, make similar statements, as do the assessment systems used in schools to evaluate and counsel beginning teachers.

A concept of an effective teacher is also central to writing a book about learning to teach and influences its plan, its organization and unifying themes, and the choice of topics to include and exclude. The following section describes the point of view of *Learning to Teach.*

A View of Teaching

The concept of effective teaching that has guided the planning and writing of *Learning to Teach* does not include any of the stereotypes embodied in Mr. Chips or Miss Brooks; neither does it include an argument about whether academic competence is more important than nurturance or vice versa. Effective teaching requires as its baseline individuals who are academically able, who have command of the subjects they are required to teach, and who care about the well-being of children and youth. It also requires individuals who can produce results, mainly those of student academic achievement and social learning. These characteristics are prerequisites for teaching, but they are insufficient without four higher-level sets of attributes:

Figure 1-3 A view of effective teaching

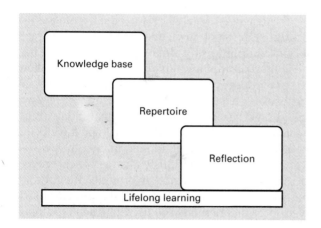

- Effective teachers have control of the **knowledge bases** on teaching and learning and use this knowledge to guide the science and art of their teaching practice.
- Effective teachers command a **repertoire** of best teaching practices (models, strategies, procedures) and can use these to instruct children in classrooms and to work with adults in the school setting.
- Effective teachers have the dispositions and skills to approach all aspects of their work in a **reflective,** collegial, and problem-solving manner.
- Effective teachers view learning to teach as a **lifelong process** and have dispositions and skills for working toward improving their own teaching as well as improving schools.

These four attributes are illustrated in Figure 1-3.

In *Learning to Teach* these four attributes of an effective teacher are crucial themes and have been woven into each of the chapters in the book. The word *theme* is used here as it is used to describe a theme song in a Broadway musical—a song that recurs often throughout the production and becomes associated with the main ideas and characters in the play. Readers will find the four themes summarized here referred to again and again throughout the book.

Knowledge Base to Guide the Art of Practice

Effective teachers have control over a knowledge base that guides what they do as teachers, both in and out of the classroom. In fact, professionals by definition have control over information (the knowledge base) that allows them to deal with certain matters with more insight and more effectively than the average person. At the same time, no professionals, including doctors, engineers, and lawyers, have a complete knowledge base from which to find answers to every question or problem. Furthermore, not every problem can be solved by the use of best practice—patients die, design ideas fail, and legal cases are lost. The same is true in teaching. Despite the use of best practice, some students do not learn and others drop out of school.

It is important for those learning to teach to understand what is meant by the knowledge bases for teaching and to understand the strengths and limitations of the scientific research that informs current knowledge bases for teachers. It is also important to point out that, though the knowledge bases for teaching are still young and not yet complete, in contrast to the fragmentary and inconsistent knowledge bases of two or three decades ago, the situation today is vastly improved.

Three questions about the knowledge base for teaching are important to the beginning teacher: (1) What does it mean to have a knowledge base about teaching, and what domains of knowledge are most relevant? (2) How do teachers access and use knowledge? and (3) What are the limits of current knowledge and research on teaching and learning?

DOMAINS OF KNOWLEDGE

Scientific knowledge is essentially knowledge about relationships between variables. In the social sciences or applied sciences (such as education) this means that knowledge exists about how one variable is related to another and, in some instances, how one set of variables under certain conditions affects others. In education, the variables that have been most studied, and those most relevant to learning to teach, are those associated with student learning and with how student learning is related to teacher behavior. Lee Schulman (1987) has attempted to organize the important domains of knowledge for teachers into seven categories:

1. *Content knowledge,* or knowledge of the particular subjects to be taught such as mathematics, English, history
2. *Pedagogical content knowledge,* that is, the special amalgam of content and pedagogy that is uniquely the province of teachers; their own special form of professional understanding
3. *Knowledge of learners* and their characteristics
4. *General pedagogical knowledge,* with special reference to those board principles and strategies of classroom management and organization that appear to transcend subject matter
5. *Knowledge of educational contexts,* ranging from the workings of the group or classroom, to the governance and financing of school districts, to the character of communities and cultures
6. *Curriculum knowledge,* with particular grasp of the materials and programs that serve as "tools of the trade" for teachers
7. *Knowledge of educational ends, purposes, and values* and their philosophical and historical grounds (pp. 2–3)

Learning to Teach has been built primarily on the knowledge bases associated with categories 3, 4, and 5. In particular, it synthesizes and describes the enormous body of knowledge that has been created in the past 20 years and that informs our understanding of how students learn, the factors that motivate learning, how leadership can be provided to manage complex instructional settings, and specifically the links that have been found between teacher expectations and behaviors and student achievement. At one time what we knew about these topics and relationships was very limited. Currently, we can be confident of considerable knowledge across several areas, some of which have been validated experimentally and replicated under varying conditions.

TEACHER USE OF KNOWLEDGE

Educational philosopher Gary Fenstermacher (1986) has taken the position that the major value of educational research for teachers is that it can lead to the improvement of their **practical arguments.**

His own argument for this position goes something like the following.

For teachers, as well as for other professional practitioners, the knowledge and beliefs held are not only important for their own sake but also because they prompt and guide action. Actions taken by practitioners are guided by a number of premises—beliefs held to be just and true and linked together in some logical format. Sometimes these premises and the underlying logic have been made explicit by the practitioner; many times, however, they are not consciously aware of their practical arguments. Fenstermacher provides the following example of a teacher's practical argument used to support the methods she used to teach reading.

1. It is extremely important for children to know how to read.
2. Children who do not know how to read are best begun with primers.
3. All nonreaders will proceed through the primers at the same rate (the importance of learning to read justifies this standardization).
4. The skills of reading are most likely to be mastered by choral reading of the primers, combined with random calling of individual students.
5. This is a group of nonreaders for whom I am the designated teacher.

Action: (I am distributing primers and preparing the class to respond in unison to me.) (p. 46)

In this example, premise 1 is a statement of value, on which most people would concur. Premise 5 is a statement of fact, presumed to be accurate. Premises 2, 3, and 4, however, are beliefs held by the teacher about how children learn and about pedagogy. These beliefs influence the actions of using primers and choral reading. In this particular instance, these beliefs are simply not supported by the research on reading instruction.

Fenstermacher points out that the results of research, if known, could lead this teacher to doubt her beliefs and subsequently rethink the premises undergirding her pedagogical behavior and instructional practices. Knowing about and using research, then, becomes a process of understanding, doubting, and challenging the beliefs we hold about how children learn and about the best practices to employ to enhance this learning. It is in contrast to taking actions based on tradition, conventional wisdom, or folklore. In fact, it could be said that educational research produces information that helps describe relationships and phenomena more accurately than folklore and popular impressions.

Research on teaching, then, can dispel old wives' tales about teaching, just as other research can dispel myths about aspects of the physical and social world outside of education. For this reason it is important for teachers to have a firm grasp of the knowledge base on teaching, including its application in various settings. Everyone, however, should be cautious and remember that teaching is a tremendously complex process that continually departs from fixed recipes and formulas. We should also remember the limits of educational research and current knowledge about teaching.

THE LIMITS OF RESEARCH

There are several reasons why research can inform classroom practice in some instances and not in others.

No Fast Formulas.   Finding relationships does not mean things work all the time. Even though principles and guidelines for best practice exist for today's teachers, the beginning teacher should not jump to the conclusion that principles based on research will work all the time, for all students, in all settings. That simply is not true. Research knowledge explains what happens most of the time and under particular conditions. Examples from medical research can help illustrate this important point.

During the past decade, many studies have shown strong relationships between cigarette smoking and various diseases—particularly heart disease and cancer. However, you all know people who have smoked all their lives and have not had heart attacks. You also know people who did not smoke but who died of cancer. Similarly, suppose it has been shown that hypothetical drug X is strongly related to the cure of disease Y, and medical researchers can cite many instances when patients using drug X were cured. However, doctors can also cite known instances where drug X has been administered, and the patient has died.

Explanations Are Not Recommendations.   Practicing teachers often ask researchers to make practical recommendations based on their research. Some examples of the types of questions they ask include: "Should we use ability groupings in third-grade classrooms?" "What are the best concepts to teach in tenth-grade social studies?" "How can I motivate John, who comes to school tired every morning?" The reply to these types of questions has to be that research alone cannot provide answers to such specific practical problems. For example, take the question about what to teach in tenth-grade social studies. Even though a researcher might provide empirical information about what other school districts teach in the tenth grade, or about the abilities of most 15-year-olds to understand historical concepts, this would not help a teacher decide what concepts to teach, given a particular group of students, the goals of a particular social studies curriculum or teacher, and the community values—all crucial factors to consider.

Explanations Are Not Recipes.   Research on teaching is very young. Many questions of interest have not been studied and many that have been studied still lack complete or adequate answers. The explanations provided by research do not normally translate directly into recipes that can be safely followed. Instead, research explanations help describe relationships between variables in a model of classroom teaching. These explanations can provide guidelines for teachers who are knowledgeable about their own abilities and skills, those of their students, and the contextual features of a particular classroom, school, and community.

Explanations Are Not Inventions.   A final limitation of research is that it tends to focus on practices currently employed by teachers, not those yet to come. The descriptions and explanations about what teachers currently do, although valuable, should not be confused with the invention or discovery of new practices. Two examples of this idea may help to highlight its importance.

Many of the research-based practices for classroom management stem from studies where researchers compared the classroom management procedures used by researcher-defined effective teachers with those used by less effective teachers. From this research, patterns of effective classroom management practices have emerged. However, these results do not mean that better practices are yet to be invented. It simply means that, compared to the range of current practices, some classroom management procedures can be said to be better than others under certain conditions.

Along the same line, much of the research on effective teaching has been done in classrooms that represent the more traditional patterns of teaching —a single teacher working with whole groups of students for the purpose of achieving traditional learning objectives, student acquisition of basic information and skills. Although this research, like the classroom management research, can inform us about best practices within the confines of the traditional paradigm, it does not tell us very much about worthwhile innovations that may exist in the future.

Repertoire of Effective Practice

The second theme about effective teaching is that effective teachers have a repertoire of best practices. *Repertoire* is a word used mainly by people in the theater and in music that refers to the number of pieces (such as readings, operas, musical numbers) a person is prepared to perform. Obviously, more experienced and expert performers have larger, more diverse repertoires than do novices. This is also true for teachers.

This book emphasizes that effective teachers have diverse repertoires and are not restricted to a few pet practices. This is in contrast to some arguments from earlier eras intended to prove the superiority of one approach over another, for example, inductive versus deductive teaching or the lecture versus discussion method. The result of all this debate was futile and misdirected because no one approach was found to be consistently superior to any other. Instead, many teaching approaches were found to be appropriate and the selection of a particular model depended on the teacher's goals and the characteristics of a specific group of learners.

The teaching practices described in this book comprise a minimum number of models, strategies, and procedures that should be in the beginning teacher's repertoire. Some are large and complex models of teaching; others are rather simple proce-

Figure 1-4 Repertoire for three aspects of teaching

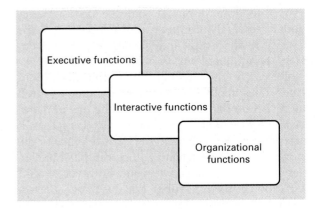

dures and techniques. The practices described are obviously not all that exist; effective teachers add to their repertoires throughout their careers.

The concept of repertoire carries with it the idea that things one can do are linked to various aspects of the job. To use the music analogy again, an accomplished musician may have one repertoire for performances of classical music, one for appearances in nightclubs or pop concerts, and perhaps another for family get-togethers. Just as this text has been built around a particular perspective of teaching, so too has it been constructed around a conception of what teachers do and the repertoire required for three domains of their work.

Teachers, regardless of their grade levels, their subject areas, or the types of schools in which they teach, are asked to perform three important functions. They are asked to provide leadership to a group of students, the **executive functions of teaching;** they are asked to provide direct, face-to-face instruction to students, the **interactive functions of teaching;** and they are expected to work with colleagues, parents, and others to perform the **organizational functions of teaching.** These three functions are illustrated in Figure 1-4. Obviously, these functions are not always discrete, nor does the teacher always perform one independently of the others. These functions, however, are convenient organizers for helping beginning teachers make sense out of the bewildering array of events associated with teaching in a complex school setting.

THE EXECUTIVE FUNCTIONS OF TEACHING

In many ways the contemporary teacher's roles are similar to those of leaders who work in other types of organizations. Leaders are expected to provide leadership, to establish procedures for effective motivation, and to coordinate the activities of various people working interdependently to accomplish organizational goals. Berliner (1982b) has called this aspect of teachers' work the executive functions of teaching and tells a story about what prompted him to start considering teaching from this perspective:

> During a break while attending a meeting on reading instruction at a prominent hotel, it was discovered that a business management seminar was underway in an adjoining room. The seminar was conducted under the auspices of the American Management Association. . . . The seminar leader was overheard saying: "One of the most crucial skills in management is to state your objectives—you have to have clearly stated objectives to know where you are going, to tell if you are on track, and to evaluate your performance and that of others." That sounded very familiar to an educational psychologist. I stayed to listen, eventually spending the day as a free-loader and spy at their meeting and abandoning my own.
>
> This group of managers, receiving in-service training, spent an hour on the topic of management by objectives. The instructors quoted Mager and Popham, names familiar to almost everyone in education. Their second topic was the use of time. They called this the greatest single management problem. Again, the relevance of their concerns and the concerns of educators seemed clear. The third topic they dealt with was motivation. They had two subtopics: First was a presentation consisting of lecture and case history on the benefits of positive reinforcement, the negative effects of criticism and punishment, the use of graphing and the beneficial effects of contracts; the second part of the motivational program was introduced by a film featuring a person well known to educators and psychologists—Robert Rosenthal. Rosenthal told these executives about the positive effects of high expectations. The last topic of the day was evaluation. The parallels between the training provided to business and public executives and some of the knowledge and skills needed to run a classroom . . . seemed obvious. (pp. 2–3)

Berliner (1982b) also reminds his readers of the historical link between the concepts of teacher and

manager that grew out of the industrialization process in western societies. Although this image has been embraced by some educators, it has also been criticized for its tendency to make people think about schools the same way they think about factories; for its overemphasis on the technical and skill sides of teaching; and for its excessive attention to control, orderliness, and efficiency at the expense of creativity and spontaneity.

Regardless of past misuse of the teacher-as-leader metaphor, there are indeed many parallels between the work they perform. *Learning to Teach* presents these executive skills in a manner that does not violate the artistic side of teaching, that is, teacher creativity and spontaneity.

THE INTERACTIVE FUNCTIONS OF TEACHING

When most people think about what teachers do, they think of the day-by-day instruction of students. This aspect of teachers' work is labeled the interactive function of teaching. The overall framework for thinking about this aspect of teaching comes mainly from three sources: (1) the "models of teaching" concept developed by Bruce Joyce and Marsha Weil (1972), (2) the teaching strategies and procedures that have resulted from the teacher effectiveness research of the past two decades, and (3) the wisdom of practice contained in the repertoire of experienced teachers.

Over the years many different teaching approaches have been created. Some have been developed by educational researchers investigating how children learn and how teaching behavior affects student learning. Others have been developed by classroom teachers experimenting with their own teaching in order to solve specific classroom problems. Still others have been invented by psychologists, industrial trainers, and even philosophers such as Socrates. In the late 1960s, Bruce Joyce and Marsha Weil began tracking down the various teaching approaches available. In the process of recording and describing each approach, they developed a taxonomy, or classification system, to analyze the basic characteristics of a particular approach in terms of its theoretical base, its educational purposes, and the teacher and student behaviors required to successfully execute the approach.

Joyce and Weil (1972) and Joyce, Weil, and

Showers (1992) labeled each of these approaches a **teaching model.** A model as defined by Joyce and Weil, and as used here, is more than a specific method or strategy. It is an overall plan, or pattern, for helping students to learn specific kinds of knowledge, attitudes, or skills. A teaching model, as you will learn later, has a theoretical basis or philosophy behind it and also encompasses a set of specific teaching steps designed to accomplish desired educational outcomes.

You can think of teaching models as similar to forms of government. In the modern world there are several dominant forms, or models, of government—monarchies, dictatorships, theocracies, and democracies. Each of these forms has been created to reflect certain values and accomplish specific goals various societies deem important. The specific procedures for each form of government, like each teaching model, differ in important ways. There is great variety in the basic ideologies behind forms of government, the goals considered most important, who becomes leader, who gets to vote. Each form of government, however, has some similarities with other forms. For example, all have systems for defining power relationships, for defining the role of citizen, or for making judgments about the innocence or guilt of those who break laws. The same is true for the various teaching models. Each model differs in its basic rationale or philosophical base and in the goals it has been created to achieve. Each model, however, shares many specific procedures and strategies, such as the need to motivate students, define expectations, or talk about things.

Teachers need many approaches to meet their goals with a diverse population of students. A single approach or method is no longer sufficient. With sufficient choices, teachers can select the model that best achieves a particular objective, the model that best suits a particular class of students, or the models that can be used in tandem to promote student motivation, involvement, and achievement.

In *Models of Teaching* (1992), Joyce, Weil, and Showers identify and describe 20 major models or approaches to teaching. But how many of these should there be in a beginning teacher's repertoire? Obviously, it would be unrealistic to ask a beginner to master all the models—that is a lifelong process. To require command of only a single model would be equally unrealistic. It seems fair and practical to ask beginning teachers to acquire a modest repertoire during the initial stages of their career. Therefore, six models have been selected that, if learned well, can meet the needs of most teachers. These are: presentation using advance organizers, concept teaching, direct instruction, cooperative learning, discovery teaching, and discussion.

The rationale for selecting the presentation model is that a major goal of teaching is to help students acquire new information in the form of facts and principles for which presenting and lecturing are most appropriate. Teachers use this approach more than any other, so it seems reasonable to expect beginning teachers to be skilled in its use.

Concept teaching and the discovery and discussion models were chosen because they are the most effective approaches for helping students to think critically and to process the information they already have. These models have well-developed research literatures and can be learned reasonably well after initial instruction and practice.

The direct instruction model is important because much of a teacher's work is aimed at helping students acquire procedural knowledge and specific skills: how to write a sentence, perform a mathematical operation, or read a map. Teachers also want their students to develop study skills such as underlining, taking notes, or test taking. Acquiring procedural knowledge and skills mostly consists of mastering a set of specific and sequential tasks. The direct instruction model can help do this, and it has a rather extensive research base. Its straightforward explication makes it very easy to learn.

The cooperative learning model, one of the newest models, has been effective in improving race and ethnic relations within multicultural classrooms and relationships among regular and handicapped students. In addition, it has been effective in increasing students' academic learning. As you will find, there are several variations of cooperative learning, some of which are rather simple and can be readily learned. Other variations are more complex and not easily mastered at first.

THE ORGANIZATIONAL FUNCTIONS OF TEACHING

The common view of teaching focuses mostly on classroom interactions between teachers and students, and as such it is insufficient for understanding the reality of teaching in contemporary schools.

Teachers not only plan and deliver instruction to their students; they also serve as organizational members and leaders in a complex work environment. Tasks associated with this aspect of teaching are called the organizational functions of teaching.

Not only are schools places where children learn; they are also places where adults carry out a variety of educational roles—principal, teacher, resource specialist, aide, and so forth. Schools are both similar to and different from other workplaces. Similarities include the ways coordination systems (for example, hierarchical authority and division of labor) are designed to get the work of the school accomplished. Beginning teachers will find that adults who work in schools are pretty much like adults who work in any other organization. They strive to satisfy their own personal needs and motives in addition to achieving the mission of the school. At the same time, those of you who have worked in other organizations (perhaps during the summer or in a previous career) will find some unique aspects to the school workplace. These include norms that give teachers a great deal of autonomy in their work but isolate them from their colleagues; clients (students) who do not voluntarily participate in the organization; and because the school is highly visible politically, diverse and unclear goals that reflect the multiple values and beliefs of contemporary, multicultural society.

Schools are also places, like other organizations, that need to be changed as things change in the larger society around them. Many people preparing to teach have strong idealistic drives to make education and schools better. This idealism, however, is not always supported with sound strategies for putting good ideas into practice, even though the knowledge base on educational change and school improvement has increased substantially over the past decade. A knowledge base now exists to explain why many earlier reform efforts in education failed, and this knowledge can be applied to school improvement ideas you may want to implement.

Building a repertoire of organizational skills is important for two major reasons. First, your ability to perform organizational functions and to provide leadership within the school as well as the classroom will greatly influence your career. It is through performing organizational functions well that beginning teachers become known to other teachers, to their principals, and to parents. It is also

how they become influential professionally with their colleagues and beyond the confines of their schools. Conversely, a beginning teacher's inability to perform organizational functions effectively is the most likely reason for dismissal. Many teachers who are terminated in their early years are dismissed not for instructional incompetence but for their inability to relate to others or to attend to their own personal growth and psychological well-being within a complex organizational setting.

A final reason for learning organizational skills is because researchers and educators are starting to understand that student learning is not only related to what a particular teacher does but also to what teachers within a school do in concert. To work toward schoolwide effectiveness requires such organizational skills as developing good relationships with colleagues, engaging in cooperative planning, and agreeing on common goals and common means for achieving those goals. The effective teacher is one who has a repertoire for entering into schoolwide dialogue about important educational issues.

Reflection and Problem Solving

A firm grasp of educational research alone will not make someone a skilled and reflective teacher. This is true for two reasons. First, the knowledge produced by educational researchers relates to the way things work in general, not to specific cases, whereas the problems faced by teachers in real classrooms are characterized by their uniqueness. The same is true for other professionals, such as doctors, lawyers, and architects, as this observation made by Donald Schön (1983) illustrates:

> The situation of practice is characterized by unique events. Erik Erikson, the psychiatrist, has described each patient as a "universe of one," and an eminent physician has claimed that "85 percent of the problems a doctor sees in his office are not in the book." The unique case calls for an *art of practice* which "might be taught," if it were constant and known, but it is not constant. (pp. 16–17)

Much of the frustration for beginning teachers stems from having to teach groups of students who are unique and about whom they know very little. The effective teacher is one who learns to approach these situations with a problem-solving orientation and who learns the art of teaching through reflection about his or her own practice.

A second reason that research alone cannot guide effective teaching practice is that research knowledge takes many years to produce and, consequently, tends to focus on traditional patterns of practice. The world of teaching, however, calls for new patterns of practice that reflect the complexity, instability, and value conflicts of the present.

Finally, as described earlier, many of the problems facing teachers become problems of values and priorities that scientific knowledge can help explain but cannot help decide. A second observation from Schön (1983) underscores the value-laden world of practicing teachers.

> Practitioners are frequently embroiled in conflicts of values, goals, purposes and interests. Teachers are faced with pressure for increased efficiency in the context of contracting budgets, demands that they rigorously "teach the basics," exhortation to encourage creativity, build citizenship, and help students to examine their values. (p. 17)

If scientific knowledge cannot provide a complete guide for effective practice, how do practitioners become skilled and competent in what they do? Again Schön (1983) provides valuable insights:

> If it is true that there is an irreducible element of art in professional practice, it is also true that gifted engineers, teachers, scientists, architects, and managers sometimes display artistry in their day-to-day practice. If the art is not invariant, known and teachable, it appears nonetheless, at least for some individuals, to be *learnable*. (p. 18)

Learning to Teach strives to present its textual information in such a way as to alert you to the areas of teaching where our knowledge is fragmented and incomplete and to alert you to possible teaching situations in which you will be required to exhibit individual problem solving and reflection. Many of the learning aids found at the end of each chapter are also aimed at assisting you in becoming problem solving in your orientation and reflective about your teaching practice. Reflection and problem solving are complex dispositions and skills and are not easily learned. However, as described above, the art of professional practice is learn-

able, and it is experience, coupled with careful analysis and reflection, that produces this learning.

Lifelong Learning Process

The final theme developed in *Learning to Teach*, perhaps the most important in the long run, is that learning to teach is a lifelong process. This book describes much of the research on teaching as well as specific skills and procedures that can be used by beginning teachers. You will be able to understand this research and, with practice, will learn to execute the various models and procedures. Command of the knowledge base and a sufficient repertoire of practice, however, will not make any beginner an accomplished teacher. Becoming accomplished is a complex process and takes a long time. The next section of this chapter explores the developmental process associated with learning to teach and provides specific information about how you can begin.

LEARNING TO TEACH

Some teachers, like fine wines, keep getting better with age. Others do not improve their skills after years of practice and remain about the same as the day they walked into their first classrooms. Why is it that some teachers approach the act of teaching critically and reflectively; are innovative, open, and altruistic; are willing to take risks with themselves and their students; and are capable of critical judgment about their own work? Conversely, why do others exhibit exactly the opposite traits?

Becoming truly accomplished in almost any human endeavor takes a long time. Many professional athletes, for example, display raw talent at a very early age, but they do not reach their athletic prime until their late twenties and early thirties and then only after many years of dedicated learning and practice. Many great novelists have written their best pieces in their later years only after producing several inferior and amateurish works. The biographies of talented musicians and artists often describe years of pain and dedication before the subjects reached artistic maturity. Becoming a truly accomplished teacher is no different. It takes purposeful actions fueled by the desire for excellence; it takes an attitude that learning to teach is a lifelong developmental process in which one gradually discovers one's own best style through reflection and critical inquiry.

This section describes some of the things we know about the process of learning to teach and emphasizes three basic premises. Learning to teach is a lifelong and developmental process, not one limited to the period of time between the first methods class and the date a teaching license is acquired. Few effective teachers are born that way. Rather they become increasingly effective through attention to their own learning and development of their own particular attributes and skills. The second is that early experiences in schools influence our conceptions about teaching. However, the memories beginning teachers have of favorite teachers they hope to model themselves after may not be the route to effective teaching. And third, becoming a truly effective teacher requires replacing naive and sometimes incorrect conceptions of teaching with more complete knowledge structures and understanding about teaching and learning.

Models of Teacher Development

One area of research about how people learn to teach comes from the field of developmental psychology. There is a growing consensus among leading theorists and researchers that humans develop cognitively and affectively through stages. Sprinthall and Thies-Sprinthall (1983) summarized this perspective and listed the following assumptions of developmental theory:

1. All humans process experience through cognitive structures called stages—Piaget's concept of schemata.
2. Such cognitive structures are progressively organized . . . into stages from the less complex to the more complex.
3. Growth occurs first within a particular stage and then progresses to the next stage in sequence. This latter change is a qualitative shift—a major leap to a significantly more complex system of processing experience.
4. Growth is neither automatic nor unilateral but occurs only with appropriate interactions between the human and the environment.
5. Behavior can be determined and predicted by an individual's particular stage of development. Predictions, however, are not exact. (p. 16)

What this means is that becoming a teacher, like becoming anything else, is a process in which development progresses rather systematically through stages with a chance of growth remaining static unless appropriate experiences occur. The following are specific developmental theories about how people learn to teach.

FULLER'S STAGES OF CONCERN

The late Frances Fuller studied student teachers, beginning teachers, and more experienced teachers at the University of Texas in the late 1960s and early 1970s. Through her research (1969) she developed a theory that describes three **stages of concern** teachers go through as they learn to teach.

1. **Survival concerns:** When people first begin thinking about teaching and when they have their first classroom encounters with children from in front of rather than behind the desk, Fuller's research suggests, they are most concerned about their own personal survival. They wonder and worry about their interpersonal adequacy and whether or not their students and their supervisors are going to like them. Also, they are very concerned about classroom control and worry about things getting out of hand. In fact, many beginning teachers in this initial stage have dreams about students getting out of control.
2. **Teaching situation concerns:** At some point, however, and this varies for different individuals, beginning teachers start feeling more adequate. Various aspects of controlling and interacting with students become somewhat routinized. At this stage teachers begin shifting their attention and energy to the teaching situation itself. They start dealing with the time pressures of teaching and with some of the stark realities of the classroom, such as too many students, inappropriate instructional materials, and perhaps their own meager repertoire of teaching strategies.
3. **Pupil concerns:** Eventually, individuals mature as teachers and find ways of coping or dealing with survival and situation concerns. It is only then, according to Fuller, that teachers reach for higher-level issues and start asking

questions about the social and emotional needs of students, being fair, and the match between the teaching strategies and materials and pupil needs and learning.

The Fuller model is useful for thinking about the process of learning to teach. It helps to put present concerns in perspective and to prepare beginners to move on to the next and higher level of concern. For example, a beginning teacher who is overly worried about personal concerns might seek out experiences and training that build confidence and independence. If class control takes too much mental and emotional energy, ways to modify that situation can be sought. An aid that can help you to measure your concerns at this point in your career is included at the end of the chapter.

FEIMAN-NEMSER'S STAGES OF DEVELOPMENT

Sharon Feiman-Nemser (1983), a researcher at Michigan State University, has also identified several stages that teachers go through in the process of becoming teachers. These are similar to those described by Fuller, but are included here nonetheless to provide another set of lenses through which to view the development process.

1. **Beginning survival stage:** This is the stage that beginners are in when they start their teaching careers. A beginner's knowledge of teaching and schools is limited to what he or she has picked up over the years as a student.
2. **Consolidation stage:** According to Feiman-Nemser, beginners eventually pass beyond the survival stage and become more confident in their ability to teach and to deal with students. Their personal and teaching goals become clearer and more concise, and many of the routines required for effective classroom management and instruction became habitual.
3. **Mastery stage:** During this stage of development, teachers master the fundamentals of teaching and of classroom management. These become effective and routine. As in Fuller's pupil concern stage, teachers now focus their energy and talent on pupil needs and strive to provide improved instruction from an ever-broadening repertoire of methods and strategies and an ever-deepening understanding of the subjects taught.

IMPLICATIONS OF DEVELOPMENTAL MODELS FOR LEARNING TO TEACH

As beginning teachers go through the process of learning to teach, the developmental models conceptualized by Sprinthall and Theis-Sprinthall, Fuller, and Feiman-Nemser have numerous implications. First, these models suggest that learning to teach is a developmental process in which each individual moves through stages that are simple and concrete at first and later, more complex and abstract. Developmental models thus provide a framework for viewing your own growth.

Second, you can use the models to diagnose your own level of concern and development. This knowledge can help teachers to accept the anxiety and concerns of the beginning years and, most important, to plan learning experiences that will facilitate growth to more mature and complex levels of functioning. For example, some developmental theorists, such as Hunt (1970, 1974), argue that growth is a result of interaction between a person's level of development and environmental conditions. Optimal development occurs only when environmental conditions provide a stimulus to a person's cognitive and emotional growth. When environmental conditions are not optimal, that is, are either too simple or too complex, then learning is retarded. In other words, as people learning to teach become more complex themselves, their environments must also become correspondingly more complex if they are to continue developing at an optimal rate. Although it is not possible to readily change many of the environments you will experience as you learn to teach, you can, nonetheless, try to seek out environments and experiences that will match your level of concern and development as a teacher.

Early Influences on Teaching

It appears that some aspects of learning to teach are influenced by the experiences that people have with important adult figures, particularly teachers, as they grow up and go through school. In the early 1970s Dan Lortie, a sociologist at the University of

Chicago, spent several years studying why people become teachers, what kind of a profession teaching is, and what experiences affect learning to teach. As part of his study, he interviewed a rather large sample of teachers and asked them what experiences most influenced their teaching. Many experienced teachers told Lortie that early authority figures, such as parents and teachers, greatly influenced their concepts of teaching and their subsequent decision to enter the field. Lortie's study and his results are summarized in Research Summary 1–1.

This is the first example of research summaries found in each chapter of *Learning to Teach*. These summaries have been provided to help you get a feel for some of the research that has been carried out in education and to help you develop an appreciation for the knowledge base on teaching. The boxed research summaries, such as the Lortie study, were chosen either because they are considered classics in particular fields or because they illustrate the variety and richness of method found in educational research.

The format used to present Lortie's research is one that will be followed throughout the book when research reports are summarized. The problem the researcher was addressing is presented first, followed by brief descriptions about who was studied and the types of procedures used. When needed, pointers are provided to help you read the research. Each research summary concludes with a description of important findings and statements about the implications of the research for practice.

This format is used because it is important that you become knowledgeable about the research base on teaching and learning, and it is equally important that you learn how to read and use research. At the end of this book there is a special section in the Resource Handbook called "Reading and Using Research." This section provides further insight into the nature of research on teaching and a practice exercise for reading research; you may want to read it before going on.

EARLY INFLUENCES: FOUR EXAMPLES

Prior to becoming teachers, most of us spent somewhere between 14,000 and 17,000 hours watching teachers teach. Obviously, as you saw in Lortie's study, these experiences influence the way we view

teaching. But what do we learn from all this watching? Four teachers are profiled below as examples of memories many beginning teachers hold of their favorite teachers. As you read about Jack Ramsey, Jane Middleton, Donald Chavez, and Mr. Chase, ask yourself: Did I have teachers like this? Do they serve as models for me? And, most important, are these teachers effective?

Jack Ramsey.   In a small rural town in northeastern Kansas, Jack Ramsey walks into his twelfth-grade social studies class promptly at 8:45 A.M. Ramsey is a stout, robust man. His ex-marine bearing and reputation for toughness bring every eye in class to the front as he makes his predicted entrance. With the flair of the drill sergeant, he calls roll. Each student responds with a crisp "Here" to his or her name as it is precisely pronounced, always preceded by the formal title of Mr. or Miss. "Ms." is a modern invention Ramsey refuses to recognize.

Instruction for the day starts with current events. Calling students at random, Ramsey asks what they read in newspapers or news magazines during the past 24 hours. TV news is not allowed. Ramsey usually comments on each report; sometimes he "kids" a bit; sometimes he responds with slight ridicule or cynicism to a particular student's comments before moving on suddenly to someone else.

The formal lesson for the day grows from the text the class is using, and Ramsey's favorite teaching strategy consists of a brief lecture on some issue discussed in the text, followed by pointed questions to members of the class. On a normal day after several questions, a controversial issue is defined by Ramsey and for the remainder of the class Ramsey and three or four of the brighter students carry on an extended and spirited debate. Class ends with the next day's assignment and a reminder from Ramsey of the upcoming test for Friday.

Ramsey is a legend in the school. Bright students look forward to the challenge of twelfth-grade social studies, and the less able worry and fret but still like him. Ramsey is tough and hard-nosed, but is considered fair, interesting, and provocative. His debates with students are notorious for the entertainment they provide. His Friday tests cover every imaginable detail and are the reason, in a school where homework normally is accomplished in class

RESEARCH SUMMARY 1-1

Lortie, D. (1975). *School-teacher: A sociological study.* Chicago: University of Chicago Press.

PROBLEM: Lortie was interested in a variety of issues about teaching as an occupation, particularly the organization of the teacher's work, the sentiments teachers hold toward their work, and the "ethos" of the teacher's occupation as contrasted to other occupations.

SAMPLE AND SETTING: Lortie collected information from a number of sources. The focus here is on the data he collected through extensive interviews with 94 teachers from five towns in the Boston metropolitan area and from a national survey conducted by the National Education Association in the late 1960s.

PROCEDURES: By Lortie's own account his methods included "historical review, national and local surveys, findings from observational studies by other researchers, and content analysis of intensive interviews" (p. ix). His sample from the five towns around Boston included selecting school systems that were broadly representative of American education; he then randomly selected teachers from within the five systems. He interviewed the teachers about the attractions of teaching and various other features of their careers using techniques he had developed in earlier studies on the legal profession.

POINTERS FOR READING RESEARCH: The researchers who carried out many of the studies used in this book reported their results in numeric form and summarized them in data tables. Lortie's data are presented not in tabular format but, instead, as direct quotes from the people he interviewed. Information quoted directly from interviews is quite easy to read and to understand. However, readers of this type of research information always need to ask themselves questions about the data, such as: Did the researcher conduct the interviews in such a way that respondents provided honest and accurate information? From many possibilities, did the researcher select quotes that were representative of what the total sample reported, or did he or she select quotes to represent a particular point of view or bias? Are the conclusions reached by researchers using interview data consistent with the information the data contain?

RESULTS: Lortie's study is large and complex and has many insights into teaching and teachers. Here are some of his findings about why people go into teaching and the influence of early experiences on their teaching.

Interview Data: One teacher interviewed shows the influence of early adult figures on her decision to teach:

---

or study halls, for every student to burn the late-night oil. Parents love him.

Jane Middleton. Urbane and sophisticated, Jane Middleton is an English teacher in Roosevelt Middle School. Her trademarks—bright scarves and chic designer clothes, outspoken criticism of bureaucratic rules, and unorthodox ideas—make her eighth-grade humanities class a "must" for every bright student at Roosevelt. Ms. Middleton's room

My mother was a teacher, her sisters were teachers—it's a family occupation. I always wanted to go into teaching. I can't remember when I didn't want to. . . . I remember as a little girl sometimes seeing teachers have a hard time. I thought, well, I will be careful because some day I'll be on the other side of the desk. (p. 61)

Lortie also found that teaching is one of the few professions where the practitioner has been in the client (student) role for an extended period (several hours each day for 16 years) before switching to the professional role. It comes as no surprise that teachers told Lortie that their own teaching was greatly influenced by the teaching they had received as students. The following excerpts from Lortie's interviews illustrate this influence.

The teacher I had in sixth grade was good, interesting. There are a few things I used this year that I remember having done in her room. (p. 63)

There was one particular teacher in my eighth and ninth grades. She was very hard, very strict, and used to say, "I know some of you don't like me since I'm so strict; but when you get out of school and think back, a lot of you will probably think of me as being the best teacher." She really was. She probably taught me how important classroom discipline was. (p. 64)

My second-grade teacher was kind. She knew it was a terrific change for me to come all the way from Iowa and she'd take the time to talk to me, to take away some of the fright. I never forgot that and when new youngsters come into my room I always try to team them up with someone. I have a special word for them. (p. 64)

I had a college professor. . . . This is the man who had more to do with my techniques than any other person. (p. 64)

I had her in United States history and she whetted my appetite for history. . . . I may be one of her products. I think I am. (p. 64)

DISCUSSION AND IMPLICATIONS: It is obvious that prior experiences with their own teachers have affected and will continue to influence the ways teachers think and act about teaching. In some ways this is positive, since it provides beginners with many models over the years. However, relying too completely upon these early experiences may make teachers rather conservative in trying new approaches. Many of the standard practices used by former teachers may not represent best practices, given current knowledge about teaching and learning. Also, if beginning teachers rely too heavily on their prior experiences, that may prevent them from being sufficiently reflective and analytical toward their work. This latter point will be discussed later in the chapter.

is colorfully decorated with a wall-size map of the world and many prints of works by the old masters. An expensive Oriental rug (purchased by Middleton) provides a setting for intimate discussions and readings. Each day is a new and stimulating experience for students. It might bring a Shakespeare reading by Middleton herself, or an opportunity to listen attentively to classical music, or a provocative guest speaker—normally an artist who is a personal friend of Middleton's. Tests are not given in Middleton's class, but students are motivated to work hard, primarily by Middleton's own love of the humanities and her compelling, charismatic personality.

Donald Chavez.   Dr. Chavez teaches a sophomore class in United States history in a large university on the East Coast. Each class period is a delightful experience for his students. An eloquent speaker, Dr. Chavez has prepared over the years a series of lectures that fill the time to the minute and are sprinkled with jokes that have become notorious around campus and are familiar to students long before they set foot in his class. Chavez's lectures center for the most part on great men (more recently, women, too) in American history. His own research has produced a vast knowledge about many American leaders, particularly information about their vanities and personal lives. The high and mighty, both living and dead, seldom escape Chavez's biting tongue; nor do their illicit dealings and love affairs, a Chavez specialty. Tests on the lectures are the primary means of grading in a Chavez class, and these tests are considered very difficult because Chavez expects students to remember every detail he covers, including his jokes.

Chavez's sections of United States history are always overenrolled. Twice during the past 15 years he has been given the university's award for excellence in teaching.

Mr. Chase.   Mr. Chase is a fifth-grade teacher at Elmwood Elementary School. Slightly overweight and with a bit of tummy always showing through the gap in the bottom of his shirts, Chase is a favorite among students and parents of Elmwood. He knows all the students in his class and their families and, in fact, knew several parents of current students when they were in his class years ago. Chase plays ball with the boys at recess and loves to stand in the hall before and after school saying "Hi" to students and teasing them (in playful ways) about their boyfriends and girlfriends. Chase prides himself on how he has individualized instruction for his students, relying heavily upon commercial texts and workbooks. Students love to hang around his desk asking for help and kidding with him. He never refuses to stay after school to help students.

Mr. Chase befriends every new student (and new teacher) in the school and helps him or her adjust to their new environment. The principal relies on Chase and seeks his advice often. She even appoints him acting principal when she has to be away from Elmwood.

No doubt you can conjure up from your own school experiences images of teachers like Ramsey, Middleton, Chavez, and Chase. They represent the popular concepts of great teachers—persons characterized by charismatic qualities and the ability to motivate or befriend students. Oftentimes memories of such teachers become a kind of vague model for people learning to teach. But is it possible for all teachers to become like these teachers? In fact, are Ramsey, Middleton, Chase, and Chavez really effective teachers?

In truth, most individuals cannot learn to teach in these charismatic styles. For example, how many people can have the bearing and the commitment to discipline and command of Ramsey? How many have a knack for the dramatic stage presence of Middleton and Chavez? How many can know their students' personal lives as well as Chase, who also had some of his students' parents in his classes?

Most people preparing to teach have less colorful personalities that lead to subtler, less pronounced teaching styles. Does that mean that they cannot become great teachers? The answer is no, not at all. Those of you with normal talents, but perhaps without charismatic personalities, can become effective teachers if you have a strong grasp of your subject field, a knowledge of pedagogy, and a reflective mind.

In truth, some of the teachers remembered most vividly because of their charismatic qualities may not have been as effective as they seemed. Many times a very charismatic teacher like Middleton works best with the most talented and academically able students—students who already possess strong verbal and information processing skills. But what about the less able and less motivated students who populate the classrooms of most schools? They are the students most in need of good teachers. Similarly, some of the friendly and popular teachers you remember befriended the lonely and were fun to be around, but did they challenge the able? Did less able students learn those basic skills so vital to later success in school from them? Often entertaining and informative lecturers such as Chavez are popular with students, and students leave thinking they have learned a lot. But have they? Have they learned to think critically? Have they been encouraged to construct their own knowledge and to form their own points of view? These are questions that must be pondered in the process of developing teaching skills and styles.

Cognitive Processes of Expert and Novice Teachers

There are many approaches to thinking about teaching and about learning to teach. One is to focus on the specific things teachers do and how these affect student performance. The emphasis here is on trying to figure out how teachers learn to execute particularly effective techniques or procedures. Another approach is to examine the complex cognitive processes (thinking) engaged in by teachers as they plan and make decisions about what they are going to do. Some of this research (Borko and Niles, 1987; Peterson, Marx, and Clark, 1978; Shavelson, 1976) will be discussed in Chapter 2 because it shows how teachers think as they plan for instruction. The emphasis in this chapter, however, is on an interesting line of inquiry that has emerged in the past few years about the differences between the cognitive performances of expert teachers and those of novice teachers.

This line of inquiry has been influenced substantially by cognitive psychology and schema theory. Cognitive psychologists use the word **schemata** to describe an individual's knowledge structure and how information is stored and processed in memory. Four important principles from schema theory have major implications for learning how to teach:

1. Individuals store and organize knowledge in memory through knowledge structures or schemata.
2. A person's schemata and prior knowledge about any topic greatly influence what can be learned.
3. To be meaningful, new information must be structured in such a way as to hook into and activate existing schemata.
4. Differences in schemata account, in part, for performance differences in complex tasks such as teaching.

These principles will be elaborated on in later chapters, and their implications for how new information should be presented to students will be described. Here the implications for learning to teach are explored.

Researchers such as Borko and Niles (1987), Calderhead (1988), and Leinhardt and Greeno (1986) have investigated how a teacher's knowledge structure (schemata) works and how schema may differ among beginning **novice** and experienced **expert teachers.** Their research points out how expert and novice teachers think differently about problems and how they use different problem-solution strategies. Their research also suggests that information found to be useful for an experienced teacher may not take on the same meaning for a beginning teacher. This research is important and has value for beginning teachers because if beginners can gain insights into the knowledge structures and thinking processes of experienced teachers, these insights can advance their own efforts.

SUMMARY

- Teaching has a scientific basis which can guide its practice; it also has an artistic side.
- The role of the teacher is a complex one that has been shaped by historical and contemporary forces. Expectations for teachers have changed: In the nineteenth century the primary concern was the teacher's moral character, whereas today we are more concerned about the teacher's pedagogical abilities.
- Today almost one-third of our students come from non-western-European backgrounds and many speak English as their second language, a situation that is currently reshaping the teacher's role. Teachers are expected to work in complex multicultural educational settings and to provide good educational experiences for all children.
- Increasingly teachers are expected to have advanced preparation and to demonstrate their knowledge of both subject matter and pedagogy.
- Effective teachers are those who understand the knowledge base on teaching, can execute a rep-

ertoire of best practices, have attitudes and skills necessary for reflection and problem solving, and consider learning to teach a lifelong process.

- The scientific basis of teaching is learned mainly through studying research and the wisdom of practice accumulated by the profession. From scientific knowledge certain teaching principles and propositions have been derived which can inform "best" teaching practices. Principles based on research, however, cannot be translated directly into fixed recipes and formulas that will work all the time.

- Repertoire refers to the number of strategies and processes teachers are prepared to use. Effective teachers develop a repertoire of methods and skills to successfully carry out various aspects of their work.

- A teacher's work can be conceptualized around three main functions: the executive, the interactive, and the organizational. The executive functions of teaching refer to the leadership roles teachers are expected to play in their classrooms, such as providing motivation, planning, and allocating scarce resources. The interactive functions refer to methods and processes teachers employ as they provide day-by-day instruction to students. The organizational functions refer to teachers' work in the school community, including work with colleagues, parents, and school leadership personnel.

- Effective practice includes abilities to approach classroom situations in reflective and problem-solving ways.

- Learning to teach is developmental, and teachers go through predictable stages. At first they are concerned about survival, later about their teaching situation, and finally about the social and academic needs of their pupils.

- Learning to teach is a complex process, and information that is useful to experienced teachers may not have the same value for beginners.

- Parents and teachers often influence a person's decision to enter teaching and affect a teacher's vision of teaching. Memories of favorite teachers, however, may not be the best models for developing one's own teaching style, because these teachers may not have been as effective as they seemed.

KEY TERMS

best practice
scientific basis of teaching
art of teaching
pedagogy
academic learning
objectivist perspective
constructivist perspective
demographic assumptions
accountability
knowledge base
repertoire
reflection
practical arguments
executive functions of teaching
interactive functions of teaching
organizational functions of teaching
teaching model
stages of concern
schemata
expert teacher
novice teacher

BOOKS FOR THE PROFESSIONAL

Barzun, J. (1991). *Begin here: The forgotten conditions of teaching and learning.* Chicago: University of Chicago Press. This little book features various essays and articles written by Jacques Barzun during his long career which describe his vision about what it means to teach and to learn and what is required of teachers and schools if they are to be effective.

Fenstermacher, G. D., and Soltis, J. F. (1986). *Approaches to teaching.* New York: Teachers College Press. Drawn from classical conceptions of teaching, this book can help beginning teachers analyze alternative approaches to teaching.

Fosnot, C. T. (1989). *Enquiring teachers, enquiring learners.* New York: Teachers College Press. This book does a wonderful job of taking concepts such as constructivist perspectives, teacher empowerment, and reflection and showing how they relate to classroom learning and how they can be put into practice for helping beginners learn to teach.

Gage, N. L. (1978). *The scientific basis of the art of teaching.* New York: Teachers College Press. This book discusses the value of educational research and how it has produced useful knowledge that supports practice.

Joyce, B., Weil, M., Showers, B. (1992). *Models of teaching* (4th ed.). Englewood Cliffs, N.J.: Prentice-Hall. This book is a must. It provides more information on the models of teaching described here, plus many others.

Lieberman, A., and Miller, L. (1984). *Teachers, their world, and their work.* Alexandria, Va.: Association of Supervision and Curriculum Development. This little book gives insightful descriptions of the day-to-day work of classroom teachers.

Lortie, D. C. (1975). *School-teacher: A sociological study.* Chicago: University of Chicago Press. A definitive and provocative book on the nature of teaching and the teaching profession. Although a complicated sociological study, Lortie's book is written so as to be understood by beginning teachers.

Reynolds, M. C. (ed.). (1989). *Knowledge base for the beginning teacher.* New York: Pergamon Press. A book of readings which attempts to define the kind of knowledge and understandings beginning teachers should have.

Richardson-Koehler, V. (ed.). (1987). *Educators' handbook: A research perspective.* New York: Longman. This book provides an excellent review of the research on classroom teaching and effective schooling. It was written for teachers and administrators and includes such topics as classroom management, teacher planning, school effectiveness, and computers and education.

Russell, T. and Munby, H. (eds.). (1992). *Teachers and teaching: From classroom to reflection.* New York: The Falmer Press. A very timely book of readings on reflective teaching with particular attention to Schön's concept of "reflection-into-action." Contributors represent the United Kingdom, the United States, Australia, and Canada.

Schön, D. A. (1983). *The reflective practitioner.* San Francisco: Jossey-Bass. This book explores the complexity of learning to become a professional and emphasizes the importance of developing skills for "reflection in action."

Warren D. (ed.). (1989). *American teachers: Histories of a profession at work.* New York: Macmillan. This collection of essays provides excellent insight into the history of teaching in the United States including efforts to reform the profession over a period of time encompassing two centuries. Essays provide a perspective about how current reforms efforts in education are linked to the past.

Wittrock, M. C. (ed.). (1986). *Handbook of research on teaching* (3d ed.). New York: Macmillan. This book is the most authoritative review of the mountain of research on teaching. Beginning teachers will find many of the chapters tough going; however, it is an invaluable reference work.

LEARNING AIDS FOR PLANNING, OBSERVATION, AND REFLECTION

- Assessing My Efforts for Learning to Teach
- Assessing My Teaching Concerns, Part 1
- Assessing My Teaching Concerns, Part 2
- Interviewing Teachers about the Scientific Basis of the Art of Teaching
- Observing the Three Teaching Functions

ASSESSING MY EFFORTS FOR LEARNING TO TEACH

PURPOSE: One of the most important goals of this text is to inspire your continuing efforts at professional development. This aid will help you to gain an overall impression of your efforts in pursuing the four attributes of effective teaching described in this chapter and to reflect on and plan for the next steps in your own professional growth.

DIRECTIONS: Circle the response that best corresponds to your level of agreement with the statement, then list the relevant activities under each category. Use the information to pinpoint gaps in your professional development activities.

1. I am actively engaged in developing my command of the knowledge base for teaching. (*Circle one.*)

Agree strongly   Agree   Neither agree nor disagree   Disagree   Disagree strongly

Topics I feel comfortable with

Topics I am currently working on

Topics I will work on next

_____   _____   _____

_____   _____   _____

_____   _____   _____

_____   _____   _____

2. I am actively engaged in reflecting on myself as a teacher and in problem solving around educational issues. (*Circle one.*)

Agree strongly   Agree   Neither agree nor disagree   Disagree   Disagree strongly

Ways I currently reflect on and solve problems about teaching:

_____

_____

_____

_____

New ways I want to learn to help me reflect on and solve problems about teaching:

_____

_____

_____

_____

3. I am actively engaged in expanding my repertoire of teaching practices. (*Circle one.*)

Agree strongly   Agree   Neither agree nor disagree   Disagree   Disagree strongly

Practices I know

Practices I am currently learning

Practices I will study next

_____   _____   _____

_____   _____   _____

_____   _____   _____

_____   _____   _____

4. I am actively engaged in the lifelong process of learning to teach. (*Circle one.*)

Agree strongly   Agree   Neither agree nor disagree   Disagree   Disagree strongly

Past actions I have taken to help me learn about teaching:

_____

_____

Actions I am currently taking to help me learn about teaching:

_____

_____

Actions I plan to take in the future to help me continue to learn about teaching:

_____

_____

ASSESSING MY TEACHING CONCERNS, PART 1

Frances Fuller and Archie George

PURPOSE: Learning to teach is a developmental process—people progress through stages, and awareness of the stage you're in can facilitate this process. This aid will help you develop awareness of your level of concern about teaching.

DIRECTIONS: Read each statement, then ask yourself: When I think about my teaching, how much am I concerned about this?

1 Not concerned   2 A little concerned   3 Moderately concerned
4 Very concerned   5 Extremely concerned

Being concerned about something is not the same as thinking it is important. Being concerned means you think about it frequently and would like to do something about it personally. Thus you can be concerned about problems or opportunities, current or anticipated issues, and so on. For each statement mark the number that best corresponds to your level of concern.

1. Lack of instructional materials	1	2	3	4	5
2. Feeling under pressure too much of the time	1	2	3	4	5
3. Doing well when a supervisor is present	1	2	3	4	5
4. Meeting the needs of different kinds of students	1	2	3	4	5
5. Too many noninstructional duties	1	2	3	4	5
6. Diagnosing student learning problems	1	2	3	4	5
7. Feeling more adequate as a teacher	1	2	3	4	5
8. Challenging unmotivated students	1	2	3	4	5
9. Being accepted and respected by professional persons	1	2	3	4	5
10. Working with too many students each day	1	2	3	4	5
11. Guiding students toward intellectual and emotional growth	1	2	3	4	5
12. Whether each student is getting what he or she needs	1	2	3	4	5
13. Getting a favorable evaluation of my teaching	1	2	3	4	5
14. The routine and inflexibility of the teaching situation	1	2	3	4	5
15. Maintaining the appropriate degree of class control	1	2	3	4	5

Analysis and Reflection: One way to reflect would be to arrange your concerns in order of importance and compare them with those of others. You may think of other ways to help you reflect on your teaching concerns.

SOURCE: Adapted from H. J. Freiberg, J. M. Cooper, and K. Ryan (1980), *Those who can, teach: Learning guide*, 3d ed., pp. 21–22. Copyright © by Houghton Mifflin Company. Adapted by permission.

ASSESSING MY TEACHING CONCERNS, PART 2

PURPOSE: Experience coupled with reflection is a powerful combination for learning. This aid will help you to begin to systematically observe and reflect on teaching.

DIRECTIONS: In the space below keep a log for 5 days, each day writing a brief paragraph about the concerns you have experienced about teaching or your anticipation of teaching.

Day 1 _____

_____

_____

Day 2 _____

_____

_____

Day 3 _____

_____

_____

Day 4 _____

_____

_____

Day 5 _____

_____

_____

_____

Analysis and Reflection: In the space below write about the common patterns you find in your concerns. Write a paragraph about what your concerns mean to you.

INTERVIEWING TEACHERS ABOUT THE SCIENTIFIC BASIS OF THE ART OF TEACHING

PURPOSE: Teaching is both science and art. This aid will help you to uncover an experienced teacher's perceptions about the scientific basis of the art of teaching and to develop your own appreciation of teaching as art and science.

DIRECTIONS: Use the following questions to guide you as you interview a teacher about his or her understanding and application of the scientific basis of the art of teaching. (Note: Many experienced teachers may not be aware of the research base and yet may be using best practice. Some effective teaching research is based on what excellent experienced teachers do.)

1. To what extent has the way you plan your teaching been influenced by: (*Estimate the percentage contribution of each.*)

   _____ research on planning

   _____ your own experience and intuition

   _____ other (*please specify*) _____

2. Can you give an example of a planning principle you have learned from each source?

   Research: _____

   Experience: _____

   Other: _____

3. Do you find you sometimes need to modify these principles in practice? If so, in what way(s)?

   _____

   _____

4. To what extent has the way you allocate resources like time and space in your classroom been influenced by: (*Estimate the percentage contribution of each.*)

   _____ research on allocating time and space

   _____ your own experience and intuition

   _____ other (*please specify*) _____

5. Can you give an example of a principle of allocating resources that you have learned from each source?

   Research: _____

   Experience: _____

   Other: _____

6. Do you find you sometimes need to modify these principles in practice? If so, in what way(s)?

_____

_____

_____

7. To what extent has the way you organize your classroom to create a productive learning environment been influenced by: (*Estimate the percentage contribution of each.*)

_____ research

_____ your own experience and intuition

_____ other (*please specify*) _____

8. Can you give an example of a principle underlying the creation of productive learning environments you have learned from each source?

Research: _____

Experience: _____

Other: _____

9. Do you find you sometimes need to modify these principles in practice? If so, in what way(s)?

_____

_____

_____

10. To what extent has the way you manage your classroom been influenced by: (*Estimate the percentage contribution of each.*)

_____ research

_____ your own experience and intuition

_____ other (*please specify*) _____

11. Can you give an example of a classroom management principle that you have learned from each source?

Research: _____

Experience: _____

Other: _____

12. Do you find you sometimes need to modify these principles in practice? If so, in what way(s)?

_____

_____

_____

13. To what extent are the teaching strategies you use influenced by: (*Estimate the percentage contribution of each.*)

_____ research

_____ your own experience and intuition

_____ other (*please specify*) _____

14. Can you give an example of a teaching strategy that you have learned from each source?

Research: _____

Experience: _____

Other: _____

15. Do you find you sometimes need to modify these strategies in practice? If so, in what way(s)?

_____

_____

_____

16. To what extent is the way you work with other adults in the school influenced by: (*Estimate the percentage contribution of each.*)

_____ research

_____ your own experience and intuition

_____ other (*please specify*) _____

17. Can you give an example of a principle underlying adult interaction in the workplace that you have learned from each source?

Research: _____

Experience: _____

Other: _____

18. Do you find you sometimes need to modify these principles in practice? If so, in what way(s)?

_____

_____

_____

19. To what extent is the way you work toward school improvement influenced by: (*Estimate the percentage contribution of each*.)

_____ research

_____ your own experience and intuition

_____ other (*please specify*) _____

20. Can you give an example of a school improvement principle that you have learned from each source?

Research: _____

Experience: _____

Other: _____

21. Do you find you sometimes need to modify these principles in practice? If so, in what way(s)?

_____

_____

_____

Analysis and Reflection: Are there any patterns to where this teacher obtains ideas or principles for teaching? Are there any patterns to how this teacher modifies these ideas or principles in practice? Write a paragraph about any patterns you perceive and their relevance to your own teaching.

OBSERVING THE THREE TEACHING FUNCTIONS

PURPOSE: Teaching is a complex, multifaceted activity. This aid will help sensitize you to the multiple functions of teaching.

DIRECTIONS: Shadow a teacher for at least half a day. Make sure you have a chance to observe him or her either before school starts or after class is let out. Make a "tick" whenever you see the teacher perform one of the listed activities. At the same time, estimate the amount of time the teacher spends on that activity, and jot down any other observations you make. Perhaps certain activities tend to occur at certain times, or a particular emotional tone is evident, or several activities occur simultaneously. Make note of anything you think will help you refine your understanding of the three teaching functions.

FUNCTION	OBSERVED	TIME	COMMENTS
Executive			
Planning	———	——	———
Allocating time and space	———	——	———
Organizing for a productive learning environment	———	——	———
Managing the classroom	———	——	———
Assessing or evaluating	———	——	———
Interaction			
Using the presentation model	———	——	———
Using the direct instruction model	———	——	———
Using the cooperative learning model	———	——	———
Using discovery or discussion models	———	——	———
Using concept teaching models	———	——	———
Using other strategies (*specify*)	———	——	———
	———	——	———
Organizational			
Interacting with other adults to carry out the work of the school	———	——	———
Working alone on nonclassroom task	———	——	———
Working toward school improvement	———	——	———

Analysis and Reflection: Tally up the number of ticks for each category, and add the amount of time spent on each category. What did this teacher spend the most time doing? What did he or she do most often? How much time is spent on average on any one episode within a category? (Divide time spent by number of ticks.) Does this seem to be the most productive allocation of the teacher's time? Why or why not?

THE EXECUTIVE FUNCTIONS OF TEACHING

INTRODUCTION

This section of *Learning to Teach* is about the executive functions of teaching. Teachers, like executives in other settings, are expected to provide leadership to students and to coordinate a variety of activities as they and students work interdependently to accomplish the academic and social goals of schooling. The executive functions of teachers are critical because if students are not motivated to participate in and persist with academic learning tasks, or if they are not managed effectively, all the rest of teaching can be lost. Yet these complex functions must be performed in classrooms characterized by fast-moving events and a large degree of unpredictability, and unlike many of the instructional functions of teaching that can be planned ahead of time, many of the executive functions require on-the-spot judgments.

This section focuses on six important leadership functions: planning, allocating scarce resources, motivating students and building productive learning environments, creating multicultural classrooms, managing classroom groups, and assessing and evaluating student progress. Even though each function is described and discussed separately, in the real day-to-day life of teaching the distinctions are not nearly so tidy. When teachers plan, as described in Chapter 2, they are also setting conditions for allocating time, motivation, and building productive

learning environments, the subjects of Chapters 3, 4, and 5. The way students behave and how they are managed on any particular day, the focus of Chapter 6, cycles back to influence future plans and resource allocation decisions, as does evaluation and grading, the focus of Chapter 7.

There is a substantial knowledge base on each aspect of teacher leadership that can provide a guide for effective practice. There is also considerable wisdom that has been accumulated by teachers over the years to help beginning teachers get started with learning to plan, to allocate resources, and to deal with students in group settings. Information from both of these sources is presented and discussed.

You will discover as you read and reflect on the executive functions of teaching that providing leadership in classrooms is no easy matter and cannot be reduced to simple recipes. Instead, leadership is tightly connected to specific classrooms and schools, and what works in general may not work in any specific case. Learning to read specific situations and to act on them effectively in real classrooms through reflection and problem solving is one of the most important challenges facing beginning teachers. When mastered, this is a most rewarding ability.

Chapter Outline

PERSPECTIVE AND RATIONALE

• Planning—The Traditional View • Planning—
An Alternative Perspective

SAMPLING THE KNOWLEDGE BASE

• Consequences of Planning • Planning and the
Experienced Teacher • Planning and the Beginning Teacher

PLANNING DOMAINS

• The Phases of Teaching • Attending to Planning Cycles

THE SPECIFICS OF PLANNING

• Instructional Objectives • Taxonomies for Helping
Choose Instructional Objectives • Lesson Plans • Choosing
Curriculum Content • Choosing Activity Structures

CHAPTER 2

Planning

Even though planning and making decisions about instruction are demanding processes that call for rather sophisticated understanding and skills, a beginning teacher does not have to feel overwhelmed. Most of you have planned trips that required complicated travel arrangements. You have planned college schedules, made to-do lists, and survived externally imposed deadlines for term papers and final examinations. Graduation celebrations and weddings are other events most people have experienced that require planning skills of a high caliber. Planning for teaching may be a bit more complex, but the skills you already have can serve as a foundation on which to build.

This chapter describes some of what is known about the processes of teacher planning and decision making. The rationale and knowledge base on planning, particularly the impact of planning on student learning and on the overall flow of classroom life, are described, as are the processes experienced teachers use to plan and make decisions. Also included is a rather detailed explanation of specific planning procedures and a number of aids and techniques used for planning in education and other fields. The discussion that follows strives to capture the complexity of teacher planning and decision making and to show how these functions are performed by teachers under conditions of uncertainty. Although the chapter's emphasis is on the planning tasks carried out by teachers in solitude prior to instruction, attention is also given to the varied in-flight decisions teachers make in the midst of lessons.

PERSPECTIVE AND RATIONALE

People today express great confidence in their ability to control events through sophisticated planning. The importance given to planning is illustrated by the many special occupational roles that have been created for just this purpose. For example, a professional cadre of land-use planners, marketing specialists, systems analysts, and strategic planners, to name a few, work full-time putting together detailed, long-range plans to influence and direct the economy, control industrial output, stimulate labor-power production, and ensure appropriate military offensive and defensive initiatives. Family planning, financial planning, and career planning are topics taught to students in high schools and universities and to adults in many settings. The skills associated with these topics are deemed important and become commonplace to many adults.

Thinking about and conducting research on the teacher's role as a planner has recently gained attention in education. It is motivated by the same assumptions that inspire a wish to understand planning in other areas of life—namely, the drive to control what happens through purposeful, organized activities that lead to targeted outcomes. Planning and decision making are vital to teaching and interact with all the other executive functions of teachers. One measure of the importance of planning is illustrated when you consider the amount of time teachers spend on this activity. Clark and Yinger (1979), for example, report that teachers estimate they spend between 10 percent and 20 percent of their working time each week on planning activities. The importance of planning is illustrated in another way when you consider the wide variety of educational activities affected by the plans and decisions made by teachers, as described by Clark and Lampert (1986):

> Teacher planning is a major determinant of what is taught in schools. The curriculum as published is transformed and adapted in the planning process by additions, deletions, interpretations, and by teacher decisions about pace, sequence, and emphasis. And in elementary classrooms, where a teacher is responsible for all subject matter areas, planning decisions about what to teach, how long to devote to each topic, and how much practice to provide take on additional significance and complexity. Other functions of teacher planning include allocating instructional time for individuals and groups of students, composing student groupings, organizing daily, weekly, and term schedules, compensating for interruptions from outside the classroom and communicating with substitute teachers. (p. 28) Indeed, the process of learning to teach is described by some (Doyle, 1990, for example) as one where teacher candidates learn to decide what curriculum content is important for students to learn and how that curriculum can be enacted in classroom settings through the execution of learning activities and events.

Planning—The Traditional View

The planning process in all fields, including education, has been described and studied by many researchers and theorists. The dominant perspective that guides most of the thinking and action on this topic has been referred to as the **rational-linear model.** This perspective puts the focus on goals and objectives as the first step in a sequential process. Modes of action and specific activities are then selected from available alternatives to accomplish prespecified ends. The model assumes a close connection between those who set goals and objectives and those charged with carrying them out. It also assumes that the social environments for which plans are made are somewhat static over time and that an information base can be established to show the degree to which goals and objectives have been accomplished. Figure 2-1 illustrates the basic linear planning model.

This model owes its theoretical base to planners and thinkers in many fields. In education the basic concepts are normally associated with early curriculum planners and theorists, such as Ralph Tyler (1950), and with later instructional designers, such as Mager (1962, 1984), Popham and Baker (1970), and Gagné and Briggs (1979). For both groups, good educational planning is characterized by carefully specified instructional objectives (normally stated in behavioral terms), teaching actions and strategies designed to promote prescribed objectives, and careful measurements of outcomes, particularly student achievement.

Planning—An Alternative Perspective

During the last decade many observers (Clark et al., 1980, 1981, for example) have questioned whether the rational-linear model accurately describes planning in the real world. Its view that organizations and classrooms are goal-driven has been challenged, as has its view that actions can be carried out with great precision in a world characterized by complexity, change, and uncertainty. For example, Weick (1979) observed the following about organizational goals and goal-based planning:

> Organizational actions at best seem to be goal-interpreted. Goals are sufficiently diverse, the future is sufficiently uncertain, and the actions on which goal statements should center are sufficiently unclear that goal statements explain a relatively small portion of the variance in action. It is probable that goals are tied more closely to actual activities than is commonly recognized

Figure 2-1   Rational-linear planning model

GOALS ────────────→ ACTIONS ────────────→ OUTCOMES

and that they are more productively understood as *summaries of previous actions*. (p. 239)

Weick's model for planning and the relationship of goals to actions could be illustrated as in Figure 2-2.

Note that Weick turns the rational-linear model found in Figure 2-1 upside down. He argues for a **nonlinear model** where what planners really do is start with actions that in turn produce outcomes (some anticipated, some not) and finally summarize and explain their actions by assigning goals to them. Proponents of this model of planning argue that plans do not necessarily serve as guides for actions, but instead become symbols, advertisements, and justifications for what people have already done. As will be shown later, this model probably describes the way many experienced teachers actually approach some aspects of planning. Although they set goals and strive to get a sense of direction for themselves and their students, teachers' planning proceeds in a cyclical, not a straight linear fashion, with a great deal of trial and error built into the process. Indeed, experienced teachers pay attention to features of both the linear and nonlinear aspects of planning and accommodate both.

SAMPLING THE KNOWLEDGE BASE

The research on teacher planning and decision making is substantial and has grown significantly in the past two decades. It provides teachers with insights about the effects of planning on students. It also provides critical information about how experienced teachers approach planning and how environmental cues influence their in-flight decisions. The studies summarized in this section have been selected to represent the work of several major researchers in the field of teacher planning and decision making. They also illustrate the complexity of

teacher planning and how certain kinds of planning can produce unanticipated and surprising results.

Consequences of Planning

Both theory and common sense suggest that planning for any kind of activity improves results. Research also favors instructional planning over undirected events and activities, but as you will see, some types of planning may lead to unexpected results.

The literature in the fields of both management and education suggests that planning that leads to shared understanding and acceptance of clear and attainable goals enhances employee or student performance. David McClelland and his colleagues (1958, 1961, 1965), who have studied motivation for many years, take the position that all people, including children, are motivated toward action in the quest to fill three basic needs: the need to have influence, to experience affiliation with others, and to achieve. Achievement appears to be the dominant motivation, particularly in our society, and the one that has been most studied. It is also the one most important to discussions of teacher planning because the need for achievement is satisfied in students when they work toward and reach challenging, but attainable, goals.

Planning processes initiated by teachers can give both students and teachers a sense of direction and help students become aware of the goals that are implicit in the learning tasks they are asked to perform. Two important studies done at about the same time highlight the effects of planning on teacher behavior and its consequence for students.

Duchastel and Brown (1974) were interested in the effects of instructional objectives on student learning. At the time of their study, previous research results were contradictory, and some had failed to support the contention that clear objectives

Figure 2-2   Nonlinear planning model

ACTIONS ────────────→ OUTCOMES ────────────→ GOALS

led to higher student achievement. The researchers randomly assigned college students taking a course in communications at Florida State University into two groups. Subjects were asked to study several units on the topic of mushrooms. Twenty-four objectives had been written for each unit and a specific test item had been written to correspond to each objective. Students in group 1 were given 12 of the 24 objectives to use as a study guide. Students in group 2 were not given any of the objectives, but they were told to learn as much as they could from the mushroom materials.

When the subjects were tested later, the researchers found that both groups scored the same on the total test. What is interesting and important, however, is the fact that the students who were given 12 of the 24 objectives to focus their learning outscored other students on test items associated with these 12 objectives. Of equal interest is that students without any objectives as study aids outscored their counterparts on the items associated with the other 12 objectives.

Duchastel and Brown concluded that learning objectives have a focusing effect on students, which leads to the recommendation that teachers make students aware of the objectives they have for their lessons. On the other hand, the researchers caution teachers to be careful because the study also illustrated how focusing too much on objectives may limit other important student learning.

John Zahorik (1970), working about the same time as Duchastel and Brown, was interested in the effects of planning on *teacher behavior*, particularly planning behaviors associated with identifying objectives, diagnosing student learning, and choosing instruction strategies. He wanted to find out if teachers who planned lessons were less sensitive to pupils in the classroom than teachers who did not plan.

Zahorik studied 12 fourth-grade teachers from four suburban schools near Milwaukee, Wisconsin. The 12 teachers in the study were randomly divided into two groups designated "teachers who planned" and "teachers who did not plan." Teachers in the planning group were given a lesson plan with objectives and a detailed outline on the topic of credit cards. They were asked to use it with their classes. Teachers in the nonplanning group were asked to reserve an hour of classroom time to carry out some unknown task—the task later to be announced as teaching about credit cards. All lessons were tape-recorded and teacher behaviors were coded using a system designed to categorize the teachers' sensitivity to students.

Zahorik found *significant* differences between the teachers who had planned and those who had not planned. Teachers who planned were less sensitive to student ideas and appeared to pursue their own goals regardless of what students were thinking or saying. Conversely, teachers who had not planned displayed a higher number of verbal behaviors that encouraged and developed student ideas. Zahorik concluded that goal-based planning may inhibit teachers from being as sensitive to students as they could be.

The question that immediately arises from this study is: If goal-based planning makes teachers less sensitive to students, should teachers eliminate planning? Zahorik concluded that the answer is obviously no. Elimination of planning might "also bring about completely random and unproductive learning. If a lesson is to be effective, it would seem that some direction in the form of goals and experiences, no matter how general or vague, is needed" (p. 150).

Both the Duchastel and Brown and the Zahorik studies are interesting because together they show the importance of goal-based planning; but they also warn that this type of planning can lead to unanticipated consequences that are not always desirable. To resolve this dilemma, Zahorik recommends that teachers establish goals that focus on their own behavior. He states: "Along with the typical plan, which can be described as a plan for pupil learning, develop a teaching plan that identifies types and patterns of teacher behaviors to be used during the lesson" (p. 150).

Another consequence of teacher planning is that it produces a smoothly running classroom with fewer discipline problems and fewer interruptions. A full chapter is devoted to classroom management later, so the research on this topic will not be highlighted here. It is important to note, however, that educational research for the past three decades has consistently found that planning is the key to eliminating most management problems. Beginning teachers who plan well find they do not have to be police officers because their classrooms and lessons are characterized by a smooth flow of ideas, activities, and interactions. Such planning encompasses the rules and goals teachers establish for their classrooms and emphasizes how responsible and businesslike classroom behavior is an integral part of learning.

Planning and the Experienced Teacher

A new body of research that has flourished over the past few years focuses on the planning and decision-making processes used by experienced teachers. Although this research does not provide clear-cut guidelines for teacher planning, it does provide many insights and provocative issues for study and reflection.

For a number of years researchers (Joyce and Hartoonian, 1964, for example) have tried to understand teacher planning and decision-making behavior and have been particularly interested in whether or not the real-life behavior of experienced teachers actually corresponds to the planning processes prescribed in the rational-linear model. In general, this research shows only a limited adherence to the model and indicates that, instead of focusing on objectives, teachers often focus on the content to be taught and specific instructional activities. Only rarely are objectives formally considered by experienced teachers.

In 1978, Peterson, Marx, and Clark studied the planning process of experienced teachers in a controlled laboratory setting, and their study has become widely accepted as confirmation of earlier speculations and findings. A portion of this study is described in Research Summary 2-1.

Planning and the Beginning Teacher

Researchers and educators also have puzzled over why it seems so difficult for beginning teachers to learn some of the important planning skills. One insight gleaned over the past few years is that it is difficult to learn from experienced teachers, not only because they think differently about planning, but also because they approach planning and interactive decision making differently. Two interesting studies have highlighted these differences.

Housner and Griffey (1985) were interested in comparing differences in planning and decision making of experienced and inexperienced teachers.

They studied 16 physical education teachers. Eight of the subjects had more than 5 years' experience; the other eight were preservice teacher candidates. The teachers were given 60 minutes to plan a lesson on how to teach soccer and basketball dribbling to 8-year-olds. The teachers then taught their lessons and were videotaped. Later the teachers viewed their lessons and told the researchers what they were thinking and the decisions they made while teaching.

Housner and Griffey found that experienced teachers planned ahead for more adaptations that might be needed as lessons got under way and were more concerned than inexperienced teachers with establishing rules for activities. In contrast, inexperienced teachers devoted a large percentage of their planning to the type of verbal instructions they would use. While the lesson progressed, the researchers also found differences between the two groups. The experienced teachers were more attentive to student performance and worked hard to keep the children focused on the performance goals. Inexperienced teachers, on the other hand, attended more to student interest and on keeping students on task in general.

Gael Leinhardt (1989) conducted a similar study and compared planning and lesson execution skills of experienced and inexperienced math teachers. Leinhardt found that experienced teachers had much more complete "mental notepads" and agendas as compared to inexperienced teachers. They also built in and used many more checkpoints to see if students were understanding the lesson than did the inexperienced teachers. The experienced teachers, according to Leinhardt,

weave a series of lessons together to form an instructional topic in a way that consistently builds upon and advances materials introduced in prior lessons. Experts also construct lessons that display a highly efficient within-lesson structure, one that is characterized by fluid movement from one type of activity to another. . . . Novice teachers' lessons, on the other hand, are characterized by fragmented lesson structures with long transitions between lesson segments. . . . Their lessons do not fit well together within or across topic boundaries. (p. 73)

The fact that experienced teachers do not always follow the planning procedures emphasized

RESEARCH SUMMARY 2-1

Peterson, P. L., Marx, R. W., and Clark, C. M. (1978). Teacher planning, teacher behavior and student achievement. *American Educational Research Journal, 15,* 417– 432.

PROBLEM: Peterson, Marx, and Clark were interested in how experienced teachers approach the planning process and how teacher planning is related to student achievement and attitudes. The part of their study that investigated the extent to which teachers attend to various planning categories, such as clarifying objectives, attending to learners' abilities, selecting instructional strategies, and other planning tasks, is summarized here.

SAMPLE AND SETTING: The researchers studied 12 elementary teachers (8.3 years average experience) and 288 junior high students, who were paid to participate in the study. The teachers included 6 women and 6 men.

PROCEDURES: The teachers were given materials (text and slides) and asked to plan for and teach (any way they wanted) three lessons on the topic of a town in France to students randomly assigned to groups of eight. The teachers were also given 11 cognitive and affective student objectives. Each day before class, teachers were given 90 minutes to plan and were asked to "think aloud" as they planned. Statements made in the "think-alouds" were tape-recorded and later coded using the category system described in Table 2-1.

RESULTS: Table 2-2, in which the results of the study are given, shows the mean and percentages of teacher planning statements coded into each of the categories. The table also shows means and percentages for teacher productivity of statements.

TABLE 2-1   Definitions of Teacher Planning Categories

CATEGORY	DEFINITION
Productivity	Total number of statements coded
Objectives	Statements about the end products or intended student outcomes toward which the teacher is working
Subject matter	Statements dealing with information found in the text, or concepts, principles, etc., that are clearly derived from material found in the text
Instructional process	Statements describing an activity or move that the teacher intends to use during instruction, including parts of large, complex strategies
Materials	Statements about instructional or noninstructional materials and their use, or about other aspects of the physical environment
Learner outcomes	Statements that account for one or more specific aspects of students' cognitive development, cognitive ability, ability to respond to a cognitive task, or their equivalents in the affective domain
Miscellaneous	Statements that do not fit into any of the above categories

SOURCE: From P. L. Peterson, R. W. Marx, and C. M. Clark (1978), p. 419.

TABLE 2-2 **Total Planning Productivity and Mean Proportions of Planning Time Devoted to Various Planning Categories for the Three Experimental Days**

	DAY		
PLANNING CATEGORY	1	2	3
Productivity (mean)	199.75	124.25	112.08
Objectives	.039	.039	.044
Subject matter	.399	.334	.210
Instructional processes	.244	.316	.309
Materials	.064	.050	.101
Learner outcomes	.052	.071	.084
Miscellaneous	.202	.189	.259

SOURCE: Adapted from P. L. Peterson, R. W. Marx, and C. M. Clark (1978), p. 423.

DISCUSSION AND IMPLICATIONS: As can be observed in Table 2-2, teachers in the study made more planning statements during the first day and fewer on each subsequent day. The largest number and proportion of planning statements focused on subject matter content, followed by instructional processes. Very small numbers of planning statements fell into the categories of materials and learner outcomes, and the smallest planning category was statements associated with objectives.

Although the results of this study do not translate into specific guidelines for beginning teachers, they do have some serious and important implications for the beginning teacher to think about.

- **Starting with objectives**   Even though beginning teachers may be required to write lesson plans that begin with objectives, they should not feel guilty if their innate sense tells them to plan for content and instructional activities first and then come back to objectives. That is what experienced teachers appear to do. As the researchers concluded: "Even though the teachers were provided with a list of desired cognitive and affective student objectives, they did not refer to them in their planning, nor did they relate their choices of instructional processes to learning objectives" (p. 424).
- **Experienced teachers as models**   The beginning teacher should also consider whether the experienced teachers in this study are, in fact, good models to follow. It may be that the planning patterns of experienced teachers do not represent best planning practice.
- **Planning time**   The beginning teacher who is spending many hours planning for the next day's lesson can take heart from the results of this study, which seem to suggest that as teachers become more familiar with a topic and with its materials, they feel more comfortable and do less planning.

in most linear models and that they attend to different planning tasks and cues from those attended to by inexperienced teachers presents some challenging problems for the beginning teacher. Unlike other acts of teaching, most teacher planning occurs in private places like the teacher's home or office. Also, by their very nature, planning and decision making are mental, nonobservable activities. Only the resulting actions are observable by others. Even when written plans are produced, they represent only a very small portion of the actual planning that has gone on in the teacher's head. The private nature of planning thus makes it difficult for beginning teachers to learn from experienced teachers. Beginning teachers may ask to look at lesson plans or they may talk to experienced teachers about planning and decision-making processes. However, many experienced teachers cannot describe in words the novice can understand the thinking that went into specific plans and decisions. This is particularly true of moment-to-moment planning decisions that characterize the rapid flow of classroom life such as those described in the studies by Housner and Griffey and by Leinhardt. Teacher planning and decision making may be one of the teaching skills where research can be of most assistance in helping beginning teachers learn about the hidden mental processes of the experienced expert.

PLANNING DOMAINS

The following sections explore several domains, or areas of teaching, for which teachers need to plan and also describes specific planning procedures for beginning teachers. Each of these topics must be mastered if positive classroom life and student learning are to be achieved.

The Phases of Teaching

Those who study teacher planning and decision making normally consider these functions as they relate to the periods before instruction, during instruction, and after instruction. These three phases of teacher planning and the types of decisions associated with each are summarized in Table 2-3.

The important point to understand here is that teacher planning is multifaceted, and many aspects of teaching in addition to those associated with deciding on the purposes and content of a lesson require planning. It is also important to note that the mental processes involved vary from one phase of teaching to the next. For example, choosing content can be done after careful analysis and inquiry about students' prior knowledge, the teacher's understanding of the subject, and the nature of the subject matter itself. Many postinstructional decisions, such as the type of test to give or how to assign grades, can also be made after careful consideration. Planning and decision making during instruction itself, on the other hand, often must be done spontaneously and on the spur of the moment.

The remainder of this chapter focuses mainly on those planning tasks and decisions associated with the **preinstructional phase. Interactive** and **postinstructional** planning and decision making will be highlighted later in relation to each of the particular teaching models described in Chapters 8 through 13. A special chapter also gives information about a most important postinstructional planning task: testing and evaluating student performance.

Attending to Planning Cycles

Teachers must plan for different **planning cycles** or time spans, ranging from the next minute or hour to the next week, month, or year. If schoolwide planning or one's own career planning is involved, time spans may even cover several years. Obviously, planning what to do or to accomplish tomorrow is much different from planning for a whole year. However, both are important. Also, plans carried out on a particular day are influenced by what has happened before and will in turn influence plans for the days and weeks ahead.

Robert Yinger (1980) of the University of Cincinnati conducted an interesting and important study a few years ago that can provide beginning teachers with a model for thinking about the time dimensions of teacher planning. Yinger made a detailed study of one first- and second-grade elementary school teacher in Michigan. Using participant-observation methods, he spent 40 full days over a 5-month period observing and recording the teacher's activities. From this work, Yinger was able

Table 2-3 Three Phases of Teacher Planning and Decision Making

PREINSTRUCTIONAL PHASE	INTERACTIVE PHASE	POSTINSTRUCTIONAL PHASE
Choosing content	Presenting	Checking for understanding
Choosing approach	Questioning	Providing feedback
Allocating time and space	Assisting	Praising and criticizing
Determining structures	Providing for practice	Testing
Determining motivation	Using wait time	Grading
	Making transitions	Reporting
	Assisting	
	Managing	

to identify the five time spans that characterized this teacher's planning: daily planning, weekly planning, unit planning, term planning, and yearly planning. Figure 2-3 illustrates these five basic levels of planning and plots their occurrence across the school year.

Yinger also found that for each level of planning the teacher attended to the following four items: goals of planning, sources of information, form of the plan, and criteria for judging the effectiveness of planning. Table 2-4 summarizes these four aspects of planning for each of the five levels.

In the sections that follow, Yinger's model is elaborated and specific information about the tasks and purposes associated with the various time dimensions of planning is provided in some detail.

THE SPECIFICS OF PLANNING

By now it must be obvious that planning is important and that a broad range of planning tasks must be considered. In this section the primary tasks associated with teacher planning are described in some detail, starting with the use of instructional objectives and followed by the use of long-range

Figure 2-3 Five levels of planning

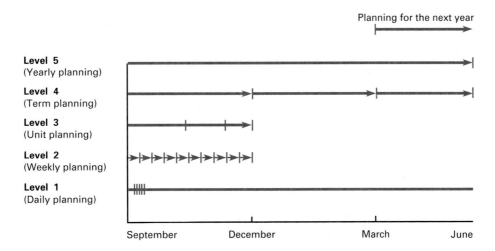

SOURCE: From R. J. Yinger (1980), Study of teacher planning. *The Elementary School Journal, 80,* 113. Copyright 1980 The University of Chicago Press. Used with permission.

Table 2-4 Planning at Each Level of the Model

	GOALS OF PLANNING	SOURCES OF INFORMATION	FORM OF THE PLAN	CRITERIA FOR JUDGING THE EFFECTIVENESS OF PLANNING
Yearly planning	1. Establishing general content (fairly general and framed by district curriculum objectives) 2. Establishing basic curriculum sequence 3. Ordering and reserving materials	1. Students (general information about numbers and returning students) 2. Resources available 3. Curriculum guidelines (district objectives) 4. Experience with specific curricula and materials	General outlines listing basic content and possible ideas in each subject matter area (spiral notebook used for each subject)	1. Comprehensiveness of plans 2. Fit with own goals and district objectives
Term planning	1. Detailing of content to be covered in next 3 months 2. Establishing a weekly schedule for term that conforms to teacher's goals and emphases for the term	1. Direct contact with students 2. Time constraints set by school schedule 3. Resources available	1. Elaboration of outlines constructed for yearly planning 2. A weekly schedule outline specifying activities and times	1. Outlines—comprehensiveness, completeness, and specificity of elaborations 2. Schedule—comprehensiveness and fit with goals for term, balance 3. Fit with goals for term
Unit planning	1. Developing a sequence of well-organized learning experiences 2. Presenting comprehensive, integrated, and meaningful content at an appropriate level	1. Students' abilities, interests, etc. 2. Materials, length of lessons, set-up time, demand, format 3. District objectives 4. Facilities available for activities	1. Lists of outlines of activities and content 2. Lists of sequenced activities 3. Notes in plan book	1. Organization, sequence, balance, and flow of outlines 2. Fit with yearly and term goals 3. Fit with anticipated student interest and involvement

and short-range plans and the tools available to teachers to accomplish planning tasks.

Instructional Objectives

By definition, teaching is a process of attempting to promote change in students. The intended change may be far-reaching, such as developing a whole new conceptual framework for thinking about science or acquiring a new appreciation for literature. It may be as precise and simple as learning how to tie a shoestring. **Instructional objectives** are statements which describe the teacher's intent about how students should change. Instructional objectives are like road maps: They help teachers and their students know where they are going and when they have arrived at their location. Like different kinds of road maps, some instructional objectives are simple. They are easy to make and read. Others are more complex. For this reason, there are several different approaches to guide the writing of instructional objectives and a variety of formats to use. A major issue (sometimes controversial) has been differences among theorists and teachers about how

Table 2-4   Planning at Each Level of the Model *(Continued)*

	GOALS OF PLANNING	SOURCES OF INFORMATION	FORM OF THE PLAN	CRITERIA FOR JUDGING THE EFFECTIVENESS OF PLANNING
Weekly planning	1. Laying out the week's activities within the frame-work of the weekly schedule 2. Adjusting schedule for interruptions and special needs 3. Maintaining conti-nuity and regularity of activities	1. Students' perform-ance in preceding days and weeks 2. Scheduled school interruptions (for example, assem-blies, holidays) 3. Materials, aides, and other resources	1. Names and times of activities in plan book 2. Day divided into four instructional blocks punctuated by A.M. recess, lunch, and P.M. re-cess	1. Completeness of plans 2. Degree to which weekly schedule has been followed 3. Flexibility of plans to allow for special time constraints or interruptions 4. Fit with goals
Daily planning	1. Setting up and ar-ranging classroom for next day 2. Specifying activity components not yet decided upon 3. Fitting daily sched-ule to last-minute in-trusions 4. Preparing students for day's activities	1. Instructions in mate-rials to be used 2. Set-up time re-quired for activities 3. Assessment of class "disposition" at start of day 4. Continued interest, involvement, and enthusiasm	1. Schedule for day written on the chalkboard and discussed with stu-dents 2. Preparation and ar-rangement of mate-rials and facilities in the room	1. Completion of last-minute prepara-tions and decisions about content, ma-terials, etc. 2. Involvement, enthu-siasm, and interest communicated by students

SOURCE: R. J. Yinger, A study of teacher planning, *The Elementary School Journal*, 80, (1980), pp. 114–115. Copyright © 1980 by University of Chicago Press. Used with permission.

specific or general instructional objectives should be.

THE MAGER FORMAT OF BEHAVIORAL OBJECTIVES

In 1962, Robert Mager wrote a little book titled *Preparing Instructional Objectives* which set off a debate over the most desirable "form of a usefully stated objective" (p. i). The general message of Mager's work was the argument that for instructional objectives to be meaningful, they must clearly communicate the teacher's instructional intent and should be very specific. Objectives written in the Mager format became known as **behavioral objectives** and required three parts:

- **Student behavior:** What the student will be doing or the kinds of behavior the teacher will accept as evidence that the objective has been achieved

- **Testing situation:** The condition under which the behavior will be observed or expected to occur
- **Performance criteria:** The standard or performance level defined as acceptable

A simple mnemonic for remembering the three parts of a behavioral objective is to think of it as the STP approach: student behavior (S), testing situation (T), and performance criteria (P). Table 2-5 illustrates how Mager's three-part approach works and provides examples of each.

When teachers write behavioral objectives using the Mager format, the recommendation is to use precise words that are *not* open to many interpretations. Examples of precise words include *write, list, identify, compare.* Examples of less precise words are *know, understand, appreciate.* There are also recommendations about how to link the three parts of

Table 2-5   Sample Behavioral Objectives Using Mager's Format

PARTS OF THE OBJECTIVE	EXAMPLES
Student behavior	Identify nouns
Testing situation	Given a list of nouns and verbs
Performance criteria	Mark at least 85 percent right
Student behavior	List five causes of the Civil War
Testing situation	Essay test without use of notes
Performance criteria	Four of five reasons

the instructional objective together using the following steps: Begin by noting the testing situation, follow this by stating the student behavior, and then write the performance criteria. Table 2-6 illustrates how behavioral objectives written in this format might look.

Mager's behavioral approach has been widely accepted among teachers and others in the educational community over the past three decades. Well-written behavioral objectives give students a very clear statement about what is expected of them, and they help teachers when it comes time to measure student progress, as you will see in Chapter 7. The behavioral approach, however, has not been free of criticism.

Critics have argued that Mager's format leads to reductionism and, when used exclusively, it leads to neglect of many of the most important goals of education. Putting an emphasis on precision and observable student behaviors forces teachers to be very specific in their objectives. To accomplish this specificity, they must break larger, more global educational goals into very small pieces. The number of objectives for almost any subject or topic could run well into the thousands, an unmanageable list

for most teachers. The teacher also runs the risk of paying attention only to specific objectives, which are of minor importance in themselves, while neglecting the sum total, which is more important than all the parts.

Critics have also pointed out, and rightfully so, that many of the more complex cognitive processes are not readily observable. It is easy, for instance, to observe a student add two columns of numbers and determine if the answer is correct. It is not easy to observe the thought processes or the mathematical problem solving that went into this act. Along the same line, it is rather easy to observe students recall the major characters in a Tolstoy novel. It is not as easy to observe and measure their appreciation of Russian literature or the novel as a form of creative expression. Critics worry that the emphasis on behavior objectives may lead to the neglect of the more important aspects of education merely because the latter are not readily observed and measured.

MORE GENERAL APPROACHES

Several curriculum theorists, as well as measurement specialists, have developed alternative approaches to the behavior objective. Gronlund (1978, 1982), for example, has illustrated how objectives can be written first in more general terms, with appropriate specifics added later for clarification. Gronlund, unlike the strict behaviorists, is more willing to use words such as *appreciate, understand, value,* or *enjoy* with his approach. He believes that although these words are open to a wide range of interpretations, they nonetheless communicate more clearly the educational intents of many teachers. Table 2-7 illustrates how an objective might look using the Gronlund format.

Table 2-6   Three Parts of Behavioral Objectives Applied

TESTING SITUATION	STUDENT BEHAVIOR	PERFORMANCE CRITERIA
Given a map . . .	The student will be able to:	At least 85 percent
Without notes . . .	Identify	Four of five reasons
With the text . . .	Solve	Correct to nearest percentages
	Compare	
	Contrast	
	Recite	

Table 2-7   More General Approach to Writing Objectives

FORMAT	EXAMPLE
Overall objective	Understands and appreciates the diversity of the people who make up American society
Subobjective 1	Can define diversity in the words of others and in his or her own words
Subobjective 2	Can give instances of how diverse persons or groups have enriched the cultural life of Americans
Subobjective 3	Can explore in writing how maintaining appreciation for diversity is a fragile and difficult goal to achieve

Notice how the initial objective is not very specific and perhaps not very meaningful or helpful in guiding lesson preparation or measuring student change. It does, however, communicate the overall intent the teacher wants to achieve. The subobjectives help clarify what should be taught and what students are expected to learn. They provide more precision, but yet are not as precise as the three-part behavior objective.

WHICH APPROACH FOR BEGINNING TEACHERS?

The form and use of instructional objectives, as with many other aspects of teaching, are likely to remain subject to controversy and inquiry for a long time. The approach used by beginning teachers will be influenced somewhat by schoolwide policies on this topic, but in most instances considerable latitude will exist for individual preference and decisions. It is important to remember that the purposes behind instructional objectives are to communicate clearly to students the teacher's intents and to aid the teacher in evaluating student growth. Common sense, as well as the research summarized earlier, would suggest adopting a middle ground between objectives stated at such a high level of abstraction that they are meaningless and a strict adherence to the behavioral approach. Gronlund's approach of writing the more global objective first and then clarifying it and getting as specific as the subject matter allows is probably the best advice at this time.

Taxonomies for Helping Choose Instructional Objectives

Taxonomies are devices which help classify and show relationships among things. You already know about a variety of **taxonomies,** for instance, those that classify plants and animals in science. One very useful taxonomy, which serves as a tool for helping make decisions about instructional objectives, is Bloom's *Taxonomy of Educational Objectives* (1956). Working with colleagues at the University of Chicago in the 1950s, Benjamin Bloom created a scheme that classifies educational objectives in a systematic fashion. Bloom's taxonomy has been widely used as an aid in planning as well as for other aspects of teaching. For example, it can be used to assist in test construction and also for choosing a questioning strategy, as will be described in later chapters. Bloom's taxonomy is divided into three large domains: the cognitive, the affective, and the psychomotor.

THE COGNITIVE DOMAIN

Objectives in the **cognitive domain** are divided into six levels, according to Bloom's classification system. Each level specifies the type of cognitive (thinking) process required of students, ranging from the simple to the more complex. The six levels in the cognitive domain and the associated cognitive processes expected of the learner are listed and described below.

Knowledge: The student can recall, define, recognize, or identify specific information presented during instruction. The information may be in the form of a fact, a rule, a diagram, a sound, and so on.

Comprehension: The student can demonstrate understanding of information by translating it into a different form or by recognizing it in translated form. This can be through giving a definition in his or her own words, summarizing, giving an original example, recognizing an example, etc.

Application: The student can apply the information in performing concrete actions. These actions may involve figuring, writing, reading, handling equipment, etc.

Analysis: The student can recognize the organization and structure of a body of information, break this information down into its constituent parts, and specify the relationships between these parts.

Synthesis: The student can bring to bear information from various sources to create a product uniquely his or her own. The product can take a variety of forms—written, oral, pictorial, etc.

Evaluation: The student can apply a standard in making a judgment on the worth of something—a concerto, an essay, an action, an architectural design, etc.

THE AFFECTIVE DOMAIN

Schools spend most of their time on objectives related to cognitive matters. However, it is important to remember that other objectives for education exist that fall into the affective domain (for example, emotional responses to tasks). Bloom's taxonomy divides affective objectives into five categories. Each category specifies the degree of commitment or emotional intensity required on the part of students. The five categories in the **affective domain** and the associated level of student response are described below.

Receiving: The student is aware of or attending to something in the environment.

Responding: The student displays some new behavior as a result of experience and responds to the experience.

Valuing: The student displays definite involvement or commitment toward some experience.

Organization: The student has integrated a new value into his or her general set of values and can give it its proper place in a priority system.

Characterization by value: The student acts consistently according to the value and is firmly committed to the experience.

THE PSYCHOMOTOR DOMAIN

Although we normally associate psychomotor activity most closely with physical education and athletics, in fact, many other subjects require physical movement of one kind or another. Obviously,

handwriting and word processing are tightly connected to all subjects. Work in laboratories for science students requires intricate use of complex equipment. Eye coordination is required for viewing all forms of visual art; hand coordination is required for producing this art. Moving from student to student, using audiovisual equipment, and communicating intentions with facial and hand gestures are examples of skills in the psychomotor domain required of teachers. Below are the six categories of objectives in the **psychomotor domain.** Notice that the categories range from simple reflex reactions to complex actions which communicate ideas and emotions to others.

Reflex movements: Student's actions can occur involuntarily in response to some stimulus.

Basic fundamental movements: Student has innate movement patterns formed from a combination of reflex movements.

Perceptual abilities: Student can translate stimuli received through the senses into appropriate desired movements.

Physical abilities: Student has developed basic movements that are essential to the development of more highly skilled movements.

Skilled movements: Student has developed more complex movements requiring a certain degree of efficiency.

Nondiscursive communications: Student has the ability to communicate through body movement.

Bloom's taxonomies have not been free from criticism. The scheme, as you can see, classifies objectives from the most simple to the most complex. Some have misinterpreted this classification system, believing that it implies that simple (for example, knowledge objectives) are not as important as the more complex (for example, synthesis objectives). This was not Bloom's intent. Others have challenged the hierarchical ordering of the instructional objectives in Bloom's taxonomies. They argue, and rightfully so, that this ordering does not fit all fields of knowledge equally well. Finally, critics have pointed out that even experts in particular fields cannot distinguish objectives among the various levels. This has been particularly true for the higher levels in the cognitive domain, where the cognitive processes of analysis and synthesis commonly overlap.

Regardless of the criticism and identified weaknesses in the taxonomies, they remain popular with teachers. Perhaps like all taxonomies, the taxonomies of instructional objectives do not describe reality completely. Nonetheless, they provide a way of thinking about different kinds of instructional intents and thus become a valuable planning tool for teachers. They provide a good reminder that we want our students to learn a variety of skills and be able to think and act in a variety of straightforward as well as complex ways.

Lesson Plans

Instructional objectives are used in conjunction with **lesson plans,** and, as you saw from Yinger's research, teachers construct both short-term and long-term plans.

DAILY PLANNING

The teacher's daily plan is the one that receives most attention. In some schools it is required. In other schools even the format for daily plans is prescribed. Normally, daily plans outline what content is to be taught, motivational techniques to be used, specific steps and activities for students, needed materials, and evaluation processes. The amount of detail can vary. During student teaching, cooperating teachers may require the beginning teacher to write very detailed daily plans, even though their own plans may be more brief.

Most beginning teachers can understand the logic of requiring rather detailed daily plans at first. Think of the daily lesson plan as similar to the text of a speech to be delivered to a large audience. Speakers giving a speech for the first time need to follow a set of detailed notes or perhaps even a word-for-word text. As they gain experience or as their speeches are gradually committed to memory from repeated presentations, they find less and less need for notes and can proceed more extemporaneously. Or think of the plan as being similar to a road map. Going to a location the first time requires careful and continuous attention to the map. After several trips, it can be put away in the car's map pocket.

Figure 2-4 Sample lesson plan format

Lesson topic/subject——————— Grade level———————

PREINSTRUCTIONAL PLANNING

Objectives: Domains:
————————————————— Cognitive
————————————————— Affective
————————————————— Motor/Skill

Materials/special arrangements/individual modifications:

DURING INSTRUCTION

Introduction/establishing set:

Sequence (syntax) of learning activities:

Closure:

Assignment:

POSTINSTRUCTIONAL

Evaluation of student learning:

    Formal:

    Informal:

Evaluation of the lesson (How did the lesson go? Revisions needed.)

SOURCE: Dr. Ann Fleener, Augsburg College, Minneapolis, Minn.

Daily plans can take many forms. The features of a particular lesson often determine the lesson plan format. For example, each of the teaching models described in Chapters 8 through 13 requires a somewhat different format, as you will see. The beginning teacher will find, however, that some schools have a preferred format that they require of all teachers. Normally that format contains most, if not all, of the features included in the sample lesson plan developed by faculty at Augsburg College and illustrated in Figure 2-4.

Observe that this lesson format includes a clear statement of objectives and a sequence of learning activities for the lesson, beginning with a way to get students started and ending with some type of closure and assignment. The lesson format also provides a means to evaluate student learning as well as the lesson itself.

WEEKLY AND UNIT PLANNING

Most schools and teachers organize instruction around weeks and units. A unit is essentially a chunk of content and associated skills that are perceived as fitting together in a logical way. Normally more than one lesson is required to accomplish a unit of instruction. The content for instructional units might come from chapters in books or from major sections of curriculum guides. Examples of units could include such topics as sentences, the Civil War, fractions, thermodynamics, the heart, Japan, or the short stories of Hemingway.

Unit planning is, in many ways, more critical than daily planning. The unit plan links together a variety of goals, content, and activities the teacher has in mind. It determines the overall flow for a series of lessons over several days, weeks, or perhaps even months, and often reflects the teacher's understanding of both the content and processes of instruction.

Most people can memorize plans for an hour or a day, but they cannot remember the logistics and sequencing of activity over several days or weeks. For this reason teachers' unit plans are generally written in a fair amount of detail. When unit plans are put into writing they also serve as a reminder later that some lessons require supporting materials, equipment, motivational devices, or evaluation tools that cannot normally be obtained on a moment's notice. If teachers are working together in teams, unit planning and assignment of responsibilities for various unit activities are most important.

Unit plans can also be shared with students because they provide the overall road map that explains where the teacher or a particular lesson is going. Through the communication of unit goals and activities students can recognize what they are expected to learn. Knowledge of unit plans can help older students allocate their study time and monitor their own progress.

Over time, experienced teachers develop unit plans and supporting materials that can be reused. However, most beginning teachers will have to rely on textbooks and curriculum guides. There is nothing wrong with doing this, and the beginning teacher should not feel guilty about it. Most curriculum guides have been developed by experienced teachers, and even though their approach to subjects cannot be expected to fit the preferences of an individual teacher, they do provide a helpful overall design to follow.

Two notes of caution are worth mentioning, however. First, some beginning teachers, particularly in middle schools and high schools, rely heavily on their college textbooks or the course and unit plans of their college instructors. These plans and materials are always inappropriate for younger learners, who are not ready for the advanced content found in college courses. Second, there are teachers who, after several years of experience, still rely on textbooks for planning and sequencing their instruction. Teaching and learning are creative, evolutionary processes that should be keyed to a particular group of students at a particular point in time. Only when this is done can lessons rise above the humdrum and provide intellectual excitement to students.

YEARLY PLANS

Yearly plans are also critical but, because of the uncertainty and complexity in most schools, cannot be done with as much precision as daily or unit plans. The effectiveness of yearly plans generally revolves around how well they deal with the following three features:

Overall Themes and Attitudes. Most teachers have some global attitudes, goals, and themes they would like to leave with their students. Perhaps a teacher in a mixed-race elementary classroom would like his or her students to end the term with a bit less bias or misunderstanding and a bit more tolerance of people who are racially different. No specific lesson or unit can teach this attitude, but many carefully planned and coordinated experiences throughout the year can. Or perhaps a high school biology teacher would like students to understand and embrace a set of attitudes associated with scientific methods. A single lesson on the scientific method will not accomplish this goal. However, personal modeling and formal demonstrations showing respect for data, the relationships between theory and reality, or the process of making inferences from information can eventually influence students to think more scientifically. As a last example, a history teacher may want students to leave his or her class with an appreciation of the very long time frame associated with the development of democratic traditions. Again, a single lesson on the Magna Carta, the Constitution, or the Fourteenth Amendment will not develop this appreciation. However, building a succession of lessons that come back to a common theme on the "cornerstones of democracy" can achieve this end.

Coverage. There are few teachers who run out of things to do. Instead, the common lament is that time runs out with many important lessons still to be taught. Experienced teachers carry many of their yearlong plans in their heads. Beginning teachers, however, will have to take care to develop yearlong plans if they want to get past the Civil War by March. Planning to cover desired topics requires asking what is really important to teach, deciding on priorities, and attending carefully to the instructional hours actually available over a year's time. In most instances teachers strive to teach too much, too lightly. Students may be better served if a reduced menu is planned. In short, most beginning teachers overestimate how much time is actually available for instruction and underestimate the amount of time it takes to teach something well. Careful planning can help minimize this error in judgment.

Cycles of the School Year. Experienced teachers know that the school year is cyclical, and that some topics are better taught at one time than another. School cycles and corresponding emotional or psychological states revolve around the opening and closing of school, the days of the week, vacation periods, the changes of season, holidays, and important school events. Some of these can be anticipated; some cannot. Nonetheless, it is important to plan for school cycles as much as possible. Experienced teachers know that new units or important topics are not introduced on Friday or the day before a holiday break. They know that the opening of school should emphasize processes and structures to facilitate student learning later in the year. They know that the end of the school year will be filled

with interruptions and decreasing motivation as students anticipate summer vacation. They also know that it is unwise to plan for a unit examination the night after a big game or the hour following the Halloween party.

As beginning teachers you know something about these cycles and corresponding psychological states from your own student days. You can use this information, along with information provided by experienced teachers in a school, as you proceed with making long-range, yearly plans.

TIMETABLING TECHNIQUES TO ASSIST UNIT AND YEARLY PLANNING

There are several techniques for assisting beginning teachers in making clear and "doable" instructional plans that go over several days or weeks or where many specific, independent tasks must be completed prior to moving on. One such technique is **timetabling.** A timetable is a chronological map of a series of instructional activities, or of some special project, the teacher may want to carry out. It describes the overall direction of activities and any special products which may be produced within a time frame. The most straightforward timetabling technique consists of constructing a special chart called a Gantt chart. A **Gantt chart** allows you to see the work pieces in relation to each other—when each starts and finishes. Two Gantt charts, one devised by a social studies teacher to plan a semester's study in American government and the second constructed by an elementary teacher for planning the logistics of a field trip to a local museum, are shown in Figures 2-5 and 2-6.

There are many formats for making timetables. Some teachers believe in evolving processes and prefer a more open and nonspecific approach. Others prefer just the opposite and write everything down in great detail. One's own personal philosophy and work style influence the exact approach and level of detail required. Regardless of the extent to which you choose to make timetables a part of your planning, it is at least important to consider their use because they help planners recognize the limits of a very important and scarce resource— time. Aids at the end of the chapter are provided to help you practice timetabling techniques and consider them in more detail. Chapter 3 returns to the

Figure 2-5 Gantt chart, social studies

TASK	TIME								
	SEPT	OCT	NOV	DEC	JAN	FEB	MAR	APRIL	MAY
Background to Settlement	xx●								
The Colonial Era	xxxx●								
The Revolutionary War	xxxx●								
Constitutional Deliberations	xxxxxxxx●●								
The Early Republic	xxxxx●								
The Civil War	xxxxxxxx●								
● Unit exams									
●● Midterm exams									

topic of time and the importance of using it effectively.

Choosing Curriculum Content

Another important domain of teacher planning is the way decisions are made about the content of instruction. The curriculum in most elementary and secondary schools is currently organized around the academic disciplines (history, biology, mathematics, and so forth) used by scholars to organize information about the social and physical world. And even though some curriculum reformers have repeatedly argued that this is an inappropriate way to organize content for young people, the current structures are likely to remain for some time. Consequently, an important planning task for teachers will continue to be choosing the most appropriate content from the various subject matter areas for a particular group of students. This is no small feat

Figure 2-6 Gantt chart, museum trip

TASK	TIME			
	MAR 10–15	MAR 18–23	MAR 26–31	APRIL 3–7
Call museum director	xx			
Talk to principal	xx			
Request bus for field trip	xx			
Introduce unit on art history	xxxxxxx			
Prepare field trip permission slips	xx			
Send permission slips home		xx		
Require slips to be returned			xx	
Teach unit on art history	xxxxxxxxxxxxxxxxxxxxxxxx			
Go over logistics of field trip				xxxxxxx
Discuss what to look for on trip				xxxx
Take trip				x
Follow-up trip in class				xxxx
Write thank-you letters				xxx

because there is already much more to teach on any topic than time allows and new knowledge is being produced every day. Consequently, most schools assume that beginning teachers, by themselves, cannot make major content decisions but that they should be guided by textbooks and curriculum guides. Thus content decisions are normally made by experienced teachers and curriculum specialists long before the student teacher, or first-year teacher, steps into a classroom. When textbooks have been carefully selected and curriculum guides planned and prepared with wisdom, they provide excellent tools for the beginning teacher to use. The experts who prepare these materials have taken considerable time to ask what should be taught and how various topics should be sequenced over time—both over the course of a year and over several years. The job of beginning teachers becomes mainly that of making sure they understand the scope and sequence of this content and finding ways to interpret and teach it effectively to a particular group of students, adding and deleting material as needed.

However, some beginning teachers may find themselves facing the time-consuming task of having to select content. For instance, textbooks in some schools may be out of date in terms of the new knowledge that beginning teachers have learned in college. If this is true, then it is the beginning teachers' responsibility to plan ways to incorporate that knowledge into their lessons. Adding new knowledge normally requires taking something else out of the already crowded curriculum.

A beginning teacher may also find instances where curriculum guides do not exist, or if they do, consist only of a brief list of topics. Again, when a beginning teacher faces this situation, content decisions will have to be made without much assistance and will require considerable understanding of the subject matter and of how students at a particular age level learn. Three ideas and tools can provide assistance in making content decisions.

KNOWLEDGE STRUCTURES

In every field there is much more to learn than it is possible to master in a single year, or even a lifetime. Teachers must choose content based on the basic ideas and **structures of knowledge** for a par-

Figure 2-7   Hypothetical knowledge structure

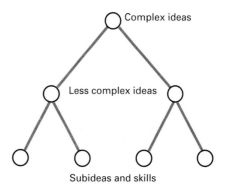

ticular field, taking into account, of course, their students' prior knowledge and abilities. In all fields of knowledge advanced concepts and understandings are built more or less pyramid fashion on simpler ones, as illustrated in Figure 2-7.

Notice in Figure 2-7 how information is divided into more complex and abstract ideas and into simpler, less complex concepts and skills. Notice also that relationships exist among various subsets of ideas and understandings. We will discuss knowledge structures in more detail in later chapters.

BEHAVIORAL CONTENT MATRIX

Taxonomies such as those developed by Bloom and his colleagues help teachers choose from among an array of possible instructional objectives for any particular unit or course. A list of instructional objectives, however, needs to be operationalized into content the teacher wishes to emphasize and the expected behaviors (specific and general) of his or her students. The **behavioral content matrix** is a planning tool that has been developed to help integrate objectives, student behaviors, and course content. Like the taxonomies, the behavioral content matrix has value for lesson planning and, in a slightly revised format, for student evaluation. Table 2-8 is an example of a behavioral content matrix developed by a health teacher for a unit on nutrition.

Making a behavioral content matrix like the one illustrated in Table 2-8 is a rather straightforward process. In this instance, the teacher has placed the categories of the cognitive domain along the top of

Table 2-8 A Sample Behavioral Content Matrix for a Unit on Nutrition

CONTENT/TOPICS	STUDENT BEHAVIORS							
	KNOWLEDGE		COMPREHENSION PRINCIPLES	APPLICATION PRINCIPLES	ANALYSIS	SYNTHESIS	EVALUATION	TOTAL OBJECTIVES
	TERMS	FACTS						
Basic food components	2		1					3
The balanced diet			1	1		1	1	4
Four food group plan	1				1			2
Dietary deficiencies	1		1		1			3
Special needs		1	1					2
Making changes					1	1	1	3
Total objectives	4	1	4	1	3	2	2	17

the matrix. Other domains could have been included. Running along the left side of the matrix is a list of the important topics the teacher wants to emphasize in this unit on nutrition. The numbers within the matrix represent the number of objectives the teachers has deemed desirable for each of the topics and in relation to the various levels of cognitive processes. Building a behavioral content matrix during the planning phase of a unit of work or a course of study takes time. However, it ensures well-balanced instruction. Like learning to use any other tools, practice and familiarity lead quickly to increased proficiency.

CONGRUENCE WITH TESTS

A third guide for choosing content is to base it on the type of test students will be expected to perform well on. Berliner (1982a) notes that "students may learn what they are given to learn, and *rarely* learn what they are not given to learn" (p. 202). The point here is obvious. If a teacher or school system plans to test students on certain information, it is only logical that content decisions be based on the body of knowledge to be covered on the tests. Sometimes this is not done, however. To illustrate this problem of matching content with tests, look at the information in Figure 2-8 adapted by Berliner (1982a) from

research done by Freeman et al. (1980) at Michigan State University. Note a lack of congruence between the content of selected achievement tests and that of the textbooks being used by teachers in this particular instance.

Choosing Activity Structures

Activity structures are those patterns of behavior that characterize what teachers do as they teach and what students do as they engage in learning tasks. These patterns of behavior can range from specific steps or phases associated with a particular lesson (described in some detail in Chapters 8 through 13) to the overall patterns that characterize a particular classroom, teacher, or group of students. Activity structures also consist of planning decisions associated with large- or small-group instruction, use of films or microcomputers, reading circles, cooperative learning groups, individual seatwork, or silent reading.

Yinger (1980) observed from his research that activities are "the basic structural units of planning and action in the classroom" and that nearly "all classroom action and interaction occurred during activities; the remaining time was used for preparing for activities or making transitions between activities" (p. 111). The research described previously

Figure 2-8   Congruence between what is tested and what is taught

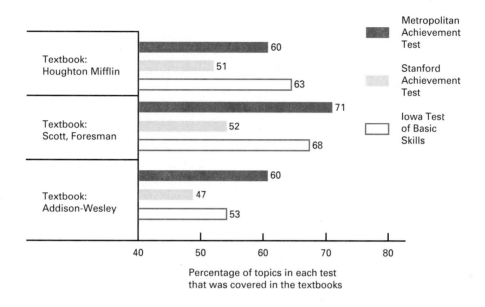

Percentage of topics in each test
that was covered in the textbooks

SOURCE: From D. C. Berliner (1982a), Recognizing instructional variables. In D. E. Orlosky (ed.), Introduction to Education. Columbus, Ohio: Charles E. Merrill. Used with permission.

showed how experienced teachers spend considerable time planning for this domain of instruction. It is likely that these planning tasks do more than anything else to establish the climate in a particular classroom. Important activity structures for beginning teachers to think about include activities that accomplish routines, build group cohesion and morale, and provide appropriate sequence and variety for accomplishing instructional tasks. Each of these is described briefly here and revisited later in a different context and in more detail.

ACTIVITIES TO ESTABLISH ROUTINES

In both elementary and secondary classrooms teachers and students are expected to perform certain housekeeping activities such as taking attendance; keeping the classroom space safe and livable; making assignments; collecting papers; and distributing or storing books, equipment, and the like. Even if teacher aides have been employed to assist with many of these tasks, they still require careful planning by the teacher. Experienced teachers plan housekeeping tasks so thoroughly and efficiently that the naive observer may not even notice they are

occurring. A beginning teacher who has not planned efficient ways to accomplish housekeeping routines will suffer from ongoing confusion and wasted instructional time. From experience and from observing effective teachers, the following planning guidelines for routines are provided for beginning teachers:

Guideline 1:   Make sure detailed written plans exist for taking roll, giving assignments, collecting and distributing papers, and storing books and equipment.

Guideline 2:   Distribute these written plans and procedures to students the first time a housekeeping activity occurs in a particular year or with a particular class.

Guideline 3:   Post copies of the housekeeping plans on the bulletin board or on chart paper to serve as public reminders about how particular activities are to be carried out.

Guideline 4:   Train student helpers immediately to provide leadership and assistance in carrying out routines. Students at all ages can and like to be in charge of taking roll, picking up books, getting and setting up the movie projector, and the like.

Guideline 5:   Follow the plan that has been developed consistently, and make sure that plenty of time exists to carry out each activity, particularly early in the year.

Guideline 6:   Be alert to ways housekeeping activities can become more efficient and seek feedback about how students think the housekeeping activities are going.

ACTIVITIES TO ESTABLISH GROUP MORALE AND COHESION

Good teachers who work with classes of students at any age (3-year-olds to adults) recognize the need to plan some classroom activities whose objectives are not to increase student learning but to build the morale and cohesion of the classroom group itself. In elementary schools favorite activities consist of weekly or daily meetings in which students share their reactions about what is going on in the class, reading parts of a favorite story after lunch each day, or taking a morning break to talk informally with friends. Parties in celebration of holidays and birthdays are also used to build group cohesion.

In high schools and with older students, this task becomes a bit more difficult, but it is just as important. Taking a break to tell a joke or to recognize a particular student's accomplishment outside of class is one technique effective high school teachers use. Devoting periods of time for students to get to know one another or to plan for the next unit of instruction is another. Regardless of the activity, group morale and cohesion affect classroom behavior, attitudes, and achievement. Developing a cohesive group requires every bit as much planning as any other classroom activity. In fact, these kinds of activities are known to get out of hand rather quickly in beginning teachers' classrooms if appropriate planning has not taken place. Some beginning teachers, report that they were ready to quit teaching after their first Halloween party.

ACTIVITIES TO SEQUENCE INSTRUCTION AND TO PRODUCE VARIETY

Other activity structures teachers must attend to are those that provide overall sequence and choreography to instructional events. These activities often present beginning teachers with the most trouble. Planning for sequence deals with how instructional activities begin, develop, and end. When planning is done well, events flow smoothly from one phase or step to another. To the novice observer and to students themselves, the transitions are hardly noticeable. Experience gradually provides teachers with a sense of how much to cover and how quickly, how to start a lesson and end it, and how to modify it if things are not going as planned. In the beginning, however, there is no substitute for careful planning.

Maintaining variety in instruction, as in life, is the spice that makes things interesting. The effective teacher is one who plans for variety. Instructional models are varied from day to day, just as are the activities associated with homework and group work. Daily and unit plans are designed to include a mixture of teacher talk, student talk, large- and small-group work, reading, working with computers, and using games and simulations. The variety that can be provided by beginning teachers depends upon their repertoire of teaching models and techniques.

SUMMARY

- Planning and making decisions about instruction are among the most important aspects of teaching because they are major determinants of what is taught in schools and how it is taught.
- It is sometimes difficult to learn planning skills from experienced teachers because most of their planning activities are hidden from public view.
- The traditional perspective of planning is based on rational-linear models characterized by setting goals and taking specific actions to accomplish desired outcomes. The knowledge base suggests that teacher planning and decision making do not always conform to rational-linear planning models. Newer perspectives on planning put more emphasis on planners' actions and reflections.
- Studies have shown that planning has consequences for both student learning and classroom behavior. It can enhance student motivation, help focus student learning, and decrease classroom management problems. Planning can

have unanticipated negative effects as well; for example, it can limit self-initiated learning on the part of students and make teachers insensitive to student ideas.

- Experienced teachers and beginning teachers have different planning approaches and needs. Experienced teachers are more concerned with establishing structures ahead of time to guide classroom activities and plan ahead for the adaptations needed as lessons get under way. In general, beginning teachers need more detailed plans than do experienced teachers. They devote more of their planning to the verbal instructions to be given and respond more often to student interests.

- Teacher planning is multifaceted but relates to three phases of teaching: the preinstructional phase, in which decisions are made about what will be taught and for how long; the instructional phase, in which decisions are made about questions to ask, wait time, and specific orientations; and the postinstructional phase, in which decisions are made about how to evaluate student progress and what type of feedback to provide.

- Planning cycles include not only daily plans but also plans for each week, month, and year. The details of these various plans differ, however. Plans carried out on a particular day are influenced by what has happened before and will in turn influence future plans.

- Specific tools to assist with teacher planning consist of instructional objectives, lesson plans, taxonomies, behavioral content matrices, and timetabling techniques.

- Instructional objectives are statements which describe the student changes that should result from instruction. They can be written in behavioral or more general forms. A good behavioral objective includes statements about expected student behavior, the testing situation in which the behavior will be observed, and performance criteria. An objective written in the more general form communicates the teacher's overall intent but lacks the precision of a behavioral objective.

- Taxonomies are devices which help classify and show relationships between things. Bloom's taxonomy, which is the most widely used device in the field, classifies objectives in three important

domains: the cognitive, the affective, and the psychomotor.

- Formats for lesson plans can vary, but in general a good plan includes a clear statement of objectives, a sequence of learning activities, and a means of evaluating student learning.

- Timetabling techniques, such as making a chronological map of a series of instructional activities, can assist with long-range planning tasks.

- The behavioral content matrix is a planning tool for helping teachers integrate their instructional objectives, course content, and expectations for student learning.

- Critical aspects of planning include choosing content, selecting activities, establishing routines, and building group morale and cohesion.

- Effective teachers know how to make good formal plans. They have also learned how to make adjustments when plans prove to be inappropriate or ineffective.

KEY TERMS

rational-linear planning model
nonlinear planning model
preinstructional phase
interactive instruction
postinstructional planning
planning cycles
instructional objectives
behavioral objectives
testing situation
performance criteria
taxonomies
cognitive domain
affective domain
psychomotor domain
lesson plans
timetabling
Gantt chart
structures of knowledge
behavioral content matrix
activity structures

BOOKS FOR THE PROFESSIONAL

Beane, J. A., Toepfer, C. F., and Alesi, S. J. (1986). *Curriculum planning and development.* Newton, Mass.: Allyn and Bacon. This book provides a thorough explication of the many issues and problems associated with curriculum planning and how curriculum planning can be applied in classrooms and schools.

Gardner, H. (1983). *Frames of mind*. New York: Basic Books. This is the initial book to spell out the author's theory of multiple intelligence. An understanding of Gardner's ideas and theories is essential to effective teacher thinking and planning.

Gardner, H. (1985). *The mind's new science*. New York: Basic Books. This book explores the history and foundations of the cognitive sciences. Although not written specifically for teachers, it is highly readable and applicable.

Gardner, H. (1991). *The unschooled mind: How children think and how schools should teach*. New York: Basic Books. Gardner's attempt to provide specific advice to educators based on his theoretical work.

Gronlund, N. E., and Linn, R. L. (1990). *Measurement and evaluation in teaching* (6th ed.). New York: Macmillan. The most thorough treatment available on issues related to classroom measurement and evaluation. Filled with practical advice and tools for teachers to assist with both planning and evaluation tasks.

Lerup, L. (1977). *Building the unfinished: Architecture and human action*. Beverly Hills, Calif.: Sage Publications. Written by an architect, this book is not about teaching. It does, however, explore clearly and precisely the interaction between people and their environments and the impact of planning on this process. With examples from studies of fishing villages in Scandinavia and student housing at Berkeley, Lerup shows how planning processes, if they are to serve people, must be conceived as cyclical and interactive and remain open with a touch of the unfinished.

Mager, R. F. (1984). *Preparing instructional objectives* (2d rev. ed.). Palo Alto, Calif.: D. S. Lake. This book, now a classic, makes a strong case for instructional objectives and tells why they should be stated clearly and precisely. It provides detailed instructions on how to become proficient in writing objectives.

Posner, G. J., and Rudnitsky, A. N. (1986). *Course design: A guide to curriculum development for teachers* (3d ed.). New York: Longman. This book provides many excellent examples and step-by-step instructions for course design and unit planning.

LEARNING AIDS FOR PLANNING, OBSERVATION, AND REFLECTION

- Assessing My Planning Skills

- Writing Objectives

- Constructing a Behavioral Content Matrix

- Timetabling Techniques

- Interviewing Teachers about In-Flight Decision Making

- Observing Lesson Activities and Segments

ASSESSING MY PLANNING SKILLS

PURPOSE: To help you assess your level of understanding and skill in various aspects of planning.

DIRECTIONS: Check the level of understanding or skill you perceive you have for the various concepts and teaching tasks associated with planning for instruction.

UNDERSTANDING OR SKILL	LEVEL OF UNDERSTANDING OR SKILL		
	HIGH	MEDIUM	LOW
My understanding of			
Perspective on planning	_____	_____	_____
Consequences of planning	_____	_____	_____
Planning domains and cycles	_____	_____	_____
Role of instructional objectives	_____	_____	_____
Taxonomies of instructional objectives	_____	_____	_____
My ability to			
Write instructional objectives	_____	_____	_____
Construct daily lesson plans	_____	_____	_____
Construct unit plans	_____	_____	_____
Construct yearly plans	_____	_____	_____
Make a Gantt chart	_____	_____	_____
Make a behavior content matrix	_____	_____	_____
Plan for routines	_____	_____	_____
Plan to establish morale and cohesion	_____	_____	_____
Plan to provide variety	_____	_____	_____

WRITING OBJECTIVES

PURPOSE: Even though objectives are not always written by experienced teachers, they are still an important aspect of teaching practice. Beginners may need to focus their lessons more carefully than experts. For this reason, you must gain facility in writing objectives. This aid will give you practice in writing and evaluating objectives.

DIRECTIONS: Write ten objectives for your grade level or subject area. Evaluate them using the guide below.

1. _____
_____

2. _____
_____

3. _____
_____

4. _____
_____

5. _____
_____

6. _____
_____

7. _____
_____

8. _____
_____

9. _____
_____

10. _____
_____

Rate each objective good, fair, or poor according to how well it (1) defines the student behavior, (2) prescribes the testing situation, (3) sets the performance criteria.

	OBJECTIVE NUMBER									
	1	2	3	4	5	6	7	8	9	10
Student behavior										
Testing situation										
Performance criteria										

Analysis and Reflection: Now revise each objective as needed. Was there any aspect of objective writing that was especially difficult? What was it? How could you make it easier?

CONSTRUCTING A BEHAVIORAL CONTENT MATRIX

PURPOSE: A question that confronts all teachers is how to choose what to teach. The behavioral content matrix is one device developed to assist with this important task. This tool has been designed to give you practice with making a behavioral content matrix.

DIRECTIONS: Select a unit from a curriculum guide in your subject area or perhaps two or three chapters from a textbook that you might use. If you have previously developed a unit of work on your own, you may wish to use it. Using the table below, place in the left-hand column the major content or topics you choose to emphasize. The various categories of student understanding and cognitive processing have been listed along the top of the table. You will notice it follows Bloom's taxonomy in the cognitive domain. After you have listed the major topics, make decisions about how many objectives you might allocate among the topics and the various levels of understanding.

Unit of work covered: _____

Anticipated time: _____

Student Behaviors

| TOPICS/CONTENT | KNOWS/RECALL OF | | | HIGHER LEVEL | | |
	TERMS	FACTS	PRINCIPLES	COMPREHENSION	APPLICATION/ SYNTHESIS	EVALUATION

TIMETABLING TECHNIQUES

PURPOSE: Gantt charts can be very helpful time management devices. This aid is to assist you in gaining facility in using Gantt charts.

DIRECTIONS: Use the guidelines below to plan three different kinds of activities: getting ready for school or work, writing a paper, and arranging a field trip.

1. Think about each activity you must do to get ready for school or work each day. List each activity along the left side of the chart below. Then draw a line horizontally from the beginning to ending time of each activity.

ACTIVITY	6:00	6:15	6:30	6:45	7:00	7:15	7:30	7:45	8:00	8:15	8:30

2. Think about all the tasks that need to be done when you are writing a paper for a class. This time, make your own chart. Again, list the activities on the left. Then decide if your time demarcations should be days, weeks, or months and draw a line between the beginning and ending times for each activity.
3. Finally, think about all the things that would need to be done if you were planning a field trip for a class you were teaching. Make your own chart, list the activities, and mark the beginning and ending times for each activity.

Analysis and Reflection: Do you notice any patterns in the way you plan? Are there ways you can facilitate your own planning? For example, are you able to plan efficiently in snatches of time on the subway, waiting in the doctor's office, or waiting for the kettle to boil? Or do you need to set aside a quantity of time and arrange for peace and quiet in order to get your planning done? Write a paragraph on your planning style.

INTERVIEWING TEACHERS ABOUT IN-FLIGHT DECISION MAKING

PURPOSE: Not all planning and decision making can be slow and deliberate. Some must happen on the spur of the moment, in the midst of a lesson. This aid is to assist you in understanding this type of decision making.

DIRECTIONS: Observe a lesson and interview the teacher as soon as possible about it. Ask the questions in the order shown on the flowchart. You will need another piece of paper to note the teacher's answers.

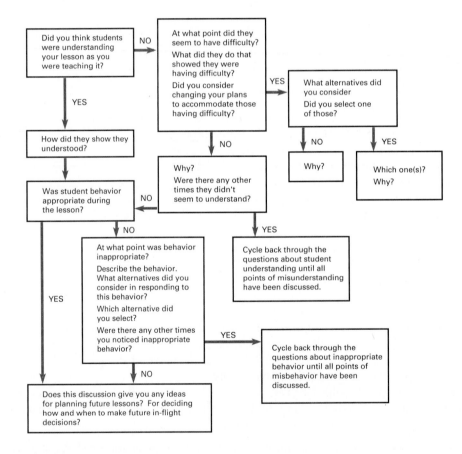

SOURCE: Adapted from P. H. Winne and R. W. Marx, Students' and teachers' views of thinking processes for classroom learning, *Elementary School Journal, 82* (1980), p. 499. Copyright© 1982, by the University of Chicago Press. Used with permission.

OBSERVING LESSON ACTIVITIES AND SEGMENTS

PURPOSE: Activity structures, or lesson segments, form the basic structural units of a lesson. Becoming sensitive to these structures will assist you in your own planning. The purpose of this aid is to help you uncover the internal structure of an experienced teacher's lesson.

DIRECTIONS: Each time the teacher begins a new lesson segment, record the time the segment begins and the type of activity that occurs during that segment. You may see activities like "lecturing," "checking for understanding," "conducting a discussion," "giving an exam," "demonstrating"; you may see other activities. Also note the teacher's transition statements and/or actions.

TIME	ACTIVITY	TRANSITION STATEMENT/ACTION

Analysis and Reflection: Figure the amount of time the teacher spent on each segment and each type of activity. Which activities took more time? Which took less? Which transition statements and actions were the most common? Which seemed to work the best?

CHAPTER 3

Time and Space

Virginia Richardson, University of Arizona

O ne aspect of teacher leadership is the allocation and management of scarce resources to create productive learning environments. But what resources does a teacher have control over? States and school districts are mandating objectives and curricula, principals make decisions about which students should be in which classes, and textbook decisions are made by school district or state-level textbook committees. The furniture is already in the classroom, and unless the teacher is in an open-space school, the size of the classroom is fixed.

It turns out that the most important resource a teacher controls is *time:* not only how much time to spend on a particular subject, but how to manage and focus students' time on academic issues in general. Another important resource is the classroom *space:* how to move around in it; where to place students, materials, and desks; and how to create an ambience for learning.

The management of classroom time is extremely complex. It requires knowledge of the curriculum, of learning principles, of individual students in the classroom, and of good management practices. Above all, it requires a commitment to cover specific academic topics and a belief that students can learn.

Whereas the research base on the management of time is quite well developed, much less is known about the management of space. Consequently, when considering the use of classroom space it is important to remain flexible regarding the placement of desks and tables and the grouping of students. However, it is difficult, given the research base, to predict how decisions regarding these matters will affect student behavior and learning. Although some principles emerge, it is also the case that effective teachers often experiment with desk placement and space arrangements. Management of these important resources is the focus of this chapter.

PERSPECTIVE AND RATIONALE

Time is clearly important to classroom teachers, just as it is to all workers. Some workers look upon time as something to get through: "I can't wait till quitting time." For most professionals, however, it is a commodity that is scarce and in high demand: "If only I had more time."

In teaching, time can be seen as a critical resource that, in combination with other resources, produces student learning. There are more and less efficient ways of using time, and more and less effective ways as well. It is one thing to efficiently race through a topic in as little time as possible, but if students do not learn, this coverage is not effective. This suggests that some particular *amount* of time spent on a topic in combination with an *effective use* of that time will maximize student learning.

Current interest in the nature of classroom time began with the publication of an article by John B. Carroll (1963) called "A Model of School Learning." In his model, Carroll posited that student learning, or "degree of learning," is a function of five factors. Three of the factors are related to the student:

1. *Aptitude,* or the amount of time it takes a student to learn a task under optimal conditions
2. *Ability* to understand instruction
3. *Perseverance,* or the amount of time the student is willing to remain actively engaged in learning

In addition, two elements are external to the student:

4. *Quality of instruction*
5. *Opportunity* time allowed for learning

Carroll mentioned three types of time in his model: time needed, time allowed, and time spent. Carroll (1978) later elaborated on his model to provide a fuller picture of time and the learning process. His complete model is shown in Figure 3-1.

Carroll explained that quality of instruction depends on the clarity with which task demands are communicated, how adequately tasks are presented, how adequately the subtasks are sequenced and paced, and how well student needs and characteristics are accounted for. His model also suggests that perseverance is not just an individual student trait but can be altered by the teacher and instructional quality. In other words, students can be motivated to persevere longer.

One of the most difficult problems faced by teachers is how much time is "needed." As Figure 3-1 shows, this depends upon knowledge of students' abilities and aptitudes as well as the particular learning task. As Carroll's model makes obvious, a teacher's use of time is not the simplistic matter that some might think it is.

The arrangement of *space* and other resources is not a simple matter either. Consider, for example, how a teacher might conduct a discussion with students. The teacher and students could be arranged in a circle that permits equal communication between all parties or, as is more usual, the students could be arranged in straight rows with all information directed to and from a central figure (the teacher).

In the latter arrangement, the discussion does not occur among participants, but between the participants and the teacher. The way space is designed influences both communication patterns and power relationships among teachers and students. Power relationships are important because they may affect the degree to which students take ownership of the content and become independent learners.

Arrangements of students, desks, and chairs not only help determine classroom communication patterns and interpersonal relationships but also influence a variety of daily decisions teachers must make concerning how scarce resources are managed and used. These are not easy choices. Fortunately, a substantial body of research can provide guidelines for beginning teachers as they think about these decisions.

SAMPLING THE KNOWLEDGE BASE

Research on Time

Research has been conducted on the way teachers manage their students' use of classroom time and also their own personal time across many different professional activities. This chapter focuses specifically on teachers' use of classroom time. Other aspects of teachers' use of time, such as time on school activities, are described in Chapter 14.

DIFFERENT TYPES OF TIME

The Carroll model described above is a compelling way of thinking about effective instruction. It was a way of organizing his thinking after years of scholarly involvement in educational psychology. During the 1970s several researchers began to test Carroll's model using a number of different concepts of time, which included:

1. **Planned time:** When teachers fill in plan books, they set aside a certain amount of time for the different subjects and activities. This is called planned time.

Figure 3-1 Carroll's model of school learning

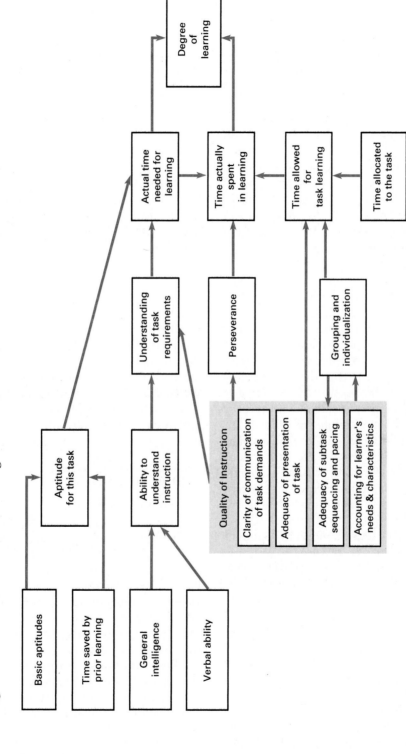

SOURCE: From A. Harnischseger and D. Wiley (1978), Model of school learning, *Journal of Curriculum Studies*, p. 216.

Figure 3-2 The relationship among four types of classroom time

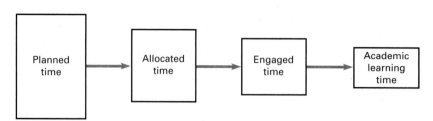

2. **Allocated time:** The amount of time the teacher actually spends on a particular subject, task, or activity in the classroom is called allocated time. This is also called **opportunity to learn** and is measured in terms of the amount of time teachers have their students spend on a given academic task.

3. **Engaged time:** The amount of time students actually spend on an activity or task is called engaged time (also called **time on task**). This type of time is measured in terms of on-task and off-task behavior. If a teacher has allocated time to seatwork on math problems, and the student is working on these problems, the student's behavior is on task. Conversely, if the student is doodling, or talking about football with another student, the behavior is counted as off task.

4. **Academic learning time (ALT):** The amount of time a student spends engaged in a task at which he or she is successful is called academic learning time. As described below, this concept is the one most closely related to student learning (Fisher et al., 1980).

5. **Time needed:** The time an individual student actually needs to master a task is called time needed. This feature of time is usually determined on the basis of ability and aptitude.

These concepts of time are all different and yield different results in their measurement. In general, the time decreases in moving from planned time to academic learning time. This is depicted in Figure 3-2. For example, suppose a teacher plans 40 minutes for a math lesson, but an observer notes that the transition from reading to math takes 5 minutes. Further, suppose several discipline problems reduce the amount of time another 5 minutes, while loudspeaker announcements and lunch money collection account for another 8 minutes. Al-

located time is, therefore, 23 minutes as contrasted to the 40 minutes of planned time. Further, assume the observer notes that the students are quite restless. During their seatwork assignments they talk and giggle with their fellow students while the teacher is working with individual students. In addition, a number of students are not paying attention when the teacher is explaining new material on the board. The average engaged time for the students thus becomes only 12 minutes. Further, a number of students really need a full hour for this particular task in order to master it. One could predict, then, that a large number of students will not master the task. Equally problematic is a situation in which the teacher allocates time to a topic that the students have already mastered. Time is valuable, and unnecessarily repeating material means that other important topics are not covered.

RELATIONSHIP BETWEEN TIME AND ACHIEVEMENT

Several important studies in the 1970s investigated the relationships between various aspects of time and student learning. Is student learning related to the amount of time allocated to a task, or the amount of time students are engaged on task, or both? The answer in most studies of regular classroom teaching was both. The more time teachers allocate to a particular academic topic and the more students are engaged in that topic, the more they will learn about it.

Researchers also learned from the various time studies that there was considerable variation from teacher to teacher in the amount of allocated time given to different subject areas. Even in those school districts where the amounts of time teachers were supposed to devote to math and reading were prescribed, the variation in allocated time from classroom to classroom was extreme. The time studies discovered that the engaged time varied from classroom to classroom even when allocated time was the same. Some of this variation was related to the teachers' classroom management skills and to the types of students found in the different classrooms.

In the late 1960s and early 1970s, a major program was initiated at the federal level. This program, called Project Headstart, supplied school districts with funds to develop early childhood programs for disadvantaged children. Despite the social and academic gains made in these Headstart classrooms, researchers soon found that the Headstart children lost many of their initial gains once they entered a regular classroom environment. Therefore, Project Follow Through was developed to supply funds for ongoing special services to the same group of disadvantaged students for whom Headstart had been designed. Project Follow Through consisted of a number of programs developed from theories of how children, particularly low-socioeconomic-status children, learn. These programs ranged from highly structured, basic-skills orientations to open-classroom and independent learning approaches. An individual school could choose to implement one of several approaches offered.

Given the amount of federal money provided for these programs, legislators soon inquired as to whether they were working. If so, which of the programs was working best, and which aspects of the programs seemed to be the most effective in raising student achievement? The second of these two questions was tackled in a study by Stallings and Kaskowitz (1974).

The study involved 108 first-grade and 58 third-grade classrooms taught by teachers who were implementing one of seven approaches. Teachers were observed three times, and then selected students in those Follow Through classrooms were observed. Students were tested for learning gains in mathematics and reading. The analysis determined which of the seven approaches produced the strongest learning gains and which aspects of teaching across the seven approaches seemed to contribute the most to learning gains.

The approaches that emphasized structured learning of the basic skills produced the strongest learning gains. However, attendance in these classrooms was below average, as were students' self-concepts.

Many findings emerged from this study, but the most pronounced was that opportunity to learn (or allocated time) on academic content was strongly related to student achievement. In other words, no matter what specific approach was used, in classrooms where teachers spent the most time on academic work, student gains in reading and mathematics were the highest. Students who spent a lot of time on nonacademic activities, or who were expected to learn by themselves, gained less.

This study was extremely important in the time-on-task literature. First, the time variable was no longer a feature found only in laboratory studies about which one could speculate. It affected real classrooms across the United States. The sample was reasonably large, and the observation measure detailed and objective. It emphasized what many people felt they already knew: if you want to learn something, you have to spend time studying it.

This study was the first in a number of studies of this sort to suggest that student learning in mathematics and reading is dependent upon direct instruction in these subjects. A second study done a few years later by Barak Rosenshine (1980) pinpointed the need to think not only about the time teachers allocate for instruction but also about actual engaged time. While allocated time affects student learning, an even more important type of classroom time relates to whether or not students are engaged in the tasks. This important study is highlighted in Research Summary 3-1.

MAINTAINING HIGH ENGAGEMENT RATES

The Beginning Teacher Evaluation Study in California showed that in classrooms where the teachers allocated more time to a particular content area, the students learned more in that area; that engagement rate (the percentage of allocated time that students are engaged) is also related to student learning; and that students who perform tasks at a high success rate learn more than those who perform at a low success rate. Finally, researchers determined that five teaching functions were important in promoting high academic learning time: diagnosis, prescription, presentation, monitoring, and feedback. These functions are displayed in Figure 3-3.

RESEARCH SUMMARY 3-1

Rosenshine, B.   (1980). How time is spent in elementary classrooms. In C. Denham and A. Lieberman (eds.), *Time to learn.* Washington, D.C.: U.S. Department of Education.

PROBLEM: Given the relationship of allocated and engaged time to student learning, how much time do elementary teachers spend in teaching reading and mathematics, the two basic skills that are of most interest to parents and others? And what do teachers do with the rest of their time? Barak Rosenshine analyzed a data base from an important study conducted in the state of California called the Beginning Teacher Evaluation Study. He looked specifically at the time variable from each of the classrooms in the study.

SAMPLE AND SETTING: One phase of the Beginning Teacher Evaluation Study involved 25 second-grade and 25 fifth-grade teachers in schools located in urban, suburban, and rural school districts. These teachers were identified as more or less effective on the basis of how much their students learned in reading and mathematics during the school year. In each classroom three male and three female students were selected for intensive observation.

PROCEDURES: The teachers were intensively observed for a period of weeks, as were their six students. In addition, the teachers kept logs of their time use, and they were interviewed by the researchers. Rosenshine analyzed information on the average amounts of time teachers allocated to reading, mathematics, and other subjects, and the amounts of time their students were engaged in these tasks.

TABLE 3-1   **Average Allocated Time per Day in Different Activities**

TIME CATEGORY	GRADE 2			GRADE 5		
	TIME PER DAY	COMBINED TIME	COMBINED PERCENTAGE	TIME PER DAY	COMBINED TIME	COMBINED PERCENTAGE
Academic activities		2h 12min.	57%	1h 50min.	2h 51min.	60%
Reading and language arts	1h 28min.			1h 50min.		
Mathematics	36min.			44min.		
Other academic	8min.			47min.		
Nonacademic activities	55min.	55min.	24%	1h 05min.	1h 05min.	23%
Noninstructional activities		44min.	19%		47min.	17%
Transition	34min.			34min.		
Wait	4min.			4min.		
Housekeeping	6min.			9min.		
Major in-class time	3h 51min.	3h 51min.		4h 44min.	4h 44min.	
Lunch, recess, breaks	1h 15min.	1h 15min.		1h 17min.	1h 17min.	
Length of school day	5h 06min.	5h 06min.		6h 00min.	6h 00min.	

SOURCE: Adapted from B. Rosenshine, (1980), p. 125.

FINDINGS: Table 3-1 gives the teachers' average allocated time per day in different activities in grades 2 and 5. The total allocated time on academic activities, including reading, mathematics, and such "other academic" subjects as science and social studies was 2 hours and 12 minutes in grade 2, and 2 hours and 51 minutes in grade 5. Time allocated to nonacademic pursuits that included art, music, physical education, flag salutes, sharing, and storytelling was 55 minutes in grade 2 and 1 hour and 5 minutes in grade 5. Noninstructional time took up 19 percent of the major in-class time in grade 2, and 17 percent in grade 5.

Teachers varied considerably on the amounts of time spent in reading and mathematics. Table 3-2 lists the allocated time, engaged minutes, and engagement rate of the three teachers in each grade who obtained the highest engaged time, the average for all teachers, and for the lowest three teachers. Note that there are considerable differences in engaged minutes between the highest and lowest three teachers. In the grade 2 sample, for example, some students were engaged 1 hour and 25 minutes in reading, and others, 43 minutes. There was more than an hour's difference in the combined engaged minutes in grade 5.

DISCUSSION AND IMPLICATIONS: Since the publication of this and similar studies, a number of programs have been developed to help teachers increase time on task. It is possible that if such a study were conducted today, the time on task would be considerably higher than it was in this study. Nonetheless, there are undoubtedly differences among teachers in engaged time. Given the relationship between engaged time and student learning, these differences are important. Students receiving the lesser amount of instruction are still expected to do well on the standardized tests given at the end of the year and are compared with students whose teachers maintain high engagement time. It therefore behooves teachers to maximize allocated time on academic subjects and to manage their classrooms so that the engagement rate is also high.

TABLE 3-2 Highest, Average, and Lowest Teachers in Academic Engaged Minutes

	READING			MATHEMATICS			TOTAL	
	ALLOCATED	ENGAGE-MENT RATIO	ENGAGED TIME	ALLOCATED TIME	ENGAGE-MENT RATIO	ENGAGED TIME	ALLOCATED TIME	ENGAGED TIME
				GRADE 2				
High 3	1h 45min.	81%	1h 25min.	35min.	82%	30min.	2h 20min.	1h 55min.
Average	1h 30min.	73%	1h 04min.	36min.	71%	26min.	2h 06min.	1h 30min.
Low 3	1h 00min.	72%	43min.	30min.	75%	22min.	1h 30min.	1h 05min.
				GRADE 5				
High 3	2h 10min.	80%	1h 45min.	53min.	86%	45min.	3h 03min.	2h 30min.
Average	1h 50min.	74%	1h 20min.	44min.	74%	35min.	2h 25min.	1h 55min.
Low 3	1h 25min.	63%	1h 05min.	38min.	63%	22min.	2h 03min.	1h 25min.

SOURCE: Adapted from B. Rosenshine (1980), p. 114.

Figure 3-3 Five instructional functions in the academic learning time model of classroom instruction

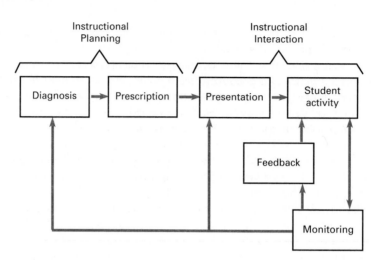

SOURCE: From Fisher et al. (1980), Teaching behavior, academic learning time, and student achievement: An overview. In C. Denham and A. Lieberman (eds.), *Time to learn*. Washington, D.C.: National Institute of Education, Department of Education, p. 10.

This type of active involvement may be particularly important for low-achieving students, although they may be the ones who receive it less. Stallings (1985) described a study that she and a colleague (Stallings and Robertson, 1979) conducted in high school mathematics classrooms. They found that teachers in general mathematics class provided less direct instruction or review of seatwork than did those in geometry and calculus classes. Further, the general math students were off task more than the geometry and calculus students. Stallings concluded that the low-achieving students need instruction from teachers to stay on task: "programmed workbooks will not help them learn the mathematical relationships necessary to cope in life" (p. 190).

The researchers found that although each of these functions that contribute to direct instruction and high ALT needed to be carried out well, they could be combined in various instructional approaches that were equally successful; no one method of instruction was found to be more effective than another. Effective teachers approached their tasks and functions in different ways, but they all approached them very well and managed to maintain their students' attention on the academic tasks at hand and to motivate them to persevere while working on these tasks.

EXTENDING LEARNING TIME: HOMEWORK

While there is a finite amount of time in the school day, teachers may extend the amount of time students spend on a topic by providing homework assignments. While some states and many school districts require teachers to provide homework, the research on its results is mixed. Recently, Harris Cooper (1989) reviewed the research on the effects of homework and found, among other things, that:

- The effect of homework on achievement was strongest for high school students, a little less strong but still positive for junior high students, and absent for upper elementary students.
- Homework related to the learning of simple tasks is more effective than that related to complex tasks.
- Homework's effects on standardized tests were similar to those on teacher-made tests.
- Homework that focused on preparation for new content or practice of old content was more ef-

fective than homework that related solely to the content of the present day's work.

This research suggests that while homework may be useful for some students at some grade levels, it should not be seen as a solution for the time pressures that teachers may feel during the school day. More complete quidelines for the use of homework will be provided later in this chapter.

Research on Space

The way space is managed has important cognitive and emotional effects on students. Although teachers do not control the amount of space provided, they have considerable leeway concerning its management.

PLACEMENT OF RESOURCES

In a classic study of classroom activities, Adams and Biddle (1970) found that in most lessons and at all grade levels there was a central group of actively participating students. The teachers talked to them and asked them questions; they responded and also asked questions and contributed to discussions. The others did not actively participate; they either withdrew, talked with neighbors, or worked.

It turned out that these active students were always located in one section of the classroom that was called the **action zone.** The action zone consisted of the front three middle students and the three down the middle aisle. These students received 64 percent of the questions. This was, of course, partially due to the position of the teacher —front and center.

One question asked by researchers was whether more motivated students choose action zone seats, or whether the action zone affects the participation rates of students regardless of who they are. Schwebel and Cherlin (1972) conducted several experiments and concluded that the action zone does affect the participation rates of students. Other researchers suggested that an important ingredient in this puzzle is teachers' eye contacts. Teachers establish better eye contact with those students in the action zone, which in turn causes them to participate more in classroom activities and discussion.

DESK AND STUDENT ARRANGEMENT

There is some evidence that teachers' personal needs affect their placement of desks and students. Feitler, Weiner, and Blumberg (1970) found that preservice teachers with a high need for control liked classroom arrangements in which the teacher was in an obvious position of control, while preservice teachers with a low need for control selected settings in which the teacher was less visible and obvious.

Although the arrangement of desks, tables, and students appears to influence certain types of student behavior and attitudes, no study has yet demonstrated a relationship between desk and furniture placement and student achievement. For example, Horowitz and Otto (1973) found no differences in student achievement between those taking a course in a traditional classroom and those taking the same course in an alternative classroom with moveable panels and flexible, comfortable seats. They did, however, find differences in student behavior. Attendance was higher, as was group cohesion and participation and visits to the instructor's office, in the alternative room. The behaviors researchers have studied to date include attendance, attention, participation levels, student movement patterns, student-to-student interactions, and group cohesion.

Carol Weinstein (1977) was able to demonstrate how students' behavior in a primary classroom changed as a result of changes in physical space. The teachers and researchers were concerned that students were not evenly distributed across the room, which meant overcrowding in some areas and underutilization in others. Further, girls were avoiding the games and science centers, and too much undesirable behavior was occurring in the reading areas. By reorganizing the room arrangement—for example, by providing more storage area in the science centers—the researchers were able to change students' choice of and participation in the centers.

Of interest to a number of researchers has been the placement of desks and students in different

RESEARCH SUMMARY 3-2

Rosenfield, P., Lambert, N., and Black, A. (1985). Desk arrangement effects on pupil classroom behavior. *Journal of Educational Psychology, 77,* 101–108.

PROBLEM: Desks in classrooms are no longer nailed to the floor. In most settings, they can be moved around with some ease. Are there better or worse arrangements for desks? Do some arrangements facilitate certain classroom tasks such as discussions? The purpose of this study was to compare student on- and off-task discussion behavior in rooms where the desks were arranged in a circle, in a row, or in clusters.

SAMPLE AND SETTING: Students in two fifth-, two fifth-sixth-, and two sixth-grade regular classrooms in several elementary schools in California participated in the study. In each of the six classrooms, eight students (four girls, four boys) were observed: two high-ability, two low-ability, two high interactors, and two low interactors. They were observed while brainstorming ideas for reading assignments. Brainstorming is a process used in a writing program called Project Write. All teachers had been trained in brainstorming techniques.

PROCEDURES: The classroom of each grade level was a control classroom and was organized in a circle, in a row, or in clusters. The three experimental classrooms were organized in all three structures at different times. The eight students in all classrooms were observed in on- and off-task behaviors, and the behaviors of the students in the different structures were compared.

RESULTS: Table 3-3 lists the frequency of observed behavior of the students in the three different structures in the experimental classrooms. As can be seen from the table, the arrangement least conducive to on-task and most related to off-task behavior during discussion is with the desks in rows. Desks in rows seem to be more related to student withdrawal than desks in clusters or circles. In addition, the circle arrangement was related to more on-task, out-of-order comments than rows and clusters.

DISCUSSION AND IMPLICATIONS: Most of the past research on arrangement of desks or chairs took place in highly artificial, experimental situations. This experiment took place in regular classrooms in connection with the type of writing task often seen in elementary schools.

---

patterns, for example, in a circle, traditional straight rows, or a horseshoe pattern. Circles appear to be extremely useful for some instructional functions. For example, one study found that when students crowd around a teacher during story-reading time they are less attentive than when they are sitting in a semicircle around the teacher (Krantz and Risley, 1972). Further, it would appear from a recent study conducted by Peter Rosenfield and his colleagues that a circle formation enhances interaction in dis-

cussions. The study is described in Research Summary 3-2.

NOISE, DENSITY, AND THE PHYSICAL ENVIRONMENT

Many teachers and principals place a premium on maintaining a quiet atmosphere in the classrooms and halls. A quiet atmosphere is generally thought to contribute to effective learning. However, research has found that students seem to adjust to

TABLE 3-3   **Average Frequency of Observed Behavior by Desk Arrangement**

BEHAVIOR	ROWS	CLUSTER	CIRCLE	SIGNIFICANT CONTRASTS*
		ON-TASK BEHAVIOR		
Hand-raising	2.82	3.40	2.35	cluster > circle
Listening	11.85	11.72	12.40	ns
Discussion comment	0.50	0.50	0.68	ns
On-task out-of-order comment	0.67	1.25	1.60	circle > rows
On-task oral response	1.18	1.76	2.28	circle > rows
Total	15.78	16.89	17.03	cluster > rows circle > rows
		OFF-TASK BEHAVIOR		
Disruptive behavior	0.62	0.68	0.69	ns
Withdrawal	3.54	2.43	2.28	rows > cluster rows > circle
Total	4.17	3.11	2.97	rows > circle

NOTE: Average frequency was based on number of observed behaviors during a total of 540 minutes of observation.
* Tukey's tests were used to calculate those significant contrasts: $p < .05$.
SOURCE: P. Rosenfield, N. Lambert, and A. Black (1985), p. 105.

It appears that discussions, such as brainstorming, should take place with desks arranged in a circle. In clusters, students raise their hands more than in circles. In circles they also make on-task, out-of-order comments more often than in clusters or rows. This indicates more active participation in circles than in rows and clusters. In rows, more students withdraw.

normal school noises, such as students pushing and yelling in the halls or power mowers outside windows. There appears to be no clear-cut relationship between fairly common school noise, even at a high level, and student performance on tasks.

On the other hand, extremely high levels of noise outside of a school, such as a nearby train or a low-flying airplane, do appear to affect achievement. Some hypothesize that such noise bothers teachers more than students, causing teachers to al-

locate less classroom time to academic content (Kyzar, 1977).

Intuition about density is not always backed by research evidence. Many people would hypothesize that a crowded classroom would affect achievement, but this is not always true. There are two types of density: social density, in which the size of the group varies in a given space, and spatial density, in which the size of the group remains constant, but the size of the space varies. In terms of social density, the achievement of students in classes with 40 or more students is negatively affected, but in classes with 18 or fewer students it is positively affected (Glass, Cahen, Smith, and Filby, 1982). However, varying classroom populations from between 20 to 30 students does not seem to affect achievement consistently. One explanation may be that teachers learn to compensate for moderate variations of density.

Finally, the atmosphere of a classroom itself can influence student attitudes and behaviors. Classroom atmosphere is not discussed here, however, since Chapter 4 is devoted to this topic.

SCHOOL-LEVEL PHYSICAL CHARACTERISTICS

Certain physical characteristics of the school have been found to be important in promoting achievement. These characteristics relate to reducing vandalism and graffiti and ensuring a well-lit and clean atmosphere. Johnston and dePerez (1985) studied effective middle schools and found that the physical aspects were probably the least important climate considerations. However, they did note that each of the effective schools that they studied were well-lit and bright and there was no graffiti in or on any of the schools. Bossert (1985) refers to the lack of vandalism in the various studies of effective secondary schools, and Rutter et al. (1979) noted that decoration and care of school classrooms were associated with higher student achievement in secondary schools.

Other aspects of school and classroom atmosphere will be discussed in Chapters 4 and 14.

USING TIME AND SPACE EFFECTIVELY

Time and space are two resources over which teachers have considerable control. Although they must still abide by the concept of a school period of fixed duration, at least in secondary schools, and cannot make their classrooms larger, teachers still have a wide variety of options available to them. There is, however, an interesting difference between time and space. Both are finite and limited, but time is the more crucial and coveted resource in terms of academic goals. Time pressures lead to considerations of efficiency, such as, "How can I maximize instruction to increase student time on task?" Space, although also finite, is in less demand for most teachers and is less likely, therefore, to produce considerations of efficiency. The primary concern with space is not to race with it as it is with time, but to experiment reflectively with rearranging the design of the classroom.

Effective, experienced teachers often make decisions about time and space almost automatically. They seem to know how to arrange a room for the most effective learning and management. They seem to know how much time is required for students to master a difficult idea or task. Beginning teachers, however, are less sure when performing these important executive functions. This section provides specific guidelines for managing time and space.

Using Time

In planning, beginning teachers must consider how long to spend on each subject and activity. They must constantly ask themselves, "Is there enough time to cover another activity? Am I spending too much time on that task?"

The time research described in the previous section provides teachers with a method for determining whether students are learning. It is sometimes difficult to know this without using a test. But because studies have correlated student achievement with academic learning time, teachers can gauge whether their students are learning by quick scans to determine whether they are on task, and whether their success rates at the tasks are high. If academic learning time is high, the students are probably learning the material that is being presented to them. If it is low, changes should be made in the amount of time spent on the topic, in management of instruction, or in the difficulty level of the content.

HOW TO INCREASE TIME ON TASK

Maximizing time on task requires, first and foremost, a teacher attitude that says student learning of the academic material is the goal of instruction, and that the responsibility of the teacher is to provide conditions conducive to learning. Time is not something to get through; it is a valuable resource that should be used to maximum advantage. The findings from the Beginning Teacher Evaluation Study (Fisher et al., 1980) provide some guidelines to use in maximizing academic learning time.

These guidelines are presented as research findings rather than as prescriptions (statements about what a teacher should do). Their purpose is to help beginning teachers keep their minds on the goal of maximizing time and to think about the use of time in relationship to their own classrooms. Such thinking should encourage the teacher to experiment with different management systems and evaluate them in order to increase academic learning time. The effective systems, however, will differ from classroom to classroom, which is why specific prescriptions for behavior are not always useful. The following research findings relate to the concept of academic learning time:

- **Allocated and engaged time:** Students in classrooms in which both the allocated time and the proportion of student engaged time is high learn more than in any other type of classroom.
- **Success level:** If the tasks presented by the teachers are performed at a high level of success by the students, the students will learn more than if the tasks are performed at a low level of success.

The following management and interaction behaviors of teachers help to maximize academic learning time and thus student achievement:

Accurate **diagnosis** of student skill level

Prescription of appropriate tasks

Substantive interaction (as compared with social, disciplinary, or procedural interaction) with students

Provision of **academic feedback** to students, particularly when they make an error

Structuring the lesson and providing directions on task procedures

Creating a **learning environment** in which students take responsibility for their work and cooperate on academic tasks

The following teacher behaviors were negatively related to maximizing academic learning time and student achievement:

Explanation in response to student need

Frequent reprimands for inappropriate behavior

The second-to-the-last finding is curious, is it not? Does it mean that a teacher should not answer students' questions when they are having difficulty completing a task? More likely, it means that if students need to ask many questions in order to complete a task, the teacher either has not explained the task well to the students or the task is set at an inappropriate level. Remember, it is important for students to be successful in their task performance. If it is too difficult for them, they will ask many questions. Therefore, when the students ask the teacher many questions related to completing the task, the teacher should consider changing the amount of direct instruction on that task or the level of difficulty of the task. This important issue will be discussed in more detail in Chapters 4 to 7.

Another curious finding relates to the reprimands for inappropriate behavior. What does one do if a student behaves inappropriately? In well-managed classrooms, teachers catch problem behavior before it disrupts the classroom. Therefore, a significant number of reprimands in a classroom indicates that the classroom is not well managed.

This picture of the well-managed classroom indicates that teachers require skills in diagnosis and prescription; they must be sensitive to individual differences and be able to present material at an appropriate level. Above all, effective teachers must value student achievement and emphasize academic goals.

HOW TO USE HOMEWORK TO EXTEND LEARNING TIME

One way to achieve **extended learning time** is to give students homework. If students practice their skills at home, more time will be available during the school day for academic instruction. But homework cannot be given out carelessly or frivolously. If the teacher doesn't value it, the students won't. Here are three general guidelines for homework:

1. Students should be given homework that they can perform successfully. Homework should not involve the continuation of instruction, but the continuation of practice or preparation for the next day's content.

2. Parents should be informed of the level of involvement expected of them. Are they expected to help their sons or daughters with answers to difficult questions or simply to provide a quiet atmosphere in which the students can complete their homework assignments? Are they supposed to check it over? Do they know the approximate frequency and duration of homework assignments?

3. Feedback should be provided on the homework. Many teachers simply check to determine whether the homework was performed. What this says to the students is that it doesn't matter how it is done, as long as it is done. Students soon figure out that the task is to get something—anything—on paper. One method for providing feedback is to involve other students in correcting the homework.

What if the students do not perform their homework? This is a difficult problem in schools that have not communicated the importance of completing homework assignments or in schools where parents do not value homework. The rules for doing homework must be fair and clear, and the consequences for not doing it should be laid out during the first week of class. One consequence, for example, might be a lower grade for a certain number of assignments missed, and if the student goes beyond that level, the teacher might involve the parents.

The consequences must also be fairly and consistently applied in cases in which students do not perform their assignments. Consistency is important, but so is compassion. A truly reasonable excuse should be accepted, although it is also helpful to demand some evidence, such as a note from a parent.

In summary, time is an important and scarce commodity that has sparked a continuing research effort over the past two decades. The importance of this body of research is that it focuses teachers' goals on maximizing academic learning time and provides a rationale for insisting on a task-oriented

classroom. Above all, it provides teachers with a way of thinking about their classrooms. One teacher (Muir, 1980) who had been involved in a research study academic learning time put it this way:

> ALT [academic learning time] is a powerful tool, not a prescription for how and when to use the tool. ALT as a concept is dynamic and ever-changing in each classroom because it focuses on ever-changing and growing human beings. A teacher must make constant adjustments in practices within the year as well as from year to year. Teachers do make a difference through their sensitivities and perceptions of their students, as well as with their academic knowledge. Only a teacher, a growing human being, can use tools such as ALT and utilize the skills mentioned in the study to synthesize a program and environment that are flexible, personalized, and appropriate for both teacher and student. . . .
>
> I suggest that teachers "play" with the issues and concepts presented in BTES [Beginning Teacher Evaluation Study]. Experiment with the ideas and the variables that appear relevant for your grade level and classroom. Primary and upper elementary classrooms are very different. Measure your ALT and transition time. Challenge yourself to increase ALT and decrease transition time regardless of your basic educational philosophy. Interesting changes may occur for you. (p. 212)

Using Space
FURNITURE ARRANGEMENT

A major decision that most teachers make at the beginning of the school year relates to the configuration of furniture in a room. (In secondary schools, this is not always the case, as some teachers move from classroom to classroom.) The way in which the furniture is arranged can influence academic learning time and, thus, student learning.

The first step in this decision-making process is to assess the quantity and type of furniture that is available. Are there chairs with desks attached? This is often the case in secondary schools. Are there tables and chairs? Are there larger tables available for activity centers? Are there more tables and chairs than students? Are there bookcases? Bulletin boards? It may be useful to talk to the person in the school responsible for furniture to determine if there is a storage room with extra furniture.

The second step is to assess your own style of teaching. Will you like to see all the students at once? Will you use small group activities? Centers? Will you lecture with recitation most of the time?

The form of the classroom should match its functions, with different formations being used for different functions. Here are the three most used formations:

- **Row and column:** This is the most traditional formation. In fact, not too long ago (and perhaps in some schools today), the desks were attached to the floor in rows. This formation is best suited to situations where the teacher wants attention focused in one direction, for example, on him or her during lecture or recitation, or during independent seatwork. A variant on the row and column arrangement is the horizontal row formation in which students sit quite close to each other in a fewer number of rows. This arrangement is useful for demonstration because the students are sitting quite close to the teacher. Neither of these arrangements is conducive to class discussion, however, or to small-group activities.
- **Circles:** As described in the research section, circles are useful for class discussion and independent seatwork. They are not the best arrangement for presentations or demonstrations because some students would inevitably face the teacher's back. For early elementary situations in which the teacher is reading to the students, students should sit in a semicircle rather than randomly sitting on a rug.
- **Clusters:** Seating clusters of four or six, such as those illustrated in Figure 3-4, are useful for group discussion, cooperative learning, or other small-group tasks. If this arrangement is used, students may have to be asked to move their chairs for lectures or demonstrations so that all students will be facing the teacher. Movement, however, as will be described in Chapter 6, can lead to disruption and cause management problems.

A particularly inventive approach for flexibility has been developed by Lynn Newsome, a reading teacher at Owen Brown Middle School in Howard County, Maryland. She uses a seating arrangement that allows her to "swing" from frontal teaching to cooperative learning groups (to be described in Chapter 11) in a very brief period of time. Her desks are arranged in a wing formation, as shown in the top of Figure 3-5. On cue students at the shaded wing desks move their desks to an arrangement shown in the lower part of Figure 3-5. Newsome reports that in both formations she can "maintain eye contact with all students, and the room appears spacious" (*MAACIE Cooperative News*, p. 5).

Finally, beginning teachers who are organizing rooms so that a number of independent activities can take place simultaneously should keep the following six guidelines in mind:

1. If there are not enough clearly marked paths from one activity center to another, the students will push and pull in their attempts to move to another center. Research indicates that one-third to one-half of the classroom should be devoted to paths (Prescott, Jones, and Kritchevsky, 1967).
2. Play units should not be hidden from students' sight or they will fall into disuse.
3. Large, empty spaces encourage students to roughhouse.
4. At all centers, the number of students should be limited to the amount of material available.
5. Storage space for materials should be easily reached by the students and should be close to the surfaces on which they work.
6. In order to supervise all activities at once, the teacher should be able to see what is going on in the activity centers. Therefore, barriers should be low and centers should not be hidden from sight.

But what happens when a classroom is not big enough or there is not enough furniture to have different configurations at the same time? One way to handle this is to determine what teaching model is employed most frequently and then to match the basic configuration of the classroom to it. Does the teacher lecture, provide group activities, or conduct discussions with the students? For example, if the teacher provides a lot of group or individual seatwork tasks, the students can sit in clusters of four. When the teacher lectures to the whole group, one of the students in each cluster can shift his or her

Figure 3-4 Four- and six-cluster seating arrangements

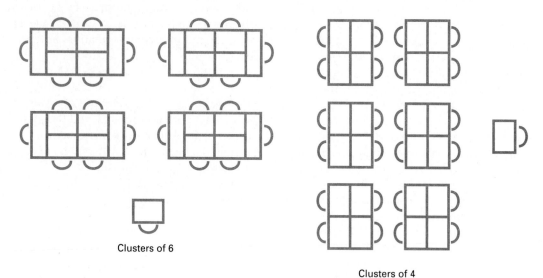

Clusters of 6

Clusters of 4

chair around so that it is facing the teacher. Further, students can be provided with hinged cardboard separators that they can place on their desks during tests or during individual seatwork when they do not want to be disturbed.

Figure 3-5 Seating arrangement for frontal teaching and cooperative learning

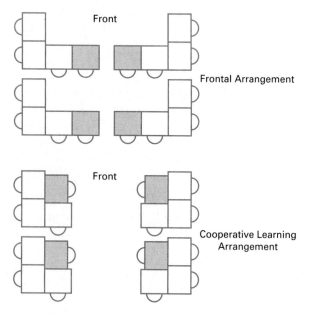

Front

Frontal Arrangement

Front

Cooperative Learning Arrangement

SOURCE: *MAACIE Cooperative News*, Vol. 3, Issue 3, February 1990, p. 5.

Above all, teachers should be flexible and experiment with different seating arrangements. It is important to highlight, however, that each configuration has its own rules of participation, and these need to be clearly spelled out to students. For example, during presentations, teachers generally ask students to raise their hands before they ask or answer questions; in a circle-discussion session, students may be encouraged to speak out without raising their hands. Therefore, too much experimentation can confuse students who have just learned the rules from a preceding form. Rules and procedures for various classroom activities must be taught to students like any other topic. Procedures for moving from one arrangement to another must also be taught and practiced. All of this will be described in more detail in Chapters 5 and 6.

CLASSROOM AMBIENCE

Although evidence about **classroom ambience** is not conclusive, experienced teachers know that it is important. Studies in later chapters illustrate how cheerful rooms affect students' concentration. You know from other experiences that some environments are warm and inviting places while others are cold and sterile places you try to avoid.

The teacher does not have to be an artist or interior designer to decorate a classroom and make it a pleasant place for students to be. Nor does it require large amounts of money. In fact, students can even help produce an interesting-looking, warm-feeling room. Many students feel good about seeing their work on the walls, and such displays can be used as an incentive system. For example, the teacher can institute a "drawing of the week" or an "essay of the week" to hang on a colorful bulletin board. Or groups of students can draw murals to illustrate a story they have read. This is just as important in secondary classrooms as it is in elementary classrooms.

SOUND

As explained previously, there is not a direct relationship between school and classroom noise and student learning. For example, a buzzing in the classroom could indicate that the students are working together on an academic task despite noise in the hall. In fact, it is important for students to talk to each other when learning new skills and concepts and to help each other with important classroom tasks. Classroom noise per se is not a problem. Only certain types of noise made at inappropriate times should be viewed as a classroom problem—that is, as a deterrent to the academic task at hand. What is important is what the students are talking about and when. If two students are having a social conversation, even if they are quiet about it, they are not maintaining high academic learning time. If a number of students are talking while the teacher is talking, other students' concentration may be disrupted. This issue will be explored more fully in Chapter 6 and in the chapters on the interactive functions of teaching.

SUMMARY

- Time and space are scarce commodities in teaching, and their use should be planned with care and foresight.
- The research on the management of time is quite well developed, whereas much less is known about the use of classroom space.
- Research on time shows that there is considerable variation from teacher to teacher on the amount of allocated time devoted to different

subject areas. The amount of time students spend on a task is related to how much they learn. Students in classrooms in which the allocated time is high, and a large proportion of students are engaged, learn more than in other classrooms.
- There are several different types of time that teachers should attend to: planned time, allocated time, engaged time, academic learning time, and time needed.
- Such teacher actions as accurate diagnosis of student skill level, prescription of appropriate tasks, substantive interactions, provisions for monitoring, and appropriate lesson structuring help maximize learning time and, in turn, student achievement.
- One very important way to extend learning time for students is through homework. Homework, however, must be carefully planned and considered. It is not a device to solve all time pressure problems.
- Good homework is characterized by practice (not instruction), parent involvement, and effective feedback from the teacher.
- Space—which has to do with the arrangement of materials, desks, and students—is another important resource managed by teachers.
- The way space is used affects the learning atmosphere of classrooms, influences classroom dialogue and communication, and has important cognitive and emotional effects on students.
- Desk arrangement affects communication patterns and student classroom behavior. Students seated in the "action zone" (the front and center of a teacher's classroom) normally get more attention than those seated elsewhere. Row-and-column arrangements are the most traditional and are best suited when the lesson demands attention focused in one direction. This arrangement can also lead to student withdrawal. Circle arrangements encourage more participation but can also lead to off-task behaviors. Cluster arrangements encourage small-group work and student involvement but can also lead to disruptions.
- The atmosphere and ambience of the classroom can influence student attitudes and behaviors. Effective teachers strive to have environments that are warm, cheerful, and inviting.

- There appear to be no direct relationships between sound, noise, and student learning. Appropriate noise levels depend upon what the teacher is trying to accomplish and the specific tasks in which students are involved.
- The uses of time and space are related to each other around learning tasks. Effective teachers develop an attitude of flexibility and experimentation about these features of classroom life. They know that every class is different, and therefore plans about the use of time and space must often be adjusted to particular circumstances.

KEY TERMS

aptitude
planned time
allocated time
opportunity to learn
engaged time
time on task
academic learning time
time needed
action zone
success level
diagnosis
prescription
extended learning time
cluster seating
classroom ambience

BOOKS FOR THE PROFESSIONAL

American Association of School Administrators. (1982). *Time on task*. Alexandria, Va.: Author. This little booklet describes the time-on-task research and provides pointers for observing the different types of time in the classroom. While this booklet was prepared for administrators, it is also extremely useful for teachers.

Cooper, H. (1989). *Homework*. New York: Longman. This book presents careful review of the research on the effects of homework along with the implication this research has for school policies and teachers' practices.

Denham, C., and Lieberman, A. (eds.). (1980). *Time to learn*. Washington, D.C.: U.S. Department of Education. This book contains a description of the study that led to the concept of academic learning time and a set of responses to the concept by scholars and practitioners.

Fisher, C. W., and Berliner, D. (eds.). (1985). *Perspectives on instructional time*. New York: Longman. The book of readings provides a variety of perspectives for looking at how time is used in school and classrooms and the implication of this important instructional variable. It also looks at some of the ways the results of research can be abused.

LEARNING AIDS FOR PLANNING, OBSERVATION, AND REFLECTION

- Assessing My Thinking about Using Time and Space Effectively
- Observing Off-Task Time in Classrooms
- Observing Differences between Planned Time and Allocated Time
- Analysis of Classroom Space Arrangements
- Observing Space Arrangements in Different Classrooms
- Planning Guide for Homework Assignments

ASSESSING MY THINKING ABOUT USING TIME AND SPACE EFFECTIVELY

PURPOSE: Time and space are scarce resources that can require complex management strategies. This aid is to help you clarify your thinking about managing time and space.

DIRECTIONS: Write a paragraph on how you think about time for teaching. You can project ahead and imagine how you will feel as a teacher, or you can think about actual teaching experiences in fieldwork or microteaching. How many times did you feel that there was not enough time? How many times did you worry about filling in time? Did you sense that the time was filled with academic tasks? With management concerns?

Write a paragraph on your favorite activities in class; again, imagine yourself in your own classroom or think about actual teaching experiences you've had. Describe the space arrangements in the classroom. Do space arrangements mesh with the activities? What do you like to do most in the classroom: lecture, allow students to learn independently or do seatwork, allow students to work together in groups, and so on? Now consider the space arrangement in the classroom. Does that arrangement allow for the types of activities with which you feel most comfortable?

OBSERVING OFF-TASK TIME IN CLASSROOMS

PURPOSE: Time on task is one of the most important variables in student learning. It is vital that teachers learn how to spot off-task behavior. This aid will help sensitize you to the signs that students are off task. It has been designed around some of the ideas of Stallings, whose research was described earlier in the chapter.

DIRECTIONS: Fill in the first two lines of the form below. In the space, draw a map of the seating arrangement in the classroom. Draw a box for each student, leaving space below the line for four marks. At 5-minute intervals, make marks below the names of students who are off task. To describe their activities, use the codes below. Before each mark, write 1, 2, 3, 4, to record the observation number. Also, fill in the top of the form to describe the teacher activity.

Students' Off-Task Seating Chart

Date _____ Teacher _____

Activity 1 _____ Time _____

Activity 2 _____ Time _____

Activity 3 _____ Time _____

Activity 4 _____ Time _____

front of classroom

CODES: S = Socializing
U = Uninvolved
W = Waiting for assistance

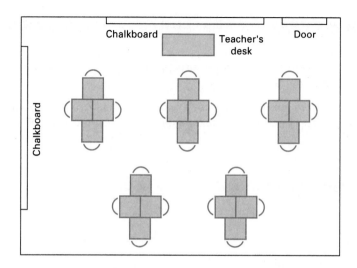

3. Ms. Scarlet has a small third-grade classroom with 26 children. She believes in learning centers and lots of independent reading in an inviting and comfortable area. She established three learning centers along one side of the classroom, a small-group reading table, and a library with a rug on the floor.

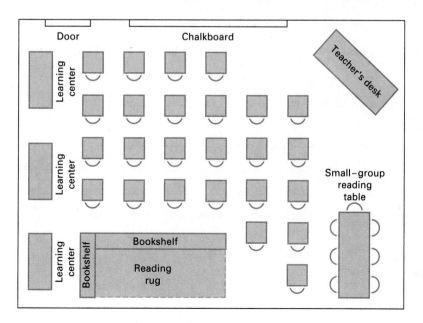

Analysis and Reflection: Reflect on what you consider to be your own emerging teaching style. What space arrangements will best suit it?

OBSERVING SPACE ARRANGEMENTS IN DIFFERENT CLASSROOMS

PURPOSE: This aid will give you further practice in making the link between classroom activities and space arrangements.

DIRECTIONS: Observe the use of space in two different classrooms at the same grade level or, if in a secondary school, the same subject. Draw a diagram of the classrooms. Observe students' movements in the space. Compare the two arrangements by answering the following questions for each:

1. What are the dominant modes of instruction in the classroom?

   _____

   _____

2. How much do students move around? During what periods of time?

   _____

   _____

3. Does there appear to be congestion in the classroom? At what points?

   _____

4. How much is each classroom area used during the course of the day?

   _____

5. How much decoration is there in the room? Does it relate to the subject? Is it student-made?

   _____

   _____

   _____

Analysis and Reflection: Which room achieves a better use of space? Why?

PLANNING GUIDE FOR HOMEWORK ASSIGNMENTS

PURPOSE: Assigning homework is an important element in proper use of instructional time. Different homework policies have different impacts on the teacher. This aid will help you clarify your beliefs about homework, so that whatever policy you select can be implemented properly.

DIRECTIONS: Answer the following questions about homework to help you establish your own future homework policies.

1. Do you believe homework should be given every night? (This means that you are willing to correct it or have the other students correct it every day.) If not, how many times per week?

   _____

   _____

2. Should students be allowed to begin and possibly finish their homework in class?

   _____

3. How long should students spend on homework in class? _____

   _____

4. What type of homework do you think should be given students? Practice work? Creative work? Library work? Other work? _____

   _____

5. Would you plan any long-term assignments that require parents' help to make sure that students obtain information at libraries or other sources? _____

   _____

6. What incentives would you provide for doing homework? _____

   _____

7. Will you grade the homework or just make sure it is completed?

   _____

   _____

8. What happens if a student does not bring in his or her homework? Will you listen to excuses? (For example, "I left it at home" or "The dog ate it.") _____

   _____

9. What percentage of the grade should be homework? _____

_____

10. In what ways should parents be involved in helping students with their homework? (For example, will you want them to correct it or just ensure that it is completed?) _____

_____

Analysis and Reflection: Now that you have thought about and answered the above questions about homework, draft a sample letter to parents explaining your policies and indicating their responsibilities. This letter should not be overly prescriptive or heavy-handed. Further, it should be written in such a way as to be understood by all parents. Finally, it should suggest a partnership between you and them to work on their children's homework. You may wish to include a survey to gauge parents' knowledge about their childrens' homework. Possible questions include: "How many nights per week does your son or daughter bring home homework from this class?" "On nights he or she does have homework, how much time does your son or daughter spend on it?"

CHAPTER 4

Learning Environments and Motivation

Students and teachers spend roughly half of their waking hours in the social arrangement we call a classroom, and, as in all social settings, they interact with each other. Teachers interact with students and students with teachers; students interact with each other and with various academic materials. As these individuals work with one another, a group develops. Teachers report that each class takes on a "distinct personality." Students report that their class is "great" or "not so great," and they remember for years their third-grade class, their fifth-period English class, or their homeroom. What classroom participants remember most often is not necessarily what the teacher taught. Instead, they describe and remember the social-psychological dimensions of the classroom. Luft (1970) described this unique dimension in the following way:

> A [classroom] group may be thought of as a developing system with its own structure, organization and norms. Classes may look alike from a distance or on paper, but actually each class is as unique as a fingerprint. Each class develops its own internal procedures and patterns of interactions and its own limits. It is as if imaginary lines were guiding and controlling behavior within the group. In spite of day-to-day variation there is a certain constancy in each class which emerges from its individual history. (p. 81)

The structures and processes teachers choose to build in classrooms influence how a class develops and the norms it establishes for social and academic learning. Providing leadership for building productive **classroom environments** is a critical leadership function performed by teachers and provides the focus for this chapter. The chapter first introduces a set of conceptual frameworks to help you understand classroom environments, then presents a sample of the research on this topic.

The overall intent of this chapter is to provide a set of wide-angle lenses for viewing and understanding classroom life in more general ways. Many of the ideas introduced in this chapter will be revisited later in Chapters 5 and 6. There we focus specifically on issues associated with building productive learning environments in classrooms populated with students of various backgrounds and needs and issues connected to classroom management.

The chapter concludes with specific procedures teachers use to build productive learning environments plus several learning aids.

PERSPECTIVE AND RATIONALE

A productive learning environment is characterized by (1) an overall climate where students feel positive about themselves, their peers, and the

Figure 4-1 Four dimensions of classroom environment

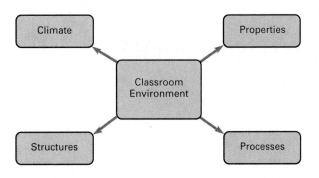

classroom as a group; (2) structures and processes where students' needs are satisfied and where students persist with academic tasks and work in cooperative ways with the teacher and other students; and (3) a setting where students have acquired the necessary group and interpersonal skills to accomplish the academic and group demands of the classroom.

Many of the concepts needed to understand classroom environments cannot be readily observed. They are psychosocial processes that are carried around in the minds of classroom members (teachers and students) and in the "ethos" of their group life. So, to understand classroom structures and processes one must acquire conceptual "lenses" with which to interpret what is observed. Increasingly scholars have tried to describe and understand what happens in classrooms. Four basic ideas emanating from this work can help you understand the complexity of the classroom and how to build a more productive learning environment. These four ideas include **classroom climate, classroom properties, classroom processes,** and **classroom structures** (see Figure 4-1).

Classroom Climate

Classroom climate is a fairly abstract concept that nevertheless helps researchers and teachers comprehend the atmosphere or ethos of classrooms. The theoretical basis for the concept of **classroom climate** emanates mainly from the work of Kurt Lewin and his many colleagues, who showed how the interactions between individuals' needs and environmental conditions were key factors in explaining human behavior. Getzels and Thelen (1960) applied

some of these ideas by developing a framework to clarify what goes on in classrooms. They described, in broad terms, the following characteristics of classroom groups: (1) a group that comes together for the purpose of learning; (2) a group where the participants are, for the most part, randomly selected and required to be group members; and (3) a group where formal leadership is given by law to one group member, the teacher. It was Getzels and Thelen's premise that understanding the relationships within such settings requires an explicit conceptual framework.

Getzels and Thelen's model of classroom groups has two important dimensions. The first dimension of the model describes how, within a classroom, there are individuals with certain personalities and needs. This psychological perspective can be labeled the *personal dimension* of classroom life. From this perspective, behavior is determined as a result of individual needs, motives, and attitudes, regardless of the institutional role.

The second dimension of the model describes how classrooms exist within the school and how certain roles and expectations develop within that setting to fulfill the goals of the system. This dimension can be labeled the *social dimension* of the classroom. From this perspective classroom behavior is determined by the shared expectations (norms) that are part of institutional roles.

It is the interaction of both the social and personal dimensions that determines behavior within a classroom setting and shapes a particular classroom's climate. Or, to simplify matters a bit, classroom social interaction is a result of individually motivated people responding to each other in a social setting. It is out of this self-other interaction that classroom climate evolves, sustains itself, and produces certain student behaviors for social and academic learning. This concept of classroom climate and its relationship to behavior can be diagramed as in Figure 4-2.

Classroom Properties

The framework developed by Getzels and Thelen helps teachers think about some of the global aspects of classroom life. In particular it shows teachers that some of classroom behavior is the result of human interaction within a social system

Figure 4-2   The class as a social system

where each part of the system affects what goes on in other parts. This framework alone is not very specific about the properties that teachers might find in classrooms. Recent scholars have developed more detailed and helpful insights.

Among others, Walter Doyle (1979, 1980, 1986) has studied and described the nature of classroom groups. The framework and perspective he has proposed views classroom settings as **ecological systems** where inhabitants (teachers and students) interact within their environment (the classroom). This ecological system, according to Doyle, has several distinctive **properties** that shape behavior regardless of how students are organized for learning or what approach a particular teacher may be using. Doyle (1986, pp. 394–395) described six properties. His ideas are paraphrased as follows:

1. **Multidimensionality:** The classroom is a crowded place in which many people with preferences and abilities compete for scarce resources. Many events must be planned and orchestrated. For example, records must be kept, schedules met, supplies organized, and student work collected and evaluated.
2. **Simultaneity:** Many things happen at once in classrooms. While helping an individual student during seatwork, a teacher must monitor the rest of the class, handle interruptions, and keep track of time. During a discussion, a teacher must listen to student answers, watch other students for signs of comprehension or confusion, formulate the next question, and scan the class for possible misbehavior.
3. **Immediacy:** Classroom events proceed at a rapid pace. Teachers have hundreds of exchanges with their students every day. They are continuously praising and reprimanding. This immediacy gives teachers little leisure time to reflect before acting.

4. **Unpredictability:** Classroom events often take unexpected turns. Distractions and interruptions are frequent. In addition, events are jointly produced; thus, it is often difficult to anticipate how an activity will go on a particular day with a particular group of students.
5. **Publicness:** The classroom is a public place, and events—especially those involving the teacher—are always witnessed by a large portion of the students.
6. **History:** Classes meet five days a week for several months and thus accumulate a common set of experiences, routines, and norms. Early meetings often shape events for the rest of the year. A class is also affected by seasonal variations and the addition of new members.

Doyle's six properties directly affect the overall classroom environment and shape the behaviors of both teachers and students. As will be described later, some classroom properties can be altered by teachers; others cannot—at least not very easily.

Classroom Processes

Working with concepts and research on interpersonal relations and group dynamics, Richard and Patricia Schmuck (1988) developed a slightly different framework for looking at classrooms. Classroom climate is an important concept in the Schmucks' framework just as it was for Getzels and Thelen. The Schmucks' unique contribution, however, is the way they define climate and the way they view interpersonal and **group processes** as important factors contributing to positive climates. The Schmucks define a positive climate as follows:

A positive climate is one in which the students expect one another to do their intellectual best and to support one another; where the students share high amounts of potential influence—both with one another and with the teacher; in which high levels of attraction exist for the group as a whole and between classmates; where norms are supportive for getting academic work done, as well as for maximizing individual differences; where communication is open and featured by dialogue; and where the processes of working and developing together as a group are considered relevant in themselves for study. (p. 24)

For the Schmucks, positive classroom climates are created by teachers when they teach students important interpersonal and group process skills and when they help the classroom develop as a group. The Schmucks identify six group processes that, when working in relation to one another, produce a positive classroom climate.

1. **Expectations:** In classrooms, people have expectations for each other and for themselves. The Schmucks are interested in how expectations become patterned over time and how they influence classroom climate and learning.
2. **Leadership:** This refers to how power and influence are exerted in classrooms and their impact on group interaction and cohesiveness. The Schmucks view leadership as an interpersonal process rather than as a characteristic of a person, and they encourage leadership to be shared in classroom groups.
3. **Attraction:** This refers to the degree to which people in a classroom have respect for one another and how friendship patterns within classrooms affect climate and learning. The Schmucks encourage teachers to help create classroom environments characterized by peer groups free from cliques, with no student left out of the friendship structure.
4. **Norms:** Norms are the shared expectations students and teachers have for classroom behavior. The Schmucks value classrooms with norms that support high student involvement in academic work but at the same time encourage positive interpersonal relationships and shared goals.
5. **Communication:** Most classroom interaction is characterized by verbal and nonverbal communication. The Schmucks argue for communication processes that are open and lively and have a high degree of participant involvement.

Figure 4-3   Structures and how they organize classroom life

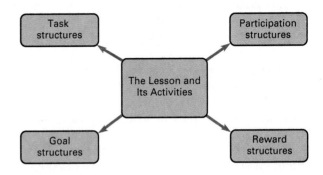

6. **Cohesiveness:** The final process refers to the feelings and commitments students and teachers have to the classroom group as a whole. The Schmucks advocate peer group cohesiveness but point out that it is important for this cohesiveness to be in support of academic work and member well-being.

Unlike the *properties* described by Doyle, classroom *processes* are highly influenced by the teacher's actions and can be altered to build productive classroom environments, as you will see later in this chapter.

Classroom Structures

The structures that shape classrooms and the demands particular lessons place on students offer a final perspective on classrooms. Researchers, such as Gump (1967), Kounin (1970), and, more recently, Doyle (1979) and Doyle and Carter (1984), have held to the view that behavior in classrooms is partially a response to the structures and demands of the classroom environment. This view of classrooms pays close attention to the kinds of structures that exist within classrooms and to the activities and tasks students are asked to perform during particular lessons, the basic unit of instruction. Figure 4-3 shows how the lesson and its activities can vary in four important ways: the nature of the learning task, structures for participation, and structures for establishing goals and providing rewards.

Unlike the classroom properties described earlier, which are mostly fixed, or the classroom processes, which are highly alterable, the four structures highlighted in Figure 4-3 are sometimes fixed by tradition, but they can also be altered if the teacher chooses to do so. In fact, one might compare classroom structures to the designs of houses. The way space in a house is designed and partitioned could be called the house's structure. This structure influences how people in the house normally interact with one another. For example, if all the rooms are small and closed off, it is difficult to have a party where lots of people can move around and interact easily. Conversely, if the house is wide open, it is difficult for individuals to find privacy. While these structures influence certain types of behavior, they do not guarantee or prevent specific behaviors. For example, you know of instances where good parties have occurred in small spaces; you also know of instances where ideal structural conditions have not produced positive interactions. Structures, however, can be changed. Using the house analogy again, walls can be removed to encourage wider interaction, or screens can be stationed to provide privacy. Classroom structures can also be changed. Each of the four classroom structures is described in more detail below.

CLASSROOM TASK STRUCTURES

The academic and social tasks and activities planned by teachers determine the kind of work students carry out in classrooms. In this instance **classroom tasks** refer to what is expected of students and the cognitive (information processing) as well as social demands placed upon them to accomplish the task. Classroom activities, on the other hand, are the things students can be observed doing: participating in a discussion, working with other students in small groups, doing seat-work, listening to a lecture, and so forth. Classroom learning tasks not only help shape the way teachers and students behave but also help determine what students learn.

Task structures differ according to the various activities required of particular teaching strategies or models used by teachers. As described in later chapters, lessons organized around lectures place far different demands on students than do lessons organized around small-group discussions. Similarly, the demands of students during discussion periods differ from those associated with seatwork.

Whereas some learning tasks and the demands they place on teachers and students stem from the nature of the learning activities themselves, others are embedded in the subjects being taught. Sometimes the academic disciplines (their concepts, organizing frameworks, and methods of revealing new knowledge) provide the basis for these differences. To understand this idea, think about the college classes you have taken in various disciplines and the demands placed upon you as a learner in various situations. For instance, the task demands and your behavior when you were doing an experiment in the chemistry lab were different from the demands placed on you as you provided thoughtful analysis of a Shakespearean tragedy. Similarly, the task demands placed on you in anthropology to understand preliterate cultures were different from those required of you to understand the industrial revolution in European history.

Sometimes different task demands exist within particular academic subjects. A lesson aimed at teaching the multiplication tables in arithmetic, for instance, makes a different set of demands on learners than does a lesson aimed at increasing skill in mathematical problem solving. Learning the names and locations of the major cities of the world requires different behaviors and actions for learners and teachers than does a geography inquiry lesson exploring the importance of location in determining standard of living. A literature lesson on character development makes different demands than does a spelling lesson.

The important thing to remember is that classroom task structures influence the thoughts and actions of classroom participants and help determine the degree of student cooperation and involvement. As will be emphasized at various places in later chapters, students need to be taught specific and appropriate learning strategies which will help them satisfy the task demands being placed on them in classrooms.

CLASSROOM GOAL STRUCTURES

A second important classroom structure is one labeled classroom **goal structures.** In Chapter 2, the concept of instructional goals was introduced. Johnson and Johnson (1975, 1987) define an instructional goal "as a desired state of future affairs . . . such as ability to spell a list of words, the successful completion of a mathematics problem or . . . understanding a basic set of concepts within a subject area" (p. 5). The goal structure of the classroom, not to be confused with instructional goals, specifies the type of *interdependence* sought among students. It specifies the ways in which students relate to each other and to the teacher while working toward instructional goals. The Johnsons (1975) defined three different types of goal structures:

1. **Cooperative goal structures** A **cooperative goal structure** exists when students perceive that they can obtain their goal if, and only if, the other students with whom they are linked can obtain their goals. . . . A cooperative goal structure requires the coordination of behavior necessary to achieve the mutual goal.
2. **Competitive goal structures** A **competitive goal structure** exists when students perceive that they can obtain their goal if, and only if, the other students with whom they are linked fail to obtain their goals.
3. **Individualistic goal structure** An **individualistic goal structure** exists when the achievement of the goal by one student is unrelated to the achievement of the goal by other students; whether or not a student achieves her goal has no bearing upon whether other students achieve their goals. . . . Usually there is no student interaction in an individualistic situation. (p. 7)

A later section of this chapter will discuss how classroom goal structures are related to student motivation. In Chapter 11, a model of teaching developed specifically around cooperative goal structures will be described.

CLASSROOM REWARD STRUCTURES

Classroom environments and behaviors can also be influenced by classroom **reward structures.** Just as goal structures can be competitive, individualistic, or cooperative, so too can reward structures. Slavin (1983) has written that competitive reward structures are those that reward students for their own individual efforts in comparison with other students. Grading on a curve would be an example of a competitive reward structure, as is the way winners

are defined in most track and field events. In contrast, cooperative reward structures are situations where individual effort helps others to be rewarded. Slavin (1983) gives the following examples: "If three people traveling in a car help push the car out of the mud, all of them benefit from each other's effort (by being able to continue the trip). A football team also is an example of a cooperative reward system, even though the team as a whole is in competition with other teams" (p. 4).

Most importantly, classroom goal and reward structures are at the core of life in classrooms and influence greatly both the behavior and learning of students. Regardless of the teacher's personal philosophy toward the use of rewards, the current reality is that student motivation centers around the dispensation of grades. In fact, Doyle (1979) argues that the primary features of classroom life are the way students engage in academic work and how they "exchange [their] performance for grades." The way teachers organize goal and reward structures determines which types of goals are accomplished and how the exchange occurs.

CLASSROOM PARTICIPATION STRUCTURES

Finally, teaching and learning are influenced by classroom **participation structures.** Participation structures, according to Cazden (1986), determine "who can say what, when, and to whom" (p. 437). These structures include the way students take turns during group lessons and the way they ask questions and respond to teacher queries. These structures also vary from one type of lesson to another. During a lecture, for example, student participation is limited to listening to the teacher and perhaps individually taking notes. A discussion or recitation connected to a lecture, on the other hand, requires students to answer questions and to give their ideas. Listening to one another is another expectation for students during a discussion or a recitation, as is raising one's hand to get a turn. When the teacher plans seatwork for students, the prescribed participation is normally to work alone and to interact one-on-one with the teacher when help is required. Small-group and cooperative learning activities obviously require a different kind of participation on the part of students. Small-group activities require that students talk to each other, and cooperative learning activities require joint production of academic tasks. Chapter 13 will provide additional information about participation structures and describe several teaching strategies recently developed for the purpose of increasing the amount of student participation during classroom learning activities.

Key Features of Classroom Life

This section has described key features of classroom life. Frameworks provide a view of classrooms as complex social and ecological systems where students' and teachers' behaviors result from the interactions of individual needs and institutional roles. The climate created in classrooms from this two-way interaction helps determine the degree of student cooperation and involvement in learning. Some features of classrooms, such as the properties of multidimensionality or immediacy, probably cannot be influenced very much by the teacher. Classrooms will remain crowded places and teachers will have to learn to deal with the rapid pace, at least in the near future. However, other features of classrooms, such as the group processes and basic task, participation, goal, and reward structures, are strongly under the control of the teacher. It is the way processes and structures are developed and maintained by teachers that determines whether or not a classroom environment is productive. Ways of doing this are described in later sections.

SAMPLING THE KNOWLEDGE BASE

The research literature supporting the topic of productive classroom environments is extensive and represents scholarship from many fields: the social psychology of education, group dynamics, motivation; the social context of teaching; and organizational psychology. It is not the aim of this section to review all of this research. Instead, interesting studies are provided to give beginning teachers insights into the way some of this research is carried out and to provide examples of some important findings. The studies cover a span of a half century and focus on the effects of classroom environments on motivation, how teacher behaviors influence group life, and how students themselves can influence each other and their teachers.

Effects of Classroom Environment on Student Motivation

It is difficult to motivate students to persist at learning tasks. Some students persist longer than others, and some tasks appear to be more interesting to some students than do other tasks. Researchers have been interested for a long time in how classroom environments influence student motivation. The general finding has been that environments characterized by mutual respect, high standards, and a caring attitude are more conducive to student persistence than other environments.

In an interesting and unique study that was conducted in the 1970s, Santrock studied the relationships between some of the dimensions of the classroom environment—happy and sad moods—and students' motivation to persist on learning tasks. Santrock randomly assigned first- and second-grade children into several different treatment groups. On the way to a classroom, students were told either a happy story, a sad story, or no story at all. The experimenter acted happy in relating a happy story, sad in relating the sad story, and neutral for no story. The various rooms were decorated in one of three ways: happy pictures, sad pictures, or neutral pictures. In the room, the children were asked to work at a task at which they were interrupted from time to time and asked to think either a happy, sad, or neutral thought. Students could stop working on the task whenever they liked.

Students thinking happy thoughts who experienced a happy experimenter in a happy room persisted much longer at the learning task than did students thinking sad thoughts with a sad experimenter in a sad room. This type of result is important because it indicates that persistence at a task for a student is not simply a function of the child's self-control or interest but can be influenced by the environment and by aspects of the environment under the teacher's control—room decor and happy moods.

Effects of Teacher Behavior on Students

For many years teachers have known that what they do has an influence on the behaviors of their students. In fact, teaching by definition is an attempt to

RESEARCH SUMMARY 4-1

Lippitt, R., and White, R.   (1958). An experimental study of leadership and group life. In E. E. Macoby, T. M. Newcomb, and F. L. Hartley (eds.), *Readings in social psychology.* New York: Holt, Rinehart & Winston.

PROBLEM: The researchers were interested in the general problem of how different types of leadership behaviors would influence both individual and group behavior.

SAMPLE AND SETTING: The sample consisted of 11-year-old children who volunteered to form small boys' clubs and participate in a series of club projects and activities.

PROCEDURES: The researchers matched children according to their leadership and friendship patterns and placed them into four clubs: Sherlock Holmes Club, Dick Tracy Club, Secret Agents Club, and Charlie Chan Club. Adult club leaders (teachers) were taught to exhibit three different types of leadership behaviors.

1. **Authoritarian leadership**   When using this role, the club leader made all policies about activities and procedures and remained aloof from club members.
2. **Democratic leadership**   When using this role, the club leader made all policies and procedures a matter of group discussion and decision. The leader strived to be a part of the group in spirit and encourage club members.
3. **Laissez faire leadership**   When using this role, the club leader was passive and left complete freedom to the group.

The researchers carefully observed the boys' behavior on a number of different variables and collected a vast amount of information on both leadership and group member behavior. The researchers also arranged for the leader to be called away at a designated point in time and the boys' work behavior (without any adult in the room) was recorded by a hidden observer. This behavior was subsequently compared to behavior when the leader was present.

POINTERS FOR READING RESEARCH: Most researchers of previous research summaries in this book have reported their information in data tables. Sometimes researchers choose to show their results in graphs and charts. Graphs and charts are actually quite easy to read, and most of you are very familiar with them. However, when several variables have been included in a graph, as is the case in this study, readers must inspect each aspect of the graph carefully to make sure they accurately understand the relationships being illustrated.

---

influence the behavior and learning of students. Also, from the beginning of formal schooling in western societies many educators have held the belief that a teacher's behavior should be "democratic" in character, thus reflecting the larger societal value about the way people should interact with one another. Take, for example, these comments written by John Dewey almost 75 years ago:

> We can and do supply ready-made "ideas" by the thousand; we do not usually take much pains to see that the one learning engages in significant situations

RESULTS: Below are two graphs showing some of the effects of the three types of leader behavior on the climate of the boys' group. Figure 4-4 shows how the three different types of leadership produced four patterns of reactions on member behavior.

Figure 4-4   Four patterns of group reaction to the three types of leadership

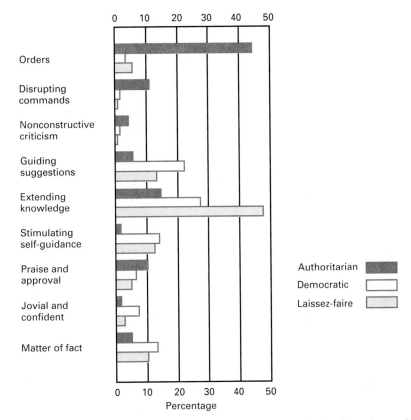

SOURCE: From R. Lippitt and R. White (1963), An experimental study of leadership and group life. In E. E. Macoby, T. M. Newcomb, F. L. Hartley (eds.), *Readings in social psychology,* New York: Holt, Rinehart & Winston, p. 146.

(Continued on page 112)

where his own activities generate, support, and clinch ideas—that is, perceived meanings or connections. This does not mean that the teacher is to stand off and look on; the alternative to furnishing ready-made subject matter and listening to the accuracy with which it is reproduced is not quiescence, but participation, sharing, in an activity. In such shared activity the teacher is a learner, and the learner is, without knowing it, a teacher—and upon the whole, the less consciousness there is, on either side, of either giving or receiving instruction, the better. (Dewey, 1916, p. 176)

But what effects do more democratic procedures or behaviors have on students? In what

RESEARCH SUMMARY   4-1   (Continued)

Figure 4-5 shows the activity patterns of the boys when their leader was present, when he was out of the room, and when he returned.

Figure 4-5   Percentage of time spent in high-activity involvement

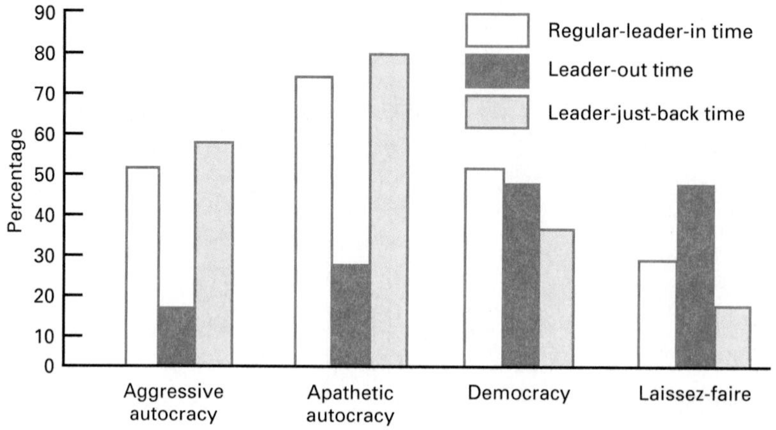

SOURCE: From R. Lippitt and R. White (1963), An experimental study of leadership and group life. In E. E. Macoby, T. M. Newcomb, and F. L. Hartley (eds.), *Readings in social psychology*, New York: Holt, Rinehart & Winston, p. 147.

has become a set of classic studies, Lewin, Lippitt, and White asked that question a half century ago. Actually, Lewin, Lippitt, and White conducted a series of studies, and the first results appeared under their names in 1939. The part of their work summarized in Research Summary 4-1 appeared later and was authored by Lippitt and White.

Effects of Student Behavior on Each Other and on Teachers

Studies such as the ones by Lewin, Lippitt, and White provide evidence that what teachers do influences what their students do. Influence in classrooms, however, does not always flow just from the teacher. Students influence each other and

can even influence the behavior of the teachers. One particularly interesting line of inquiry over the years has been research that investigates how the student peer group, through both formal and informal interactions, affects attitudes and achievement. Peer group influences have been documented in studies of college dormitories and living houses (Newcomb, 1961, for example), and in many different public and private school settings. Much of the research shows that many students conform to peer group norms and that all too often these norms are in contradiction to those held by educators and teachers. James Coleman (1961) studied ten American high schools in the 1950s. He found many instances where the adolescent peer group supported norms for being popular and being athletic over the

DISCUSSION AND IMPLICATIONS: The researchers found that the boys reacted to autocratic leadership in one of two ways: aggressive (being rebellious and critical) and apathetic, (being turned off and noninvolved). Figure 4-4 indicates that in the clubs with autocratic leadership members were more dependent on the leaders' actions, showed more discontent, were less friendly to one another, made fewer suggestions and fewer requests for information, and carried on less conversation with each other than did members in clubs with more democratic leaders.

Figure 4-5 shows the involvement pattern for the two types of autocratic groups, the democratic groups, and the laissez faire groups when the leader was present, when the leader was absent, and immediately after the leader returned. Members of the group with the democratic leader used about the same proportion of their time when the leader was present as when the leader was absent. Laissez faire group members were more involved when the leader was gone. The researchers concluded this was because certain boys were stepping in and providing leadership during this period. For the autocratic groups, it can be observed that the involvement dropped drastically when the leader left the room and then rose correspondingly upon the leader's return.

The Lewin, Lippitt, and White studies showed rather convincingly that leader (or teacher) behavior has important influences on children's willingness to cooperate and stick to learning tasks. Many have concluded from this study (and others like it) that teachers who are overly strict and autocratic may get a lot of work from their students if they are physically present, but that involvement will drop once close supervision is removed because of the dependency group members develop under autocratic leadership. The results from this study have also led to the conclusion that laissez faire teachers present problems to students in that leaderless groups or classrooms have difficulty persisting at tasks and defining expectations for accomplishment.

school's norms in support of academic achievement. This finding has been replicated in American high schools in every decade since Coleman's original work. Today peer group pressure is used often to explain high dropout rates and low achievement of many inner city youth.

Richard Schmuck (1963) also studied classroom peer groups, particularly friendship patterns in elementary schools. From a sample of 27 classrooms and over 700 students in rural, urban, and suburban Michigan, Schmuck found that the friendship patterns of students in elementary schools varied from classroom to classroom. In some classrooms many students liked one another and were highly involved with their classmates. In other classrooms students were very cliquish, with a few students identified as very popular and others rejected by their peers. In classrooms with broad peer-liking structures, Schmuck found that students were more likely to have higher feelings of self-esteem and to make more use of their academic abilities as contrasted with students in the cliquish classrooms.

Finally, student and peer group norms can even influence the behavior of their teachers. This idea was illustrated in a unique and very interesting study conducted by Willis Copeland (1980). Copeland turned around the traditional research question, "What do teachers do to influence students?" and asked, "What do students do to influence the behaviors of their teachers?" Participants in Copeland's study were students in two middle-grade school classrooms (Classrooms A and B) and two student teachers assigned to those classrooms (Beth and Al). Classroom A was located in a racially and ethnically mixed school and had a large proportion of underachieving pupils. Classroom B was located in a school in an affluent, upper-middle-class neighborhood and had highly able and motivated students. After 2 months of observation of students and teachers in these classrooms, the student teachers switched assignments. Al in Classroom A went to Classroom B; Beth in Classroom B went to Classroom A. Again student and teacher behaviors were observed.

Copeland found that regardless of who the teacher was (Al or Beth) in Classroom A, he or she adopted a more forceful questioning and responding style toward the students. Similarly, in Classroom B, regardless of whether Al or Beth was teaching, a more indirect questioning and responding style was used. Copeland concluded from his study that behavior in classrooms is bidirectional, that is, behaviors of the participants are influenced not only by what the teacher does but also by what students do. In this situation, the academic abilities and development of the students themselves served to influence the student teachers' behaviors. Certain teacher behaviors (direct and forceful) seemed to work (at least were used) with the less able and less motivated students found in Classroom A, while other behaviors (indirect) seemed to work and were used with the more able and motivated students found in Classroom B.

STRATEGIES FOR BUILDING PRODUCTIVE LEARNING ENVIRONMENTS

Building productive learning environments—places where students have positive attitudes toward themselves and their classroom group and where they display a high degree of achievement motivation and involvement in academic tasks—is a difficult and complex process for most beginning teachers. Experienced teachers who have skills in working with the alterable aspects of group and motivational processes are not always able to communicate these skills clearly to novice teachers. Experienced teachers, however, usually emphasize to beginning teachers that there is no one list of

"things to do," no single dramatic event that will produce a productive learning environment. Instead, as with so many of the leadership functions of teaching, success depends on doing a lot of "little things" well.

You saw in Getzels-Thelen's social system perspective of classroom life that major determinants of student behavior were their personal needs and the individual interests they bring with them to school as well as the social group which develops as students interact with each other and with their teacher. You saw in Doyle's ecological perspective how the lesson and its activities become the central components of classroom life. Both of these perspectives stress the importance of establishing productive learning environments—places where students are working cooperatively with the teacher and where they are engaged in important academic tasks. This condition is rather simple to prescribe, yet teachers find the task of getting students engaged in academic work among the most difficult of the leadership functions of teaching. It is no easy undertaking to motivate students who are "turned off" to school, just as it is no easy task to create learning activities that will challenge the able and at the same time sustain the interest of the less able. The strategies teachers use to motivate individual students and the work they do to help the classroom develop as a group are the ingredients for building productive learning environments. How effective teachers do these things provides the content for the remainder of this chapter.

Student Motivation

Figure 4-2 illustrated how student behavior results from an interaction of both personal and social dimensions of classroom life. The consideration of students' needs in the personal dimension leads to a discussion of **motivation,** a very important topic for teachers. Motivation is a rather abstract concept that is not easy to define. It is internal to the person and thus cannot be observed. Nonetheless, experienced teachers know the importance of motivation and know that it is one of the important forces that guides students' actions. Three major ideas guide contemporary thinking on motivation. Each can be translated into practical strategies for teachers to consider.

NEED DISPOSITION THEORY

Developed in the 1950s and 1960s (Alschuler et al., 1970; Atkinson, 1958; Atkinson and Feather, 1966; McClelland, 1958), **need disposition theory** presents the point of view that people are motivated to take action and invest energy in pursuit of three outcomes: achievement, affiliation, and influence. The desire for achievement is evident when students are trying hard to learn a particular subject or when they are striving to reach the objectives of a particular teacher. **Achievement motives** manifest themselves in teachers as they strive to provide good instruction and act as competent professionals. **Affiliative motives** become important when students and teachers come to value the support and friendship of their peers. The motivation toward **influence** can be seen in those students who strive to have more control over their own learning and in those teachers who strive to have a larger say in the way schools are run. Students' feelings of self-esteem are related to feelings they have about their competence, affiliation, and influence. When these emotional states are frustrated by the activities in a classroom or a school, students may become less involved in the school. When these states are frustrated for teachers they are likely to feel incompetent, lonely, and powerless.

Achievement motivation or the student's "intent to learn" is the most important aspect of this theory of motivation for classroom teaching and has been the focus of other theorists and researchers as they have refined and extended some of McClelland's and his colleagues' original ideas.

ATTRIBUTION THEORY

Much of the early research on achievement motivation found strong relationships between the child-rearing practices of parents and a child's achievement motivation. Parents who encourage their children to try new things and who reward them for high performance establish in their children a need to achieve and a willingness to take risks. On the other hand, parents who overly protect their children and punish them for failure tend to raise children with low achievement motivation. The assumption that achievement motivation is an unalterable result of early childhood experiences means teachers have little hope of changing a child's aspiration to learn. This led Bernard Weiner and several of his colleagues in the 1970s to propose **attribution theory** as an alternative explanation of achievement motivation. Attribution theory is a rather major reinterpretation of need disposition theory and is based on the proposition that the way persons come to *perceive* and to *interpret* the causes of their successes or failures are the major determinants of their achievement motivation, rather than fixed early experiences. According to Weiner (1974, 1979), success or failure can be attributed to four causes: ability, effort, luck, and the difficulty of the learning task. Some people tend to associate their success with their abilities and their failures with their lack of effort. Conversely, other people attribute their success to luck and their failures to their lack of ability. People with high achievement motivation seem to fall mostly in the first category; people with low achievement motivation in the second.

Attribution theory offers hope for teachers because, as is described later, teachers can do things to change students' perceptions of themselves and the things around them, and this in turn can lead to a corresponding increase in student effort.

FLOW

A third perspective on motivation stems from the work of University of Chicago psychologist and educator Mihaly Csikszentmihalyi (1990). For over two decades, Csikszentmihalyi has studied what he calls "states of optimal experience" defined as times in persons' lives when they are experiencing total involvement and concentration as well as strong feelings of enjoyment. These types of experiences are called **flow experiences** because the respondents Csikszentmihalyi studied often reported that what they were doing during the experience was so enjoyable "it felt like being carried away by a current, like being in a flow" (p. 127).

Perhaps you can think about a time in your life when you were doing something and became totally involved. It could have been climbing a mountain, reading a novel, working on an old car, playing chess, engaging in a challenging run, or writing a poem. If you were experiencing flow you would have been totally absorbed and concentrating on the activity alone even to the point of losing track of time. In Csikszentmihalyi's words, "actor and action become one" (p. 127) and participation is sustained because of intrinsic rather than extrinsic motivation.

Obviously, the concept of flow has implications for education and for teaching. In fact, Csikszentmihalyi has concluded that the main obstacles to student learning do not stem from cognitive abilities of students but instead from the way we structure schools and from learning experiences that inhibit intrinsic motivation and corresponding flow experiences. Emphasis on external rules and evaluation and on rewards such as grades deters flow experiences for students. Similarly, standardized curricula and lessons that keep students in passive roles inhibit involvement and enjoyment.

Schools and teachers who can structure learning activities so students become totally involved and experience flow are much more likely to enable students to excel in academic and social learning. This type of total involvement, however, is only possible in learning experiences that have certain characteristics.

First, flow experiences require that the challenge of a particular learning activity corresponds to the learner's level of skill. All the learner's skill is required, yet the activity cannot be so difficult that the participant becomes frustrated. Perhaps rock climbing can provide the best example of the need to match the degree of challenge and skill. If you were an advanced beginning rock climber, you would be bored if asked to climb the slightly sloping, 15-foot-high rock in your backyard. This would not require use of your skills nor provide you with challenging practice. On the other hand, as an advanced beginner you would become very frustrated and stressed if asked to climb El Capitan, one of the most challenging climbs in the United States. You will read later how experienced teachers plan lessons in which they balance the level of difficulty and the amount of challenge.

The definition of clear and unambiguous goals is a second characteristic of learning experiences likely to produce flow. As you read in Chapter 2, lessons that make clear to students what is expected of them and what they are supposed to accomplish are more likely to produce extended engagement and involvement than are lessons with unclear goals and expectations.

Finally, persons who report having had flow experiences say they gained relevant and meaningful feedback about their activity as they were doing it. Feedback on good performance provides intrinsic motivation. Feedback on poor performance gives the person needed information to improve. How teachers can facilitate feedback and knowledge of results in lessons will be described in the next section.

In summary, Csikszentmihalyi's theory of motivation emphasizes the importance of designing learning experiences that students will find enjoyable and appropriately challenging. This type of learning experience will be intrinsically rather than extrinsically motivating and will be characterized by activity with clear goals and opportunities for feedback.

ALTERABLE FACTORS AND MOTIVATION

You saw in the Getzels-Thelen model that one major determinant of students' behavior was their personal needs and the individual attributes and interests they bring with them to the classroom. You also saw in the explanations of need disposition and attribution theories that there are some aspects influencing student motivation, such as early childhood experiences, over which teachers can have little influence. Unfortunately, many teachers attend only to these aspects of student motivation. Often the lunchroom conversations of teachers focus on the social backgrounds of students: "He comes from a broken home"; "She lives in poverty"; "His family has never been to college"; "Her mother is a social climber and has unrealistic expectations for her." Psychological analysis is also a favorite topic of discussion: "John is insecure"; "Richard is overly dependent"; "Mary is anxious"; "Ben is afraid to risk failure." Even though these observations and diagnoses may be accurate, there really isn't very much teachers can do to alter or influence past events. There are, however, specific steps teachers can take in their classrooms that will increase their students' motivation to learn. In this section several concrete factors contributing to motivation that *can* be influenced by the beginning teacher are described. Several of these have been borrowed from the work of Madeline Hunter (1982) and her translation of Weiner's attribution theory. Others come from ideas discovered by teachers themselves.

Figure 4-6   Balancing difficulty and stress

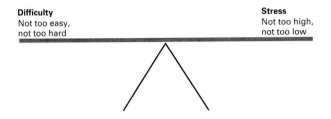

Difficulty	**Stress**
Not too easy, not too hard	Not too high, not too low

Madeline Hunter (1982) concluded that there are several factors associated with motivation that teachers can modify and control. These factors are not discrete, nor is one more important than the other. Instead, they interact with one another and together can increase students' motivation to learn.

Level of Concern.   One aspect of motivation is the **level of concern** students have toward achieving some learning goal. Concern is also associated with stress. If students find a task too easy or the present level of performance satisfactory, they will feel little need to achieve and will put out little effort. On the other hand, if a task is too difficult or if it causes too much stress, then the stress itself becomes dominant and little energy will be expended on learning. Figure 4-6 illustrates the balance needed for a learning task to be at the right level.

Hunter (1982) reported that a "moderate level of concern stimulates effort to learn" (p. 12) and offered the following examples of ways teachers can raise or lower students' levels of concern toward learning tasks:

a. Stand next to a student who is not participating to raise concern, or move away from an anxious student to lower concern.

b. Announce that "This will probably be on the test," or reassure your class that "Everyone has trouble with this at first but, as we work, it will become increasingly clear."

c. Give a test that you grade, or give a test followed by the answers so students can check their own learning.

d. Announce that "This part is difficult and a high level of concentration and effort is required," or that "This is difficult but we will work on it for several days before you are expected to know it." (p. 12)

Closely connected to the strategy of adjusting students' level of concern is that of helping students set realistic and achievable goals. Students who set very high goals which are unachievable can be encouraged to rethink what might be more realistic goals for themselves. Similarly, students who always set low goals can be encouraged to raise their sights.

Feeling Tone.   As observed in Santrock's study, students put forth more or less effort according to the pleasantness or unpleasantness of the learning environment and the particular learning situation. Hunter (1976) provided the following examples of things teachers can say to establish a positive, neutral, or negative **feeling tone:**

Positive	"You write such interesting stories, I'm anxious to read this one."
Negative	"That story must be finished before you're excused for lunch."
Neutral	"If you aren't finished, don't worry, there'll be plenty of time later."

(p. 32)

An important point for teachers to consider, if they choose to use unpleasant feeling tones to motivate students to complete a difficult learning task, is to return as soon as possible to a positive one. Again Hunter (1982) provides some good examples: "I really put a lot of pressure on you and you've responded magnificently," or "I know you were angry about the demands being made, but you should be proud of the improvement in your performance" (p. 13).

Feeling tones in the classroom are not only the result of specific things teachers say at a particular moment; they are also the result of many other structures and processes created by teachers to produce productive learning environments. Some of these will be described in later sections of this chapter.

Success.   A third factor that can influence a student's achievement motivation, feelings of success, is associated with the degree of difficulty of a task and the amount of effort expended. Tasks that are too easy require too little effort and produce no feelings of success and, consequently, are unmotivational. At the same time, tasks that are too difficult for students, regardless of the effort they expend, will also be unmotivational. Effective teachers learn how to adjust the level of difficulty of learning tasks for particular students. Sometimes this means providing special challenges for the brightest in the class and providing more support and assistance for those who find a particular task too difficult.

Effective teachers also help students see the connections between the amount of effort they put into a learning task and their successes and accomplishments. This is done by discussing with students why particular efforts led to success and conversely why in other instances they led to failure.

Interest. The interest level students have in a particular learning task is certainly associated with their motivation to achieve. The teacher can do a number of things to relate learning materials and activities to students' interests. Hunter (1982) provided the following examples:

> Relating materials to students' lives and using the students' names: "Suppose John, here, were presenting an argument for electing his friend and Charles wished to challenge his position. . . ." Or, "Mary, here, has the pigmentation most commonly associated with Nordic races while Sue's is more typical of the Latinos." (p. 19)
>
> Making materials vivid and novel: "When you order your favorite McDonald's milkshake, it won't melt even if you heat it in the oven. That's the result of an emulsifier made from the algae we're studying." Or, "Suppose you believed in reincarnation. In your next life what would you need to accomplish that you didn't accomplish satisfactorily in this life?" (pp. 19–20)

Using games, puzzles, and other activities which are inviting and carry their own intrinsic motivation is another means that teachers use to make lessons interesting for students. Similarly, variety of activities (field trips, simulations, music, guest speakers) and instructional methods (lecture, seatwork, discussion, small-group) keep students interested in school and their schoolwork.

Two cautions need to be highlighted about using student interests for motivational purposes. Stressing the novel or vivid can sometimes distract

students from learning, a topic that will be discussed in more detail in Chapter 8. Similarly, new interests are formed through learning about a new topic. Teachers who expose their students only to materials in which they are already interested prevent them from developing new interests.

Knowledge of Results. Getting feedback about performance is a fifth motivational factor described by Hunter (1982). This includes feedback about areas in which students are doing well in addition to those that need improvement. **Knowledge of results** needs to be more specific and immediate than the grades teachers put on report cards every 6 to 9 weeks. In Chapter 10 specific guidelines for giving feedback are provided. This topic is also covered in the chapter on testing and evaluation. It is enough to say here that feedback needs to be as immediate as possible (handing back tests the next day), as specific as possible (comments in addition to an overall grade on a paper), and nonjudgmental ("Your use of the word 'that' is incorrect—you should have used 'which' instead," rather than, "What's wrong with you? We have gone over the difference between 'that' and 'which' a dozen times").

Assignments can also be designed with built-in feedback features. The use of videotaping and the microcomputer is particularly good for assignments and practice with built-in feedback.

Classroom Goal and Reward Structures. Competitive goal and reward structures lead to comparisons and win-lose relationships among students and make a student's ability, rather than effort, the primary factor for success. Cooperative goal and reward structures lead to social interdependence, and shared activity makes student effort the primary factor for success. Chapter 11 will go into greater detail about how to set up cooperative goal and reward structures.

Attending to Influence and Affiliation Motives. Most motivational research has focused on achievement motivation. Although less is known about influence and affiliation motives, they too play a role in determining the type of effort students will expend on learning tasks and how long they will persist. In general, students' influence needs

Table 4-1   Pluses and Wishes Chart

PLUSES	WISHES
The lecture on cells was clear.	We wish we had had more time on the experiment.
The group work was interesting.	We wish more students would cooperate.
We enjoyed the principal's visit.	We wish the test had been fairer.

are satisfied when they feel they have some power or say over their classroom environment and their learning tasks, as illustrated in the Lewin, Lippitt, and White (1939) studies. Here are a few specific examples of how teachers can use influence needs to motivate students:

- Hold weekly planning sessions with students, assessing how well the previous week has gone and what they would like to see included in next week's lessons. Some experienced teachers use a technique called "pluses and wishes." On large newsprint or butcher paper the teacher makes two columns and labels them as shown in Table 4-1. Together students and teachers list their suggestions for all to consider. The teacher can use information on this list in his or her own planning and can come back to it to show students that particular lessons and activities have been influenced by their input.
- Assign students to perform important tasks, such as distributing and collecting books and papers, taking care of the aquarium, taking roll, acting as tutors to other students, taking messages to the principal's office, and the like.

In most schools, it is the peer group that students look to for satisfying their affiliation needs. Unfortunately, norms for peer group affiliation often conflict with the strong achievement norms teachers would like to see. In some instances, very competitive cliques that exclude many students from both the academic and social life of the school are found. In other instances, peer group norms exist that apply negative sanctions to those students who try to do well in school work. Teachers can

make needs for affiliation work in a positive way by following some of these procedures.

- Make sure that all the students in the class (even in high school) know one another's names and some personal information about each student.
- Initiate cooperative goal and reward structures, as described in Chapter 11.
- Take time to help the students in the classroom develop as a group, using procedures described in the following section.

Group Development

Chapter 1 described the developmental stages teachers go through in learning to teach. Groups, like individuals, also develop, grow, and pass through discernible stages in this process. The Schmucks (1988) have adapted general theories about **group development** and have created a four-stage developmental model for classroom groups. These four stages are summarized in Table 4-2.

The Schmucks are quick to point out, and rightfully so, that the stages of classroom development are not always sequential. Instead, they are often cyclical in nature, with many of the stages repeating themselves several times during the school year. When new students are placed in classrooms, membership issues again become important. Student growth in interpersonal skills keeps influence issues unstable and in constant flux. Larger societal issues cause change and a need to renegotiate norms associated with academic goals and performances.

The stages of classroom group development also have no *definite* time frames associated with them. The time it takes each group to work out issues associated with membership, influence, and task accomplishment will depend upon the skill of individual members within the class and the type of leadership the teacher provides. *General* time frames, however, can be inferred from the statements of experienced teachers. They report that membership issues consume students during the first month of school and that the most productive period for student learning and attention to academic tasks is between November and early May.

Teachers can assist the development of their classroom group in two important ways. They can teach students that groups grow and learn in some

Table 4-2   Schmucks' Stages of Classroom Development

STAGE	GROUP AND MEMBER NEEDS AND BEHAVIORS
Stage 1: Inclusion and membership	Early in classroom life students seek to find a niche for themselves in the peer group. Students want to present a good image and are on their good behavior. Teachers have great influence during this period because of their assigned authority. Everyone is sizing up one another, and the issues of inclusion and membership must be resolved before the group can move along to the next state.
Stage 2: Influence and collaboration	Members of the class enter into two types of power struggles. One struggle tests the authority of the teacher; the other establishes the peer group pecking order. Tensions will exist between the students and the teacher and between the students themselves during this stage. If these tensions cannot be resolved and power relationships balanced, the group cannot move along very productively to the next stage.
Stage 3: Individual and academic goals	The classroom enters a stage of development for working productively on academic goals. Students during this stage can set and accomplish goals and work together on tasks. The classroom can also be pulled back into earlier stages during this stage.
Stage 4: Self-renewal/adaptive change	This stage is one in which members can think about their continuous growth and about taking on new and more challenging tasks. This is also a stage that can produce conflict because change in tasks will perhaps upset earlier resolutions of issues around membership and power.

SOURCE: Based on material from R. A. Schmuck and P. A. Schmuck, pp. 178–187. Copyright © 1988 Wm. C. Brown. All rights reserved. By permission.

of the same ways individuals do. They can also explain and help students learn how to work in groups and provide leadership to group efforts.

Teachers can help students resolve membership and inclusion issues by having lessons that help students learn each other's names and find out information about one another. When new students enter the group special efforts can be made to ensure their acceptance. Influence issues can be resolved by using many of the techniques described later in relation to classroom management. Communicating goals and expectations to students can help groups aspire to high individual and group achievement.

Finally, positive communication and discourse is perhaps the single most important variable for building groups and productive learning environments. It is through classroom discourse that norms are established and classroom life defined. It is through discourse that the cognitive and social aspects of learning unite. Much more about this important topic is included in Chapter 13.

SUMMARY

- Classrooms can be viewed as social and ecological systems that include and influence the needs and motives of individuals, institutional roles, and the interaction between member needs and group norms.
- A productive learning environment is characterized by an overall climate where students feel positive about themselves and their peers, where their individual needs are satisfied so they persist in academic tasks and work cooperatively with the teacher, and where students have the requisite interpersonal and group skills to meet the demands of classroom life.
- Four important features which help us understand classrooms include classroom climate, classroom properties, classroom processes, and classroom structures. Classroom climate refers to the overall ethos or atmosphere of the classroom. Climate evolves from the interaction of individual needs and motives with institu-

tional roles and expectations. Classroom properties are distinctive features of classrooms that help shape behavior. Six important properties include multidimensionality, simultaneity, immediacy, unpredictability, publicness, and history. Classroom processes define interpersonal and group features of classrooms and include expectations, leadership, attraction, norms, communication, and cohesiveness. Classroom structures are the foundations which shape particular lessons and behaviors during those lessons. Four important structures include task, goal, reward, and participation structures.

- Some classroom features can be altered by the teacher; others cannot. Some of the classroom properties, such as multidimensionality or immediacy, cannot be influenced readily by the teacher. Group processes and the classroom goal, task, reward, and participation structures are more directly under the teacher's control.
- Studies on classroom environment show that student motivation and learning are influenced by the types of processes and structures teachers create in particular classrooms.
- Studies have also uncovered important relationships between teacher behaviors, student engagement, and learning. In general, students react more positively and persist on academic tasks in classrooms characterized by democratic as opposed to authoritarian processes.
- Influence in classrooms does not flow just from the teacher. Studies have shown that students influence each other and also the behavior of their teachers.
- Effective teachers create productive learning environments by focusing on things that can be altered, such as increasing student motivation and encouraging group development.
- Factors associated with motivation that teachers can modify and control include students' level of concerns, feeling tones, task difficulty and success rates, students' interests, knowledge of results, classroom goal and reward structures, and students' achievement, influence, and affiliation motives.
- Teachers assist the development of their classrooms as a group by teaching students how groups grow and learn and by helping students learn how to work in groups.

- Time allocated to building productive learning environments will reduce many of the frustrations experienced by beginning teachers and extend their abilities to win student cooperation and involvement in academic tasks.

KEY TERMS

classroom environments
classroom climate
personal dimension
social dimension
classroom properties
multidimensionality
group processes
expectations
leadership
attraction
norms
classroom structures
task structures
goal structures
cooperative goal structure
competitive goal structure
individualistic goal structure
reward structure
participation structure
achievement motive
affiliation motive
influence motive
attribution theory
level of concern
feeling tone
knowledge of results
group development

BOOKS FOR THE PROFESSIONAL

Csikszentmihalyi, M. (1990). *Flow: The psychology of optimal experience*. New York: Harper and Row. This book describes Csikszentmihalyi's research and his theories about flow, or optimal, experiences. It is not written specifically for teachers; however, it is very readable and will be of interest to the beginning teacher who wants to explore theories of motivation in some depth.

Egan, G. (1974). *The skilled helper: A model for systematic helping and interpersonal relationships*. Monterey, Calif.: Brooks/Cole. This is an excellent presentation of theory behind helping relationships and good specific examples that can be adapted by teachers.

Johnson, D. W., and Johnson, F. P. (1987). *Joining together: Group theory and group skills* (3d ed.). Englewood Cliffs, N.J.: Prentice-Hall. This book is an excellent introduction to group theory with many practical exercises that can be used by teachers in the classroom.

Marzano, R. J. (1992). *A different kind of classroom: Teaching with dimensions of learning*. Alexandria, Va.: Association for Supervision and Curriculum Development. This excellent new book considers what we need to do to make classrooms into learning-centered environments that support student learning and growth.

Morine-Dershimer, G. (1985). *Talking, listening, and learning in elementary classrooms*. New York: Longman. This book looks at classroom interaction patterns and pupils' perceptions of classroom language.

Schmuck, R. A., and Schmuck, P. (1988). *Group processes in the classroom* (5th ed.). Dubuque, Iowa: W. C. Brown. This book provides a thorough review of group dynamics literature as it applies to the classroom as a learning group and includes many activities and ideas to help teachers build productive learning environments.

Stipek, D. J. (1988). *Motivation to learn: From theory to practice*. Englewood Cliffs, N.J.: Prentice-Hall. Stipek provides a good survey of theory and research on the various approaches for understanding motivation and also presents concrete suggestions on how to apply motivational theories to classroom practices.

LEARNING AIDS FOR PLANNING, OBSERVATION, AND REFLECTION

- Assessing My Ability for Building Productive Learning Environments
- Surveying Students about Classroom Climate
- Interviewing Teachers about Classroom Goal and Reward Structures
- Motivation Questionnaire for Students

ASSESSING MY ABILITY FOR BUILDING PRODUCTIVE LEARNING ENVIRONMENTS

PURPOSE: To help you assess your level of understanding ad skill for building productive learning environments.

DIRECTIONS: Check the level of understanding or skill you perceive you have for the various concepts and teaching tasks listed for building productive learning environments.

UNDERSTANDING OR SKILL	LEVEL OF UNDERSTANDING OR SKILL		
	HIGH	MEDIUM	LOW
My understanding of			
Classroom climate	_____	_____	_____
Classroom properties	_____	_____	_____
Classroom processes	_____	_____	_____
Classroom structures	_____	_____	_____
Expectations	_____	_____	_____
Motivation	_____	_____	_____
My ability to			
Promote positive expectations	_____	_____	_____
Increase student motivation by adjusting			
Level of concern	_____	_____	_____
Feeling tone	_____	_____	_____
Success	_____	_____	_____
Interest	_____	_____	_____
Knowledge of results	_____	_____	_____
Goal and reward structures	_____	_____	_____
Influence and affiliation motives	_____	_____	_____
Facilitate group development by attending to			
Inclusion and membership issues	_____	_____	_____
Influence and collaboration issues	_____	_____	_____
Individual and academic goals	_____	_____	_____
Self-renewal and adaptive change	_____	_____	_____

SURVEYING STUDENTS ABOUT CLASSROOM CLIMATE

PURPOSE: A positive classroom climate can facilitate learning. This aid will give you a means of determining students' perceptions about classroom climate.

DIRECTIONS: Ask a teacher if you can conduct the survey in his or her class. Then distribute the survey to students for them to fill out in class. If you are working with younger children or those with reading difficulties, you may wish to read each item aloud and have students fill out answer sheets with happy, indifferent, or frowning faces. Add other questions that may be of special interest to you.

Classroom Life

Here is a list of some statements that describe life in the classroom. Circle the letter in front of the statement that best tells how you feel about this class. *There are no right or wrong answers.*

1. Life in this class with your regular teacher has:
   a. All good things
   b. Mostly good things
   c. More good things than bad
   d. About as many good things as bad
   e. More bad things than good
   f. Mostly bad things

2. How hard are you working these days on learning what is being taught at school?
   a. Very hard
   b. Quite hard
   c. Not very hard
   d. Not hard at all

3. When I'm in this class, I usually am:
   a. Wide awake and very interested
   b. Pretty interested, kind of bored part of the time
   c. Not very interested, bored quite a lot of the time
   d. Bored, don't like it.

4. How hard are you working on schoolwork compared with the others in the class?
   a. Harder than most
   b. A little harder than most
   c. About the same as most
   d. A little less than most
   e. Quite a bit less than most

5. How many of the pupils in this class do what the teacher suggests?
   a. Most of them do
   b. More than half do
   c. Less than half do
   d. Hardly anybody does

6. If we help each other with our work in this class, the teacher:
   a. Likes it a lot
   b. Likes it some
   c. Likes it a little
   d. Doesn't like it at all

7. How good is your schoolwork compared with the work of others in the class?
   a. Much better than most
   b. A little better than most
   c. About the same as most
   d. Not quite as good as most
   e. Much worse than most

8. How often do the pupils in this class help one another with their schoolwork?
   a. Most of the time
   b. Sometimes
   c. Hardly ever
   d. Never

9. How often do the pupils in this class act friendly toward one another?
   a. Always
   b. Most of the time
   c. Sometimes
   d. Hardly ever

Analysis and Reflection: Tabulate and examine the results of the survey to obtain a broad view of the classroom's feeling tone, of student motivation, and the norms and expectations of the group. Look for classroom trends and for individuals or subgroups that may deviate from the classroom. Write a paragraph about this classroom's climate and its strong and weak points; suggest ways it might be improved.

SOURCE: Adapted from R. Fox, M. B. Luszki, and R. Schmuck, *Diagnosing classroom learning environment,* Chicago: Science Research Associates, 1966, pp. 11–13.

INTERVIEWING TEACHERS ABOUT CLASSROOM GOAL AND REWARD STRUCTURES

PURPOSE: Goal and reward structures can have a significant impact on the learning environment. This aid is to help you examine how goal and reward structures are exhibited in classrooms.

DIRECTIONS: Use these questions as a guide in interviewing teachers about how they use classroom goal and reward structures.

(Remember that goal structures can be individualistic, competitive, or cooperative; that is, students' attainment of a goal can be unrelated to others' attainment, dependent on the failure of others, or dependent on the success of others, respectively. Reward structures are distinct from goal structures in that they refer to the rewards students receive for attaining their goals. Reward structures can also be individualistic, competitive, or cooperative. As in goal structures, if rewards are given individually and independently of the rewards others receive, then the reward structure is individualistic; if one's reward is dependent on the failure of others to receive the reward, the reward structure is competitive; and a reward structure in which one's reward is dependent on the success of another is a cooperative reward structure. Think about a track meet as an example. If the goal is to win the race, then one person winning means others fail. This is a competitive goal structure. The ribbon or trophy is the reward. If only the winner receives the ribbon, then the reward structure is competitive. If everyone receives a ribbon, say for participation, then the reward structure is individualistic.)

1. What activities do you have students do in which their ability to complete the activity or attain the goal of the activity is unrelated to whether other students complete it?

   _____

   _____

   _____

2. What activities do you have students do in which their ability to complete the activity or attain the goal of the activity depends on other students not completing it or attaining the goal?

   _____

   _____

   _____

3. What activities do you have students do where they must work together, where one student's ability to complete the activity to attain the goal depends on other students also being able to complete it or attain the goal?

   _____

   _____

   _____

4. In what ways do you reward students so that one student's reward is unrelated to rewards for any other students?

_____

_____

_____

5. In what ways do you reward students so that one student's reward depends on another student not receiving the award?

_____

_____

_____

6. In what ways do you reward students so that one student's reward hinges on whether other students also receive the reward?

_____

_____

_____

Analysis and Reflection: What are the predominant goal and reward structures in these teachers' classes? Are all three types of structures represented? Is the mix of structures appropriate? What would be a better mix?

MOTIVATION QUESTIONNAIRE FOR STUDENTS

PURPOSE: Motivation is a critical element in building productive learning environments. This student questionnaire can help uncover strengths and weaknesses around motivation.

DIRECTIONS: Ask a teacher if you can survey his or her students about motivation. Distribute the survey and have students rate each statement on a scale of 1 to 5, agree strongly to disagree strongly.

**1 Agree strongly   2 Agree   3 Neither agree nor disagree
4 Disagree   5 Disagree strongly**

1. Sometimes I get a little nervous about my work in this class.	1 2 3 4 5
2. I want to do really well in this class.	1 2 3 4 5
3. I usually have to do boring things in this class.	1 2 3 4 5
4. This is a very pleasant class.	1 2 3 4 5
5. If I try, I can usually manage the work in this class.	1 2 3 4 5
6. I really don't care about grades very much.	1 2 3 4 5
7. My teacher is the only one who decides what happens in this class.	1 2 3 4 5
8. My teacher takes a long time to grade my papers, and seldom writes comments on them.	1 2 3 4 5
9. This class is way too easy for me.	1 2 3 4 5
10. I worry a lot all the time about my work in this class.	1 2 3 4 5
11. We never work in groups in this class.	1 2 3 4 5
12. I feel like I have a say in what happens in this class.	1 2 3 4 5
13. Sometimes we work and get graded in groups in this class.	1 2 3 4 5
14. This class makes me feel unhappy.	1 2 3 4 5
15. Interesting things happen in this class.	1 2 3 4 5
16. This class is way too hard.	1 2 3 4 5
17. My teacher almost always tells me why I got the grade I got right away.	1 2 3 4 5

Find the mean score for each item. Fill in the accompanying form with the mean score for each item. The items are sorted out according to the different domains, or elements of motivation. A high score on the positively worded items indicates a good job has been done in motivating students in that domain. A high score on the negatively worded items indicates a need for improvement.

DOMAIN	POSITIVELY WORDED	NEGATIVELY WORDED
Level of concern	1 _____	10 _____
Feeling tone	4 _____	14 _____
Success	5 _____	9 _____
		16 _____
Interest	15 _____	3 _____
Knowledge of results	17 _____	8 _____
Goal and reward structures	13 _____	11 _____
Influence needs	12 _____	7 _____
Achievements	2 _____	6 _____

Analysis and Reflection: Write a paragraph detailing the ways students are motivated in this class and suggesting ways motivation could be improved.

Chapter Outline

PERSPECTIVE AND RATIONALE
• Examining the Problem • Why Teach
Multiculturally? • Philosophical Roots
SAMPLING THE KNOWLEDGE BASE
• Race and Ethnicity • Language • Gender • Social
Class • Exceptionality
CREATING CLASSROOMS THAT ARE MULTICULTURAL
• Personal and Professional Development • Teacher
Expectations • Curriculum Development • Instructional
Development • Classroom Organization and
Management • School Organization

CHAPTER 5

Multicultural and Mainstreamed Classrooms

Dr. Nancy Winitzky, University of Utah

Multicultural education is an important topic for teachers. At its heart is a concern about equity and fair treatment for groups that have traditionally experienced discrimination. Originally restricted to minority racial groups, multicultural education now applies to differences based on language, gender, class, and exceptionality as well as racial and ethnic differences. Given the diversity of contemporary society, increasing international interdependence, and past histories of discrimination, it is critical for beginning teachers to become culturally aware and instructionally effective with diverse groups of students.

This chapter will help lay the groundwork for you as you begin your study of multicultural education. Its history and rationale will be traced, research in each multicultural domain will be sampled, and recommendations for practice will be advanced.

PERSPECTIVE AND RATIONALE

For most educators, the term **multicultural education** has come to signify recognizing, understanding, and appreciating all cultural groups and the development of skills in working with diverse groups of students. Some scholars, however, prefer a more activist view of the term, one that goes beyond the development of sensitivity, understanding, and interpersonal skills and advocates, in addition, some form of direct political action.

Examining the Problem

Many of the same forces that gave rise to the civil rights movement and movements throughout the world for greater equity and freedom have provided the impetus for the evolving concept of multicultural education. The realization of injuries suffered by minority groups, the desire to right those wrongs, and the resurgence of pride in racial and ethnic heritage all converged on the classroom in the post-World War II era and intensified concern for multicultural education. As described in Chapter 1, the growing awareness that the United States is increasingly a multicultural society, the fact that minority groups will soon constitute a majority of the school population, and the increasing necessity for all subcultures to understand and appreciate each other are all factors sustaining teachers' interest in multicultural education.

It is easy to become complacent about these issues when we see examples of handicapped people becoming successful comedians and actors, women and minorities being elected to prominent

Figure 5-1   Persons earning incomes over $25,000 in the United States

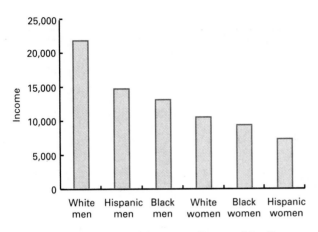

SOURCE: U.S. Department of Commerce, Bureau of the Census, *Statistical Abstract of the United States,* 112th ed., p. 453.

posts, and bilingual programs being provided for new immigrants. However, as Sleeter and Grant (1988) caution, these signs of progress can be deceiving. The fact that the income of black high school graduates is still 40 percent below that of white graduates is disturbing to many. Inequalities are also evident in differential health, unemployment, poverty, political representation, and crime statistics, with blacks, Hispanics, and other minority ethnic groups consistently suffering more adverse conditions than whites.

The picture is almost as bleak for women. Female earning power is still only about 70 percent that of men, even when mitigating factors such as experience and education are taken into consideration. That gap has been widening in recent years. A recent United Nations analysis reports that American women make only 65 percent of what men earn. Coupled with the fact that women are increasingly becoming heads of households, this has led to greater poverty levels for women and children. For example, while 16 percent of all children lived below the poverty line in 1970, 21 percent did so in 1985. That number is projected to rise to 27 percent by the year 2020 (Pallas, Natriello, and McDill, 1989). Figures 5-1 and 5-2 show how women and children suffer poverty disproportionately.

Social class stratification is an invisible problem

to most Americans, but one that seems to be worsening in recent years. The overall poverty rate has been increasing and the middle class is shrinking. Recent Bureau of the Census estimates of poverty indicate that 35.7 million Americans live below the poverty line, a 28-year high, and that most of them are children. Reed and Sautter (1990) report that the United States has the highest rate of childhood poverty among industrial nations. Homelessness is also a troubling problem. Families now account for one-third of the homeless; as many as 500,000 children in this country are homeless. While beliefs about rugged individualism incline us to blame the individuals for their distressing situations, studies indicate that economic achievement is best predicted by educational achievement, which in turn depends primarily on family socioeconomic status (Sleeter and Grant, 1988). This means that if you are poor, the educational and economic deck is stacked against you, making success much more difficult to attain.

The handicapped are yet another disadvantaged group. Statistics on the physically and mentally disabled are not as complete as for other groups, but it is known that unemployment and underemployment rates are very high. Unemploy-

Figure 5-2   Children in U.S. schools who live below the poverty line

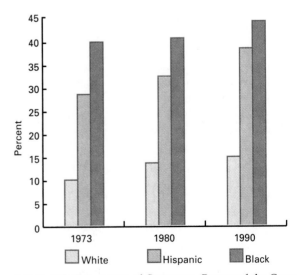

SOURCE: U.S. Department of Commerce, Bureau of the Census, *Statistical Abstract of the United States,* 112th ed., p. 456.

ment rates as high as 36 percent have been cited, and the poverty rate for the disabled is estimated to be 26 percent.

Why Teach Multiculturally?

Some may ask why schools should concern themselves with these larger social problems. It may be unfair, even unrealistic, to expect schools to remedy such inequities. There are at least three arguments that could be advanced in response. The first is that these issues should be of major concern to every citizen, that it is incumbent upon us as citizens to work toward the public good by trying to ameliorate these problems. Since we are citizens who happen to be educators, we can do our part through multicultural education.

The second argument is that Americans have a strong belief in the power of education as the route to later success in life—economically, politically, and culturally. This belief is supported by research, which consistently shows that education is related to income. The argument has intuitive appeal as well, in that educated persons are equipped with the tools to escape from poverty and to participate fully in our economic and political systems.

Finally, many believe that we really have no choice. We simply live in a multicultural world, and our schools should reflect that aspect of modern life. Children in today's schools come from an enormous range of backgrounds, languages, and abilities. To meet their educational needs, teachers must understand and promote teaching that is multicultural.

Philosophical Roots

The philosophy underlying multicultural education is cultural pluralism. Horace M. Kallen (1924), one of its major theorists, saw cultural pluralism as a step beyond two other competing ideologies— **Americanization** and the **melting pot**. Americanization was strongly promoted by prominent educators and politicians from the turn of the century well into the 1920s. Advocates believed that there existed an American race, culture, and value system that was based on the mores of northern Europe, and that minority groups should forsake their own cultures and assimilate completely into this dominant American culture. Elwood P. Cubberley, a noted

educator of the period, succinctly described the Americanization position:

> The southern and eastern Europeans are a very different type from the north Europeans who preceded them. Illiterate, docile, lacking in self-reliance and initiative and possessing none of the Anglo-Teutonic conceptions of law, order and government, their coming has served to dilute tremendously our national stock, and to corrupt our civic life. . . . Our task is to break up their groups or settlements, to assimilate and to amalgamate these people as part of our American race, and to implant in their children, so far as can be done, the Anglo-Saxon conceptions of righteousness, law and order and popular government, and to awaken in them reverence for our democratic institutions and for those things in our national life which we as a people hold to be of abiding worth. (Quoted in Krug, 1976, pp. 7–8)

The melting pot idea, although often confused with Americanization, was very different. Proponents of the melting pot believed that all ethnic groups had strengths and that in the "crucible" of America, these strengths would be merged into a new, superior culture. Rather than being contemptuous of cultural diversity, melting pot advocates welcomed diversity as a source of strength.

> They believed that the new emerging American culture must be built not on the destruction of the cultural values and mores of the various immigrant groups but on their fusion with the existing American civilization. . . . In the burning fires of the melting pot, all races were equal—all were reshaped, and molded into a new entity. (Krug, 1976, p. 12)

Cultural pluralism rejects both the racism of Americanization and the conception of a single culture emerging from the melting pot. Cultural pluralism, while acknowledging the existence of a dominant American culture, also recognizes the strength and permanence of its subcultures. In Kallen's (1924) conception, subcultures should accept the common elements of the dominant culture but should be constantly interacting with it and injecting into it new elements, to the benefit of all. The melting pot metaphor, with its implications of homogeneity, has been replaced with the salad metaphor, in which each ingredient is distinct and valued by itself, while at the same time contributing to the whole and bound together with a common dressing, that is, the dominant culture.

SAMPLING THE KNOWLEDGE BASE

Although values and philosophical perspectives influence classroom practice of multicultural education, there is at the same time a substantial knowledge base which describes what actually happens to children from diverse cultures when they attend school and which provides insights into the best practices for working with these children. In this section, research from each multicultural category —race and ethnicity, language, gender, social class, and exceptionality—will be sampled to see what guidance research has to offer.

It must be pointed out that the categories used to organize this section are social constructions. That is, while membership in any one category may be based on physical characteristics like skin color or disability, these characteristics may signify different categories in different societies. For example, in the United States, a person with any African ancestry is usually considered black; in Puerto Rico, however, the same person may be classified as white if his or her social standing is high. A disability, too, may or may not constitute a handicap, depending on social factors. Ease in manipulating symbols, for example, is important in technological societies, but less so in agrarian communities; a person lacking this skill would be considered learning disabled in one society, but not in the other. It is important to remember, as you read the sampled research, that these classifications are being used more for social purposes than because they have an independent basis in reality.

Race and Ethnicity

The racial and ethnic inequalities that persist in society are mirrored in schools and classrooms. Over the years, accumulated evidence has shown that minority students receive a lower-quality education as a result of differing enrollment patterns, an unequal curriculum, tracking, and differential classroom interactions with teachers. Minorities are disproportionately placed in vocational and special education programs but are underenrolled in col-

lege preparation and gifted programs. Even when the coursework is ostensibly the same, there are inequalities. For example, the College Entrance Examination Board (1985) found that blacks who had taken 3 or more years of mathematics were less likely than whites to have covered algebra, geometry, and calculus. The curriculum covered in vocational courses differs, too, with blacks receiving training for low-paying jobs such as cosmetology and mill work, and whites gaining experience with business finance and management concepts (Oakes, 1985).

Tracking represents a more formalized version of these curricular inequalities. While tracking per se has fallen out of favor in many school districts, de facto tracking through advising in or out of college preparatory coursework is common. Many investigators have demonstrated the deleterious effects of tracking on classroom life and learning for minority students (Goodlad, 1984; Oakes, 1985; Rosenbaum, 1976). For example, the content and cognitive demands differ, with emphasis on memorization of basic facts and skills in lower-track classes and lower-ability groups, and emphasis on critical thinking, problem solving, and conceptual understanding in the upper tracks. Interestingly, heterogeneous and middle-track classes more closely resemble the higher track in learning goals and activities; in other words, minority students are more likely to receive a higher-quality education in mixed-ability classes and groups.

Finally, teachers exhibit differential interaction patterns with minority and majority students. These differential patterns hold no matter the teacher's race. Minority students are asked fewer questions of all types, are given less wait time, and are less often praised or encouraged (Gay, 1974). We will return to the topic of teacher expectations and differential treatment later in this chapter.

Language
CULTURAL DEFICIT VERSUS CULTURAL DIFFERENCE

Are the teachers and administrators who treat minority students in this miseducative manner bad, racist people? Not usually. They are responding in ways that are reasonable given mainstream beliefs about teaching, learning, and the uses of language and given the ways the students behave. School staff and students often occupy different cultures with different ways of communicating and different beliefs and values. For example, Phillips (1972) studied the way Native American children learned at home and compared it to the way they were expected to learn in school. She observed that these children were silent in classroom lessons, sometimes even when asked a direct question by the teacher. Most Americans would assume that these children were extremely shy or that they had learning or linguistic disabilities—in the latter case referring them to low-ability or special classes would make sense. However, Phillips found that within their own culture, they were expected to learn by watching adults, not interacting with them; that they were to turn to older siblings, not adults, when they needed assistance; and that they were accustomed to a great deal more self-determination at home than was permissible in the school environment. In light of this information, their classroom behavior can be properly interpreted as an instance of cross-cultural miscommunication rather than as a deficiency.

Another example of cultural discontinuity comes from a landmark study of several years ago. Heath (1983) documented the diverging communicative styles of working-class African Americans, middle-class African Americans and Euro-Americans in the Piedmont region of the Carolinas. One of the many cultural differences she found involved the use of questions. At home, working-class African-American adults didn't ask children very many questions, and when they did, they were real questions, really seeking information that the adult didn't have. In school, however, teachers expected children to answer questions all the time, and the questions themselves were artifical in that the adults already knew the answer. From the students' perspective these questions didn't make any sense at all, and there was difficulty bridging the cultural gap.

Villegas (1991) has elaborated on the **cultural difference theory** to account for the achievement difficulties minority students experience in schools. The vehicle for interaction in school is language, and if language is used by a subculture in ways different from the mainstream, then members of the subculture are at a disadvantage, as these and other studies document. As Villegas explains:

> Children whose language use at home corresponds to what is expected in the classroom have an advantage in the learning process. For these students, prior experience transfers to the classroom and facilitates their academic performance. In contrast, minority children frequently experience discontinuity in the use of language at home and at school. They are often misunderstood when applying prior knowledge to classroom tasks. (p. 7)

The cultural difference theory has come to replace the **cultural deficit theory** as the most viable explanation for the difference in achievement between minority and majority students. Various deficit theories have posited that minorities are genetically deficient in IQ or have some other inherent defect that interferes with their ability to be successful in school. These theories have become discredited, partly because studies such as Heath's and Phillips' above, as well as many others, have shown just how much children of all cultures learn, linguistically, intellectually, socially, and culturally, before they enter school. Further, if the achievement differential were due to a deficiency, we would expect the gap in achievement to be widest when children begin school, and then to narrow as time went on. In fact, the opposite happens; the longer minority children spend in school, the farther they fall behind their mainstream peers (Persell, 1977).

DIALECTS

Clearly, language is a big factor in schooling. Not surprisingly, the United States enjoys a rich diversity of languages and dialects. Black English and Hawaiian Creole are a few of the major indigenous dialects. In the past, these and other dialects were considered inferior to English, and school people blamed the use of these "substandard" languages for childrens' poor academic performance (another manifestation of the cultural deficit theory). The school's remedy was to attempt to eliminate the use of the home dialect. This approach has not worked. Children do not improve academically when their language is suppressed and, in fact, may suffer negative emotional and cognitive consequences.

It is important to emphasize that people speaking a dialect are not speaking an error-ridden form of standard English. They are using a distinct language with its own complexity and its own rules.

Use of the double negative, for example, anathema in standard English, is correct in black English, as it is in many romance languages. Here is a further sampling of rules for black English (Jordan, 1988):

- Use a minimal number of words for every idea; this is the source for the aphoristic and poetic force of the language.
- Eliminate use of the verb *to be* whenever possible. This leads to the deployment of more descriptive and, therefore, more precise verbs.
- Never use the *-ed* suffix to indicate the past tense of a verb. (*Standard English:* She closed the door. *Black English:* She close the door. Or, she have close the door.)
- In Black English, unless you keenly want to underscore the past tense nature of an action, stay in the present tense and rely on the overall context of your ideas for the conveyance of time and sequence. (pp. 368–369)

Teachers must be careful not to make negative judgments about students' abilities based on such uses of English; that is, teachers should not assume that users of nonstandard English lack the intellectual capital to be academically successful. The goal should be to support the home dialect while at the same time helping students gain a firm command of standard English.

SECOND LANGUAGE ACQUISITION

In addition to dialect diversity, the United States is home to a number of people for whom English is a second language. These students are referred to as **ESL** (English as a second language) or **LEP** (limited English proficiency) students. There are over 200 Native American languages spoken in the United States, and a large minority of the U.S. population speaks Spanish. The influx of immigrants in recent years has brought many speakers of Vietnamese, Farsi, Korean, Russian, and many others. For millions of American students, English is not the native tongue.

How do these children approach the problem of learning English? It is not an easy task; communicative competence in any language consists of more than simply knowing its phonology (pronunciation), morphology (word formation), syntax (gram-

mar), and lexicon (vocabulary). The speaker also needs to understand how to organize speech beyond the level of single sentences; how to make and interpret appropriate gestures and facial expressions; about the norms surrounding using the language in accordance with roles, social status, and in different situations; and finally, how to use the language to acquire academic knowledge (cognitive-academic language proficiency).

In first-language learning, these abilities are acquired over an extended period of time and in meaningful social interaction with others. Cummins (1981) estimates that non-English speakers require 2 years to attain basic communication skills but need 5 to 7 years to develop cognitive-academic language proficiency (CALP). That is, children can get along on the playground and in social situations very readily, but to become skillful in learning academic content in the medium of English takes much longer.

It appears that the task of learning a second language is a creative one. Second-language learners do not passively soak up a new language; they must listen attentively, rely on social and other context cues to help them make guesses about how to use the language, test out their guesses, and revise accordingly (Allen, 1991). Wong Fillmore (1976) studied the strategies five Mexican children used to learn English. She found that they quickly developed several stock expressions ("gimme," "my turn," "what's that?") that they could apply in numerous situations, that they looked for patterns, that they made the most of what they did know, and that they worked on getting meaning across, supplementing speech with mime and gestures, and didn't worry too much about the finer points. In another study, Wong Fillmore (1982) compared good language learners with poor language learners and found that what distinguished them was their level of engagement in the classroom. Good learners did much observing, listening, and some interacting, while poor learners did little.

LANGUAGE IN THE CLASSROOM

Schools are legally required to assist language-different children in learning English and in learning school subjects. This came out of the 1974 Supreme Court ruling in *Lau v. Nichols*, arising from a class action suit by Chinese students in San Francisco against the school district. The Court reasoned that instruction presented in a language students could not understand amounted to denying them equal access to the educational system. The district's practice, common to many districts, had been simply to place LEP students in regular classrooms with native speakers. This **submersion approach,** allowing language minority students to sink or swim on their own, is no longer permissible.

Schools have responded to the *Lau v. Nichols* mandate in a variety of ways. The most common is to provide ESL instruction in a pull-out program. ESL students are placed in regular classrooms for most of the day but attend separate classes part of the day for English instruction. Another approach is to provide a **transitional bilingual program** for non-English-speaking students. In these programs, instruction is initially provided in the native language, with gradual increases in English until the student is proficient. ESL is a part of these programs, too. **Full bilingual programs,** in which the goal is full oral proficiency and literacy in both languages, are rare. Interestingly, research suggests that bilingualism brings with it several cognitive advantages, including heightened cognitive flexibility and a greater ability to analyze language (McCown and Roop, 1992).

Happily, researchers have also illuminated some methods that more effective teachers use to help language-minority students learn English and subject matter. Allen (1991) summarized this research:

> They simplified their language, used gestures, and linked talk to a strong context. While the child's native language was used occasionally to explain concepts that were difficult to make clear in English, direct translation was not used, nor were the two languages mixed. These teachers were making their language comprehensible by keeping the learner's special needs in mind, involving the children in talk, and judiciously using the native language when necessary.

Guidelines for teachers can also be gleaned from the second-language learning literature. To learn to speak, read, and write in English requires a high input of English speech and print. Teachers that structure learning tasks and classroom interaction to maximize comprehensible English input help their students master the language. For example, effective teachers would structure more teacher-student interaction and less peer interaction in a classroom in which most of the students were LEP, but in a classroom that was evenly divided between native speakers and LEP students, more peer interaction would be appropriate.

Gender

Education has long been a field dominated by women. During the 1920s, for example, more than half of all elementary school principals were women. However, as schools and districts became larger and more urban, the percentage of women administrators declined; in the 1970s, only 13 percent were women. Current trends are again reversing this picture, and the proportion of women in administration is on the rise (Sadker, 1985). Classroom teaching has been done primarily by women for well over a century.

Even though women predominate, gender bias has been a problem in the classroom. Complicating matters has been the controversy in recent years over whether gender differences exist in verbal and mathematical abilities and whether these differences are the result of differential socialization and education provided for boys as compared to girls. In a timely and persuasive meta-analysis (a technique for synthesizing and summarizing results from many individual studies), Linn and Hyde (1989) concluded that differences between boys and girls "were always small, that they have declined in the last 2 decades, that differences arise in some contexts and situations but not in others, and that educational programs can influence when differences arise" (p. 17). This is encouraging news for educators, because it fortifies our sense that we can and do make a difference in our students' lives.

Unfortunately, current differences in how males and females fare in schools are disturbing. Girls begin school ahead of boys on many cognitive, social, and physical factors, but by secondary school, they fall behind in achievement on standardized tests. Girls at the academic extremes are less likely to be identified and provided special assistance than boys (Cushner, McClelland, and Safford, 1992). In the classroom itself, teachers interact with girls less, give them less praise and other forms of feedback, and ask them fewer complex questions (Sadker and Sadker, 1990).

Researchers have identified both curricular and instructional elements of gender bias in classrooms, and have suggested improvements in practice based on these research findings. In analyzing curriculum materials, we can identify six forms of sex bias.

1. *Linguistic bias,* in which masculine terms and pronouns are used to refer to all people, is easy to spot and easy to remedy. Simply replacing *he* with *they, mankind* with *people,* and so on, corrects the problem.
2. *Stereotyping* is another problem. In many textbooks and basal readers, boys are depicted in typically male ways—brave, active, successful—while girls are shown as being timid, passive, and dependent. The bias extends into how adult males and females are featured, with men shown in traditionally male roles and careers, and women in traditionally female ones.
3. *Invisibility* is another way sex bias finds its way into teaching. Women are simply omitted or are greatly underrepresented in both text and illustrations.
4. *Imbalance* is a related problem and refers to the situation where only one aspect or interpretation of an issue or group of people is presented.
5. *Unreality* is another form of bias found in some textbooks and curriculum materials. In an attempt to avoid controversy, texts sometimes present an unrealistic picture of modern life, showing a nuclear family as typical, perhaps, instead of a single-parent or blended family.
6. *Fragmentation* is the last form of bias. Often information about women is not integrated into the body of a text, but is given in a separate chapter or box, conveying the idea that women's contributions are tangential to the mainstream and not important.

When teachers are working with materials that contain these biases, they need to supplement them with other books or illustrations that give balance to their instructional program. Teachers can also directly confront the curriculum biases with their students and use them as an opportunity to discuss their impact on all of us. Research has shown that attitudes are influenced by how females are depicted in materials. When children see the pronoun *he* used in a universal sense, they don't see people in their mind's eye, they see men. On the other hand, when children read about men and women behaving nonstereotypically, their attitudes about gender-appropriate behavior broaden (Scott, 1986). Of course, these same forms of bias can also be found with other cultural groups.

Social Class

Two research studies show dramatically the differences that **socioeconomic status** (SES) can make on school learning. Cazden (1972) examined speech patterns, specifically sentence length, under differing contexts for a working-class (low-SES) child and a middle-class (middle-SES) child. She found that while they each gave their shortest utterances in the same context, an arithmetic game, their longest-sentence context varied: for the middle-class child, during a formal, story-retelling situation, and for the working-class child, during an informal, out-of-school conversation. In an earlier study, Heider, Cazden, and Brown (1968) found that while working-class and middle-class students' descriptions of animal pictures contained the same number of key attributes, working-class students required more prompts from the adult interviewer than middle-class students. If the interviewer hadn't persisted in requesting more information, student knowledge would have been underestimated.

These findings indicate that low-SES students have verbal abilities that may not be accessed by typical classroom tasks. As with any cultural group, people of each socioeconomic status behave in ways appropriate to their subculture. Middle-class teachers expect middle-class behavior, and when low-SES students behave differently, as the above studies document, teachers' expectations about their abilities are negatively affected. Differing expectations result in differential student-teacher interactions, which result in poorer academic performance for low-SES students.

Another problem working-class students, and minority children, face is ability grouping and tracking. Low-SES students are disproportionately placed in low-ability groups and low-track classes. Instructional quality is poorer in these groups than in the higher groups. The criteria used to guide placement decisions are sometimes of dubious merit. Most often used are standardized aptitude test scores (the type administered in large groups, deemed least valid by test developers), and teachers' judgments. Unfortunately, teachers' judgments are influenced by race and class, and even when ability and teacher recommendation are equivalent, race and class are determining factors in placing children. The research highlighted in Research Summary 5-1 is a landmark study conducted by Ray Rist in 1970. He documented the impact of social class on grouping and instruction. In the 20-year span since the publication of Rist's study, other researchers (Anyon, 1980; Goodlad, 1984; Hallinan and Sorensen, 1983; Oakes, 1985; Rosenbaum, 1976; Sorensen and Hallinan, 1986) have corroborated his disturbing findings.

POVERTY

The picture does not improve when the focus is on schools that serve poor communities. Haberman (1991) has described the "pedagogy of poverty" that characterizes instruction in these schools. This pedagogy consists almost entirely of rote learning, of drill and practice, of teacher commands and student compliance. There is nothing wrong with drill and practice in and of itself, but when it is conducted to the exclusion of all other teaching behaviors, there is a problem. Haberman elaborates:

> The pedagogy of poverty does not work. Youngsters achieve neither minimum levels of life skills nor what they are capable of learning. The classroom atmosphere created by constant teacher direction and student compliance seethes with passive resentment that sometimes bubbles up into overt resistance. Teachers burn out because of the emotional and physical energy that they must expend to maintain their authority every hour of every day. (p. 291)

An increasingly large group of poor children are homeless. Their extremely stressful life situation causes special problems in the school. For example, because they move and change schools often, their records may not be available when they enter the school. They may also lack a feeling of control over

their own life and may react to that by clinging to objects or by acting out aggressively. Their living conditions may be very crowded, so that they come to tune out other people. Most distressing, of course, is the lack of the basics of decent food and clothing, leaving them susceptible to illness and to stigmatizing by their peers. The Stewart B. McKinney Homeless Assistance Act (P. L. 101-645, reauthorized in 1990) mandates that homeless children receive the same services as other students and that school districts remove any barriers to equal educational access, such as requiring school or immunization records prior to enrolling a student (Linehan, 1992).

Exceptionality

Public schools handle exceptional children primarily through **mainstreaming.** Legally the concept of mainstreaming came into existence in 1975 with the passage of Public Law 94-142, the Education for All Handicapped Children Act. This legislation was a response to inequalities and discrimination in educational services provided to handicapped children. In some jurisdictions handicapped children had been barred from attending school because of their special needs. The aim of the law was to ensure a free public education for all children.

Mainstreaming, however, would be important even if it weren't mandated by law. Other educational benefits accrue besides alleviating discrimination. For example, handicapped children have the opportunity to learn appropriate social and academic behavior from observing and modeling nonhandicapped children. The nonhandicapped children also benefit in that they are able to see firsthand the strengths and potential contributions, as well as the limitations, of their handicapped peers. The school environment and society at large are thereby enriched.

Public Law 94-142 has several provisions, among them: (1) students should be educated in the least restrictive environment, (2) each handicapped child should have an individual education plan (IEP), and (3) evaluation procedures should be nondiscriminatory. These are discussed below.

Children are to be educated within the **least restrictive environment.** This means that, to the extent possible, children with handicaps should be in-

RESEARCH SUMMARY 5-1

Rist, R. C. (1970). Student social class and teacher expectations: The self-fulfilling prophecy in ghetto education. *Harvard Educational Review, 40,* 411–451.

PROBLEM: Previous studies had shown that academic achievement was highly correlated with social class. However, researchers weren't sure how schools helped reinforce that relationship. Rist conducted an observational study to find out how teachers contributed to the achievement differential between social classes.

SAMPLE: Rist studied a single class of children, located in an urban ghetto area. All the teachers, administrators, and students were black. Half the population of the school received some form of public assistance.

PROCEDURES: Data for this study were collected by means of 90-minute observation periods conducted twice weekly. Observations were conducted throughout the year while the children were in kindergarten and again when the same children were in the first half of their second-grade year. The classroom was also visited informally four times during first grade. Observers made a continuous handwritten account of classroom interaction and activity as it occurred. Additionally, a series of interviews were held with both the kindergarten and second-grade teachers.

RESULTS: Rist documented that the kindergarten teacher used nonacademic data—namely, who was on welfare, a behavioral questionnaire completed by children's mothers, the teacher's own experience with and other teachers' reports about siblings, medical information, and the family structure—to make placement decisions. The teacher used this information, together with observations of the children's dress, physical appearance, and verbalizations during the first few days of school, to place children in low-, middle-, and high-ability groups on the eighth day of kindergarten. Children of like "ability" were seated together and received like instruction throughout the year. The teacher gave more positive attention to the children in the high group and spent more instructional time with them. She reprimanded the lows more often. The children in the low group were situated in the room such that when material was presented at the chalkboard, they could not see it. Children labeled high ability frequently ridiculed those labeled low ability.

When the students entered first grade, their new teacher also divided them into low-, middle-, and high-ability groups and seated them together. All of the kindergarten highs

---

tegrated into the regular classroom. Those with very mild physical, emotional, and learning disabilities are to spend their entire school day in the regular classroom. Those with slightly more serious problems are to receive extra assistance from a special educator, either in or out of class. As the disabilities grow more serious, the responsibility of the regular classroom teacher is further reduced, and the child is to receive a larger portion of his or her education in more specialized settings, culminating in a full-time residential school. In practice, the majority of

handicapped children who are mainstreamed are those who attend regular classes for at least part of the day and who have mild physical or learning disabilities. Table 5-1 displays the levels of severity of handicap and the recommended school environment.

As mentioned above, each handicapped child is to have an **individualized educational plan** (IEP). IEPs are to be developed by a committee composed of the regular classroom teacher, the child's parents, the special education teacher, and any other staff became first-grade highs (Group A), the former middle and low children became middle children (Group B), and children who were repeating first grade constituted the new low group (Group C). Only the Group A children had completed the kindergarten curriculum and were able to start right away with the first-grade material. Groups B and C children spent the early part of their first-grade year completing kindergarten lessons.

The second-grade teacher continued the low-middle-high grouping practice. Group A students became "Tigers," Groups B and C students became "Cardinals," and repeating second-graders became "Clowns." By now, however, the teacher had test score data on which to base her decisions, as well as parental occupation and other social-class information. Of course, low children were at a disadvantage on these tests because they had not been exposed to the same curriculum as the high children. The different groups were assigned different books for reading instruction and could not advance to the next book until the previous one was completed. Further, the teacher allowed no independent reading in which a child could finish a book on his or her own and move ahead. Thus, low children were locked into the low group, with no way of ever advancing into the higher group. Rist summed up his results with this statement: "The child's journey through the early grades of school at one reading level and in one social grouping appeared to be pre-ordained from the eighth day of kindergarten" (p. 435).

DISCUSSION AND IMPLICATIONS: Rist's findings shocked the educational community. He demonstrated that teachers' expectations and instructional decisions and actions were profoundly influenced by the social-class characteristics of children and that children who did not fit the middle-class mold suffered academically and emotionally. He concluded, "It appears that the public school system not only mirrors the configurations of the larger society, but also significantly contributes to maintaining them. Thus the system of public education in reality perpetuates what it is ideologically committed to eradicate—class barriers which result in inequality in the social and economic life of the citizenry" (p. 449).

Rist's purpose was to expose the problem, not solve it, and thus he did not offer suggestions to teachers about how to avoid falling into the practices of those in his study. The last section of this chapter will, however, tackle this problem in some detail.

that may be helpful, such as psychologists, speech therapists, or medical personnel. IEPs should contain information about the child's current level of academic performance, a statement of both long- and short-term educational goals, a plan for how these goals will be achieved, the amount of time the child will spend in the regular class, and an evaluation plan. The IEP is to be revised annually. Figure 5-3 shows a typical IEP format.

Evaluation procedures are to be nondiscriminatory. In screening children for special services, school officials are required to use a variety of tests and to consider the child's cultural background and language. The involvement of parents in the evaluation process is mandated, and no major educational decisions may be made without their written consent. Parents must be informed of intended school actions in their own language.

Children may require special services for a number of reasons. Those who have been exposed prenatally to cocaine, alcohol, or other drugs, for example, may exhibit characteristic behaviors, such

Table 5-1 Educational Options for Exceptional Students

TYPE OF CLASS	PERCENT OF STUDENTS	WHOSE RESPONSIBILITY
1. Student is in regular classroom with no special assistance.		Regular teacher has primary responsibility
2. Student is in regular classroom entire day with help from special education resource teacher.	88%	Regular teacher has primary responsibility; special education teacher assigned to support and help.
3. Student attends regular classroom most of the day; pulled out to resource room for special instruction	6%	Regular teacher has primary responsibility; special education teacher leads in the resource room.
4. Student is placed in special education classes for majority of the day; may attend regular classes in special subjects.		Special education teacher has primary responsibility.
5. Student is placed in a separate school for the handicapped.	5%	Special education teacher has primary responsibility.
6. Student is educated at home or in a hospital.		Special education teacher has primary responsibility.

SOURCE: Adapted from M. L. Hardman, C. J. Drew, and M. W. Egan, *Human exceptionality,* Boston, Mass.: Allyn & Bacon, 1984, p. 56.

as low tolerance for frustration, inability to predict the consequences of their actions, self-regulatory problems (for example, temper tantrums, physical aggression), or hyperactivity (Burgess and Streissguth, 1992; Griffith, 1992). Exposure to lead in the environment, through chipped paint, air, water, and other sources, is estimated to adversely affect the neurological functioning of 16 percent of American children (Needleman, 1992). Family violence can result in cognitive and social problems. Genetic factors, illness, or accidents may also necessitate special services.

Whatever the cause, for students to be deemed eligible for special services, their exceptionality must first be categorized as one of the following:

Mental retardation or developmental handicaps
Learning disabilities
Behavior disorders or emotional disturbance
Communication (speech and language) disorders
Hearing impairments
Visual impairments
Physical and other health impairments
Severe and multiple handicaps
Gifted and talented

School systems receive special federal funds for each labeled handicapped child, so the process of categorizing looms large in schools. Controversy reigns, however, about the desirability of labeling per se and the validity of current means for evaluating exceptionality. Advocates of labeling contend that it helps educators meet the special needs of the student and brings additional funding to bear where it is most needed. While they acknowledge the weaknesses of the current system of evaluation and placement, they argue that eliminating labeling amounts to throwing the baby out with the bath water.

Opponents counter that labeling creates more problems than it solves. For example, questions about equity arise because of the differential placement of boys, lower-SES students, and minorities into special education programs and because the incidence of handicap varies widely from state to state and district to district. Labels also cause perceived problems to be viewed as deficiencies inherent in the child, possibly causing deficiencies in the learning environment to be overlooked. Labels tend to become permanent; once placed in a special education program, students tend to stay there. Other students may ridicule labeled children, and these children may suffer diminished self-esteem as a consequence. Classifying special children also requires a lot of time, which might be better allocated directly on instruction. Finally, there exist few well-validated methods of instruction which are tied to the categories, and distinctions between the catego-

Figure 5-3 Sample individualized learning plan

CHILD'S NAME: _____   DATE: _____

ELIGIBILITY CERTIFIED: _____ (date)

IEP COMMITTEE MEMBERS: _____

_____

Child's current placement and level of performance? _____

_____

_____

Long-term goals	Actions	Person responsible	Evaluation

Short-term goals	Actions	Person responsible	Evaluation

How much time will child spend in regular class? _____

This plan to be revised by _____ (date)

Parents' signature: _____   Date _____

_____   Date _____

---

ries are blurry. There are no special interventions for the mildly mentally retarded, for instance, that are distinct from those that might be used with any students experiencing academic difficulty (Reynolds, Wang, and Walberg, 1987).

What about gifted and talented children? Some of the same problems crop up for this population, too. Minority students are underrepresented in programs for the gifted. Methods for assessing giftedness are not well validated. Many of the strategies used with these students, such as group investigation (described in Chapter 11) and higher-level thinking strategies (described in Chapters 9 and 12), would be appropriate for regular students as well. Unlike special education programs, though, most school systems with gifted programs receive no additional monies from the federal government.

Teachers must shoulder several responsibilities for assisting exceptional children, but many of these overlap with their regular duties. Teachers need to

be able to identify potentially handicapped or gifted children and make referrals for them. They need to participate in IEP meetings and be able to work in a team with other professionals to serve the special student. They may also need to assist handicapped children with special equipment. As always, they must accommodate individual differences and maintain communication with parents. And they must help exceptional and regular students work and play together.

Most beginning teachers worry about what can be done in the classroom to assist special students. First, familiarize yourself with district policies and procedures for referral and screening. Be alert for students with problems or special potential. Do you have any students whose academic work is well below or well above grade level? Do you have students whose behavior is well below or above the maturity level of age-mates? Do any of your students demonstrate especially low or high persistence at learning tasks? Are any of your students exceptionally creative? Typically, districts expect teachers to refer students exhibiting these characteristics—unusual academic performance, behavior, persistence, or creativity—to the appropriate colleague for further evaluation. More specific strategies for working with exceptional children will be described in the next section.

CREATING CLASSROOMS THAT ARE MULTICULTURAL

There are clearly a wealth of options available for developing classrooms that are multicultural. In fact, the array of options may be so large that they bewilder rather than assist the beginner in implementing multicultural reforms. In this section, multicultural strategies are organized and summarized to ease that process. Beginning teachers are encouraged to work on their own knowledge and attitudes; to improve classroom management and organization; to enhance instruction, interaction, and expectations; to enrich the curriculum; and to alter the school organization in a comprehensive strategy for accomplishing multicultural goals. Underlying these recommendations for practice are two themes: value and challenge. Claude Steele in a recent piece in *The Atlantic* (1992) argued that "If what is meaningful and important to a teacher is to become meaningful and important to a student, the student must feel valued by the teacher for his or her potential and as a person" (p. 78). If anything going on in the school—curriculum cast as remediation, or instruction cast as the pedagogy of poverty—diminishes students' sense of themselves as valued people, students will be disinclined to identify with the goals of the school. Intellectual challenge goes hand in hand with valuing. "A valuing teacher-student relationship goes nowhere without challenge, and challenge will always be resisted outside a valuing relationship" (Steele, 1992, p. 78). Part of communicating that someone is valued is communicating high expectations.

Personal and Professional Development

Personal and professional development form the first part of this strategy. Teachers can improve their own knowledge and attitudes toward people of dif-

ferent cultures as a first step in developing multicultural competence. They must take the initiative to learn about the subcultures in their area, strive to uncover and conquer their own biases, and master the dynamics of intercultural interaction.

To familiarize yourself with local subcultures, find and read books, magazines, and research articles, and take courses. To give you an idea of what can be gleaned from the literature on cross-cultural education, here are three excerpts from research that shed light on the effects of culture in the classroom. They provide those in the mainstream culture a glimpse of what the mainstream culture looks like to a member of a minority culture.

A Navajo woman describes her first experience of school:

> Well, my first deal is just getting to school. Just when you live all Navajo culture and you first start school and first see the brick buildings, you don't know what's inside them buildings. Especially when you've only been to trading post twice in your life before school. It's when you get there you see these long lines of kids with their mamas. All the kids throwing fits and cryin, hangin onto their mom. And your mom's standin there beside you sayin, "You can't be like them. You can't cry cause you're big girl now. You gotta go to school. Don't, don't shame me at the beginning. You gotta make me proud." . . .
>
> So she took all of us to school, and she dropped me off there. . . . The ceilings were so high, and the rooms so big and empty. It was so cold. There was no warmth. Not as far as "brrr I'm cold," but in a sense of emotional cold. Kind of an emptiness, when you're hanging onto your mom's skirt and tryin so hard not to cry. And you know it just seems so lonely and so empty. Then when you get up to your turn, she thumbprints the paper and she leaves and you watch her go out the big, metal doors. The whole thing was a cold experience. The doors were metal and they even had this big window, wires running through it. And these women didn't smile or nothin. You watch your mama go down the sidewalk, actually it's the first time I seen a sidewalk, and you see her get in the truck, walk down the sidewalks. You see her get in the truck and the truck starts moving and all the home smell goes with it. You see it all leaving. (Quoted in McLaughlin, in press, pp. 13–14)

An educational anthropologist describes elementary classrooms in Mexico:

Characteristic of instruction in the *Primaria* was its oral, group interactive quality. . . . Students talk throughout the class period; teachers are always available to repeat, explain, and motivate; silent seat work is rare; and often a crescendo of sound . . . is indicative of instructional activity. The following observation of a first-grade classroom illustrates this pattern of verbal and physical activity:

As she instructs children to glue sheets of paper in their books and write several consonant-vowel pairs, the teacher sometimes shouts her directions to compete with the clamor of kids asking for glue, repeating instructions to each other, sharing small toys, sharpening pencils, asking to go to the bathroom, etc. This activity and "noise" is compounded by the large number in the classroom, 35, but things somehow seem to get done by some, if not all, students. Then teacher has the children recite the word pairs taped to the chalkboard. They shout these out loudly as a group as she points to each combination with an old broken broom handle. Sometimes she calls out the pairs in order; other times, out of order to check their attention. Then she calls individual children to the board, gives them the stick, they choose a pair of sounds, but then have to pronounce them loudly and quickly as she presses them for correct responses. (Macias, 1990, p. 304)

An example of cultural discontinuity in the classroom comes from a study of Hmong adults enrolled in an English language class (Hvitfeldt, 1986). These students refused to accept any democratic decision making, even of the most trivial kind. On one occasion, the teacher wanted to begin a review lesson by having the students draw numbers from a cup. When he held out the cup and said, "Who's first?" no one responded. After a long pause, one student said, "You teacher. You say." In Hmong culture, families and clans are extremely close and cooperative, viewing themselves as a single economic unit and looking exclusively to the male family head for all decisions. Given this background, it is not surprising that they resisted individual input into decisions.

Another avenue for familiarizing yourself with subcultures is to reach out to people in the community to try to understand their points of view. Talk to your students and get to know them. The following story illustrates how participation in a community event helped one school principal develop an important insight into the behavior of a large minority group in her school. Experiences like hers,

coupled with observation and reflection, can help you bring your own biases to the surface and deal with them.

I'm a principal at an urban elementary school with a high percentage of Pacific Islander kids. They often have a hard time in school—rowdy, easily distracted, quick-tempered—and I got some insight into why when their community invited me to a special ceremony at their church, a ceremony to recognize those kids who were doing well in school.

I got there a few minutes early, and they showed me to the stage where guests of honor were to sit. I settled down expectantly for the event to begin. The starting time came and went, friendly people wandered in and out, and punctual me started getting nervous. Finally, things seemed to gel and they got under way, almost an hour late.

They put on a very nice ceremony, showcasing each child individually on the stage, applauding each one, giving each a little remembrance. It was quite touching, and the kids were just beaming.

The children all went back and sat down in the audience again, and the meeting continued on to several more items on the agenda. Well, the kids were fine for awhile, but as you might imagine, they got bored fast and started to fidget. Fidgeting and whispering turned into poking, prodding, and open chatting. I became a little anxious at the disruption, but none of the other adults appeared to even notice, so I ignored it, too. Pretty soon several of the children were up and out of their seats, strolling about the back and sides of the auditorium. All adult faces continued looking serenely up at the speaker on the stage. Then the kids started playing tag, running circles around the seating area and yelling gleefully. No adult response—I was amazed, and struggled to resist the urge to quiet the children. Then some of the kids got up onto the stage, running around the speaker, flicking the lights on and off, and opening and closing the curtain! Still nothing from the Islander parents! It was not my place, and I shouldn't have done it, but I was so beyond my comfort zone that with eye contact and a pantomimed shush, I got the kids to settle down.

I suddenly realized then that when these children, say, come to school late, it doesn't mean that they or their parents don't care about learning or that they're a little bit lazy—that's just how all the adults in their world operate. When they squirm under desks and run around the classroom, they aren't trying to be disrespectful or defiant, they're just doing what they do everywhere else. Now I'm better equipped to help them develop the knowledge and skill they need to be successful in our school and our society, and I'm learning what it takes to get along in theirs. (Personal communication)

Beginning teachers will also find it helpful to develop understanding of intercultural interaction. Brislin, Cushner, Cherrie, and Yong (1986) have devised training for helping people from any culture cope effectively with cross-cultural interaction. They maintain that there are three broad areas of concern and potential misunderstanding when people of different cultures come together: people's intense feelings, knowledge about cultural differences, and bases for cultural differences.

Whenever people meet and interact with others from a different culture, they experience predictable emotional reactions. When you find students in your class from a culture unfamiliar to you, you will likely feel anxiety, you may become upset because of disconfirmed expectations, and you will probably feel very discomfitted by the ambiguity of the situation. This **culture shock** is a normal reaction, however unpleasant, and will pass with time, as long as you make the effort to understand and accommodate the cultural gulf between you and your students, as the principal in the above story did. The danger is that people can react to their extreme discomfort by entrenching themselves in their prejudices, an unhelpful response.

There are a number of areas of cultural difference that seem to consistently cause trouble. Beginning teachers need to be alert to these. Cultures differ, for instance, in their attitudes toward work and the appropriate balance between being on task and socializing. Middle-class Americans tend to be very task-oriented, while many other cultures give more attention to social interaction. Cultures also vary in their sense of time. For Americans, punctuality is an unquestioned virtue, and children in school are penalized for tardiness, turning work in late, and so on. But in many nonwestern cultures, people are much more relaxed about time, do not regard punctuality as particularly sacred, and do not pay strict attention to deadlines. The amount of physical space deemed proper between people when conversing and norms about making eye contact are other key areas of difference.

Another important area is the relative weight put on the needs of the group versus the needs of the individual. American culture is very oriented to the individual, while in Japanese and in some Native American cultures more emphasis is placed on the group. Many Native American children, for example, do not want to be singled out for praise and attention, a situation which can be very disconcerting to their teachers. Finally, peoples' values differ, as Brislin et al. (1986) describe.

> As part of their socialization, people learn to accept as proper a small set of ideas within such broad areas as religion, economics, aesthetics, political organization, and interpersonal relationships. Such learning becomes internalized and it affects attitudes, preferences, and views of what is desirable and undesirable. Understanding these internalized views . . . is critical in cross-cultural adjustment. (p. 41)

Teachers also need to be aware of the bases of cultural differences, the underlying reasons behind these outward manifestations of cultural difference. One of these is that people of different cultures categorize and differentiate information differently; that is, they chunk information, combining and separating bits, in a variety of ways. A simple example comes from language comparisons. In English, there are the separate verbs *to like* and *to love,* while in French one word, *aimer,* means both, and in Italian, no verb meaning "to like" exists. Speakers of these different languages categorize and differentiate experiences differently. It is easy to imagine the difficulties in communicating clearly when the parties interacting, even though they may both be speaking English, are relying on such divergent conceptions.

Another especially important area for teachers to be aware of is learning style variations across cultures. While teaching and learning clearly occur in all cultures, preferred styles differ. In particular, in some cultures and domestic subcultures, teaching and learning are conducted in context, while in mainstream American schools, the predominant mode is out of context. What does "in-context learning" mean? It means that children acquire skills and knowledge at the point that they are needed and in real-life situations. For example, children may learn to use a paring knife in the context of helping their parents prepare meals, or may learn how to multiply fractions in the context of doubling a recipe when company is coming. Out-of-context learning means that learning is unconnected to a real, immediate need. When parents play "what's this" games with infants, or when math is broken down into discrete algorithms, each drilled separately before application to real math problems, then out-of-context learning is happening. While both kinds of teaching and learning can clearly "work," children accustomed to in-context learning are confused by out-of-context teaching.

Finally, cultures differ in their attributions, or judgments about the causes of behavior. A polite smile construing friendliness in one culture may constitute a cold rebuff in another. Giving a friend academic assistance can mean helpfulness to one person, cheating to another. Erroneous attributions can obviously hinder the development of rapport between people of different cultures.

With so many areas of divergence, it is easy to see how students and teachers from different cultures could come into conflict with each other. Simply being aware of these potential sources of misunderstanding will reduce the risk that miscommunication will occur. When students and parents observe your efforts, they will feel that you do indeed value their experience.

Teacher Expectations

Earlier in the chapter we documented teachers' differential interaction patterns with various groups of students—minority versus majority, boys versus girls, lower SES versus higher SES, and regular versus exceptional students. As we also pointed out, many times these patterns are determined by the **expectations** teachers hold for students from various groups. Becoming aware of one's expectations and learning how to minimize differential interactions is probably the single most important action beginning teachers can take to create classrooms which are free from bias and instructionally effective.

SELF-FULFILLING PROPHECY

In 1968, Robert Rosenthal and Lenore Jacobson published *Pygmalion in the Classroom*. This little book, instantly popular with professional and lay audiences, introduced the concept of the **self-ful-filling prophecy** and set off two decades of research and controversy about the effects of teacher expectations on student achievement and self-esteem. Rosenthal and Jacobson's research consisted of providing teachers in a particular elementary school information about several students in each of their classes. Teachers were told that a few students had been identified through a new test as "bloomers," and that these students could be expected to make large achievement gains during the coming year. In fact, the students for whom teachers had been given information had been identified at random, and no special test information existed. As the year progressed, however, the identified bloomers, particularly those in the early grades, made significant gains in achievement. Rosenthal and Jacobson argued that these gains could be attributed to differential treatment received from the teachers as a result of their false expectations—thus the **self-fulfilling prophecy,** a situation where inaccurate perceptions of students' abilities and subsequent acting on these perceptions make them come true over the years.

Rosenthal and Jacobson's original study has been faulted because of its methodological weaknesses. (See Brophy and Good, 1974; Claiborn, 1969.) Their study, however, aroused the interest of the research community in the effects of teacher expectation on student achievement, and over the past two decades researchers have found that though the effects of teacher expectations on students are not quite as straightforward as suggested in the Rosenthal-Jacobson study, they are, nonetheless, real.

Teacher expectations for individual students, as well as for whole classes of students, do indeed affect the kinds of interactions and relationships teachers establish with students and, in some instances, what students learn. Teacher expectations create a cyclical pattern of behaviors on the part of both teachers and students. Drawing from the work of Good and Brophy (1987) this cyclical process is illustrated in Figure 5-4.

There are two important questions to ask about this process and teacher expectations. How are expectations created in the first place, and how do they get communicated to students?

In the classroom, as in all other aspects of life, people make impressions on us. The way students

Figure 5-4 Cyclical process of teacher expectations

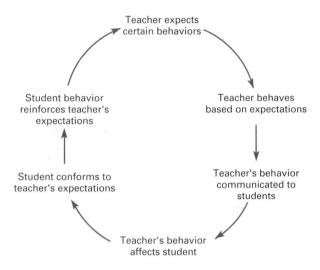

dress, the language they use, their physical features, as well as their interpersonal skills, influence the teacher. Information about a student's family or information gleaned from the school's records, even before the teacher meets a student, can also create impressions and expectations, as Rist's study demonstrated (Research Summary 5-1). As long as initial impressions are accurate, there is no problem. But when initial impressions are translated into inaccurate expectations about students and then used subsequently in differential treatment toward them, there is a problem.

Once expectations (positive or negative) are formed, they are communicated to students in numerous ways. You can probably think of several instances when a particular teacher communicated expectations to you which influenced your attitude and work in that teacher's class. You may remember high expectations a teacher held for you. From the first day of class, she chose to single you out for important assignments; she wrote positive comments on your papers; and she called on you to answer difficult questions. It is likely that you worked hard for this teacher, perhaps even beyond your potential. Or you may remember an instance when a teacher had low expectations for you. Your work was seldom acknowledged publicly, and even though you raised your hand, you were seldom called upon. If this behavior on the part of the teacher persisted, it is likely that you started to ig-

nore your work in this class and concentrated your energies elsewhere.

Table 5-2 lists some of the ways that teachers communicate their expectations to students and how they behave differentially toward those for whom they hold high and low expectations. After you read the summary of teacher behaviors in Table 5-2, you will likely vow not to communicate low expectations to students in your classroom. This is a worthy goal but also one that requires more than just good intentions. It is good to know, however, that the goal can be achieved. *Differential treatment* does not occur in all teachers' classrooms. In fact, there is considerable difference among teachers in the degree to which they hold inaccurate expectations for students and act differentially toward students. Conversely, achieving a classroom free of inaccurate expectations and differential treatment is difficult. Sometimes false expectations form because of the unconscious biases and stereotypes we have. It is difficult to take action on things done unconsciously. Other times students for whom teachers have low expectations are also those who are disruptive. Disruptive students often require more verbal and nonverbal interactions from the teacher which are negative or critical in their tone. Similarly, the contributions of disruptive students can often be of low quality or careless. It is difficult, therefore, to call on low achievers or to use their ideas when their responses may disrupt the overall flow of a lesson, also an important goal for teaching. Later a set of guidelines will be provided to help teachers overcome some of these difficulties.

SUSTAINING EXPECTATION EFFECT

The discussion up to this point has focused on the self-fulfilling prophecy, a situation where teachers hold inaccurate beliefs about particular students and act toward students based on these inaccurate beliefs, and where over time students conform in their own behavior to the teacher's expectation. There is actually a second kind of expectation effect that can occur. Labeled **sustaining expectation effect,** this condition exists when the teacher accurately reads a student's ability and behaves toward the student with this information but does not alter the expectation when a student improves or regresses over time. You can probably recall instances

Table 5-2 Teacher Differential Treatment of High and Low Students

CATEGORIES OF BEHAVIOR	TEACHER BEHAVIORS
Praise and feedback	Rewarding inappropriate behaviors by lows
	Criticizing lows more often than highs for failure
	Praising lows less frequently than highs for success
	Failing to give feedback to the public responses of lows
	Differential administration or grading of tests or assignments
	Briefer and less informative feedback to questions of lows
Verbal interactions	Waiting less time for lows to answer
	Giving lows answers or calling on someone else
	Calling on lows less often to respond to questions
	Asking lows only easier, nonanalytic questions
	Less acceptance and use of lows' ideas
Interpersonal interactions	Generally paying less attention to lows
	Interacting with lows less frequently
	Demanding less from lows
	Interacting with lows more privately than publicly
	Seating lows farther away from the teacher
	Less friendly interactions with lows
	Less eye contact with lows
	Less nonverbal communication and responsiveness to lows
Instructional strategies	Less use of effective but time-consuming methods with lows
	More seatwork and low-level academic tasks for lows
	Leaving lows out of some instructional activities

SOURCE: Adapted from T. L. Good and J. E. Brophy, *Looking in classrooms* (4th ed.), New York: Harper & Row, 1987, pp. 128–129.

of this happening to you in classrooms as well as in other places. Perhaps you were an excellent English student. The essays you wrote for the teacher were always meticulously done. They were written with clarity, and you showed considerable creativity in the ways you created beautiful images with words. You always received an A for your effort. One week, however, you were recovering from the flu and were overwhelmed with other schoolwork. You had to write your essay in haste and with little thought or care. At this point you simply didn't care about your grade; you just wanted to get it done. When the paper was returned marked A and a comment from the teacher, "Another superb piece of writing," you knew that your work had been judged, not on its current value, but on your prior history of producing good essays. The teacher sustained his or her high expectations for you even though your work was at a lower level.

You can also probably think of instances when sustaining expectation effect worked the other way. Perhaps you were notorious for not keeping up with your reading assignments in history. Every time the teacher called on you, you answered with silly and careless answers. This behavior made your classmates laugh. It also covered up your unpreparedness. You decided one day to stop this behavior. You started to read your assignments very carefully, and you came prepared to discuss your ideas in class. You raised your hand in response to the teacher's questions over and over, but someone else was always selected to recite. When you did get your chance everyone started to laugh, including the teacher, before you could complete your point. This is another instance where you had changed your behavior; you were working at a higher level, but past expectations were sustained by others (students and teachers) preventing them from accurately perceiving your improvement. Cooper and Good (1983) report that sustaining effects are actually more common in classrooms than are self-fulfilling prophecies, thus presenting yet another challenge to the teacher striving to create a productive, multicultural classroom.

GUIDELINES FOR TEACHERS

In the classroom, as in all aspects of life, people make impressions on us, and we act on these impressions. In the classroom, the challenge obviously is to develop strategies to avoid negative expectations and to emphasize positive expectations. Several guidelines listed below can help teachers accomplish this goal.

1. Remember that a teacher's job is to teach all students and assume an attitude that all students can learn. Communicate this positive belief in students to them.
2. Be very careful about how information from other teachers or information in the student's file is used.
3. During classroom discussions, strive to give all students equal access to public time. One way to do this is to prepare a stack of index cards with students' names. Shuffle the cards so the names come up at random; as you call on students, mix their cards back into the deck.
4. Systematically monitor the frequency and nature of verbal interactions with highs and lows, with members of different racial and ethnic groups, with boys and girls, with regular and exceptional students. Having another person observe and record these interactions provides the best objective record for analysis. Alternatively, you may want to videotape yourself and view the tape later to assess your actions.
5. Systematically monitor the frequency and nature of nonverbal interactions with highs and lows, with members of different racial and ethnic groups, with boys and girls, with regular and exceptional students. Again, observers or videotape provide effective means for analyzing your interactions.
6. If ability grouping is used, find ways for it to remain flexible and open to change. Review group membership continuously. Argue with

yourself that a student in a low or high group does not belong there.
7. Strive to be fair and consistent in the way student work is evaluated. On work that calls for subjective judgment (such as essays), periodically check for sustaining effect by taking the paper of a student who normally gets an A and argue with yourself that it really should be a C. Conversely, take a C paper and argue that it merits an A.
8. Strive to distribute rewards and privileges in a fair and consistent manner for high and lows; for members of different racial and ethnic groups; for boys and girls; for regular and exceptional students.
9. Survey members of the class about how fairly they think the teacher treats them. A learning aid at the end of this chapter exists for this purpose.
10. Ask yourself whether your actions communicate value and challenge. Are you showing your students that you have confidence in their abilities by expecting excellence from them?

Curriculum Development

In addition to attending to their own personal and professional development, teachers have a number of curricular strategies they may turn to as they develop multicultural classrooms. A prerequisite to any curricular change is for teachers to broaden their conceptions about what is important to teach; teachers need to move beyond the standard canon and become more inclusive in their choice of content. For example, including literary works by prominent nonwhite authors in an American literature class is one action English teachers might take.

Next, teachers can evaluate the textbooks and other materials they use for bias. Recall the forms of bias—linguistic, stereotyping, invisibility, imbalance, unreality, and fragmentation. (See the learning aid at the end of the chapter to help you evaluate materials.) Teachers can supplement learning activities with additional materials to redress bias. By the same token, when teachers make presentations, they need to supply examples and illustrations that are grounded in a variety of cultures. Finding such examples and illustrations will demand great initiative. One resource is the practitioner journal; journals for teachers such as *Instructor* (the February 1991 issue is devoted to multicultural resources for elementary teachers), *Arithmetic Teacher, Art Education, Social Studies, Mathematics Teacher,* and others, provide much helpful information. For example, one issue of *Arithmetic Teacher* (February 1991) describes a unit on teaching the geometry concept "tessalation" through Native American art forms. Associations devoted to promoting multicultural education comprise another useful resource. Interracial Books for Children (1841 Broadway, New York, NY 10023) publishes a bulletin containing articles about and reviews of resources for elementary through adult education, mostly in the areas of literature and history.

Alternatively, teachers can raise the issue of bias and discuss it directly with their students. Students themselves can analyze curriculum materials for bias and share their findings with peers. Class discussions can focus on the emotional impact of the various forms of bias, on the political conditions that give rise to bias, or on action that can be taken to correct it. Chapter 12 of this book provides guidelines for organizing effective discussions.

In addition to these minimal curricular reforms, there are three general approaches to incorporating multicultural aims and topics into the curriculum. One is the **single-group curriculum approach,** in which teachers set aside courses or units that present information on specific groups or cultures. Another method is called the **topical approach.** It, too, consists of recognizing and teaching about nondominant cultures. However, it does so in a more limited way than does the single-group approach: by devoting lessons to the heroes of various cultures; celebrating holidays of various cultures; and recognizing the art, music, literature, cuisine, and language of different cultures. For example, a third-grade teacher might have a Mexican-American theme party on Cinquo de Mayo with a piñata and tacos and might teach the children a few words in Spanish. Although these can be worthwhile educational activities, both approaches have problems. They emphasize differences between groups, not similarities, and so may have the undesired side effect of widening cultural gaps, rather than bringing cultures closer together. The topical approach can

be quite superficial, and both approaches can be fragmented.

A third curricular strategy is called the **conceptual approach.** When teachers use this method, they incorporate a series of concepts associated with cultural pluralism into ongoing lessons. A set of key multicultural concepts identified by one group of teachers is illustrated in Figure 5-5. These are not the only concepts that could be used; you may come up with other concepts that better suit your subject area or grade level.

Here are a few examples of lessons using these concepts. The concept of pluralism could be infused into an intermediate school lesson on bar graphs, in which students plot the proportions of various ethnic and other groups in their community. The concept of interdependence could be infused into an elementary science unit on ecology. A secondary social studies lesson on voting rights could infuse the concept of exploitation.

Teachers using the conceptual approach would first consider which of these concepts are complementary to material they are already teaching. Then, as opportunities arose, they would incorporate the appropriate concepts into their lessons. In planning for such lessons, teachers should couple the multicultural concept with the regular instructional objective and should specify learning materials and activities that achieve both goals. This means, obviously, teaching toward multiple goals, a topic covered in some detail in several other chapters.

Teachers may find that different approaches are appropriate depending on the grade level or subject area they teach, or their own level of teaching experience. But no matter which approach is pursued at any given time, teachers need to review their curricular decisions to ensure that they demonstrate to their students they are valued people and to ensure that they provide a complex curriculum, one that is challenging to students. From the eyes of young black students, a curriculum lacking black faces tells them that they don't count, and it gives students of other groups the same message. Minority children who are assigned to remedial education because their prior knowledge is different from that of majority children are not being challenged to the level of their ability. Complex curricula convey both value and challenge; are often thematic, integrating

Figure 5-5 Concepts to guide multicultural education

- **Individuality:** Refers to the personal characteristics that are unique to an individual and distinguish him/her from others. Respect for individuality leads to positive concepts of self and others.
- **Cultural patterns:** Common elements such as values, norms, beliefs, customs, and rituals that unite members of a group and distinguish them from other groups.
- **Subsistence:** Refers to the essential needs common to all people—food, clothing, and shelter.
- **Social structure:** The organization of any society through the development of family and of educational, political, religious, and social institutions.
- **Interdependence:** The reliance of one or more individuals or groups upon one another for a successful, cooperative existence.
- **Communication:** The process by which individuals or groups transmit messages through the use of language, symbols, signs, or behavior.
- **Exploitation:** The taking advantage of one person or group for the benefit of another individual or group. There are different forms of exploitation within a society such as prejudice, discrimination, and stereotyping.
- **Pluralism:** A state of society in which members of diverse ethnic, racial, religious, or social groups maintain participation in their specific groups while functioning effectively within a common civilization.

SOURCE: Charles County Maryland, Teacher Corp Project, no date.

subject areas and intellectual goals; and often arise out of students' own questions. The group investigation model described in Chapter 11 provides a good structure from which a challenging curriculum can be developed.

Instructional Development

There are a number of instructional strategies teachers can use to develop classrooms that are multicultural. For instance, teachers can anchor instruction in students' prior knowledge and help them construct links between what they know and what they are to learn. By so doing, teachers will help students see commonalities and differences between cultures and will assist them in becoming multicultural. To do this effectively, though, teachers must actively seek out information about students' prior knowledge.

When teachers group students for instructional purposes, they can lean heavily on heterogeneous grouping and minimize ability grouping. The dele-

terious effects of tracking and the poor-quality instruction generally found in lower-ability groups and classes are well documented. Make sure that there are students of high, middle, and low ability in each learning group and strive to achieve racial and ethnic balance.

Teachers can also design learning activities that mesh with a variety of learning styles. There are several style dimensions along which teachers can vary their instruction. One route is to incorporate visual, auditory, tactile, and kinesthetic modalities into lessons. Teachers can also apply cooperative as well as individualistic task and reward structures. Further, teachers can vary their lessons by making them more or less concrete or abstract, more or less formal or informal, and by emphasizing in-context as well as out-of-context learning.

A related consideration in planning and presenting lessons is to capitalize on students' existing abilities. This is particularly crucial for exceptional or culturally different children, who may be ascribed low status by their mainstream peers.

Teachers can use a technique called **assigning competence** with these low-status students (Lotan and Benton, 1990). To assign competence, teachers first carefully observe their students while they work at a variety of tasks, focusing on the low-status children, and then identify the special abilities that these students have. They may be skilled in verbal reasoning, drawing, visual or spatial abilities, or others. Teachers then publicly and specifically draw the class's attention to the low-status student's special competence. Children that have been troubled by a lack of motivation and low achievement often bloom after teachers assign them competence. The story presented in Figure 5-6 illustrates the impact of assigning competence on one student.

An instructional element that should comprise an important part of your teaching is strategy instruction. One of the characteristics that distinguishes good learners from poor ones is their ability to use a variety of strategies to read and write, to solve problems involving numbers, and to learn successfully. When teachers help at-risk students acquire the strategies needed to learn effectively, they give them the tools for school success. There are a large number of programs available to support teachers in this goal; we will focus on one of these, reciprocal teaching (Palincsar and Klenk, 1991).

Reciprocal teaching has been used with elementary and secondary students; with regular, special education, and at-risk students; and for teaching subject matter and reading comprehension. Research has documented the effectiveness of the approach. The method promotes the use of four strategies identified as critical in reading comprehension and in reading to learn: asking questions, summarizing, clarifying, and predicting. Teachers (or student discussion leaders) work with groups of six to eight students, reading and discussing a piece of text together. Teachers initially model the strategies and then gradually place more responsibility on the students to generate the strategies they need to learn from the text. Here is an excerpt from a first-grade reading class using reciprocal teaching:

> Mrs. D.: (Reading) . . . The bear cubs rolled over and over, growling fiercely. Baby Bear was bigger than his sister, and he began to play too rough. . . .
> Kendra: (Clarifying) What's rough?
> Mara: Like you say rough texture.

> Mrs. D.: Well, that's one kind of rough.
> Robert: The other one is like they beat you up.
> Mrs. D.: That's another kind of rough. Let me read the sentence and see which one you think it is. If it's the way you feel, the texture, or the beating up part. (Palincsar and Klenk, 1991, p. 118)

Teacher and students are using the clarifying strategy, one that is used as needed when a word or concept is not understood. The teacher is showing that to fix the misunderstanding, you have to look back to the text. Here is another excerpt, this time from a seventh-grade geology class, in which summarizing and predicting are used to facilitate textbook learning:

> The text concludes, "Below the crust is a large layer called the mantle. It is a much heavier layer. The part of the mantle just below the crust is a strange place. Pressure there is very great, and the temperatures are very high."

> Doug: (Leading the discussion and summarizing) This told about the second layer of the earth, the one that is under the first one.
> Sara: The one under the crust.
> Doug: Yeah, the crust. It told about what it is like, like how heavy it is and what the temperature is. My prediction is that they will tell us about the next layer because this picture shows another one, and I'll bet it will be cooler because dirt gets colder when you dig.
> Chris: That doesn't make sense to me because, because as it's been goin' down, it's been gettin' hotter.
> Stephanie: And heavier, too.
> Chris: Pretty soon, we'll get to the gooey stuff, and it's real hot.
> Sam: That's the lava.
> Mr. M.: Well, let's read on and see who's right in their predictions. What will the next layer be like? Who will be the teacher? (Palincsar and Klenk, 1991, pp. 120–121)

These older students have become more adept at using reading comprehension strategies and now take on leadership roles in the discussion. This aspect of the approach has been shown to be highly motivating, even for disruptive students.

Motivation is itself a major concern. You learned in Chapter 4 about need disposition theory and attribution theory and about the alterable factors impinging on students' willingness to engage

Figure 5-6   A story about assigning competence

Alicia, a rather tall, bilingual Spanish-English-speaking second grader, was the type of youngster whom people barely noticed. She was not a discipline problem; she did not make demands on the teacher or the other students, nor did she actively participate in interactions. Alicia seldom raised her hand to answer questions, and she rarely voiced her opinions.

One day in April, while videotaping group interactions in Alicia's classroom, we focused on students who frequently exhibited low-status behavior. While working on the coordinates and measurement unit, Alicia had teamed up with another child in her group, Aneke. Their task was to draw life-sized representations of their bodies. The girls took turns, lying on large sheets of butcher paper and then outlining each other's bodies with a thick, felt-tip pen. After making the outlines, the children had to cut out the replicas and then color in their features and clothing.

Aneke had possibly the highest academic status in this second-grade classroom. She was petite, precocious, and popular. She knew the answer to almost every question the teacher asked. Her hand flew up at every opportunity. She was a delightful, outgoing child, who seemed to be skilled at everything she was asked to do.

Among the important skills needed by students in the second grade is the ability to use scissors and to cut accurately. However, as Alicia and Aneke set about to cut out their butcher paper bodies, it become apparent that Aneke, who was so accomplished academically, did not know how to use scissors properly, nor did she know how to follow the outline of the body to cut it out accurately. Aneke was distressed. She feared she would cut off her paper arms and legs. Patiently and expertly, Alicia guided Aneke through the procedure, coaching her exasperated partner on how to use the scissors and follow the outline.

When Alicia's teacher viewed the videotape of this incident with one of the authors, the teacher commented on the fact that this was the first time since school started that she had seen Alicia show real mastery on a skill relevant to a classroom task. During the next orientation, the teacher shared her observation with the class. She wanted all the children to realize that Alicia was particularly skilled at using scissors and that if ever they needed help cutting, they could turn to Alicia as a resource.

Coincidentally, the school was getting ready to present a musical called "Let George Do It." This colonial play required that each class be responsible for making a number of three-cornered hats. The second grade teacher decided to put Alicia in charge of making these hats for her class. Alicia was to pick children to be on the committee, decide on what materials were needed, get the pattern from the teacher in charge of costumes, and see to it that the hats were made to specification. Since Alicia was perceived as the most accomplished "cutter" in her classroom, the committee looked to her for guidance.

Alicia took to the making of the three-cornered hats with tremendous enthusiasm. Again, it was the first time since September that her teacher had seen Alicia talking and working with other children in such an animated and empowered way. Alicia was now raising her hand more often during wrap-up, answering questions frequently and accurately. During this same period of time, the teacher also discovered that Alicia had good spatial reasoning and visual thinking skills. For example, when the task for her group was to draw a map of the classroom to scale, Alicia drew the map and then created an impressive three-dimensional model of the room. The teacher made sure that Alicia was assigned competence for this accomplishment also.

After the beginning of the next academic year, the opportunity arose to talk with Alicia's third-grade teacher. This teacher said that she would have never guessed that Alicia had been a low-status student for a large part of her second grade. Particularly during Finding Out/Descubrimiento, but also during many other parts of the day, Alicia interacted frequently and effectively with her classmates, raised her hand and answered questions correctly, and expressed her opinions readily. Children listening to Alicia were often observed going along with her suggestions. Alicia was greatly valued by her teachers and her classmates for her artistic and organizational skills. It appeared that Alicia was also performing better academically in almost every curricular area.

SOURCE: R. A. Lotan and J. Benton (1990). Finding out about complex instruction: Teaching math and science in heterogenous classrooms. In N. Davidson (ed.), *Cooperative learning in mathematics: A handbook for teachers*. Menlo Park, Calif.: Addison-Wesley, pp. 60–62.

and persist in learning tasks. Researchers have also studied specific strategies that promote motivation for at-risk students. The HOTS program (Pogrow, 1990) was developed for elementary students in remedial pull-out programs. Rather than providing additional drill on basic skills, as most pull-out programs do, students were challenged with difficult, ambiguous problems and were expected to discuss, question, and resolve problems for themselves with only modest help from the teacher. The program has been very effective in helping underachievers succeed in school, and part of the reason is that students find challenge and interaction much more motivating than "drill-and-kill." Abi-Nader (1991) described a successful program for Hispanic high school students that focused on priming them for college in part through future-oriented classroom talk. These students had been oriented to getting by day-by-day, and they were unaccustomed to planning and goal-setting. Program classes are filled with references to the future, from specific lessons that prepare them for future experiences (like filling out sample financial aid forms), to describing situations they may encounter in college or in a professional career, to telling stories about graduates from the program and their successes in college and careers.

One other factor should be considered in every lesson: assessment of student learning. Through both teacher-made and standardized tests, bias is often introduced into the classroom. To circumvent this bias, teachers need to do two things: (1) rely on a variety of methods for evaluating student learning—through written or oral tests, student reports and projects, observations, interviews, and discussions with parents and others who know the student and (2) test at a variety of levels—recall, comprehension, application, analysis, synthesis, and evaluation. The goals of schooling are not high scores on culturally biased tests, after all, but rather are outcomes like the ability to read independently for information and enjoyment, to solve problems involving numbers, to apply the lessons of history to current social problems, and so on. Whenever possible, assess students directly for achievement of these real goals, not just for the goal's proxy. Many teachers are beginning to use portfolios of student work to document student learning as an alternative to traditional tests. Analogous to artist's portfo-

lios, students' portfolios are collections of student work samples that demonstrate progress in learning over time. Artwork, writing samples, research projects, journal entries, video clips of interaction in small groups, as well as tests and other materials, can make up the contents of portfolios. These are also very useful in parent-teacher conferences.

Teachers also have available to them many well-validated strategies to help all students accomplish learning goals. Cooperative learning has been mentioned several times; models such as STAD, Jigsaw, and group investigation, described in Chapter 11, have a remarkable research base backing their efficacy in increasing achievement, prosocial behavior, problem-solving abilities, and intergroup acceptance.

Community problem solving, a strategy similar to group investigation described in Chapter 11, has also been found effective in multicultural classrooms. When using this strategy teachers encourage students to identify concerns they have about their community or neighborhood and help them plan and carry out independent projects. In one case, students at a low-income-area elementary school decided to tackle the problem of a hazardous waste site in their neighborhood. In the process of confronting this problem, students had to plan, read up on environmental issues and understand the danger of the various chemicals on their doorstep, write to their legislators and investigate the political process, organize and present their arguments for action effectively to a variety of audiences, and raise and manage money. In the context of a meaningful, important, and engaging activity, then, students developed skills in reading, writing, math, social studies, science, design and layout, and interpersonal communication. Figure 5-7 lists the five steps teachers follow in implementing a community problem solving approach.

A special note is needed about strategies to employ with handicapped and exceptional students. As with all types of students, exceptional students model teachers' intended and unintended behaviors and often live up to teachers' expectations, whether positive or negative. Positive, even-handed regard for exceptional students is a prerequisite to effective teaching. Teachers also need to carefully think through the physical layout of their classrooms and make any changes that will facilitate

Figure 5-7 Steps in a community problem-solving project

Step 1: Identify concerns. Have the students identify areas of concern in their community, neighborhood, or school boundary which affects their lives in some way. Make a list of all the ways the problem affects them and other people whom they know. Have each student present the problem in a class discussion.

Step 2: List ideas for problem solving, choose one. Have the students make a list of ideas which would positively affect the area of concern they have identified. Have each student present his or her ideas in a class discussion.

Step 3: List steps to solving problems. In a class discussion, identify ways students could, with some assistance, actually implement some of the ideas they have for change. For instance, the class could clean up a vacant lot, but couldn't build a mass-transit system, though they could write letters to the mayor.

Step 4: Begin steps to solve problem. Turn the problem into a class project, making students responsible for carrying through with the steps they identified in step 3. This is their chance to get actively involved and learn how to effect change in their community.

Step 5: Identify your audience. Have the students identify sources they can contact for further assistance or information, such as community advocacy organizations, newspapers, or government agencies. Utilize the available resources in getting attention for the project, finding out how to influence a decision or change a bad situation.

SOURCE: Copyright © Project 2000 with Stephen Goldsmith.

easy movement for all students, particularly those who may require wheelchairs or special walking devices. They need to think through scheduling and time constraints and how these might affect special students. For example, transition time between lessons may need to be extended for a student who is physically hampered, and the downtime thus created for the nonhandicapped students properly managed. Likewise, highly able students will accomplish learning tasks very quickly, and thought must be given to the meaningful use of their extra time. Routines and procedures for such contingencies must be planned and taught to the whole class.

Regarding specific lessons, teachers can develop learning materials and activities commensurate with handicapped or gifted children's abilities, much as they adapt lessons to the individual differences of all students. In doing so, they should expect to work closely with resource teachers and other support personnel. Most schools have such support services readily available.

Cooperative learning strategies can also be used often, both to facilitate achievement and to help exceptional and regular students accept and appreciate each other. Finally, the following tips for teaching the mildly learning-disabled or behaviorally disabled students most likely to be mainstreamed have been adapted from recommendations offered by the National Information Center for Handicapped Children and Youth:

1. Use highly structured materials. Tell students exactly what is expected. Avoid distractions, such as colorful bulletin boards, in work areas.
2. Allow alternatives to the use of written language, such as tape recorders or oral tests.
3. Expect improvement on a long-term basis.
4. Reinforce appropriate behavior. Model and explain what constitutes appropriate behavior.
5. Provide immediate feedback and ample opportunities for drill and practice.

Note that these actions are not very different from many of the effective teaching behaviors described in Chapter 10. Careful task analysis and use of direct instruction will be important tools for helping handicapped students. Behavior modification, in which desired behaviors are positively reinforced and undesired behaviors are negatively reinforced or punished, will also be a helpful strategy.

Not all agree, however, that these are the only effective teaching strategies for this population. Curtis and Shaver (1980) conducted an experimental study with low-track secondary students in which strategies similar to group investigation and community problem solving were used in social studies classes. The researchers obtained significant results indicating that the treatment increased experimental students' interest in social issues, their ability to think critically, and their self-esteem. In some cases, reading comprehension was also improved. Interestingly, the teaching methods used in the Curtis and Shaver study closely resemble strategies researchers recommend for gifted children. Group investigation, community problem solving, and strategies emphasizing independent process-oriented learning are often advocated for these students.

In their instructional decisions, teachers have many opportunities to demonstrate that they value all their students and to provide intellectually challenging experiences for them. Approaches such as cooperative learning and reciprocal teaching tell students that they all can learn, that they all can make a contribution to the learning process, and that all perspectives are valued. Community problem solving tells students that teachers care about their lives and their communities and provides opportunities for complex, meaningful, and motivating academic work. Instructional strategies such as these form the starting point of an effective multicultural repertoire for beginning teachers.

Classroom Organization and Management

A related instructional concern is classroom management. Management frequently poses problems for new teachers, and these problems are exacerbated when cultural differences are present. One means to alleviate the problem is to foster classroom democracy, following Glasser's classroom meeting

model described in Chapter 6. When students have the opportunity to air their views, many problems can be solved. Such an approach also communicates that all students are valued members of the classroom community.

Researchers have found that classroom climate and teacher affect are vitally important to at-risk students. Schlosser (1992) studied 31 culturally diverse high school students who had been identified as potential dropouts by the district. For two years, she interviewed and observed both the students and their teachers in an attempt to identify those teaching practices most effective with this population. Students said that good teachers displayed the following behaviors:

> (a) noticing you and asking if you're in any trouble, (b) including topics of interest to students in classroom discussions, and telling you that you can come back after class if you want to talk more, and (c) listening to what you say without jumping at you. (Schlosser, 1992, p. 133)

Teachers who demonstrated that they cared about students by talking with them, finding out about their lives, and applying that information in the way they structured their classrooms were the most effective with at-risk students. These actions help create personalized learning environments, which are more successful because teachers "know more about student lives and backgrounds, are better able to draw on their students' experiences to bridge the gap between the known and unknown, and are more likely to understand what knowledge must be made explicit for students" (Schlosser, 1992, p. 138).

Problems will inevitably arise, however, and teachers may feel some conflict about how to approach difficulties with diverse students. For example, does enforcing school rules amount to denying respect for students' culture? Experienced teachers come to understand that respecting the culture of all students does not mean abandoning the rules of the school. Punctuality and other aspects of dominant culture may not be regarded as important elsewhere, but they are important in mainstream culture, and in order to be successful within that culture, all students must learn to abide by these norms when circumstances warrant it. Not enforcing such rules at school would be to perform a disservice to all students. However, the attitude and spirit with which rules are enforced need not be demeaning or punitive. Teachers can explain rules and consequences in a neutral way to students and parents and offer suggestions on how they might cope with such rules. Teachers can also make clear that rules at school apply only at school and that students are certainly free to express their own values within the context of their subcultures. By the same token, teachers and schools should be open to examining and changing their rules and policies, if these no longer serve the learning needs of their students and community.

Some students, because of particularly difficult life circumstances like acute poverty, homelessness, or fetal alcohol syndrome, may pose especially taxing classroom management and discipline problems for teachers. There are a number of actions teachers can take to ease these difficulties. One is to reframe the student's disruptive action. Adults tend to interpret the aggressive or challenging behaviors these children may display as malicious, when they may represent the only mechanism the student has for expressing overstimulation, frustration, or some other message as simple as "I need to go to the bathroom." The first step for teachers, then, is to figure out what the behavior means to the student. One tool to help develop hypotheses about the function of disruptive behavior is to maintain a behavioral log, tracking what kinds of behaviors happen under what circumstances. Others are close observation and referrals to specialists. Then teachers can help students develop nondisruptive alternatives to cope with their frustrations. This vignette by a clinical psychologist illustrates how children's coping behaviors may interfere with smooth classroom functioning:

> [A] 4-year-old child was referred to me because he was "out of control in the classroom," had been cocaine-exposed prenatally, and was becoming increasingly aggressive toward the teacher.
>
> When this little boy arrived for testing, my first impression was that he was nothing like what the teacher had described. He was friendly, polite, and . . . extremely cooperative. However, after about five minutes . . . the child announced he was done. I tried to persuade him otherwise by redirecting his attention to different items, pushing the table a little closer to him, and asking him to try a few more things. This attempt to make him continue when he wanted to quit was met

> with a behavioral outburst . . . screaming, kicking, and shoving. . . . I immediately pulled the table away, at which time the child ran out of the room.
>
> I assumed the testing phase of the evaluation was over and started writing a few notes. . . . A few minutes later, however, the little boy returned . . . and said that he was ready to continue. After another 10 minutes or so . . . the child again said, "I'm done now," to which I replied, "That's fine." The child calmly got out of his chair, walked around the room for a minute, and then sat down to resume testing. This pattern was repeated. . . .
>
> It was easy to see in a one-to-one testing situation that this child recognized the limits to his concentration and coped with increasing frustration by briefly removing himself. . . . It is equally easy to see, however, how this behavior created problems in the classroom. By wandering around, he would be disrupting the learning of other children. When the teacher tried to make him sit back down, she was increasing his frustration by removing from him the one method he had developed for coping. (Griffith, 1992, p. 34)

Griffith goes on to suggest that one solution to this impasse might be for the teacher to mark out a space on the floor with masking tape at the back of the room so the child would have a place to pace without disturbing others while they developed a larger repertoire of coping strategies.

Rootlessness, stress, and lack of sense of control over their lives can also lead to special problems for homeless and extremely poor students. They may exhibit low tolerance for frustration and stimulation, short attention span, and distractability, typical of reactions to high stress. These students, too, may benefit from instruction in alternate ways of coping with stress and frustration. Linehan (1992) offers several additional guidelines to make classroom life more hospitable for these students:

- Let the student "own" something in the classroom, perhaps a plant or a game—something that others must get their permission to handle.
- Give the student a classroom job to be responsible for, a stake in the life of the classroom.
- Don't confiscate their things or deny recess/physical activity as a punishment or to allow time for makeup work; they need a sense of personal control and their outlets for activity may be limited.

- They may not have any quiet space to study in at their living quarters; if so, allow them to complete and store homework assignments at school.
- Transportation may be problematic; if so, don't penalize them for being late.
- Make sure students and parents are aware of the special services the school may offer—free lunch, free breakfast, bilingual activities, and other programs should be made readily available.
- Keep students' life circumstances confidential.

Most of these special needs students will require extra teaching in communication skills, in social skills, and in making choices.

It is in the area of classroom organization, management, and discipline that teachers can most emphatically demonstrate an attitude of caring and valuing their students. Warmth, friendliness, asking questions about students' lives—these actions tell students you are concerned about what happens to them and help engender cooperation in times of conflict. Accommodating children with special needs and respecting cultural differences, within the boundaries of maintaining high expectations and promoting biculturalism, also foster feelings of mutual trust and respect.

School Organization

In addition to reflecting on and modifying their own classroom practice, teachers can help effect multicultural reforms at the school level. A number of programs and practices of demonstrated effectiveness are available.

One of the most consistent findings from research is that tracking by ability does not promote achievement. Further, it has damaging consequences for minority students. A good place to start multicultural reforms, then, is to reduce or eliminate tracking. Many schools are beginning to experiment with reorganizing into teams of teachers and students, with developing interdisciplinary curricula, with relying heavily on cooperative learning in heterogeneous groups, and with alternatives to standardized testing (Oakes, 1992).

There are also several school-level actions teachers can take to address the difficult life circumstances of students considered "at risk" due to poverty. Most schools offer free and reduced-price lunches for students, but only about 50 percent of these schools also offer free and reduced-price breakfasts. A smaller number of districts provide meals over the summer through the Summer Food Service Program. The connection between student learning and basic nutrition is not only self-evident but also well documented, so it behooves schools and districts that lack these basic programs to implement them. To launch lunch, breakfast, or summer food projects, contact the responsible administrator within the district, usually the person in charge of food services. Ask that the district work with the appropriate state agency, usually the state office of education, to make application to the United States Department of Agriculture, Food and Nutrition Service.

School programs that target early intervention are also helpful. The effectiveness of programs like Head Start is well established. For every dollar invested in Head Start, many more are saved later on in reduced need for discipline and remediation, welfare, and criminal justice. Yet only about 20 percent of eligible children are served. The process of establishing a Head Start center is long and complex, but beginning teachers can lend their support to existing centers by promoting awareness among colleagues and parents and by lobbying for increased funding so that more low-income children can be served. Early identification and intervention with children who have been exposed prenatally to drugs and alcohol is also very important. To establish new programs or support existing ones, link with health and special education professionals in your school or district.

Recently a move toward interagency collaboration has begun among educators concerned with at-risk students. As Guthrie and Guthrie (1991) argue: "A wide assortment of social service agencies has been organized to serve children and youth at risk; but the services often overlap, agencies are compartmentalized, and children are incorrectly referred" (p. 17). To improve services, they advocate that these agencies coordinate their work with schools to provide assistance that is comprehensive, preventive, and child-centered. Again, linking with health, special education, and social service professionals is the first step in streamlining interagency collaboration.

Another important avenue to improve the educational outcomes of low-income students is community involvement. When parents and other community members are involved in the life of the school through tutoring programs, mentoring programs, school improvement committees, parent education, site-based governance, or other activities, students benefit (Epstein, 1991; Nettles, 1991).

Three schoolwide intervention programs are especially noteworthy: *Accelerated Schools* (Levin, 1987), *Success for All* (Madden, Slavin, Karweit, Dolan, and Wasik, 1992), and Yale psychiatrist James Comer's program initiated in New Haven, Connecticut, schools (Comer, 1988). These programs share characteristics such as parent involvement, decentralized decision making, and application of research-based instructional innovations. All three have proved highly effective in raising the achievement of at-risk students.

A word about being a new teacher and an agent for change at the same time. All of the programs and practices described in this chapter are worthwhile, important, and ought to be put into place in the public schools. Indeed, there is much public support for action to alleviate racial intolerance in the schools (71 percent of Americans in favor, according to a recent Gallup poll). Unfortunately, because of a variety of factors (lack of funds, time, awareness), many schools have inadequate programs or lack them entirely. We urge you to make working for multicultural reform part of your professional agenda. You probably have concerns about your ability to successfully carry out these reforms. As a newcomer to a large, complex organization, you will not have a lot of clout, but you will have some. When you make proposals that are backed by solid research, administrators and colleagues will be more likely to listen. When you talk with parents and patrons and enlist their support, you will be more likely to effect change. It is also wise to prioritize your reform goals and focus your limited energy on only one or two projects at a time. Chapter 14 presents more detailed information on the processes of individual and organizational change and of improving schools.

SUMMARY

- The term *multicultural education* involves learning to recognize, understand, and appreciate all cultural groups—whether based on racial, ethnic, language, gender, or other differences—and the development of skills in working with diverse groups of students. Today's classrooms are characterized by diversity. It is critical for teachers to develop classrooms which treat all students equally, regardless of their gender, racial or ethnic heritage, or learning difficulties. In creating multicultural classrooms effective teachers adopt an ecological perspective and view their classrooms as a system of interconnected elements—students, teachers, learning materials, instruction, and goals—all of which interact to produce or inhibit student learning.
- The knowledge base on multicultural education can help teachers to understand particular cultures, what happens to children of different cultures in school, and how to develop a strong multicultural teaching repertoire.
- Studies over the years have shown that minority students receive a lower-quality education as a result of enrollment patterns, tracking and grouping patterns, and differential interactions with teachers.
- Language diversity must be respected, and bilingual skills must be encouraged and developed for students who do not speak the dominant language.
- Gender bias exists in schools and classrooms because of linguistic bias and stereotyping.
- Socioeconomic status has rather dramatic effects on school learning, mainly because of tracking and grouping and because of differential interactions with teachers.
- Traditionally, handicapped students have received inferior education. Current efforts to mainstream handicapped students are aimed at correcting this situation.
- As with many other aspects of teaching, knowledge, self-understanding, and reflection about intercultural interactions are essential for teachers in developing multicultural classrooms and schools.
- Teachers attend to their personal and profes-

sional development by improving their own knowledge and attitudes toward people of different cultures and by becoming aware of their cultural biases.

- Teachers' expectations affect relationships with students, what they learn, and students' perceptions of their own abilities.
- Teachers can learn to be aware of, and minimize, their biases about students of different backgrounds.
- There is a robust set of curricular materials and instructional strategies teachers can use to accomplish multicultural goals.
- The most widely used approaches to incorporate multicultural topics into the curriculum include the single-group curriculum approach, the topical approach, and the conceptual approach.
- Teaching processes that can be employed to promote multicultural education include anchoring instruction to student's prior knowledge, meshing learning activities to students' learning styles, and capitalizing on students' existing abilities.
- Specific teaching models and strategies available to accomplish multicultural learning goals include cooperative learning and community problem solving.
- Teachers must evaluate and adapt their curriculum, instruction, and schools in keeping with the dual goals of valuing and challenging all their students.

KEY TERMS

multicultural education
Americanization
melting pot
cultural pluralism
linguistic bias
socioeconomic status
mainstreaming
least restrictive environment
individualized educational plan (IEP)
teacher expectations
self-fulfilling prophecy
differential treatment
sustaining expectation effect
single-group curriculum
topical approach
conceptual approach
assigning competence
community problem solving

BOOKS FOR THE PROFESSIONAL

Biklen, D. (1985). *Achieving the complete school.* New York: Teachers College Press. Through numerous case studies, this book describes principles and methods for teachers to achieve mainstreaming in their classrooms.

Cushner, K., McClelland, A., and Safford, P. (1992). *Human diversity in education: An integrative approach.* New York: McGraw-Hill. This book gives a thorough presentation of the issues surrounding multicultural education in the broadest sense and further develops sensitivity to problems inherent in intercultural interaction in schools through didactic presentation, case studies, and critical incidents.

Dilworth, M. E. (ed.). (1992). *Diversity in teacher education: New expectations.* San Francisco: Jossey-Bass. This timely collection of essays focuses on the importance of diversity in our schools and classrooms and the challenges currently being faced by teachers and teacher educators.

Heath, S. B. (1983). *Ways with words: Language, life and work in communities and classrooms.* Cambridge, England: Cambridge University Press. This classic and fascinating study of the cultural mismatch of race and class in the American south will give you a clearer understanding of the impact of culture on teaching and learning.

Means, B., Chelemer, C., and Knapp, M. S. (1991). *Teaching advanced skills to at-risk students: Views from research and practice.* San Francisco: Jossey-Bass. This book gives an excellent, detailed explanation about how to teach high-level, complex goals to at-risk students. Strategies for language arts and mathematics at both elementary and secondary levels are described.

LEARNING AIDS FOR PLANNING, OBSERVATION, AND REFLECTION

- Observing and Interviewing Teachers with Special-Needs Children

- Evaluating Curriculum Materials for Bias

- Interviewing a Student from a Different Culture

- Assessing My Multicultural Teaching Skills

- Teacher Expectations Questionnaire for Students

OBSERVING AND INTERVIEWING TEACHERS WITH SPECIAL-NEEDS CHILDREN

PURPOSE: It's relatively simple to vow to treat all children equitably, but it's sometimes difficult to put such ideals into practice. This learning aid will help you learn how experienced teachers actually accomplish the goal of fair and effective treatment of exceptional and limited-English students.

DIRECTIONS: First observe, then interview, a teacher about how he or she manages a classroom with special-needs children, using the observation and interview form below as a guide. Observe and note the following:

1. How has the teacher arranged the furniture in the room?

   _____

   _____

2. What has the teacher placed on the walls? Are they brightly and busily decorated or more subdued? Are rules, procedures, or other cues posted?

   _____

   _____

3. Note the teacher's use of time. How much time is devoted, on average, to each lesson segment? Do students move around much between lesson segments? How much time does the teacher provide for transitions?

   _____

   _____

4. How has the teacher grouped students for instruction? Whole class? Individual? Small groups? Do the students stay in the same grouping pattern, or do they change from one arrangement to another?

   _____

   _____

5. What rules and procedures do students observe in this classroom?

   _____

   _____

6. Note peer interaction. Tally the number of positive and negative statements students make to each other.

   _____

   _____

7. What teaching strategy is the teacher using?

_____

_____

Now that you've observed the class, use the questions below to guide an interview with the teacher.

8. What is your strategy for dealing with the wide range of academic ability and diverse language abilities in your classroom?

_____

_____

9. How did you come to this strategy? Where did you get your ideas? What else have you tried, and how successful was it?

_____

_____

10. How have you helped special-needs students be accepted by other children?

_____

_____

11. Do you have pull-out programs in your school (a program in which a child with special needs is "pulled out" of his or her regular classroom for instruction by a special teacher)? If so, how do you work around learning disabled and handicapped students going in and out? Gifted and talented students? Limited-English students?

_____

_____

12. Describe your working relationship with the resource teacher(s).

_____

_____

Reflection and Analysis: Based on what you have read, observed, and discussed with teachers, briefly outline your own plan for how you will accommodate special-needs children in your own class. What obstacles are you likely to run into in implementing your plan? How might you circumvent them?

EVALUATING CURRICULUM MATERIALS FOR BIAS

PURPOSE: The purpose of this aid is to systematically assess bias in textbooks and other learning materials.

DIRECTIONS: Select an elementary or secondary school textbook to evaluate, either from a school in which you are doing fieldwork or from the university curriculum library. Read it, paying special attention to the content, examples, and visual material in it. Then fill out the charts below; write a "Y" for "yes" in the appropriate cell if the book exhibits that particular form of bias for that particular group.

1. Look at the *content* of the book, the information conveyed. Are any of these forms of bias present: stereotype, imbalance, invisibility, unreality, linguistic, fragmentation?

   Race/ethnicity: _____
   Gender: _____
   Low-SES: _____
   Handicap: _____

2. Look at the *examples* used to elaborate on and clarify the content. Are any of these forms of bias present: stereotype, imbalance, invisibility, unreality, linguistic, fragmentation?

   Race/ethnicity: _____
   Gender: _____
   Low-SES: _____
   Handicap: _____

3. Look at the *visuals* used to illustrate the content. Are any of these forms of bias present: stereotype, imbalance, invisibility, unreality, linguistic, fragmentation?

   Race/ethnicity: _____
   Gender: _____
   Low-SES: _____
   Handicap: _____

Reflection and Analysis: Does the book contain bias? Would you use it in your own classroom? Why or why not? If you did use it, how would you raise the issue of bias with your students? Alternatively, how would you supplement the text to provide a bias-free curriculum?

INTERVIEWING A STUDENT FROM A DIFFERENT CULTURE

PURPOSE: Part of developing knowledge and skill in teaching multiculturally is learning about different cultures, especially about how people from different cultures fare in schools. You can use this aid to learn more about culturally diverse students.

DIRECTIONS: Use the questions below to guide an interview with a student from a sub-culture.

1. What are the similarities you've noticed between your own culture and the mainstream culture?

_____

_____

2. What are some of the differences you've noticed between your culture and the main-stream?

_____

_____

3. What do you especially like about school? _____

_____

_____

4. What problems have you run into at school? _____

_____

_____

5. How did you deal with those problems? _____

_____

6. What have your teachers done in the past that helped you learn and get along with other students?

_____

_____

7. What else could teachers do to help you learn and get along better at school? _____

_____

Reflection and Analysis: Make a list of actions teachers could take to ease learning for culturally diverse students. Share your list with fellow students and/or cooperating teachers, and discuss the pros and cons of each suggestion.

ASSESSING MY MULTICULTURAL TEACHING SKILLS

PURPOSE: This aid is designed to help you gauge your abilities in implementing a multicultural classroom. Use it to assist you in planning your own professional development.

DIRECTIONS: Check the level of effectiveness you feel you have attained in each of the following areas.

UNDERSTANDING OR SKILL	LEVEL OF UNDERSTANDING OR SKILL		
	HIGH	MEDIUM	LOW
I understand and can articulate a strong rationale for multicultural education.	_____	_____	_____
I understand and can describe the research base underlying each multicultural domain.	_____	_____	_____
I am examining and correcting my own biases about other groups.	_____	_____	_____
I can teach to multiple goals, incorporating information about a diversity of groups.	_____	_____	_____
I can evaluate curriculum materials for bias and supplement them when necessary.	_____	_____	_____
I can uncover and correct dysfunctional teacher-student interaction patterns.	_____	_____	_____
I can group students heterogeneously.	_____	_____	_____
I can use a variety of teaching techniques and strategies.	_____	_____	_____

Analysis and Reflection: What are your strengths? What are your weaknesses? Write a one-paragraph action plan describing specifically what you will do to improve in one of your weak areas.

TEACHER EXPECTATIONS QUESTIONNAIRE FOR STUDENTS

PURPOSE: The nature of teacher expectations is an important variable in building positive learning environments. The questionnaire can help you assess your treatment of students.

DIRECTIONS: Distribute the questionnaire and have students rate each statement on a scale of 1 to 3. Use the smiley face version for younger students.

1   Seldom   2   Sometimes   3   Always

The Way You See Me Working with You

1. Do I praise you for good work?	1	2	3
2. Do I like you?	1	2	3
3. Am I friendly?	1	2	3
4. Do I call on you when you raise your hand?	1	2	3
5. Do I criticize you when you don't deserve it?	1	2	3
6. Am I unfriendly?	1	2	3
7. Do I work with you as much as with other students?	1	2	3
8. Do I treat you fairly?	1	2	3
9. Do I smile at you?	1	2	3
10. Do I grade your work fairly?	1	2	3
11. Do I help you when you need help?	1	2	3
12. Do I pay attention to you?	1	2	3
13. Do I understand your problems?	1	2	3
14. Do I like your work?	1	2	3
15. Do I give you enough responsibility?	1	2	3
16. Do you like the way I look at you?	1	2	3
17. Do I give you enough time for your work?	1	2	3
18. Do I ask you "hard" questions?	1	2	3
19. Do you think I am friendly toward you?	1	2	3
20. Do I ask enough from you?	1	2	3

Analysis and Reflection: Find the class mean for each item. Compare the class mean with the mean score for the five most positive students and the five least positive students. Reflect on the differences you see between students who see you most positively and those who see you least positively. Are there racial differences? gender differences? social class differences?

Chapter Outline

PERSPECTIVE AND RATIONALE

SAMPLING THE KNOWLEDGE BASE

• Focus on the Individual • Classroom Ecology and Group Processes • Effective Teaching Research

PREPARING FOR EFFECTIVE CLASSROOM MANAGEMENT

• Preventive Classroom Management • Managing Inappropriate and Disruptive Behavior • Exhibiting Confidence and Exerting Influence • Assertive Discipline

WORKING TOWARD SELF-MANAGEMENT

• Dreikurs' Logical Consequences • Glasser's Classroom Meeting

CHAPTER 6

Classroom Management

When teachers talk about the most difficult problems they experienced in their first years of teaching, they mention **classroom management** and discipline most often. Although a rich knowledge base on classroom management has been developed over the past two decades, as well as a spate of management training programs, beginning teachers continue to feel insecure about managing their first classrooms.

Many of these anxieties are, in fact, similar to the anxieties experienced by people in any field when they are asked to assume positions of leadership and to exert influence and authority for the first time. Nonetheless, gaining a set of basic management understandings and skills will do much to reduce the anxiety that naturally accompanies one's first classroom assignment. Describing the important concepts and skills associated with classroom management is the aim of this chapter. The first section of the chapter builds on the conceptual frameworks introduced in Chapter 4 and then presents a sampling of key research studies from the classroom management literature. In the final section of the chapter are specific and concrete procedures beginning teachers can use as they prepare for effective classroom management.

PERSPECTIVE AND RATIONALE

Many of the conceptual frameworks for understanding classroom management have been presented in previous chapters and do not need to be repeated here. There are, however, a few more ideas that can provide additional perspective and provide a focus for the preventive management approach taken in this chapter.

First, *classroom management and instruction are interrelated*. Classroom management is not an end in itself; it is merely one part of a teacher's overall leadership role. In this regard, classroom management cannot be separated from the other executive functions of teaching. For example, when teachers plan carefully for lessons, as described in Chapter 2, they are doing much to ensure good classroom management. When teachers plan ways to allocate time to various learning activities or consider how space should be used in the classroom, they are again making important decisions that will affect classroom management. Similarly, all the strategies for building productive learning environments described in Chapter 4, such as helping the classroom develop as a group, attending to student motiva-

173

tion, or facilitating honest and open discourse, are also important components of classroom management.

Second, *it is impossible to totally separate the managerial and instructional functions of teaching.* Each teaching model or strategy a teacher chooses to use has its own social system and its own task demands that influence the behaviors of both teachers and learners. The instructional tasks associated with giving a lecture, for example, call for behaviors on the part of students that are different from those needed for tasks associated with learning a new skill. Similarly, behavioral demands for students working together in groups are different from those required for working alone on a seatwork assignment. Instructional tasks are integrally related not only to the problem of instruction but also to the problems of order and management. An important theme stressed in this chapter is what Brophy and Putnam (1979) and Evertson and Emmer (1982) have called preventive management. Teachers who plan appropriate classroom activities and tasks, who make wise decisions about time and space allocation, and who have a sufficient repertoire of instructional strategies will be building a learning environment that minimizes management and discipline problems.

Finally, *classroom management is possibly the most important challenge facing beginning teachers,* since their reputation among colleagues, school authorities, and even students will be strongly influenced by their ability to perform the managerial functions of teaching, particularly creating an orderly learning environment and dealing with student behavior. Sometimes, beginning teachers think this is unfair and argue that schools and principals put too much emphasis on order as contrasted to learning. Perhaps it is unfair. Nonetheless, teachers' leadership ability is tested in the arena of management and discipline, and when something goes wrong it is known more quickly than other aspects of teaching. More importantly, without adequate management little else can occur. Dunkin and Biddle (1974) pointed out this important fact two decades ago when they wrote that "management of the classroom . . . forms a necessary condition for cognitive learning; and if the teacher cannot solve problems in this sphere, we can give the rest of teaching away" (p. 135).

SAMPLING THE KNOWLEDGE BASE

The research on maintaining order in the classroom has been guided by at least three major orientations: focus on the individual, classroom ecology and group processes, and effective teaching.

Focus on the Individual

Research that focuses on the individual student seeks to understand the causes of behavioral problems and recommends specific interventions and discipline procedures for teachers to use. This tradition has been led mainly by clinical and counseling psychologists, such as Dreikurs (1968), Grey (Dreikurs and Grey, 1968), and Glasser (1969), and by behavioral psychologists and those who apply behavioral theory, such as Canter and Canter (1976). Their research or practice has focused on such psychological causes as insecurity, need for attention, anxiety, and lack of self-discipline, as well as sociological causes such as parent overprotection, bad peer relationships, or disadvantaged backgrounds. Their recommendations to teachers normally emphasize ways to help individual students through counseling or behavior modification and show less concern for managing the classroom group. This tradition is mentioned only briefly for two reasons. First, many of the psychological and sociological causes of student behavior are beyond the influence of classroom teachers, and second, the management of classroom groups is a more pressing issue for the beginning teacher.

The final section of this chapter does, however, include a description of Driekurs', Glasser's, and the Canters' approaches to classroom management. Driekurs and Glasser both put the responsibility of behavior on the student, and Glasser incorporates concrete procedures for helping students develop self-management skills within a group setting.

Classroom Ecology and Group Processes

In Chapter 4, several ideas were described that help explain classroom life from an ecological perspective and the work of such researchers as Barker (1968), Doyle (1979), Gump (1967), and Kounin (1970) were cited. The ecological perspective ad-

Preventive Classroom Management

Many of the problems associated with student misbehavior are dealt with by effective teachers through preventive approaches. Much of this section is based on the research emanating from Kounin's work and that of the Texas project, summarized earlier. The ideas and procedures are introduced here and they are revisited in Chapter 15 in connection with starting the first year of teaching because one of the important findings from the work at the University of Texas is the importance of establishing routines for effective management at the start of the school year. In fact, there is evidence that later in the year, when teachers who are having problems try to create better management practices, student cooperation then is difficult, if not impossible, to achieve (Evertson, Emmer, Sanford, and Clements, 1983).

ESTABLISHING RULES AND PROCEDURES

In classrooms, as with most other settings where groups of people interact, a large percentage of potential problems and disruptions can be prevented by planning rules and procedures beforehand. To understand the truth of this statement, think for a moment about the varied experiences you have had in nonschool settings where fairly large numbers of people come together. Examples most people think about include driving a car during rush hour in a large city, attending a football game, going to Disneyland, or buying tickets for a movie or play. In all of these instances established rules and procedures indicated by traffic lights and queuing stalls help people who do not even know each other to interact in regular, predictable ways. Rules, such as "the right of way" and "no cutting in line," help people negotiate rather complex processes safely and efficiently.

Think for a moment of what happens when procedures or rules suddenly break down or disappear. You can probably recall an instance when a power outage caused traffic lights to stop working or when a large crowd arrived to buy tickets for an important game before the ticket sellers set up their queuing stalls. Recently, a teacher was in Detroit for a conference, and her return flight was booked on an airline that had merged with another airline on that particular day. When the two airlines combined their information systems, something went wrong with the computers. This computer malfunction made it impossible for the ticket agents to know who was on a particular flight and prevented them from issuing seat assignments. Disruptive behavior and bedlam resulted. People were shoving each other as individuals tried to ensure a seat for themselves; passengers were yelling at each other and at the cabin crew. At one point members of a normally well-disciplined crew were even speaking sharply to each other. The story turned out okay, because a seat was found for everyone. The boarding process, however, had not proceeded in the usual orderly, calm manner because some well-known procedures were suddenly unavailable.

Classrooms are not too different from busy airports or busy intersections. They, too, require rules and procedures to govern important activities. As used here, **rules** are statements that specify the things students are expected to do and not do. Normally, rules are written down, are made clear to students, and are kept to a minimum. **Procedures,** on the other hand, are the ways of getting work and other activity accomplished. They are seldom written down, but effective classroom managers spend considerable time teaching procedures to students in the same way they teach academic matter. Student movement, student talk, and what to do with downtime are among the most important activities that require rules to govern behavior and procedures to make work flow efficiently.

Student Movement. In many secondary classrooms, such as a science laboratory, the art room, or the physical education facility, and in all elementary classrooms, students must move around to accomplish important learning activities. Materials have to be obtained or put back, pencils need sharpening, small groups are formed, and so on.

Effective classroom managers devise ways to make needed movements by students flow smoothly. They devise queuing and distribution procedures that are efficient; they establish rules that minimize disruptions and ensure safety. Examples of rules might include those that limit the number of students moving at any one time or those that specify when to be seated. How to line up, move in the halls, and go unattended to the library are procedures that assist with student movement.

Student Talk. Students talking at inappropriate times or asking questions to slow down the pace of a lesson pose a classroom management problem that is among the most troublesome to beginning teachers. This problem can vary in severity, from a loud, generalized classroom clamor that disturbs the teacher next door to a single student talking to a neighbor when the teacher is explaining an important idea.

Effective classroom managers have a clear set of rules governing student talking. Most teachers prescribe when no talking is allowed (when the teacher is lecturing or explaining), when low talk is allowed and encouraged (during small-group work or seatwork), and when anything goes (during recess and parties). Effective classroom managers also have procedures that make classroom discourse more satisfying and productive, such as talking one at a time during a discussion, listening to other people's ideas, raising hands, and taking turns.

Downtime. A third area of classroom life for which rules and procedures are required is during **downtime.** Sometimes, lessons are completed before a period is over, and it is inappropriate to start something new. Similarly, when students are doing seatwork some finish before others. Waiting for a film projector to arrive for a scheduled film is another example of downtime.

Effective classroom managers devise rules and procedures to govern student talk and movement during these times. Examples include: "If you finish your work, you can get a book and engage in silent reading until the others have finished." "While we wait for the film to start, you can talk quietly to your neighbors, but you cannot move around the room."

TEACHING RULES AND PROCEDURES

Rules and procedures are of little value unless participants learn and accept them. This requires active teaching. Effective classroom managers generally establish only a few rules and procedures, then teach them carefully to students and make them routine through their consistent use. In most classrooms only a few rules are needed, but it is important for the teacher to make sure students understand the purpose for the rule and its moral or practical underpinnings. Concepts and ideas associated with rules have to be taught just the same as any other set of concepts and ideas. For instance, very young children can see the necessity for keeping talk low during downtime, when it is explained that loud talk disturbs students in neighboring classrooms who are still working. Taking turns strikes a chord with older students who have heightened concerns with issues of fairness and justice. Potential injury to self and others can be explained as the reason why movement in a science laboratory has to be done a certain way. One point of caution about teaching rules should be noted, however. When teachers are explaining rules, they must walk a rather thin line between providing explanations that are helpful to students and sounding patronizing or overly moralistic.

Most movement and discourse procedures have not only a practical dimension but also a skill dimension that must be taught, like academic skills. In Chapter 13 several strategies will be described to teach students how to listen to other people's ideas and how to participate in discussions which can be used by beginning teachers to help manage student talking. Student movement skills also need to be taught. Even with college-age students, it takes instruction and two or three practices to make getting into a circle, a fishbowl formation, or small groups move smoothly. Effective classroom managers devote time in the first week or so of the school year to teaching rules and procedures and then provide periodic review as needed.

Effective classroom managers are consistent in their enforcement of rules and their application of procedures. If they are not, any set of rules and procedures soon dissolves. For example, a teacher may have a rule for student movement that says, when you are doing seatwork and I'm at my desk, only one student at a time can come for help. If a student is allowed to wait at the desk while a first student is being helped, soon several others will be there too. If this is an important rule for the teacher, then whenever more than one student appears, he or she must be firmly reminded of the rule and asked to sit down. Another example would be when a teacher has a rule that no talking is allowed when he or she is giving a presentation or explaining important ideas or procedures. If two students are then allowed to whisper in the back of the room, even if they are not disturbing others, soon many students will follow suit. Similarly, if the teacher wants students to raise their hands before talking during a discussion and then allows a few students to blurt out whenever they please, the hand-raising rule is soon rendered ineffective.

It is difficult for beginning teachers to establish consistency for at least two reasons. One, rule breaking normally occurs when more than one event is going on simultaneously. The novice teacher cannot always maintain total awareness of the complex classroom environment and thus does not always see what is occurring. Two, it takes considerable energy and even personal courage to enforce rules consistently. Many beginning teachers find it easier and less threatening to ignore certain student behavior rather than to confront and deal with it. Experienced teachers know that avoiding a difficult situation only leads to more problems later.

PREVENTING DEVIANT BEHAVIOR WITH SMOOTHNESS AND MOMENTUM

A second dimension of preventive classroom management involves pacing instructional events and maintaining appropriate momentum. The research by Doyle and Carter (1984) described how students can delay academic tasks, and Kounin's research (1970) pointed out the importance of keeping lessons going in a smooth fashion. Kounin also described how teachers sometimes do things themselves that interfere with the flow of activities. For example, sometimes a teacher might start an activity and then leave it in midair. Kounin labeled this type of behavior a **dangle.** A dangle occurs, for example, when a teacher asks students to hand in their notes at the end of a lecture and then suddenly decides that he or she needs to explain one more point. Teachers also slow down lessons by doing what Kounin labeled **flip-flops.** A flip-flop is when an activity is started and then stopped while another is begun and then the original started again. A flip-flop occurs, for example, when a teacher tells students to get out their books and start reading and then interrupts the reading to explain a point and then resumes the silent reading. Dangles and flip-flops interfere with the smoothness of classroom activities, cause confusion on the part of some students, and most importantly, present opportunities for noninvolved students to misbehave.

Teachers also do things that slow down the momentum of lessons. Kounin described two types of important slow-down behaviors—**fragmentation** and **overdwelling.** A teacher who goes on and on after instructions are clear to students is overdwelling. A teacher who breaks activities into overly small units, such as "sit up straight, get your papers out, pass them to the person in front, now pass them to the next person," and so on is fragmenting a set of instructions. Slowing down momentum disrupts smoothness and gives noninvolved students opportunities to interrupt classroom activities.

Minimizing disruptive and slow-down behaviors is difficult for beginning teachers to learn, as are many other effective management skills. Smoothness and momentum definitely vary with the nature of individual classes— what may be a dangle in one classroom may not be so in another, or what may be overdwelling with one group of students may be appropriate for another group.

ORCHESTRATING CLASSROOM ACTIVITIES DURING UNSTABLE PERIODS

A third important dimension of preventive classroom management involves planning and orchestrating student behavior during unstable periods of the school day—periods of time when order is most difficult to achieve and maintain.

Opening Class.   The beginning of class, whether it is the first few minutes of the morning in an elementary classroom or the beginning of a period in secondary schools, is an unstable time. Students are coming from other settings (their homes, the playground, another class) where a different set of behavioral norms apply. The new setting has different rules and procedures as well as friends who have not been seen since the previous day. The beginning of class is also a time in most schools where several administrative tasks are required of teachers, such as taking roll and making announcements.

Effective classroom managers plan and execute procedures that help get things started quickly and surely. For example:

1. They greet their students at the door, extending welcomes to build positive feeling tones, and also to keep potential trouble outside the door.
2. They train student helpers to take the roll, read

announcements, and do other administrative tasks, so they can be free to start lessons.

3. They write instructions on the board or on newsprint so students can get started on lessons as soon as they come into the room.

4. They establish routine and ceremonial events that communicate to students that serious work is about to begin.

Transitions.   Citing research of Gump (1967, 1982) and Rosenshine (1980), Doyle (1986) says that "approximately 31 major **transitions** occur per day in elementary classrooms, and they account for approximately 15 percent of classroom time" (p. 406). There are fewer transitions in secondary classrooms, but they still are numerous and take considerable time. It is during transition periods (moving from whole group to small groups, changing from listening to seatwork, getting needed materials to do an assignment, getting ready to go to recess) that many disruptions occur. Learning to handle transitions is difficult for most beginning teachers. Prior planning and the use of cuing devices are two techniques that can help.

Planning is crucial when it comes to managing transitions. Chapter 2 described how transitions must be planned just as carefully as any other instructional activity. At first, beginning teachers should conceive of each transition as a series of steps they want students to follow. These steps should be written down in note form and in some instances given to the students on the chalkboard or on newsprint charts. For example, making the transition from a whole-class lecture to seatwork might include the following steps:

Step 1:   Put your lecture notes away and clear your desk.

Step 2:   Make sure you have pencils and a copy of the work sheet being distributed by the row monitor.

Step 3:   Begin your work.

Step 4:   Raise your hand if you want me to help you.

As beginning teachers become more experienced with managing transitions, they will no longer need to list the steps for minor transitions

and may instead rely on clear mental images of what is required.

Cuing and signaling systems are used by effective teachers to manage difficult transition periods. The best way to understand cuing is to think of it as a warning device similar to the yellow light on a traffic signal or the "Slow" sign on a curving road. Cues are used by teachers to alert students that they are about to change activities or tasks and to start getting ready. Here are some examples of cues.

- During a small-group activity, a teacher goes around to each group and announces, "You have five minutes before returning to the whole group."
- During a discussion activity, a teacher tells students, "We must end the discussion in a few minutes, but there will be time for three more comments."
- During a laboratory experiment, the teacher says, "We have been working for 20 minutes now, and you should be at least halfway done."
- In getting ready for a guest speaker, the teacher tells the class, "Our speaker will arrive in 3 minutes, let's straighten up the chairs and get ready to greet her."

Many teachers also develop a signal system for alerting students to a forthcoming transition or for helping them move through the steps of a transition smoothly. Signal systems are particularly effective with younger children and in classrooms where the activities are such that it is difficult to hear the teacher. The band instructor raising his or her baton is an example of a signal for students to get quiet and ready their instruments to play the first note. Figure 6-1 shows a set of hand signals developed by one experienced teacher to alert and assist his students with difficult transitions and to check their understanding of what is being taught.

Closing Class.   The closing of class is also an unstable time in most classrooms. Sometimes the teacher is rushed to complete a lesson that has run over its allocated time; sometimes materials such as tests or papers must be collected; almost always students need to get their own personal belongings ready to move to another class, the lunchroom, or the bus. Effective teachers anticipate the potential

Figure 6-1 Examples of signals for communicating with students

Rhythm or echo clapping can be used to get attention of the students in the classroom. When the teacher claps four beats, the students respond with a two-clap echo, and this signals that all activity stops.

Bell signaling can be used to gain the attention of the students. Just a short ring will cue the students to stop all activities and listen (small hand bell).

Light signaling is often used by teachers and can be affective. The light switch is flicked once, quickly.

Arm signals can be used at times to gain the attention of students without having to use an audible signal. When children are in the hallway, lining up, or in the playground, the teacher raises an arm and this will cue the students to do the same and become quiet.

Finger signals can be used effectively in managing small groups, dismissing students, or conducting other tasks. When dismissing groups of students by areas, code the groups numerically and dismiss by signals.

Looks are often effective in gaining a student's attention. A quizzical or firm look may be all that is needed.

Charts can signal directions and important messages. Use a smiley face or sad face suspended from the ceiling. Flip to sad face when students' behavior is unacceptable; return to a smiley face when acceptable behavior occurs.

Charts that can tell students what to do when they finish work are very useful, and assist students in becoming more independent and involved in purposeful activities. The ideas on these charts should be varied and changed frequently.

Thumb signals can be used to respond to yes-no situations, to signal choices, and to communicate when things aren't clear.

Signal with extended thumb

Examples: Do you agree? (Thumbs up); Do you disagree? (Thumbs down); Not clear? (Thumbs sideways)— Is this an example of the problem?

Finger signals can be used to respond to numerical answers, multiple-choice, and true-false questions. Signal with hand against chest.

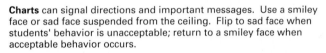

Examples: Show us how many tens are in 64. Which word means land surrounded by water? 1. peninsula 2. island 3. continent Which word means land surrounded by water on three sides? 1. peninsula 2. island 3. continent Share the answer by forming the beginning symbol or letter to the answer with your fingers. (Be as creative as you can in developing signals.)

(Continued on page 184)

Figure 6-1 *(Continued)*

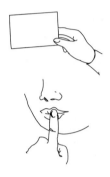

Think pads/response cards can be used to let every student answer. These responses can be written on scrap paper cut into quarters and placed in envelopes on the children's desks. Children write answers on pads or cards and hold them up to be checked by the teacher. Responses can be adapted to any subject area, and any type of question. This information can serve as a pretest, a check on prior day's work, or as a diagnostic informal assessment.

    Example: "Write the names of the seven (7) continents on your pads—then let me see.

Whisper signal can provide general feedback to the teacher.

    Examples: Point to the word as we all whisper it. Place your finger on the part that proves the answer. Whisper the number of the paragraph where the answer is found.

Head signaling can also be used to respond to a question or direction.

    Example: Put your head on your desk and imagine what I am describing. Lift your head when you have the answer.

Help cards can be used to signal for assistance from the teacher or a student. When the student encounters a problem or has difficulty, he/she goes on to the next problem or activity but signals for help by placing a card on the corner of the desk. This signal will alert the teacher or a student helper to provide assistance as soon as possible. Loss of time from waiting with the hand raised is avoided and the student learns to better utilize his or her time.

    Example: A student cannot spell a word, posts the help card, and continues work.

SOURCE: From M. Bozeman (1985), Signaling in the classroom. (Mimeographed.) Salisbury, Md.: Salisbury State College.

management problems associated with closing class by incorporating the following procedures into their classroom organizational patterns:

1. Leaving sufficient time to complete important closing activities, such as collecting books, papers, and the like
2. Making homework assignments early enough so that possible confusion can be cleared up prior to the last minute of class
3. Establishing routine procedures for collecting student work (such as placing a box by the door), so class time does not have to be used for this activity
4. Using alerting and cuing procedures to give students warning that the end of the class is approaching and that certain tasks need to be completed before they leave
5. Teaching older students that class will be dis-

missed by the teacher, not by the school bell or buzzer

DEVELOPING STUDENT ACCOUNTABILITY

A final dimension of preventive classroom management involves the procedures effective teachers develop to hold the students accountable for their academic work and for their classroom behavior. Carolyn Evertson and Edmund Emmer have identified six areas that teachers should attend to for developing **student accountability.** These are listed in Figure 6-2.

Managing Inappropriate and Disruptive Behavior

Preactive planning and skilled orchestration of classroom activities can prevent many of the management problems faced by beginning teachers, but

Figure 6-2 Evertson and Emmer's procedures for developing student accountability

---

1. **Clarity of work assignments**: The teacher must have a specific set of expectations for student performance, covering such details as the form of student work, expectation regarding neatness, completeness, due dates, and procedures for make-up work. The specific requirements in these areas may vary greatly from teacher to teacher, according to subject matter and age level of the students, and the personal preferences of the teacher. The teacher must decide what is reasonable, given the teaching context, and what will aid students in the development of good work habits. . . .

2. **Communicating assignments**: Assignments should be clear, so that every student understands what to do. This can be accomplished in several ways. Establishing a routine for posting assignments in a particular place or having students copy assignments onto their worksheet or paper assures that everyone will at least be able to find out what the assignment is, even when the teacher is not available to point it out to them. Grading requirements should be spelled out to students, so that they know exactly what the teacher considers important in assessing achievement. . . .

3. **Monitoring student work**: Once assignments are made and students begin work, it is again essential that the teacher be aware of student progress. This can be accomplished by circulating throughout the classroom and systematically checking each student's work. The teacher should scan the class for a minute or two at the beginning of a seatwork activity to make sure that everyone has begun. . . . Once the teacher is sure that everyone understands the task and has begun work, then he or she may circulate around the room and assist individual students. During recitation or discussion activities, as well as small-group work, the teacher should also monitor student involvement.

4. **Checking work**: Once assignments have been completed, the teacher needs a system for checking work. Assignments that have specific answers may be checked by students. This provides quick feedback to each student, although the teacher should be sure to establish procedures for checking. A procedure is also needed for students to turn in their papers. Certain assignments may be put in a basket at the front of the room, and a special area may be designed for collecting and returning assignments of absent students.

5. **Giving feedback to students**: It is through practice and feedback that most instruction begins to pay off in learning. When students receive information about their performance, they obtain the basis for improvement. Regular routines for checking work and returning it to students are useful. It is also helpful if teachers set aside some time after assignments have been returned for the students to review their papers and make corrections. . . . The feedback older students receive is usually tied in with a grading system; therefore, the teacher needs an overall basis for grading consistent with the instructional goals.

6. **Clarity of instructions**: Most effective managers give clear and specific instructions, which is an instructional and a managerial asset. Clear instruction of academic content helps students succeed and learn; unclear instruction can produce failure, frustration, and task avoidance. Clarity is aided by a number of factors. First, the teacher must have a very good idea of what is to be taught and how. Therefore, planning is essential. Second, the teacher must communicate information so that students understand it. Thus, the teacher's awareness of student comprehension is critical. Third, the precision and clarity of the teacher's oral expression are important. Sloppy speech habits lead to vagueness and confusion.

SOURCE: From C. Evertson and E. Emmer (1982), Preventive classroom management. In D. Duke (ed.), *Helping teachers manage classrooms*. Alexandria, Va.: Association for Supervision and Curriculum Development, pp. 28–29. Used with permission.

not all. As in other social settings, every classroom will have a few students who will choose not to involve themselves in classroom activities and, instead, be disruptive forces. Disruptions can, of course, range from students talking when they are supposed to be listening to the teacher or refusing to go along with a small-group activity to yelling at the teacher and stomping out of the room. Managing disruptive behavior calls for a special set of understandings and also a special repertoire of skills.

THE CAUSES OF MISBEHAVIOR

Because beginning teachers have observed disruptive behavior in classrooms for many years, most can readily list the major causes of student misbehavior. These are the causes that appear on most lists: (1) students find schoolwork boring and irrelevant and try to escape it; (2) students' out-of-school lives (family or community) produce psychological and emotional problems that they play out in school; (3) students are imprisoned within schools that have authoritarian dispositions, which causes them to rebel; and (4) student rebelliousness and attention seeking are a part of the growing-up process.

Beginning teachers will want to think about the causes of inappropriate behavior, but they should beware of spending too much time on this type of analysis for two reasons. One, knowing the cause of student misbehavior, although helpful in analyzing the problem, does not necessarily lead to any change in that behavior. Two, dealing too much with psychological or sociological causes of misbehavior, particularly those that are not under the teacher's influence, can lead to acceptance and/or resignation. William Glasser (1986) made this point clearly:

> When a student is doing badly in school, we often point our finger at a dismal home when the reason really is that the student does not find school satisfying enough for him to make an effort. There is no doubt that a student who cannot satisfy his needs at home may come to your class hungry for love and recognition and impatient that he can't quickly get what he wants. Rather than become discouraged, you should realize that if he can begin to satisfy his needs in your class, and if you are patient enough with his impatience, he has a good

chance to learn enough to lead a productive life despite his home life. (p. 21)

DEALING WITH MISBEHAVIOR

The general approach recommended to beginning teachers for dealing with disruptive behavior is not to search zealously for causes but, instead, to focus on the misbehavior itself and to find ways to change it, at least during the period of time the student is in the classroom. This approach emphasizes the importance of teachers accurately spotting misbehavior and making quick, precise interventions.

Being With It and Overlapping.   You can all remember a teacher from your own school days who seemed to have "eyes in the back of her head." Kounin calls this skill **with-itness.** Teachers who are with it spot deviant behavior right away and are almost always accurate in identifying the student who is responsible. Teachers who lack this skill normally do not spot misbehavior early and they often make mistakes when assigning blame.

Overlappingness is a second skill teachers use to spot and deal with deviant behavior. Overlapping means being able to spot a student acting inappropriately and inconspicuously deal with it so the lesson is not interrupted. Moving close to an offender is one overlapping tactic effective classroom managers use. Putting a hand on the shoulder of a student who is talking to his neighbor while continuing with instructions about how to do a lab project is another. Integrating a question intended to delay instruction or a "smart" remark right into an explanation about Edgar Allan Poe's syntax is a third example of overlappingness.

With-it and overlapping skills are difficult for beginning teachers to learn because they call for quick, accurate reading of classroom situations and the ability to perform several different teaching behaviors simultaneously. Once learned, however, they ensure more smoothly running lessons and classrooms.

Responding Quickly to Desist Incidences.   In classrooms, just as in any social setting, there are some participants who commit deviant acts. An example of deviant behavior on the freeway would be driving more than 5 miles an hour above the speed

Figure 6-3   Examples of teacher desist behaviors

Clarity
The degree to which the teacher specifies what is wrong.

Unclear desist:	"Stop that!"
Clear desist:	"Do not sharpen your pencil while I am talking"

Firmness
The degree to which the teacher communicates "I mean it."

Unfirm desist:	"Please don't do that."
Firm desist:	"I absolutely will not tolerate that from you!"

Roughness
The degree to which the teacher expresses anger.

Unrough desist:	"You shouldn't do that anymore."
Rough desist:	"When you do that I get angry and I intend to punish you."

---

limit; in church it might be falling asleep during the sermon; in a library it is talking while others are trying to study. Those charged with the responsibility of enforcing rules and procedures may or may not choose to respond to each occurrence of deviancy. For example, most highway patrol officers will not stop a motorist for going 60 miles an hour on the freeway; most ministers will not choose to confront a single parishioner who falls asleep; and those who talk very softly in libraries will probably not elicit a response from the librarian. There are times, however, when those in charge will choose to respond to deviant behaviors. Kounin calls this a **desist incident,** meaning an incident serious enough so that, if not dealt with, it will lead to further and widening management problems. The way that desist incidents are identified and dealt with is the business of classroom management.

The way teachers respond to desist incidents can vary widely. Kounin (1970) identified several teacher **desist behaviors.** Three of these behaviors are illustrated in Figure 6-3. Extending the research of Kounin and drawing on their own work, Carolyn Evertson and Edmund Emmer provided a set of guidelines for the use of desist behaviors by teachers. Their guidelines are shown in Figure 6-4.

Exhibiting Confidence and Exerting Influence

To be effective in classroom management, a beginning teacher cannot rely totally on rules, procedures, and techniques. There is also a leadership dimension to classroom management that is closely connected to a teacher's interpersonal style and perhaps even to his or her inner strength. This is a difficult dimension to describe and one that is even more difficult for beginning teachers to do something about. An aspect of teaching that has not been studied carefully of late, it is nonetheless important and deserves some attention.

Success in providing leadership to others depends on the degree to which a person exhibits confidence and the degree to which he or she is willing and able to exert interpersonal influence. The precise relationships between these personal traits and effective classroom management have not been studied carefully. However, most principals and others who interview and hire new teachers say they are important.

CONFIDENCE

A high correlation between teacher confidence and effective classroom management was observed in Sanford's research described earlier. But what does confidence mean, and what are the characteristics of a confident teacher? This is a difficult question to answer precisely. However, some of your own experiences may provide some helpful insights.

Think for a moment about people you know whom you would consider confident. There is a good chance that you are thinking of a person who always seems to be in charge, who talks with conviction, and who does not shy away from difficult situations. Similarly, if you think about people who

Figure 6-4 Evertson and Emmer's guidelines for managing inappropriate behavior

---

1. Ask the student to stop the inappropriate behavior. The teacher maintains contact with the child until the appropriate behavior is correctly performed.

2. Make eye-contact with the student until appropriate behavior returns. This is suitable when the teacher is certain the student knows what the correct response is.

3. Restate or remind the student of the correct rule or procedure.

4. Ask the student to identify the correct procedure. Give feedback if the student does not understand it.

5. Impose the consequence or penalty of the rule or procedure violation. Usually, the consequence for violating a procedure is simply to perform the procedure until it is correctly done. When the student understands the procedure and is not complying in order to receive attention or for other inappropriate reasons, the teacher can use a mild penalty, such as withholding a privilege.

6. Change the activity. Frequently, off-task behavior occurs when students are engaged too long in repetitive, boring tasks or in aimless recitations. Injecting variety in seatwork, refocusing the discussion, or changing the activity to one requiring another type of student response, is appropriate when off-task behavior spreads throughout a class.

SOURCE: From C. Evertson and E. Emmer (1982), Preventive classroom management. In D. Duke (ed.), *Helping teachers manage classrooms.* Alexandria, Va.: Association for Supervision and Curriculum Development, p. 27. Used with permission.

lack confidence, you probably think of a person who perhaps is shy, tentative, and indecisive. Beginning teachers obviously vary tremendously in this respect. There is not space here to go into detail about how to build confidence if the reader does not have it. However, it is important to point out some of the characteristics of confident people and list a few actions that help build more confident behaviors if these are lacking. Some common characteristics of confident people include:

Voice: Confident people speak with sufficient volume to be heard and express their ideas and wishes with conviction.

Posture: Confident people stand straight, walk forcefully, and look people in the eye.

Conviction: Confident people believe in themselves, their ideas, and their decisions.

Dress: Confident people use dress to draw attention to themselves.

As with so many other aspects of human behavior, it is important to point out the situational aspects of confidence. For example, a person may feel confident in one setting and not another. Even very confident people will feel less confident in new settings, such as student teaching and the first job, than in more familiar situations. Confidence may also be a function of how other people are perceiving one's behavior. For instance, speaking or dressing in certain ways only projects confidence if others see it that way.

Beginning teachers will find few college classes in building confidence, but there are a variety of community workshops and seminars devoted to this goal. Some that readily come to mind include public speaking classes, assertiveness training seminars, workshops on dressing for success, support workshops and networks for shy people, and acting and stage presence workshops. A beginning teacher who believes he or she lacks confidence and finds this detrimental to effective classroom management should seek out learning experiences of this type.

INTERPERSONAL INFLUENCE

You saw in the Doyle and Carter study described earlier how students used questions and other tactics to delay certain academic work. They were in a sense testing the teacher's instructional system and trying to advance their own agendas. Put another

Table 6-2   Influence in Classrooms

SOURCES OF INFLUENCE	TEACHERS	STUDENTS
Reward influence	Teachers have control of grades and can reward students with good grades.	Students can control their own behavior and can reward teachers with good behavior.
Coercive influence	Teachers can withhold good grades and special privileges and impose penalties.	Students can withhold involvement and cooperative behavior.
Legitimate influence	The position of teacher has legally vested power.	Students have little legitimate power; they do have considerable rights.
Expert influence	Teachers by training have special knowledge that is valued by many students.	Some students, "the real smart ones," have expert power that can in some instances compete with the teacher's.
Referent influence	Teachers have referent influence with students through their own charisma.	Popular students have a great deal of referent power within the peer culture.

way, students, like people in any social setting, strive to have influence over their environments. In many ways the job of the teacher is one of exerting **interpersonal influence** over students. Such influence should be used only to achieve positive academic and social goals and never for purposes of personal domination.

Over three decades ago, French and Raven (1959) thought about the processes of interpersonal influence and postulated that people have five ways to influence others in social settings: (1) one's ability to control and distribute valued rewards, (2) one's ability to withhold rewards, (3) one's authority legally vested in a position, (4) one's expertise or special knowledge, and (5) one's personal attractiveness or membership in a primary reference group. According to French and Raven, all persons in social situations have some sources of influence, and one of the dominant facts of group life is the subtle but constant negotiation that occurs as individuals play out their own personal agendas and strive to influence a group's goals and procedures. Table 6-2 describes sources of influence for teachers and students in classrooms. These ideas are important for beginning teachers because they describe how teachers can use various kinds of influence to shape classroom events.

As can be observed in Table 6-2, teachers have legitimate influence based on the teaching position itself and expert influence based on their greater knowledge and skill. Some teachers, as a result of personal attractiveness and charisma, also have referent influence with students. They can, for example, get students to relate to important goals, impart a sense of importance and urgency about these goals, and give students a sense of personal efficacy.

Much attention has been paid by educators to the way teachers use reward and coercive influence. Some ideas emanating from this interest are described here.

USING REWARDS

A rather well-established principle in psychology is that when certain behaviors are **reinforced,** they tend to be repeated; conversely, behaviors that are not reinforced tend to decrease or disappear. This principle holds true for classrooms and provides teachers with one means for managing student behavior. The key to using reinforcement principles to influence student behavior obviously rests on the teacher's ability to (1) identify desirable behaviors, (2) identify appropriate reinforcers, and (3) skillfully use these reinforcers to strengthen and encourage desired behaviors.

Praise.   The reinforcer most readily available to the classroom teacher is **praise.** However, there are important guidelines for the effective use of praise. For example, general praise, such as "great job," "oh, that's wonderful," or "excellent," is not very effective. Nor is insincere praise apt to have the desired effect. Jere Brophy, a researcher at Michigan State University, reviewed a massive amount of research on the subject of praise and came up with the guidelines for teachers described in Figure 6-5.

Figure 6-5 Brophy's guidelines for effective praise

Effective Praise	Ineffective Praise
1. Is delivered contingently	1. Is delivered randomly or unsystematically
2. Specifies the particulars of the accomplishment	2. Is restricted to global positive reactions
3. Shows spontaneity, variety, and other signs of credibility; suggests clear attention to the student's accomplishment	3. Shows a bland uniformity that suggests a conditioned response made with minimal attention
4. Rewards attainment of specified performance criteria (which can include effort criteria)	4. Rewards mere participation, without consideration of performance processes or outcomes
5. Provides information to students about their competence or the value of their accomplishments	5. Provides no information at all or gives students information about their status
6. Orients students toward better appreciation of their own task-related behavior and thinking about problem solving	6. Orients students toward comparing themselves with others and thinking about competing
7. Uses student's own prior accomplishments as the context for describing present accomplishments	7. Uses the accomplishments of peers as the context for describing students' present accomplishments
8. Is given in recognition of noteworthy effort or success at difficult (for this student) tasks	8. Is given without regard to the effort expended or the meaning of the accomplishment (for *this* student)
9. Attributes success to effort and ability, implying that similar successes can be expected in the future	9. Attributes success to ability alone or to external factors such as luck or (easy) task difficulty
10. Fosters endogenous attributions (students believe they expend effort on task because they enjoy it and/or want to develop task-relevant skills)	10. Fosters exogenous attributions (students believe they expend effort on the task for external reasons—to please the teacher, win a competition or reward, etc.)
11. Focuses students' attention on their own task-relevant behavior	11. Focuses students' attention on the teacher as an external authority figure who is manipulating them
12. Fosters appreciation of, and desirable attributions about, task-relevant behavior after the process is completed	12. Intrudes into the ongoing process, distracting attention from task-relevant behavior

SOURCE: From J. E. Brophy (1981), Teacher praise: A functional analysis. *Review of Educational Research,* Spring: 26. Copyright 1981, AERA, Washington, D.C.

Rewards and Privileges. Teachers can also encourage desirable behaviors through granting **rewards** and **privileges** to students. Rewards teachers have at their disposal include:

1. Points given for certain kinds of work or behavior that can enhance a student's grade

2. Symbols such as gold stars, happy faces, or certificates of accomplishment

3. Special honor rolls for academic work and social conduct

Privileges that are at the command of most teachers to bestow include:

1. Serving as a class leader or helper who takes notes to the office, collects or passes out papers, grades papers, runs the movie projector, and the like
2. Extra time for recess
3. Special time to work on a special individual project
4. Being excused from some required work
5. Free reading time

A carefully designed system of rewards and privileges can help immensely in encouraging some types of behavior and reducing others. However, rewards and privileges will not solve all classroom management problems, and beginning teachers should be given two warnings. First, what is a reward or a privilege for some students will not be perceived as such by others. The age of students obviously is a factor; family and geographical background are others. Effective teachers generally involve their students in identifying rewards and privileges in order to ensure their effectiveness. Second, an overemphasis on extrinsic rewards can interfere with the teacher's efforts to promote academic work for its own sake and to help students practice and grow in self-discipline and management.

COERCIVE PUNISHMENT AND PENALTIES

Rewards and privileges are used to reinforce and strengthen desirable behaviors. **Punishments** and penalties are used to discourage infractions of important rules and procedures. Socially acceptable punishments and penalties available to teachers are, in fact, rather limited and include:

1. Taking points away for misbehavior which, in turn, affects students' grades
2. Making the student stay in from recess or stay after school for detention
3. Removal of privileges
4. Expulsion from class or sending a student to a counselor or administrator

Beginning teachers should be careful about the types of punishments and penalties they establish. Researchers from the University of Texas offer the guidelines found in Figure 6-6.

Assertive Discipline

Some classroom management and discipline programs have been built around the central concepts of the teacher acting in confident and assertive ways toward student misbehavior and administering predetermined penalties for infractions of classroom rules. During the past 15 years one of the more popular programs based on these ideas has been developed by Lee and Marlene Canter. Called **assertive discipline,** the Canters' program maintains that teachers can gain control of their classrooms by insisting on appropriate student behavior and by responding assertively to student infractions.

Teachers (and sometimes whole schools) trained in assertive discipline start by developing a set of classroom and school rules deemed necessary for learning to occur. Consequences for disobedience are also clearly specified in advance. Students and their parents are then given clear explanations of these rules and the consequences for infractions are explained. The Canters stress the importance of teachers following through with their rules, being consistent with administering consequences, and expecting support from parents.

THE ASSERTIVE RESPONSE STYLE

At the center of the Canters' approach is their belief that teachers should respond to student misbehavior with an assertive style instead of responding passively or in hostile ways. Responding to student misbehavior with a rhetorical question such as "Why are you doing that?" is an example of a passive style. The passive teacher, according to the Canters, is not using interpersonal influence effectively and appears wishy-washy to students. The hostile teacher, on the other hand, often responds angrily to student misbehavior and makes threats such as "You'll be sorry you did that," or tries to produce guilt such as "You should be ashamed of yourself." Passive and hostile styles are not effective, according to the Canters. Teachers who use a passive style are not communicating clearly to students what they expect, and the hostile style often produces meaningless threats that are difficult to enforce.

The assertive style calls for teachers to be very clear about their expectations and to respond to student misbehavior firmly and confidently. Teachers

Figure 6-6   Guidelines for the use of penalties

---

1. Use reductions in grade or score for assignment- or work-related behaviors such as missing or incomplete work. Other penalties, such as detention or fines, are usually not needed. When a problem of missing work becomes chronic, contact the student's parents, talk with the student, and try to get at the source of the problem.

2. Use a fine or demerit system to handle repeated violations of rules and procedures, particularly those involving willful refusal to comply with reasonable requests. Such behaviors might include continued talk during whole-class instruction, or leaving one's seat. You will not need penalties to handle occasional occurrences of these types of inappropriate behaviors . . . ; however, students who persist in such behavior need a penalty for a deterrent. Give them one warning, and if the behavior persists, assess a fine or demerit.

3. If you have a student who frequently receives penalties, try to set a more positive tone. Help the student formulate a plan to stop the inappropriate behavior, and be sure he or she understands what is and is not acceptable behavior.

4. Limit the use of penalties such as fines or checks to easily observable behaviors that represent major or chronic infractions of rules and procedures. The reason for this limitation is that penalty systems work only when they are used consistently. In order for this to take place, you must be able to detect the misbehavior when it occurs. If you cannot, you will find yourself constantly trying to catch students who misbehave. For example, don't try to "fine" each student who whispers during seatwork. You can handle such events in simpler ways, and you certainly don' t want to spend all your time checking for whispering behavior. However, you could use a fine if the student does not stop when you request it.

5. Keep your classroom positive and supportive. Penalties should serve mainly as deterrents and should be used sparingly. Try to rely on rewards and personal encouragement to maintain good behavior.

SOURCE: From Emmer/Evertson/Sanford/Clements/Worsham, *Classroom management for secondary teacher,* ©1984, p. 64. Adapted by permission of Prentice-Hall, Inc. Englewood Cliffs, N.J.

are counseled to specify the misbehaving student by name and to keep eye contact with the student. The Canters maintain that teachers should not accept excuses from misbehaving students. They argue that even though a student may have inadequate parenting, special health problems, or heavy stress in their lives, these unfortunate circumstances should not excuse students from acting appropriately in the classroom or taking responsibility for their own behavior.

CONSEQUENCES

Under the Canter approach, consequences are kept simple and are designed so their implementation will not cause severe disruption to ongoing instructional activities. Cangelosi (1988) reports one example of an assertive discipline program in a particular junior high school.

1. Each classroom teacher specifies for students the rules for classroom conduct. During the course of the year, new rules may be decided upon. . . . An up-to-date list of rules is always displayed in the classroom.

2. The first time each day a student violates a rule during a particular class session, the teacher writes the student's name on a designated area of a chalkboard. The number of the rule that was violated is put next to the name. The teacher does not say anything about the transgression; she or he only writes the name and numeral on the board and continues with the planned activities.

3. The second time a student violates a rule (not necessarily the same rule), the number of that rule is added to the name appearing on the board. Again, the teacher makes no other response to the off-task behavior.

4. Upon the third violation of the rules in the same

class period, the student must leave the class and report to detention room. Again, the teacher does not take class time to talk to the student about the matter. The teacher only indicates that a third violation has occurred and the student is already aware of the consequences.

5. There are no penalties or requirements for students who have no more than one violation during any one class period.

6. Students with two violations are required to meet with the teacher after school to discuss the misbehavior and map out a plan for preventing recurrences.

7. The parent of students with three violations must appear at school to discuss the misbehavior and make plans for preventing recurrences with the student, the teacher, and another school official. The student may not return to the class where the violations occurred until a plan has been worked out with the parents. (pp. 32–33)

Though the Canters' approach has been very popular, it also has its critics. Some teachers find it difficult to administer consequences without significantly disrupting their instructional programs. It takes time and energy, for instance, to write names on the chalkboard and to keep track of rule infractions. Also, some believe that assertive discipline puts too much emphasis on penalties and teacher-made rules and not enough emphasis on involving students in establishing their own classroom rules and learning how to be responsible for self-discipline. Finally, assertive discipline has not been evaluated thoroughly, and its effectiveness remains unclear.

WORKING TOWARD SELF-MANAGEMENT

The final classroom management approaches described in this chapter go beyond planning and orchestrating classroom activities or dealing with specific disruptive acts. These approaches are aimed at helping students take responsibility for their own behavior and helping them work toward **self-management.**

Dreikurs' Logical Consequences

Chapter 4 provided a thorough description about how people's behavior can be attributed to goal-directed activity aimed at satisfying human motives and needs. In the 1960s, Dreikurs and his colleagues developed an approach to classroom discipline based on the idea that most student behavior (acceptable and unacceptable) stems from the fundamental need to belong and to feel worthwhile. According to Dreikurs, when the need to belong or feel worthwhile is frustrated through socially acceptable channels, students misbehave. Dreikurs categorized this misbehavior into four types: (1) attention getting, (2) power seeking, (3) revenge seeking, and (4) displays of inadequacy. Teachers trained in the Dreikurs approach learn how to identify the type of student misbehavior and administer **logical consequences** for this misbehavior.

Logical consequences are punishments related directly to the misbehavior rather than the more general penalties such as detention or reprimands used in many classrooms. Making a student who had written on the bathroom wall repaint the wall is a classic example of a logical consequence.

The Dreikurs approach emphasizes the importance of democratic classrooms in which students have a say in making the rules. He views the logical consequence of misbehavior as more than just arbitrary punishment. He encourages teachers to administer logical consequences in a friendly and matter-of-fact manner, without elements of moral judgment. The long-range goal of this approach to discipline is to have students understand the reasons for their misbehavior and find ways to satisfy their self-worth and affiliation needs in socially acceptable ways.

The difficulties teachers have with the Dreikurs approach are twofold. Without extensive training, some find it difficult to develop the skill in identifying the specific motive that is causing the student to misbehave. Others find it difficult to identify logical consequences for many misbehaviors that occur in classrooms. For instance, what is the logical consequence for speaking out of turn? for sassing the teacher? for smoking in the halls or carrying a weapon to school? Nonetheless, some teachers who possess the necessary counseling skills have found the Dreikurs approach a powerful tool for dealing with disruptive students and helping them develop self-management skills.

Glasser's Classroom Meeting

Trained first as a chemical engineer, and later as a physician and clinical psychologist, William Glasser

Table 6-3   Syntax for the Glasser Classroom Meeting

PHASE	TEACHER BEHAVIOR
Phase 1: Establish the climate	Using many of the strategies and procedures described in Chapters 4 and 12, the teacher establishes a climate such that all students feel free to participate and to share opinions and feedback.
Phase 2: Identify problems	Teacher asks students to sit in a circle. Either the teacher or the students can bring up problems. Teacher should make sure that problems are described fully and in nonevaluative ways. Specific examples of the problems are encouraged.
Phase 3: Make value judgments	After a specific problem has been identified, the teacher asks students to express their own values about the problem and the behaviors associated with it.
Phase 4: Identify courses of action	Teacher asks students to suggest alternative behaviors or procedures that might help solve the problem and to agree on one to try out.
Phase 5: Make a public commitment	Teacher asks students to make a public commitment to try out the new behaviors or procedures.
Phase 6: Provide follow-up and assessment	At a later meeting, the problem is again discussed to see how effectively it is being solved and whether commitments have been kept.

(1969, 1986) has devoted much of his professional life to finding ways to make schools more satisfying and productive for students. Like Dreikurs, Glasser believes that most classroom problems stem from a failure to satisfy the basic need of students. In his early work Glasser emphasized students' need for love and feelings of self-worth; in his later work he expanded his list of basic needs to include survival and reproduction, belonging and love, power and influence, freedom and fun. Whereas Dreikurs proposes counseling and individual attention as a way to help students find ways to satisfy their needs, Glasser believes that school structures need to be modified. He has proposed the **classroom meeting,** a regular 30-minute nonacademic period in which teachers and students discuss and find cooperative solutions to personal and behavior problems and where students learn how to take responsibility for their own behavior and their personal and social development.

RUNNING CLASSROOM MEETINGS

A Glasser classroom meeting consists of six steps or phases (see Table 6-3). Note that for each phase there are specific things teachers need to do to make the meeting go successfully. In addition, there are several aspects of the total learning environment that need attention. When the classroom meeting is first being introduced and taught to students, the

teacher keeps the learning environment tightly structured. More and more freedom can be given to students as they become successful in meetings. The teacher must maintain the responsibility for ensuring participation, for keeping student problem solving focused, and for providing overall leadership. Normally, the teacher acts as discussion leader and asks students to sit in a circle during the classroom meetings. However, with younger students, participants sometimes sit on the floor, and with older students, the role of discussion leader is sometimes assumed by a student in the class.

SUGGESTIONS FOR STARTING AND RUNNING CLASSROOM MEETINGS

Effective execution of classroom meetings requires specific teacher actions before, during, and after the meeting. As much care and concern must go into planning and executing meetings as any other aspect of instruction.

Planning.   In preparation for classroom meetings, teachers will need to think through what they want the meeting to accomplish and have some problems ready for discussion in case none come from students. Most important, overall planning must allow time for classroom meetings on a regular basis.

In elementary schools many teachers who use classroom meetings start each day with this activity;

others schedule it as a way to close each day; still others schedule classroom meetings on a weekly basis. In most middle and high schools, teachers schedule meetings less frequently, perhaps 30 minutes every other Friday, with special meetings if serious problems arise. The frequency of meetings is not as important as their regularity.

Conducting the Meeting. On the surface the classroom meeting may look fairly simple and easy to conduct. In reality it is very complex and calls for considerable skill on the part of the teacher. If the beginning teacher is in a school where classroom meetings are common and students already understand their basic purposes and procedures, then the teacher can start meetings at the beginning of school. If not, then the recommendation is for beginning teachers to wait for a few weeks before introducing classroom meetings to students.

Most of the student and teacher skills needed for successful meetings are described elsewhere in *Learning to Teach*, particularly in Chapters 13 and 15. Some are repeated here, as they specifically relate to each phase of the classroom meeting.

1. *Establishing climate:* Before classroom meetings can be successful, the overall climate must be one that encourages participation in free and nonpunitive ways. Students also must be prepared in the appropriate mindset to make meetings productive. Although classroom meetings can be used to build this kind of productive environment, some degree of trust must exist before meetings can be implemented. Many of the activities described in Chapter 4 are preludes to implementing classroom meetings.

2. *Identifying problems:* Students who have not been involved in classroom meetings need to be taught what constitutes a legitimate problem for the meeting. Problem-solving techniques can be taught, including giving students time to practice stating a problem, giving examples of a problem, and identifying the descriptive and value dimensions of a problem.

3. *Dealing with values:* The values surrounding most classroom behavior problems are very important, especially differences regarding the value of academic work. Put bluntly, some students do not value academic work as much as teachers do. At the same time, teachers may find an amazing similarity of values across racial, ethnic, and social-class lines regarding other aspects of classroom behavior. For example, most students, even at a very young age, see the moral and practical necessity of such rules as taking turns, listening, and showing respect to others. They also readily embrace most procedures that ensure safety and fairness. The classroom meeting can become an important forum for talking about value similarities and differences.

4. *Identifying alternative courses of action:* Except for very young children, most students can readily identify courses of action they, their teacher, or their classmates can take to resolve all kinds of classroom management problems. They know the reasons for rewarding desirable behavior and punishing disruptive behavior and they also know the shortcomings of relying too heavily on these strategies. They even know what sort of alternative actions are available in classroom settings. During this phase of the classroom meeting, the teacher's primary role is to listen to alternative proposals, make sure everyone understands each one, and push for some type of consensus about which action students are willing to take. The teacher must also be clear and straightforward with students if a proposed action is definitely unacceptable, particularly those proposals that go against school policy. However, this does not exclude student efforts to get school policies changed.

5. *Making a public commitment:* A public commitment is nothing more than a promise by students, and in some instances the teacher, that certain attempts are going to be made to correct difficult situations. Many teachers write these promises on newsprint charts so that everyone in the class can remember them.

6. *Follow-up and assessment:* Once students have made a commitment to try out a new set of procedures and behaviors, it is very important that these commitments be followed and assessed. Specifically, teachers must remember the public commitments that were made and periodically come back to them in future classroom meetings. If commitments are not being kept or if the

planned actions are not solving the problem, then additional time and energy must be given to the problem.

SUMMARY

- Classroom management is not an end in itself but a part of the teacher's overall leadership role.
- Managerial and instructional aspects of teaching are highly interrelated and in real life teaching cannot be clearly separated.
- Unless classroom management issues can be solved the best teaching is wasted, thus making it possibly the most important challenge facing beginning teachers.
- A well-developed knowledge base on classroom management provides guidelines for successful group management as well as ways of dealing with disruptive students.
- A large portion of disruptive student behavior can be eliminated by using preventive classroom management measures such as clear rules and procedures and carefully orchestrated learning activities.
- With-itness, momentum, overlapping, smoothness, and group alerting all increase student work involvement and decrease off-task behavior and management problems.
- Effective managers have well-defined procedures that govern student talk and movement, make work requirements clear to students, and emphasize clear explanations.
- Effective managers establish clear rules and procedures, teach these rules and procedures to students, and carefully orchestrate classroom activities during such unstable periods as the beginning and end of class and transitions.
- Effective managers develop systems for holding students accountable for their academic work and classroom behavior.
- Regardless of planning and orchestration skills, teachers are still often faced with difficult or unmotivated students who will choose to be disruptive forces rather than involve themselves in academic activity.
- Effective managers have intervention skills for dealing quickly with disruptive students in direct but fair ways.
- Effective managers recognize the importance of interpersonal influence which stems from several sources: ability to distribute and withhold valued rewards, vested authority, expertise and special knowledge, and personal attractiveness and membership in a primary reference group.
- Teachers can encourage desirable behaviors by giving praise and granting rewards and punishments.
- Specific approaches to classroom management, such as assertive discipline, emphasize the importance of being clear about expectations and consistent in administering consequences.
- In the long run, effective teachers find ways to reduce management and discipline problems by helping students learn self-management skills.
- As with other teaching functions, effective teachers develop an attitude of flexibility about classroom management because they know that every class is different and plans, rules, and procedures must often be adjusted to particular circumstances.
- Although many aspects of thinking about classroom management can be learned from research, some of the complex skills of classroom orchestration will come only with extended practice and serious reflection.

KEY TERMS

classroom management
classroom ecology
downtime
smoothness
momentum
dangle
flip-flop
fragmentation
overdwelling
transitions
cuing
signaling
student accountability
with-itness
overlappingness
desist incident
desist behaviors
interpersonal influence
reward influence
coercive influence
legitimate influence
expert influence
referent influence
reinforcement
praise

rewards
privileges
punishment
assertive discipline
logical consequences

BOOKS FOR THE PROFESSIONAL

Bramson, R. M. (1981). *Coping with difficult people.* New York: Random House. Classrooms are not the only settings where we find people who are difficult to deal with. This little book describes a variety of strategies for dealing with these people in all aspects of life. It is well written and will give beginning teachers concrete suggestions and also the encouragement of knowing that their problems are not too different from those of managers and leaders everywhere.

Cangelosi, J. S. (1988). *Classroom management strategies: Gaining and maintaining students' cooperation.* New York: Longman. This book is a very readable overview of various approaches to classroom management and is filled with reports by practicing teachers on how to deal with a wide range of problem situations.

Emmer, E., Evertson, C., Sanford, J., Clements, B., and Worsham, W. E. (1989). *Classroom management for secondary teachers.* (2d ed.). Englewood Cliffs, N.J.: Prentice-Hall.

Evertson, C., Emmer, E., Clements, B., Sanford, J., and Worsham, M. (1989). *Classroom management for elementary teachers.* (2d ed.). Englewood Cliffs, N.J.: Prentice-Hall. These two volumes, one aimed at secondary teachers, the other for elementary teachers, describe in more detail many of the procedures and techniques described in this chapter. Growing out of a decade of research at the University of Texas, these books offer a comprehensive approach to classroom management from the perspective of teacher effectiveness. They stress the importance of teacher planning and organization as preventive management approaches.

Glasser, W. (1969). *Schools without failure.* New York: Harper & Row. Although close to 25 years old now, this is still one of the best analyses of why students misbehave and fail in school. Glasser's recommendation that schools themselves need restructuring is presented powerfully, and his description of the use of the classroom meeting model will provide beginning teachers with more details than are presented in this chapter.

Glasser, W. (1986). *Control theory in the classroom.* New York: Harper & Row. Glasser's most recent work extends some of the basic ideas presented in *Schools without Failure.* Most important are Glasser's recommendations for how schools can be restructured to provide more powerful settings for learning and how teachers can use the learning team and the cooperative learning strategies described in Chapter 12 of *Learning to Teach* to accomplish this restructuring.

Weinstein, C. S., and Mignano, A. J., Jr. (1992). *Elementary classroom management: Lessons from research and practice.* New York: McGraw-Hill. This highly readable new book on classroom management combines both the research and the wisdom of practice on this topic. It shows how various learning tasks make different demands on the management structure and how different management approaches are required.

LEARNING AIDS FOR PLANNING, OBSERVATION, AND REFLECTION

- Assessing My Classroom Management Skills
- Observing Teachers' Management Behavior
- Observing Students' Influence on Academic Tasks
- Interviewing Teachers about Rules and Procedures
- Observing Management Practices during Unstable Periods
- Observing Teacher Responses to Student Misbehavior

ASSESSING MY CLASSROOM MANAGEMENT SKILLS

PURPOSE: The aids for this chapter begin with an assessment device designed to help you to gauge your level of effectiveness in applying classroom management skills.

DIRECTIONS: Check the level of effectiveness you feel you have attained for each of the following skills.

UNDERSTANDING OR SKILL	LEVEL OF UNDERSTANDING OR SKILL		
	HIGH	MEDIUM	LOW
My ability to			
Establish and teach rules and procedures			
Student movement	_____	_____	_____
Student talk	_____	_____	_____
Downtimes	_____	_____	_____
Ensure smoothness and momentum	_____	_____	_____
Orchestrate unstable periods			
Planning thoroughly	_____	_____	_____
Cuing and signaling	_____	_____	_____
Develop student accountability	_____	_____	_____
Manage inappropriate and disruptive behavior			
With-itness	_____	_____	_____
Overlappingness	_____	_____	_____
Using the desist response	_____	_____	_____
Project confidence	_____	_____	_____
Exert interpersonal influence			
Using rewards	_____	_____	_____
Using punishment	_____	_____	_____
Use the classroom meeting model	_____	_____	_____

OBSERVING TEACHERS' MANAGEMENT BEHAVIOR

PURPOSE: As discussed in the chapter, Kounin has contributed much to our understanding of classroom management. This aid is to help you develop awareness of the teacher in-class behaviors described by Kounin that have an impact on classroom management.

DIRECTIONS: Observe a teacher for about an hour. As you observe, note instances where the lesson seems to go especially well—students are orderly and on task—and instances where the lesson seems to go especially poorly—students are disorderly and off task. After the observation, answer the questions below.

1. Did the teacher exhibit with-itness? _____

    If so, give an example of it that appeared in the lesson. _____

    _____

    Describe how students behaved in this example. _____

    _____

    If not, how might he or she have done so? _____

    _____

2. Did the teacher exhibit overlappingness? _____

    If so, give an example of it that appeared in the lesson. _____

    _____

    Describe how students behaved in this example. _____

    _____

    If not, how might he or she have done so? _____

    _____

3. Did the teacher exhibit smoothness? _____

    If so, give an example of it that appeared in the lesson. _____

    _____

    Describe how students behaved in this example. _____

    _____

    If not, how might he or she have done so? _____

    _____

4. Did the teacher exhibit momentum? _____

   If so, give an example of it that appeared in the lesson. _____

   _____

   Describe how students behaved in this example. _____

   _____

   If not, how might he or she have done so? _____

   _____

5. Did the teacher exhibit group alerting? _____

   If so, give an example of it that appeared in the lesson. _____

   _____

   Describe how students behaved in this example. _____

   _____

   If not, how might he or she have done so? _____

   _____

6. Did the teacher exhibit accountability for students? _____

   If so, give an example of it that appeared in the lesson. _____

   _____

   Describe how students behaved in this example. _____

   _____

   If not, how might he or she have done so? _____

   _____

7. Did the teacher exhibit challenge arousal? _____

   If so, give an example of it that appeared in the lesson. _____

   _____

   Describe how students behaved in this example. _____

   _____

   If not, how might he or she have done so? _____

   _____

8. Did the teacher exhibit variety? _____

   If so, give an example of it that appeared in the lesson. _____

   _____

   Describe how students behaved in this example. _____

   _____

   If not, how might he or she have done so? _____

   _____

Analysis and Reflection: Write a paragraph about how you might apply these management principles while teaching in your own subject area or grade level.

7. Which ones seem easiest for students to follow? Why? Which ones seem hardest? Why?

_____

_____

_____

_____

8. What do you do to maintain and enforce them? _____

_____

_____

9. What are the rules and procedures in your class that govern downtime?

_____

_____

_____

10. How did you initially teach those rules and procedures? _____

_____

_____

11. Which ones seem easiest for students to follow? Why? Which ones seem hardest? Why?

_____

_____

_____

_____

12. What do you do to maintain and enforce them? _____

_____

_____

Analysis and Reflection: What seem to be the common elements of rules and procedures at any grade level? Are there any rules and procedures that occur in each level? Are there any common ways they are taught, maintained, and enforced? Are there any common areas of difficulty? Conversely, what did you uncover about rules and procedures that seems to apply only to a particular age group or a particular teacher's style? How will you apply what you have learned to your own teaching?

OBSERVING MANAGEMENT PRACTICES DURING UNSTABLE PERIODS

PURPOSE: Unstable periods in classroom life pose the most difficult management challenges. This aid is to help you to gain practical knowledge about how to manage these difficult periods.

DIRECTIONS: Observe an elementary classroom for a few hours from the opening of the school day or a secondary classroom for an entire period. Check the actions you see the teacher take in managing unstable periods.

	Yes	No

1. **Opening Class**
   In order to open class smoothly and efficiently, did the teacher do the following:

   a. Greet students at the door? _____ _____

   If so, give an example: _____

   _____

   b. Use student helpers for routine administrative tasks? _____ _____

   If so, give a example: _____

   _____

   c. Write start-up activities on the board? _____ _____

   If so, give a example: _____

   _____

   d. Use routine or ceremonial events that set the proper tone? _____ _____

   If so, give an example: _____

   _____

   e. Other (specify): _____

2. **Transitions**
   Keep a tally of the number of transitions you observe.

   _____

   Describe one of the transitions you observed.

   _____

   _____

	Yes	No
In order to move students smoothly and efficiently from one activity to the next, did the teacher do the following:		

a. Rely on routinized procedure?　　　　　　　　　_____　_____

   If so, give an example: _____

   _____

b. Cue or signal the students in some way?　　　　_____　_____

   If so, give an example: _____

   _____

c. Other (specify): _____

3. **Closing Class**
   In order to close class smoothly and efficiently, did the teacher do the following:

   a. Leave sufficient time to collect books and papers?　_____　_____

   b. Make assignments early enough to avoid last-minute confusion?　_____　_____

   c. Rely on routine procedures for collecting papers and materials?　_____　_____

   　If so, give an example: _____

   　_____

   d. Cue students that close of class was approaching?　_____　_____

   e. Other (specify): _____

Analysis and Reflection: Which elements of effective management of unstable periods did this teacher rely on? Which elements were missing? How might this teacher incorporate these missing elements into his or her management routines? Write a paragraph about how you will manage unstable periods in your own classroom.

OBSERVING TEACHER RESPONSES TO STUDENT MISBEHAVIOR

PURPOSE: How to respond to student misbehavior is one of the greatest concerns of beginning teachers. This aid is to help you to gain practical knowledge about how to respond to such misbehavior.

DIRECTIONS: Observe a classroom for 45 to 60 minutes. Whenever you observe an instance of student misbehavior, quickly describe the incident, then use the codes given below to code the type of misbehavior and the teacher's response. (You may use more than one code per incident, if necessary.)

INCIDENTS	STUDENT MISBEHAVIOR	TEACHER RESPONSE
1. _____	_____	_____
2. _____	_____	_____
3. _____	_____	_____
4. _____	_____	_____
5. _____	_____	_____
6. _____	_____	_____
7. _____	_____	_____
8. _____	_____	_____
9. _____	_____	_____
10. _____	_____	_____

Codes for Student Behavior
A. Minor misbehavior
B. Serious misbehavior

Codes for Teacher Responses
A. With-itness: spotted misbehavior early and accurately
B. Overlapping: while teaching,
    1. Moved closer to problem student
    2. Made and held eye contact with problem student
    3. Rested hand on student's shoulder
    4. Integrated off-task remark into teaching activities
    5. Other (specify)
C. Used a desist, that is, told the student to stop the misbehavior. The desist was
    1. Clear
    2. Firm
    3. Rough
D. Restated the rule or procedure for the student
E. Had the student identify the rule or procedure
    1. Gave corrective feedback to the student if he or she did not understand the rule
F. Imposed a consequence
G. Changed activity

Analysis and Reflection: What were the teacher's most common responses to instances of minor misbehavior? Were these successful? Why or why not? What were the teacher's most common responses to instances of serious misbehavior? Were these successful? Why or why not? Think through the range of options you will be likely to have for responding to misbehavior. Write at least two paragraphs about these options, and the kinds of situations in which they would be appropriately applied.

Chapter Outline

PERSPECTIVE AND RATIONALE

SAMPLING THE KNOWLEDGE BASE

• Effects of Grades on Students • Teacher Bias in Assessment and Grading • Importance of Grades

SCHOOLWIDE ASSESSMENT PROGRAMS

• Schoolwide Use of Standardized Tests • Standardized Tests • Norm-Referenced and Criterion-Referenced Tests • Advantages and Disadvantages • Communication of Standardized Test Results

THE TEACHER'S ASSESSMENT PROGRAM

• Diagnosing Prior Knowledge • Providing Corrective Feedback • Testing for Summative Evaluation

SPECIFICS OF TESTING AND GRADING

• General Principles • Test Construction and Use • Grading • Summary Guidelines

A LOOK TO THE FUTURE

• Performance Assessment • Authentic Assessment • Student Portfolios and Narrative Descriptions
• Assessing Group Effort and Individually Contracted Work • Experimenting with New Approaches

CHAPTER 7

Assessment and Evaluation

Leaders in almost all situations are responsible for assessing and evaluating the people who work for them. So too are teachers responsible for the assessment and evaluation of students in their classrooms, an aspect of their work that some find unpleasant. Nonetheless, assessment, evaluation, and grading are of utmost importance to students and parents, and the way these processes are performed have long-term consequences. Assessment and evaluation processes also consume a fairly large portion of teachers' time. For instance, a review by Shaefer and Lissitz (1987) reported that teachers spend as much as 10 percent of their time on matters related to assessment and evaluation. Stiggins (1987) found that teachers could spend as much as one-third of their time on "assessment-related" activities. For these reasons, it is critical that beginning teachers build a repertoire of effective strategies for performing the executive functions of student assessment and evaluation.

Although certain measurement techniques associated with assessment and evaluation are beyond the scope of this book, many basic concepts and procedures are well within the grasp of the beginning teacher. The first section of this chapter provides a perspective about why assessment and evaluation are important and defines several key concepts. This is followed by a section that samples the knowledge base on this topic. The final sections describe specific procedures beginning teachers can use for developing an overall assessment plan, making tests, and grading students, as well as a discussion about schoolwide assessment and evaluation processes. A discussion also is included about some newer approaches to student assessment that are emerging in some schools. The chapter concludes with a set of learning aids to help you solidify your knowledge of these topics.

PERSPECTIVE AND RATIONALE

If you will think back to your own school days, you will recall the excitement (and the anxiety) of getting back the results of a test or of receiving your report card. When these events occurred, they were almost always accompanied by the student question, "Wad-ja get?" You also remember (in fact, you still hear) another favorite student question, "Is it going to be on the test?" These questions and the emotion behind them highlight the importance assessment and evaluation play in the lives of students.

Importance of Assessment and Evaluation

Probably since the time the first test or the first grade was given, there has been controversy surrounding their use. For instance, some have argued that grades dehumanize education and establish distrust between teachers and students. Others have said that grading and comparing students leads to harmful anxiety and to low self-esteem for those who receive poor grades. Even those who acknowledge the importance of assessment and evaluation have often condemned current practices for the emphasis on testing basic skills out of context and the excessive competition which results. Still others have commented that grades are really a "rubber yardstick," measuring the whims of particular teachers rather than mastery of important educational goals. Regardless of the criticism and controversy surrounding this topic, the process of assessing and evaluating students has persisted and basic practices have remained essentially constant for most of this century. Two important conditions of schools and teaching help explain this fact.

SORTING FUNCTION OF SCHOOLS

Sociologists have observed on numerous occasions that schools in large complex societies are expected to help sort people for societal roles and occupational positions. Although some may wish for the day when better and fairer means are found for making these judgments, at present the larger society assigns the job of assessing and evaluating student growth and potential, in large part, to teachers. How well students perform on tests, the grades they receive, and the judgments their teachers make about their potential have important, long-run consequences for both students and society. These judgments can determine who goes to college, the type of college they attend, the type of career open to them, and their first jobs, as well as the lifestyles they maintain. Enduring perceptions about self-worth and self-esteem can also result from the way students are evaluated in school. For these reasons, of all the executive functions of teaching, assessing and evaluating student growth and potential may be the most far-reaching. Teachers who do not take this aspect of their work seriously (regardless of re-

forms they may desire) are doing their students a great disservice.

GRADE-FOR-WORK EXCHANGE

Chapter 4 pointed out how classroom reward structures influence the overall learning environment and how much of what students choose to do, or not do, is determined by what Walter Doyle labeled the "grade-for-work exchange." This idea, you may remember, described how students, like the rest of us, can be motivated to do certain things for extrinsic rewards. We may work hard and do what employers want so we will receive a merit raise; we may volunteer for community service hoping to receive public recognition for our work. This does not mean that our work has no intrinsic value or that altruistic reasons do not prompt us to help others. It simply means that for many human beings extrinsic rewards are valued and provide a strong incentive to act in particular ways.

Academic tasks such as completing assignments, studying for tests, writing papers, and carrying on classroom discourse is the work of students. Many teachers want their students to perform this academic work for the intrinsic value of learning itself. Although this is an admirable, and in many instances an attainable goal, the importance of grades, the primary extrinsic reward available to teachers, should not be overlooked. It is important to remember that, just as adults work for a salary, students work for grades, and that these exchanges are critically important and help explain much of classroom life.

Key Assessment and Evaluation Concepts

Assessment and evaluation are functions carried out by teachers to gather information needed to make wise decisions, and it should be clear by now that the decisions teachers make are important to students' lives. These decisions should be based on information that is relevant and as accurate as possible. Several key concepts can help you understand this topic more fully.

ASSESSMENT

The term **assessment** usually refers to the full range of information gathered and synthesized by teachers about their students and their classrooms. Information can be gathered on students in informal ways such as through observation and verbal exchange. It can also be gathered through formal means such as homework, tests, and written reports. Information about classrooms and the teacher's instruction can also be part of assessment. The range of information here can also vary from informal feedback provided by students about a particular lesson to more formal reports resulting from course evaluations and standardized tests.

EVALUATION

Whereas assessment focuses on gathering and synthesizing information, the term **evaluation** usually refers to the process of making judgments, assigning value, or deciding on worth. A test, for example, is an assessment technique to collect information about how much students know on a particular topic. Assigning a grade, however, is an evaluative act because the teacher is placing a value on the information gathered on the test.

Most evaluation specialists talk in terms of either formative or summative evaluations, depending on the use of the evaluation information. **Formative evaluations** are collected prior to or during instruction and are intended to inform teachers about their students' prior knowledge and skills in order to assist with planning. Information from formative evaluations is not used to make judgments about a student's work; it is used to make judgments about such matters as student grouping, unit and lesson plans, and instructional strategies. **Summative evaluations,** on the other hand, are efforts to use information about students or programs after a set of instructional activities has occurred. Its purpose is to summarize how well a particular student, group of students, or the teacher has performed on a set of learning goals or objectives. Summative evaluations are designed so that judgments can be made about accomplishments. Information obtained from summative evaluations are those used by teachers to determine grades and inform the reports sent to students and their parents.

INFORMATION QUALITY

If teachers make important decisions about students and about their teaching, it is only common sense that the information they use to make these decisions should be of high quality. Measurement and evaluation specialists use two technical terms to describe the quality of assessment information: reliability and validity.

A test is said to be **reliable** when it produces dependable, consistent scores for persons who take it more than once over a period of time. For instance, if a single student took a test on Friday and then again the next Friday and received the same score, it is likely the test is reliable. If a group of students took the test one week and repeated the same test the following week and the rankings of the various students stayed about the same, it is even more likely that the test is reliable. A reliable test, thus, is one that measures a student's ability on some topic or trait consistently over time. A reliable test gives teachers accurate and dependable assessment information; however, it is important to remember that no single test can be expected to be perfect. Factors such as student guessing, mistakes made by teachers in scoring, as well as the students' feeling of well-being on the testing day all introduce error, inconsistency, and unreliability. Later, we will describe procedures that can cut down on the amount of error in tests.

A test is said to be **valid** when it measures what it claims to measure. For example, a test which claims to measure students' attitudes toward mathematics would be invalid if it really measured their attitude toward their current mathematics teacher. Obviously, if a test is not measuring what it is intended to measure the information it produces is of no value for teacher decision making. As you will see later, it is possible to increase the validity of teacher-made tests.

SAMPLING THE KNOWLEDGE BASE

The knowledge base for assessment and evaluation is immense. The underlying concepts used for measuring all kinds of traits and attributes, such as intelligence, achievement, and personality, have long intellectual traditions. Similarly, technical topics associated with test construction, grading, and the use of evaluation information have been studied thoroughly for most of this century. Three lines of inquiry important to beginning teachers will be sampled in this section: the effects of grades on students, bias in teaching assessment, and the importance of grades and evaluation information to parents.

Effects of Grades on Students

For obvious reasons, one of the most important and frequently asked questions by beginning teachers is, Do grades and grading procedures influence student learning? Fortunately, this has also been a question of interest to educational researchers. Much is known about the effects of grades and other **extrinsic rewards** on students. However, a note of caution is in order about this research, because the issues involved are complex and intricate. As you will see, simple recipes do not exist.

One line of research stemmed from natural experiments which occurred in the late 1960s and the 1970s. During this period several colleges and universities began the practice of giving students the choice of taking classes on a grade or a pass-fail basis. Several studies (for example, Gold et al., 1971) compared the students' performance, and the findings were pretty consistent: students performed better in graded situations than they did in pass-fail situations.

These findings, however, were with college-aged students and failed to answer the question, What about younger students in elementary or high schools? Fortunately, the effects of grades and extrinsic rewards on their performance have also been studied. In a particularly interesting study, Cullen, Cullen, Hayhow, and Plouffe (1975) compared the performance of three groups of high school students when different kinds of extrinsic rewards were present. Their study is highlighted in Research Summary 7-1.

COMPLEXITY OF THE INFLUENCE OF GRADES

As illustrated in the Cullen, Cullen, Hayhow, and Plouffe study, grades can be a strong incentive for performing work. The beginning teacher, however, should be careful in interpreting this finding, because factors other than grades can affect performance. One key factor is how interesting or intrinsically motivating the assignment is in the first place.

For example, in a rather well-known study, Lepper and her colleagues (1973) compared three groups of preschool children. Children were told they could draw pictures (an intrinsically interesting task for young children) during their free-play time. Children in one group were promised a reward if they drew a picture. Children in another group were told they would receive a surprise. Those in the third group were promised nothing. After this reward structure was introduced, the children were observed, and the amount of time they spent drawing pictures during free play was recorded. Those students who were promised a surprise or no reward at all spent almost twice as much time drawing as did students who had been promised a reward. These results, as you can see, are quite different from those of the Cullen, Cullen, Hayhow, and Plouffe study. Lepper and her colleagues explained their findings by pointing out that giving extrinsic rewards for something that is intrinsically interesting may actually have the opposite effect. This does not mean, however, as Lepper (1973) and others have explained, that extrinsic rewards should not be used. They are still needed for tasks that do not have high intrinsic motivation.

Another factor that influences the effects of grades on student learning is how students themselves perceive these grades in relation to the work they have performed. You remember reading in Chapter 4 that some students attribute their success or failure to their own hard work or lack thereof, whereas other students attribute it to luck. The grade and what it means will obviously be interpreted differently by each type of student.

A student's past history with grades can also be a factor. Students who have a history of receiving high grades, for instance, have likely developed a positive view of themselves and will continue to aspire to and work for high grades. On the other hand, students who have histories of low grades come to see themselves as failures, and another low grade only confirms this perception. Obviously the status parents and close friends attach to grades also influences students' attitudes.

Teacher Bias in Assessment and Grading

From your own student experiences you undoubtedly know how important it is for teachers to be perceived as fair and impartial in their treatment of young people. Being free from bias is particularly important when judging student work and assigning grades. Teacher bias is also a topic that has been extensively researched. In fact, some of the most interesting studies were done by Starch and Elliot (1912, 1913), who showed the subjectivity of teachers in assessing and assigning grades to essay exams. In their first study, the researchers asked teachers in a number of different schools to grade student-produced essay exams in English. Later the researchers asked history and mathematics teachers to perform the same task. Starch and Elliot found that teachers used many different criteria when assessing essays, and consequently the scores or grades they gave to the same paper varied widely. On one English essay, for instance, the percentage of points awarded varied from 50 to 97. Similar studies conducted over the years continue to show that teachers hold different criteria for judging student work and that they are influenced by numerous subjective factors, such as the student's handwriting, whether or not the opinions expressed agree with those of the teacher, and the expectations teachers hold for a particular student's work. (Remember the concept of self-fulfilling prophecy described in Chapter 5.) Fortunately, a number of strategies have been devised to reduce bias and subjectivity in assessment and grading. These procedures and techniques will be described more fully later in this chapter.

Importance of Grades to Parents

Finally, parents are very concerned about their children's grades because they, more than their children, understand fully the important sorting function going on in schools. For instance, most parents can recall critical judgments made about their work and the consequences these had for them. Similarly, they are keenly aware of the judgments being made when their child is placed in a lower-level reading group or a general math class instead of algebra.

Teachers have been known to complain about this type of parental concern, and sometimes these complaints are justified. For instance, some parents let unrealistic expectations for their children interfere with the teacher's professional judgment about the most appropriate level of work for their child. Conversely, other parents seem indifferent to their children's academic evaluation and offer little encouragement at home for doing good work or getting good grades.

Most parental concern, however, is natural and can be potentially beneficial. There is a growing research literature showing that parental concern can be tapped and used by effective teachers for the purpose of enhancing student learning. Recall in Chapter 3 how involving parents through homework was described as a way of extending instructional time. Several studies (Cooper, 1989, for example) have also shown that when teachers show regard for parental concerns by using more frequent reporting procedures and by getting parents to support the school's reward systems at home, these actions can result in more homework completed, better attendance, more academic engagement, and generally increased student output.

SCHOOLWIDE ASSESSMENT PROGRAMS

The following sections focus directly on strategies beginning teachers can use to make assessment and evaluation both fair and productive. The topic of schoolwide assessment programs is described first, followed by specific procedures associated with classroom testing and grading. The chapter concludes with a look to the future by describing several emerging approaches to student assessment.

Schoolwide Use of Standardized Tests

Currently, it is common practice for school systems to use standardized tests to diagnose and evaluate students' academic progress. In larger school systems whole units of specially trained personnel exist to coordinate and manage this important educational activity. It is a rare school where students are not tested, at least on a yearly basis, in such topics as study skills, reading, language acquisition, mathematical operations, verbal reasoning, and concept development. Sometimes schools use tests developed and distributed by national test publishers. Others use tests developed and distributed by state or district testing authorities. There appears to be a growing trend to require all students to pass a state-mandated functional literacy or minimal competency test of achievement before they are granted a high school diploma. The results of testing are used to make judgments about the effective-

RESEARCH SUMMARY 7-1

Cullen, F. T., Cullen, J. B., Hayhow, V. L., and Plouffe, J. T. (1975). The effects of the use of grades as an incentive. *Journal of Educational Research. 68, 277–279.*

PROBLEM: A persistent problem for teachers is how to get students to do their homework. In this study, Francis Cullen and colleagues experimentally manipulated two types of incentives to see what effects they would have on getting students to complete a rather simple library assignment.

SAMPLE AND SETTING: Subjects for the study consisted of 233 students who made up 14 high school classes in three suburban schools. Students were mainly middle class. In School A, subjects were enrolled in ten freshman health classes; in School B, subjects were enrolled in three junior-level psychology classes; subjects in one freshman English class were used in School C. Within each school, the same instructor taught all the classes.

PROCEDURES: All students in the study were asked to complete a one-page library assignment. Although the assignment varied according to the subject of the class, it was the same in terms of length and difficulty. The 14 classes were randomly assigned to three different conditions.

1. **Positive-incentive group:** Students in this group were told if they handed in the assignment, they would receive X amount of points on their final grade. If they did not complete the assignment, no points would be taken away.
2. **Negative-incentive group:** Students in this group were told that if they did not hand in the assignment they would lose X amount of points on their final grade.
3. **Control group:** Students in this group were told that completion or noncompletion of the assignment would not affect their grade.

POINTERS FOR READING RESEARCH: There are no new concepts or procedures introduced in this study. The chi square (χ^2) statistic was used to determine significant differences among groups.

RESULTS: Table 7-1 shows the results from the Cullen et al. study.

As can be observed from the data displayed in Table 7-1, using grades as an incentive secured greater participation in this particular assignment than when no incentives were present. Note that less than 14 percent of the students completed the assignment when told it would not affect their grade in any way. These data also confirmed the researcher's hypothesis that grades used as *negative incentives* would be more powerful than grades used as *positive incentives*. Almost two-thirds of the students completed the assignment when told not doing so would lower their grade (negative incentive), compared to only 42 percent who completed the assignment when told they would receive "extra points" toward their grade (positive incentive).

TABLE 7-1 Percentage of Students Completing and Not Completing Assignments under Positive, Negative, and No Incentives*

INCENTIVE	STUDENTS COMPLETING ASSIGNMENT		STUDENTS NOT COMPLETING ASSIGNMENT	
	N	%	N	%
Positive incentive	45	41.7	63	58.3
Negative incentive	66	64.1	37	35.9
No incentive	3	13.6	19	86.4

* $\chi^2 = 24.379$, df = 2, p < .01

DISCUSSION AND IMPLICATIONS: Obviously, this study did not control for many other variables which might potentially influence assignment completion. The researchers acknowledged this weakness in their study. They suggested that intelligence, achievement motivation, and the learning environment, as well as the intrinsic aspect of the assignment, can potentially interact with and influence student work. However, the results of this study remain consistent with other studies that have been done and tend to reinforce what many experienced teachers know: given the current grading and evaluation procedures used in schools, students perform more work if that work is tied to a grade.

The finding that negative incentives are more effective than positive incentives is also consistent with other research. Again, many factors obviously come into play. Several reasons have been offered to explain this phenomenon. It may be that positive incentives such as "extra points" will not enhance the grade of students already doing well, so why bother? Or, peer culture may deter students from working for extra points. For example, a student doing extra work runs the risk of being perceived by other students as a "rate or curve buster" and subject to sanctions from friends.

However, when students are faced with losing points (negative incentives) this is another matter. They must complete the assignment or risk having their overall grade for the course lowered. Even close friends are unlikely to scoff at this action.

Finally, there is an interesting question stemming from this study which the researchers did not address, but which is of interest to beginning teachers: Why did one-third to one-half of the students, regardless of positive or negative incentives, choose not to complete the assignment?

ness of schools and teachers and, most importantly, to decide the future educational and job opportunities available to students.

Beginning teachers will not be required to select the tests to be used on a schoolwide basis, nor will they be held responsible for the administration, scoring, or initial interpretations of these tests. They will, however, be expected to understand the nontechnical aspects of the testing program, and they will be expected to use test results and communicate these clearly to students and their parents.

Standardized Tests

Standardized tests, as contrasted to tests made by teachers, are those that have been designed and validated by professional test makers for specific purposes such as measuring academic achievement or literacy levels. They can normally be administered in many different settings and still produce reliable information. In some instances, standardized tests also provide information about how some nationwide "norm group" performed on the test, thus providing a basis of comparison for students subsequently taking the test. Examples of standardized tests include the Stanford Achievement Test, the California Achievement Test, or the well-known Scholastic Aptitude Test (SAT) used by many colleges and universities in making entrance selections. Many of you took the SAT and soon will be taking the National Teachers Examination (NTE), which is another example of a standardized test.

Norm-Referenced and Criterion-Referenced Tests

Today, two major types of standardized tests are used to measure student abilities and achievement. These are called norm-referenced and criterion-referenced tests. It is important to understand the differences between these two approaches to testing and to be able to communicate to others the assumptions, the advantages, and the disadvantages of each approach.

Norm-referenced tests attempt to evaluate a particular student's performance by comparing it to the performance of some other well-defined group of students on the same test. Most of the achievement tests you have taken as students were norm-referenced. Your score told you how you performed on some specific topic or skill in comparison with

students from a national population who served as the "norming" group for the test. Most norm-referenced tests produce two types of scores—a raw score and a percentile rank. The raw score is the number of items on the test a student answers correctly. The percentile-rank score is a statistical device that shows how a student compares to others, specifically the proportion of individuals who had the same or lower raw scores for a particular section of the test. Table 7-2 shows how raw scores are converted to percentile ranks on standardized, norm-referenced tests. Look at the student who answered 38 out of the 48 test items correctly. You can see this score placed the student in the 71st percentile, meaning that 71 percent of the students in the norm group scored 38 or lower on the test. If you look at the student who had a raw score of 30 on the test, you can see this converts to a percentile score of 22, meaning that only 22 percent of the students in the norm group scored 30 or below.

Whereas norm-referenced tests measure student performance against that of other students, **criterion-referenced tests** measure it against some agreed-upon level of performance or criterion. To show the major difference between a norm-referenced and criterion-referenced test, let us use as our example a runner's speed on the 100-yard dash. If a runner were compared to a larger group of runners using concepts from norm-referenced testing, the tester would report that a student who ran the 100-yard dash in 13 seconds was in the 65th percentile for all other students in his or her age group. Using concepts from criterion-referenced testing, the tester would report that the established criterion for running a 100-yard dash was 12 seconds and that the student can now run it in 13 seconds, 1 second short of criterion.

Normally the content and skills measured on criterion-referenced tests are much more specific than on norm-referenced tests. Obviously each provides different types of information for teachers to use. Figures 7-1 and 7-2 illustrate some of these differences. Notice that the criterion-referenced test indicates the level of mastery for very specific word-attack skills as contrasted to the more general category of reading comprehension found in the norm-referenced test. You will read later in this chapter how performance and authentic assessment advocates take both of these approaches to task.

Table 7-2 Conversion of Raw Scores to Percentile Ranks

RAW SCORE	PERCENTILE RANK	RAW SCORE	PERCENTILE RANK
48		34	44
47		33	40
46		32	36
45	99+	31	30
44	96	30	22
43	93	29	18
42	90	28	15
40	81	27	11
39	76	26	7
38	71	25	4
37	65	24	3
36	56	23	1
35	49	22	1−

SOURCE: From W. R. Borg and M. D. Gall, *Educational research: An introduction* (4th ed.), New York: Longman, 1983, p. 274.

Note also that results from the norm-referenced tests are reported in percentile ranks, whereas the results on the criterion-referenced test show the degree to which a particular student has mastered a specific word-attack skill.

Advantages and Disadvantages of Different Approaches

If the teacher is interested in how his or her students compare to students elsewhere, results from norm-referenced tests are obviously called for. Norm-referenced tests allow comparisons within a particular school, district, or state. For example, achievement levels in all third grades in a particular district might be compared with those from other districts. Norm-referenced tests, however, will not tell very much about how well a specified set of school or teacher objectives are being accomplished; nor will they tell how students are currently doing in comparison to past performance on locally derived objectives.

Criterion-referenced tests, on the other hand, can provide information about a student's level of performance in relation to some specified body of knowledge or list of agreed-upon objectives. This is important information to have when making judgments about the effectiveness of particular instructional programs and activities. The results of criterion-referenced tests, however, do not allow for comparisons of students in a particular locale with

national norms. More and more schools and teachers are using criterion-referenced tests because their information is better for diagnosing student difficulties and for assessing the degree to which schoolwide or systemwide purposes are being achieved.

Communication of Standardized Test Results

It is important that teachers be able to explain the results of both norm-referenced and criterion-referenced tests in honest and straightforward ways. They may be asked to go over test scores with students, to explain test results to parents, and to interpret test scores that are published in the newspaper. Students and their parents need to know that a single score on a test does not pretend to measure all aspects of a person's abilities. At the same time, they need to know how standardized tests scores are used to make decisions that can affect students' lives.

Community members often need to be reminded of the strengths and limitations of particular testing programs and of the assumptions underlying all standardized tests. Educators have not done a very good job of explaining, in nontechnical terms, the assumptions behind norm-referenced testing and their limitations for judging the effectiveness of a particular school's educational program, nor have they explained the severe limita-

Figure 7-1   Student profile on selected topics of the California Achievement Test

CAT CALIFORNIA ACHIEVEMENT TESTS, FORMS E&F	CTB/MCGRAW–HILL

INDIVIDUAL TEST RECORD

CLASS :
SCHOOL : UMCP
DIST   : COLLEGE PARK

STUDENT:
BIRTH DATE:

NATIONAL PERCENTILE

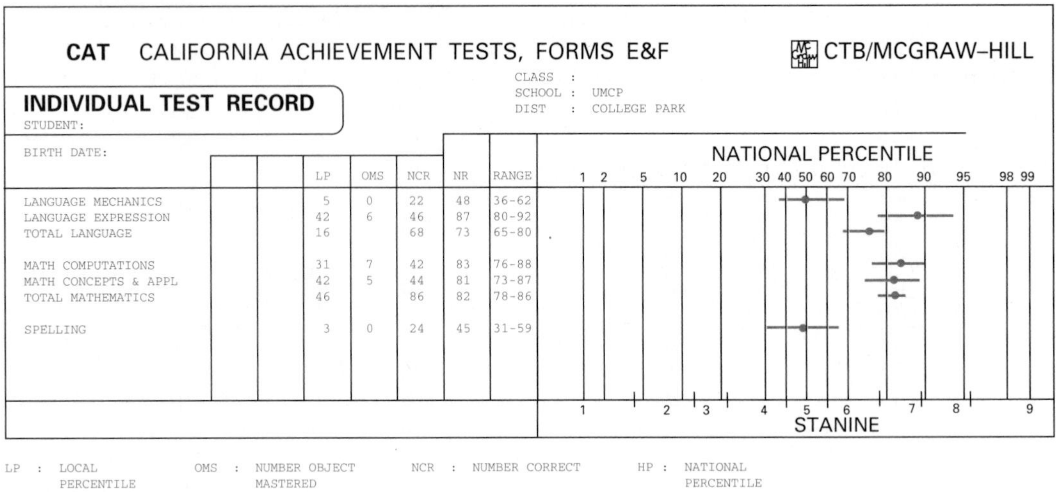

		LP	OMS	NCR	NR	RANGE
LANGUAGE MECHANICS		5	0	22	48	36-62
LANGUAGE EXPRESSION		42	6	46	87	80-92
TOTAL LANGUAGE		16		68	73	65-80
MATH COMPUTATIONS		31	7	42	83	76-88
MATH CONCEPTS & APPL		42	5	44	81	73-87
TOTAL MATHEMATICS		46		86	82	78-86
SPELLING		3	0	24	45	31-59

National Percentile scale: 1 2 5 10 20 30 40 50 60 70 80 90 95 98 99

STANINE: 1 2 3 4 5 6 7 8 9

LP : LOCAL   OMS : NUMBER OBJECT   NCR : NUMBER CORRECT   HP : NATIONAL
     PERCENTILE   MASTERED   PERCENTILE

SOURCE: From B. S. Bloom, T. J. Hastings, and G. F. Madaus, *Handbook on formative and summative evaluation of student learning*, p. 104. Copyright 1971 McGraw-Hill. Used with permission.

tions of most paper and pencil standardized tests for making judgments about the multiple intelligences and skills found in human beings. Knowledgeable teachers can find ways to communicate to parents and others that norm-referenced tests only compare students against a norm group and do not necessarily provide a good measure for how well a particular teacher, school, or system is achieving particular objectives. Teachers can also communicate to parents and the community that students'

Figure 7-2   Level of mastery of various word-attack skills in the Gary public school system

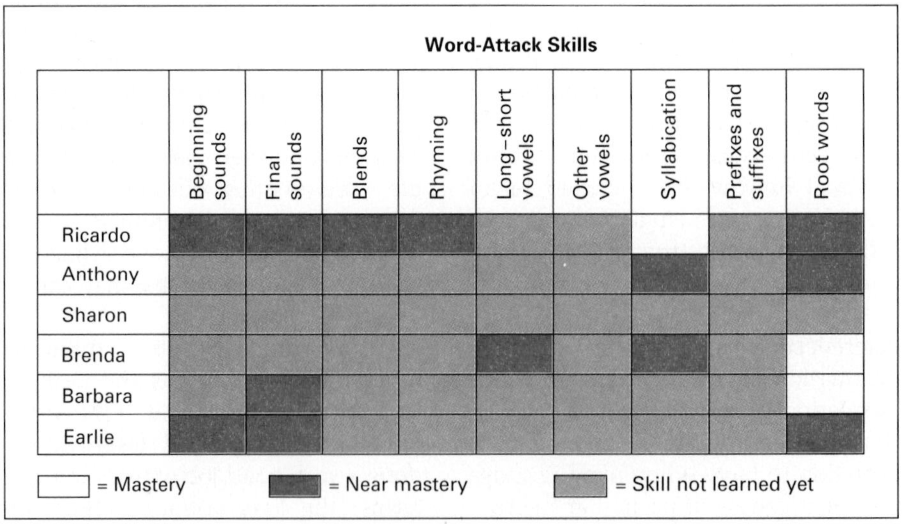

Word-Attack Skills

	Beginning sounds	Final sounds	Blends	Rhyming	Long–short vowels	Other vowels	Syllabication	Prefixes and suffixes	Root words
Ricardo									
Anthony									
Sharon									
Brenda									
Barbara									
Earlie									

☐ = Mastery   ■ = Near mastery   ▓ = Skill not learned yet

SOURCE: From B. S. Bloom, T. J. Hastings, and G. F. Madaus, *Handbook on formative and summative evaluation of student learning*, p. 104. Copyright 1971 McGraw-Hill. Used with permission.

abilities and dispositions toward learning help determine how well they do on standardized tests, and that a school with a predominance of less motivated students will never perform as well as schools with a predominance of highly motivated students.

THE TEACHER'S ASSESSMENT PROGRAM

Whereas testing specialists have the major responsibility for systemwide testing, classroom teachers are responsible for the assessment, testing, and grading related to their own specific courses. In general the teacher's assessment activities are aimed at one of the following three goals: diagnosing **prior knowledge** and skills, providing corrective feedback, and making judgments and grading student achievement. These three purposes have some similarities but also some important differences.

Diagnosing Prior Knowledge

To individualize instruction for specific students or to tailor instruction for a particular classroom group requires reliable information about students' capabilities and their prior knowledge. Both norm- and criterion-referenced standardized tests attempt to measure many areas of student achievement but are most highly developed and most readily available in reading, language development, and mathematics. Unfortunately, they are less available in other subject areas.

In many school systems, beginning teachers will be assisted by test and measurement personnel or by counseling and special education staff who have been specifically trained to help diagnose student capabilities and achievement. In other school systems this type of assistance may not be available. If formal diagnostic information is not available, beginning teachers will have to rely on more informal techniques for assessing prior knowledge. For example, teachers can observe students closely as they approach a particular task and get some sense about how difficult or easy it is for them. Similarly, by listening carefully to students and by asking probing questions, teachers can get additional cues about students' prior knowledge on almost any topic. In fact, teacher and student questions are a major means of ascertaining student understanding. Verbal responses help teachers decide whether to move forward with the lesson or to back up and review. Nonverbal responses such as frowns, head nodding, puzzled looks, and the like also provide hints about how well students understand a topic. However, beginning teachers should be aware that sometimes these nonverbal behaviors can be misinterpreted.

Because many students will not admit their lack of knowledge or understanding in large groups, some teachers have found that interviewing students in small groups can be a good way to get the diagnostic information they need. This technique is particularly useful for getting information from students who do not participate regularly in classroom discussions or who give off few nonverbal signals. Constructing student portfolios, to be described later, can also be used for diagnosing prior knowledge.

Providing Corrective Feedback

A second important purpose of assessment and evaluation is to provide students with feedback on how they are doing. As with diagnosing students' prior knowledge, this is easier to do for some topics and skills than others. Test makers have developed rather sophisticated and reliable procedures for measuring discrete skills such as word recognition or simple mathematical operations. It is also quite easy to collect information on how fast a student can run the 100-yard dash or how long it takes to climb a 30-foot rope. Biofeedback techniques are also available to help students monitor their own physical reactions to stress and certain types of exertion. However, as instruction moves from a focus on such basic skills and abilities to a focus on more complex thinking and problem-solving skills, the problem of providing corrective feedback becomes more difficult because there are fewer reliable tests and acceptable procedures for these more complex processes.

Chapter 10 provides some principles for giving feedback to students and explains the importance of feedback for student improvement. It also emphasizes that for corrective feedback to be useful it must be immediate, frequent, and communicated in nonjudgmental ways.

Table 7-3   Three Major Purposes of Classroom Assessment

	DIAGNOSTIC	FEEDBACK	REPORTING
Function	Placement, planning, and determining the presence or absence of skills and prior knowledge	Feedback to student and teachers on progress	Grading of students at the end of a unit or semester
When used	At the outset of a unit, semester or year or during instruction when student is having problems	During instruction	At the end of quarter, semester, or year's work
Type of test	Standardized diagnostic tests; observations and checklists	Quizzes and special tests or homework	Final exams
Scoring	Norm- and criterion-referenced	Criterion-referenced	Norm- or criterion-referenced

Testing for Summative Evaluation and Reporting

For most beginning teachers, the bulk of their assessment time and energy is for the purpose of assessing student progress, determining grades, and reporting progress. Although some teachers do not like this aspect of their work, it must be done and done well for reasons enumerated earlier. First, students expect their work to be evaluated, and they perform academic work for grades, as you have seen. Teachers who take this work-for-grade exchange lightly, or who do it poorly, are normally faced with serious classroom problems. Second, the larger society has assigned the job of making judgments about student achievement and ability to teachers. The key concepts and procedures associated with the three major purposes of classroom assessment are summarized in Table 7-3. The next section will provide more specific information about this aspect of the teacher's assessment program.

SPECIFICS OF TESTING AND GRADING

The most important aspect of student evaluation in most classrooms involves the tests teachers make and give to students. Good test construction requires both skill and a commitment to this aspect of teaching. The general principles which follow offer beginning teachers some much-needed guidelines for constructing their own paper and pencil tests.

Constructing more complex performance tests is discussed later.

General Principles

Gronlund (1982) provides six basic principles that should guide teachers as they design an assessment system and create their own tests. These principles, which have been reduced here to five, are summarized below.

MEASURE ALL INSTRUCTIONAL OBJECTIVES

An often-heard student complaint is that the test did not "cover what we covered in class." For whatever reasons, students who say this believe that they have been unfairly judged. Thus Gronlund's first principle is that teachers should construct their test so it measures clearly the learning objectives they have communicated to students. In short, the test should be in harmony with the teacher's instructional objectives. For example, if the teacher has just completed a unit of work on the American colonial period and wants students to understand all aspects of this era, then the test should cover more than just the religious leaders of the period.

COVER ALL LEARNING TASKS

Most lessons and units of instruction contain a variety of learning objectives ranging from the recall of factual information to the understanding, analysis, and creative application of specific principles. A good test does not focus entirely on one type of objective such as factual recall; rather, it should measure a representative sample of the teacher's learning objectives. Remember, however, that measuring more complex skills such as higher-level reasoning is more costly and time-consuming.

USE APPROPRIATE TEST ITEMS

There are, as you know from your own experiences, many different kinds of test items and testing formats available to teachers. Some types of test items, such as matching or fill-in-the-blanks, are better for measuring recall of specific information; others, such as essay items, are better for tapping higher-level thinking processes and skills. A good test includes items that are most appropriate for a particular objective. More about this aspect of constructing tests will be provided later.

MAKE TESTS VALID AND RELIABLE

A test is said to be reliable when it produces dependable, consistent scores for persons who take it more than once over a period of time. A test is said to be valid when it measures what it claims to measure. Teacher-made tests that are clearly written and that minimize guessing are generally more reliable than are ambiguous ones that encourage guessing. Likewise, tests containing a fairly large number of items are generally more reliable than those with just a few items. A test that is well planned and that covers the full range of objectives and topics is most likely to ensure validity. Teaching students the necessary skills to take the test also increases validity because, in some instances, students may know the information being tested but simply cannot read or interpret the questions. No single test, however, can give a completely accurate picture of what a student knows or can do. Thus, there is always the need to interpret results with caution and to rely on multiple sources of assessment information before making final judgments about student's work.

USE TESTS TO IMPROVE LEARNING

This final principle is meant to remind teachers that although tests may be used primarily to diagnose or assess student achievement, they can also be learning experiences for students. Going over test results, for instance, provides teachers with opportunities to reteach important information students may have missed. Debate and discussion over "right" answers can stimulate further study about a topic. Effective teachers integrate their testing processes into their total instructional programs for the purpose of guiding and enhancing student learning.

Test Construction and Use

PLANNING THE TEST

In almost any class, teachers attempt to teach many different things. Some of what they teach is influenced by curriculum guides that have been developed in their district and by the textbooks available to them. Some things that are taught stem from a teacher's own interest and judgment about what is important; still others are influenced by what students are interested in and what they choose to study. Also, the instructional objectives of a particular course can cover a range of behaviors, including important facts about a topic, major concepts and principles, simple and complex skills, appreciations, and the ability to think critically and analytically. Obviously, every piece of information, skill, or higher-level process cannot be included on a particular test. Thus, decisions must be made about what to include and what to leave out. The **table of specifications** is a device invented by evaluation specialists (Bloom, Hastings, and Madaus, 1971; Gronlund, 1982, for example) to help teachers make these decisions and to determine how much space to allocate to certain topics and to the different levels of student cognitive processes. Table 7-4 shows a sample table of specification.

As you can see from Table 7-4, the teacher has listed the major topics covered in the left-hand column. This particular table of specifications covers a unit of study on colonial America. It could have covered a day's work, a week's, or a whole course of study. Along the top of the table, the teacher has listed the cognitive processes or student behaviors associated with the unit. Although other category systems could have been used, the teacher who constructed this table relied upon Bloom's taxonomy, which was introduced in Chapter 2. Finally, within the table itself, the teacher has placed numbers. These numbers represent the teacher's

Table 7-4   Table of Specification

Unit of work covered: _____

Anticipated time for taking the test: _____

| | STUDENT BEHAVIORS AND COGNITIVE PROCESSES | | | | | |
| | KNOWS/RECALL OF | | | HIGHER-LEVEL | | |
TOPICS/CONTENT	TERMS	FACTS	PRINCIPLES	COMPREHENSION	APPLICATION	EVALUATION
Colonial life	1			1	1	
New England town		1		1	1	
Southern plantation			2	1	2	
Clergy		1				
Transportation systems			1	1	2	
Children and education			1	1		1
Indian warfare		2			1	1
France and Spain		1	1			1
Westward expansion	2			1	1	2
Total number of test items	3	5	5	6	8	5

judgment about how many test items to include on the test for each of the topics and under each of the cognitive processes.

MAKING THE TEST

Once the teacher has decided which topics and cognitive processes to cover on a test, the next step is to decide on the test's format and the type of test items to use. A major question is, Will the test be objective or essay? These are terms you are very familiar with from your prior experiences. However, it is important to point out that the term *objective,* as used here, means that answers to the items can be scored relatively free from bias. Like most other aspects of teaching, the choice on whether to use an objective or an essay test has important trade-offs. These will be described below.

CONSTRUCTING AND SCORING OBJECTIVE TESTS

True-false, matching, multiple-choice, and fill-in-the-blanks are examples of test items that may be used on an **objective test.** The advantages of these types of test items are obvious. They allow greater coverage of the various topics a teacher has taught, and they can be easily and objectively scored. One

disadvantage of objective tests is that unless a teacher has considerable skill, it is difficult to write objective items that measure higher-level cognitive skills and processes. Another disadvantage is that good objective tests take a long time to construct. They simply cannot be put together in a few minutes the night before. Also, teachers always worry about the "guessing factor" associated with objective tests. This is particularly true when matching or true-false items are used. Finally, objective test items, regardless of how well constructed, can measure only a very limited range of understandings and skills. If the decision is made to use the objective format, several factors should be considered as test items are prepared.

True-False Items.   When the content of instruction or a learning objective calls for students to compare alternatives, true-false tests can be a useful means to measure their understanding. True-false tests are also useful as an alternative to a multiple-choice item if the teacher is having trouble coming up with several distracters. A good true-false item should be written so the choice is clear and the answer unambiguous. Look for instance at the examples of good and poor true-false items below:

Good   An island is a land mass that is smaller than a continent and is surrounded by water.

Poor   Islands have been more important in the economic history of the world than have peninsulas.

The first example requires students to know the definition of the concept *island* as compared to other land forms. The answer is unambiguous. The second example, however, is very ambiguous. The word "important" would likely be interpreted in many different ways by students. An obvious shortcoming with true-false items is that students, whether they know the material or not, have a 50 percent chance of getting the correct answer.

Matching.   When the teacher wants to measure student recall over a fairly large amount of factual information, matching items can be useful. Students are presented with two lists of items (concepts, dates, principles, names) and asked to select an item from one list which most closely matches an item from the other list. Most evaluation specialists caution against making either list too long—perhaps no more than six to eight items—or having more than one match for each set of items. Like true-false items, there is an element of guessing that the teacher needs to consider when choosing to use matching items. Below is an example of a matching question used by an English teacher who wanted to see if students knew the authors of the various literary works they have studied.

Directions: Match the author listed in Column B with the work he wrote, listed in Column A.

1. ____ *Leaves of Grass*	A.	Thoreau
2. ____ *Nature*	B.	Hawthorne
3. ____ *Walden*	C.	Cooper
4. ____ *The Scarlet Letter*	D.	Emerson
5. ____ *Moby Dick*	E.	Melville
6. ____ *The Pathfinder*	F.	Whitman

Fill-in-the-Blanks.   A third popular type of objective test item is fill-in-the-blank. This type of item is rather easy to write, and it does a good job of measuring students' abilities to recall factual information. The element of guessing is virtually eliminated because choices of possible correct answers are not provided. The tricks of writing good fill-in-the-blank items are to avoid ambiguity and to make sure questions have no more than one correct response. To show how two correct answers are possible, take the example below:

The Civil War battle of Antietam was fought in _____.

Some students might write in "Maryland" (the place), while others might write in "1862" (the date). Some subjects and instructional objectives lend themselves to clarity better than others.

Multiple Choice.   Multiple-choice items are considered by most evaluation specialists to be the best type of objective test item. Multiple-choice items are rather robust in their use, and if carefully constructed, they minimize guessing. Also, if appropriately written, multiple-choice items can tap some types of higher-level thinking and analytical skills.

Multiple-choice items consist of providing students with three types of statement: a **stem,** which poses a problem or asks a question, the *right answer,* which solves the problem or answers the question correctly, and **distracters,** several statements which are plausible, but wrong. Although the number of distracters can vary, normally three or four are recommended.

Good multiple-choice items are difficult to write. The stem must provide enough contextual information so students thoroughly understand the problem or question being posed. At the same time, it must be written so that the correct answer is not easily revealed. Distracters must be such that they provide plausible solutions to students who have a vague or incomplete understanding of the problem, yet must be clearly recognized as the "wrong" answer by students who have command of a topic. General guidelines for writing multiple-choice items include recommendations to (1) make the stem specific but with sufficient contextual information, (2) make all the distracters plausible and grammatically consistent with the stem, and (3) make all aspects of the item clear so that students will not read more than was intended into the answer. Below are several examples which highlight these guidelines.

Stems should be straightforward and specific

but provide sufficient context. Here is an example of a good stem.

> Historians attached historical significance to the Battle of Antietam because
> A. So many people were killed in the bloodiest battle of the Civil War.
> B. It gave Lincoln the victory he needed to issue the Emancipation Proclamation.
> C. Strategically it was the strongest victory to that point by the Confederate Army.
> D. It showed how vulnerable the North was to invasion by forces from the South.

And here is an example of a poor stem.

> Antietam was
> A. The bloodiest battle of the Civil War.
> B. The battle that gave Lincoln the victory he needed to issue the Emancipation Proclamation.
> C. The strongest victory to that point by the Confederate Army.
> D. The battle that showed how vulnerable the North was to invasion by forces from the South.

Most Civil War historians point out that the Battle of Antietam was tactically a draw. Strategically, however, it was a Confederate defeat and it did give Lincoln a victory he thought he needed before formally issuing the Emancipation Proclamation. The stem in the good example alerts students that it is the "historical significance" of the battle that they should consider. Those who had a good understanding of this specific era of the Civil War would know the link between Antietam and the Emancipation Proclamation. Without that context, however, distracter A might also be a very plausible answer, because the Battle of Antietam was the most costly in human life for a single day's engagement during the Civil War.

Just as the stem for a multiple-choice question needs to be carefully constructed, so too do the distracters. Two common errors made when writing distracters are lack of grammatical consistency and implausibility. Look at the example below.

> Historians attached historical significance to the Battle of Antietam because

> A. So many people were killed.
> B. It gave Lincoln the victory he needed to issue the Emancipation Proclamation.
> C. The Confederate Army.
> D. Most Americans love bloody battles.

As you can see, several things are wrong with the distracters in this example. Distracters A, C, and D are much shorter than B. This may cue students to the right answer. Distracter C does not complete the sentence started in the stem. Thus it is grammatically different than distracters A, B, and D. Finally, for the serious student distracter D could be eliminated almost immediately.

Essay Tests. Many teachers and test experts agree that essay tests do the best job of tapping students' higher-level thought processes and creativity. Obviously, this is a decided advantage of an essay test over an objective test. Another advantage is that it normally takes less time to construct. A note of caution, however. Good, clear essay questions don't just happen. And bear in mind the time it takes to construct sample answers and read and grade essay questions.

Essay tests have been criticized because they cover fewer topics than objective tests and they are difficult to grade objectively. The first criticism can be partially resolved by using a combination of items—objective items to measure student understanding of basic knowledge and essay items to measure higher-level objectives.

As for grading bias, several guidelines have been developed by experienced teachers and evaluation specialists which help reduce this danger.

1. *Write the essay question so it is clear and explains to students what should be covered in the answer.* For example, if the teacher wants students to apply information, the questions should say that; if the teacher wants students to compare two different ideas or principles, the question should state that clearly. For instance, "Discuss the Civil War" is too broad and does not tell students what to do. Consequently, answers will vary greatly and will be difficult for the teacher to score. On the other hand, "Describe and compare economic conditions in the North and the South during the 1840s and 1850s, and explain how these conditions influenced deci-

sions by both sides to engage in civil war" describes more clearly the topics to be covered in the essay and the type of thinking about the topic the teacher wants.

2. *Write a sample answer to the question ahead of time and assign points to various parts of the answer.* Writing a sample answer can become a criterion on which to judge each of the essays. Points assigned to various aspects of the answer (for instance, 5 points for organization, 5 points for coverage, and perhaps 5 points overall) helps deal with the problem of uneven quality that may exist across a given answer. Students should be made aware of the point distribution, if this technique is used by the teacher.

3. *Use techniques to reduce expectancy effects.* In Chapter 5 you were introduced to the concept of expectancy effects—a phenomenon whereby teachers expect some students to do well and others to do poorly. Having students write their names on the back of their essays is one technique used to prevent this type of bias. However, this strategy has limited value because most teachers soon find they readily recognize a particular student's handwriting. If the essay test has two or three questions, reading all the responses to a single question and then shuffling the papers before reading responses to the next question is another procedure teachers use to reduce expectancy effects. If teachers are working in teams, checking each other's grading is also helpful.

4. *Consider using holistic scoring.* Some evaluation specialists have argued that the best procedure for scoring essay questions and other types of student writing (reports, essays, etc.) is one they have labeled **holistic scoring.** The logic behind this procedure is that the total essay written by a student is more than the sum of its parts and should be judged accordingly. Teachers who use this approach normally skim through all the essays and select samples that could be judged as very poor, average, and outstanding. These samples then become the models for judging the other papers. Some teachers use this same process but add a second procedure of stacking the papers in appropriate piles as they read, for instance, an A pile, a B pile, and so on. They then reread selected papers from the various piles to check their initial judgments and to

check for comparability of papers within a given pile.

Obviously, constructing essay items and making judgments about students' work this way can be difficult and time-consuming. The use of essay questions, however, remains one of the best means for measuring the more complex and higher-level abilities of students. Subjective grading will probably always be an unattractive feature of essay testing, but by employing the safeguards described above, this factor can be greatly reduced.

GIVING THE TEST

The format of the test and the kind of coverage it provides are important ingredients. The conditions under which students take the test are equally important. As with many other aspects of teaching, having appropriate structures and routines can help make test taking a less stressful and more productive activity for students. Several guidelines stemming from the practices of effective teachers should be considered.

1. *Find ways to deal with test anxiety.* When confronted with a test, it is normal, and even beneficial, for students to be a little bit anxious. However, some students (often more than teachers suspect) experience a degree of test anxiety that prevents them from doing as well as they could. Effective teachers learn to recognize such students and help reduce anxiety in a number of ways. One way is to simply help students relax prior to a testing situation. Some teachers use humor and the release from tension it provides. Other teachers use simple relaxation methods, such as a few moments for reflection or deep breathing. Sometimes anxious students lack the requisite test-taking skills. Setting aside periods of instruction to help students learn how to pace themselves, how to allocate time during a test, how to make an outline for an essay question prior to writing, or how to skip over objective questions for which they do not know the answers, has been shown to reduce **test anxiety** and to improve test performance.

2. *Organize the learning environment for conducive*

test taking. In Chapter 3, you read how critical the use of space is for instruction. In Chapter 4, other aspects of the overall learning environment were discussed. The physical environment for test taking should allow students ample room to do their work; this in turn helps minimize cheating. Obviously, the test environment should be quiet and free from distractions.

3. *Make routines and instructions for the test clear.* Common errors made by beginning teachers include lack of carefully developed test-taking routines and unclear instructions. Most experienced teachers routinize the process of getting started on a test. They pass out the tests face down and ask students not to start until told to do so. This procedure is important for two reasons. One, it gives each student the same amount of time to complete the test. Two, it allows the teacher a chance to go over the instructions for the whole group. In giving instructions for the test, experienced teachers know that it is important to go over each section of the test and to provide students with guidelines for how long to spend on each part. If a new format or type of question is being introduced, procedures and expectations need to be explained. Checking to make sure students understand the tasks they are to perform is another critical feature of getting students ready to take the test.

4. *Avoid undue competition and time pressures.* Unless teachers are using the cooperative learning strategies described in Chapter 11, there is always going to be some competition among students. Competition comes into focus most clearly during testing situations. Experienced teachers use a variety of means to reduce the effects of harmful competition such as grading to a criterion instead of on a curve (explained later), making the final grade for the course dependent upon many samples of work, not just one or two tests, and having open discussions with students about competition and its effects on learning.

Insufficient time is another factor which produces poor test performance. In fact, teachers often hear students complain, "I knew the stuff, but I didn't have enough time." Except in instances where time is the criterion (for example, running the 100-yard dash), tests should be constructed so that students will have ample time to complete all aspects of the test. Beginning teachers often have trouble predicting the amount of time required for a particular test. Until these predictions become more accurate, a safe rule of thumb is to err on the side of having too much time as contrasted to too little time. Making some of the tests "take-homes" is another way to avoid the pressures of time associated with test taking.

Grading

The logic behind norm-referenced and criterion-referenced testing also applies to the two major approaches to grading. The concept of **grading on a curve** is a commonly used procedure in secondary schools and colleges where students compete with each other for positions along a predetermined grading curve. A teacher following a strict interpretation of the grading-on-a-curve concept would give 10 percent of the students As, 20 percent Bs, 40 percent Cs, 20 percent Ds and 10 percent Fs. Under this grading scheme, even students with a high degree of mastery over the testing material sometimes fall into one of the lower grading areas and vice versa.

An alternate approach to grading on a curve is **grading to criterion** or mastery. Teachers using this approach define rather precisely the content and skills objectives for their class and then measure student performance against that criterion. For example, in spelling, the teacher might decide that the correct spelling of 100 specified words constitutes mastery. Student grades would then be determined and performance reported in terms of the percentage of the 100 words a student can spell correctly. A teacher using this approach might specify the following grading scale: A = 100 to 93 words spelled correctly; B = 92 to 85 words spelled correctly; C = 84 to 75 words spelled correctly; D = 74 to 65 words spelled correctly, and F = 64 or fewer words spelled correctly.

Table 7-5 illustrates the differences between these two approaches for a particular group of students. As can be observed, the two approaches produce different grades for individuals within the same class of students. Both grading on a curve and

Table 7-5 Assigning Spelling Grades from Test Scores Using Two Approaches

	GRADING ON A CURVE		GRADING TO CRITERION	
Eric	98	A	98	A
Mary	97		97	
Ruth	96	B	96	
John	96		96	
Helen	96		96	
Sam	95		95	
Denise	92	C	92	B
William	90		90	
Louise	90		90	
Elizabeth	90		90	
Betty	87		87	
Marcos	87		87	
Martha	86		86	
Tom	83		83	C
Bob	80	D	80	
Dick	78		78	
Beth	73		73	D
Lane	69		69	
Mark	50	F	50	F
Jordon	50		50	

grading on mastery present some troublesome dilemmas for teachers. When grading on a curve the teacher is confronted with questions about the relationship of grades to native ability. For example, should 10 percent of a class of very able students be given Fs? Should 10 percent of a class of very slow students be given As?

Criterion testing and grading also present troublesome issues for teachers. If criterion levels are set in relation to what is realistic for a particular group of students, then able students should be expected to perform more work and at higher levels than their less-talented peers. However, when grades are assigned the question arises: Should students who complete all work accurately, even though it is at a lower level, be given the same grade as students who complete all work accurately at a higher level?

Some schools and teachers have tried to resolve this dilemma by using a criterion-referenced report card that lists all the major objectives of the course. Rather than assigning a single grade for the entire course, the teacher assigns a number of grades or verbally describes a child's performance for each

objective. This approach is also not trouble-free for teachers. Many parents are accustomed to the five-letter grading scale, because it is what they experienced when they were in school. Departures are confusing to them. Also, since a student's GPA is traditionally used to determine admissions to colleges and jobs, it is difficult to report a long list of performance measures that people in the outside world can understand.

Summary Guidelines for Testing and Grading

This section concludes with four summary guidelines that can assist beginning teachers as they approach the task of working out their own testing and grading procedures.

TEST AT ALL LEVELS

A common mistake made by some teachers is to focus most test items on simple recall of information. It is easier to write and score this type of question because there is usually a single correct answer. However, if the teacher wants to extend student thinking and promote higher-level thought processes, then test questions must require higher-level thinking. Bloom's taxonomy and a table of specification, described previously, are devices to assist the beginning teacher in constructing test items at various levels.

COMMUNICATE CLEARLY TO STUDENTS WHAT THEY WILL BE TESTED ON

A favorite question from students is, "Will we be tested on this?" Effective teachers make it very clear to students which of the ideas presented in a lecture or found in the textbook will be included on the test. Some teachers will write key ideas from a lecture on the board or give them to students as a handout. Some provide the same type of tool for information in the text. This communicates to students exactly what they are responsible for on the test. Other teachers spend time in review, outlining key ideas to be covered on the test. Still others provide study sheets with sample questions. The goal in each case is to alert students to what is expected of them.

Effective teachers also communicate to students the various levels of knowledge which they will need to demonstrate and the amount of detail expected. If the students are expected to commit a list of facts to memory, they are told so; if they are expected to evaluate one idea and contrast it with another, they are told so. Starting with the fifth or sixth grades, students can be taught Bloom's classification system and can use it as a guide for their own study, just as teachers use it as a guide for test construction.

TEST FREQUENTLY

Some teachers will wait until the end of an instructional unit to test students' knowledge acquisition. It is better to test students frequently for two reasons. First, frequent tests pressure students to keep up with what they are learning and provide them with feedback on how they are doing. Second, frequent testing provides the teacher with feedback on how well students are doing on key instructional objectives and allows reteaching of ideas students are not learning.

MAKE GRADING PROCEDURES EXPLICIT

Regardless of the approach a teacher chooses to use in assigning grades, the exact procedures should be written down and should be communicated clearly to students and to their parents. Taking the mystery out of grading is one way to help students accomplish the work expected of them and is also a means of getting students to see the "fairness" of the grading system.

A LOOK TO THE FUTURE

This chapter has described the importance of assessment and evaluation mainly from the perspective of traditional practices. The effects of testing and grading on student learning have been explored, as has the importance these processes hold for parents and the long-run consequences they have for students.

This chapter has also pointed out that many aspects of testing and grading are controversial and have been for a long time. Perhaps your generation of teachers will find better and fairer ways to make judgments about the work of students. Perhaps methods will be invented which will keep the posi-

tive aspects of assessment and evaluation intact—providing feedback to students and their parents about work accomplished—but will eliminate the more destructive aspects of current practices. Some innovative processes and procedures currently exist. These may provide foundations on which to think about the future of evaluation and grading.

Currently there appears to be a nationwide demand for more accountability for schools and for teachers as well as a call for higher standards. There is a general belief that the emphasis over the past decade of focusing on minimal competencies measured with multiple-choice, standardized tests perhaps has raised the basic skill level of students slightly but has failed to promote and measure higher-level thinking and problem-solving skills. Many educators, parents, and test and measurement experts believe that this situation can be corrected by introducing new approaches to student assessment such as the use of performance tasks, authentic assessment, student portfolios, and grading for team effort.

Performance Assessment

Instead of having students respond to multiple-choice questions on paper and pencil tests, advocates of **performance assessments** would have students demonstrate that they could *perform* particular tasks such as writing an essay, doing an experiment, interpreting the solution to a problem, playing a song, or painting a picture. Notice that the emphasis here is on testing procedural knowledge as contrasted to declarative knowledge as described in Chapter 2. Figures 7-3 and 7-4 display examinations that would be considered good examples of performance assessments.

Figure 7-3 shows the procedures developed by the State of Maryland to test students' abilities to perform particular tasks in reading and writing. Note how students are asked to perform particular tasks, how the performance assessment is spread over several days, and how efforts are made to examine the broader connections between the reading and writing process as compared to measuring discrete reading or writing skills.

Figure 7-4 is the scoring form used to grade a performance task developed by Richard Shavelson and his colleagues at the University of California in

Figure 7-3   Maryland's reading-writing examination

Maryland is using performance assessment as a lever to improve programs. Assessments were developed by the State Education Department and Maryland teachers with the technical assistance of CTB/McGraw-Hill. Following is an example from the reading-writing examination.

Maryland has taken the natural parallel between reading and writing to the point where they are integrated into one assessment. The entire process models how to teach reading and writing together, directly in opposition to the skills approach, which breaks down reading (and then writing) into tiny steps, tests each through workbook drills, and uses basal readers with controlled vocabulary. To show how it works, I will describe the sample grade 8 reading-writing/ language use assessment.

Each student is given a reading book, which contains a map of North America on the first page, with Canada, Alaska, and Yukon Territory marked on it; a short story by Jack London entitled "To Build a Fire"; and an excerpt from *Hypothermia: Causes, Effects, Prevention*, by Robert S. Pozos and David O'Born, published by New Century Publishers in 1982. Students also have response books into which they write answers.

The assessment begins with a prereading activity, which focuses students on the topic—the deadly cold of the Yukon Territory and its dangers—by asking them to think about their own experiences of being cold. They are asked to spend 10 minutes writing a journal entry describing their experience on the appropriate page of their books. Then they read London's "To Build a Fire" and respond to a series of questions probing their comprehension of the story. The first question can be answered with a drawing of the scene of the action if the student prefers to draw rather than write. A question later in the sequence asks the students to compare their own experience, described in the journal entry, with that of the man in the story who dies in the extreme cold. The final three questions probe the students' reading abilities by asking them to assess the difficulty of the story and explain why they rated it "very easy," "somewhat easy," "about average," "somewhat hard," or "very hard" and describe their reading strategies, that is, what they do to make sense of the story when they come to a word or a reference they do not understand.

On the second day of the assessment, the students begin by writing a 5-minute letter to the man in London's story giving him some advice that might have saved his life. Before they read the excerp *Hypothermia: Causes, Effects, Prevention*, there is class discussion about the topic, with the teacher writing on the board a cluster of the students' ideas as they respond to the words (succumb, insidious) that they will find in the excerpt. After they read the piece, they respond to a series of questions, again including the option to draw a picture or a diagram for at least one of them.

On the third day of the assessment, the students are expected to integrate the information from the two pieces into a written response to one of three situations: informing a group of friends of what they will need to do to stay safe on a winter weekend trip; writing a poem, story, or short play expressing their feelings about extreme states, not only cold but also heat, hunger, or fatigue; or writing a speech to persuade people to avoid travel in the Yukon. As in the case of Arizona and California, teachers will cover these three kinds of writing because they know that one of them—but they do not know which one—will be used in the assessment.

In each case, the student is asked to go through a process of first brainstorming ideas and either listing them or making a web of words with lines connecting them to major ideas. (These graphic organizers are now a recognized part of teaching the writing process.) Students write a rough draft, pause to consider whether it meets the needs of the situation, and then revise the piece. Finally, they use a proof-reading guidesheet supplied in the response book to prepare a final copy. . . . The material is graded according to two rubrics: one for the answers to the questions designed to measure reading comprehension and the other for the persuasive or informative writing. The prereading and prewriting activities and the class discussion are recorded but not scored.

SOURCE: From R. Mitchell (1992); *Testing for learning: How new approaches to evaluation can improve American schools,* pp. 47–49. Copyright The Free Press.

Figure 7-4   Paper towels investigation—hands-on scoring form

Student _____ Observer _____ Score _____ Script _____

1. **Method**	A. Container Pour water in/put towel in Put towel in/pour water in 1 pitcher or 3 beakers/glasses	B. Drops	C. Tray (surface) towel on tray/pour water on pour water on tray/wipe up

2. **Saturation**   A. Yes B. No C. Controlled

3. **Determine Result**
    A. Weigh towel
    B. Squeeze towel/measure water (weight or volume)
    C. Measure water in/out
    D. Time to soak up water
    E. No measurement
    F. Count # drops until saturated
    G. See how far drops spread out
    H. Other _____

4. **Care in Measuring**   Yes   No

5. **Correct Result**   Yes   No

Grade	Method	Saturate	Determine Result	Care in Measuring	Correct Answer
A	Yes	Yes	Yes	Yes	Yes
B	Yes	Yes	Yes	No	Yes/No
C	Yes	Yes/Controlled	Error		Yes/No
D	Yes	No	Missing		Yes/No
F	– – – – – – – – – – – – – – No Attempt – – – – – – – – – – – – – – –				

SOURCE: From R. J. Shavelson and G. P. Baxter (1992), What we've learned about assessing hands-on science. *Educational Leadership.* 49, 8, p. 21. Used with permission.

Santa Clara. The task presented to students was to "determine which of three paper towels held the most and least water" (Shavelson and Baxter, 1992, p. 21). Students could use any equipment they wanted to (of that available) in their science laboratory. Notice that the scoring form strives to measure performance not only in terms of outcomes, but also in terms of scientific processes.

The reading and writing tasks developed in Maryland and the paper towel experiment developed in California are efforts to measure rather complex intellectual skills and processes. Obvious questions which might be asked are, Why aren't these approaches used more often? and, why did it take us so long to invent them? Most measurement experts agree (as do teachers who have tried to devise and use performance assessments) that per-

formance tests take a great deal of time to construct and administer and that in most instances they are much more expensive. Think, for instance, how long it would take and the cost that would be involved to administer performance assessments to cover all the traditional topics currently found on the SAT. Further, the creation of good performance assessments requires considerable technical knowledge perhaps beyond that currently held by most teachers.

Authentic Assessment

Whereas performance assessment asks students to demonstrate certain behaviors or skills in a testing situation, **authentic assessment** takes these demonstrations a step further and asks that the demon-

Figure 7-5   Examples of performance and authentic assessment

---

Performance assessment and authentic assessment are often used interchangeably, but do they mean the same thing? Although both labels might appropriately apply to some types of assessment, they are not synonymous. We must be clear about the differences if we are to support each other in developing improved assessments.

To distinguish between the two terms, let's look at a familiar form of assessment with which we have a wealth of experience. Following are two examples of a direct writing assessment in which students produce writing samples.

CASE 1

Every May school district X conducts a direct writing assessment. For four days, all students at selected grade levels participate in a standardized series of activities to produce their writing samples. Using a carefully scripted manual, teachers guide students through the assessment with limited teacher directions and extended student writing time (up to 45 minutes) each day: Topic Introduction and Pre-writing (Day 1), Rough Drafting (Day 2), Revising and Editing (Day 3), and Final Copying and Proofreading (Day 4). The assessment clearly supports the Writing-as-a-Process intructional model.

CASE 2

School district Y also conducts a direct writing assessment annually in May. Each student has a conference with his or her teacher to determine which paper from the student's portfolio to submit for assessment purposes. The papers in the portfolio have not been generated under standardized conditions but, rather, represent the ongoing work of the student for the year. All the papers were developed by the student, with as much or as little time allocated to each of the Writing-as-a Process stages as he or she saw fit.

ASSESSING THE CASES

Is Case 1 an example of an authentic assessment? Yes. The students are asked to perform specific behaviors that are to be assessed: to prove that they can write, the students produce a writing sample. Is Case 2 an example of a performance assessment? Yes also. The portfolio contains numerous examples of actual student performance, although much of the structure associated with testing has been removed.

Is Case 1 an example of an authentic assessment? No. While the students are asked to perform the specific behavior to be assessed, the context is contrived. In real life, individuals seldom write under the conditions imposed during a standardized direct writing assessment. Is Case 2 an example of an authentic assessment? Yes. Performance is assessed in a context more like that encountered in real life; for example, students independently determined how long to spend on the various stages of the writing process, creating as many or as few rough drafts as they saw necessary to complete their final copies.

SOURCE: From C. A. Meyer (1992). What is the difference between authentic and performance assessment? *Educational Leadership*, 49, 8, pp. 39–40. Used with permission.

Figure 7-6   The learning experiences form

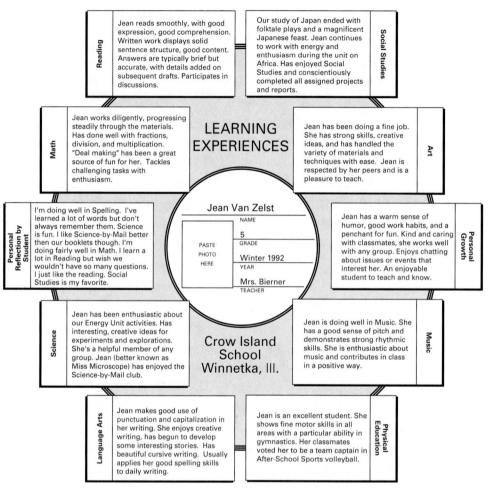

SOURCE: From E. A. Hebert (1992). Portfolios invite reflection—from students and staff, *Educational Leadership*, 49, 8, p. 60. Used with permission.

stration be in a real-life setting. Carol Meyer, an evaluation expert from the Beaverton, Oregon, Public Schools provides two examples to show the difference between authentic and regular performance assessments. These are illustrated in Figure 7-5.

Student Portfolios and Narrative Descriptions

Closely related to performance and authentic assessment is the use of student **portfolios.** Many of you are already aware of the portfolio process in that it has been used in various fields of the visual

arts for a long time. It is common practice for painters, graphic designers, and cartoonists, for example, to select illustrative pieces of their work and organize it into a portfolio which can be used to demonstrate their abilities to potential clients or employers. Often actors, musicians, and models use the same process.

Some schools, such as those in Winnetka, Illinois, and Manhatten, Kansas, have students develop portfolios to both assess and to report student achievement. The portfolio in these schools consists of a sample of artifacts, journal entries, and reflections that represent what the student has done and can do across all subject areas. In both Winnetka and Manhatten students prepare their portfolios to be shared with parents and are guided by such questions as:

How has my writing changed since last year?

What do I know about numbers now that I didn't know in September?

What is unique about my portfolio?

The idea here is to have students prepare their portfolios so that students "reflect on their own learning" (Hebert, 1992, p. 61). In addition, the teachers in Winnetka have combined portfolios, student reflections, and their own judgments into a visual reporting device, which is illustrated in Figure 7-6.

Assessing Group Effort and Individually Contracted Work

In Chapter 11, you will read about cooperative learning procedures where students are awarded points and grades for their work in teams and for their individual work. These procedures hold good potential for reducing the destructive process of comparing students with their peers and for reducing excessive competition.

There is also more and more interest among educators today in using criterion-referenced evaluations. For instance, the creators and developers of mastery learning (Bloom, 1976; Guskey and Gates, 1986), the Keller plan (Keller, 1966), or individualized prescribed instruction (IPI) have shown how learning materials for some subjects can be broken down into smaller units of study and how students can be given the opportunity to work toward a specified objective (criterion) until they have mastered it. Grades under these systems are determined not by comparing students with their peers but by the number of objectives they have mastered. Systems where teachers make contracts with individual students allow each student to compete with himself or herself on mutually agreed-upon criteria rather than compete with others. Grading for team effort and for individually contracted work, however, are difficult processes for teachers to implement by themselves. These experiments run strongly against current norms and traditions, and they require schoolwide policies and collegial support to be successful.

Experimenting with New Approaches

Some beginning teachers will find themselves in schools where a great deal of experimentation is going on with alternative assessments procedures. Others will find more traditional approaches being used. Alone, without the assistance of colleagues, it is doubtful that beginning teachers can implement a complete alternative classroom assessment system. They can, however, experiment with pieces of alternative assessments. For instance, a science teacher could devise a few performance tests, such as the paper towel experiment described earlier, or a language arts or English teacher could make part of a student's grade depend on the performance of particular authentic writing tasks. Some use of portfolios would benefit almost every grade level in every subject area. These steps would be movements in the right direction as your generation of teachers works to find better and fairer ways to assess and make judgments about the work of students.

SUMMARY

- Assessment and evaluation can be defined as functions performed by teachers to make wise decisions about their instruction and about their students. A fairly large portion of the teacher's time is consumed with assessment and evaluation processes. The consequences of testing and grading students are immense. They can determine the colleges students attend, the careers open to them, and the lifestyles they ultimately maintain.
- There is an extensive knowledge base about the technical aspects of assessment and evaluation.
- Evaluation specialists make key distinctions between formative and summative evaluation. Formative evaluation information is collected prior to or during instruction and is used to inform teachers about their students' prior knowledge and to make judgments about lesson effectiveness. Summative evaluation information is collected after instruction and is used to summarize how students have performed and to determine grades.
- Because the decisions made are so important, it is essential that the information used by teachers to make judgments be of high quality. Measurement specialists use two technical terms to de-

scribe the quality of assessment and evaluation information: reliability and validity. Reliability refers to the ability of a test or measurement device to produce consistent scores or information for persons who take the test more than once over a period of time. Validity refers to the ability of a test or other device to measure what it claims to measure.

- Studies have shown that external rewards, such as grades, can provide a strong incentive for students to perform work and can affect student learning. Studies have also shown that external rewards can sometimes have negative effects, particularly with tasks students find intrinsically interesting anyway.

- Schoolwide assessment programs include the use of norm- and criterion-referenced tests normally chosen and administered by district specialists. Norm-referenced tests evaluate a particular student's performance by comparing it to the performance of some other well-defined group of students. Criterion-referenced tests measure student performance against some agreed-upon criterion.

- It is important that teachers understand the advantages and disadvantages of various types of schoolwide assessment procedures and be able to communicate these to students and their parents.

- The teacher's own classroom assessment program includes features for collecting information which can be used to diagnose students' prior knowledge and skills, to provide students with corrective feedback, and to make accurate judgments about student achievement.

- A variety of guidelines exist for teachers to follow as they construct tests to measure student learning and as they make judgments and assign grades for student work. General principles for test construction consist of making test items in harmony with instructional objectives, covering all learning tasks, making tests valid and reliable, interpreting test results with care, and using the appropriate test items.

- A table of specification is a device invented by evaluation specialists to help teachers determine how much space to allocate to various topics covered and to measure various levels of student cognitive processes.

- Teacher-made tests can consist of true-false, matching, fill-in-the-blanks, multiple-choice, and essay items. Each type has its own advantages and disadvantages.

- Teacher bias in judging student work from essay questions is an important issue. To reduce bias, teachers should make their expectations for essay answers clear to students, write sample answers ahead of time, and use techniques to reduce expectancy effects.

- When giving tests, effective teachers find ways to reduce test anxiety on the part of students, organize their learning environments for conducive test taking, make instructions clear, and avoid undue competition.

- Grading "on a curve" and grading to "criterion or mastery" are the two major approaches to grading used by classroom teachers. Each approach has its advantages as well as its shortcomings.

- Guidelines such as making sure there is congruence between test items and what is being taught, testing frequently, testing at all levels, being fair and impartial, and communicating clearly about testing and grading procedures help teachers devise effective assessment and evaluation programs in their classrooms.

KEY TERMS

assessment
evaluation
formative evaluation
summative evaluation
reliability
validity
extrinsic rewards
standardized tests
norm-referenced tests
criterion-referenced tests
prior knowledge
table of specifications
objective test
essay test
holistic scoring
grading on a curve
criterion-referenced grading
performance assessment
authentic assessment
student portfolio

BOOKS FOR THE PROFESSIONAL

American Educational Research Association, American Psychological Association, and National Council on Measurement in Education (1985). *Standards for educational and psychological testing.* Washington, D.C.: American Psychological Association. This important resource for teachers outlines the technical standards for test construction and for using test results.

Gronlund, N. E., and Linn, M. (1990). *Measurement and evaluation in teaching* (6th ed.). New York: Macmillan. One of the most well-written and complete works on classroom evaluation, this book includes rationale and principles behind testing, as well as ample practical advice.

Mehrens, W. A., and Lehmann, I. J. (1984). *Measurement and evaluation in education and psychology* (3d ed.). New York: Holt, Rinehart & Winston. This book introduces the topic of measurement and evaluation with a good section devoted to helping teachers develop their own tests.

Mitchell, R. (1992). *Testing for learning: How new approaches to evaluation can improve American schools.* New York: The Free Press. This highly readable and up-to-date account of new approaches to student evaluation includes examples of best practice and presents the issues raised by different approaches to evaluation.

Perrone, V. (1991). *Expanding student assessment.* Alexandria, Va.: Association for Supervision and Curriculum Development. "The message underlying all the chapters of this book is that we must move assessment activities closer to the actual work of teachers and children; we must make classrooms the starting point for linking learning to large educational social purposes" (p. 164).

LEARNING AIDS FOR PLANNING, OBSERVATION, AND REFLECTION

- Assessing My Assessment and Evaluation Skills
- Interviewing Teachers about Their Evaluation and Grading Procedures
- Constructing a Table of Specification
- Analyzing Teacher-Made Tests
- Reflecting on the Future of Assessment and Evaluation

ASSESSING MY ASSESSMENT AND EVALUATION SKILLS

PURPOSE: To help you assess your level of understanding and skill in various aspects of assessment and evaluation.

DIRECTIONS: Check the level of understanding or skill you perceive you have for the various concepts and teaching tasks associated with classroom evaluation and grading.

UNDERSTANDING OR SKILL	LEVEL OF UNDERSTANDING OR SKILL		
	HIGH	MEDIUM	LOW
My understanding of			
Effects of grading	————	————	————
Teacher bias in grading	————	————	————
Importance of grades to parents	————	————	————
Schoolwide use of standardized tests	————	————	————
Norm- and criterion-referenced tests	————	————	————
Principles of testing and grading	————	————	————
My ability to			
Diagnose students' prior knowledge	————	————	————
Provide corrective feedback to students	————	————	————
Construct essay tests	————	————	————
Construct objective tests	————	————	————
Score tests free from bias	————	————	————
Help reduce test anxiety for students	————	————	————
Develop a "fair" grading system	————	————	————

INTERVIEWING TEACHERS ABOUT THEIR EVALUATION AND GRADING PROCEDURES

PURPOSE: Using appropriate testing and grading procedures is an important challenge for beginning teachers. This tool is to help you to gain practical knowledge about the testing and grading practices currently being used by teachers.

DIRECTIONS: Interview several teachers using the questions listed below. You may wish to select teachers at different levels: for example, one elementary, one middle school or junior high, and one high school teacher. Or you may wish to select teachers from different subject areas: for example, history, English, physical education, math, biology.

1. What would you say is the overall philosophy that guides your evaluation and grading program?

   _____

   _____

   _____

2. What aspects of testing and grading do you find most difficult?

   _____

   _____

   _____

3. How much of what you do in testing and grading is influenced by schoolwide or district policies? Can you give me examples? May I see (or have) a copy of the report card used in your school?

   _____

   _____

   _____

4. Since you have been teaching, have you observed any changes in attitudes and procedures associated with testing and grading? How about students—have their attitudes
changed?

_____

Have parents' attitudes changed? _____

_____

Have specific procedures used in your school changed?

_____

_____

5. If you had a magic wand and could make anything happen, what would you decree in
regard to student evaluation and testing? Why do you choose these actions?

_____

_____

_____

CONSTRUCTING A TABLE OF SPECIFICATION

PURPOSE: A question that confronts all teachers is what to cover on a test. Students want to know what will be on the test so they know what to study. Teachers want to make sure they test various levels of student understanding; they also want to make their tests congruent with their instructional objectives. The table of specification is one device developed by evaluation specialists to assist with test construction. This tool has been designed to give you practice with making a table of specification.

DIRECTIONS: Select a unit from a curriculum guide in your subject area or two or three chapters from a textbook that you might use. If you have previously developed a unit of work on your own, you may wish to use it. Using the table below, place in the left-hand column the major content or topics covered in the guide, textbook, or unit of work. The various categories of student behaviors and cognitive processing have been listed along the top of the table. After you have listed the major topics, go into the table and make decisions about how many items you might allocate among the topics and the levels of understanding.

Unit of work covered: _____

Anticipated time for taking the test: _____

	STUDENT BEHAVIORS AND COGNITIVE PROCESSES					
	KNOWS/RECALL OF			HIGHER-LEVEL		
TOPICS/CONTENT	TERMS	FACTS	PRINCIPLES	COMPREHENSION	APPLICATION	EVALUATION
_____	____	____	_____	_____	_____	_____
_____	____	____	_____	_____	_____	_____
_____	____	____	_____	_____	_____	_____
_____	____	____	_____	_____	_____	_____
_____	____	____	_____	_____	_____	_____
_____	____	____	_____	_____	_____	_____
_____	____	____	_____	_____	_____	_____
_____	____	____	_____	_____	_____	_____

INTRODUCTION

The next six chapters of *Learning to Teach* focus directly on what most people think of as teaching—the actual face-to-face interaction between the teacher and the learner. Each chapter considers one of the following six basic approaches to instruction: (1) teaching information through presentation, (2) teaching concepts for higher-level thinking, (3) teaching skills through direct instruction, (4) teaching social and academic skills through cooperative learning, (5) promoting verbal interaction through discussion, and (6) higher-level thinking through inquiry teaching.

These approaches are labeled **teaching models,** although one of several other terms—such as *teaching strategies, teaching methods*, or *teaching principles*—could have been chosen. The label "teaching model" was selected for two important reasons.

First, the concept *"model"* implies something larger than a particular strategy, method, or procedure. For example, as used here, the term *teaching model* encompasses a broad, overall approach to instruction rather than a specific strategy, such as discussion or seatwork, that can be used with any of the models. Models of teaching have some attributes that specific strategies and methods do not have. The attributes of a model are a coherent theoretical basis and rationale made explicit by its creators and developers; a point of view and an orientation about what students should learn and how they learn; and recommended teaching behaviors and classroom structures for bringing about different types of learning.

Second, the concept of the teaching model can serve as an important communication device for teachers. Joyce, Weil, and Showers (1992), as you saw in Chapter 1, classified various approaches to teaching according to their instructional intents, their syntaxes, and the nature of their learning environments. Instructional intents are the types of learning goals a model has been designed to achieve. The use of a particular model helps the teacher achieve some goals, but not others. A model's **syntax** is the overall flow of a lesson's activity. The **learning environment** (called social system by Joyce, Weil, and Showers) is the context in which any teaching act must be carried out.

Although there is nothing magic about these words or this classification system, they provide a language for communicating about various kinds of teaching activities, when they should occur, and why. Take the idea of syntax, for instance. It is used to define the major steps or phases of a lesson based on a particular model. It specifies what kind of teacher and student actions should occur and in what order. The syntaxes of the various models differ, and it is these differences that must be understood if the models are to be used effectively.

In describing the six models in the chapters that follow, we might seem to suggest that there is only one correct way to use a particular model. In some respects this is true. If teachers deviate too far from the model's syntax or environmental demands, they are not using the model. On the other hand, once teachers have mastered a particular model, they often need to adapt it to their own particular teaching styles and to the particular group of students with whom they are working. As with most other aspects of teaching, models are guides for thinking and talking about teaching. They should not be viewed as recipes to follow.

There is a substantial knowledge base for the interactive functions of teaching that can provide a guide for practice. To carry out the interactive functions of teaching, however, you will also rely on the wisdom that has been accumulated by experienced teachers over the years. You will find that many of the interactive functions of teaching overlap with what has already been described in previous chapters. Part of the excitement and challenge in learning to teach is to figure out the complexities of teaching, which the organizational pattern of a book cannot portray with complete accuracy.

Chapter Outline

PERSPECTIVE AND RATIONALE
* Structure and Organization of Knowledge * Meaningful
Verbal Learning * Cognitive Psychology of Learning
SAMPLING THE KNOWLEDGE BASE
* Prior Knowledge and Set Induction * Using Advance
Organizers * Teacher Clarity * Teacher Enthusiasm
MAIN FEATURES OF PRESENTATION
* Instructional Effects of the Model * Syntax of the
Model * Structure of the Learning Environment
PROCEDURES FOR EFFECTIVE PRESENTATION
* Preinstructional Tasks * Conducting the Lesson
* Postinstructional Tasks

CHAPTER 8

Presentation

Formal presentations by teachers comprise one-sixth to one-fourth of all classroom time. The amount of time devoted to presenting and explaining information increases at the higher grade levels of elementary school, in middle schools, and in high schools (Dunkin and Biddle, 1974). Some educators have argued that too much time is devoted to teachers talking, and over the past two decades considerable effort has gone into creating models aimed at decreasing the amount of teacher talk. Nonetheless, formal presentation of information remains the most popular model of teaching, and the amount of time devoted to it has remained relatively stable over time.

The popularity of presenting and explaining is not surprising since the most widely held objectives for education at the present time are those associated with the acquisition and retention of information. Curricula in schools have been structured around bodies of information organized as science, mathematics, English, and the social sciences. Consequently, curriculum guides, textbooks, and tests routinely used by teachers are similarly organized. Experienced teachers know that exposition is an effective way of helping students acquire the array of information society believes it is important for them to know.

The purpose of this chapter is to introduce the **presentation teaching model** and tell how to use it effectively. Judgments will not be made about the ideal amount of time a teacher should devote to this model. Instead, the model will be described as a valuable teaching approach that can be used in all subject areas and at all grade levels. The point of view taken here is that the appropriate use of the presentation model is situational; that is, its use depends on the objective the teacher is striving to achieve and the particular students with whom the teacher is working.

Fortunately, the knowledge base on teacher presentation and explanation is fairly well developed. Beginning teachers can learn this model quite easily. As you read this chapter and study the model, you will find much that is familiar. Some of the material you already know from speech classes taken in high school or college. Some of the difficulties of presenting you know from informal talks or speeches you have made. Although the goals of public speaking and classroom presentations are quite different, many of the basic communication skills are the same. As in previous chapters, this chapter first provides a framework for thinking about presenting and explaining information to students, followed by summaries of some of the research that supports this model. The chapter concludes with a discussion of procedures for teachers and learning aids to help you understand and practice the model.

PERSPECTIVE AND RATIONALE

Three complementary ideas have come together over the past three decades to provide the rationale and the pedagogy for the presentation model of teaching. These include: (1) the concept of **structure of knowledge,** (2) the psychology of **meaningful verbal learning,** and (3) ideas from **cognitive psychology** associated with the representation and acquisition of knowledge. It is important to understand the ideas underlying these three topics because they provide the basis on which teachers choose, organize, and present information to students. They also support several features of the other models presented later in this section.

Structure and Organization of Knowledge

Knowledge of the world has been organized around various subject areas called disciplines. History is an example of a discipline that organizes knowledge using temporal concepts; biology organizes information and ideas about living things and physics about the physical world. The clustering of courses by academic departments in college catalogs is one illustration of the wide array of disciplines which currently exist. The classification of books in libraries according to subject matter under the Dewey decimal or Library of Congress system is another.

The disciplines, as they are defined at any point in time, constitute the resources on which most teachers and curriculum developers draw in making decisions about what knowledge should be taught to students. Over two decades ago Ralph Taylor made this observation in a speech at a conference on curriculum:

> From the standpoint of the curriculum, the disciplines should be viewed primarily as a resource that can be drawn upon for the education of students. Hence, we want to understand these resources at their best. And we, I think properly, are often fearful that some of the second-hand treatment that we get of these subjects really prostitutes them—does not represent them at their best. Certainly these disciplines at their best are not simply an encyclopedic collection of facts to be memorized but rather they are an active effort to make sense out of some portion of the world or of life. (Ford and Pugno, 1964, p. 4)

During the 1950s several scholars and curriculum theorists started to study how disciplines were organized and what that organization meant to instruction. A little book written by Jerome Bruner in 1960 called *The Process of Education* highlighted this research. This inquiry produced the idea that each discipline has a structure consisting of key concepts that define the discipline. Figure 8-1 shows a partial knowledge structure for information about American government.

Note that the illustration shows how the structure of government can be viewed as having several major ideas with a variety of subideas such as citizen rights, powers given to the states, and the various branches of government. It is not appropriate here to go into detail about the knowledge structures of various disciplines. However, it is important to emphasize that such structures exist and that they become a means for organizing information about topics, for dividing information into various categories, and for showing relationships among various categories of information.

The teaching implications of this structuring of knowledge are clear—the key ideas supporting each structure should be taught to students instead of lists of disparate facts or bits of information. For example, Bruner (1962) argued that knowing about a house "is not a matter of knowing about a collection of nails, shingles, wallboards, and windows" (p. 77). It is the total concept of house that is significant and important. The same could be said with examples from mathematics, economics, or botany.

Meaningful Verbal Learning

David Ausubel (1963), an educational psychologist, did some interesting ground-breaking work at about the same time. He was particularly interested in the way knowledge is organized hierarchically and how the human mind organizes ideas. He explained that at any point in time a learner has an existing "organization, stability, and clarity of

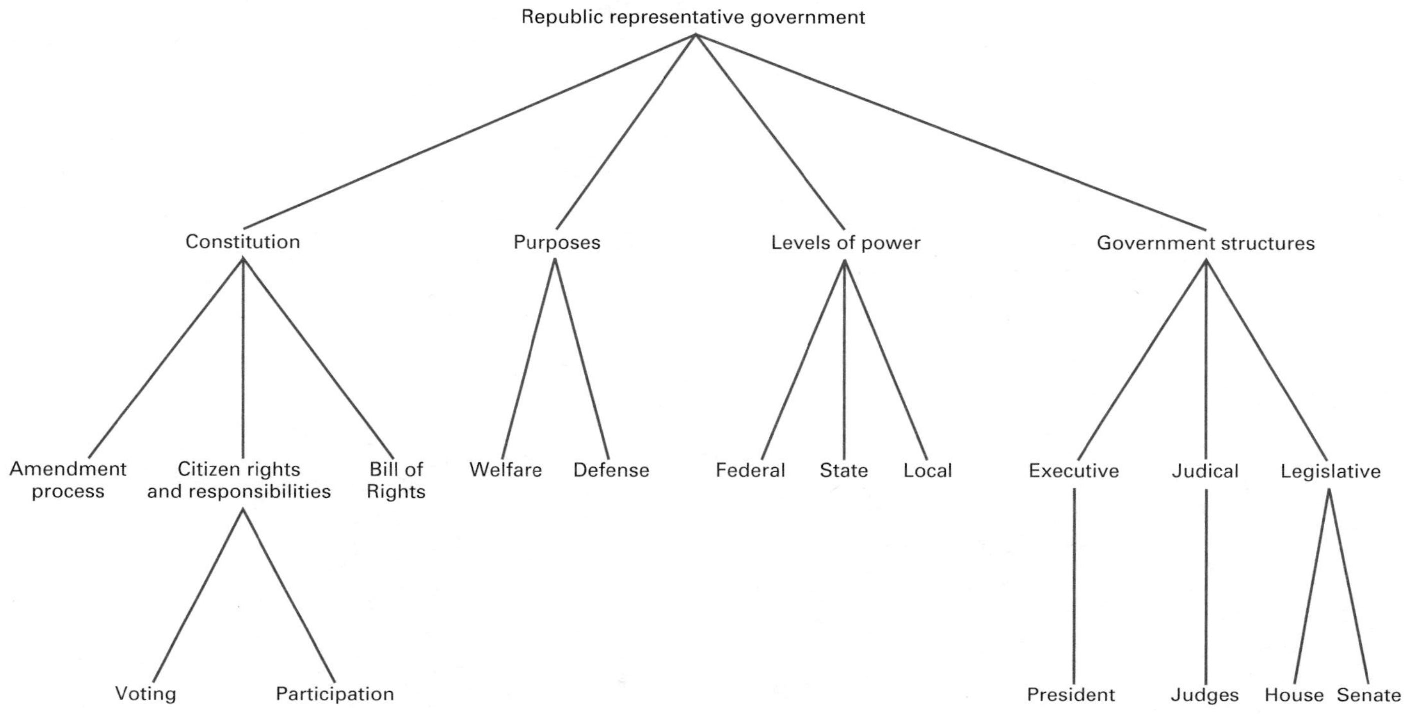

Figure 8-1 A partial structure of knowledge for representative government

knowledge in a particular subject-matter field" (p. 26). He called this organization a **cognitive structure** and believed that this structure determined the learner's ability to deal with new ideas and relationships. Meaning can emerge from new materials only if they tie into existing cognitive structures of prior learning.

Ausubel saw the primary function of formal education as the organizing of information for students and the presenting of ideas in clear and precise ways. The principal function of pedagogy, according to Ausubel, is "the art and science of presenting ideas and information meaningfully and effectively—so that clear, stable and unambiguous meanings emerge and . . . [are] retained over a long period of time as an organized body of knowledge" (Ausubel, 1963, p. 81). For this learning to occur, according to Ausubel, the teacher should create two conditions: (1) present learning materials in a potentially meaningful form, with major and unifying ideas and principles, consistent with contemporary scholarship, highlighted rather than merely listed as facts; and (2) find ways to anchor the new learning materials to the learners' prior knowledge and cognitive structures and ready the students' minds so that they can receive new information.

The major pedagogical strategy proposed by Ausubel (1963) is the use of **advance organizers.** It is the job of an advance organizer to "delineate clearly, precisely, and explicitly the principal similarities and differences between the ideas in a new learning passage, on the one hand, and existing related concepts in cognitive structure on the other" (p. 83). More specific details about how to construct and present advance organizers will be provided later in this chapter.

Cognitive Psychology of Learning

A third stream of inquiry that helps explain how information should be presented to students grew out of the rapidly expanding field of cognitive psychology. Its frame of reference is important to teachers because it provides ways for thinking about how knowledge is represented, and it emphasizes that one of the important goals of teaching is to facilitate active thinking and mental processing. As you read the key ideas below, you will ob-

serve how they are connected in many ways to Bruner's earlier concept of structure of knowledge and Ausubel's ideas about meaningful verbal learning.

Also, not unlike Ausubel's ideas about knowledge structure is a currently formulated theory called schema theory. Cognitive psychologists use the label "schema" to define the ways people organize information about particular subjects and how this organization influences their processing of new information and ideas. Individuals' schema differ in important ways, and **schemata** held about math or science or any other topic, for example, prepare the learner to process new information and to see relationships. The more complete knowledge structures become on a particular topic the easier it becomes to see connections and more abstract relationships.

Ellen Gagné (1985) organized the ideas and research in the field of cognitive psychology that apply directly to teaching. The discussion that follows relies heavily on her important work and her definitions of three concepts: knowledge types, knowledge representation, and information processing.

TWO TYPES OF KNOWLEDGE

Attributing the idea to Gilbert Ryle (1949) and Robert Gagné (1977), Ellen Gagné distinguished between two types of knowledge: declarative knowledge and procedural knowledge. **Declarative knowledge** is knowledge about something or knowledge that something is the case. **Procedural knowledge** is knowledge about how to do something. Examples of declarative knowledge, again using the illustration of government presented in Figure 8-1, would be information about the legislative branch of government; for example, it has two chambers, the House and the Senate, and senators are elected for 6-year terms. Procedural knowledge about the same subject would be knowledge about how to go to the polling place to vote on Election Day or how to write a letter to a senator.

This distinction between the two types of knowledge is an important one for teachers. Declarative and procedural knowledge are acquired differently by students and require different teaching approaches. This chapter, for instance, deals mainly with what teachers do to help students acquire de-

Figure 8-2   Hypothetical propositional network

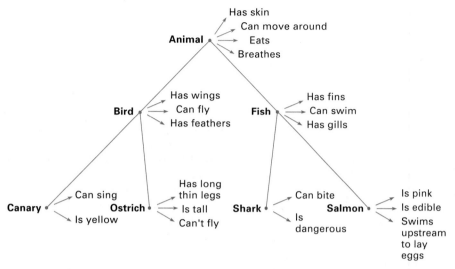

SOURCE: From A. M. Collins and M. R. Quillian (1969), Retrieval time from semantic memory. *Journal of Verbal Learning and Verbal Behavior, 8,* 241. Used with permission.

clarative knowledge—new information about some topic, for instance. Conversely, Chapter 10 focuses on what teachers do to help students acquire procedural knowledge.

KNOWLEDGE REPRESENTATION

Cognitive psychologists say that humans process knowledge in terms of basic units, called propositions or ideas. According to Gagné (1985):

> One of the most important characteristics of any given unit of information is its relationship to other units. Our knowledge of such relationships underlies our ability to make analogies and to see other types of connections. Such abilities are important in novel problem-solving situations.
>
> Because the relationships among sets of information are a crucial aspect of intelligence, it is important to have a way of representing them. One way is the form of **propositional networks,** which are sets of interrelated propositions. (p. 40)

Figure 8-2 shows a hypothetical propositional network for information about certain categories of living things. The illustration in Figure 8-2 is similar to the structure of knowledge concept introduced earlier and to Ausubel's concept of meaningful verbal learning. Without going into further detail on this topic, it is important to note that just as scholars organize academic disciplines according to a structure, so too do learners organize knowledge into propositions and networks. Although cognitive psychologists are not in complete agreement about the exact nature of these networks, the important point for teachers is that information is stored in some type of propositional network and, as will be described later, these networks actively filter new information and thereby determine how well new information presented by teachers will be integrated and retained by learners.

PRIOR KNOWLEDGE: WORKING AND LONG-TERM MEMORY

A final concept from cognitive psychology that is important to teachers as they plan and present new information to students is the concept of working and long-term memory.

New ideas and information enter the mind

through one of the senses—eyes or ears, for example—and are noted first by the learner's **working memory.** Working memory, according to Gagné (1985), is the "place where conscious mental work is done. For example, if you are solving the problem 26 × 32 mentally, you would hold the intermediate products 52 and 78 in working memory and add them together there" (p. 10). That part of the environment and mental activity of which the learner is actually aware at a particular moment is working memory.

Information in working memory may soon be forgotten unless stored more deeply in **long-term memory.** Long-term memory can be likened to a computer. Information must first be coded before it can be stored and, although stored for perhaps a lifetime, cannot be retrieved unless first given appropriate cues. Information or ideas stored in long-term memory must also be retrieved to working memory before it can be used.

According to Gagné and White (1978), long-term memory stores four types of information: verbal knowledge, intellectual skills, images, and episodes. Verbal knowledge is the declarative and propositional knowledge described above. Intellectual skill is the procedural knowledge for performing intellectual tasks such as the skill to write a sentence. Images and episodes are pictorial representations of certain information and memories of certain events in which the learner has participated. Figure 8-3 shows how working and long-term memory interact in instructional settings.

Teaching principles about presenting information growing out of ideas from cognitive psychology are important for teachers in four ways. One, it is important to know that knowledge is organized and structured around basic propositions and unifying ideas. However, individuals differ in the way their knowledge about particular topics is organized. Two, students' abilities to learn new ideas depend on their prior knowledge and existing cognitive structures. Three, the primary tasks for teachers in helping students acquire knowledge are: (1) organizing learning materials in a thoughtful and skillful way, (2) providing students with advance organizers that will help anchor and integrate new learning, and (3) providing them with cues for drawing information from their long-term to their working memories. Finally, remember that cognitive structures change as a result of new informa-

tion and thus become the basis for developing new cognitive structures.

SAMPLING THE KNOWLEDGE BASE

The knowledge base on presenting and explaining information to learners has been developed by researchers working in several different fields, especially cognitive psychology and information processing, as described in the previous section. Other research comes from the study of teaching and has focused on such topics as set induction, use of prior knowledge, and advance organizers. Still other work has looked at teacher clarity and enthusiasm and how these attributes affect student learning. Since it is impossible to provide full coverage of this extensive research base, only selected works have been highlighted in this section.

Prior Knowledge and Set Induction

Research has been conducted, particularly during the past 10 years, on the influence of **prior knowledge** for learning to read, learning to use new information, and learning to write. In general this research points toward the importance of prior knowledge for learning new information and new skills. For example, a particularly interesting study on the influence of prior knowledge on children's production of narrative was conducted by Mosenthal and his colleagues (1985). The researchers selected a representative group of fourth-grade teachers and picked two whose teaching styles were characterized by asking questions to elicit prior learning from students and two who did not do much of this. Each teacher was then asked to conduct a writing lesson in his or her class. The lesson consisted of presenting students with a series of 13 pictures representing a baseball episode and asking students to write a story about the picture sequences. The results from this study showed that students in the classrooms where teachers made use of their students' prior knowledge produced stories that were generally more complex and creative than those produced by students in the other classrooms.

One important teaching skill for helping students use their prior knowledge is a skill called **set induction.** Set induction is a technique used by teachers at the beginning of a presentation to pre-

Figure 8-3   An example of working and long-term memory

Suppose that a second-grade teacher wants Joe to learn the fact that the capital of Texas is Austin. The teacher asks Joe, "What is the capital of Texas?" and Joe says, "I don't know." At the same time Joe may set up an expectancy that he is about to learn the capital of Texas, which will cause him to pay attention. The teacher then says, "The capital of Texas is Austin." Joe's ears receive this message along with other sounds such as the other pupils' speech and traffic outside the school.

All of the sounds that Joe hears are translated into electrochemical impulses and sent to the sensory register. The pattern that the capital of Texas is Austin is selected for entry into working memory, but other sound patterns are not entered.

Joe may then code the fact that the capital of Texas is Austin by associating it with other facts that he already knows about Austin (e.g., that it is a big city and that he once visited it). This coding process causes the new fact to be entered into long-term memory. If Joe has already developed special memory strategies (which is somewhat unlikely for a second grader), his executive control process would direct the coding process to use these special strategies.

The next day Joe's teacher might ask him, "What is the capital of Texas?" This question would be received and selected for entry into WM. There it would provide cues for retrieving the answer from LTM. A copy of the answer would be used by the response generator to organize the speech acts that produce the sounds, "Austin is the capital of Texas." At this point Joe's expectancy that he would learn the capital of Texas has been confirmed.

SOURCE: From E. D. Gagné, *The cognitive psychology of school learning*, p. 12. Copyright © 1985 by D. Reprinted by permission of Little, Brown and Company.

---

pare students to learn and to establish a communicative link between the learners and the information about to be presented. Several informative studies have been conducted on this topic. One of the most interesting was conducted in Australia by R. F. Schuck in the early 1980s. In a rather sophisticated experimental study, Schuck (1981) randomly assigned 120 ninth-grade biology students to two groups. Teachers for the experimental group were given 4 hours of training on set induction techniques. When the experimental students' achievement was compared to that of the control students, Schuck found that the use of set induction had a clear impact on student achievement. This impact existed not only immediately following instruction but held up when students were tested 24 to 26 weeks later.

As you will see later, set induction is not the same as an advance organizer, although both serve the similar purpose of using students' prior knowledge. Through set induction, teachers help students retrieve appropriate information and intellectual skills from long-term memory and get it ready for use as new information and skills are introduced.

More information about and examples of set induction will be provided later.

Using Advance Organizers

As you read in the previous section, Ausubel saw the use of an **advance organizer** as a means to help make information meaningful to students. For Ausubel, an advance organizer consists of statements made by teachers just prior to actual presentation of the learning materials. These statements are at a higher level of abstraction than the subsequent information. Later in this chapter advance organizers are defined more precisely; however, here it is important to say that advance organizers help students use prior knowledge just as establishing set does. They differ, however, in that they are tied more tightly to the subsequent information and provide an anchor for later learning.

Research Summary 8-1 presents Ausubel's seminal work on advance organizers, first published in 1960.

Since David Ausubel first published his results,

RESEARCH SUMMARY 8-1

Ausubel, D. P.   (1960). The use of advance organizers in the learning and retention of meaningful verbal material. *Journal of Educational Psychology, 51, 267–272.*

PROBLEM: Does giving students an advance organizer to serve as an intellectual scaffold really facilitate learning and retention of unfamiliar but meaningful verbal learning materials? David Ausubel asked and studied this question over 30 years ago. This original study sparked a research interest in this problem and subsequently led to a substantial knowledge base on the effects of using advance organizers and the importance of tying learning materials to the existing cognitive structures of students.

SAMPLE AND SETTING: Ausubel studied 110 senior undergraduate students (78 women and 32 men) at the University of Illinois. The students were in teacher education and were enrolled in a course in educational psychology when they were asked to participate in the study.

PROCEDURES: The researcher designed a 2,500-word learning passage on the topic of the "metallurgical properties of carbon steel." Emphasis of the content of the learning materials according to the researcher was on "basic principles of the relationship between metallic grain structures, on the one hand, and temperature, carbon content, and rate of cooling on the other." This topic was chosen because it had been determined that it was one that most liberal arts and teacher education majors would not be familiar with, an important condition if the central hypothesis was to be tested. Subjects were divided into two groups, experimental and control. The groups were matched on the basis of ability to learn unfamiliar material (test score on another passage of comparable difficulty). Each group then received the following treatments.

- **Experimental group:**   The introduction to the steel learning materials for students in the experimental group contained a 500-word introductory passage with a substantive advance organizer—background material presented at a higher level of abstraction than information in the content of the materials to follow.
- **Control group:**   The introduction to the steel learning materials for students in the control group provided historically relevant material and information in a 500-word passage, but no advance organizer.

Both groups studied the learning materials for 35 minutes and then took a test on the materials 3 days later. The test consisted of 36 multiple-choice items covering the major principles and facts in the learning materials.

---

other psychologists and educational researchers have been actively testing his hypothesis. Walberg (1986) reported that from 1969 to 1979 advance organizers were the subject of 32 studies. Walberg also described a synthesis of research done by Luiten, Ames, and Aerson (1980) that identified over 135 studies on the effects of advance organizers. Although not all of the studies show the effectiveness of advance organizers, the findings seem to be consistent enough over time to recommend that teachers use advance organizers when presenting information to students.

TABLE 8-1 Retention Test Scores of Experimental and Control Groups on Learning Passage

GROUP	TYPE OF INTRODUCTION	MEAN	STANDARD DEVIATION
Experimental	Advanced organizer	16.7*	5.8
Control	Historical overview	14.1	5.4

* Significant at the .05 level.

POINTERS FOR READING RESEARCH: There are no new concepts introduced in Table 8-1. Ausubel's study is rather straightforward. However, as with many studies during this era, Ausubel's subjects were college students. Results stemming from this type of population do not necessarily generalize to younger students and those with varying backgrounds typical of most elementary and secondary schools. It was not until the 1970s that large numbers of researchers left their own college classrooms and conducted investigations in the schools themselves. This study is included here, regardless of its weaknesses, because of Ausubel's close association with the advance organizer model of teaching and because it has influenced so much later research.

RESULTS: Table 8-1 shows the test scores made by students in the experimental and control groups.

DISCUSSION AND IMPLICATIONS: As can be observed in Table 8-1, students who were given advance organizers before they read the 2,500-word passage on steel retained more information 3 days later as compared to students who were introduced to the learning materials with a historical passage. The weakness in Ausubel's study, as a test for the effectiveness of the advance organizer, is that the information was given to students in text, not verbally. Nonetheless, the idea is still the same. A word of caution: Ausubel's study should not be interpreted as proof that historical information is unimportant. Historical perspectives can be used, but they are not as effective as conceptual organizers in helping students integrate and retain meaningful verbal information.

Teacher Clarity

Using advance organizers, establishing set, and attending to prior learning all affect student learning. Another variable associated with the presentation of information that has been shown to influence student learning is teacher clarity. An important early study on the topic of teacher clarity was conducted by Hiller, Gisher, and Kaess (1969). They asked teachers to deliver two different 15-minute presentations to their students—one on Yugoslavia and the other on Thailand. Teachers were encouraged to make the presentations in their normal fashion. They studied five teacher presentation variables: verbal fluency, amount of information, knowledge structure cues, interest, and vagueness. The researchers found significant relationships on two factors: verbal fluency (clarity) and vagueness. The examples of vagueness or lack of clarity provided by the researchers were particularly enlightening.

> And the young author's name, although this isn't too important a thing to remember, is that it was a young author who wrote this. I'll put his name on the board anyway. Mihajlov wrote these articles. And someone has done something, that is like someone very similar had done, and there was another author whose name is, um, let's just remember there's another author. . . .
>
> But at the same time it's a relatively new country, rebuilding you see, and they put a lot of money into building roads and factories and so on and so you don't have a lot of consumer goods—shoes and so on. So, there are not a lot of these things available. There are, is a lot of money and so the dollar became worth a lot less. (p. 672)

It should be clear that teachers who present information in the above ways will give their students little chance of learning the materials. The researchers suggested that vagueness in a presentation most often indicates that the speaker does not know the information well or cannot remember the key points. This, of course, suggests several steps for teachers who are about to present information to their students: (1) make sure the content is thoroughly understood, (2) practice and commit the key ideas to memory prior to presentation, or (3) follow written notes very carefully.

In a review of the research done in the 1950s and 1960s, Rosenshine and Furst (1973) reported that "teacher clarity" was a specific teaching trait that showed up consistently as having an impact on student achievement. Similarly, when Walberg, Schiller, and Haertel (1979) reviewed the research from 1969 to 1979 they found seven studies that focused on teacher clarity. All seven showed a strong relationship between teacher clarity and student achievement.

Teacher Enthusiasm

A final aspect of presentation is **teacher enthusiasm.** This is an interesting concept for two reasons. First, enthusiasm is often confused with theatrics and its associated distractions, and second, the research on the relationship between teacher enthusiasm and student learning is mixed. The topic gives an opportunity to provide a concrete example of how conflicting evidence from research on an important aspect of teaching can lead to different guidelines for practice.

EFFECTS OF ENTHUSIASM

In 1970 Rosenshine reviewed the research on teacher enthusiasm and reported that it showed pretty consistent relationships between teacher enthusiasm and student learning. Since that time researchers have tried to study teacher enthusiasm with more precise designs and have developed training programs to help teachers become more enthusiastic in their presentations. For example, Collins (1978) developed and tested a training program that looked at a specific set of enthusiastic behaviors: rapid, uplifting, varied local delivery; dancing, wide-open eyes; frequent, demonstrative questions; varied, dramatic body movements; varied emotive facial expressions; selection of varied words, especially adjectives; ready, animated acceptance of ideas and feelings; and exuberant overall energy (Collins, 1978). Collins found that students in classes of enthusiasm-trained teachers did better than those in classes of untrained teachers.

However, in 1979 Bettencourt, one of Mark Gall's students at the University of Oregon, replicated Collins's study and could find no differences in achievement between enthusiasm-trained and untrained teachers. This led Bettencourt and Gall to go back and review several of the earlier studies on enthusiasm. Borg and Gall (1983) reported the following about this review:

> Four of the previous experiments had demonstrated a positive effect of teacher enthusiasm on student achievement. Only one . . . had found an absence of effect. We discovered that the few experiments with positive results have one feature in common. The comparison treatment (the no-training condition) in each

study required the teacher to purposefully act in a non-enthusiastic manner. For example, in one of the comparison treatments the teacher "read an entire speech from a manuscript" and "made no gestures or direct eye contact and held vocal inflection to a minimum" (Coats and Smidchens, 1966). In the two experiments reporting no effect, however, the comparison group were . . . allowed to use their natural teaching style. (p. 38)

It appears that some evidence exists that points to the importance of enthusiasm as an influence on student learning. However, the studies showing effects have pitted enthusiasm against "depressed enthusiasm," not against natural teaching styles. The exact nature of enthusiasm and how much of it to use remain unknown at the present time.

MAIN FEATURES OF PRESENTATION

The specific presentation model highlighted here is an adaptation of Ausubel's advance organizer model. This model requires the teacher to provide students with advance organizers prior to presenting new information and to make special efforts during and following a presentation to strengthen and extend student thinking. This particular approach was chosen for two reasons. One, the approach is compatible with current knowledge from cognitive psychology about the way people organize, process, and learn new information. Two, various components of the model have been carefully studied over the past 20 years, thus giving the model a substantial, if not always consistent, knowledge base.

As with other models of teaching presented in this book, the presentation model can be described by (1) its instructional effects, (2) its syntax, and (3) the structure of its learning environment. Each of these features was described in the introduction to this section and is used now to organize information about presentations made by teachers.

Instructional Effects of the Model

The **instructional effects** of the presentation model are clear and straightforward, namely, to help students acquire, assimilate, and retain information. The model also helps students build and expand their conceptual structures and develop specific habits for thinking about information. Objectives for teachers when they are using the presentation model are targeted toward what was described earlier as declarative knowledge as contrasted to procedural knowledge.

Syntax of the Model

There are four phases, or steps, for teachers to follow when presenting information to students. The flow proceeds from the teacher's initial introduction to the lesson by establishing set and presenting his or her objectives, through presentations of the advance organizer and the learning materials, to the conclusion with interactions aimed at extending and strengthening student thinking. Each phase and appropriate teacher behavior is described in Table 8-2.

Structure of the Learning Environment

In the presentation model, the teacher strives to structure the learning environment tightly. Except in phase 4, where the environment must facilitate student interaction, the teacher is an active presenter and expects students to be active listeners. Successful use of the model requires good conditions for presenting and listening, including appropriate facilities for use of audio and visual aides. The success of the model depends upon students' being sufficiently motivated to listen to what the teacher is saying. During formal presentations students should not be sharpening pencils, talking to neighbors, or working on other tasks. Creating an appropriate learning environment for this type of activity can in some settings be a very difficult task.

PROCEDURES FOR EFFECTIVE PRESENTATION

Understanding the theoretical and research bases underlying the teacher presentation model is not sufficient for its effective use. That requires expert execution of a set of decisions and behaviors during the preinstructional, interactive, and postinstruc-

Table 8-2 Syntax of the Presentation Model

PHASE	TEACHER BEHAVIOR
Phase 1: Present objectives and establish set	Teacher goes over the objectives of the lesson and gets students ready to learn.
Phase 2: Present advance organizer	Teacher presents advance organizer, making sure that it provides a framework for later learning materials and is connected to students' prior knowledge.
Phase 3: Present learning materials	Teacher presents learning materials, paying special attention to their logical ordering and meaningfulness to students.
Phase 4: Extend and strengthen student thinking	Teacher asks questions and elicits student responses to the presentation to extend student thinking and encourage precise and critical thinking.

tional phases of teaching. In this section guidelines for using the presentation model appropriately and effectively are described.

Preinstructional Tasks

Except for people who are really shy, it is quite easy to get up in front of a class of students and talk for 20 to 30 minutes. *Talking, however, is not teaching.* Making decisions about what content to include in a presentation and how to organize content so it is logical and meaningful to students takes extensive preparation by the teacher. Three planning tasks are most important: (1) choosing objectives and content for the presentation, (2) determining students' prior knowledge and cognitive structures, and (3) selecting appropriate and powerful advance organizers and procedures for set induction.

CHOOSING CONTENT

Most beginning secondary school teachers will still be learning the subjects they teach; many elementary teachers will never completely master all the subjects included in the contemporary elementary curriculum. For teachers who are still in the process of mastering their teaching specialties, the recommendation for choosing content is to rely on the frameworks and structures provided in curriculum guides. Most guides have been written by subject matter specialists to conform to the subject's knowledge structure and are based on experienced teachers' estimates of students' prior knowledge. If good guides do not exist in a particular school sys-

tem, they can be found in the libraries of most major universities or resource centers within state departments of education. Whether beginning teachers use their own knowledge of the subject or knowledge that has been organized by others, several principles can assist in choosing content for a particular presentation or series of presentations.

Economy. It has been observed that most presentations by teachers contain too much information and too much information that is irrelevant. Students are hampered from learning key ideas because of verbal clutter. Bruner (1962), among others, says teachers should strive for economy in their presentations and explanations. Economy means being very careful about the amount of information presented at any one time; it also means providing concise summaries of key ideas several times during the presentation. The economy principle argues for taking a difficult concept and making it clear and simple for students, not taking an easy concept and making it difficult through vagueness and the use of too many words. It means helping students examine a few critical ideas in depth rather than bombarding them with unrelated facts which have little chance for impacting learning.

Power. Bruner also describes how the principle of power should be applied when selecting content for a presentation. A powerful presentation is one where basic concepts from the subject area are chosen and presented in straightforward and logical ways. It is through logical organization that students come to see relationships between specific

Figure 8-4 The causal factors affecting rice growing

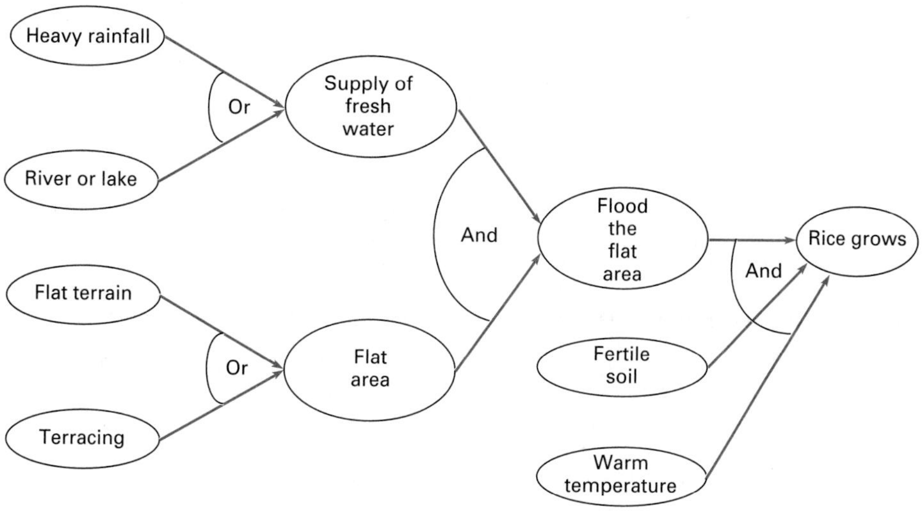

SOURCE: From A. Collins (1977), Processes in acquiring knowledge. In R. C. Anderson, R. J. Spiro, and W. E. Montague (eds.). *Schooling and the acquisition of knowledge.* Hillsdale, N.J.: Lawrence Erlbaum Assoc. Publishers, Fig. 1, p. 341.

facts and the interrelationships among the important concepts that make up any topic. To achieve economy and power in a presentation depends not so much on the delivery style of the teacher as it does on planning. In fact, a carefully organized presentation read in monotone might be more effective in producing student learning than a dynamic presentation void of powerful ideas and logical organization, even though students may enjoy the latter more.

Conceptual Mapping. A third idea that is useful in helping decide what to teach is that of **conceptual mapping**. Posner and Rudnitsky (1986) have written that "conceptual maps are like road maps, but they are concerned with relationships among ideas, rather than places. Conceptual maps . . . help you to 'get your bearings' . . . to clarify the kinds of ideas you want taught—so you can proceed toward your destination of real student learning" (p. 25). To make a conceptual map, you identify the key ideas associated with any topic and arrange these ideas in some logical pattern. Sometimes conceptual maps are hierarchical diagrams, like the one in Figure 8-1, displayed earlier in this chapter. Sometimes they focus on causal relations, such as the conceptual map displayed in Figure 8-4.

Conceptual maps are fun to make. They can help you decide which important ideas to teach and they also can serve as a pictorial to help students understand relationships among various ideas a teacher may want to explain.

DETERMINING STUDENTS' PRIOR KNOWLEDGE

Information given in a presentation is based on teachers' estimates of their students' existing cognitive structures and their prior knowledge of a subject. As with many other aspects of teaching, there are no clear-cut rules or easy formulas for teachers to follow. There are, however, some ideas that can serve as guides for practice and also some informal procedures to be learned from experienced teachers.

Cognitive Structures. For new material to be meaningful to students, teachers must find ways to connect the new material to what students already know. Students' present ideas on a particular topic determine which new concepts are potentially meaningful. Figure 8-5 illustrates how a student's cognitive structure might look in relation to a set of concepts about government. Note that the information in Figure 8-5 is the same as the information

Figure 8-5 An individual's cognitive structure with respect to representative government

Republic representative government

- Constitution
  - Amendment process
  - Citizen rights and responsibilities
    - Voting
    - Participation
  - Bill of Rights
- Purposes
  - Welfare
  - Defense
- Levels of power
  - Federal
  - State
  - Local
- Government structures
  - Executive
    - President
  - Judical
    - Judges
  - Legislative
    - House
    - Senate

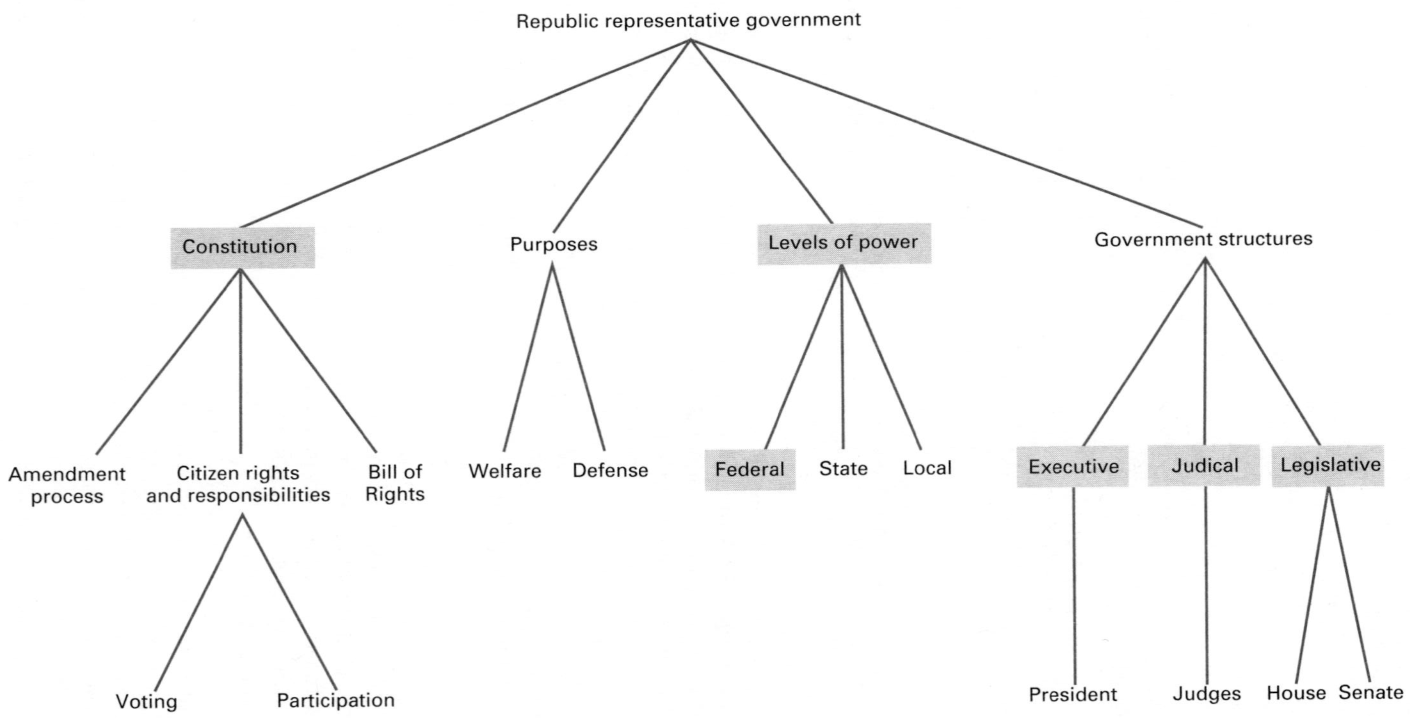

illustrated in Figure 8-1 except Figure 8-5 is being used to show that some concepts have been learned and others have not. Note also the illustrator's judgment (shaded areas) about which concepts will be relevant because of the student's prior knowledge.

Intellectual Development. Cognitive structures are influenced by students' prior knowledge. They are also influenced by maturation and development. Chapter 1 introduced the idea of emotional and cognitive development and described the developmental stages of teachers. Several theorists have put forth developmental theories, including Hunt (1974), Piaget (1963), and Perry (1969). Space does not allow a full discussion of the similarities and differences among developmental theories, but they agree that learners do go through developmental stages ranging from very simple and concrete structures at early ages to more abstract and complicated structures later. It is important that teachers tailor the information they present to the level of development of the learner.

Ideas about how students develop intellectually can provide assistance to teachers as they plan for a particular presentation; however, they cannot provide concrete solutions for several reasons. As experienced teachers know, development is uneven and does not occur precisely at any given ages. Within any classroom, the teacher is likely to find students at extremely varied stages of development. The teacher will also find some students who have developed to a high level of abstraction in some subjects, say history, and still be at a very concrete level in another subject, such as mathematics.

Another problem facing the teacher striving to apply developmental theories to planning for a particular presentation is the problem of measuring the developmental levels of students. Specific tests exist (such as Hunt's Paragraph Completion Test, or Perry's Test), but these are difficult for teachers to use and are better suited for older students. Most teachers must rely on more informal assessments. For example, teachers can watch students as they approach specific problem-solving tasks and make a rough assessment of the degree to which they use concrete or abstract operations. By listening carefully to students and asking probing questions, teachers can determine whether or not the information they are presenting is meaningful. Watching for nonverbal cues during a presentation, such as silence, or frowns, or expressions of interest, can provide insights into what students are integrating into their knowledge structures. Silence, for example, can mean that students are bored; most often it means they do not understand what the teacher is saying. It may be that part of the "art of teaching" and a major difference between expert and novice teachers is expert teachers' abilities to read subtle communication cues from students and then adapt their presentations so that new learning materials become meaningful.

CHOOSING ADVANCE ORGANIZERS

The third planning task associated with the presentation model is choosing appropriate advance organizers. Remember, advance organizers become the hooks, the anchors, the "intellectual scaffolding" for subsequent learning materials. They must be constructed with care. Two major guidelines are important to consider. The advance organizer should be:

- Presented at a higher level of abstraction than the content of the learning materials
- Designed to relate to the students' prior knowledge

One point should be repeated here: The advance organizer is not the same as other techniques used by teachers to introduce a lesson, such as reviewing past work, establishing set, or giving an overview of the day's lesson. All of the above are important for effective presentations, but they are not advance organizers. Below are three examples of advance organizers teachers have used in particular presentations to give you an idea of what an advance organizer is.

Example 1. Say a history teacher is about to present information about the Vietnam war. After reviewing yesterday's lesson, telling students the goals of today's lesson, and asking students to recall in their minds what they already know about Vietnam (establishing set), the teacher might present the following advance organizer:

I want to give you an idea that will help you understand why the United States became involved in the Vietnam war. *The idea is that most wars reflect conflict between peoples over one of the following: ideology, territory, or access to trade.* As I describe for you the United States's involvement in Southeast Asia between 1945 and 1965, I want you to look for examples of how conflict over ideology, territory, or access to trade may have influenced later decisions to fight in Vietnam.

Example 2.   Suppose a science teacher is about to present information about foods the body needs to function well. After going over the objectives for the lesson, the teacher might ask students to list all the food they ate yesterday (establishing set) and then present the following advance organizer:

> In a minute I am going to give you some information about the kinds of foods the body needs to function well. Before I do that, however, *I want to give you an idea that will help you understand the different kinds of food you eat by saying they can be classified into five major food groups: fats, vitamins, minerals, proteins, and carbohydrates.* Each food group contains certain elements, such as carbon or nitrogen. Also, certain things we eat (potatoes, meat) are the sources for each of the elements in the various food groups. Now as I talk about the balanced diet the body needs, I want you to pay attention to the food group to which each thing we eat belongs.

Example 3.   Or, finally, suppose an art teacher is going to show and explain to students a number of paintings from different historical eras. After giving an overview of the lesson and asking students to think for a minute about changes they have observed between paintings done during different historical eras, the teacher presents the following advance organizer:

> In a minute I am going to show and talk about several paintings—some painted in France during the early nineteenth century, others during the late nineteenth and early twentieth century. Before I do that I am going to give you an idea to help you understand the differences you are going to see. *That idea is that a painting reflects not only the individual artist's talent but also the times in which it is created. The "times" or "periods" influence the type of techniques an artist uses as well as what he or she paints about and the type of colors used.* As I show you the various paintings, I want you to look for differences in color, subject of the painting, and specific brush techniques used by the artists and see how they reflect the artist's time.

Conducting the Lesson

As you read, the syntax for the presentation model consists of four basic phases. These include explaining goals and establishing set, presenting the advance organizer, presenting the learning materials, and extending and strengthening student thinking. Behaviors associated with effective teaching practice for each of these steps are described below.

EXPLAINING GOALS AND ESTABLISHING SET

Effective teaching using any instructional model requires an initial step by the teacher aimed at motivating students to participate in the lesson. Behaviors consistently found effective for this purpose are sharing the goals of the lesson with students and establishing a set for learning.

Explaining Goals.   In the discussion on motivation and flow, you learned that students need a reason for participating in particular lessons and they need to know what is expected of them. Effective teachers telegraph their goals and expectations by providing abbreviated versions of their lesson plans on the chalkboard or with newsprint charts. Some teachers prefer newsprint charts because they can be made up the night before and posted on the wall, leaving the chalkboard free for other use; then they can be stored for future use. Effective teachers also outline the steps or phases of a particular lesson and the time required for each step. This allows the students to see the overall flow of a lesson and how the various parts fit together. Sharing the time parameters for the lesson also encourages students to help keep the lesson on schedule. Figure 8-6 shows how a social studies teacher shared her goals and the phases of her presentation with a group of eleventh-grade students.

Making students aware of what they are going to learn will help them make connections between a particular lesson and its relevance to their own lives. This motivates students to exert more effort. It also helps them to draw prior learning from long-term memory to working memory, where it can be used to integrate new information provided in a presentation.

Figure 8-6   Aims and overview of lesson on World War II

Today's Objective: The objective of today's lesson is to help you understand how events circumstances bring about change in the way people think about things.

Agenda:

5 minutes	Introduction, review, and getting ready
5 minutes	Advance organizer for today's lesson
20 minutes	Presentation on the demise of the battleship and the concept of decisive engagement
15 minutes	Discussion for critical thinking
5 minutes	Wrap-up and preview of tomorrow's lesson

Establishing Set.   To get runners ready and off to an even start in a foot race, the command from the starter is "Get ready. . . . Get *set*. . . . Go!" The *get set* alerts runners to settle into their blocks, focus their attention on the track ahead, and anticipate a smooth and fast start.

Establishing set for a lesson in school is very much the same. Effective teachers have found that a brief review that gets students to recall yesterday's lesson or perhaps a question or anecdote that ties into students' prior knowledge is a good way to get started. Note the words used by the teacher in Figure 8-7 as he establishes set for his students.

Set activities also help students get their minds off other things they have been doing (changing classes in secondary schools; changing subjects in elementary schools; lunch and recess) and begin the process of focusing on the subject of the forthcoming lesson. These activities can also serve as motivators for lesson participation. Each teacher develops his or her own style for establishing set, but no effective teacher eliminates this important element from any lesson.

PRESENTING THE ADVANCE ORGANIZER

A previous section explained the planning tasks associated with choosing an appropriate advance organizer. Now consider how an advance organizer should be presented.

Effective teachers make sure the advance organizer is set off sufficiently from the introductory activities of the lesson and from the presentation of learning materials. As with the lesson goals, it is effective to present the advance organizer to stu-

dents using some type of visual format such as a chalkboard, a newsprint chart, or an overhead projector. The key, of course, is that students must understand the advance organizer. It must be taught just as the subsequent information itself must be taught. This requires the teacher to be precise and clear.

PRESENTING THE LEARNING MATERIALS

The third phase of the model is the presentation of the learning materials. Remember how important it is for the teacher to organize learning materials in their simplest and clearest form using the principles of power and economy. The key now is to present previously organized materials in an effective manner, giving attention to such matters as clarity, examples and explaining links, the rule-example-rule technique, the use of transitions, and finally, enthusiasm.

Clarity.   As described in the research section of this chapter, a teaching behavior that has consistently been shown to affect student learning is the teacher's ability to be clear and specific. Common sense also tells us that students will learn more when teachers are clear and specific rather than vague. Nonetheless, researchers and observers of both beginning and experienced teachers can find many instances of presentations that are vague and confusing. According to Hiller and his colleagues (1969), "Vagueness occurs when a performer . . . does not sufficiently command the facts or the understandings required for maximally

Figure 8-7 Establishing set through review

SOURCE: From E. D. Gagné, *The cognitive psychology of school learning,* p. 45. Copyright © 1985 by Ellen D. Gagné. Reprinted by permission of Little, Brown and Company.

effective communication'' (p. 670), or when a speaker tries to present information he or she has forgotten or never really knew.

Clarity of presentation is achieved through planning and organization, as already explained. It is also achieved through practice of the suggestions provided by Rosenshine and Stephens (1986) in Figure 8-8. These suggestions are based on the review of the research of Brophy (1980), Emmer et al. (1982), Kennedy, Bush, Cruickshank, and Haefele (1978), and Lard and Smith (1979).

One of the learning aids at the end of this chapter has been designed to help you observe teacher clarity.

Explaining Links and Examples. Effective presentations contain precise and accurate explaining links and examples. According to Rosenshine (1971a), **explaining links** are prepositions and conjunctions that indicate the cause, result, means, or purpose of an event or idea. Examples of such links would include ''because,'' ''since,'' ''in order to,'' ''if . . . then,'' ''therefore,'' and ''consequently.'' Explaining links help students see the logic and relationships in a teacher's presentation and increase the likelihood of understanding.

Examples are another means used by successful presenters to make material meaningful to students.

Good examples are, however, difficult for beginning teachers to think up and use. Hunter (1982) has provided the following guidelines that experienced teachers have found useful in selecting examples:

- Identify the critical attribute(s) of the present learning.
- Select from students' own lives some previous knowledge or experience that exemplifies the same critical attribute.
- Check your example for distracters.
- Present the example.
- Label the critical attributes or elements in the example.
- Present exceptions.

Here is an example of an example. Say the teacher has been explaining the differences between mammals and reptiles to a group of young learners. She might state an important generalization, such as ''All mammals have warm blood.'' Then she would move to her examples and say, ''Examples of mammals you know about in your everyday lives would include human beings, dogs, and cats. All of these animals are mammals and have warm blood. Reptiles, on the other hand, are cold-blooded. One of the best-known reptiles is the snake. Can you think of others?''

Figure 8-8 Aspects of clear presentation

---

1. Clarity of goals and main points
   a. State the goals or objectives of the presentation.
   b. Focus on one thought (point, direction) at a time.
   c. Avoid digressions.
   d. Avoid ambiguous phrases and pronouns.

2. Step-by-step presentations
   a. Present the material in small steps.
   b. Organize and present the material so that one point is mastered before the next point is given.
   c. Give explicit, step-by-step directions (when possible).
   d. Present an outline when the material is complex.

3. Specific and concrete procedures
   a. Model the skill or process (when appropriate).
   b. Give detailed and redundant explanations for difficult points.
   c. Provide students with concrete and varied examples.

4. Checking for students' understanding
   a. Be sure that students understand one point before proceeding to the next point.
   b. Ask the students questions to monitor their comprehension of what has been presented.
   c. Have students summarize the main points in their own words.
   d. Reteach the parts of the presentation that the students have difficulty comprehending, either by further teacher explanation or by students tutoring other students.

SOURCE: From B. Rosenshine and R. Stephens, Teaching functions. Reprinted with the permission of Macmillan Publishing Company from *Handbook of research on teaching*, 3d ed., M. C. Wittrock, ed. Copyright © 1986 by the American Educational Research Association.

Another example of a teacher using an example follows:

When we talk about weather we mean the day-to-day changes in the hotness, coldness, dryness, and wetness of a place. Climate means the kind of weather a place has over many months or even years.

Here is an example that will show you the difference between weather and climate. Sometimes the weather is very hot in Chicago. The summer Diana, Vito, Gina, and Sammy were asked to describe Chicago, temperatures rose into the high 90s on many days. (Perfect swimming weather!) But, even though the weather sometimes is very hot in Chicago, still we don't say that Chicago has a hot climate. Let's see why not. (Scott, Foresman, *Third Grade Social Studies*, 1979, p. 105)

Presenting material clearly and using precise and accurate explaining links and examples requires that teachers thoroughly understand both the materials being presented and the structure of the subject area being taught. For the beginning teacher having trouble, no solution exists except studying the content and the subject until mastery is achieved.

Rule-Example-Rule Technique. A third technique used by effective presenters is the **rule-example-rule technique.** In this technique:

1. A key rule or principle, such as "prices in a free market are influenced by supply and demand," is presented.

2. Examples of this rule are provided, such as: "When Americans in the 1980s chose to use less oil (decrease in demand), and new oil fields were opened in coastal waters (increase in supply), the price of Middle Eastern oil went down." Or, "When there was a drought in the

Midwest in the 1990s (decrease in supply), the price of corn went up."

3. The passage is concluded with a summary and restatement of the original rule: "So, as you can see, the fluctuation of supply, along with people's desire for a product, influence what the price of a product will be."

Signposts and Transitions.   Particularly in longer presentations which contain several key ideas, effective presenters help learners capture main ideas and move from one part of the lesson to another by using **verbal signposts** and transitional statements. A signpost tells the learner what is important. Examples might include statements such as, "This is the main point I have been trying to make." "Please remember this point." "The most important point to remember is. . . ."

Sometimes a transitional statement may be used to alert listeners to important points just made, such as, "Now let me summarize the important points for you before I move on." In other instances, a transitional statement telegraphs what is to follow, for example, "We have just covered the important eras in Hemingway's life. Let's now turn to how his involvement in the Spanish Civil War influenced his writings." Or, "Now that we know the purposes of a conjunction, let's see how they work in some sample sentences." Transitional statements are important because (1) they highlight the relationships among various ideas in a presentation and (2) they help display the internal organization of the information to learners.

Enthusiasm.   As discussed in the research section, some evidence exists that points to the importance of enthusiasm as an influence on student learning. However, results are somewhat contradictory.

Many teachers, particularly in secondary schools and colleges, argue that the key to effective presentation is for the presenter to use techniques and strategies borrowed from the performing arts. In fact, books have been written describing this approach, such as Timpson and Tobin's *Teaching as Performing* (1982). Emphasis is given to wit, energy, and charisma. Presentation is full of drama, anecdotes, and humor. However, this type of presentation can produce a positive evaluation from student audiences without regard for learning outcomes.

This was seen in one well-known study where a charismatic lecturer purposely gave an entertaining lecture without any real substance (see Naftulin et al., 1973) and got a very positive evaluation from a student audience. This type of presentation does not necessarily lead to student acquisition of important information.

Although making presentations interesting and energizing for learners is desirable, the beginning teacher who has the skills to make such presentations should consider a note of caution. Too many theatrics may, in fact, detract from the key ideas a teacher is trying to convey and focus students' attention on the entertaining aspects of the presentation. This does *not* mean that teachers should not display enthusiasm for their subjects and/or a particular lesson. There is a fine line between the teacher who uses humor, storytelling, and involvement to get major ideas across to students, and the teacher who uses the same techniques for their entertainment value. A learning aid at the end of this chapter will assist you in observing the use of teacher enthusiasm and in reflecting about this attribute of effective presentations.

CHECKING FOR UNDERSTANDING AND EXTENDING STUDENT THINKING

The final phase of a presentation lesson is to check to see if students understand the new learning materials and to extend their thinking about these new ideas.

Checking for Understanding.   It is obvious that if teachers do a lot of teaching but students are not learning, nothing has been accomplished. Periodically (weekly, unit-by-unit, each quarter), effective teachers use homework, tests, and other formal devices to find out what students understand and what they don't understand. For each lesson, however, teachers should also use informal methods to check for understanding. Watching for verbal and nonverbal cues, described earlier, is one method teachers can use. When students ask questions that don't seem to connect to the topic, they are sending a verbal message signaling they are confused. Puzzled looks, silence, and frowns are nonverbal signs that students are not "getting it." Eyes wide open in amazement, smiles, and positive head nodding all signal that understanding is occurring.

Experienced teachers become very effective in reading verbal and nonverbal cues; however, a surer means to **check for understanding** is to ask students to make direct responses to statements or questions. Several easy-to-use techniques can become a valuable piece of the beginning teacher's repertoire. One is the technique of posing a question about the materials just presented and having students as a group signal their responses. Here are examples of how this works, as described by Madeline Hunter (1982):

> "Thumbs up if the statement I make is true, down if false, to the side if you're not sure."
>
> "Make a plus with your fingers if you agree with this statement, a minus if you don't, and a zero if you have no strong feelings."
>
> "Show me with your fingers if sentence 1 or sentence 2 has a dependent clause."
>
> "Raise your hand each time you hear (or see) an example of. . . ." (p. 60)

Note in the examples just provided that Hunter encourages students to use the signal system to report confusion or things they are not quite sure of. These are areas, obviously, where teachers need to provide additional explanation. Hunter also reports that "occasionally, some teachers feel that this is 'baby stuff' and (older) students will feel silly or resent this type of . . . probing" (p. 60). However, she claims, as do many experienced teachers, that even when used at the college level, students are in fact appreciative of having their misconceptions cleared up immediately rather than having them revealed later on an important test. Choral responses (having students answer in unison) is another means to check for understanding, as is sampling several individuals in the class.

There are also several methods used by experienced teachers which are *not* very effective. For instance, sometimes a teacher will conclude a presentation and ask, "Now, you all understand, don't you?" Students normally perceive this as a rhetorical question and consequently do not respond. Asking more directly, "Now, does anyone have any questions?" is an equally ineffective way to check for student understanding. Most students are unwilling to admit publicly to confusion, particularly if they think they are the only ones who didn't understand what the teacher said or if they are afraid of being accused of not listening.

Extending Student Thinking. Although an effective presentation should transmit new information to students, that is not the only goal for presenting and explaining information to students. More importantly, teachers want students to use and strengthen their existing cognitive structures and to increase their ability to monitor their own thinking. The best means for extending student thinking following a presentation of new information is through classroom discourse, primarily by asking questions and having students discuss the information. It is through this process that students integrate new knowledge with prior knowledge, build more complete knowledge structures, and come to understand more complex relationships. The techniques of asking appropriate questions and conducting effective discussions are among the most difficult for beginning teachers to master and thus become the subject matter for a whole chapter later on (Chapter 12).

Postinstructional Tasks

Chapter 2 described a view of teaching that included preinstructional, instructional, and postinstructional tasks. The most important postinstructional tasks connected to the presentation model are testing and grading students on the information presented. Tests and grades are perhaps the most important feedback that teachers give to students, to parents, and to others associated with the schools, as you read in Chapter 7.

The presentation model is particularly adept at transmitting new information to students and at helping them retain that information. Therefore, the testing of students' knowledge acquisition and retention is the appropriate evaluation strategy for the model. This type of testing lends itself nicely to the paper-and-pencil tests with which you are very familiar. In testing for student knowledge, however, there are several factors that should be considered. Teachers should test at all levels of knowledge and not for simple recall of information. Furthermore, teachers should communicate clearly to students what they will be tested on. Finally, it is better to test frequently than to wait for midterm or final testing periods, particularly with younger students.

SUMMARY

- Presentations, explanations, and lectures by teachers comprise a large portion of classroom time primarily because curricula in schools have been structured around bodies of information which students are expected to learn.
- The presentation teaching model draws its rationale from three streams of contemporary thought: concepts about the way knowledge is structured, ideas about how to help students acquire meaningful verbal learning, and concepts from the cognitive sciences that help explain how information is acquired and processed.
- Bodies of knowledge have logical structures from which key concepts and ideas are drawn for teachers' presentations.
- Knowledge can be broken into two main categories: declarative and procedural. Declarative knowledge is knowledge about something or knowledge that something is the case. Procedural knowledge is knowledge about how to do something.
- People process information in terms of basic units, sometimes called propositions or ideas. The way that new knowledge is processed is heavily dependent on the learner's prior knowledge.
- People take in information and knowledge through their senses and transform it into working and long-term memory.
- Meaningful verbal learning occurs when teachers present major unifying ideas in ways that connect these ideas to students' prior knowledge.
- The knowledge base on the presentation model is well developed. Studies have shown the positive effects of using advance organizers, connecting new information to students' prior knowledge, and presenting the information with clarity, enthusiasm, economy, and power.
- The instructional effects of the presentation model are mainly to help students acquire, assimilate, and retain information.
- The general flow or syntax for a presentation consists of four main phases: presenting objectives and establishing set, presenting an advance organizer, presenting the learning materials, and using processes to help extend and strengthen student thinking.
- Successful presentations require a fairly tightly structured learning environment which allows the teacher to effectively present and explain new information and the students to hear and acquire the new information.
- The preinstructional tasks for the presentation model include carefully selecting content, creating advance organizers, and matching both to students' prior knowledge.
- Presenting information to students requires preparing students to learn from presentations as well as delivering learning materials.
- Clarity of a presentation depends on both the teacher's delivery and the teacher's general mastery of the subject matter being presented.
- Advance organizers serve as intellectual scaffolding on which new knowledge is built.
- Specific techniques used in presenting new material include explaining links, rule-example-rule, elaborations, and verbal transitions.
- Teachers can help students extend and strengthen their thinking about new materials through discussion, questioning, and dialogue.
- Postinstructional tasks of the presentation model consist mainly of finding ways to test for student knowledge acquisition. Because students will learn what is expected of them, it is important to test for major ideas. If testing is limited to the recall of specific ideas or information, that is what students will learn. If teachers require higher-level cognitive processing on their tests, students will also learn to do that.

KEY TERMS

teaching models
presentation teaching model
structure of knowledge
meaningful verbal learning
cognitive psychology
cognitive structure
advance organizer
schema
declarative knowledge
procedural knowledge

propositional network
working memory
long-time memory
set induction
teacher clarity
instructional effects
structure of learning environment
conceptual mapping
establishing set
explaining links
rule-example-rule technique
verbal signposts
checking for understanding

BOOKS FOR THE PROFESSIONAL

Bruner, J. (1960). *The process of education.* Cambridge, Mass.: Harvard University Press. A classic that influenced the curriculum reform movement of the 1960s, particularly in regard to the "structure of knowledge."

Gagné, E. D. (1985). *The cognitive psychology of school learning.* Boston: Little, Brown. An excellent review of the research in cognitive psychology with particular attention to learning and how teachers can use this research in their day-to-day instruction.

LEARNING AIDS FOR PLANNING, OBSERVATION, AND REFLECTION

- Assessing My Presentation Skills
- Lesson Plan for Presentation
- Observing a Presentation in Microteaching or Classrooms
- Observing Teacher Clarity
- Observing Teacher Enthusiasm

ASSESSING MY PRESENTATION SKILLS

PURPOSE: This aid provides an overall indication of your skill in the presentation model. The key components of the model, as given in the text, have been highlighted here. This could be used just after reading the chapter to pinpoint areas of confusion or after a practice presentation to assess your own performance.

DIRECTIONS: Check the level of skill you perceive that you have for the various teaching tasks associated with the presentation model.

UNDERSTANDING OR SKILL	LEVEL OF UNDERSTANDING OR SKILL		
	HIGH	MEDIUM	LOW
Preinstructional tasks			
Choosing content	_____	_____	_____
Determining prior knowledge of students	_____	_____	_____
Selecting an advance organizer	_____	_____	_____
Instructional tasks			
Phase 1: Explaining goals and establishing set	_____	_____	_____
Phase 2: Presenting the advance organizer	_____	_____	_____
Phase 3: Presenting the learning materials			
Clarity	_____	_____	_____
Explaining links and examples	_____	_____	_____
Enthusiasm	_____	_____	_____
Phase 4: Extending and strengthening thinking			
Questioning	_____	_____	_____
Conducting discussions	_____	_____	_____
Postinstructional tasks			
Testing and grading	_____	_____	_____
Assessing my own performance	_____	_____	_____

LESSON PLAN FOR PRESENTATION

PURPOSE: This is a suggested format for making a lesson plan tailored specifically to the presentation model. You can try it out as you plan a presentation microteaching assignment or in field placements. As you do so, maintain an attitude of flexibility and experimentation. Revise the format as you see the need.

DIRECTIONS: Follow the guidelines below as you plan a presentation lesson.

Planning phase

Content to be taught: _____

_____

Advance organizer: _____

_____

Objectives

1. Given _____ , the student will be
   (Situation)

   able to _____ with
   (Target behavior)

   _____ .
   (Level of performance)

2. Given _____ , the student will be
   (Situation)

   able to _____ with
   (Target behavior)

   _____ .
   (Level of performance)

Conducting the lesson

Time	Phase and Activities	Materials
____	Lesson goals, rationale, and set: _____	
	_____	
	_____	
____	Advance organizer: _____	
	_____	
	_____	

_____   Presenting information: _____

_____

_____

_____   Extending student thinking: _____

_____   _____

_____   _____

Pitfalls to avoid

During Introduction   **During Transitions**   **During Ending**

Analysis and Reflection: How well did this format work for you? Did some elements seem to be extraneous to you? Did some important elements seem to be missing? How will you revise this format the next time you give a presentation? Write a paragraph in response to these questions.

OBSERVING A PRESENTATION IN MICROTEACHING OR CLASSROOMS

DIRECTIONS: This form highlights the key aspects of a presentation lesson. It can be used to observe a peer in a microteaching laboratory or an experienced classroom teacher. It can also be used to assess a lesson you have taught and videotaped. As you observe the lesson, check the category you believe describes the level of performance of the teacher you are observing. Also answer the general questions about the lesson at the bottom of the form.

TEACHER BEHAVIOR	LEVEL OF PERFORMANCE			
	EXCELLENT	ACCEPTABLE	NEEDS IMPROVEMENT	NOT NEEDED
Planning				
How appropriate was the content of the lesson?	_____	_____	_____	_____
How well prepared was the teacher overall?	_____	_____	_____	_____
Execution				
How well did the teacher				
Explain goals and purposes?	_____	_____	_____	_____
Establish set?	_____	_____	_____	_____
Provide the advance organizer?	_____	_____	_____	_____
Speak with clarity?	_____	_____	_____	_____
Use explaining links and examples?	_____	_____	_____	_____
Display appropriate enthusiasm?	_____	_____	_____	_____
Extend and strengthen student thinking?	_____	_____	_____	_____

Overall planning

What did you like best about the way the lesson was planned and organized? _____

_____

What could be improved? _____

_____

Lesson execution

Think about teaching style and delivery. What did you like best about the way the lesson was presented?

_____

What could be improved? _____

_____

If you were a student in peer microteaching, how did you feel about the teacher's interaction with you?

_____
_____

SOURCE: Adapted from plan used by faculty at Augsburg College.

OBSERVING TEACHER CLARITY

PURPOSE: This aid refines understanding of how to achieve clarity. As described earlier in the chapter, clarity has several ingredients, such as checking for student understanding and avoiding vagueness. These ingredients are listed below.

DIRECTIONS: Observe a teacher during a presentation for 10 to 15 minutes, then check how effectively you feel the teacher incorporated these indicators of clarity into his or her presentation.

INDICATORS OF CLARITY	LEVEL OF EFFECTIVENESS			
	HIGH	MEDIUM	LOW	NOT DONE
Stated objectives	___	___	___	___
Made content organization explicit	___	___	___	___
Used explaining links	___	___	___	___
Gave appropriate examples	___	___	___	___
Used the rule-example-rule technique	___	___	___	___
Used a variety of media	___	___	___	___
Made smooth transitions from one point to the next	___	___	___	___
Checked with students to verify understanding	___	___	___	___
Avoided vagueness	___	___	___	___
Other (specify)	___	___	___	___
_____	___	___	___	
_____	___	___	___	

Analysis and Reflection: Write specific examples from the teacher's presentation that reflect each indicator of clarity. Can you apply any of these examples to your own subject area or grade level? How might you adapt the others to fit your subject or grade level? Keep these ideas on file for future use.

OBSERVING TEACHER ENTHUSIASM

PURPOSE: Enthusiasm is an important part of lecturing but should not be confused with theatrics. Enthusiasm makes learning exciting, but theatrics can interfere with learning. The following elements of enthusiasm were taken from Collins (1978). This tool is intended to demonstrate in concrete ways how enthusiasm can be communicated to students.

DIRECTIONS: Observe a teacher during a presentation for 10 to 20 minutes, then check how effectively you feel the teacher incorporated the following elements of enthusiasm.

ELEMENTS OF ENTHUSIASM	LEVEL OF EFFECTIVENESS			
	HIGH	MEDIUM	LOW	NOT DONE
Vocal delivery Varied, lilting, uplifting intonations, many changes in tone, pitch	✓			
Eyes Shining, frequently opened wide, eyebrows raised, eye contact with total group		✓		
Gestures Frequent movements of body, head, arms, hands and face, sweeping motions; clapping hands; head nodding rapidly			✓	
Movements Makes large body movements, swings around, changes pace, bends body		✓		
Facial expression Changes denoting surprise, sadness, joy, thoughtfulness, awe, excitement			✓	
Word selection Highly descriptive, many adjectives, great variety		✓		
Acceptance of ideas and feelings Accepts ideas and feelings quickly with vigor and animation; ready to accept, praise, encourage, or clarify in a nonthreatening manner; many variations in responding to pupils		✓		
Overall energy High degree of spirit throughout lesson		✓		

Analysis and Reflection: Did any elements of enthusiasm seem more important than others in communicating excitement for learning? Which elements do you think most easily suit your own personality? Which elements do you think need improvement?

1,7   1,4   overall — nervousness

Chapter Outline

PERSPECTIVE AND RATIONALE

• Concepts and Higher-Level Thinking • The Nature of Concepts

SAMPLING THE KNOWLEDGE BASE

• Human Development and Concept Learning • Presentation and Sequencing of Examples • Use of Best Examples • Use of Visual or Mental Images • Guidelines from Research

MAIN FEATURES OF THE MODEL

• Instructional Effects of Concept Teaching • Two Approaches to Concept Teaching • Syntax of Concept Teaching • Structure of the Learning Environment

PROCEDURES FOR TEACHING CONCEPTS

• Preinstructional Tasks • Conducting the Lesson • Postinstructional Tasks

CHAPTER 9

Concept Teaching

Richard Jantz, University of Maryland

Most experienced teachers would agree that conveying information to students is very important but that teaching students how to think is even more important. Experienced teachers also know that concepts are the basic building blocks for thinking, particularly higher-level thinking, in any subject. Concepts allow individuals to classify objects and ideas and to derive rules and principles; they provide the foundations for the idea networks that guide our thinking. The process of learning concepts begins at an early age and continues throughout life as people develop more and more complex concepts, both in school and out. The learning of concepts is crucial in schools and in everyday life, because concepts allow mutual understanding among people and provide the basis for verbal interaction.

The focus of this chapter is on **concept teaching** and how teachers can help students attain and develop the basic concepts needed for further learning and higher-level thinking. The first section deals with the nature of concepts and their importance in education, the next section summarizes research that underlies and supports concept teaching, and the final sections focus on the model itself and describe specific teaching and evaluation procedures associated with two approaches to concept teaching.

PERSPECTIVE AND RATIONALE

"Ball." "Chair." "Box." "Table." "Crayon." Kim is naming things and placing objects into groups or classes. She is developing concepts. Combining something concrete, such as a ball, with an abstract quality, such as roundness, enables Kim to identify classes of objects, events, and ideas that differ from each other. By repeatedly sorting and classifying different balls she can eventually form an abstract concept for these similar objects that allows her to think about them and, eventually, to communicate with others about them.

Concepts and Higher-Level Thinking

Concept learning is more than simply classifying objects and forming categories. It is also more than learning new labels or vocabulary to apply to classes of objects and ideas. Instead, concept learning involves the process of constructing knowledge and organizing information into comprehensive and complex cognitive structures.

As has been described in previous chapters, students come into classrooms with a variety of prior experiences from which they have formed conceptions (schemata) about the physical and social worlds. These schemata are a student's way of

281

looking at the world. They help students explain and interpret what is happening in their lives. Sometimes the conceptions students hold are accurate; many times they are intuitive, naive, and, in fact, misrepresentations of reality. Misconceptions cannot be changed by simply presenting new information. Instead, change requires teaching processes which enable students to become aware of their existing schemata and which help them to develop new concepts and reformulations of existing ways of thinking.

The Nature of Concepts

In everyday usage the term **concept** is used in several ways. Sometimes it refers to an idea someone has, such as "My concept of how a president should act is straightforward." At other times it is used like a hypothesis, for example, "My concept is that we are always in debt because we spend too much on frills." When the term *concept* is used in connection with teaching and learning it has a more precise meaning and refers to the way knowledge and experience are categorized.

Concept learning is essentially "putting things into a class" and then being able to recognize members of that class (R. M. Gagné, 1985, p. 95). This requires that an individual be able to take a particular case, such as his or her pet dog Lucky Lady, and place it into a general class of objects, in this case a class termed *dog*, that shares certain attributes. This process requires making judgments about whether a particular case is an instance of a larger class.

CONCEPTS THEMSELVES CAN BE PLACED INTO CATEGORIES

Concepts, like most other objects or ideas, can be categorized and labeled. Knowing the different types of concepts is important because, as will be illustrated later, different types of concepts require different teaching strategies. One way of classifying concepts is according to the rule structures that define their use.

Some concepts have constant rule structures. The concept of island, for example, always involves land surrounded by water. A triangle is a plane, closed figure with three sides and three angles. The rule structures for these concepts are constant. Their

critical attributes are combined in an additive manner and are always the same. This type of concept is referred to as a **conjunctive concept**.

Other concepts are broader and more flexible and permit alternative sets of attributes. Their rule structures are not constant. For example, the concept of a strike in baseball is based upon a number of alternative conditions. A strike may be when a batter swings and misses, when an umpire determines that the pitch was in the strike zone even though the batter did not swing at the ball, or when the batter hits a foul ball. This type of concept is called a **disjunctive concept**, that is, one that contains alternative sets of attributes. The concept "noun" is another example of a disjunctive concept. It may be a person, a place, or a thing, but it cannot be all three at the same time.

A third type of concept is one whose rule structure depends on relationships. The concept "aunt" describes a particular relationship between siblings and their offspring. The concepts "time" and "distance" are also **relational concepts**. To understand either of these concepts, one must know the other, plus the relationship between them. For example, "week" is defined as a succession of days that has as its beginning point day 1 (usually Sunday) and as its ending point day 7 (usually Saturday) and a duration of 7 days.

CONCEPTS ARE LEARNED THROUGH EXAMPLES AND NONEXAMPLES

Learning a particular concept involves identifying both examples and nonexamples. For instance, a cow is an example of a mammal but is a nonexample of a reptile. Australia is an example of a country in the southern hemisphere, but it is a nonexample of a developing country. Cotton and silk are examples of the concept "fabric," but leather and steel are nonexamples. As will be described later, the way examples and nonexamples are identified and used by teachers is important in a concept lesson.

CONCEPTS ARE INFLUENCED BY SOCIAL CONTEXT

The critical attributes of a conjunctive concept, such as "equilateral triangle," are fixed across social contexts. However, disjunctive or relational concepts, such as "poverty" or "literacy rate," change from one social context to another. Concepts with changing critical attributes are often found in the behavioral and social sciences and need an operational definition depending on the social context or cultural environment in which they are used. Consider the concept "aunt." In some societies, "aunt" or "auntie" refers to any adult in the society who has some responsibility for caring for a particular child and has nothing to do with actual blood relationship. Consider also the geographical concepts "north" and "south" as they relate to climate. Children in the northern hemisphere are taught that as one goes south, the climate gets warmer. Obviously this would not hold true for children in Australia or Argentina. The labeling of concepts is also influenced by context. In England a car's windshield is called a "windscreen," and the trunk is called the "boot." In this instance, the concepts are the same; the label is different.

CONCEPTS HAVE DEFINITIONS AND LABELS

All concepts have names or labels and more or less precise definitions. For example, a relatively small body of land surrounded on all sides by water is labeled an island. Labels and definitions permit mutual understanding and communication with others using the concept. They are prerequisites for concept teaching and learning. Labels, however, are human inventions and essentially are arbitrary. Knowing the label does not mean a student understands the concept. This is what makes teaching concepts difficult.

CONCEPTS HAVE CRITICAL ATTRIBUTES

Concepts also have attributes that describe and help define them. Some attributes are critical and are used to separate one concept from all others. For example, an equilateral triangle is a triangle with three equal sides. The **critical attributes** are that it must be a triangle and that each of the sides must be equal. Triangles without three equal sides are not equilateral triangles. In addition, if the concept is a subset of a broader concept, then it must also include the critical attributes of the broader concept. An equilateral triangle is a member of the class of concepts called triangles and thus must contain all the critical attributes of a triangle.

CONCEPTS HAVE NONCRITICAL ATTRIBUTES

Some attributes may be found in some but not in all members of the class. These are called **noncritical attributes**. For example, size is a noncritical attribute of an equilateral triangle. All concepts have both critical and noncritical attributes, and it is sometimes difficult for students to differentiate between the two. For example, the concept "bird" is typically associated in most people's minds with the noncritical attribute, flying. Robins, cardinals, eagles, and most other birds can fly. Flying, however, is not a critical attribute of birds, since ostriches and penguins cannot fly yet they are still classified as birds. Focusing exclusively on critical attributes and typical members of a class can sometimes cause confusion when learning new concepts. Although flying is a noncritical attribute of birds, it is nonetheless typical of most birds and must be accounted for in teaching about them.

CONCEPT LEARNING INVOLVES BOTH CONCEPTUAL AND PROCEDURAL KNOWLEDGE

Conceptual knowledge is the learner's ability to define a concept based on some criteria (for example, physical characteristics or relationships) and to recognize the concept's relationship to other concepts. It implies understanding of the typical or best instance of the class, based on defining attributes. For example, if you were to identify the typical or best example of the adult male in terms of height, you would probably use as your prototype someone about 6 feet tall. You would not use the 7-foot 6-inch basketball player or the 4-foot 8-inch jockey.

Procedural knowledge of a concept refers to the student's ability to use the concept in a discriminating fashion. This involves the ability to use a concept's defining attributes to compare and contrast it with similar but different concepts. Procedural knowledge about males would allow comparison with similar concepts, such as "female," "girls," "boys," "old men," "young men," and "tall men."

To understand the difference between conceptual and procedural knowledge, think again about the concept "equilateral triangle." Learning this concept involves both the acquisition of conceptual knowledge and the development of procedural knowledge. Conceptual knowledge exists when a student knows the defining attributes of an equilateral triangle and can speak with clarity about them. A student with a conceptual knowledge of an equilateral triangle would define it as a plane, closed figure with three equal angles and three straight sides of equal length. This student would be able to generalize a single instance of an equilateral triangle to the whole class. The student with procedural knowledge, however, could *apply* the definition and could *discriminate* the class of triangle from other classes of triangles and other closed, simple plane figures, such as rectangles or octagons. The student could also generalize to and discriminate among newly encountered instances of equilateral triangles.

SAMPLING THE KNOWLEDGE BASE

The knowledge base on concept teaching and learning is very extensive and covers a wide range of topics. This is because concept development and its relation to how the mind works have held the interest of theorists, philosophers, and researchers for centuries. Recently this work has centered mainly in psychology and includes the contributions of Jean Piaget, Jerome Bruner, David Ausubel, and Howard Gardner, among others. Their studies showed how conceptual thinking develops in children and youth and how certain approaches to concept teaching affect these learning processes. To sample ideas from the research tradition, a few topics of particular importance to teachers have been selected for review.

Human Development and Concept Learning

One important set of ideas underlying concept teaching comes from the field of human development. This research specifies how age and stages of intellectual development interact and influence students' readiness to learn various types of concepts. This research has shown that children begin learning concepts at a remarkably early age. Starkey (1980), for example, identified the beginnings of concept formation with the object-sorting and object-preference behavior found in children between 9 and 12 months of age. These initial sorting activities gradually lead to classifying and generalizing, which are the basis for concept learning. Children around 26 months of age can sort concepts into simple genus-species relationships, such as the fact that cats and dogs are animals. At about 4 1/2 years of age they can comprehend hierarchical relationships, such as people-lady-nurse or food-fruit-orange (Welch and Long, 1940).

Research has also shown that young children can develop complex spatial and temporal concepts. Friedman (1980) found that children between 3 and 5 years of age could comprehend such spatial terms as *ahead of, behind, beside, together with, above, between,* and such temporal terms as *before, after,* and *at the same time.* Although concept learning continues throughout life, the way concepts are learned is affected by the learner's age, language development, and level of intellectual development.

Bruner (1966) identified three distinct modes of learning: (1) learning by doing, called the *enactive mode,* (2) learning by forming mental images, called the *iconic mode,* and (3) learning through a series of abstract symbols or representations, called the *symbolic mode.* As children grow older and progress through the grades, they depend less on the enactive mode and more on mental imagery and symbolic operations. In general, children under age 7 rely mainly on doing, or the enactive mode, for learning concepts. Children between the ages of 7 and 11 still rely on the enactive mode but begin learning concepts by forming mental images. Older children and early adolescents still use the iconic mode but increasingly rely on abstract symbols and mental imagery.

Presentation and Sequencing of Examples

The research on human development can assist teachers as they make decisions about the types and complexity of concepts to teach. Other research has focused more specifically on the components of the concept lesson itself and how these components can best be approached. One particular component that has been studed is how best to present and sequence the examples and nonexamples of the concept being taught.

Although there are several ways to do this, they

can be categorized into two basic methods: expository, or the **rule-to-example** method, and interrogatory, or the **example-to-rule** method. The rule-to-example method, as you will see later, consists of the teacher's first defining the concept for students and then providing them with examples and nonexamples to reinforce their understanding of the concept. The focus is on labeling and defining the concept.

The example-to-rule method consists of turning this process around. Examples and nonexamples are given first, and students discover or attain the concept themselves through a process of inductive reasoning. The rule-to-example approach normally is best for the development of knowledge about a concept for which students have little or no previous understanding. The example-to-rule approach is best when students have some understanding of the concept, and the goals of the lesson are to explore the presence or absence of critical attributes of particular concepts and to learn the processes of inductive reasoning. Sometimes both approaches are used when students are learning complicated concepts.

Whether examples and nonexamples of the concept are presented in random or logical fashion is also important. Bruner and his colleagues (1956) studied this problem, as have many others since (for example, Petty and Jannson, 1987). The results seem to be pretty consistent on two points: The way examples and nonexamples are sequenced does influence concept attainment, and a logical or rational sequence is better than a random sequence. This finding obviously requires teachers to do a thorough analysis of the concept being taught and to deliberate about what constitutes the most logical sequencing of examples and nonexamples.

Use of Best Examples

The work of Bruner and others demonstrated the importance of examples and nonexamples and how these should be presented in a lesson. But what about the examples themselves? What should their characteristics be, and how should they be selected and used?

In general, initial examples should be selected on the basis of their familiarity to the class. Students need to see typical examples clearly before they are ready to consider atypical ones. Similarly, students normally find it easier to identify a concept with its most immediate neighbors before relating it to more distant ones. If a robin is used as the best (most familiar) example of the concept "bird," it is easier for the learner to distinguish close neighbors to robins, such as cardinals, sparrows, or bluebirds, than to distinguish more distant members, such as ducks, chickens, or penguins.

The importance of best examples was highlighted in an interesting study conducted by Tennyson and his colleagues a few years ago. In a carefully controlled study, the researchers tested the effectiveness of two approaches to teaching the concept "regular polygon" to a sample of third-grade students. Some groups of students received a definition of regular polygon and then were presented with some best examples of this concept, such as the ones in Figure 9-1. Another group received a definition of the concept and an operational rule about regular polygons. The operational definition used in the study is shown in Figure 9-2.

The group of students given the best examples achieved higher than did the group given the operational rule. This study clearly showed that the use of best examples can aid the learning of concepts. The use of best examples prevents misconceptions that might occur if more distant or atypical examples are used. It also appears that the use of best examples can minimize classification errors that often occur when students are only given a definition as the basis for making judgments as to whether an instance is a member of the class or not.

Use of Visual or Mental Images

Using visual or mental images also affects the learning of concepts and supports the old adage that "a picture is worth a thousand words." Tennyson (1978) tested three types of pictorial support with elementary children as aids for concept learning. In one case the children were given drawings highlighting the relevant features of the concept. In the second case the students were guided to produce their own drawings highlighting the relevant features. In the third instance students were asked to generate mental images of the relevant features. The

Figure 9-1 Best examples of regular polygons

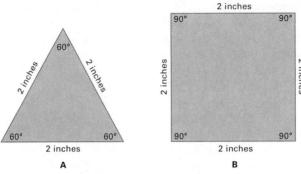

SOURCE: Adapted from R. Tennyson et al. (1983), Concept learning by children using instructional presentation forms for prototype formation and classification-skill development. *Journal of Educational Psychology, 75,* 282. Copyright 1983 by the American Psychological Association. Adapted by permission of the publisher and author.

students were divided into two groups. The first group received full pretraining in one of the three techniques; the second group was given only practice items without training.

This study concluded that for young children learning concepts and rules can be assisted by providing pictorials or by having students generate their own pictorials to accompany the text and by providing specific instructions for these tasks. This study was conducted with third- and fourth-grade students using mathematical concepts, but it holds promise for other instruction as well.

For example, Anderson and Smith (1983) studied how children come to understand science concepts such as light and color. They had 113 children in five classrooms study the following passage:

Bouncing Light

Have you ever thrown a rubber ball at something? If you have, you know that when the ball hits most things, it bounces off them. Like a rubber ball, light bounces off most things it hits.

When light travels to something opaque, all the light does not stop. Some of this light bounces off. When light travels to something translucent or transparent, all the light does not pass through. Some of this light bounces off. When light bounces off things and travels to your eyes, you are able to see.

Figure 9-2 Operational rule for regular polygons

Read the following addition to the definition of regular polygons:

Regular polygons have:

1. All sides of equal length
2. All equal angles

They are:

3. Planes
4. Closed
5. Simple

SOURCE: Adapted from R. Tennyson et al. (1983), Concept learning by children using instructional presentation forms for prototype formation and classification-skill development. *Journal of Educational Psychology, 75,* 283. Copyright 1983 by the American Psychological Association. Adapted by permission of the publisher and author.

Figure 9-3 Visual depiction of the role of light in seeing

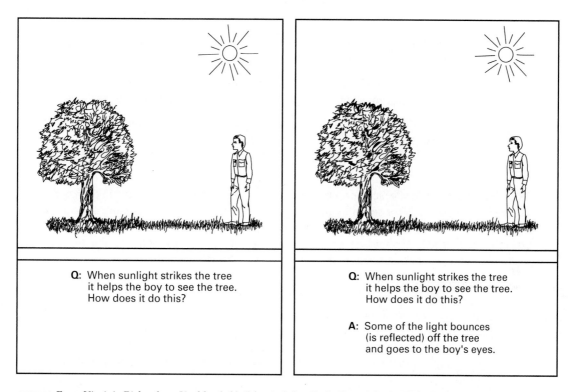

SOURCE: From Virginia Richardson-Koehler (ed.), *Educator's handbook.* Copyright ©1987 by Longman.

They found that only 20 percent of the students could understand that seeing is a process of detecting light which has been reflected off some object. However, in a second experiment they used a visual aid such as the one illustrated in Figure 9-3. In contrast to the 20 percent who learned the concepts from reading about light, 78 percent of the students understood the concepts the teachers were trying to teach when visual aids were used to illustrate the concepts.

Graphic organizers and webs are other forms of visual representation. These devices can help highlight the critical attributes of a concept and help make the concept more concrete for students. They can also provide students with an effective means for retrieving information from long-term memory so new concepts can be more easily understood. More information about how to make webs will be provided later in the chapter. The effects of graphic organizers are explored in Research Summary 9-1.

Guidelines from Research

The research on concept teaching and learning indicates that particular teaching strategies can help students learn concepts more effectively. Eight guidelines are offered here from the research just summarized and from the work of Martorella (1982), who did an extensive review of research related to instructional applications of the principles of concept learning:

1. Teachers should begin with a clear definition of the concept.
2. At some point, instruction should include a definition of the concept and a statement of the concept's critical attributes.
3. The teaching of some concepts requires both expository and interrogatory presentations.
4. The use of best examples can increase concept learning.

RESEARCH SUMMARY 9-1

Hawk, P. (1986). Using graphic organizers to increase achievement in middle school life science. *Science Education, 70,* 81–87.

PROBLEM: The purpose of this study was to determine the effectiveness of graphic organizers in aiding concept learning among sixth- and seventh-grade students in life science.

SAMPLE AND SETTING: Subjects for this study were seventh-graders enrolled in seven classes of life science at four middle schools, and sixth-graders enrolled in eight classes of life science at four other middle schools. All eight schools were within the same school system.

PROCEDURES: The life science course in which the subjects were enrolled was the required course of study for seventh-graders. In an effort to accelerate the science program in the school system, half of the schools were designated to pilot a revised science curriculum using high-ability sixth-graders. This revised curriculum was essentially the seventh-grade life science curriculum. Students were divided into two groups.

- **Experimental group:** Sixth-grade students were given specially developed graphic organizers to accompany the first seven chapters of a life science text published by Holt, Rinehart & Winston. An example of one of these organizers is found in Figure 9-4. The content covered in the chapters was the scientific method, the living world, and life support processes. The organizers had been developed by a group of teachers, and teachers in the study were given a 2-day workshop on their use.
- **Control group:** Seventh-grade students served as the control group. These students did not receive the graphic organizers during instruction. Teachers in this group were told to teach using their regular methods.

An analysis of covariance design was used to control statistically any initial differences in the students that might confound differences caused by the treatment. Present were an experimental variable (graphic organizers), a covariate variable (pretest), and a depen-

Figure 9-4 Graphic organizer for protoplasm

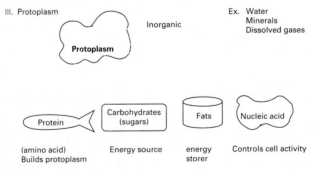

SOURCE: Adapted from P. Hawk (1986), Using graphic organizers to increase achievement in middle school life science. *Science Education,* 70:84. Copyright 1986 John Wiley & Sons. Reprinted by permission of John Wiley & Sons.

dent variable (posttest). Teachers for both groups were provided with a list of activities to include during the instruction of each chapter and a time line to follow.

Identical pretests and posttests containing 50 items were used in the study. This test is standardized and published by Holt, Rinehart & Winston for use with their life science curriculum.

POINTS FOR READING RESEARCH: All research studies have limitations. One of the limitations of this study was teacher control. All the teachers used their usual pedagogy, and obviously they varied in ability and style. This is always a limitation in actual classroom research. However, in the opinions of the system supervisors there was no significant difference in the two groups of teachers. You must decide if you agree with this.

RESULTS: The results in Table 9-1 clearly support the use of graphic organizers as a teaching strategy for improving concept learning. The 213 students in the sixth-grade classes of life science that used the organizers had an adjusted percentage difference between the pretest and posttest of 43 percent, while the 177 students in the seventh-grade classes that did not use graphic organizers had an adjusted percentage difference of 24 percent. The adjusted percentage difference between the two treatments was statistically significant.

TABLE 9-1   **Mean Percentage Scores for Pretests and Posttests by Treatment Group**

TREATMENT GROUP	PRETEST	POSTTEST	
	Obtained	Obtained	Adjusted
Graphic	26%	68%	69%
Control	28%	54%	52%

SOURCE: P. Hawk (1986), p. 85.

DISCUSSION AND IMPLICATIONS: The significant findings in this study support previous studies on the effectiveness of using graphic organizers. There are a number of reasons why graphic organizers enhance learning. First, the graphic organizer provides an overview of the material to be learned. It says, "This is where we are going and these are the things we need to know to get there." Second, the graphic organizer provides a framework and reference points that aid the learner in assimilating new vocabulary and in organizing the main concepts into a logical pattern. Third, the graphic organizers cue students as to what to look for as they read printed materials. The organizers direct students to look for cause and effect, for comparison and contrast, for sequence of events, and a variety of other relationships. Fourth, as a review instrument, the graphic organizer is succinct and informative. It appears to strengthen the learner's retention. Finally, the graphic aspect of the organizers used in this study provided visual aids with specific frameworks to assist in learning new vocabulary and concepts.

It would appear that classroom teachers could aid their students' concept learning by using graphic organizers without changing any other aspects of their pedagogical style except for explaining the use of the organizers.

5. Unless students know the critical attributes of a concept, they should be taught them prior to or concurrently with instruction.

6. Some opportunities to experiment with identifying examples and nonexamples should be incorporated in a concept lesson, along with feedback on the correctness or incorrectness of the responses.

7. The use of visuals such as graphics, charts, diagrams, and webs can aid in the learning of concepts by making them more concrete and by depicting relationships among concepts and their critical attributes.

8. The use of graphic organizers can facilitate the learning of concepts described in text-based materials.

Many of these principles, as you will see, are incorporated in the specific teaching procedures described in the following section.

MAIN FEATURES OF THE MODEL

Instructional Effects of Concept Teaching

Concept teaching models have been developed primarily to teach key concepts that serve as foundations for student higher-level thinking and to provide a basis for mutual understanding and communication. Such models are not designed to teach large amounts of information to students. However, by learning and applying key concepts within a given subject, students are able to transfer specific learnings to more general areas. In fact, without mutual understanding of certain key concepts, subject area instruction is nearly impossible.

Two Approaches to Concept Teaching

There are numerous approaches to concept teaching, but two basic ones have been selected for this chapter: direct presentation and concept attainment.

DIRECT PRESENTATION

Direct presentation employs the rule-to-example approach defined earlier. Once the teacher has presented a definition of the concept, identified its critical attributes, and shown examples and nonexamples, students practice the concept and, through guided questioning by the teacher, acquire conceptual ownership. Built upon the work of Tennyson, Youngers, and Suebsonthi (1983), the approach includes some of the same principles as the direct instruction model described in Chapter 10.

CONCEPT ATTAINMENT

Heavily influenced by the work of Bruner and his colleagues (1956), the **concept attainment** approach is used when students already have some idea about a particular concept or set of concepts. Through consideration of multiple examples and nonexamples of a particular concept, teachers promote inductive thinking by students and help them monitor their own thinking processes.

Distinctions between these two approaches and specific teaching behavior will be described in more detail later in this chapter.

Syntax of Concept Teaching

There are four major phases or steps in each of the concept teaching approaches described in this chapter. There are, however, variations in the internal sequencing of activities, as you will see later. The overall sequence of activities is summarized in Table 9-2.

Structure of the Learning Environment

The learning environment for concept teaching is one that might be described as moderately structured. Transitions into and out of a concept lesson should be planned. The teacher makes judgments about which concepts to teach and where concept lessons should be sequenced within a larger unit of study. The teacher also selects the best examples and nonexamples of the concept based upon the background and experiences of the students. During a concept lesson, there are numerous occasions when the teacher's main role becomes one of responding to student ideas, encouraging student participation, and supporting students as they develop their reasoning abilities. Checking for understanding and giving students opportunities to ex-

Table 9-2   Syntax for Concept Teaching

PHASE	TEACHER BEHAVIOR
Phase 1: Presenting goals and establishing set	Teacher explains the goals and procedures for the lesson and gets students ready to learn.
Phase 2: Input of examples and nonexamples	In the direct presentation approach, teacher names the concepts, identifies the critical attributes, and illustrates with examples and nonexamples. In concept attainment, examples and nonexamples are given and students inductively arrive at the concept and its attributes.
Phase 3: Testing for attainment	Teacher presents additional examples and nonexamples to test students' understanding of the concept. Students are asked to provide their own examples and nonexamples of the concept.
Phase 4: Analysis of thinking and integration of learning	Teacher gets students to think about their own thinking processes. Students are asked to examine their decisions and the consequences of their choices. Teacher helps students integrate new learning by relating the concept to other concepts in a unit of study.

plore their own thinking processes also call for the teacher's support and encouragement. The learning environment for concept teaching, just as with the presentation model described in Chapter 8, requires students to pay close attention to the lesson. While a concept lesson is in progress, there is no time for casual talk with neighbors, studying other subject areas, or any other activity that might take attention away from the lesson.

PROCEDURES FOR TEACHING CONCEPTS

Preinstructional Tasks

In the following story, entitled the "League of the Iroquois," two generalizations serve as the focus of the lesson. These two generalizations, or "big ideas," and the key concepts within them permit comparisons of different cultures at different time periods. The key concepts are in italics:

1. *People* unite to form *governments*.
2. *People* take different *roles* and *responsibilities* in their government.

League of the Iroquois

At a meeting of the colonies in Albany, New York, in 1754, Franklin presented a "plan of union." According to his plan, each colony would choose representatives to a "grand council." This council would pass laws that all the colonies would follow. Where did Franklin get the idea for such a plan? Very possibly, from the Iroquois Indians.

About 200 years before the Albany meeting, the six nations of Iroquois joined together to form the League of the Iroquois. The original aim of the League was to promote peace among the Iroquois. Later, joined together in the League, the Iroquois became powerful opponents in war.

Women and men played different parts in this League government. Women chose the men who were the representatives, or chiefs, from each tribe to the Great Council of the Iroquois, called the Longhouse. Women decided what would be discussed at the Great Council. Often the chief had to decide on ways to solve problems. This sometimes involved making rules for the people in all the tribes. If the chiefs did not do their jobs well, women could remove them from the Council.

Benjamin Franklin's plan of government was not accepted by the colonists at the Albany meeting in 1754. But the government of the United States that was formed thirty-three years later was like the Longhouse Council in many ways. Can you think how? (Scott, Foresman, *Third Grade Social Studies*, 1979, pp. 194–195)

In order to understand these two generalizations above and use them to solve problems, students must first understand the concept embedded in them. For instance, they must understand the concept of role before they can identify the roles and responsibilities that women had in the League of the Iroquois or before they can compare the roles of women today with those of the Iroquois. Consequently, a teacher's first decisions when planning a concept lesson involve selecting, defining, and analyzing concepts to be taught.

SELECTING CONCEPTS

The curriculum is the primary source of key concepts for instruction. These concepts may be embedded in a textbook, as illustrated above, or contained in local curriculum guides. In the story of "The League of the Iroquois," the concepts of role, responsibilities, and government are implied within the text, but they also need to be taught. Reading the text and being able to apply the generalization, "People unite to form governments," is dependent on the learner's conceptual and procedural knowledge of the key concepts.

The teacher's edition for most textbook series provides guidance in selecting key concepts for instruction. For example, in the same third-grade social studies textbook, the teacher's edition identifies the main idea for Lesson Two (excerpted below) as "weather and climate can affect your choices." Knowledge of the concepts of weather, climate, and choices is crucial to understanding this main idea. In this instance the concepts of weather and climate are clearly stated as learning outcomes (key concepts) and are developed within the lesson.

> Just as the location of your community can affect your choices, so can its weather and climate. Suppose, for example, that you plan to go on a picnic Saturday. But, suppose when Saturday comes, it brings "thunder" and "storms." You decide to cancel your picnic because of bad weather. Weather has influenced your choices.
>
> When we talk about weather we mean the day-to-day changes in the hotness, coldness, dryness, and wetness of a place. Climate means the kind of weather a place has over many months or even years.
>
> Here is an example that will show you the difference between weather and climate. Sometimes the weather is very hot in Chicago. The summer Diana, Vito, Gina, and Sammy were asked to describe Chicago, temperatures rose into the high 90s on many days. (Perfect swimming weather!) But, even though the

> weather sometimes is very hot in Chicago, still we don't say that Chicago has a hot climate. Let's see why not. (Scott, Foresman, *Third Grade Social Studies*, 1979, p. 105)

Local curriculum guides are another source for selecting concepts for instruction. In some cases the key concepts will be listed as vocabulary to be developed in the unit. In other cases concepts will be found within the main ideas or generalizations for a unit of study. For example, the fifth-grade curriculum guide for Howard County Public Schools, Howard County, Maryland, contains a unit on the westward movement. In this unit students study why people migrated west; in the process, they study such key concepts as migration, economic gain, religious freedom, and political freedom. They also examine other concepts related to the unit's objectives, such as expansion, self-sufficiency, heterogeneity, frontier, pioneer, pluralism, and terrain. Some of the other concepts for the unit are listed below. Obviously, they cannot all be taught, and the teacher must make decisions about which ones to single out for particular lessons.

trek	rebellion
pioneer	flatboat
territory	acre
Conestoga wagon	besiege
harsh	reservations
blockade	neutral
frontier	canal
fertile soil	treaty
compromise	expedition
treaties	turnpikes

Teachers need to make decisions about which of the new vocabulary words need to be directly taught as concepts. Judgments are constantly being made as to which new terms are essential to understanding the important ideas of a lesson or a unit. If the students don't know the key concepts within a generalization or main idea, then a lesson on the unknown concept(s) should be taught. Merrill and Tennyson (1977) summarized the major conditions under which concept lessons are appropriate.

> Does the material involve *new terms?* If so, prepare a concept lesson for each important new term or related set of new terms.

Does the material require the student to define *new words?* If so, prepare a concept lesson for each important new word or related set of new words.

Does the content involve *rule using?* If so, prepare a concept lesson for each component in the rule.

Does the content involve a *series of steps or events?* If so, examine each step or event as a potential concept and prepare a concept lesson for those steps or events that are concepts.

Does the material require *identification of parts?* If so, decide if some parts should be taught as concepts and prepare a concept lesson for those that should be taught. (pp. 21–22)

In the process of selecting concepts to teach, it is important to remember a point made earlier: helping students understand a concept involves more than getting them to provide definitions of new vocabulary words.

DEFINING CONCEPTS

Critical attributes, as you read earlier, are those attributes that are present in every example of a concept and distinguish it from all other concepts. For example the concept "tree" might be defined as a "plant that lives for many years and has a single main stem that is woody." This definition includes the critical attributes "plant," "lives for many years," "single main stem," and "woody." These critical attributes define a concept and, consequently, students must understand them. However, noncritical attributes also enter into the picture. For example, size, shape, and color are noncritical attributes of trees. Blue lagoons, sandy beaches, and palm trees may be desirable on an island but they are noncritical attributes. When learning concepts, students must not confuse the noncritical attributes, no matter how common, with the critical attributes of the concept.

The source of the definition for a concept and its critical attributes is also important. In some instances concepts are defined in the glossaries of the students' textbooks, but in other cases they may be defined in the curriculum guides published by the local school districts. These definitions and critical attributes should be examined carefully. Markle (1975) warned that "some of the words in many definitions are irrelevant to classifying tasks. For in-

stance, Webster's says under 'dog,' that these were 'kept in domesticated state since prehistoric times,' an interesting fact, perhaps, but without utility in the identification task" (p. 7). Markle also cautioned against using synonyms as critical attributes and against using the illustrations in dictionaries and texts as defining examples. The best sources of definitions stem from the specialists within a particular subject area. Economists, anthropologists, mathematicians, chemists, and geographers, for example, are apt to provide more exact definitions and attributes of concepts in their fields than other less specialized sources. These definitions provided by experts, however, often require simplification, particularly for younger children.

Merrill and Tennyson (1977) offered the following three steps in defining concepts for instruction:

1. Identify the concept's name. A name is a word or symbol that is used to refer to the class as a whole or to examples of the class, for example, the word *island.*
2. List critical and noncritical attributes. A critical attribute is a characteristic shared by all members of a class, whereas a noncritical attribute is a characteristic shared by some, but not all, members of the class. In the example of an island, the identifying characteristics are *land mass, water,* and *surrounding.*
3. Write a concise definition. A definition is a statement identifying each of the critical attributes and indicating how these attributes are combined. For example, *an island is a land mass that is smaller than a continent and is surrounded by water.* (p. 30)

When translating definitions from particular academic subjects into instructional definitions, it is important not to distort or eliminate the critical attributes. The result might be to teach a false concept. It is also important to remember that memorizing a definition does not equate with understanding the concept.

ANALYZING CONCEPTS

Once a concept has been selected and defined in terms of its critical attributes, the concept needs to be analyzed for examples and nonexamples. The selection of examples and nonexamples, based on the critical attributes, is probably the most difficult and

Table 9-3 Analysis of Coordinated Concepts

CONCEPT	DEFINITION	EXAMPLE	NONEXAMPLE	CRITICAL ATTRIBUTES
Island	A land mass not as large as a continent, surrounded by water	Hawaii Cuba Greenland	Florida Lake Erie Australia	1. Land mass (not continent), AND 2. Water, AND 3. Land surrounded by water
Lake	A large inland body of water surrounded by land	Lake Huron Great Salt Lake Big Lake	Ohio River Hawaii pond	1. Large inland body of water, AND 2. Land, AND 3. Water surrounded by land
Peninsula	A land area almost entirely surrounded by water, but having a land connection to a larger land mass	Florida Italy Delmarva	Cuba Hudson Bay Big Lake	1. Land connected to larger land mass, AND 2. Water, AND 3. Land surrounded almost entirely by water
Bay	A body of water partly surrounded by land, but having a wide outlet to the sea	Chesapeake Hudson Green Bay	Florida lake gulf	1. Body of water connected to the sea by a wide outlet, AND 2. Land, AND 3. Water partly surrounded by land

tional phase of concept teaching. Examples serve as the connectors between the concept's abstraction and the learner's prior knowledge and experiences. Examples must be meaningful to the learner and must be as concrete as possible.

Charts, diagrams, and webs, as well as pictures, can be employed as visual examples of abstract concepts. They can also aid the teacher in analyzing the concept for instructional decisions. Table 9-3 contains an analysis of a set of concepts. Numbering the critical attributes and using the word *and* can be a reminder that all of the critical attributes must be present to have an example of the concept.

Look at the example "Hawaii" in Table 9-3. It is a land mass not as large as a continent, there is a body of water nearby, and the water completely surrounds it. Each of the three critical conditions of an island is met; therefore, it is an example of the concept. Teachers might also look at Florida as a nonexample of island. Land and water are present, but the land is not completely surrounded by water. All of the criteria are not met; therefore, Florida is a nonexample.

The isolation of the attributes is critical to the analysis and teaching of concepts. The teacher needs to decide if the attributes are critical and

should be presented when matching examples and nonexamples such as Hawaii and Florida, or if the attributes are noncritical and are best used in divergent examples after clear instances of the concept are presented.

It is also important in the process of isolating attributes to make some judgment as to the difficulty of the examples. What is meaningful to the teacher may be too difficult and not within the experiences of the learner. Merrill and Tennyson (1977) illustrated easy, medium, and difficult examples for teaching the concept "adverb." They indicated that an "adverb is a word that modifies a verb, an adjective, or another adverb and answers one of these questions: When? How? Where? or To What Extent?" The critical attributes are "modifies another word" and "function." Figure 9-5 presents examples and nonexamples of the concept "adverb."

Webbing can also be used to analyze a concept. A **web** provides a visual image of the characteristics and relationships generating from the core idea of the concept. Figure 9-6 is a web of the concept "equilateral triangle."

There are normally four steps in constructing a web for a particular concept. These include:

Figure 9-5 List of easy and difficult examples and nonexamples of adverbs

Easy Examples

1. You are so happy.
2. She has been absent lately.
3. Slowly, she walked home.
4. The train chugged loudly.

Medium Examples

5. Are you fighting mad?
6. Clouds gathered threateningly.
7. It was not difficult to explain.
8. The most dangerous weapon is a gun.

Difficult Examples

9. The small floral print looked pretty.
10. Cats are my No. 1 favorite pet.
11. He wants the dark purple bicycle.
12. The book had three color pictures.

Easy Nonexamples

13. Sewing makes you happy.
14. She has been late.
15. She is slow.
16. The loud train chugged.

Medium Nonexamples

17. Do you fight?
18. The threatening clouds gathered.
19. It is difficult to explain that *not* is a negative word.
20. Most guns are dangerous weapons.

Difficult Nonexamples

21. The small print looked pretty.
22. One special cat is my favorite pet.
23. He wants the dark trim to match.
24. The book had three pictures.

SOURCE: Adapted from M. D. Merrill and R. D. Tennyson (1977), *Teaching concepts: An instructional design approach.* Englewood Cliffs, N.J.: Educational Technology, pp. 50–51.

Step 1: Create the core, which is the focus of the web. This would be the name of the concept.

Step 2: Construct strands branching out from the core. These strands are critical attributes of the concept.

Step 3: Draw strand supports, which connect the critical attributes to the concept.

Step 4: Identify the strand ties, which may show relationships among the various attributes.

Learning aids have been included at the end of this chapter to provide you with practice in analyzing and webbing concepts.

CHOOSING AND SEQUENCING EXAMPLES AND NONEXAMPLES

When selecting a set of examples, teachers will often make the noncritical attributes of the concept as *different* as possible. This helps students focus on the critical attributes common to each of the examples. For instance, if teachers are developing the concept of "island" they might include Hawaii, a tropical island, and Greenland, which has a cold climate. The obvious differences in climates will help students focus their attention on the common attributes of these two examples. Likewise, when developing a set of examples for insects, teachers might include waterbugs and ants, which live in different environments but still have the same critical attributes.

When selecting a set of matched examples and nonexamples, teachers normally attempt to make the noncritical attributes of the pairs as *similar* as possible. This enables the student to focus on the differences between the example and the nonexample. The Florida peninsula and the Cuban island could serve as a matched pair because of the similarities in climate.

Figure 9-6 Web of the concept "equilateral triangle"

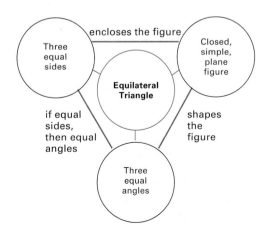

Examples and nonexamples should be sequenced for presentation in a logical fashion, and normally sets should be ordered from the easiest to the more difficult. Teachers may also want to plan to give cues to focus students' thinking before each set of three to five examples. This latter suggestion is particularly important when using the concept attainment approach with younger students.

DECIDING ON AN APPROACH

A final preinstructional decision involves choosing which approach to use. This decision depends on both the goals sought by the teacher and the nature of the concept. Remember, concept attainment is a search for critical attributes of a concept already familiar to the students and employs an inductive process. The direct presentation approach is deductive, with the teacher defining the concept for students and then helping them understand it through a presentation of examples and nonexamples. Both approaches promote higher-level thinking skills and processes.

Conducting the Lesson

The four phases of a concept teaching lesson were outlined in Table 9-2. Teacher and student behavior associated with each phase is detailed below.

PRESENTING GOALS AND ESTABLISHING SET

At the beginning of a concept lesson, just as with all types of lessons, the teacher needs to communicate clearly to students the objectives of the lesson and how the lesson will proceed. The teacher might also go over the steps of the lesson and give students reasons why the concepts about to be taught are important to learn. Establishing set for a concept lesson requires procedures no different from those described in Chapter 8. Teachers get students ready to learn with a brief review, questions about yesterday's lesson, or an interesting anecdote that ties the forthcoming lesson into students' prior knowledge.

INPUT OF EXAMPLES AND NONEXAMPLES AND TESTING FOR ATTAINMENT

The exact sequence for defining and labeling a concept or presenting examples and nonexamples varies according to the particular approach being used by the teacher. It is this internal arrangement and flow of activities which give each of the two approaches its unique character and allows each one to accomplish the particular goals for which it was designed.

Direct Presentation. In the direct presentation approach the internal flow of the lesson includes:

1. Naming the concept and providing students with a definition
2. Identifying the critical attributes and giving examples and nonexamples of the concept
3. Testing for concept understanding by getting students to provide examples and nonexamples

Taking the concept "island" as analyzed in Table 9-3, a teacher using the direct presentation approach might proceed as follows:

- Tell students that they were going to learn the concept "island" and write the name of the concept on the board so that students can see the word.
- List the critical attributes: (1) land mass (not a continent), (2) water, (3) land surrounded by water.
- Show a simple drawing that contains only the critical attributes and point out each critical attribute. This could be followed by pictures of best examples, such as Hawaii, Greenland, or Cuba. As each picture is presented, point out the critical attributes again.
- Show students both examples and nonexamples of the concept and ask questions that force judgments about whether a new instance is an example or nonexample of the concept. Have students tell why or why not. Have students come up with their own example and nonexamples.

Concept Attainment. In concept attainment, students already have some grasp of a concept or set of concepts and are asked to make decisions about whether or not particular examples are instances of a class. Teachers using the concept attainment approach would use the following steps:

1. Provide students with examples, some that represent the concept and some that do not. Best examples are clearly labeled *yes*, and carefully selected nonexamples are clearly labeled *no*.
2. Urge students to hypothesize about the attributes of the concept and to record reasons for their speculation. The teacher may ask additional questions to help focus student thinking and to get them to compare attributes of the examples and nonexamples.
3. When students appear to know the concept, they name (label) the concept and describe the process they used for identifying it. Students may guess the concept early in the lesson, but the teacher needs to continue to present examples and nonexamples until the students attain the critical attributes of the concept as well as the name of the concept.
4. The teacher checks to see if the students have attained the concept by having them identify additional examples as *yes* or *no*, tell why or why not they are examples, and generate examples and nonexamples of their own.

Concept attainment is an inductive process that assists learners in organizing data according to previously learned concepts. Unlike the direct instruction approach, the teacher provides a label and definition only after the students have engaged in the discovery of the critical attributes.

To illustrate the concept attainment approach, consider the following lesson, again using the concept "island."

• The teacher shows a picture of an island and tells students this is an example of the concept. The teacher then shows a picture of a landform that is not an island and states that this is a nonexample of the concept.
• The teacher continues displaying pictures of islands and other landforms, telling students which are and which are not examples. Students are asked to guess what they think the concept is. All hypotheses and ideas are listed on the chalkboard. The teacher continues to present examples and nonexamples and asks students to reconsider their original hypotheses.
• Students are asked to state a definition of the concept and, if possible, label it. They also list the critical attributes of the concept.

• The teacher then shows additional pictures of islands and other landforms and asks students to identify each as a *yes* or *no*. The teacher also asks students to provide examples of islands they know about and instances of landforms that are not islands. Students explain why or why not.

The major roles for the teacher during this aspect of a concept attainment lesson are to record student hypotheses and any critical attributes identified, to cue students, and to provide additional data if necessary.

ANALYZING THINKING AND INTEGRATING LEARNING

The final phase of both approaches to concept teaching emphasizes teacher-directed activities aimed at helping students to analyze their own thinking processes in order to integrate newly acquired conceptual knowledge. To accomplish this teachers ask students to think back and recount what was going through their minds as they were considering the concepts. What criteria did they use for grouping items? When did they first figure out the concept? How? What was confusing in the direct presentation lesson? How does the concept relate to other concepts they know about? Were they focusing on the concept as a whole or on a particular attribute? How did noncritical attributes affect attaining the concept? If they were going to teach the concept to a student younger than them, what would they do?

The intent of this type of questioning is to get students to think about their own thinking (termed *metacognition*) and to discover and consider the patterns they use to learn and integrate new concepts into their cognitive frameworks. This phase of a concept lesson relies, obviously, upon student discussion and participation. The guidelines for encouraging and facilitating student discussion and participation provided in Chapters 4 and 13 can also be used for this final phase of a concept teaching lesson.

Postinstructional Tasks

Many of the same ideas and strategies used in defining and analyzing concepts can be employed in evaluating students' understanding of concepts.

The critical attributes become the basis for knowing a concept. A concept analysis separates the critical attributes from the noncritical attributes, permitting discriminations and classifications to take place.

To attain the higher levels of concept learning advocated by Klausmeier (1980), the learner should be able to (1) define the concept and know its critical attributes, (2) recognize examples and nonexamples, and (3) evaluate examples and nonexamples in terms of their critical attributes. For example, with the concept "island," the learner, when given examples of islands, bays, lakes, and peninsulas could (1) properly name and identify the islands, (2) name the critical attributes of islands and discriminate them from noncritical attributes, and (3) evaluate how the islands differ from bays, lakes, and peninsulas; in terms of the critical attributes of islands, for example, peninsulas are not completely surrounded by water.

Klausmeier (1980) provided examples of multiple-choice test items for assessing students' understanding of concepts.

1. Item to measure knowledge of the definition of the concept *inferring*:

   Which of the following is the best definition of *inferring?*
   a. Using one or more of the senses to examine things carefully and to draw a conclusion.
   b. Relating a scientific observation to something which is known, and drawing a conclusion about what was observed.
   c. Drawing a conclusion about what will happen without making a scientific observation.
   d. Relating a scientific fact to something which is observed, and predicting the scientific outcome.

2. Item to measure the ability to discriminate the critical attributes of *inferring*:

   For the following questions, blacken the letter of the correct answer on your answer sheet.
   Which of the following tells about someone relating a scientific observation to something which is known?
   a. Tom looked up information about African wildlife and gave a report on lions.
   b. Mary drew pictures of three different types of clouds in the sky.
   c. Bill saw some blue speckled eggs in a nest.

He knew that robins lay blue speckled eggs.
   d. Pam heard a noise in the dark room. She thought, "It must be a monster."

3. Item to measure the ability to recognize examples and nonexamples of the concept inferring:

   Some of the following stories describe inferring. Some stories do not. You must read each story carefully and then decide whether or not the person inferred. If the story describes inferring, blacken in the space for "Yes" on your answer sheet; if the story does not, blacken the space for "No."
   a. Sandy observed many acorns underneath a tall tree. She knew that acorns fall from oak trees. Sandy concluded that the tall tree was an oak.
   b. Don looked carefully at a slice of bread and saw something green growing there. Don knew that bread mold was green.
   c. Sam went to visit his uncle on the farm. He looked in the barn to see if his uncle was there, but he did not see his uncle. Sam did not see the cows either.
   d. Joe baked a cake. The cake did not rise. Joe knew that baking powder makes cakes rise. He concluded that he had left the baking powder out of his cake. (pp. 127–130)

When evaluating students' understanding of a concept, it is important that teachers ask the students to do more than merely define the concept with words. They should also ask students to demonstrate knowledge of the critical attributes and their relationships. For example, the concept "sidewalk" might be defined as "a walkway *beside* a street." To demonstrate knowledge of the concept, the learner might "(1) identify a walkway by pointing to an actual picture of a walkway, (2) identify the street in a similar fashion, and (3) demonstrate *beside* by correctly relating the walkway to the street in the correct spatial relationship" (Gagné and Briggs, 1979, p. 66).

There are a number of principles that teachers should consider when constructing tests of the students' behaviors in the learning of concepts. For example, test items should include examples that measure the students' abilities to generalize to newly encountered examples of a concept. The test items should also assess students' abilities to discriminate among examples and nonexamples. Tests might employ different formats such as true-false, multiple choice, matching, short answer, or short essay. Practice assessment activities such as a variation of "Twenty Questions" can be used to provide practice on the students' knowledge of concepts.

Tests for concept learning can also be employed for diagnostic purposes. An analysis of students' errors can indicate whether students have misconceptions about a concept, overgeneralize the concept to include closely related nonexamples, or undergeneralize by labeling some examples as nonexamples. If any of these three conditions exists, *reteaching* should take place. Merrill and Tennyson (1977) suggested the following guidelines:

1. If a student makes an overgeneralization error, additional instruction should consist of *matched* example-nonexample pairs that emphasize the absence of the critical attribute.

2. If a student makes an undergeneralization error, additional instruction should consist of more *difficult* examples that focus attention on the presence of the critical attribute.

3. If a student makes a misconception error, additional instruction should consist of matched example-nonexample pairs that are *divergent* on the noncritical attribute causing the confusion. Attribute isolation should focus the student's attention on the noncritical nature of this attribute. (p. 82)

SUMMARY

- Concepts are the basic building blocks around which people organize their thinking and communication. A concept's critical attributes help define it and distinguish it from other concepts. The various kinds of concepts include conjunctive concepts, disjunctive concepts, and relationship concepts. Students grasp general concepts mainly by being presented with specific examples and nonexamples of the concept.
- Concept learning and logical thinking are critical goals for almost everything taught in schools. These become important scaffolding for building student understanding of school subjects. Concept learning is essentially a process of putting things into classes or categories.
- The knowledge base on concept learning and teaching is extensive. Studies have shown how

age and intellectual development influence readiness to learn concepts. Studies have also shown how examples and nonexamples should be presented to maximize student learning and how teachers can use such specific practices as visual and mental images and graphic organizers to support concept learning.

- The instructional effect of concept teaching is mainly to help learners acquire conceptual understandings of the subjects they are studying and to provide a basis for higher-level thinking.
- A concept lesson consists of four major phases: presenting goals and establishing set, providing examples and nonexamples, testing for attainment, and helping students analyze their thinking processes.
- There are several different approaches to teaching concepts. Two of the most prevalent are direct presentation and concept attainment. In direct presentation the teacher labels and defines the concept early in the lesson and then presents the best examples through exposition. In concept attainment the teacher presents examples and nonexamples of a particular concept but does not define and label the concept until the end of the lesson.
- Preinstructional tasks include concept selection and analysis, selection of examples and nonexamples, and decisions regarding the sequence in which to present the examples.
- Through questioning and discussion, teachers help students analyze their thinking and integrate new learning with old as the final phase of a concept lesson.
- As with other instructional models, a major postinstructional task requires teachers to match their testing programs to the model's particular goals.
- When evaluating students' understanding of a concept, it is important to ask students to do more than merely define the concept. Students should also be asked to demonstrate their knowledge of the concept's critical attributes and its relationship to other concepts.

KEY TERMS

concept teaching
concept
conjunctive concept

disjunctive concept
relational concept
example
nonexample
critical attributes
noncritical attributes
conceptual knowledge
procedural knowledge
rule-to-example
example-to-rule
graphic organizers
direct presentation
concept attainment
web
integration of learning

BOOKS FOR THE PROFESSIONAL

Bruner, J., Goodnow, J., and Austin, G. (1956). *A study of thinking*. New York: Wiley. This book provides an examination of thinking as the foundation for concept attainment.

Hyde, A. A., and Bizar, M. (1989). *Thinking in context: Teaching cognitive processes across the elementary school curriculum*. New York: Longman. This book provides a solid and contemporary theoretical framework about how to teach concepts and thinking skills to students. It shows how cognitive processes are linked to content in four important subject areas: reading and writing, mathematics, science, and social studies.

Klausmeier, H. (1980). *Learning and teaching concepts*. New York: Academic Press. This book includes reports on experiments and test construction for concept learning. It also contains suggestions for adapting concept teaching for individual differences.

Merrill M. D., and Tennyson, R. D. (1977). *Teaching concepts: An instructional design guide*. Englewood Cliffs, N. J.: Educational Technology. Outlined in this text are specific steps for such activities as selecting concepts, defining concepts, selecting an example pool, and teaching strategies. The final section is on putting it all together.

Tobin, K., Kahle, J. B., and Fraser, B. J. (1990). *Windows into science classrooms: Problems associated with higher-level cognitive learning*. New York: Falmer Press. Although the focus of this book is on science classrooms, much of the research that is described and interpreted can be generalized to other types of classrooms where the teacher is interested in conceptual and higher-level learning.

LEARNING AIDS FOR PLANNING, OBSERVATION, AND REFLECTION

- Assessing My Skills for Concept Teaching
- Observing a Concept Attainment Lesson in Microteaching or Classrooms
- Concept Analysis
- Webbing Exercise
- Analyzing Curriculum Guides for Concept Lessons

ASSESSING MY SKILLS FOR CONCEPT TEACHING

PURPOSE: The purpose of this aid is to give you an opportunity to assess your current level of effectiveness or understanding of concept teaching.

DIRECTIONS: Check the level of effectiveness or understanding you feel you have for the teaching tasks listed below that are associated with concept teaching.

UNDERSTANDING OR SKILL	LEVEL OF UNDERSTANDING OR SKILL		
	HIGH	MEDIUM	LOW
Preinstructional tasks			
Selecting concepts	_____	_____	_____
Defining concepts	_____	_____	_____
Analyzing concepts	_____	_____	_____
Sequencing examples and nonexamples	_____	_____	_____
Deciding on which approach to use	_____	_____	_____
Instructional tasks			
Directed presentation			
Present goals and establish set	_____	_____	_____
Name concept and provide definition	_____	_____	_____
Identify critical attributes	_____	_____	_____
Show examples	_____	_____	_____
Develop concept	_____	_____	_____
Analyze thought processes and/or integrate learning	_____	_____	_____
Concept attainment			
Present goals and establish set	_____	_____	_____
Present examples and nonexamples of concept	_____	_____	_____
Facilitate students' hypothesizing about concept and comparing attributes	_____	_____	_____
Facilitate students' describing how they arrived at the label for the concept	_____	_____	_____
Check for student understanding	_____	_____	_____
Analyze thought processes and/or integrate learning	_____	_____	_____
Postinstructional tasks			
Testing for concept learning	_____	_____	_____

OBSERVING A CONCEPT ATTAINMENT LESSON IN MICROTEACHING OR CLASSROOMS

DIRECTIONS: This form highlights the key aspects of a concept attainment lesson. It can be used to observe a peer in a microteaching laboratory or an experienced classroom teacher. It can also be used to assess a lesson you have taught and videotaped. As you observe the lesson, check the category you believe describes the level of performance of the teacher you are observing. Also answer the general questions about the lesson at the bottom of the form.

	LEVEL OF PERFORMANCE			
TEACHER BEHAVIOR	EXCELLENT	ACCEPTABLE	NEEDS IMPROVEMENT	NOT NEEDED
Planning				
How appropriate was the concept of the lesson?	______	______	______	______
How well prepared was the teacher overall?	______	______	______	______
Execution				
How well did the teacher				
Explain goals and purposes?	______	______	______	______
Establish set?	______	______	______	______
Explain the functions of yes and no categories?	______	______	______	______
Have sufficient yes and no examples?	______	______	______	______
Ask questions to focus student thinking on the essential attributes?	______	______	______	______
Ask students to compare characteristic yes examples?	______	______	______	______
Ask students to generate hypotheses about the concept?	______	______	______	______
Have the students name the concept?	______	______	______	______
Have students provide their own examples and nonexamples after concept was defined?	______	______	______	______

Have students describe the
  thinking processes they
  used in attaining the
  concept?   _____   _____   _____   _____

Have students evaluate the
  effectiveness of their
  thinking strategies?   _____   _____   _____   _____

Overall Planning

What did you like best about the way the lesson was planned and organized? _____

_____

What could be improved? _____

_____

Lesson Execution

Think about teaching style and delivery. What did you like best about the way the lesson was presented?

_____

_____

What could be improved? _____

_____

If you were a student in peer microteaching, how did you feel about the teacher's interaction with you?

_____

_____

CONCEPT ANALYSIS

PURPOSE: It is imperative that the teacher carefully analyze any concept that he or she is planning to teach. In order to communicate clearly to students what the concept is, what its attributes are, and what constitutes an example or nonexample, the teacher needs to have an unshakably clear grasp of the concept. This aid, which is adapted from P. Martorella (1985, p. 83), is a planning guide to assist you in concept analysis.

DIRECTIONS: Select a concept for analysis that it is likely you will want to teach some day. Follow the steps listed below to analyze this concept.

1. Name the concept. _____

   _____

2. Define or state the rule for the concept. _____

   _____

   _____

3. List the critical attributes of the concept. _____

   _____

   _____

4. List the noncritical attributes that are related to the concept. _____

   _____

   _____

5. Select examples that highlight the critical attributes of the concept. _____

   _____

   _____

6. Select nonexamples that are closely related to the concept. _____

   _____

Analysis and Reflection: Try teaching your concept informally to a few friends. Did you discover any parts that were difficult for them to understand? Based on your friends' feedback, refine your definition, attributes, and examples. Write a paragraph on what you learned about forming clear definitions, attributes, and examples.

CHAPTER 10

Direct Instruction

ometimes it is easy for teachers to forget that the foundation for all other types of learning is basic skills. Skills—cognitive and physical—are the foundations on which more advanced learning (including learning to learn) are built. Before students can discover powerful concepts, think critically, solve problems, or write creatively they must first acquire basic skills and information. For example, before students can acquire and process large amounts of information, they must be able to decode and encode spoken and written messages, take notes, and summarize. Before students can think critically, they must have basic skills associated with logic, such as drawing inferences from data and recognizing bias in presentation. Before students can write an eloquent paragraph, they must master basic sentence construction, correct word usage, and the self-discipline required to keep on a writing task. In essence, in any field of study, we must *learn the mechanics before the magic.*

In fact, the difference between novices and experts in almost any field is that experts have mastered certain basic skills to the point where they can perform them unconsciously and with precision, even in new or stressful situations. For example, expert teachers seldom worry about classroom management because after years of experience they are confident of their group control skills. Similarly, top

NFL quarterbacks read every move of a defense without thinking and automatically respond with skillful actions to a "safety blitz" or double coverage of prize receivers, something novice quarterbacks cannot do.

This chapter focuses on a teaching model which is aimed at helping students learn basic skills and knowledge that can be taught in a step-by-step fashion. For our purposes here, the model is labeled the **direct instruction model.** As you will see later, this model does not always have the same name. Sometimes it is referred to as a *training model* (Joyce, Weil, and Shower, 1992). Good, Grouws, and Ebmeier (1983) have called their model **active teaching.** Hunter (1982) labeled hers **mastery teaching.** And recently, Rosenshine and Stephens (1986) called this approach **explicit instruction.**

Even though you may never have thought about this model in any systematic way, you will undoubtedly be familiar with certain aspects of it. The rationale and procedures underlying this model were probably used by adults to teach you to drive a car, brush your teeth, hit a solid backhand, write a research paper, or solve algebraic equations. This model may have been used to correct your phobia about flying or wean you from cigarettes. The direct instruction model is rather straightforward and can be mastered in a relatively short time.

It is a "must" in the repertoire of the beginning teacher.

PERSPECTIVE AND RATIONALE

Several historical and theoretical roots provide the rationale for the direct instruction model, including the ideas from cognitive psychology and information processing discussed in Chapter 8. Joyce, Weil, and Showers (1992) have emphasized the contributions from training and behavioral psychology. Madeline Hunter (1987) credits the work of R. M. Gagné (1977) as the basis for the components included in her lesson design. Rosenshine and Stephens (1986) wrote that they found a book published by the War Manpower Commission in 1945 titled *How to Instruct* that included many of the ideas and steps associated with direct instruction. Much of the research presented in Chapter 3 on time and learning also supports the model, as you will soon see. Short discussions about the contributions of systems analysis, training psychology, and studies of effective teaching follow.

Systems Analysis

Systems analysis has its roots in many fields and it has influenced research on many aspects of human development—biology, organizational theory, social theory, and learning. Basically, it is the study of the various relationships that exist between the interdependent parts of some whole. Examples of two well-known *systems* are the intricate relationships among the various living organisms that make up an ecosystem or the relationships between the production, distribution, and communication parts of the incredibly complex system of international trade. People generally become aware of the part-whole relationships of systems only when they break down. For example, overpopulation of rabbits developed in Wyoming after the coyote population was systematically eliminated in that area. Similarly, there are instances when purchasers are unable to buy a Japanese car in Chicago because East Coast dock workers are on strike.

In the area of instruction and learning the systems approach has emphasized how to systematically separate complex skills and ideas into their component parts so they can be taught and learned more effectively. Two theorists and instructional designers, Gagné and Briggs (1979), represent the systems point of view in education:

> Systematically designed instruction can greatly affect individual human development. Some educational writings . . . indicate that education would perhaps be best if it were designed simply to provide a nurturing environment in which young people were allowed to grow up in their own ways, without the imposition of any plan to direct learning. We consider this an incorrect line of thinking. Unlearned and undirected learning, we believe, is very likely to lead to the development of many individuals who are in one way or another incompetent to derive personal satisfaction from living in our society of today or tomorrow. (p. 5)

Later you will see how the ideas of directed learning and task analysis (a tool used by systems analysts) have contributed to the direct instruction model.

Training Psychology

If systems analysis has provided the rationale and theory for the precision of the direct instruction model, training psychology, as applied in military and industrial settings, has motivated much of the direct application. With the rise of modern organizations, many jobs require performance of tasks far more complex than those required in earlier periods. Modern warfare has also created a demand for personnel who can operate complex and sophisticated weapon systems. For example, it is reported that the Air Force's B-1 bomber requires over 7,000 manuals totaling over 1 million pages to guide the 1,577 personnel who fix and fly this plane (*Washington Post,* August 18, 1985). Obviously, since no one person can fix the plane or even understand such complexity, a continuing problem for educators in military and industrial settings is how to prepare personnel who can master particular pieces of large complex tasks. Since traditional educational methods failed to produce the necessary precision and mastery, training methods based on behavioral psychology gradually evolved in military and industrial settings and were ultimately adopted by teachers in schools.

Studies of Effective Teachers

Teachers discovered that direct instruction could be adapted to the teaching of basic academic skills such as reading, mathematics, writing, and various science and social science skills. Much of the evidence of the model comes from studies where researchers found effective teachers who were using direct instruction on their own. When the achievement of their students was compared to that of students in classrooms where the teachers were not so direct in their instructional approaches, researchers found that the former were doing better, particularly in reading and mathematics at the elementary level.

SAMPLING THE KNOWLEDGE BASE

The knowledge base for the direct instruction model and its various components comes from many fields. Three areas are highlighted here, including studies that provide some insight into the knowledge base and the nature of the research associated with this model.

Overall Effects

Much of the research that provided the empirical base for the direct instruction model has already been introduced. Chapter 3 described the Stallings and Kaskowitz (1974) study in which the researcher found that classrooms in Project Follow Through that emphasized structured learning of basic skills produced stronger learning gains than classrooms using more informal approaches. You also read about studies showing strong relationships between structured situations where students had high time-on-task ratios and student achievement, particularly in the area of basic skills. Many of these studies used procedures that identified two groups of teachers: those who were effective in producing student achievement and those who were not. Observing these teachers in naturalistic settings gave some insight into what the effective ones were doing to promote higher student achievement; in this instance they were applying direct instruction procedures.

Some researchers started to list the behaviors used by effective teachers and to develop programs that could be used to train teachers and to test the cause and effect relationships between specific teacher behaviors and student achievement under experimental conditions. One such experiment was done by Good and Grouws at the University of Missouri. Based on earlier research, Good and Grouws developed a program for teaching mathematics in elementary school based on the direct instruction model. The instructional behaviors they deemed important are listed in Figure 10-1. Their research is summarized in Research Summary 10-1.

Behavioral Modeling and Demonstration

Some of the conceptual underpinnings for the direct instruction model come from Albert Bandura's social learning theory and **behavioral modeling** which says that much of what we learn is through modeling. Bandura (1977) wrote:

> Learning would be exceedingly laborious, not to mention hazardous, if people had to rely solely on the effects of their own actions to inform them what to do. Fortunately, most human behavior is learned observationally through modeling: from observing others one forms an idea of how new behaviors are performed, and on later occasions this coded information serves as a guide for action. Because people can learn from example what to do, at least in approximate form, before performing any behavior, they are spared needless errors. (p. 22)

Given the confines of the classroom, demonstration is usually the most practical strategy for teachers to use in promoting learning through modeling. However, demonstrations must be carefully planned and executed as described later. They must also be structured so the learner will, according to Bandura, "attend to, and perceive accurately, the significant features of the modeled behavior" (1977, p. 24). This proposition has been studied in a variety of formats and contexts over the years, including studies that date back to the 1930s and 1940s. The key principles that come out of all this research are

RESEARCH SUMMARY 10-1

Good, T. L., and Grouws, D. A. (1979). The Missouri mathematics effectiveness project: An experimental study in fourth-grade classrooms. *Journal of Educational Psychology, 71,* 355–362.

PROBLEM: In a previous study, Good and Grouws observed that certain teachers using specific direct instruction practices seemed to consistently produce high levels of achievement in their students. In this study they decided to investigate the effectiveness of these practices experimentally.

SAMPLE AND SETTING: From the Tulsa, Oklahoma, public schools, 40 classroom teachers volunteered from 27 schools that used semidepartmental structures for teaching mathematics. Good and Grouws report that most of the schools were in low socioeconomic areas of the city.

PROCEDURES: The researchers met with all the teachers in the fall of the year and randomly assigned them to two groups. Schools were used as the units for random assignment.

- **Experimental group:** The program was explained to the teachers in this group and they were provided with a short training session and a 45-page manual explaining the key teaching behaviors of the program, which are summarized in Figure 10-1.
- **Control group:** Teachers in this group were told they would not get any information about the program or the study until it was over. Their job was to continue to teach mathematics in their own style. The researchers strived to create a strong Hawthorne condition with control teachers by emphasizing how important it was to improve achievement in mathematics.

Student achievement was measured with a specially designed test of the content covered by teachers in the school system, the mathematics subtest of Science Research Associates' standardized achievement test. Students were tested in September at the beginning of the project and again in December and January.

RESULTS: The researchers observed all the teachers in the study and reported that the program as defined was implemented "reasonably well." Table 10-1 shows the impact of the experimental program on student achievement.

---

these: (1) effective demonstrations require careful attention by teachers to make sure all behaviors being demonstrated are accurately modeled, (2) conditions are present so learners can clearly perceive what is going on, and (3) explanation and discussions during demonstrations enhance later student performance. Procedures for giving effective demonstrations are elaborated later in the chapter.

Practice and Transfer

A critical feature of the direct instruction model is the use of practice, particularly practice to facilitate

Figure 10-1   Summary of key instructional behaviors

Daily Review (first 8 minutes except Mondays)
1. Review the concepts and skills associated with homework
2. Collect and deal with homework assignments
3. Ask several mental computation exercises

Development (about 20 minutes)
1. Briefly focus on prerequisite skills and concepts
2. Focus on meaning and promote student understanding by using lively explanations, demonstrations, process explanations, illustrations, etc.
3. Assess student comprehension
   (a) Using process/product questions (active questions)
   (b) Using controlled practice
4. Repeat and elaborate on the meaning portions as necessary

Seatwork (about 15 minutes)
1. Provide uninterrupted successful practice
2. Momentum—keep the ball rolling—get everyone involved, then sustain involvement
3. Alerting—let students know their work will be checked at the end of the period
4. Accountability—check the students' work

Homework Assignment
1. Assign on a regular basis at the end of each math class except Fridays
2. Should involve about 15 minutes of work to be done at home
3. Should include one or two review problems

Special Reviews
1. Weekly review/maintenance
   (a) Conduct during the first 20 minutes each Monday
   (b) Focus on skills and concepts covered the previous week
2. Monthly review/maintenance
   (a) Conduct every fourth Monday
   (b) Focus on skills and concepts covered since the last monthly review

SOURCE: From T. L. Good and D. A. Grouws (1979), The Missouri mathematics effectiveness project: An experimental study in fourth-grade classrooms. *Journal of Educational Psychology, 71,* 357. Copyright 1979 by the American Psychological Association. Reprinted by permission of publisher and author.

(Continued on page 316)

transfer. Fortunately, this topic has been studied rather extensively, so a solid base exists from which to operate. The syntax for this model brings practice into focus two times: first, when the teacher provides initial practice to see if students understand specific topics or skills, and second, when independent practice is assigned under different or more complex conditions. Both kinds of practice are intended to promote transfer of learning.

Transfer of learning is an important concept because the intention of most school learning is to promote transfer to nonschool settings. Teachers

RESEARCH SUMMARY 10-1 *(Continued)*

TABLE 10-1 Preproject and Postproject Means and Standard Deviations for Experimental and Control Classes on the SRA Mathematics Test

GROUP	PREPROJECT DATA			POSTPROJECT DATA			POSTPROJECT GAIN		
	RAW SCORE	GRADE EQUIVALENT	PERCENTILE	RAW SCORE	GRADE EQUIVALENT	PERCENTILE	RAW SCORE	GRADE EQUIVALENT	PERCENTILE
Experimental									
Mean	11.94	3.34	26.57	19.95	4.55	57.58	8.01	1.21	31.01
Standard deviation	3.18	.51	13.30	4.66	.67	18.07			
Control									
Mean	12.84	3.48	29.80	17.74	4.22	48.81	4.90	.74	19.01
Standard deviation	3.12	.48	12.43	4.76	.68	17.45			

SOURCE: Adapted from T. L. Good and D. A. Grouws (1979), p. 359.

DISCUSSION AND IMPLICATIONS: As can be observed in Table 10-1, students in the experimental group began the program with lower scores than did students in the control group. Note, however, that by the end of the program students in the experimental group had gained significantly—11.94 to 19.95 on number of questions answered correctly, as contrasted with a gain for the control group students of 12.84 to 17.74. Data in Table 10-1 also show the impressive gain in terms of national norms or percentile ranking. The achievement gains by students in the experimental group were statistically significant.

This study, among several others done since that time, supports the premise that direct instruction and training can produce fairly impressive results for the type of learning the model is aimed at accomplishing. The Good and Grouws study is also important because it shows that achievement can occur, given the right instruction, in urban, low-income schools. Good and Grouws are themselves quick to point out that all mathematics instruction should not necessarily follow this approach, because other goals can be better achieved by different approaches.

want their students to read a first-grade primer so that they can later read newspapers, magazines, and works of literature. Teachers want students to solve mathematical problems in textbooks so that later they can perform real-world mathematical functions or think mathematically in problem situations.

The concept of time for learning, introduced in Chapter 3, is also associated with practice and transfer. Researchers have studied such questions as: How much time should be devoted to practice? Should the time be spread out or concentrated? How much time should pass between practice sessions? Later in the chapter several of these issues are discussed in some detail.

MAIN FEATURES OF DIRECT INSTRUCTION

As with the case of other models, the direct instruction model can be described by its instructional effects, its syntax, and the structure of its learning environment. After providing an overview of the model, teaching behaviors required to successfully execute this model are examined.

Instructional Effects

In Chapter 8, the concepts of declarative and procedural knowledge were introduced. Declarative knowledge, remember, is knowledge learners have about something, whereas procedural knowledge is knowledge about how to do something. The direct instruction model has been specifically designed to promote student learning of the procedural knowledge needed to perform simple and complex skills and for declarative knowledge that is well structured and can be taught in a step-by-step fashion. The models described previously focused primarily on acquisition of declarative knowledge; in contrast, the direct instruction model makes important contributions to the teaching of skills. Table 10-2 contrasts the instructional objectives of models aimed at promoting **knowledge acquisition** with those of models aimed at teaching skills.

Differences can easily be observed in the two sets of objectives listed in Table 10-2. For instance, in the first set of objectives, the student is expected to know ice hockey rules. This is important declarative knowledge for students in a physical education class. However, being able to identify the rules does not necessarily mean that the student can perform any skills associated with ice hockey, like passing while on the move, the content of the procedural knowledge objective found in column 2. Another example illustrating the differences in the two types of objectives could be from the field of music. Many people can identify a French horn; some are even familiar with the history of the instrument. Few, however, have sufficient procedural knowledge to play a French horn well.

Syntax of Direct Instruction

There are five essential phases or steps in the direct instruction model. The model begins with the teacher providing rationale and establishing set. Next, it requires demonstration of the skill or knowledge being taught. And it concludes with opportunities for students to practice and receive feedback on their progress. It is always important for teachers to promote transfer to other real-life settings for skills taught in classrooms. The five phases of the training model are summarized in Table 10-3. A more detailed discussion of these steps is presented in the last section of this chapter.

Structure of the Learning Environment

Of all the models described, the direct instruction model requires the most careful structuring and orchestration by the teacher. To be effective, the

Table 10-2   Contrasting Objectives for Knowledge Acquisition and Skill Development

KNOWLEDGE ACQUISITION	SKILL DEVELOPMENT
1. The student will be able to list the basic rules of ice hockey.	1. The student will be able to pass while moving.
2. The student will be able to identify the subjects in the following sentences: a. Whose brother are you? b. Ralph always walked to school. c. Josie loves to read mysteries.	2. The student will supply an appropriate verb in the following sentences: a. Where _____ you? b. Ralph always _____ to school. c. _____ the apples to your sister.
3. Given the equation $y = 2.6x + 0.8$, the student will correctly select the number corresponding to the y intercept.	3. The student will be able to solve for x in the equation $9 = 2.6x + 0.8$.

Table 10-3 Syntax of the Training Model

PHASES	TEACHER BEHAVIOR
Phase 1: Provide objectives and establish set.	Teacher goes over objectives for the lesson, gives background information, and explains why the lesson is important. Gets students ready to learn.
Phase 2: Demonstrate knowledge or skill.	Teacher demonstrates the skill correctly or presents step-by-step information.
Phase 3: Provide guided practice.	Teacher structures initial practice.
Phase 4: Check for understanding and provide feedback.	Teacher checks to see if students are performing correctly and provides feedback.
Phase 5: Provide extended practice and transfer.	Teacher sets conditions for extended practice with attention to transfer of the skill to more complex situations.

model requires attention to every detail of defining the skill or content to be taught and the nature of the demonstration, as well as to the practice schedules provided for students. Even though there are opportunities for teachers and students to jointly identify goals, the model is primarily teacher-directed. This does not mean, as most developers of the model point out, that the learning environment has to be authoritarian, cold, or free from humor. It does mean that the environment is task-oriented and provides high expectations for student accomplishment.

PROCEDURES FOR USING DIRECT INSTRUCTION

Expert execution of the direct instruction model requires specific behaviors and decisions by teachers during the preinstructional, interactive, and postinstructional stages. Some of these required behaviors you have already learned from studying the previous models; some, however, are unique. The unique features are emphasized here.

Preinstructional Tasks

Although the direct instruction model is applicable to any subject, it is most appropriate for the performance-oriented subjects, such as reading and writing or physical education, and for the skill components of the more informationally oriented subjects like history or science. It is also effective for teaching those aspects of any subject in which the

information or skill is well-structured and can be taught in the step-by-step fashion. This probably explains its popularity among reading and mathematics teachers in elementary schools. The direct instruction model is not appropriate for teaching creativity, higher-level thinking skills, or abstract concepts and ideas, nor for teaching attitudes, appreciation, or understanding of important public issues. Table 10-2 illustrated the kinds of objectives for which the direct instruction model is most appropriate. In this section more detail is provided in how to prepare objectives for this model.

PREPARING OBJECTIVES WHEN USING THE MODEL

Previous chapters described the characteristics of objectives in some detail. In general, conceptualizing objectives for a lesson using the direct instruction model follows the same general guidelines. Remember, as described in Chapter 2 a good objective is student-based and specific, describes the testing situation, and specifies the level of performance expected. The major characteristic of objectives for lessons that are skill-oriented is that the objectives for these types of lessons normally represent easily observed behaviors that can be stated precisely and measured accurately. For example, if the objective is to have students climb a 15-foot rope in 7 seconds, that behavior can be observed and timed. If the objective is to have the student go to the world globe and point out Kuwait, that behavior can be observed. On the other hand, performance tests for more complex skills (such as your use of the various models of teaching described in this book) are very difficult to construct and sometimes nearly impossible. A learning aid at the end of this chapter has been designed to help you gain further clarity about the nature of basic skill objectives deemed important in schools.

PERFORMING TASK ANALYSIS

Task analysis is one tool used to define with some precision the exact nature of a particular skill or well-structured bit of knowledge. Some people believe that task analysis is something that is unreasonably difficult and complex, when in fact it is a rather straightforward and simple process, particularly for teachers who know their subjects well. The central idea behind task analysis is that complex understandings and skills cannot be learned at one time or in their entirety. Instead, for ease of understanding and mastery, complex skills and understandings must first be divided into significant component parts.

Task analysis helps the teacher define precisely what it is the learner needs to do to perform a desired skill. It can be accomplished through the following:

Step 1: Find out what a knowledgeable person does when the skill is performed.

Step 2: Divide the overall skill into subskills.

Step 3: Put subskills in some logical order, showing those that might be prerequisite to others.

Step 4: Design strategies to teach each of the subskills and how they are combined.

Figure 10-2 shows a simple task analysis for an objective in mathematics, subtracting whole numbers.

Sometimes a task analysis can take the form of a flowchart. This allows the skill and the relationships among subskills to be visualized. It also can show the various steps that a learner must go through in acquiring the skill. Figure 10-3 is a task analysis done this way. It shows the steps and subskills needed to perform a set of skills associated with playing ice hockey.

It would be a mistake to believe that teachers do

task analysis for every skill they teach in the detail found in Figures 10-2 and 10-3. Even though the process is not difficult, it is time-consuming. Effective teachers do, however, rely on the main concept associated with task analysis, that is, that most skills have several subskills and that learners cannot learn to perform the whole skill well unless they have mastered the parts.

As a final note about task analysis, think about the way information and tasks associated with using the various teaching models are organized in this book. First it is stated that there are a number of tasks that must be performed: planning tasks in the preinstructional phase, specific tasks associated with conducting the lesson, and tasks connected to postinstructional activities. A teacher who cannot perform all tasks well cannot use the model effectively. On the other hand, even if all tasks can be performed well, a lesson will not be well taught unless the teacher can creatively combine all the parts into a meaningful whole.

Conducting the Lesson

As outlined in Table 10-3, the direct instruction model breaks down into the following five steps: (1) providing objectives and establishing set, (2) demonstrating the skill or understanding that is the focus of the lesson, (3) providing guided practice, (4) checking for understanding and providing feedback, and (5) assigning independent practice. The first four steps, which take place in the classroom, are described below. The fifth step is dealt with as a postinstructional activity.

PROVIDING OBJECTIVES AND ESTABLISHING SET

Regardless of the instructional model being used, good teachers begin their lessons by explaining their objectives and establishing a learning set. As previously described, an abbreviated version of the objectives should be written on the chalkboard or printed and distributed to students. In addition, students should be told how a particular day's objective ties into previous ones and, in most instances, how it is a part of longer-range objectives or themes. They should also be informed about the

Figure 10-2 Task analysis for subtracting whole numbers

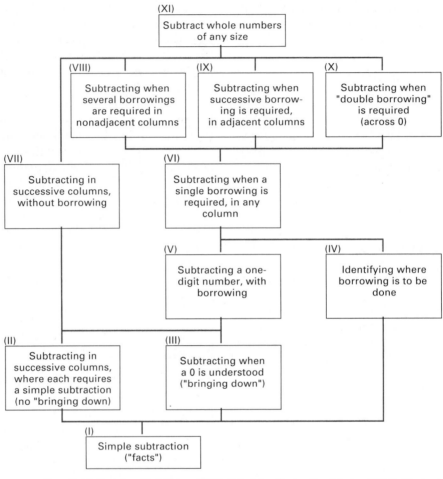

SOURCE: From R. M. Gagné and L. J. Briggs (1979), *Principles of instructional design.* © Holt, Rinehart and Winston. Reprinted by permission of Holt, Rinehart and Winston Inc.

flow of a particular lesson and about how much time the lesson is expected to take. Figure 10-4 is an example of what a science teacher provided for her students prior to a lesson on microscopes.

Giving the rationale and overviews for any lesson is important, but it is particularly so for skill-oriented lessons. Such lessons typically focus on discrete skills that students may not perceive as important but that require substantial motivation and commitment to practice on the part of students. Knowing the rationale for learning a particular skill helps to motivate and bring the desired commitment, as contrasted to such general statements as,

"It's good for you," "You'll need it to find a job," or, "It is required in the curriculum guide."

CONDUCTING DEMONSTRATIONS

The direct instruction model relies heavily on the proposition that much of what is learned and much of the learner's behavioral repertoire comes from observing others. Bandura's social learning theory specifically demonstrated and argued that it is from watching particular behaviors that students learn to perform them and to anticipate their consequences. The behaviors of others, both good and bad, thus

Figure 10-3   Flow chart of skills for ice hockey

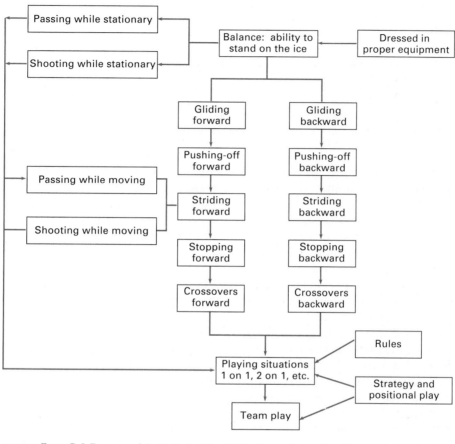

become guides for the learner's own behavior. This form of learning by imitation saves students much needless trial and error. It can also allow them to learn inappropriate or incorrect behaviors.

Demonstrating a particular concept or skill requires teachers to (1) acquire a thorough understanding or mastery of the concept or skills prior to the demonstration, and (2) carefully rehearse all aspects of the demonstration prior to the actual classroom event.

Understanding and Mastery.   To ensure that students will observe correct rather than incorrect behaviors, teachers must attend to exactly what goes into their demonstrations. The old adage often re-

peated to children by parents, "Do as I say, not as I do," is not sufficient for teachers trying to teach precise basic information or skills. Examples abound in every aspect of human endeavor where people unknowingly perform a skill incorrectly because they observed and learned the skill from someone who was doing it wrong. The important point here is that if teachers want students to do something "right," they must ensure that they demonstrate it correctly.

Rehearsal.   It is exceedingly difficult to demonstrate anything with complete accuracy. The more complex the information or skill, the more difficult it is to be precise in classroom demonstrations. To

Figure 10-4   Aims and overview of today's lesson on microscopes

Today's objective: The objective of today's lesson is to learn how to bring into focus the lens on a compound light microscope so you can make an accurate observation of plant cells.

Agenda:

5 minutes	Introduction, review, and objectives
5 minutes	Rationale
10 minutes	Demonstration of how to adjust lens on microscope—questions and answers
20 minutes	Practice with your microscope (I'll come around and help)
10 minutes	Wrap-up and assignment for tomorrow

ensure correct demonstration and modeling requires practice ahead of time. It also requires that the critical attributes of the skill or concept be thought through clearly and distinctly. For example, suppose you want to teach your students how to use the card catalog to locate information in the library and you are going to demonstrate how call numbers on a particular card correspond to a book's location. It is important to prepare and rehearse so the numbering system demonstrated is consistent with what students will find in their particular library. If the demonstration consists of such steps as going to the card catalog, looking up the book, writing down the call number, and then proceeding to the stacks, it is important that these steps be rehearsed to the point that none (such as writing down the call number) is forgotten during the actual demonstration.

PROVIDING GUIDED PRACTICE

Common sense says that "practice makes perfect." In reality, this principle does not always hold up. You all know people who drive their cars every day but who are still poor drivers, or people who have many children but who are poor parents. All too often the assignments teachers give students do not really provide for the type of practice that is needed. Writing out answers to questions at the end of a chapter, doing 20 mathematics problems, or writing an essay do not always help students master important skills.

A critical step in the direct instruction model is the way the teacher approaches **guided practice.** Fortunately for the beginning teacher, a considerable amount of research evidence now exists that can guide efforts to provide practice. For example, it

is known that active practice can increase retention, make learning more automatic, and enable the learner to transfer learning to new or stressful situations. The following principles can help teachers provide for practice.

Assign   Short,   Meaningful   Amounts   of Practice.   In most instances, particularly with a new skill, it is important to ask students to perform the desired skill for short periods of time and, if the skill is complex, to simplify the task at the beginning. Briefness and simplification, however, should not distort the pattern of the whole skill. Look again at the example of a teacher using the direct instruction model to help students learn how to use the card catalog in the library. After sufficient explanation and demonstration the teacher now wants students to practice the skill. One approach would be to send students to the library to locate 20 books listed on a work sheet. Probably a more efficient and controlled way would be to have sample sets of catalog cards in the room (simplifying the complexity of the whole catalog system) and have students look up one book at a time in the card index (shortening the practice).

Assign Practice to Increase Overlearning.   For skills that are critical to later performance, practice must continue well beyond the stage of initial mastery. Many skills associated with the performing arts, athletics, reading, and typing have to be overlearned so they become automatic. It is only through **overlearning** and complete mastery that a skill can be used effectively in new and novel situations or under stress. This ability to automatically perform a skill or combination of skills is what separates the novice from the expert in all fields.

Teachers must be careful, however, because efforts to produce overlearning can become monotonous and actually decrease students' motivation to learn.

Be Aware of the Advantages and Disadvantages of Massed and Distributed Practice.   Many schools in the United States have homework policies—the rule of thumb is about 30 minutes per night per subject for older students and at least a few minutes a night for younger students. Although homework can be valuable for extending student learning, a required amount of time each night can be harmful. The amount and timing of practice depend upon many factors. Normally psychologists have defined this issue as **massed** (continuous) **practice** versus **distributed** (divided into segments) **practice.** Although the research literature does not give direct principles that can be followed in every instance, massed practice is usually recommended for learning new skills, with the caution that long periods of practice can lead to boredom and fatigue. Distributed practice is most effective for refining already familiar skills, again with the caution that the interval of time between practice segments should not be so long that students forget or regress and have to start over again.

Attend to the Initial Stages of Practice.   The initial stages of practice are particularly critical since it is during this period that the learner can unknowingly start using incorrect techniques that later must be unlearned. It is also during the initial stages of practice that the learner will want to measure success in terms of his or her performance as contrasted to technique. This issue will be described more completely below.

CHECKING UNDERSTANDING AND PROVIDING FEEDBACK

Without knowledge of results, practice is of little value to students. In fact, the most important task of teachers using the direct instruction model is providing students with meaningful **feedback** or **knowledge of results.** Feedback to students can be done in many ways, such as verbal feedback, video- or audiotaping of performance, tests, or written comments. Without specific feedback, however, students will not learn to write well by writing, read

well by reading, or run well by running. The critical question for teachers is how to provide effective feedback for large classes of students. A learning aid at the end of this chapter has been designed to assist your observation of how experienced teachers use practice and provide feedback. Here are some important guidelines.

Provide Feedback as Soon as Possible after the Practice.   It is not necessary that feedback be provided instantaneously, but it should be close enough to the actual practice that students can remember clearly their own performance. This means that teachers who provide written comments on essays should be prompt in returning corrected papers. It means that tests gauged to measure performance should be corrected immediately and gone over with students. It also means that arrangements for verbal feedback or feedback using video or audio devices should be such that delay is kept to a minimum.

Make Feedback Specific.   In general, feedback should be as specific as possible to be most helpful to students. For example:

"Your use of the word 'domicile' is pretentious; 'house' would do nicely."

instead of:

"You are using too many big words."

Or:

"Your hand was placed exactly right for an effective backhand."

instead of:

"Good backhand."

Or:

"Three words were spelled incorrectly on your paper: 'pleistocene,' 'penal,' and 'recommendation.'"

instead of:

"Too many misspelled words."

Concentrate on Behaviors, Not Intent.   Feedback is most helpful to students and raises less defensiveness if it is aimed directly at some behavior as contrasted to one's perception of the intent behind the behavior. For example:

"I cannot read your handwriting. You do not provide enough blank space between words and you make your O's and A's identically."

instead of:

"You do not work on making your handwriting neat."

Or:

"When you faced the class in your last speech, you spoke so softly that most students could not hear what you were saying."

instead of:

"You should try to overcome your shyness."

Keep Feedback Appropriate to the Developmental Stage of the Learner.   As important as knowledge of results is, feedback must be administered carefully to be helpful. Sometimes, students can be given too much feedback or feedback that is too sophisticated for them to handle. For example, a person trying to drive a car for the first time can appreciate hearing that he or she "let the clutch" out too quickly which caused the car to jerk. The beginning driver, however, is not ready for explanations about how to drop the brake and use the clutch to keep the car from rolling on a steep hill. A young student being taught the "i before e" rule in spelling probably will respond favorably to being told that he or she spelled "brief" correctly, but may not be ready to consider why "recieve" was incorrect.

Emphasize Praise and Feedback on Correct Performance.   You all know from your own experiences that you like to receive positive more than negative feedback. In general, praise will be accepted whereas negative feedback may be denied.

Teachers, therefore, should try to provide praise and positive feedback particularly when students are learning new concepts and skills. However, when incorrect performance is observed, it must be corrected. Characteristics of effective praise were given in Chapter 6. Here is a sensible approach to the dealing with incorrect responses and performances provided by Madeline Hunter (1982, pp. 85–90). She recommended the following three teacher behaviors:

1. Dignify the student's incorrect response or performance by giving a question for which the response would have been correct. For example, "George Washington would have been the right answer, if I had asked you who was the first president of the United States."
2. Provide the student with an assist, hint, or prompt. For example, "Remember, the president in 1828 was also a hero in the War of 1812."
3. Hold the student accountable. For example, "You didn't know President Jackson today, but I bet you will tomorrow when I ask you again."

A combination of positive and negative feedback is best in most instances. For example, "You did a perfect job of matching subjects and verbs in this paragraph, except in the instance where you used a collective subject." Or, "You were holding the racket correctly as you approached the ball, but you had too much of your weight on your left foot." Or, "I like the way you speak up in class, but during our last class discussion you interrupted Ron three different times when he was trying to give us his point of view."

When Giving Negative Feedback, Show How to Perform Correctly.   Knowing that something has been done incorrectly does not help students do it correctly. Negative feedback should be accompanied with actions by the teacher demonstrating correct performance. If a student is shooting a basketball with the palm of the hand, the teacher should point that out and demonstrate how to place the ball on the fingertips; if a writing sample is filled with words used incorrectly, the teacher should pencil in words that would be more appropriate; if students are holding their hands incorrectly on the

Table 10-4   Items for Knowledge Test and Skill Test

KNOWLEDGE TEST	SKILL TEST

1. How many players are there on an ice hockey team?
  a. 6
  b. 8
  c. 10
  d. none of the above
	1. Demonstrate a pass while moving.

2. What is the subject of the following sentence? "*Mary's mother is an artist.*"
  a. Mary
  b. mother
  c. an
  d. artist
	2. Correct the verbs, as needed, in the following sentences:
	  a. Kim ran slowly to the store.
	  b. Tommy said it was time to go.
	  c. Levon sat joyfully to greet her dad.
	  d. "Please be noisier," said the teacher.

3.
 	
At what point is the intercept located?
  a. 1   c. 3
  b. 2   d. 4
	3. Solve for x in the following equations:
	  a. $2 = x + 4$
	  b. $5x = 1 + (x/2)$
	  c. $14 = 2x + 9x$
	  d. $x/3 = 9$

computer keyboard, the correct placement should be modeled.

Help Students to Focus on "Process" Rather Than Outcomes.   Many times beginners want to focus their attention on measurable performance. "I just typed 35 words per minute without any errors." "I wrote my essay in an hour." "I drove the golf ball 75 yards." "I cleared the bar at 4 feet 6 inches." It is the teacher's responsibility to get students to look at the "process" or technique behind their performances and to understand that incorrect techniques may achieve immediate objectives but will probably inhibit later growth. For example, a student may type 35 words per minute using only two fingers but will probably never reach 100 words per minute using this technique. Starting the approach on the wrong foot may be fine for clearing the high jump bar at 4 feet 6 inches, but will prevent the jumper from ever reaching 5 feet 6 inches.

Teach Students How to Judge Their Own Performances.   Chapter 1 described how important it is for beginning teachers to learn how to assess and judge their own performances by submitting their own teaching to self-review and reflection. The same advice can be given to students to help them learn and progress. Teachers can help students judge their own performances in many ways. They can explain the criteria used by experts in judging performance; they can give students opportunities to judge peers and assess their own progress in relation to others; and they can emphasize the importance of self-monitoring and goal setting and of not being satisfied with only "extrinsic" feedback from the teacher.

Postinstructional Tasks

Postinstructional tasks associated with the direct instruction model consist of the final phase in the syntax, providing for independent practice and testing student understanding and skill.

INDEPENDENT PRACTICE

Most **independent practice** for students provided by teachers using the direct instruction model is done through homework. Considerable attention about how to assign and use homework to extend learning time was provided in Chapter 3 and does not need to be repeated here. It is, however, worth mentioning again that homework or independent practice is an opportunity for students to perform newly acquired skills on their own and, as such, should not involve the continuation of instruction, but instead the continuation of the practice. Also, feedback should be provided for independent practice in the same fashion as recommended for initial practice.

TESTING

Previous chapters emphasized the importance of matching testing and evaluation strategies to the goals and objectives for particular lessons and the inherent purposes of a particular model. Since the direct instruction model is used most appropriately for teaching skills and knowledge that can be taught in a step-by-step fashion, evaluation should focus on performance tests measuring skill development rather than paper and pencil tests of declarative knowledge. For example, being able to identify the characters on the typewriter's keyboard obviously does not tell us much about a person's ability to type; however, a timed typing test does. Being able to identify verbs in a column of nouns does not mean that a student can write a sentence; it takes a test that requires the student to write a sentence to enable a teacher to evaluate that student's skill. Writing the correct steps in any of the teaching models described in this book does not tell us whether a teacher can use the model in front of 30 students; only a classroom demonstration can exhibit the teacher's mastery of that skill.

Many times, performance tests are difficult for teachers to devise and to score with precision, and they can also be very time-consuming. However, if you want your students to master the skills you teach, nothing will substitute for performance-based evaluation procedures. Table 10-4 has examples adapted from Ellen Gagné (1985) of the type of test items that would be included on a skills test and contrasts those with items on the same topic that one would find on a knowledge test. Note that the test items correspond to the sample objectives in Table 10-2.

SUMMARY

- Acquiring basic information and student skill development are important goals for every subject taught in schools. In almost any field students must learn basic skills—cognitive and physical—before they can go on to more advanced learning.

- Teachers use the direct instruction model to help students learn basic skills and knowledge. The direct instruction model draws its rationale from work in systems analysis, training psychology, and teacher-effectiveness research. It has been widely used and tested in school and nonschool settings, particularly in industry and in the military. The knowledge base on the direct instruction model is rather extensive. Many studies show its positive effects on raising student achievement, particularly with elementary students from low socioeconomic backgrounds.

- The instructional effects of the direct instruction model are mainly to promote student learning of procedural knowledge (skills) and declarative knowledge which can be organized and taught in a step-by-step fashion.

- The general flow or syntax of a direct instruction lesson consists mainly of five phases: providing objectives and establishing set, demonstrating the skill to be learned, providing guided practice, checking for student understanding and providing feedback, and providing for extended practice and transfer.

- The direct instruction model requires a highly structured learning environment and careful orchestration by the teacher. This tight structure does not mean, however, that the environment is necessarily authoritarian or uncaring.

- Preinstructional tasks associated with the direct instruction model put emphasis on careful preparation of precise objectives and performing task analysis so that complex skills can be divided and taught in significant component parts.

- Conducting a direct instruction lesson requires teachers to be proficient in demonstrating complex skills, providing students with reasons for learning these skills, and setting up appropriate conditions for practice and feedback.

- The use of practice should be guided by several

principles: assigning short, meaningful amounts of practice, assigning practice to increase over-learning, and making appropriate use of massed and distributed practice.

- For skill learning to occur, teachers must check to see if students are understanding what they are being taught and provide appropriate feedback to correct errors and misapplications.
- Postinstructional tasks of a direct instruction lesson include paying attention to the type of independent homework assignment given so students can practice under more complex conditions and constructing good performance-based tests that can accurately measure skills and provide feedback to students.

KEY TERMS

direct instruction model
active teaching model
mastery teaching model
explicit instruction
systems analysis
effective teaching
teacher-effectiveness research
behavioral modeling
transfer of learning
task analysis
demonstration
guided practice
overlearning

massed practice
distributed practice
feedback
knowledge of results
independent practice

BOOKS FOR THE PROFESSIONAL

Gagné, R. M., and Briggs, L. J. (1979). *Principles of instructional design.* New York: Holt, Rinehart & Winston. This book contains very good chapters on designing instruction, particularly in understanding task analysis and assessing student performance.

Garner, R. (1987). *Metacognition and reading comprehension.* Norwood, N.J.: Ablex. Although the focus is on reading, this book contains a good review of the research on metacognition and many ideas on how teachers can promote better student learning through direct and explicit instructional strategies.

Good, T. L., Grouws, D. A., and Ebmeier, H. (1983). *Active mathematics teaching.* New York: Longman. This book reports, for the general audience, the work of the Missouri Mathematics Program, including a summary of several research projects. Implications for teachers interested in the direct instruction model are described.

Hunter, M. (1982). *Mastery teaching.* El Segundo, Calif.: TIP Publications. This book presents a brief account of specific strategies developed by Hunter, many of which are consistent with the focus of the direct instruction model.

Posner, G. J., and Rudnitsky, A. N. (1986). *Course design. A guide to curriculum development for teachers* (3d ed.). New York: Longman. This very readable book describes many aspects of course design and is particularly helpful in explaining how to break complex information and skills into teachable units.

LEARNING AIDS FOR PLANNING, OBSERVATION, AND REFLECTION

- Assessing My Skills for Using the Direct Instruction Model
- Lesson Plan Format for a Direct Instruction Model Lesson
- Observing Direct Instruction in Microteaching or Classrooms
- Observing Teacher Use of Practice
- Reviewing Curriculum Guides for Skill Objectives

ASSESSING MY SKILLS FOR USING THE DIRECT INSTRUCTION MODEL

PURPOSE: To help you gain insight into your level of skill in using the model, use this aid after reading the chapter or after a microteaching or field assignment.

DIRECTIONS: Check the level of skill you perceive yourself having for the various teaching tasks associated with the direct instruction model.

UNDERSTANDING OR SKILL	LEVEL OF UNDERSTANDING OR SKILL		
	HIGH	MEDIUM	LOW
Preinstructional tasks			
Writing clear objectives	_____	_____	_____
Performing task analysis	_____	_____	_____
Preparing skill lessons	_____	_____	_____
Preparing for demonstration	_____	_____	_____
Instructional tasks			
Phase 1			
Explaining objectives and set	_____	_____	_____
Phase 2			
Conducting demonstration	_____	_____	_____
Phase 3			
Designing guided practice	_____	_____	_____
Phase 4			
Checking for understanding	_____	_____	_____
Providing feedback	_____	_____	_____
Postinstructional tasks			
Phase 5			
Designing independent practice	_____	_____	_____
Designing performance test items	_____	_____	_____

LESSON PLAN FORMAT FOR A DIRECT INSTRUCTION MODEL LESSON

PURPOSE: This is a lesson plan format suggested for use with the model. As with the formats suggested for other teaching models, experiment with this format to determine if it meets your requirements. Be flexible and modify it as the need arises.

DIRECTIONS: Use the following suggested format as a model for writing a training lesson.

Planning phase

Content or skill to be taught: _____

_____

Objectives

1. Given _____ , the student will be able to
   (Situation)

   _____ , with
   (Target behavior)

   _____
   (Level of performance)

2. Given _____ , the student will be able to
   (Situation)

   _____ , with
   (Target behavior)

   _____
   (Level of performance)

Conducting the lesson

Time	Phase and Activities	Materials
____	Lesson objectives and set: _____	____
	_____	____
____	Lesson demonstration: _____	____
	_____	____
	_____	____
____	Initial guided practice: _____	____
	_____	____
	_____	____
____	Checking for understanding and providing feedback: ____	____
	_____	____
	_____	____

_____   Independent practice activities: _____   _____

_____   _____

_____   _____

Pitfalls to avoid

During Introduction   **During Transitions**   **During Ending**

OBSERVING DIRECT INSTRUCTION IN MICROTEACHING OR CLASSROOMS

DIRECTIONS: This form highlights the key aspects of the direct instruction model. It can be used to observe a peer in a microteaching laboratory or an experienced classroom teacher. It can also be used to assess a lesson you have taught and videotaped. As you observe the lesson, check the category you believe describes the level of performance of the teacher you are observing. Also answer the general questions about the lesson at the bottom of the form.

TEACHER BEHAVIOR	LEVEL OF PERFORMANCE			
	EXCELLENT	ACCEPTABLE	NEEDS IMPROVEMENT	NOT NEEDED
Planning				
How appropriate was the skill selected to teach?	_____	_____	_____	_____
How well prepared was the teacher overall?	_____	_____	_____	_____
How well had the teacher performed task analysis?	_____	_____	_____	_____
Execution How well did the teacher				
Explain goals and purposes?	_____	_____	_____	_____
Establish set?	_____	_____	_____	_____
Demonstrate the skill or material?	_____	_____	_____	_____
Provide for initial practice?	_____	_____	_____	_____
Check for student understanding?	_____	_____	_____	_____
Provide feedback to students?	_____	_____	_____	_____
Try to promote transfer?	_____	_____	_____	_____
Provide for independent practice?	_____	_____	_____	_____

Overall planning

What did you like best about the way the lesson was planned and organized? _____

_____

What could be improved? _____

_____

Lesson execution

Think about teaching style and delivery. What did you like best about the way the lesson was
    presented?

_____

_____

What could be improved? _____

_____

If you were a student in peer microteaching, how did you feel about the teacher's interaction with
you? _____

_____

_____

OBSERVING TEACHER USE OF PRACTICE

PURPOSE: As emphasized in this chapter, practice is an important element in the direct instruction model and requires finesse to manage properly. Use this aid in the field to help refine your understanding of the use of practice.

DIRECTIONS: During skill lessons, observe a teacher each day for several days. Stay in the same subject area, and try to observe from the first day a skill is introduced to the last day it is covered. For example, you may watch a teacher introduce, develop, and review the skill of writing a business letter, or multiplying by 5s, or cleaning a carburetor. Whatever the skill, pay close attention to how the teacher handles student practice. Use the questions below to guide your observation and reflection.

1. On the first day the skill was introduced, what type of practice assignment did the

   teacher make: guided practice, independent practice, or both? _____

   How much time was devoted to the practice segment in class? _____

   As homework? _____

   What proportion of the total lesson was devoted to practice? _____

   Describe the teacher's behavior during the practice segment. _____

   _____

   Describe the students' behavior during the practice segment. _____

   _____

2. As the skill was developed over one or a few days, what type of practice assignment did

   the teacher make: guided practice, independent practice, or both? _____

   How much time was devoted to the practice segment in class? _____

   As homework? _____

   What proportion of the total lesson was devoted to practice? _____

   Describe the teacher's behavior during the practice segment. _____

   _____

   Describe the students' behavior during the practice segment. _____

   _____

3. As the skill was reviewed, what type of practice assignment did the teacher make: guided practice, independent practice, or both? _____

How much time was devoted to the practice segment in class? _____

As homework? _____

What proportion of the total lesson was devoted to practice? _____

Describe the teacher's behavior during the practice segment. _____

_____

Describe the students' behavior during the practice segment. _____

_____

Analysis and Reflection: How did the teacher portion out practice? In other words, did you see massed or distributed practice, or both? _____ At what points in the development of the skill were these observed: early on, during the development phase, or during review? _____

_____

Did the teacher give an indication that practice assignments were being matched to students' developing ability to perform the skill? ___ If so, how did the teacher gauge student performance? _____

_____

What kinds of teacher behavior characterized earlier skill lessons? Later skill lessons? ___

_____

What kinds of student behavior characterized earlier skill lessons? Later skill lessons? ___

_____

Do you think this teacher made wise decisions concerning provision for student practice? Why or why not? _____

_____

_____

_____

REVIEWING CURRICULUM GUIDES FOR SKILL OBJECTIVES

PURPOSE: This aid is designed to familiarize you with common skill objectives in your area or grade level and to give you practice with task analysis.

DIRECTIONS: Examine several curriculum guides in your subject area or grade level. List the skill objectives they contain. If any occur more than once, put check marks by them to keep a running tally.

1. _____

_____

_____

_____

2. _____

_____

_____

_____

_____

3. _____

_____

_____

Analysis and Reflection: Which objectives occur most frequently? _____

_____

Think through a task analysis for the three most common objectives.

Cooperative Learning

The three models of teaching described previously—presentation, concept teaching, and direct instruction—are used by teachers primarily (1) to help students acquire new information, (2) to process information already acquired from prior learning, and (3) to learn important skills. It has been emphasized that academic learning (acquiring information and thinking about that information), although extremely important, does not represent the only set of objectives for student learning. Chapter 11 presents a model of teaching called cooperative learning that goes beyond helping students learn academic content and skills to address important social goals and objectives.

PERSPECTIVE AND RATIONALE

The cooperative learning model is not the result of any single stream of pedagogical thought. Its roots go back to the early Greeks, and contemporary developments started with early-twentieth-century educational psychologists and pedagogical theorists.

John Dewey, Herbert Thelen, and Democratic Classrooms

In 1916 John Dewey, then at the University of Chicago, wrote a book called *Democracy and Education*. Dewey's conception of education was that the classroom should mirror the larger society and be a laboratory for real-life learning. Dewey's pedagogy required teachers to create within their learning environments a social system characterized by democratic procedures and scientific processes. Their primary responsibility was to engage students in inquiry into important social and interpersonal problems. The specific classroom procedures described by Dewey (and his latter-day followers) emphasized small, problem-solving groups of students searching for their own answers and learning democratic principles through day-to-day interaction with one another.

Many years after Dewey, Herbert Thelen (1954, 1960), who was also at the University of Chicago, developed more precise procedures for helping students work in groups. Like Dewey, Thelen argued that the classroom should be a laboratory or miniature democracy for the purpose of study and inquiry into important social and interpersonal problems. Thelen, with his interest in group dynamics, put more structure on the pedagogy of group investigation and, as will be described later, provided the conceptual basis for contemporary developments in cooperative learning.

The use of cooperative group work for Dewey and Thelen went beyond improving academic learning. Cooperative behavior and processes were viewed as basic to human endeavor, the foundation on which strong democratic communities could be built and maintained. The logical way to accomplish these important educational objectives for Dewey and Thelen was to structure the classroom and the students' learning activities so that they would model the desired outcomes.

Gordon Allport and Intergroup Relations

In 1954 the Supreme Court issued its historic *Brown v. Board of Education of Topeka* decision in which the Court ruled that public schools in the United States could no longer operate under a separate-but-equal policy, but must become racially integrated. This led to subsequent decisions and actions by judicial and legislative bodies all across the country calling for public school authorities to submit plans for desegregation.

At the time, thoughtful theorists and observers warned that putting people of different ethnic or racial backgrounds in the same location would not, in and of itself, counteract the effects of prejudice or promote integration and better intergroup acceptance. They knew, for example, that the cafeteria in an integrated school might still be characterized by black students sitting on one side of the room and white students on the other. They also knew that a community might be highly integrated but still have restaurants or churches patronized by an all-white or all-black clientele.

A leading sociologist of the time, Gordon Allport, argued that laws alone would not reduce intergroup prejudice and promote better acceptance and understanding. Sharan et al. (1984) summarized three basic conditions formulated by Allport to counteract racial prejudice: "(1) unmediated interethnic contact, (2) occurring under conditions of equal status between members of the various groups participating in a given setting, and (3) where the setting officially sanctions interethnic cooperation" (p. 2).

Some of the interest in the cooperative learning model in recent years has grown out of attempts to structure classrooms and teaching processes according to these three conditions. Some of Robert Slavin's work, which will be described later, was conducted in the inner cities along the eastern seaboard as part of integration efforts. The work of

Sharan and his colleagues in Israel was prompted by that country's need to find ways to promote better ethnic understanding between Jewish immigrants with European backgrounds and those with Middle Eastern backgrounds. The work of the Johnsons at the University of Minnesota explored how cooperative classroom environments might lead to better learning by and more positive regard toward handicapped students mainstreamed (integrated) into regular classrooms.

Social Psychology and Small-Group Theory

Chapters 2 through 7 provided many ideas about the nature of classroom life and a set of concepts for viewing classrooms as complex social settings where teachers perform important leadership functions. Concepts from group dynamics theory and research were described as guides for teachers' work with classroom groups. The importance of group processes on students' academic learning and socialization was discussed in some detail. Here, a few of these concepts are extended for the purpose of showing how social psychology and **small-group theory** provide the third intellectual tradition for the cooperative learning model.

GROUP EFFECTS ON INDIVIDUAL PERFORMANCE

In the early part of this century social psychologists began research on a topic most commonly referred to as "social facilitation." Classic studies in this tradition, such as Allport (1924) and Dashiell (1935), compared the performances of individuals performing both physical and intellectual tasks alone with individuals performing the same tasks with others present. The research showed that having others present has important effects on performance in some instances. Some developers of cooperative learning have used their knowledge of this research to plan specific strategies and procedures.

COOPERATION VERSUS COMPETITION

Interest in the effects that cooperative versus competitive situations have on individual and group performance also dates back to the early part of the twentieth century. Experiments conducted in laboratories, work organizations, and classrooms have consistently shown that cooperative goal structures (activities where persons are working together toward common group goals) are more productive than competitive structures. Many studies conducted across diverse settings suggest that under cooperative conditions where individuals are rewarded for group success three things happen:

1. Interdependent relationships, in which cooperation is rewarded, lead to strong motivation to complete a common task.
2. Group work develops a considerable friendliness among group members.
3. Cooperation develops a highly effective communication process that tends to promote maximal generation of ideas and greater mutual influence.

This cooperative-versus-competitive hypothesis has been tested more directly during the past decade, specifically in field tests of cooperative learning strategies, and this research will be described in detail later in this chapter.

Experiential Learning

A fourth intellectual tradition behind the cooperative learning model comes from theorists and researchers who are interested in how children learn from experience. This group rejects the idea that children (or adults for that matter) should be passive learners under the domination of the teacher. In Chapter 1, some of the principles and practices associated with **experiential learning** were introduced. The central principle introduced was that experience accounts for much of what students learn, but for best results, experience must be accompanied by systematic analysis and reflection. Cooperative learning also embraces this principle, particularly the models developed by Sharan in Israel and the Johnsons at the University of Minnesota. For example, Sharan and Sharan (1976) take the position that the teacher's task is "to increase the child's sense of efficacy by teaching him to control more of his opportunities for learning. . . . Active learning which organizes and assimilates experience through interaction with the environment will help to develop logical thought and higher order verbal communication skills" (p. x).

SAMPLING THE KNOWLEDGE BASE

Cooperative learning has a substantial research base, particularly in the field of social psychology. The study of small-group dynamics, social facilitation, and the effects of cooperative versus competitive behavior on performance provide a substantial supporting literature for the knowledge of cooperative learning. This section, however, will rely on a more recent literature, particularly the research on classroom effects of cooperative learning on (1) cooperative behavior and interethnic cooperation, (2) interactions with handicapped children, and (3) academic learning. As in previous chapters, studies have been selected that are illustrative of research in the field and that represent the work of several (but not all) major theorists and researchers.

Effects on Cooperative Behavior

Twentieth-century living is characterized by global, interdependent communities and by complex social institutions which require high degrees of cooperation among members. Consequently, most people prize cooperative behavior and believe it to be an important goal for education. Many of the schools' extracurricular activities, such as team sports and dramatic and musical productions, are justified on this basis. But what about activities within the academic classroom? Do certain types of activities, such as those associated with cooperative learning, have effects on students' cooperative attitudes and behaviors?

Shlomo Sharan and his colleagues (1984) at Tel Aviv University in Israel have sought answers to this question. For over a decade Sharan and colleagues worked on developing a particular approach to cooperative learning and testing it to see if its use would improve social relations among different Jewish subgroups in Israel, particularly between those of European and Middle Eastern backgrounds. In one study, researchers randomly assigned 33 English and literature teachers to three training groups. Teachers in group 1 were taught how to "fine-tune" their whole-class teaching skills. Those in group 2 were taught how to use Slavin's Student Teams Achievement Divisions (STAD) (explained later), and those in group 3 were taught Sharan's Group Investigation (GI) approach to cooperative learning. The investigators collected massive amounts of information before, during, and after the experiment, including data from achievement tests, classroom observations, and cooperative behavior of students.

For the test of cooperative behavior, students were selected from classrooms using each of the three instructional approaches and were asked to engage in a task called "Lego Man." In six-member teams (each with three European and three Middle Eastern members), students were asked to plan how they would carry out a joint task which consisted of constructing a human figure from 48 pieces of Lego.

Sharan's study showed clearly that the instructional methods influenced the students' cooperative and competitive behavior. Group Investigation generated more cooperative behavior, both verbal and nonverbal, than did whole-class teaching or STAD. STAD, however, produced more cooperative behavior than whole-class teaching. Students from both cooperative-learning classrooms displayed less competitive behavior than those who came from whole-class teaching classrooms. In other analyses done on these data Sharan and his colleagues showed that the cooperative-learning approaches also increased the cross-ethnic cooperation during the Lego task more than whole-class teaching.

Promoting Positive Interactions with Handicapped Children

Two decades after the Supreme Court ended separate-but-equal public schools, the Ninety-fourth Congress passed an equally historic piece of integration legislation. Titled the Education for All Handicapped Children Act, and soon to be known as Public Law 94-142, this legislation required handicapped students to be placed, whenever possible, into least-restrictive environments. Instead of placement in special schools or classrooms (the approach used for most of the twentieth century), children with handicapping conditions (approximately 12 percent of the student population) would be mainstreamed (integrated) into regular classrooms. Obviously, this meant that regular classroom teachers would now have children with physical, emotional, and mental disabilities in their classrooms.

Just as theorists knew that racial integration would not end prejudice, there was considerable evidence in 1974 that placing handicapped people (who have traditionally been perceived negatively by nonhandicapped peers) in close proximity to others would not end negative attitudes. In fact, some researchers argued that closer contact might even increase prejudice and stereotyping. A critical factor in producing more positive attitudes and behaviors seemed to be the way the interaction between handicapped and nonhandicapped students was structured. David and Roger Johnson and several of their colleagues at the University of Minnesota studied how goal structures influence interaction in a unique and interesting way. Their study is summarized in Research Summary 11-1.

Effects on Academic Achievement

One of the important aspects of cooperative learning is that while it is helping promote cooperative behavior and better group relations among students, it is simultaneously helping students with their academic learning. Slavin (1986) reviewed research and reported that 45 studies had been done between 1972 and 1986 investigating the effects of cooperative learning on achievement. These studies were done at all grade levels and included the following subject areas: language arts, spelling, geography, social studies, science, mathematics, English as a second language, reading, and writing. Studies he reviewed were conducted in urban, rural, and suburban schools in the United States and in Israel, Nigeria, and Germany. Out of the 45 studies, 37 of them showed that cooperative learning classes significantly outperformed control group classes in academic achievement. Eight studies found no differences. None of the studies showed negative effects for cooperative learning.

MAIN FEATURES OF COOPERATIVE LEARNING

Cooperative learning is a model of teaching with a set of common attributes and features. It also has several variations which will be described in this section along with explanations of the model's instructional effects, syntax, and environmental struc-

RESEARCH SUMMARY 11-1

Johnson, R., Rynders, J., Johnson, D. W., Schmidt, B., and Haider, S. (1979). Interaction between handicapped and nonhandicapped teenagers as a function of situational goal structuring: Implications for mainstreaming. *American Educational Research Journal, 16,* 161–167.

PROBLEM: The researchers wanted to find out the effects of various goal structures on the interactions between nonhandicapped junior high students and trainable mentally retarded students in a learning situation, in this instance, bowling classes.

SAMPLE: Subjects in the study were 30 junior high students (ages 13 to 16, including 15 boys and 15 girls) from three midwestern junior high schools. Nine nonhandicapped students came from a public junior high school; nine other nonhandicapped students came from a private Catholic school. The 12 handicapped students were from a school for the handicapped. The handicapped students were classified as trainable mentally retarded. This meant that they were able to communicate and understand instructions and that they did not have any physical handicaps that would prevent them from bowling.

PROCEDURES: Students were divided randomly into learning teams of five. Each team contained three nonhandicapped students and two handicapped students. Each of the learning teams was then assigned to one of three experimental conditions.

- **Cooperative condition:** Team members were instructed to "maximize" their team's bowling score at a criterion of 50 points improvement over the prior week. They were to help each other in any way possible.
- **Individualistic condition:** Students in these teams were instructed to "maximize" their individual scores by 10 points over the previous week and to concentrate only on their own performance.
- **Laissez faire condition:** Students were given no special instructions.

(Continued on page 344)

ture. After presenting an overview of the model, we will examine more thoroughly the teaching behaviors required to effectively teach a cooperative learning lesson.

Common Ingredients of Cooperative Learning

The models described in Chapters 8, 9, and 10 are characterized by task structures where teachers are working with a whole class of students at the same time or where students are working individually to master academic content or skills. The reward systems for these models are based on individual effort and performance, and their reward structures on individual competition. The cooperative learning model uses different task and reward structures.

Slavin (1984) explained that there are two important components in all cooperative learning methods: **a cooperative incentive structure** and **a cooperative task structure**. According to Slavin, "the critical feature of a cooperative incentive structure is that two or more individuals are interdependent for a reward they will share if they are successful as a group. . . . Cooperative task structures are situations in which two or more individuals are allowed, encouraged, or required to work together on some task, coordinating their efforts to complete the task" (p. 55).

RESEARCH SUMMARY 11-1 (Continued)

The three bowling instructors in the study were told what to say and were rotated across groups. All groups received the same amount of training over a 6-week period.

Trained observers, who were kept naive about the purpose of the study, watched the students bowl and recorded interactions among students into three categories: positive, neutral, and negative. Observations focused on the period of time from when a bowler stepped up to bowl until he or she stepped down from the bowling line.

POINTERS FOR READING RESEARCH: The researchers used the chi square (χ^2) to test the significance of their results. This statistic is used by researchers when their data are of a particular type. It serves the same purpose as other tests of significance introduced earlier. The results as reported in this study are straightforward and easy to read and understand.

RESULTS: Tables 11-1 and 11-2 show the results of the bowling study. Table 11-1 displays the frequency of homogeneous and heterogeneous interactions among the students in the three conditions. Table 11-2 displays data on "group cheers" for handicapped students who threw strikes and spares over the course of the study.

TABLE 11-1   **Frequency of Homogeneous and Heterogeneous Interactions within Conditions***

	POSITIVE		NEUTRAL		NEGATIVE		
	HOMO	HETERO	HOMO	HETERO	HOMO	HETERO	TOTAL
Cooperative	495	336	67	47	4	10	959
Individualistic	243	92	61	17	15	11	439
Laissez faire	265	136	75	49	9	6	540
Total	1003	564	203	113	28	27	1938

* $\chi^2 = 86.87$, $p < 01$.
NOTE: Homogeneous interactions took place between nonhandicapped students and between handicapped students; heterogeneous interactions took place between handicapped and nonhandicapped students.
SOURCE: Adapted from R. Johnson et al. (1979). p. 165.

Cooperative learning is described as having the following essential features:

- Students work in teams to master academic materials.
- Teams are made up of high, average, and low achievers.
- Teams are made up of a racially and sexually mixed group of students.
- Reward systems are group-oriented rather than individually oriented.

All of these features are explained more fully later in the chapter.

Instructional Effects of Cooperative Learning

The cooperative learning model has been developed to achieve at least three important instructional objectives.

Table 11-3   Syntax of the Cooperative Learning Model

PHASES	TEACHER BEHAVIOR
Phase 1: Provide objectives and set	Teacher goes over objectives for the lesson and establishes learning set.
Phase 2: Present information	Teacher presents information to students either through verbal presentation or with text.
Phase 3: Organize students in learning teams	Teacher explains to students how to form learning teams and helps groups make efficient transition.
Phase 4: Assist team work and study	Teacher assists learning teams as they do their work.
Phase 5: Test	Teacher tests knowledge of learning materials or groups present results of their work.
Phase 6: Recognize achievement	Teacher finds ways to recognize both individual and group effort and achievement.

Then students return to their home team and teach other members what they have learned. Following home team meetings and discussions, students take quizzes individually over the learning materials. In the Slavin version of Jigsaw, team scores are formed using the same scoring procedures as in STAD. High-scoring teams and individuals are recognized in the weekly class newsletter or by some other means.

GROUP INVESTIGATION

Many of the key features of the **Group Investigation (GI)** approach were designed originally by Herbert Thelen. More recently, this approach has been extended and refined by Shlomo Sharan and his colleagues at Tel Aviv University. Group Investigation is perhaps the most complex of the cooperative learning approaches and the most difficult to implement. In contrast to STAD and Jigsaw, students are involved in planning both the topics for study and the ways to proceed with their investigations. This requires more sophisticated classroom norms and structures than do approaches that are more teacher-centered. It also requires that students be taught the communication and group process skills described in Chapters 4 and 13.

Teachers who use the GI approach normally divide their classes into five- or six-member heterogeneous groups. In some instances, however, groups may form around friendships or around an interest in a particular topic. Students select topics for study, pursue in-depth investigations of chosen subtopics,

and then prepare and present a report to the whole class. Sharan et al. (1984) described the following six steps of the GI approach:

1. **Topic selection:** Students choose specific subtopics within a general problem area, usually delineated by the teacher. Students then organize into small two- to six-member task-oriented groups. Group composition is academically and ethnically heterogeneous.
2. **Cooperative planning:** Students and teacher plan specific learning procedures, tasks, and goals consistent with the subtopics of the problem selected in Step 1.
3. **Implementation:** Pupils carry out the plan formulated in Step 2. Learning should involve a wide variety of activities and skills and should lead students to different kinds of sources both inside and outside the school. The teacher closely follows the progress of each group and offers assistance when needed.
4. **Analysis and synthesis:** Pupils analyze and evaluate information obtained during Step 3 and plan how it can be summarized in some interesting fashion for possible display or presentation to classmates.
5. **Presentation of final product:** Some or all of the groups in the class give an interesting presentation of the topics studied in order to get classmates involved in each other's work and to achieve a broad perspective on the topic. Group presentations are coordinated by the teacher.
6. **Evaluation:** In cases where groups pursued different aspects of the same topic, pupils and

teacher evaluate each group's contribution to the work of the class as a whole. Evaluation can include either individual or group assessment, or both. (pp. 4–5)

Structure of the Learning Environment

The learning environment for cooperative learning is characterized by democratic processes and by active roles for students in deciding what should be studied and how. The teacher provides a high degree of structure in forming groups and defining overall procedures, but students control the minute-to-minute interactions within groups. If a cooperative learning lesson is to be successful, extensive resource materials must be available in the teachers' room or in the school's library or media center. Success also requires good working relationships between the classroom teacher and resource specialists in the school.

PROCEDURES FOR USING COOPERATIVE LEARNING

Preinstructional Tasks

Many functions of teacher planning described previously can be applied to cooperative learning lessons. However, there are also some unique aspects of planning when using this model. For example, time spent organizing or analyzing specific lesson skills may instead be spent gathering resource materials, texts, or work sheets so that small groups of students can work on their own. Instead of planning for the smooth flow and sequencing of major ideas, the teacher may work on how to make smooth transitions from whole-class to small-group instruction.

CHOOSING APPROPRIATE CONTENT

As with any lesson, one of the primary planning tasks for teachers is choosing content that is appropriate for the students given their interests and prior learning. This is particularly true for cooperative learning lessons, because the model requires a substantial amount of student self-direction and initiative. Without interesting and appropriately challenging content, a cooperative lesson can quickly break down.

Obviously, veteran teachers know from past experience which topics are most suited for cooperative learning, just as they know the approximate developmental levels and interests of students in their classes. Beginning teachers must depend on curriculum guides and textbooks for appropriate subject content. However, there are several questions that beginning teachers can use to determine the appropriateness of subject content.

> Have the students had some prior contact with the subject matter, or will it require extended explanation by the teacher?
>
> Is the content likely to interest the group of students for whom it is being planned?
>
> If the teacher wants to use text, does it provide sufficient information on the topic?
>
> For STAD or Jigsaw lessons, does the content lend itself to objective quizzes that can be administered and scored quickly?
>
> For a Jigsaw lesson, does the content allow itself to be divided into several natural subtopics?
>
> For a Group Investigation lesson, does the teacher have sufficient command of the topic to guide students into various subtopics and direct them to relevant resources?

FORMING STUDENT TEAMS

A second important planning task for cooperative learning is deciding how student learning teams are to be formed. Obviously, this task will vary according to (1) the goals teachers have for a particular lesson, and (2) the racial and ethnic mix and the ability levels of students within their classes. Below are some examples of how teachers might decide to form student teams.

- A fifth-grade teacher in an integrated school might use cooperative learning for the purpose of helping students to better understand peers from different ethnic or racial backgrounds. He or she might take great care to have racially or ethnically mixed teams in addition to matching for ability levels.
- A seventh-grade English teacher in a mostly middle-class white school might form student

teams according to students' achievement levels in English.

- A tenth-grade social studies teacher with a homogeneous group of students might decide to use Group Investigation and form teams according to student interest in a particular subtopic but also keep in mind mixing students of different ability levels.
- A fourth-grade teacher with several withdrawn students in her class may decide to form cooperative teams based on ability but also to find ways to integrate the isolates with popular and outgoing class members.
- Early in the year a teacher with several students new to the school might form learning teams on a random basis, thus ensuring opportunities for the new students to meet and work with students they don't yet know. Later, students' abilities could be used to form learning teams.

Obviously, the composition of teams has almost infinite possibilities. During the planning phase, teachers must delineate clearly their academic and social objectives. They also need to collect adequate information about their students' abilities so that if heterogeneous ability teams are desired, they will have the needed information. Finally, teachers should recognize that some features of group composition may have to be sacrificed in order to meet others.

DEVELOPING MATERIALS AND DIRECTIONS

When teachers prepare for a whole-class presentation, a major task is to gather materials that can be translated into meaningful verbal messages. Although teachers provide verbal information to students in a cooperative learning lesson, this information is normally accompanied by text, work sheets, and study guides.

If students are to be given text, it is important that it be both interesting and at an appropriate reading level for the particular class of students. Materials from a college textbook or other advanced text is normally inappropriate for school-aged students except, perhaps, those in advanced high school classes. If study guides are to be developed by teachers, these should be designed to highlight the content deemed most important. Good study guides and materials take time to develop and cannot be done well the night before a particular lesson is to begin.

If teachers are using the Group Investigation method, an adequate supply of materials will have to be collected for use by student learning teams. In some schools, a beginning teacher can rely on the school librarian and media specialists for gathering materials. This normally requires the teacher to communicate clearly about the goals and objectives of a particular lesson and to be precise about how many students will be involved. For librarians and media specialists to be of maximum assistance requires enough lead time for them to do their work. Again, a beginning teacher should be cautioned about last-minute requests. One of the learning aids at the end of this chapter provides you with a chance to explore the library and media resources in a school with an eye toward future cooperative learning lessons. The following guidelines are offered to get maximum assistance from school support staff when planning a cooperative learning lesson:

- Meet with the school librarian and media specialists at least 2 weeks prior to the lesson and go over your lesson objectives. Ask for their ideas and assistance.
- Follow up the meeting with a brief memo summarizing ideas, time lines, and agreements.
- Check back a few days before materials are needed to see if things are coming along as you expected and offer your assistance, if needed.
- If the materials are to be used in your room, ask the specialist to help you design a system for keeping track of materials. You may also ask the specialist to come into your room and explain the system to your students.

It is important that students have a clear understanding about their roles and the teacher's expectations for them as they participate in a cooperative learning lesson. If other teachers in the school are using cooperative learning, this task will be easier because students will already be aware of the model and their role in it. In schools where few teachers use the cooperative learning approach, beginning teachers will have to spend time describing the model to students and working with them on requisite skills. Chapters 4 and 13 describe procedures to increase communication within classroom groups and also activities to build group cohesion. These are critical skills for students in classrooms where teachers plan to use cooperative learning.

An important thing to remember for beginning teachers who have not used cooperative learning before and who are using it with students who are not familiar with the model is that at first it may appear not to be working. Students will be confused about the cooperative reward structure. Parents may also object. Also, students may not at first be very enthusiastic about the possibilities of small-group interactions on academic topics with their peers. Chapters 14 and 15 provide additional information about why this happens and what can be done about it.

Finally, special directions about the goals and activities of a particular cooperative learning lesson should be given to students in writing—on tag board displays for younger children and as handouts for older students. Included in these directions would be information about

- The goals of the lesson
- What students are expected to do while working in learning teams
- Time lines for completion of particular work or activities
- Dates of quizzes when using STAD or Jigsaw
- Dates for major presentations when using Group Investigation
- Grading procedures—both individual and group rewards
- Format for presentation of reports

Using the cooperative learning model can be most difficult for the beginning teacher because it requires the simultaneous coordination of a variety of activities. On the other hand, this model can achieve some important educational goals that other models cannot, and the rewards of this type of teaching can be enormous for the teacher who plans carefully.

Conducting the Lesson

In Table 11-3 the syntax for the cooperative learning model was divided into six steps: (1) presenting the goals for the lesson and establishing set; (2) present-ing information to students through verbal presentation, text, or other forms; (3) making the transition into learning teams; (4) managing and helping students during team study and seatwork; (5) testing over team presentation of materials; (6) recognition of student achievement. The first four steps will be discussed in this section. Testing and student recognition will be described as postinstructional tasks.

PRESENTING GOALS AND ESTABLISHING SET

Some aspects of presenting goals and establishing set are not different for cooperative learning than they were for other models. Effective teachers begin all lessons by reviewing, explaining their objectives in understandable language, and showing how the lesson ties into previous learning. Because many cooperative learning lessons extend beyond a particular day or week and because the goals and objectives are multifaceted, the teacher normally puts special emphasis on this phase of instruction.

For example, when teachers are introducing a group investigation lesson for the first time, they will want to spend sufficient time with students to make sure specific steps and roles are clearly understood. This can also be the time when a teacher may want to talk about how students can take responsibility for their own learning and not rely solely upon the teacher. It may also be a time to discuss how knowledge comes from many sources such as books, films, and one's own interactions with others.

If a teacher is about to introduce Jigsaw, he or she may want to discuss how people are required to work interdependently with others in many aspects of life and how Jigsaw gives students an opportunity to practice cooperative behaviors. Similarly, if the teacher's main objective is to improve relations between students from different ethnic backgrounds or races, he or she may want to explain this idea to students and discuss how working with people who are different from us provides opportunities to know one another better.

The important point with all these examples is that students are more likely to work toward important goals and objectives if the rationale for the lesson has been explicitly discussed. It is difficult for students to perform a task well if they are unclear about why they are doing it or if the criteria for success are kept secret.

PRESENTING INFORMATION VERBALLY OR IN TEXT

Procedures and guidelines for presenting information to students will not be repeated here because that subject was covered extensively in Chapter 8. It is important, however, to provide some information about the use of text. Most of what is described here is not unique to the cooperative learning model and can be used by the beginning teacher in many situations involving text.

Teachers of young children know that relying on text to transmit content involves helping the children learn to read the assigned materials. Teachers in the upper grades and secondary schools (and college, for that matter) often assume their students can read and comprehend the assigned materials. Many times this is an incorrect assumption. If a cooperative learning lesson requires students to read text, then effective teachers, regardless of the age level of their students or the subject taught, will assume responsibility for helping students become better readers.

MAKING TRANSITIONS FROM WHOLE CLASS TO LEARNING TEAMS

The process of getting students into learning teams and getting them started on their work is perhaps one of the most difficult steps for teachers using cooperative learning. This is the phase in a cooperative learning lesson where bedlam can result unless the transition is carefully planned and managed. There is nothing more frustrating to teachers than transitional situations where 30 students are moving into small groups, not sure of what they are to do, and each demanding the teacher's attention and help. Three simple but important strategies can be used by teachers to make transitions go smoothly.

1. **Write key steps on the chalkboard or on charts** Visual cues assist large groups of students as they move from one place in the room to another. Think of these as signs similar to those provided for people lining up to purchase theater tickets to a popular play or queuing procedures used at public events such as football games. Below is an example of such a display:

   Step 1: Move quickly to the location where your team's name has been posted on the wall.

   Step 2: Choose one team member to come up to my desk to gather needed learning materials.

   Step 3: Spend 10 minutes reading your particular assignment.

   Step 4: At my signal, begin your discussions.

   Step 5: At my signal, return to your learning team and start presenting your information.

2. **State directions clearly, and ask two or three students to paraphrase the directions** Getting several students to repeat the directions helps everyone to pay attention and also gives the teacher feedback on whether or not the directions are understood.

3. **Identify a location for each learning team and have that clearly marked** Left to their own devices, students at any age (even adults) will not evenly distribute themselves around a room. They will tend to cluster in areas of the room that are most easily accessible. For effective small-group work, teachers should clearly designate those parts of the room they want each team to occupy and insist that teams go to that particular location.

A learning aid has been included at the end of this chapter to study and reflect upon the transition process in a cooperative learning lesson.

MANAGING AND HELPING STUDENTS DURING TEAMWORK

Some rather uncomplicated cooperative learning activities allow students to complete their work with minimum interruption or assistance by the teacher. For other activities, the teacher may need to work closely with each of the learning teams, reminding them of the tasks they are to perform and the time allocated for each step. When using the Group Investigation method, the teacher must remain constantly available to assist with resource identification. There is a fine line for the teacher to follow during this phase of a cooperative learning lesson. Too much interference and unrequested assistance can be annoying to students. It can also take away opportunities for student initiative and self-direction. At the same time, if the teacher finds that students are unclear about the directions or that

Figure 11-1   Scoring procedures for STAD and Jigsaw

Step 1: Establish base line	Each student is given a base score based on averages on past quizzes.
Step 2: Find current quiz score	Students receive points for the quiz associated with the current lesson.
Step 3: Find improvement score	Students earn improvement points to the degree to which their current quiz score matches or exceeds their base score, using the scale provided below.

More than 10 points below base. . . . . .0 points
10 points below to 1 point below base . . . . .10 points
Base score to 10 points above base. . . . . .20 points
More than 10 points above base . . . . .30 points
Perfect paper (regardless of base) . . . . .30 points

SOURCE: From R. Slavin (1986), *Student team learning* (3d ed.), Center for Research on Elementary and Middle Schools, p. 19. © Johns Hopkins.

they cannot complete planned tasks, then direct intervention and assistance are required. A learning aid at the end of this chapter has been designed for beginning teachers who want to learn more about how students interact with one another during small-group work.

Postinstructional Tasks

For each of the models of teaching described previously, the importance of using evaluation strategies that are consistent with the goals and objectives of a particular lesson and consistent with the model's overall theoretical framework has been emphasized. For example, if the teacher is using presentation and explanation to help students master important ideas and to think critically about these ideas, then test questions asking students both for recall and for higher-level responses are required. If the teacher is using the direct instruction model to teach a specific skill, a performance test is required to measure student mastery of the skill and to provide corrective feedback. All of the examples and suggestions given in previous chapters, however, are based on the assumption that the teacher is operating under a competitive or individualistic reward system. The cooperative learning model changes the reward system and, consequently, requires a different approach to evaluation and recognition of achievement.

For STAD and the Slavin version of Jigsaw, the teacher requires students to take quizzes over the learning materials. Test items on these quizzes must, in most instances, be of an objective type so they can be scored in class or soon after. Figure 11-1 illustrates how individual scores are determined, and Figure 11-2 gives an example of how a quiz scoring sheet might look.

Slavin (1983), the developer of this scoring system, described it this way:

The amount that each student contributes to his or her team is determined by the amount the student's quiz score exceeds the student's own past quiz average. . . . Students with perfect papers always receive the . . . maximum, regardless of their base scores. This individual improvement system gives every student a good chance to contribute maximum points to the team if (and only if) the student does his or her best, and thereby shows substantial improvement or gets a perfect paper. This improvement point system has been shown to increase student academic performance even without teams (Slavin, 1980), but it is especially important as a component of STAD since it avoids the possibility that low performing students will not be fully accepted as group members because they do not contribute many points. (p. 24)

An elaborate scoring system does not exist for the Group Investigation approach. The group re-

Figure 11-2 Quiz score sheet (STAD and Jigsaw)

Student	Date: May 23 Quiz: Addition with Regrouping			Date: Quiz:			Date: Quiz:		
	Base Score	Quiz Score	Improvement Points	Base Score	Quiz Score	Improvement Points	Base Score	Quiz Score	Improvement Points
Sara A.	90	100	30						
Tom B.	90	100	30						
Ursula C.	90	82	10						
Danielle D.	85	74	0						
Eddie E.	85	98	30						
Natasha F.	85	82	10						
Travis G.	80	67	0						
Tammy H.	80	91	30						
Edgar I.	75	79	20						
Andy J.	75	76	20						
Mary K.	70	91	30						
Stan L.	65	82	30						
Alvin M.	65	70	20						
Carol N.	60	62	20						
Harold S.	55	46	10						
Jack E.	55	40	0						

SOURCE: From R. Slavin (1986), *Student team learning* (3d ed.), p. 20. Center for Research on Elementary and Middle Schools. © Johns Hopkins.

port or presentation serves as one basis for evaluation and students should be rewarded for both individual contributions and the collective product. The teacher has to be careful with the evaluation process for group investigation activities. Consistent with the concept of cooperative reward structure, it is important for the teacher to reward the group product. However, this can cause two kinds of problems. One, a few ambitious students may take on a larger portion of the responsibility for completing the group project and then be resentful toward classmates who made only minor contributions yet received the same evaluation. Similarly, students who have neglected their responsibilities to the group effort may develop cynicism toward a system that rewards them for work not accomplished. No place in the literature has been found where this problem is directly addressed.

Some experienced teachers have found a solution by providing two evaluations for students—one for the group's effort and one for each person's individual contribution. The latter is sometimes difficult to ascertain. This procedure also prevents less able students from making as significant contributions as are possible with the scoring system of STAD and Jigsaw based on individual improvement.

RECOGNITION OF EFFORT

A final important postinstructional task unique to cooperative learning is the emphasis given to recognizing student effort and achievement. Slavin and the Johns Hopkins developers created the concept of the weekly class newsletter for use with STAD and Jigsaw. The teacher (sometimes the class itself)

Figure 11-3 Sample weekly newsletter

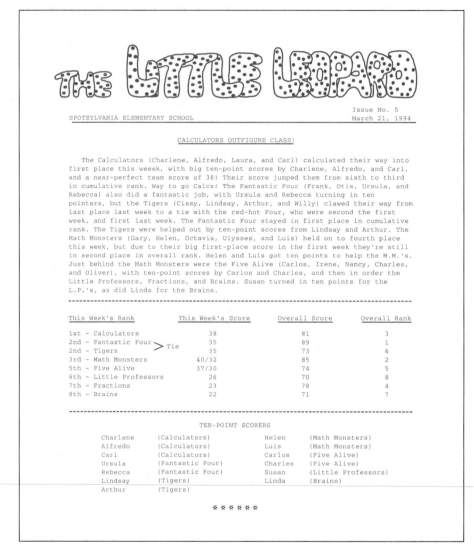

SOURCE: From R. Slavin (1986), *Student team learning* (3d ed.), p. 25. Center for Research on Elementary and Middle Schools. © Johns Hopkins.

reports on and publishes the results of team and individual learning in this newspaper. An example of a weekly newsletter is shown in Figure 11-3.

More recently, the Johns Hopkins group has tended to play down the competition among teams, and instead of determining winning teams they recommend pitting teams against preestablished criteria to evaluate team achievement. Figure 11-4 shows the criteria used by some teachers and recommended by Slavin.

The developers of the Group Investigation approach recognize team efforts by highlighting group presentations and by displaying the results of group investigations prominently in the room. This form of recognition can be emphasized even more by inviting guests (parents, students from another

Figure 11-4 Determining and rewarding team scores and team summary sheet

Step 1: Determining team scores

Team scores are figured by adding each member's individual improvement points and dividing by the number of members on the team.

Step 2: Recognizing team accomplishments

Each team receives a particular certificate based on the following point system.

Team Average	Award
15 points	Good Team
20 points	Great Team
25 points	Super Team

Team name_**Fantastic Four**

Team members	1	2	3	4	5	6	7	8	9	10	11	12	13	14
Sara A.	30													
Eddie E.	30													
Edgar I.	20													
Carol N.	20													
Total team score	100													
Team average*	25													
Team award	Super Team													

*Team average = a total team score ÷ number of team members

SOURCE: From R. Slavin (1986), *Student team learning* (3d ed.), p. 19. Center for Research on Elementary and Middle Schools. © Johns Hopkins.

class, or the principal) to hear final reports. Newsletters summarizing the results of a class's group investigation could also be produced and sent to parents and others in the school and community.

SUMMARY

- Cooperative learning is unique among the models of teaching because it uses a different task and reward structure to promote student learning. The task structure of cooperative learning requires students to work together on academic tasks in small groups. The reward structure recognizes collective as well as individual effort.

- The intellectual roots for cooperative learning grew out of an educational tradition emphasizing democratic thought and practice, active learning, and respect for pluralism in multicultural societies.

- A strong knowledge base supports the use of cooperative learning. Studies have shown the positive effects of cooperative learning on academic achievement, race relationships, cooperative behavior, and attitudes toward the handicapped.

- The instructional effects of cooperative learning go beyond academic learning and specifically aim at promoting intergroup acceptance, broader peer liking patterns, and self-esteem.

- There are several types of cooperative learning. Three of the most popular include Student Teams Achievement Divisions (STAD), Jigsaw, and Group Investigation (GI).
- Regardless of the specific approach, a cooperative learning lesson has three essential features: students work in teams, teams are heterogeneously formed, and reward systems are group-oriented.
- The general flow or syntax of a cooperative learning lesson includes six major phases: providing objectives and set, giving students information through presentation or text, organizing students into learning teams, providing time and assisting team study, testing for results, and recognizing both individual and group achievement.
- The learning environment for cooperative learning is characterized by democratic processes; students assume active roles and take responsibility for their own learning.
- Preinstructional tasks emphasize considering the best ways for organizing students for small-group work and collecting a variety of appropriate learning materials to be used during group work.
- During a cooperative learning lesson key roles for teachers include helping students make transitions from whole-class settings to learning teams and assisting teams as they do their work.
- Conducting a cooperative learning lesson changes the teacher's role from that of center-stage performer to choreographer of small-group activity. Time is spent helping students work together rather than presenting and demonstrating learning materials.
- Postinstructional tasks, particularly evaluation, stress group as well as individual rewards, along with new forms of recognition.

KEY TERMS

small-group theory
experiential learning
Education for All Handicapped Children Act
cooperative incentive structure
cooperative task structure
Student Teams Achievement Divisions
Jigsaw
Group Investigation

BOOKS FOR THE PROFESSIONAL

Aronson, E., Blaney, S. C., Sikes, J., and Snapp, M. (1978). *The Jigsaw classroom*. Beverly Hills, Calif.: Sage Publications. This book presents an in-depth discussion of the Jigsaw approach to cooperative learning, including results from research and detailed directions for teachers interested in the approach.

Davidson, N. (Ed.). (1989). *Cooperative learning in mathematics: A handbook for teachers*. Reading, Mass.: Addison-Wesley. This is a book of readings on cooperative learning strategies, written specifically for teachers and representing most of the major cooperative learning theorists and researchers.

Johnson, D. W., and Johnson, R. T. (1986). *Learning together and alone. Cooperation, competition, and individualization* (2d ed.). Englewood Cliffs, N.J.: Prentice-Hall. This book gives a detailed rationale for the goal and reward structures required of cooperative learning and also provides many good ideas for teachers who want to implement cooperative learning in their classrooms.

Kagan, S. (1992). *Cooperative learning*. San Juan Capistrano, Calif.: Resources for Teachers. A resource manual to assist teachers with using cooperative learning in their classrooms, this book is filled with lesson ideas and aids.

Slavin, R. (1983). *Cooperative learning*. New York: Longman. This book provides detailed rationale behind cooperative learning along with summaries of Slavin's research.

Slavin, R., Sharan, S., Kagan, S., Hertz-Lazarowitz, R., Webb, C., and Schmuck, R. (eds.). (1985). *Learning to cooperate, cooperating to learn*. New York: Plenum Press. This is a book of readings by the major theorists and developers of cooperative learning. Rich in theory, it also provides practical approaches for teachers to follow.

LEARNING AIDS FOR PLANNING, OBSERVATION, AND REFLECTION

- Assessing My Skills for Using Cooperative Learning
- Observing Cooperative Learning in Microteaching or Classrooms
- Observing Small-Group Interaction
- Observing Transitions and Group Management
- Visiting the School's Library and Media Center

ASSESSING MY SKILLS FOR USING COOPERATIVE LEARNING

PURPOSE: To help you assess your level of skill in using cooperative learning, this aid can be used either after reading the chapter or after a microteaching or field assignment.

DIRECTIONS: Check the level of skill you perceive that you have for the various teaching tasks associated with the cooperative learning model.

UNDERSTANDING OR SKILL	LEVEL OF UNDERSTANDING OR SKILL		
	HIGH	MEDIUM	LOW
Preinstructional tasks			
Choosing appropriate content	_____	_____	_____
Deciding on composition of learning teams	_____	_____	_____
Developing and/or gathering needed materials	_____	_____	_____
Writing clear directions	_____	_____	_____
Instructional tasks			
Explaining objectives and establishing set	_____	_____	_____
Presenting information (lecture and/or text)	_____	_____	_____
Making transition to learning teams	_____	_____	_____
Helping students during team study	_____	_____	_____
Postinstructional tasks			
Constructing appropriate tests	_____	_____	_____
Scoring tests for individuals and groups	_____	_____	_____
Devising means to recognize student achievement	_____	_____	_____

OBSERVING COOPERATIVE LEARNING IN MICROTEACHING OR CLASSROOMS

DIRECTIONS: This form highlights the key aspects of a cooperative learning lesson. It can be used to observe a peer in a microteaching laboratory or an experienced classroom teacher. It can also be used to assess a lesson you have taught and videotaped. As you observe the lesson, check the category you believe describes the level of performance of the teacher you are observing. Also answer the general questions about the lesson at the bottom of the form.

TEACHER BEHAVIOR	LEVEL OF PERFORMANCE			
	EXCELLENT	ACCEPTABLE	NEEDS IMPROVEMENT	NOT NEEDED
Planning				
How appropriate was the content for the lesson?	_____	_____	_____	_____
How appropriate were plans for team formation?	_____	_____	_____	_____
How appropriate were materials gathered to support the lesson?	_____	_____	_____	_____
How well prepared was the teacher overall?	_____	_____	_____	_____
Execution How well did the teacher				
Explain goals and purposes?	_____	_____	_____	_____
Establish set?	_____	_____	_____	_____
Explain small-group activities?	_____	_____	_____	_____
Make transition to learning teams?	_____	_____	_____	_____
Help students during team study?	_____	_____	_____	_____
Recognize individual effort?	_____	_____	_____	_____
Recognize team effort?	_____	_____	_____	_____

Overall planning

What did you like best about the way the lesson was planned and organized? _____

_____

What could be improved? _____

_____

Lesson execution

Think about teaching style and delivery. What did you like best about the way the lesson was

presented? _____

_____

What could be improved? _____

_____

If you were a student in peer microteaching, how did you feel about the teacher's interaction with

you? _____

_____
_____

OBSERVING SMALL-GROUP INTERACTION

PURPOSE: For cooperative learning to be a success, students must help each other learn. This tool will focus you on how students behave when in their teams and will enhance your ability to spot off-task behavior.

DIRECTIONS: Observe a class during the team study phase of a cooperative learning lesson. Watch one of the teams; every 15 seconds, check off which of the following behaviors it exhibits.

FREQUENCY	GROUP ACTIVITY
_____	1. Reading (finding information and so forth)
_____	2. Manipulatng equipment
_____	3. Task discussion, general participation
_____	4. Task discussion, one or two students dominate
_____	5. Procedural discussion
_____	6. Observing
_____	7. Nontask discussion
_____	8. Procedural dispute
_____	9. Substantive discussion, task relevant
_____	10. Silence or confusion
_____	11. Other (specify) _____

Analysis and Reflection: Were the students more often on or off task? _____

If on task, what did the teacher do that contributed to on-task behavior? _____

If off task, what could the teacher have done to prevent the off-task behavior? _____

SOURCE: Adapted from T. L. Good and J. E. Brophy, *Looking in classrooms* (4th ed.), New York: Harper & Row, 1987. Reprinted by permission of the publisher.

OBSERVING TRANSITIONS AND GROUP MANAGEMENT

PURPOSE: As noted in this chapter, managing the transition from large- to small-group work can be trying. This aid will help you focus on teacher behaviors that smooth transition periods.

DIRECTIONS: Make a check when you observe the teacher performing the indicated behaviors.

_____   Teacher wrote key steps of the activity on the chalkboard or on charts.

_____   Teacher stated directions clearly.

_____   Teacher summarized directions.

_____   Teacher had one or two students summarize directions.

_____   Teacher used hand signals or other visual signals or auditory signals to cue students.

_____   Teacher directed teams to the areas of the room where they were to work.

_____   Teacher labeled teamwork areas clearly.

_____   Other (specify) _____

Analysis and Reflection: What key thing did the teacher do to help with transitions? What could the teacher have done to make transition go more smoothly? Why?

VISITING THE SCHOOL'S LIBRARY AND MEDIA CENTER

PURPOSE: A vital component of the Group Investigation approach to cooperative learning is an adequate supply of resources that students can comb for information. This aid is designed to assist you in evaluating a library's resources.

DIRECTIONS: Visit a school library or other source facility and interview resource specialists. Find answers to the following questions.

1. Does the library have a substantial or minimal collection of print materials for student use? _____

   _____

2. To what degree does the media center have nonprint materials available for student use? _____

   _____

3. If you were an elementary or secondary school student, would you find the library and/or media center a pleasant and conducive place to study? Why? Why not?

   _____

   _____

4. What types of procedures does the librarian or media specialist prefer when working with a teacher on Group Investigation projects?

   a. Policy about deadlines? _____

   _____

   b. Policy about taking materials to the classroom? _____

   _____

   c. Policy about small groups of students coming to library on their own? _____

   _____

   d. Policy about resource specialists coming into the room and assisting students with their group investigations? _____

   _____

5. What are the main logistical drawbacks or weaknesses of the library or media center as a support system for group investigation? _____

   _____

Chapter Outline

PERSPECTIVE AND RATIONALE

• Inquiry Teaching • Thinking Skills and Processes

SAMPLING THE KNOWLEDGE BASE

MAIN FEATURES OF INQUIRY TEACHING

• Instructional Effects of Inquiry Teaching • Syntax of
Inquiry Teaching • Structure of the Learning Environment

PROCEDURES FOR USING INQUIRY TEACHING

• Preinstructional Tasks • Conducting the
Lesson • Postinstructional Tasks

CHAPTER 12

Inquiry Teaching

T his chapter is about inquiry teaching and its use in helping students learn to think. The model, as it will be described here, also goes by other names such as **discovery teaching** and **discovery learning.** Also, when educators discuss strategies to promote higher-level thinking they most often are describing approaches very similar to inquiry teaching. Conceptually, inquiry teaching can be considered comparable to other models described in previous chapters, such as concept attainment, direct instruction, and cooperative learning. However, unlike the models that emphasize presenting ideas or demonstrating concepts and skills, the model teacher in inquiry teaching poses problems, asks questions, and facilitates dialogue. Inquiry teaching, in fact, cannot occur unless teachers and their students are skilled in discussion techniques and unless norms exist within the classroom that allow open and honest exchange of ideas through dialogue and discussion. Therefore, as you will see, there are many parallels between this chapter and the one that follows on classroom discussion.

The first section of the chapter provides a perspective for thinking about inquiry teaching and about the intellectual processes this approach aims to develop. The second section samples some of the research that supports the knowledge base on this topic. The final sections include procedures teachers should consider as they prepare to create their own approaches to inquiry teaching.

PERSPECTIVE AND RATIONALE

To become effective in using inquiry strategies and in facilitating inquiry in classrooms demands an understanding of several important topics. As you will see, these topics and the teaching approaches growing out of them are interrelated.

Inquiry Teaching

Getting students to think, solve problems, and discover things for themselves are not new goals for education. Similarly, teaching strategies labeled discovery method, inquiry training, or inductive teaching have long and prestigious heritages. The **Socratic method,** dating back to the early Greeks, emphasized the importance of inductive reasoning and dialogue in the teaching process. John Dewey (1933) described in some detail the importance of what he labeled "reflective thinking" and the processes teachers should use to help students acquire productive thinking skills and processes. Jerome Bruner (1960, 1962, 1966) emphasized the importance of discovery learning and how teachers could help learners become "constructionists," or builders of their own knowledge.

The overall goal of inquiry teaching has been, and continues to be, that of helping students learn how to ask questions, seek answers or solutions to satisfy their curiosity, and build their own theories and ideas about the world. During the curriculum reform movement of the 1950s and 1960s several specific approaches to inquiry teaching were developed in a number of subject areas.

When discovery teaching was applied in the sciences and social sciences it emphasized the inductive reasoning and inquiry processes characteristic of the scientific method. For instance, Richard Suchman (1962) developed an approach called **inquiry training.** Teachers present students with puzzling situations or discrepant events which spark curiosity and motivate inquiry. For example:

> The teacher holds up a pulse glass. The pulse glass consists of two small globes connected by a glass tube. It is partially filled with a red liquid. When the teacher holds one hand over the right bulb, the red liquid will begin to bubble and move to the other side. If the teacher holds one hand over the left bulb, the red liquid will continue to bubble but move to the other side. The teacher asks students: Why does the red liquid move?

As students inquire and seek answers to this question, the teacher encourages them to ask for data about the pulse glass and the moving liquid, to generate hypotheses or theories that help explain the red liquid's movement, and to think of ways they could test their theories. Suchman worked mainly in the field of elementary science. Somewhat similar programs, however, have been developed for use in high school science and social science classes (Schwab, 1965, for example).

When discovery approaches are used in other fields such as the humanities or history, the processes of inquiry in those fields guide the lesson. For example, Edwin Fenton (1966) developed what he labeled "an **inductive approach**" to use in social studies and history classrooms. Fenton emphasized the importance of getting students to ask the kinds of questions that historians might ask, to participate in historical analysis, and to test ideas and theories against artifacts from the historical record.

Regardless of specific applications, what is common across subject areas is that teachers are taking an inductive rather than a deductive orientation. Instead of giving students ideas or theories about the world, which is what teachers are doing when they use the presentation or direct instruction models, teachers using inquiry or discovery approaches pose questions or problems to students and ask them to come up with their own ideas and theories. The teacher is not "instructing" students on important ideas, but instead facilitating inquiry and discovery. To do this effectively requires some knowledge of what thinking is and the nature of human discourse in the process of learning to think. Aspects of thinking will be discussed in this chapter. The nature of discourse in classrooms will be considered in Chapter 13.

Thinking Skills and Processes

There is an array of ideas and sometimes bewildering lists of terms used to describe the ways people think. But, what does thinking mean? What are **thinking skills**? What are **higher-order thinking skills**? From the many definitions that have been provided, most include statements which describe abstract intellectual processes and operations. For example,

- Thinking is a process involving such mental operations as induction, deduction, classification, and reasoning;
- Thinking is a process of dealing with abstractions and discovering the essential principles of things, as contrasted to remaining on the concrete level of facts and specific cases;
- Thinking is the ability to analyze and criticize and to reach conclusions based on sound inference or judgment.

Most contemporary statements about thinking recognize that thinking skills are not the same as skills associated with more concrete behaviors or physical activities. Furthermore, thinking processes, unlike more concrete behaviors, are complex and nonalgorithmic. Consider the following statements provided by Lauren Resnick (1987) about what she calls higher-order thinking:

- Higher order thinking is *nonalgorithmic*. That is, the path of action is not fully specified in advance.
- Higher order thinking tends to be *complex*. The total path is not "visible" (mentally speaking) from any single vantage point.
- Higher order thinking often yields *multiple solutions*, each with costs and benefits, rather than unique solutions.
- Higher order thinking involves *nuanced judgment* and interpretation.
- Higher order thinking involves the application of *multiple criteria*, which sometimes conflict with one another.
- Higher order thinking often involves *uncertainty*. Not everything that bears on the task at hand is known.
- Higher order thinking involves *self-regulation* of the thinking process. We do not recognize higher order thinking in an individual when someone else "calls the plays" at every step.
- Higher order thinking involves *imposing meaning*, finding structure in apparent disorder.
- Higher order thinking is *effortful*. There is considerable mental work involved in the kinds of elaborations and judgments required. (pp. 2–3)

Notice how Resnick has used words and phrases such as "nuanced judgment," "self-regulation," "imposing meaning," and "uncertainty." Obviously, thinking processes and the skills people need to activate them are highly complex.

Hyde and Bizar (1989) have provided another conception of thinking. Based on recent research in cognition, Hyde and Bizar write about thinking as **intellectual processes** instead of skills. Their six intellectual processes are described in Figure 12-1. Like Resnick, Hyde and Bizar point out the complexity of thinking. They also emphasize the importance of *thinking about thinking* in context. That is, although thinking processes have some similarities, they also vary according to what one is thinking about. For instance, the processes we use when thinking about mathematics differ from those used when thinking about poetry.

Because of their complexity, thinking processes cannot be taught using only approaches suitable for teaching concrete ideas and skills. Thinking skills and processes are, however, clearly teachable and most programs and curricula which have been developed rely heavily on classroom discourse and discussion.

SAMPLING THE KNOWLEDGE BASE

The knowledge base of discovery and inquiry teaching and their relationship to student thinking has been influenced by several research traditions. The first consists of the work of theoreticians, curriculum developers, and educational researchers who have tested the effectiveness of various inquiry approaches for promoting student thinking. Linguists and anthropologists have also contributed to the knowledge base by describing what goes on in classrooms where inquiry and discussion methods are being used. Research in the cognitive sciences, which helps explain how students acquire information and how cognitive growth comes about, is a final tradition that has supplied evidence that supports the use of inquiry teaching. Of late, much has been learned about inductive approaches to teaching by the research and the clinical observations made by teachers themselves. This research, too, massive to review here, fairly consistently points out that it takes inquiry teaching and strategies associated with higher-level thinking to produce growth in the thought and inquiry processes of students.

The study selected as Research Summary 12-1 is different from those found in previous chapters in two important ways: (1) it is the only example of learning from clinical observations and (2) it is the only example of the work of an actual K–12 classroom teacher.

MAIN FEATURES OF INQUIRY TEACHING

This section provides an overview of inquiry teaching as a particular approach to instruction that is similar to other models, yet distinct from all others. As with other models presented in previous chapters, the inquiry teaching model's instructional effects, syntax, and learning environment will be discussed first, followed by a description of specific procedures used by teachers when employing the inquiry teaching model.

Instructional Effects of Inquiry Teaching

As with the concept teaching model described in Chapter 9, the inquiry teaching model is not designed to cover a large amount of learning materials

Figure 12-1   An overview of intellectual processes

Schema: Using prior knowledge, relating ideas to experience, integrating the old and the new
  · Relating information to oneself
  · Using tacit knowledge
  · Looking for assumptions
  · Interpreting
  · Finding analogies, metaphors, and similes
  · Criticizing and evaluating

Focus: Breaking things down, analyzing, encoding, representing, deciding what is relevant and what are the key units to focus on
  · Identifying key aspects, attributes, features, characteristics
  · Observing events, phenomena, creatures, things
  · Comparing and contrasting
  · Collecting, recording, and representing

Pattern: Combining, putting together, synthesizing, seeing patterns, forming concepts, conceiving of the whole entity
  · Organizing information
  · Classifying and categorizing
  · Summarizing
  · Inferring and concluding
  · Predicting and hypothesizing

Extension: Using what is known to understand and act upon increasingly complex problems and situations
  · Decision making
  · Problem solving
  · Conducting investigations and inquiries

Projection: Diverging from the known to create new and different understanding of forms
  · Imagining
  · Expressing
  · Creating
  · Inventing
  · Designing

Metacognition: Thinking about one's own thinking; using executive/control processes
  · Planning or strategizing
  · Monitoring or checking
  · Regulating
  · Questioning
  · Reflecting
  · Reviewing

SOURCE: From A. A. Hyde and M. Bizar (1989), *Thinking in context: Teaching cognitive processes across the elementary school curriculum.* New York: Longman.

RESEARCH SUMMARY 12-1

Kay, H. (1991). Jason and Matt. In K. Jervis and C. Montag (eds.), *Progressive education for the 1990s: Transforming practice.* New York: Teachers College Press.

As an elementary school teacher, differences in problem-solving approaches fascinate me and I take every opportunity to explore them. One of my favorite experiences came while working with two fifth-grade boys, Jason and Matt. I wrote down this story to illustrate how diverse two children's thinking can be about the same situation.

I had worked on the chessboard problem before with groups of adults and children. On this occasion, using a chessboard and beans, I told the boys the legend from Jacobs (1970):

> There is a legend about the king of Persia and the inventor of the game of chess. According to the legend, the king of Persia, out of gratitude to the inventor of the chess, offered him anything he would like for a reward. The inventor requested that one grain of wheat be placed upon the first square of the chessboard, two grains be placed on the second square, four grains on the third square, continuing in this manner, doubling the number of grains for each successive square on the board. This request seemed reasonable enough to the king and he sent one of his servants off for a bag of wheat. As the king soon realized, one bag of wheat would simply not be enough. By continually doubling the amount of wheat on each square of the board until the sixty-fourth square is reached, more than nine quintillion grains of wheat are needed. That is enough wheat to cover the state of California with one foot of wheat. Another way to consider the amount is, 500 times the 1976 *annual* world harvest of wheat, which is probably more wheat than has been harvested by man in history! The inventor, no doubt, was compensated in another way. (p. 54)

Jason and Matt began computing straight away. Matt added first on his fingers, then on paper. Jason, in contrast, sounded like a metronome saying the numbers out loud: 1, 2, 4, 8, 16, 32, 64, his perfect rhythm broken only slightly for the next two numbers in the sequence. Matt stopped adding and counting to suggest that we figure out the number of beans for the first row of the chessboard and then multiply by 2. Jason wasted no time in telling Matt that his idea would not work and then reminded him that the number *doubled* on *each* successive square. Matt went back to counting. He counted out beans, put them in a cup, and added in the new amount. When he had filled his cup halfway. I asked him how full the cup would be when the doubled the amount in it. I knew that Matt had been working with fractions in class and was surprised when he struggled with ½ cup + ½ cup. Later it became evident that Matt had a very strong need to be precise; he was unwilling to make the mental leap from 128 beans = ½ cup of beans, 128 beans + 128 beans = 256 beans, therefore ½ cup of beans + ½ cup of beans = 1 cup of beans or 256 beans. He argued that measuring by cups was imprecise because he could not *always* be completely certain that one cup had exactly 256 beans!

(Continued on page 372)

RESEARCH SUMMARY 12-1 *(Continued)*

At one point Matt's addition and self-checking fascinated me. He added two six-digit numerals, looked at the sum, and muttered, "That can't be right." He then counted the digits in his answer for verification, said, "No, that's not right," and added again. Matt also had difficulty reading large numbers. Having only as an adult mastered reading six or seven-digit numerals. I sympathized with Matt and offered help. My offer was shunned and Matt continued to add.

Both boys became interested in calculating how many containers of beans it would take to actually fill one quarter of the room in which we were sitting. Jason sprung to action immediately: the bottom of the bean container was roughly the size of one floor tile, or one square foot, and the container's height was about one foot. He began counting the floor tiles to figure the area of the room and then multiplied to obtain the room's volume. His math was completely mental and incredibly quick. So swift, in fact, that my brow was knitted and I was saying, "Wait a minute! I need to figure this one out on paper!" Jason's arithmetic was accurate. I asked him if he could tell me what his mental process was.

In his serious way, he carefully told me that he had counted a length of 32 tiles and a width of 50 tiles. "Since half of 30 is 15, then half of 32 is 16, then add the zeros to get 1,600 square feet." I needed to write *that* down and think a bit! Jason knew that there was a connection between multiplying by five and dividing by two (did *I* know that connection?). He was very comfortable with ignoring zeros while computing mentally and inserting them when finished. My mental approach for multiplying 32 × 50 would have been to first multiply 50 × 30 = 1,500; then multiply 2 × 50 = 100; and then add 1,500 + 100 = 1,600. For me to re-create what Jason had done so quickly, I had to think about it being easier to multiply 32 by 100 instead of multiplying 32 by 50 resulting in 3,200, or twice the answer. Once double the answer is arrived at I only needed to divide 3,200 by 2 to 1,600. Since Jason ignored all zeros from the start, he multiplied by 1 instead of 100,

---

or convey huge quantities of information to students. The model has been developed primarily to accomplish three important instructional effects: (1) to help students develop the intellectual skills of asking important questions and seeking answers, (2) to help students acquire the inquiry process skills associated with various domains of human learning, and, most importantly, (3) to help students become independent, autonomous learners confident and capable of learning on their own.

Syntax of Inquiry Teaching

There are five major phases in the inquiry approach to teaching. However, skillful inquiry teachers often vary particular sequencing and overall syntax and

sometimes lessons in particular subject areas will require slight syntax changes. In general, however, the overall sequence of teacher behavior follows the syntax described in Table 12-1.

Structure of the Learning Environment

Unlike the very structured learning environment required of the presentation and direct instruction models, or the use of small groups required in cooperative learning, the learning environment during an inquiry lesson is characterized by whole-class instruction, open processes, and active student roles. In fact, the whole process of helping students become independent, autonomous learners and of assisting them in becoming confident in their own then divided his answer by 2, and then added two zeros. Jason's comment. "Since half of 30 is 15, then half of 32 is 16," puzzled me until I realized that Jason did not know immediately what half of 32 was, but he did know that half of 30 was 15; thus, $32 \div 2$ had to be 16.

The area of half the room was 1,600 square feet. To arrive at a figure for one quarter of the room's volume, Jason estimated the height of the room as 10 feet, and calculated the volume for one half of that space. To figure volume for a space that is 1,600 square feet and five feet high, Jason knew that he needed to know what five 1,600's are. His approach, once again, was to take the zeros off 1,600 and add 16 five times: $16 + 16 = 32$, $32 + 32 = 64$. $64 + 16 = 80$, replace the zeros and Jason had 8,000 cubic feet!

Matt was committed to proving Jason's square footage wrong. Matt counted tiles and argued that there were some partial tiles in the area where Jason had counted. He also pointed out that Jason had not counted every bean in the container and therefore would be unable to compute *exactly* how many beans there would be in one quarter of the room. Jason looked at him incredulously and said calmly, at first, "The exact number of beans does not matter, we have a good idea how many beans there are and who really cares with beans, anyway?" Matt continued to needle Jason until Jason left in utter disgust. I talked with Matt about the importance of accuracy in certain situations, but felt that my words fell on deaf ears. I began to wonder if Matt's demand for accuracy was a cover. He had been most comfortable doing the routine operations of addition and counting. He was less comfortable with reasoning and problem solving, and very often unsuccessful in these situations. Jason estimated a great deal and was very comfortable with ball park estimates. Matt was safe when he shifted the arena for debate from problem solving and estimation to computation based upon certain, not estimated numbers.

intellectual skills requires active involvement. Although the teacher and students proceed through the various phases of the lesson in a somewhat structured and predictable fashion, the norms surrounding the lesson are those of open inquiry and freedom of thought and expression. The teacher's role is not one of dispensing knowledge and truth but instead acting as helper and guide.

PROCEDURES FOR USING INQUIRY TEACHING

Conceptually the inquiry teaching model is quite straightforward, and it is easy for beginning teachers to grasp. Effective execution of the model, how-ever, is more difficult. It requires considerable practice, and it requires making specific decisions during the preinstructional, interactive, and postinstructional stages of the lesson. Some of the required behaviors you will find similar to those you already have learned from studying other models; some, however, are unique to the inquiry teaching model. In the discussion that follows familiar topics will be reviewed briefly while the emphasis will be put on the unique features of inquiry teaching.

Preinstructional Tasks

Since the essence of an inquiry lesson is interactive, beginning teachers sometimes believe that little planning is required. This simply is not true. Plan-

Table 12-1 Syntax for Inquiry Teaching

	PHASE	TEACHER BEHAVIOR
Phase 1:	Providing objectives and set and explaining inquiry procedures	Teacher goes over the objectives of the lesson and gets students ready to inquire. Teacher explains ground rules.
Phase 2:	Presenting the puzzling situation	Teacher describes the puzzling situation to the class using the most appropriate medium.
Phase 3:	Data gathering and experimentation by students	Teacher encourages students to ask questions about the puzzling situation with the aim of helping them gather information to assist inquiry.
Phase 4:	Hypothesizing and explaining	Teacher encourages students to make predictions and to provide explanations for the puzzling situation.
Phase 5:	Analyzing the inquiry process	Teacher gets students to think about their own intellectual processes and the inquiry process associated with a specific lesson.

ning for an inquiry lesson, as with any more indirect approach to instruction, requires as much or more effort than does planning for more direct instruction lessons. It is prior planning that facilitates movement through the syntax of an inquiry lesson and which assures that important instructional effects are accomplished.

DECIDING ON PURPOSES

Deciding on purposes for an inquiry lesson is one of two important preinstructional tasks for teachers. It is important to think through ahead of the lesson the exact intellectual skills on which to focus the lesson and to decide how a particular inquiry lesson will help develop autonomous learners.

CHOOSING AND DESIGNING A PUZZLING SITUATION

As explained earlier, an inquiry lesson is based on the premise that puzzling and mysterious situations produce disequilibrium and in turn cause students to be curious about a particular topic. This curiosity motivates students to inquire and to learn. Choosing and designing an appropriate puzzling situation, thus, becomes a critical preinstructional task. In the process of designing puzzling situations, teachers are in essence actualizing their instructional intents and combining these with the school's curriculum. What could be more important?

A **puzzling situation** is one which explores cause and effect relationships around a particular topic and one which poses "why" or "what if" questions. The number of puzzling situations in any

field is endless. As you approach choosing a particular situation for a lesson, consider the following:

1. Think about situations around a particular topic that have been or are puzzling to you. The situation must pose a question or problem that requires explanation through cause and effect analyses.
2. Decide if the particular situation has a natural interest to the particular group of students with whom you are working.
3. Consider if the puzzling situation can be presented in a fashion understandable to your particular group of students and in a way in which the "puzzling" aspect of the problem stands out.

Below are several examples of puzzling situations used by teachers at various grade levels and subject fields.

The Red Liquid. One puzzling situation devised for upper elementary science is one in which students are presented with a device called a pulse glass (described earlier in this chapter), which is displayed in Figure 12-2. As you can see, the pulse glass has two small globes connected by a glass tube. The lower portion of the glass tube holds a red liquid. When the teacher places her hand on the globe on the right side, the red liquid moves up into the left globe. When the teacher places her hand on the globe on the left side, the red liquid moves into the right globe. The puzzling situation presented to the students is: "Why does the red liquid move?"

Figure 12-2   Pulse glass

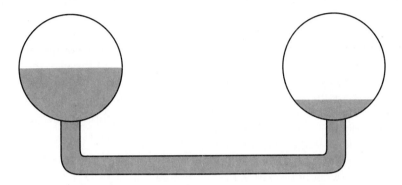

The Oxbow Incident.   You may remember from your high school reading a short story called *"The Oxbow Incident."* The story evolves around three men who rode into a small town in Montana. They are arrested, tried, and hung for a crime they didn't commit. After reading or being told this story, the American Literature teacher would present the question: "Why did this happen?"

Alka Seltzer Air.   Harvard University's Eleanor Duckworth (1991) describes a puzzling situation she likes to use in her teaching. On the left-hand side of a balance such as the one portrayed in Figure 12-3 is an airtight plastic bag containing an Alka-Seltzer tablet in a piece of plasticene at the top and

Figure 12-3   Balance apparatus

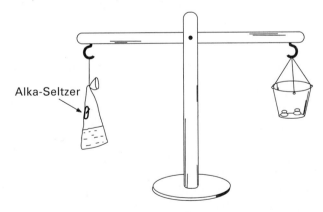

Alka-Seltzer

SOURCE: Duckworth, E. (1991). Twenty-four, forty-two, and I love you: Keeping it complex. In K. Jervis and C. Montag (eds.), *Progressive education for the 1990s: Transforming practice.* New York: Teachers College Press.

some regular water in the bag's bottom. On the right side are enough weights to balance that side of the arm. If the tablet is allowed to fall into the water, the left side of the balance goes up. The question to be posed to students is: "Why does the left side of the balance go up?"

Conducting the Lesson

The five phases of an inquiry lesson were described in Table 12-1. Desired teacher and student behavior associated with each of these phases is described below.

ESTABLISHING SET AND EXPLAINING INQUIRY PROCEDURES

At the start of an inquiry lesson, just as with all types of lessons, teachers communicate clearly to students the purposes of the lesson, get them ready to learn through motivation, and describe to students what they are expected to do during the lesson. Particularly with younger students or with students, regardless of their age, who have not been involved in inquiry lessons previously, the teacher must teach the rules and procedures governing the lesson with precision and in some detail.

Important procedures for an inquiry lesson that should be taught to students are summarized below.

1. It should be explained to students that the goal of the lesson is not to learn new information but instead to learn how to inquire and to think on their own.

2. At the beginning of the inquiry the teacher will pose a question about a puzzling situation.

There are no absolute "right" answers to the question and the teacher will not provide his or her explanation initially.

3. During the data collection phase of the lesson, students will be encouraged to ask questions aimed at seeking information. The teacher will answer these questions to the best of his or her ability and will tell students when he or she does not have the data they request.

4. During the hypothesizing and explanation phase of the lesson students will be encouraged to express their ideas openly and freely. No idea will be ridiculed by the teacher or by classmates. Everyone will be given an opportunity to contribute to the inquiry and to give their ideas.

PRESENTING THE PUZZLING SITUATION

The teacher needs to present the puzzling situation with care. The guidelines provided in Chapter 10 on how to conduct a classroom demonstration can be helpful here. The puzzling situation should be conveyed to students in as interesting and accurate a fashion as possible. Being able to feel and touch something (such as the pulse glass or the balance apparatus described previously) generates interest and motivates inquiry. Short videotapes of events are similarly motivational. The important point here is that the puzzling situation sets the stage for the remainder of the lesson, and its presentation must captivate student interest and produce disequilibrium if the lesson is to be successful.

DATA GATHERING AND EXPERIMENTATION

This phase of the lesson is very important. It is a time when the teacher encourages students to gather data and conduct mental experiments on the puzzling situation. The aim is for students to gather sufficient information to create and build on their own ideas. This phase of the lesson, however, should not become a mere question and answer game where the students play "Twenty Questions" with the teacher. Below is an actual exchange between a teacher and her students when she was conducting an inquiry lesson using the pulse glass described previously.*

* The exchanges are paraphrased from actual audiotapes and published in print in F. Newton (1972), *Facilitating inquiry in the classroom*, Portland, Oregon: Northwest Regional Education Laboratory.

Student 1:	Does the liquid go all of the way through the tube, or does it just run on the side? I mean, if the liquid just runs on this side . . . and it doesn't go through the middle, does that go all the way through the whole thing?
Teacher:	Yes, it does, it's like . . . the tube's kind of like a hose, and it goes right through the whole tube.
Student 2:	Is it colored water?
Teacher:	No, it is not colored water.
Student 3:	Is that some sort of a chemical in there?
Teacher:	What do you mean by a chemical?
Student 3:	Uh, something that would react more than water.
Teacher:	Are you asking is there something special about the liquid?
Student 3:	Yes.
Teacher:	Methylene chloride is the name of the red liquid.

As you can see, the teacher is helping students collect needed information about the pulse glass and the red liquid. As this inquiry proceeded the teacher revealed that the pulse glass was essentially airtight, that the boiling point of methylene chloride is 40.1 degrees Centigrade, and that it is more dense than water. She also pointed out, when queried, that methylene chloride is not repelled by heat.

Sometimes students ask questions or suggest experiments that could be conducted on the puzzling situation. For instance:

If you were to take that tip off the glass would it still work?

When you hold your hand on one bulb, does it get hot inside?

Would the red liquid run up when you hold the glass vertical?

If I were to put a very small hole in the top of one of the bulbs, would the red liquid still move?

When this type of question is posed by a student, it is important for the teacher to acknowledge and encourage exploration of the question by the whole class. The teacher can also provide assistance to students and help them think about how they might conduct other experiments.

HYPOTHESIZING AND EXPLAINING

After students have collected sufficient data and conducted experimentations on the phenomena, they will want to start offering explanations in the form of hypotheses and theories. During this phase of the lesson the teacher encourages all ideas and accepts them fully. Some teachers like to list these theories on the chalkboard or on newsprint charts using procedures similar to those described in Chapter 9. Below are some theories students have come up with in an inquiry lesson using the pulse glass:

- The red liquid moves because you have just the right amount of heat.
- The pulse glass is like a heart pushing blood.
- The heat of your hand makes the red liquid vaporize so that it pushes out.
- Air makes it move like that.
- The liquid moves because the heat repels it, pushes it away.

The teacher's role during this phase of the lesson is to accept students' ideas and to encourage free interchange. The teacher can also ask students to support their hypotheses with questions such as: "What data or evidence makes you have that idea?" Or, the teacher may encourage a student to be more specific: "What do you mean by 'just the right amount of heat?'"

During this phase of the lesson the teacher may also want to encourage students to probe more deeply into an idea or collect more information. For instance, "What would you need to know in order for you to feel certain that your hypothesis about the red liquid is accurate?" Or the teacher may encourage additional experimentation: "What could you do to test your idea about just the right amount of heat?"

ANALYZING THE INQUIRY PROCESS

The final phase of an inquiry lesson involves activities aimed at helping students analyze their own thinking processes and to think about the inquiry and intellectual traditions in various subject fields. This final phase of an inquiry lesson is very similar

to the final phase of a concept teaching lesson described in Chapter 9. Teachers ask students to think back and recount what was going on in their minds during the various phases of the lesson. When did they first start getting a clear explanation for the situation? Why did they accept some explanations more readily than others? Why did they reject some explanations? Did they change their thinking about the situation as the lesson progressed? What caused this change?

Postinstructional Tasks

Postinstructional tasks associated with an inquiry lesson most often consist of some type of feedback to students and perhaps assessment and evaluation. As with other lessons where the instructional intents are not the acquisition of declarative knowledge, evaluative tasks for an inquiry lesson normally do not consist of paper and pencil tests over information. Best evaluation for lessons using the inquiry model will be based on some of the alternative assessment tasks already described in length in Chapters 7 and 9.

SUMMARY

- Unlike some of the other models where the emphasis is on presenting ideas and demonstrating skills, inquiry teaching consists of the teacher presenting puzzling situations to students and getting them to inquire about the situations and theorize about cause and effect relationships.
- The inquiry teaching model is among the oldest of the models and finds its intellectual roots in the Socratic method dating back to the early Greeks.
- In modern times, and over the past three decades, considerable attention has been given to developing a set of approaches to teaching known by various names, such as discovering learning, inquiry training, and teaching thinking, but with common instructional intents — mainly helping students become independent, autonomous thinkers capable of figuring things out for themselves.
- The knowledge base on inquiry teaching and higher-level thinking is rich and complex.
- The instructional effects of inquiry teaching are

mainly to help students develop their intellectual skills, to help them acquire inquiry process skills, and to help them gain confidence in their own thinking.

- The learning environment of an inquiry lesson is characterized by openness, active student involvement, and an atmosphere of intellectual freedom.
- The general flow or syntax of an inquiry lesson consists of five major phases: establishing set and explaining procedures, presenting a puzzling situation to students, helping students gather data about the puzzling situation, helping students hypothesize and explain the puzzling situation, and helping them analyze their thinking and inquiry processes.
- Major preinstructional tasks associated with an inquiry lesson consist of getting clear about purposes and designing an interesting and appropriate puzzling situation to present to students.
- While conducting an inquiry lesson, teachers are facilitators and guides of student inquiry.
- Postinstructional tasks of inquiry lessons consist mainly of finding alternative assessment devices to measure students' inquiry skills and their intellectual processes.

KEY TERMS

discovery teaching
discovery learning
Socratic method
inquiry training
inductive approach
thinking skills
higher-order thinking skills
metacognition
intellectual processes
puzzling situation
data gathering
experimentation
hypothesizing

BOOKS FOR THE PROFESSIONAL

Costa, A. L. (1985). *Developing minds: A resource book for teaching thinking.* Alexandria, Va.: Association for Supervision and Curriculum Development. This excellent set of resources is for teachers interested in making their classrooms more inquiry- and thinking-oriented.

Duckworth, E. (1987). *The having of wonderful ideas and other essays on teaching and learning.* New York: Teachers College Press. This book provides some delightful and insightful essays on teaching and learning.

Jervis, K., and Montag, C. (eds.). (1991). *Progressive education for the 1990s: Transforming practice.* New York: Teachers College Press. This excellent and timely collection of readings considers progressive education and its traditional emphasis on teaching students how to inquire, to think, and to learn on their own.

Kaplan, M. (1992). *Thinking in education.* Cambridge: Cambridge University Press. This book provides an excellent and contemporary analysis of what it means to teach children how to think and what needs to be done at all levels of education if we are to convert our classrooms into "communities for inquiry."

Resnick, L. B. (1987). *Education and learning to think.* Washington, D.C.: National Academy Press. This book provides a review of cognitive research along with justification and means for helping students develop dispositions and skills for higher-level thinking.

Resnick, L. B., and Kloper, L. E. (eds.). (1989). *Toward the thinking curriculum: Current cognitive research.* Alexandria, Va.: Association for Supervision and Curriculum Development. The yearbook of ASCD provides an excellent review of the research in the cognitive sciences that has implications for curriculum development in the various subject areas and for teaching students how to think and inquire.

LEARNING AIDS FOR PLANNING, OBSERVATION, AND REFLECTION

- Assessing My Skills for Using the Inquiry Teaching Model
- Lesson Plan Format for an Inquiry Lesson
- Observing Inquiry Lessons in Microteaching or Classrooms
- Interviewing Teachers About Their Use of the Inquiry Model

ASSESSING MY SKILLS FOR USING THE INQUIRY TEACHING MODEL

PURPOSE: To help you gain insight into your level of skill in using the inquiry model, use this aid after reading the chapter or after a microteaching or field assignment.

DIRECTIONS: Check the level of skill you perceive yourself having for the various teaching behaviors and tasks associated with the inquiry teaching model.

UNDERSTANDING OR SKILL	LEVEL OF UNDERSTANDING OR SKILL		
	HIGH	MEDIUM	LOW
Preinstructional tasks			
Considering purpose of inquiry lessons	————	————	————
Making plans for inquiry lessons	————	————	————
Designing puzzling situations	————	————	————
Instructional tasks			
Phase 1: Establishing set and explaining inquiry procedures	————	————	————
Phase 2: Presenting puzzling situations	————	————	————
Phase 3: Helping students gather data and do mental experiments	————	————	————
Phase 4: Helping students hypothesize and explain puzzling situations	————	————	————
Phase 5: Helping students analyze their own thinking and inquiry process	————	————	————
Postinstructional tasks			
Designing appropriate assessments for inquiry lessons	————	————	————

LESSON PLAN FORMAT FOR INQUIRY LESSON

PURPOSE: This is a lesson plan format suggested for use with the inquiry model. As with the formats suggested for other teaching models, experiment with this format to determine what works best for you.

DIRECTIONS: Use the following suggested format as you prepare an inquiry lesson.

Planning phase

General topic of the inquiry: _____

Objectives (make sure they are inquiry and thinking objectives, not content objectives)

1. _____

_____

2. _____

_____

Conducting the lesson

Time	**Phase and Activities**	**Materials**
_____	Set and inquiry procedures: _____	
_____	Puzzling situation: _____	
_____	Data gathering: _____	
_____	Hypothesizing and explaining: _____	
_____	Analyzing thinking and inquiry processes: _____	

Pitfalls to avoid

During Instruction   **During Transitions**   **During Ending**

OBSERVING INQUIRY LESSONS IN MICROTEACHING OR CLASSROOMS

PURPOSE: This form highlights the key aspects of an inquiry lesson. It can be used to observe a peer in a microteaching laboratory or an experienced teacher in the classroom.

DIRECTIONS: As you observe the lesson, check the category you believe describes the level of performance of the teacher you are observing. Also answer the general questions about the lesson on the bottom of the form.

	LEVEL OF PERFORMANCE			
TEACHER BEHAVIOR	EXCELLENT	ACCEPTABLE	NEEDS IMPROVEMENT	NOT NEEDED
Planning				
How appropriate was the selected inquiry topic?	_____	_____	_____	_____
How appropriate was the puzzling situation?	_____	_____	_____	_____
How well prepared was the teacher overall?	_____	_____	_____	_____
Execution				
How well did the teacher				
Establish set?	_____	_____	_____	_____
Explain inquiry procedures?	_____	_____	_____	_____
Present the puzzling situation?	_____	_____	_____	_____
Help students gather data?	_____	_____	_____	_____
Help students hypothesize?	_____	_____	_____	_____
Help student analyze their thinking and their inquiry processes?	_____	_____	_____	_____

Overall

What did you like best about the way the lesson was planned and organized?

_____

_____

_____

What could be improved?

_____

_____

_____

Think about teaching style and delivery. What did you like best about the way the lesson was conducted?

_____

_____

_____

What could be improved?

_____

_____

_____

If you were a student in peer microteaching, how do you feel about the teacher's interaction with you?

_____

_____

_____

INTERVIEWING TEACHERS ABOUT THEIR USE OF THE INQUIRY MODEL

PURPOSE: For many years educators have promoted and tried to foster inquiry teaching and inquiry-oriented classrooms. Teachers have been admonished many, many times to spend less time teaching low-level skills and to spend more time on developing critical and higher-level thinking skills in their students. Most observers, however, do not believe much progress has been made over the years. This aid will give you the opportunity to investigate beliefs about inquiry teaching from the perspective of experienced teachers.

DIRECTIONS: Use the questions below as a guide in interviewing teachers about their use or non-use of the inquiry teaching model.

1. In what situations in your teaching do you use teaching methods that might be classified as inquiry or discovery lessons or lessons that aim at higher-level thinking?
2. What do you see as the major strength of this type of teaching?
3. What do you see as the major drawback of this type of teaching?
4. Some people believe that American schools and teachers spend too much time on basic skills and not enough time on promoting higher-level thinking. What do you think?
5. If you want to spend more time on inquiry and discovery teaching are their barriers to prevent you from doing so? On the part of colleagues? Administration? Parents? Students?

Chapter Outline

PERSPECTIVE AND RATIONALE
* Classroom Discourse and Discussion

SAMPLING THE KNOWLEDGE BASE
* Teacher Talk * Teacher Questioning * Wait-Time

MAIN FEATURES OF CLASSROOM DISCUSSION
* Common Ingredients of Discussion * Instructional Effects of Discussion * Syntax for Holding Discussions * Different Approaches for Holding Discussions * Structure of the Learning Environment

PROCEDURES FOR CONDUCTING DISCUSSIONS
* Preinstructional Tasks * Holding the Discussion * Postinstructional Tasks

IMPROVING DISCUSSION AND DISCOURSE PATTERNS
* Slowing the Pace and Broadening Participation * Increasing Interpersonal Regard and Understanding * Using Tools to Help Students Learn Discourse and Thinking Skills * Strategies for Teaching Discourse and Thinking Skills

CHAPTER 13

Classroom Discussion

In each of the previous chapters in Part 2 of *Learning to Teach*, a specific teaching model was described. However, you saw that at some point in most lessons, regardless of the model, dialogue or discussion was required between teachers and students. For instance, you read how discussion comes toward the end of presentation and concept lessons as teachers strive to check for understanding and help students extend their thinking about particular information or concepts. Discussion occurs mainly in small groups during cooperative learning lessons, while the inquiry lesson demands constant dialogue to accomplish the instructional effects intended for that model.

This last chapter of Part 2 provides a detailed presentation of what is normally labeled **classroom discussion.** Discussion, you will find, is not a unitary teaching model like those presented in previous chapters. Instead it is a particular teaching procedure or strategy which forms a part of the syntax of most other models and is used by teachers across a number of models. However, since you are accustomed to thinking about particular approaches to instruction according to their instructional effects, their learning environments, and their syntaxes, these same categories will be used to describe classroom discussion in this chapter.

As with previous chapters, this chapter will provide first a perspective for thinking about classroom discussion and the knowledge base for this strategy; this will be followed with more specific procedures required of teachers as they plan for and conduct classroom discussions. The final section highlights the importance of teaching students how to become effective participants within the classroom discourse system and describes how beginning teachers can change some of the unproductive discourse patterns that characterize many classrooms today.

PERSPECTIVE AND RATIONALE

Effective use of classroom discussion strategies requires an understanding of several important topics pertaining to classroom discourse and discussion.

Classroom Discourse and Discussion

The dictionary definitions of *discourse* and *discussion* are almost identical: to engage in an orderly verbal interchange and to express thoughts on particular subjects. Teachers are more likely to use the term *discussion* to describe the procedures they use to encourage verbal interchange among students. Scholars and researchers are more likely to use the term *discourse* to reflect their interest, not in the specific procedures but in the larger patterns of exchange and communication found in classrooms. In this section the term *discourse* will be used to provide an overall perspective about classroom communication; later the term *discussion* will be used when specific procedures are described.

DISCOURSE

Think for a moment about the many everyday situations where success depends largely on the use of language and communicative processes. Friendships, for instance, are initiated and maintained mainly through language—friends talk and share experiences with one another. Families, it is said, maintain their unique histories by building patterns of discourse (sometimes even in the form of secret codes) which appear natural to those within the family but are experienced as strange to those on the outside, such as newly acquired in-laws. Youth culture and youth gangs develop special patterns of communication which provide member identity and group cohesion. It is difficult to imagine a cocktail party, a dinner party, a church gathering, or any other kind of social event existing for very long if people could not verbally express their ideas and listen to the ideas of others. The popularity of radio talk shows and computer networking add additional evidence to the centrality of interaction through the medium of language.

Discourse through language is also central to what goes on in classrooms. Courtney Cazden (1986), one of the foremost scholars on the topic of classroom discourse, has written that "spoken language is the medium by which much teaching takes place" (p. 432). Spoken language provides the means for students to talk about what they already know and to form meaning from new knowledge as it is acquired. Spoken language affects the thought processes of students, as well as providing them with their identity as learners and as members within the classroom group.

DISCOURSE AND COGNITION

A strong relationship exists between language and logic, and both lead to the ability to analyze, reason deductively and inductively, and make sound in-

ferences based on knowledge. Discourse is one way for students to practice their thinking processes and enhance their thinking skills. Mary Budd Rowe (1986) has summarized this important point nicely. "To 'grow,' a complex thought system requires a great deal of shared experience and conversation. It is in talking about what we have done and observed, and in arguing about what we make of our experiences, that ideas multiply, become refined, and finally produce new questions and further explorations" (p. 43).

Discourse can be thought of as **externalization of thinking,** that is, exposing one's invisible thoughts. Through public discourse, then, teachers are given a partial window for viewing the thinking processes of their students and a setting for providing correction and feedback when faulty or incomplete reasoning is observed. Thinking out loud also provides students with opportunities to hear (so to speak) their own thinking and that of others and learn how to monitor their own thinking processes. This is very important because, as you read in Chapters 8 and 9, learners don't simply acquire knowledge by recording new information on a blank slate; instead, they actively construct knowledge over time as they interpret new knowledge in light of other knowledge already possessed.

SOCIAL ASPECTS OF DISCOURSE

One aspect of classroom discourse, then, is its ability to promote cognitive growth. Another aspect is its ability to connect and unite the cognitive and the social aspects of learning. As you observed in Chapter 4, the classroom discourse system is central to creating positive learning environments. It helps define participation patterns and consequently has a great deal of impact on classroom management. In other words, the talk of teachers and students provides much of the social glue that holds classroom life together.

The **cognitive-social connection** is most clear in the way social participation impacts on thinking and cognitive growth. Resnick and Kloper (1989) have observed that the

social setting provides occasions for modeling effective thinking strategies. Skilled thinkers (often the instructor, but sometimes more advanced fellow students) can demonstrate desirable ways of attacking problems, analyzing texts, or constructing argument. . . . But most important of all, the social setting may let students know that all the elements of critical thought—interpretation, questioning, trying possibilities, demanding rational justification—are socially valued. (p. 8–9)

Thus, discourse provides opportunities not only for engagement in thinking but, when properly done, helps establish thinking as a positive thing for students to do.

SAMPLING THE KNOWLEDGE BASE

The knowledge base on classroom discourse and discussion and their relationships to student thinking has been influenced by several research traditions. The first consists of an array of persons working in the fields of anthropology, linguistics, ecological psychology, and sociology. These researchers have produced descriptive studies about what goes on in classrooms, especially how spoken language is used by teachers and students. A second tradition stems from the process-product research, described in preceding chapters. Remember how researchers in this tradition tried to determine the effectiveness of various teaching processes on desired student outcomes. The final tradition, also previously introduced, is research in the cognitive sciences, which helps explain how students acquire and process information and how cognitive growth comes about. Research from each of these traditions has helped to build a rather large knowledge base, of which only a portion can be sampled here.

Teacher Talk

Working from a variety of perspectives and with a diverse set of methods, researchers who study classroom discourse have found that most teachers talk a lot and that a basic pattern of communication exists in most classrooms. Also, they have found that this pattern is not necessarily the best one for promoting student thinking. This basic pattern is called **recitation**—a teaching activity where students in a whole-class setting are drilled by the teacher using a question-answer format. Cuban (1982, 1984) has documented how the recitation pattern emerged early in the history of formal schooling and how it has persisted throughout the twentieth century at almost all levels of schooling

and across all academic subjects. Teacher dominance of classroom communication was also thoroughly documented by Ned Flanders in the late 1960s and early 1970s in numerous studies on teacher-student interaction. Flanders (1970) concluded that in most classrooms two-thirds of the talk is by teachers. John Goodlad in his extensive study of schools made essentially the same observation in 1984.

The pattern is still with us today. In 1989, Richard and Patricia Schmuck (1991) visited and collected information on rural schools in the United States. They studied 25 school districts in 21 states. They interviewed 212 teenagers about their school experience and observed lessons in over 30 high school classrooms. In 22 out of the 30 classrooms, they reported seeing mainly recitation lessons. They reported teachers talking three-fourths of the time and commented that this was more than Flanders observed two decades ago. Only twice did the Schmucks observe students talking in pairs, and only four times did they observe small-group interaction and exchange.

Teacher Questioning

Recitation relies on teachers talking and asking questions. The ways teachers ask questions and the type of questions they ask have been the focus of considerable inquiry and concern for quite some time. Mark Gall (1970), who has on several occasions reviewed the research on questioning, highlighted how frequently questions are asked in classrooms and, like Cuban, illustrated that a persistent recitation pattern has existed over time.

> Certainly teachers ask many questions during an average school day. A half-century ago, Stevens (1912) estimated that four-fifths of school time was occupied with question-and-answer recitations. Stevens found that a sample of high school teachers asked a mean number of 395 questions each day. High frequencies of questions used by teachers were also found in recent investigations: ten primary-grade teachers asked an average of 348 questions each day during a school day (Floyd, 1960); twelve elementary-school teachers asked an average of 180 questions each in a science lesson (Moyer, 1966); and fourteen fifth-grade teachers asked an average of sixty-four questions each in a 30-minute social studies lesson (Schreiber, 1967). (p. 11)

What is the effect on student learning of so many questions being asked? In particular, what is the effect of factual and higher-order questions on student learning and thinking? For many years, the conventional wisdom argued that higher-order questions lead to greater cognitive growth than more concrete, factual questions. However, reviews of research in the early 1970s (Dunkin and Biddle, 1974; Rosenshine, 1971b) reported that no clear evidence existed one way or the other. By 1976, Rosenshine was prepared to challenge the conventional wisdom when he concluded that "narrow" (factual) questions actually seemed to be best, particularly when teachers provided immediate feedback about the correct and incorrect answers. (It is important to point out that Rosenshine reviewed studies done in early-grade classrooms which had a large proportion of children from lower social and economic backgrounds.) A few years later in a review by Redfield and Rousseau (1981), the use of factual questions was again challenged, and the researchers reported that indeed asking higher-level and thought-provoking questions had positive effects on student achievement and thinking.

During the past decade, researchers have continued to attack the problem about the effects of question types on student achievement and thinking. There appears to be an emerging consensus that the type of questions teachers ask should depend on the nature of the students with whom they are working and the type of educational objectives they are trying to achieve. Gall (1984), for example, has more recently interpreted this research in the following way:

- Emphasis on fact questions is more effective for promoting young disadvantaged children's achievement, which primarily involves mastery of basic skills; and
- Emphasis on higher cognitive questions is more effective for students of average and high ability, especially as they enter high school, where more independent thinking is required. (p. 41)

In addition to the types of questions teachers ask, researchers have also been interested in the difficulty **level of questions** and in teachers' overall pattern of questioning. Level of difficulty refers to students' ability to answer questions correctly regardless of cognitive level. Research on this topic has also produced mixed results. The recommendations by Brophy and Good (1986) after their review of the research are as follows:

- It seems clear that most (perhaps three-fourths) of teachers' questions should elicit correct answers. . . .
- Most of the rest (of the questions) should elicit overt, substantive responses (incorrect or incomplete answers) rather than failures to respond at all. (pp. 362–363)

Some researchers, such as Cazden and Mehan (1989) and Edwards and Mercer (1987), have not been so concerned with the type of questions teachers ask, but instead have focused on the overall pattern of questioning. They have discovered important "unspoken classroom rules" which have been missed by other researchers. For example Cazden and Mehan (1989) write that in most classrooms: "(1) It is the teacher who asks the questions; (2) The teacher knows the answers; and (3) Repeated questions imply wrong answers" (p. 50). Cazden argues that these implicit rules must be confronted directly if teachers want discourse in their classrooms which promote inquiry and higher-level thinking. This issue will be discussed more fully later in the chapter.

Wait-Time

A final important line of research focuses on a variable known as **wait-time**. This variable was first observed and considered in the late 1960s, a time when considerable effort was made to improve curricula in almost all of the academic subjects. As described earlier, these new curricula, particularly in the sciences and the social sciences, were developed to help students learn how to inquire and discover relationships among social and natural phenomena. The recommended method for virtually all of these curricula was inquiry or discovery-oriented discussions.

Initially, curriculum developers and researchers who observed teachers working with the new curricula were disappointed because the amount and quality of discourse fell far below their expectations. Some believed that this was true because the teachers using the new curricula lacked sufficient scientific knowledge. Mary Budd Rowe

(1974a; 1974b) and her colleagues, however, had evidence which challenged this idea. For instance, they had observed that teachers who had extensive training in the new programs did not have substantially different discourse patterns from those who had little or no exposure. They also compared the discourse patterns of 54 prominent scientists and science educators who had helped to develop a particular science curriculum to the patterns of classroom teachers and found that the "patterns of questions and responses were remarkably alike" (Rowe, 1974a, p. 82).

This led Rowe and her colleagues to consider other reasons for the low quality of discourse. The pattern which emerged from their early observations was that discourse in classrooms was characterized not only by recitation but also by speed. They found that when teachers asked questions, they would wait less than 1 second for a response before moving on to another question or another student. This phenomenon was labeled **wait-time 1**. They also found that when students provided a response, teachers similarly waited less than 1 second before reacting or asking the next question. This phenomenon was labeled **wait-time 2**.

These observations concerning the rapid pace of classroom discourse led Rowe and others to develop a conception of classroom life that would explain the discourse patterns and one that would help to account for changes if wait-time patterns could be altered. Rowe's view consisted of thinking about the classroom as a system or "game" with two players: (1) the teacher and (2) the students collectively. In this game four kinds of moves were possible:

1. Structuring: giving directions, stating procedures, suggesting changes.
2. Soliciting: asking questions.
3. Responding: answering solicitations, expanding on a structuring move, reporting data, or continuing a line of reasoning.
4. Reacting: evaluating statements made by self or other players. (pp. 81–82)

Obviously, as in any game, it is not very much fun if all players can't play and some have to sit on the bench most of the time. This seemed to be happening when the pace was moving at such a rapid rate. Rowe argued that teachers dominated three of the moves in the game—structuring, soliciting, and reacting—and even though students potentially had control of the responding move, short wait-times prevented significant playing time.

Research Summary 13-1 is a description of the initial major study done by Mary Budd Rowe. As you will see, the important lesson from this research is that slowing down the pace of discourse (extending wait-times 1 and 2) gives students a chance to participate more actively in classroom life, and as a result, changes rather dramatically the communication patterns.

MAIN FEATURES OF CLASSROOM DISCUSSION

Because classroom discourse or discussion is so central to all aspects of teaching, it is difficult to examine it apart from all other executive and interactive functions of teaching. Nonetheless, this section and the one that follows will strive to provide an overview of classroom discussion as a distinct approach to teaching and will offer specific procedures for beginning teachers to consider.

Common Ingredients of Discussion

Discussion can be perceived as an approach to teaching with three common ingredients:

- Both student and teacher talk are required.
- Students are expected to enter into dialogue and conversation about academic materials.
- Students and teachers are expected to practice and publicly display their thinking.

Today, in some form or another, discussion is the most preferred method employed by teachers who choose to reduce their own talk in order to more actively involve their students in thinking processes and discovery. For many years, discussion was viewed solely as an alternative to lecture, and a lively debate existed among practicing teachers, as well as educational researchers, as to which was most effective. The contemporary view does not pit discussion against other strategies or models but instead recognizes that (1) discussion is a strat-

RESEARCH SUMMARY 13-1

Rowe, M. B. (1974). Wait-time and rewards as instructional variables, their influence on language, logic, and fate control. Part One: Wait-time. *Journal of Research in Science Teaching, 11*, 81–94.

PROBLEM: Could it be that the absence of talk (pauses by the teacher) does more to influence discourse and complex cognitive processes than its presence? This provocative question was pursued by Mary Budd Rowe and her colleagues some years ago. This now classic study, along with others that were conducted subsequently, introduced the concept of "wait-time" to the knowledge base on teaching.

SAMPLE AND SETTING: This study actually progressed through two stages: (1) systematic observation of teachers in natural settings, and (2) planned experiments where the researchers attempted to change the natural behavior of teachers.

NATURAL OBSERVATIONS: Discussion patterns were initially analyzed from 103 tapes made by 36 primary teachers in the New Jersey and New York region using the Science Curriculum Improvement Study (SCIS). The researchers also sought tapes of lessons from other parts of the country and at other grade levels. At the end of this stage of their inquiry, they had obtained over 300 tapes from rural, surburban, and urban areas and from a variety of grade levels, including high school and college classes. Analysis of these lessons showed that the pace of instruction in most classrooms was very fast. In all but three classrooms, out of the hundreds studied, teachers displayed the following pattern:

- Teacher asked a question. Student must respond in at least 1 second.
- If student did not respond in 1 second, teacher repeated, rephrased, asked a different question, or called on another student. (Wait-time 1)
- When a student did respond, the teacher reacted or asked another question within an average of 0.9 seconds. (Wait-time 2)

The investigators concluded from this phase of their work that instruction in virtually all classrooms was very fast and that sufficient wait-time was not occurring. They also concluded that in a few classrooms where they did find students engaged in inquiry, sustained conversation, speculation, and argument about ideas that the average wait-time hovered around 3 seconds. With this information, the researchers planned and conducted a series of controlled microstudies (1) to see if teachers could be taught to slow down the pace of their discussions by using wait-time, and (2) if the slower pace had an impact on discourse and cognitive processes.

PROCEDURES FOR THE MICROSTUDIES: Ninety-six teachers from two locations were recruited and trained to employ wait-times of at least 3 seconds. From a pool of lessons prepared by the researchers using various curricula and aimed at various grade levels, teachers were asked to teach six lessons to students who were assigned to four-member learning groups. Each lesson was recorded on audiotape. Tapes were transcribed and coded. The wait-time variables were measured using the following criteria:

- *Wait-time 1:* The time between when the teacher stops speaking and when either a student responds or the teacher speaks again
- *Wait-time 2:* The time between when a student stops speaking and when the teacher speaks

POINTERS FOR READING RESEARCH: The results of this study are descriptive and rather straightforward. No new research concepts are introduced. However, Rowe's study is interesting in that it was conducted in stages. This illustrates how good research often moves from casual observations of phenomena in a natural setting to more systematic observation and only then to intervention and manipulation of important variables in controlled settings for the purpose of seeing if things can be changed for the better.

RESULTS: Teacher behavior changed as a result of training to use longer wait-times. Table 13-1 shows the number of questions asked and the typical distribution of question types by teachers before and after wait-time training.

Notice the sharp drop in the number of questions asked by teachers after wait-time training. Also note that the number of informational questions declined while the number of probing and thought-provoking questions increased rather dramatically.

The researchers hypothesized that if teachers could slow down their pace, this behavior would impact on the way their students responded. Table 13-1 displays the results of Rowe's wait-time studies as they impact on what she called student outcome variables. Notice that this table compares the behaviors of only 76 of the 95 teachers who achieved criterion wait-times of 3 seconds or longer.

Table 13-2 shows these results when teachers started to use longer wait-times:

- The length of student responses increased from 8 words per response under the fast pace used by teachers to 27 words. This signifies considerably longer statements by students after teachers are trained to use wait-time.
- The number of unsolicited but appropriate responses increased from a mean of 5 to a mean of 17.

TABLE 13-1 Number of Questions and Typical Distribution of Question Types Before and After Wait-Time Training

	BEFORE TRAINING	AFTER TRAINING
Mean number of questions per 15 minutes of transcript	38	8
Typical questions (%)		
Rhetorical	3	2
Informational	82	34
Leading	13	36
Probing	2	28

(Continued on page 394)

RESEARCH SUMMARY 13-1 (Continued)

TABLE 13-2 **Student Outcome Variables: Contrasts Between Tape 1 and Tape 6 of the Training Sequence for 76 of 95 Teachers Who Achieved Criterion Wait-Times of 3 Seconds or Longer**

STUDENT VARIABLE	TAPE 1	TAPE 2
Length of response		
Mean	8	27
Range	(3–12 words)	(14–39 words)
Number of unsolicited but appropriate responses		
Mean	5	17
Range	(0–17)	(12–28)
Number of failures to respond		
Mean	7	1
Range	(1–15)	(0–3)
Number of evidence-inference statements		
Mean	6	14
Range	(0–11)	(6–21)
Number of solicitation, structuring, and reacting statements		
Mean	5	32
Range	(1–6)	(11–46)

- Failures to respond ("I don't know" or silence) decreased. In classrooms prior to training, the "no response" was as high as 30 percent of the time. This changed dramatically once teachers started to wait at least 3 seconds for students to think.
- When wait-time was lengthened, students provided more evidence type of statements to support the inferences they were making.
- With a slower pace, students asked more questions and the number of structuring and soliciting moves increased.

DISCUSSION AND IMPLICATIONS: What is striking about this study and other wait-time studies done since Rowe's initial work is (1) teachers, left to their natural inclinations, pace instruction much too fast to allow very much careful inquiry or serious dialogue, and (2) a rather simple intervention can bring rather striking changes in discourse patterns. Learning to "wait" results in fewer and different types of questions by teachers and, most importantly, different student responses. Given more time, students will less often fail to respond ("I don't know") and they will increase the length of their responses. The quality of responses will also change. Students in classrooms where teachers use wait-time engage in inquiry-oriented and speculative thinking.

egy that does not necessarily stand alone but can be employed across all models of teaching and in a variety of situations, and (2) the choices about when to use discussion depend on whether dialogue among students is needed to help the teacher accomplish particular goals and objectives, particularly those associated with higher-level thinking and discovery learning.

Instructional Effects of Discussion

Discussions are used by teachers to achieve at least three important instructional objectives.

1. **To improve student thinking and help students construct their own meaning about academic content:** As you have already learned, telling students about something does not necessarily ensure their comprehension and understanding of new materials. Discussing a topic helps students strengthen their existing cognitive structures and helps them increase their ability to think.

2. **To promote student involvement and engagement:** Research, the wisdom of experienced teachers, as well as common sense would argue that for true learning to take place students must take responsibility for their own learning and not depend solely on the teacher. Using discussion is one means of doing this. It gives students public opportunities to talk about and play with their own ideas and provides motivation to engage in discourse beyond the confines of the classroom walls.

3. **To help students learn important communication skills and thinking processes:** Because discussions are public, they provide one means for the teacher to find out what students are thinking and how they are processing the ideas and information being taught. Discussions thus provide social settings for teachers to help students analyze their thinking processes and for learning important communication skills such as stating ideas clearly, listening to others, responding to others in appropriate ways, and even learning how to ask good questions.

Syntax for Holding Discussions

Although there are several different approaches to discussion, the major phases or steps for holding discussions are described briefly in Table 13-3.

Different Approaches for Holding Discussions

Although the basic principles of discussions are generally the same, variations of the method need to be highlighted here. Since space does not permit the presentation of all variations, the four approaches deemed most important for beginning teachers are described below.

USING DISCUSSION IN CONJUNCTION WITH OTHER TEACHING MODELS

All of the teaching models described in previous chapters require discussion at some time during their execution. For instance, when using the presentation or direct instruction models, you saw the importance of getting students to talk about new knowledge or skills as a way for the teacher to check for understanding as well as to extend student thinking. Concept teaching, you remember, requires specific types of student discussion, first as they strive to attain a particular concept and later as they develop deeper understanding of the concept and use their critical thinking skills. Cooperative learning similarly requires students to verbally interact, although the emphasis is often on student-to-student exchange in small groups. Inquiry teaching requires constant exchange between teachers and learners in all phases of the lesson.

RECITATION DISCUSSIONS

Although recitation is often overused, and for some teachers it appears to be the only strategy in their repertoire, it nonetheless has its place. Many times teachers ask students to read about a particular topic. This reading may be as short as a paragraph or as long as a chapter or a whole book. It can cover a spate of topics, various literary forms such as scientific reports, historical documents, plays, poems, short stories, novels, or pieces of music. Teachers ask students to do this reading with a definite purpose in mind. Sometimes it is to glean important information about a topic; other times it is to become familiar with a particular author, a specific type of literature, or a point of view. Brief question-and-answer sessions (recitation discussions) over assigned reading materials can provide teachers with a means to check for student understanding as well as providing motivation for students to complete their reading assignments.

DISCOVERY OR INQUIRY DISCUSSIONS

As described in Chapter 12, some discussions conducted by teachers are for the specific purpose of getting students to participate directly in the pro-

Table 13-3 Syntax for Holding Discussion

PHASES	TEACHER BEHAVIOR
Phase 1: Provide objectives and set	Teacher goes over the objectives for the discussion and gets students ready to participate
Phase 2: Focusing the discussion	Teacher provides a focus for discussion by describing ground rules, asking an initial question, presenting a puzzling situation, or describing a discussion issue
Phase 3: Holding the discussion	Teacher monitors student interactions, asks questions, listens to student ideas, responds to student ideas, enforces the ground rules, keeps records of the discussion, expresses own ideas
Phase 4: Ending the discussion	Teacher helps bring the discussion to a close by helping to summarize or express the meaning the discussion has had for him or her
Phase 5: Debriefing the discussion	Teacher asks students to look at their discussion and thinking processes

cess of thinking and to be discoverers of their own ideas. Normally, this type of discussion is referred to as an inquiry or discovery lesson. Although a number of specific approaches have been developed, they all have a common syntax: the teacher gets the lesson started by presenting students with what Suchman (1962) labeled a "discrepant event" or what Palincsar and Brown (1989) more recently called "mystery spots." Both refer to puzzling situations that are not immediately explainable, such as instances where water appears to run uphill, metal changes shape under heat, social data confront conventional wisdom, and the like. Because these situations are puzzling to students and create cognitive dissonance, they provide a natural motivation to think. When teachers are using this approach, they encourage students to generate theories and hypotheses to explain the puzzling events, to ask questions, to generate data, and to put their ideas to empirical and logical tests. In this type of discussion, teachers help students become conscious about their own thinking processes and teach them to monitor and evaluate their learning strategies.

DISCUSSIONS TO CLARIFY POSITIONS AND TO SHARE EXPERIENCES

Often teachers hold discussions for the purpose of helping students develop shared meaning from common experiences or to confront one another with differences of opinion. Younger children may be asked to talk about what they learned from their visit to the zoo or the apple farm. Older students may be asked to talk about what they learned from a science experiment they all performed or a novel they read. Important current events such as a breakthrough in an arms treaty, new abortion legislation, or a natural disaster are often discussed in the classroom so that different points of view may be explored. Unlike recitation discussions—where teachers are asking for recall of specific information—or inquiry lessons—where teachers are getting students to reason—this type of discussion aims at helping students form and express independent thought and opinions. Through dialogue about shared experience and argument about what these experiences mean, ideas are refined or expanded and questions are raised for future study.

Structure of the Learning Environment

As you will see later in more detail, the structure of the learning environment surrounding discussions is incredibly important. As with cooperative learning and inquiry teaching, the environment for conducting discussions is characterized by open processes and active student roles. It also demands careful attention to the use of physical space. The teacher may provide varying degrees of structure and focus to a particular discussion, depending upon the nature of the class and the learning objectives. However, in many ways the students themselves will control the specific minute-to-minute interactions.

PROCEDURES FOR CONDUCTING DISCUSSIONS

As with the specific models of teaching described in the preceding chapters, using discussion requires a set of tasks and activities to be performed by the teacher prior to, during, and after a lesson.

Preinstructional Tasks

There are two common beliefs held by some beginning teachers: planning for a discussion requires less effort than planning for a presentation, and discussions cannot really be planned because they rely upon spontaneous and unpredictable interactions among students. Both of these ideas are wrong. Planning for a discussion requires every bit as much effort as, perhaps more than, planning for other types of lessons, and even though spontaneity and flexibility are important in discussions, it is prior planning by the teacher that makes these features possible.

CONSIDERING THE PURPOSES FOR THE DISCUSSION

Deciding that discussion is appropriate for a given lesson is the first step in planning to hold a discussion. Preparing the lesson and making decisions about what type of discussion to hold and specific strategies to employ are next. As described earlier, although discussions can stand alone as a teaching strategy, they are most frequently used in connection with other teaching models. Planning for a discussion requires deciding exactly what its purposes are. Although the particular uses of discussion are practically infinite, teachers generally want their discussion to accomplish one of the objectives just described: recitation to help check for student understanding of reading assignments or discovery

discussions to teach thinking skills or share experiences.

CONSIDERING THE STUDENTS

Knowing about students' prior knowledge is just as important in planning a discussion as it is in planning a presentation. Experienced teachers know that they must also take into consideration their students' discourse and communication skills. They consider, for instance, how particular students in the class will respond differently to various kinds of questions or foci; they predict how some will want to talk all the time, while others will be reluctant to say anything. When planning discussions it is important to devise ways to encourage participation by as many students as possible, not just the bright ones, and to be prepared with questions and ideas that will spark the interest of diverse students. More will be said about this aspect of discussion later.

MAKING A PLAN

A lesson plan for either a presentation or a discussion consists of a set of objectives and a content outline. For a discussion, however, the plan should not only include the targeted content but also a well-conceived focus statement, the description of a puzzling event, or a set of questions. If the discussion is going to follow a presentation, it is likely that the teacher already has the content firmly in mind and has explored the types of relationships which are important. When the discussion follows assigned readings, experienced teachers know that they must have read the materials themselves and in most instances have taken extensive notes not only about specific facts but, more importantly, about the main ideas, points of view, and key relationships highlighted in the reading. Sometimes beginning teachers find using the "conceptual web" technique described in Chapter 9 a useful way to organize complex concepts and relationships prior to a discussion. Beginning teachers will find that careful attention to preparation will assist immensely as they strive to keep details straight for students and help facilitate student understanding and higher-order thinking.

For some types of discussions asking students questions becomes a key feature. In preparing their questioning strategy, teachers need to consider both

Table 13-4 Six Question Types According to Bloom's Taxonomy

LEVEL	EXAMPLES OF QUESTIONS	COGNITIVE PROCESSES
Level 1: Knowledge	Which region of the United States is Ohio in? What does H_2O stand for?	Recalling factual information
Level 2: Comprehension	What is the difference between longitude and latitude? What is the book The Old Man and the Sea about?	Using information
Level 3: Application	If John has 12 feet of lumber, how many 2-foot boards can he make?	Applying principles
Level 4: Analysis	Why do you think the red liquid moves? Why do some trees lose their leaves in winter?	Explaining relationships or making inferences
Level 5: Synthesis	If the North had not won the Civil War, what would life be like in the United States today? What might happen if the Earth experienced a continuing warming trend? What if John Brown had succeeded at Harper's Ferry?	Making predictions
Level 6: Evaluation	Which novel do you think is the best piece of literature? What do you think about the recycling program?	Making judgments or stating opinions

the cognitive level of questions and their level of difficulty.

You read in the research section how researchers have studied the various types of questions asked by teachers and their effects on student learning. During the past two decades there have been many systems developed for classifying the cognitive level of teacher questions. Most of the classification systems have similarities; all consider questions in terms of the cognitive processing they require of students. In Chapter 2, Bloom's taxonomy of educational objectives was used as a means for selecting content and instructional objectives. This taxonomy has also been used by teachers to design questions for classroom discussion. Table 13-4 shows six categories of classroom questions and examples of each.

As described earlier, the research about the effects of using various types of questions is still unclear. However, the recommendations to beginning teachers would be to recognize that different questions require different types of thinking and that a good lesson should include both lower- and higher-level questions. One approach is to start by asking simple recall questions to see if students have grasped the basic ideas under consideration, followed by comprehension and analysis questions ("why" questions), and then conclude with more thought-provoking questions about the topic.

In preparing the lesson plan and questioning strategies, remember to think through the issues associated with question difficulty, described earlier. Experience helps teachers to know their students and to devise questions of appropriate difficulty.

Decisions about question type and difficulty can be better made during the quiet of advanced planning rather than during the discussion itself.

USING THE PHYSICAL SPACE

Another planning task is to make arrangements for appropriate use of the physical space. Chapter 3, you remember, described how different seating patterns affected communication patterns within the classroom. The best seating arrangements for discussion are either the U-shape or circle. Both seating patterns allow students to see each other, an important condition for verbal interaction. Both can be accommodated in most classrooms. Each, however, has some advantages and disadvantages that should be considered.

The U-shape, with the teacher situated at the open end of the U, gives a bit more authority to the teacher, an important feature when working with groups of students who lack discussion skills or where behavior management is a problem. The U-shape also allows freedom of movement for teachers. Teachers may need ready access to the chalkboard or flip charts, or they may need to move into the U to make closer contact with particular students. The disadvantage of the U is that it establishes some emotional distance between the teacher as discussion leader and the students. It also puts considerable physical distance between students who are sitting at the head of the U and those sitting at the end.

The circle, on the other hand, minimizes both emotional and physical distance among participants and maximizes opportunities for students to talk freely with one another. The disadvantage of the circle is that it inhibits the teacher from moving freely to the chalkboard or among students. There is simply something about the circle that requires the teacher to be seated along with the students.

Most elementary and secondary schools today have furniture and other features which make movement from one seating arrangement to another possible. In some instances, however, beginning teachers will be confronted with situations which will severely limit this possibility. For example, some science laboratories and shop classes have fixed tables. Some drama and English classes may be held in the school theater where seating is fixed. These conditions require special problem solving on the part of teachers. Some experienced science teachers have been known to have students stand in a U-shape during discussion sessions; drama teachers have seated their students on the floor of the stage. The specifics of the classroom space and the teacher's own personal preferences certainly are strong considerations when making planning decisions about use of the space prior to a discussion.

Holding the Discussion

For whole-class discussions to be successful, some rather sophisticated communication and interaction skills are required on the part of both teachers and students. Also required are norms that support open exchange and mutual respect. As discussion leader, the teacher should clearly focus the discussion, keep it on track by refocusing student digressions, encourage participation by listening carefully to all ideas and points of view, and help keep a record of the discussion.

FOCUSING DISCUSSIONS

Many classroom discussions are characterized by talk and more talk, much of which has little to do with either the main aims of the lesson or with extending student thinking. An effective discussion, just like an effective presentation, is clearly focused and to the point. At the beginning, teachers must explain the purposes of the discussion and get students set to participate. They must also pose a specific question, raise an appropriate issue, or present a puzzling situation associated with the topic. These activities have to be in a form which students can understand and respond to. Stating the focus question or issue clearly is one key to getting a good discussion started.

KEEPING THE DISCUSSION FOCUSED

As a whole-class discussion proceeds, many circumstances can get it off track. In some instances students will purposely try to get the teacher off the topic. One example might be students who want to talk about last Friday's ball game instead of the causes of World War I. Talking about Friday's game is fine if that is the objective of the lesson, but it is not appropriate if the aim is to extend student thinking about the causes of war.

A second example of wandering is when a student expresses an idea or raises a question that has nothing to do with the topic. This happens often, particularly with students who have trouble concentrating in school. It is also likely to happen with younger students who have not been taught good listening and discussion skills.

In both instances effective teachers acknowledge what students are doing—"We are now talking about last Friday night's game," or "You say your father had a good time in New York last weekend"—and then refocuses the class's attention on the topic with a comment, such as "Talking about the game seems to be of great interest to all of you. I will let you do that during the last 5 minutes of the class period, but now I want us to get back to the question I posed to you." Or, "I know you are very interested in what your father did in New York, and I would love it if you would spend some time during lunch telling me more. Right now we want to talk about. . . ."

KEEPING A RECORD OF THE DISCUSSION

Most experienced teachers know that verbal exchange during a discussion proceeds in more orderly fashion if some type of written record is kept of the discussion as it unfolds. Sometimes this consists of writing the main ideas or points of view made by students on the chalkboard or on flip charts. At other times it may consist of constructing conceptual webs which illustrate the various ideas and relationships being discussed.

A dilemma faced by beginning teachers keeping a discussion record is how much detail to include and whether or not all ideas should be written down. These decisions depend upon the nature of the students and the purposes of the discussion. When the teacher is working with a group which lacks confidence in discourse skills, it is probably a good idea to write down as much as possible. Seeing many ideas on the chalkboard or flip chart provides a public display of the many good ideas that exist within the group. With a more experienced and confident group, the teacher may want to list

only key words, thus affording a more open exchange of ideas and opinions.

If the teacher has asked students specifically for their theories or ideas about a topic, it is important to list all ideas and treat these equally, regardless of their quality. On the other hand, if questions focus on direct recall of right answers, then only right answers should be recorded. How to respond to incorrect responses will be discussed in a moment.

LISTENING TO STUDENTS' IDEAS

A favorite discussion technique used by many teachers at the college and high school levels is one referred to as "playing the devil's advocate." Teachers who use this technique purposely take the opposite point of view from that being expressed by individual students or groups of students. Even though this approach can create lively exchange between the teacher and a small group of students, it does not work well with younger students or with many high school students except, perhaps, for the very bright and the most verbal. Debate and argument arouse emotions, and despite their motivational potential, may divert the students' attention from the topic. It also causes many of the less verbal or shy students to shrink from participation. If the teacher's goal is to help students understand the lesson and extend their thinking, then the teacher should listen carefully to each student's ideas. The teacher should remain nonjudgmental and inquiry-oriented, rather than challenge and argue with students.

USING WAIT-TIME

You read in the research section how many teachers do not give students sufficient time to think and respond. There are probably several reasons for this. First, there is a strong cultural norm against silence. Silence is uncomfortable for many people and, consequently, they jump in to keep the conversation moving. Second, waiting for student response can be perceived by teachers as threatening to the pace and momentum of a lesson. Finally, silence or waiting can give uninvolved students opportunities to start talking or otherwise misbehave. Although many contextual conditions should influence wait-time, the general recommendations would be for beginning teachers to practice waiting at least 3 seconds for a student's response, to ask the question again or in a slightly different way if there is no response, and to never move on to a second question without some closure on the first. The amount of wait-time should probably be less for direct-recall questions and more for questions aimed at higher-level thinking and more complex content. After a student response, teachers should also wait a sufficient time before moving on.

RESPONDING TO STUDENT ANSWERS

When students respond correctly to teachers' questions, effective teachers acknowledge the correct answer with brief affirmations, such as "That's right," "OK," "Yes." They do not spend time providing overly gushy praise. Most beginning teachers learn these behaviors quite quickly. However, responding to incorrect or incomplete responses is a more complicated situation. We think the guidelines on **dignifying student errors** provided by Hunter (1982) are as sound as any. She recommends the following teacher moves:

1. *Dignify* the student's incorrect response or performance by giving a question for which the response would have been correct: for example, "George Washington would have been the right answer if I asked you who the first president of the United States was."
2. Provide the student with an *assist*, hint, or prompt: for example, "Remember the President in 1828 was also a hero in the War of 1812."
3. Hold the student *accountable:* for example, "You didn't know President Jackson today, but I bet you will tomorrow when I ask you again."

RESPONDING TO STUDENT IDEAS AND OPINIONS

Although the art of questioning is important for effective discussion, other verbal behaviors by teachers are equally important, especially those associated with responding to students' ideas and opinions. These are responses aimed at getting students to extend their thinking and to be more conscious of their thinking processes. Statements

and/or questions such as the following provide illustrations on how to do this:

- Reflecting back on student ideas
  "I heard you say. . . ."
  "What I think you are telling me is. . . ."
  "That is an interesting idea, I have never thought of it in quite that way. . . ."
- Getting students to consider alternatives
  "That is an interesting idea; I wonder, however, if you have ever considered this as an alternative. . . ."
  "You have provided one point of view about the issue. How does it compare with the point of view expressed by. . . ?"
  "Evelyn has just expressed an interesting point of view about the topic. I wonder if someone else would like to say why they agree (disagree) with her idea?"
  "Do you think the author would agree with your idea? Why? Why not?"
- Seeking clarification
  "I think you have a good idea. However, I am a bit confused. Can you expand your idea a bit to help me understand it more fully?"
- Labeling thinking processes and asking for supportive evidence
  "It sounds to me like you have been performing a mental *experiment* with these data."
  "You have made a very strong *inference* from the information given you."
  "Can you think of an *experiment* that would put that hypothesis to a good test?"
  "What if I told you (give new information)? What would that do to your *hypothesis*?"
  "That is an interesting position. What *values* led you to it?"
  "If everyone held the *judgment* you just expressed, what would be the result?"

Finally, many beginning teachers express concern about whether or not they should express their own ideas and opinions during a discussion. Although teachers do not want to dominate discussions or make it appear that they are the only ones with good ideas, expressing ideas appropriately can be very beneficial. It provides opportunities for teachers to model their own thinking processes and show students the way they tackle problems. It also communicates to students that the teacher sees himself or herself as part of a learning community interested in sharing ideas and discovering knowledge.

BRINGING THE DISCUSSION TO A CLOSE AND DEBRIEFING

As with other types of lessons, discussions need to be brought to proper closure. There are a variety of ways that effective teachers do this. In some instances they may choose to summarize what has been said in a few sentences and try to tie various ideas together or relate them to the larger topic being studied. In other instances, teachers may want to close the discussion with a short presentation highlighting new or previously studied information. Some teachers ask students to summarize the discussion by posing a final question such as, "What is the main thing you got from our discussion today?" or "What do you think was the most provocative point made during our discussion?"

From time to time discussions should be debriefed. **Debriefing** in this instance means to look back or reflect, not on the content of the discussion but on the way the discussion proceeded. To conduct a successful debriefing requires that teachers teach students the differences between the discussion itself and the debriefing and to pose questions such as: How do you think our discussion went today? Did we give everyone a chance to participate? Did we listen to one another's ideas? Were there times when we seemed to get bogged down? If so, why? What can we all do next time to make our discussion more stimulating or provocative?

Postinstructional Tasks

As with the other teaching approaches, there are instructional tasks for teachers to perform following a discussion. One is considering how a particular discussion should be followed up in subsequent lessons; the other is grading.

FOLLOW-UP

Experienced teachers make both formal and mental notes for themselves following discussions. Sometimes these notes pertain to the content of the discussion and help determine subsequent lessons. For example, perhaps a discussion identifies some serious gaps in students' knowledge about a topic. This can prompt the teacher to plan a presentation on this topic or to find suitable reading materials to assign to students. On other occasions, a discussion will identify aspects of a topic in which students are particularly interested. Teachers can use this information to plan lessons which will take advantage of this natural interest. The conduct of the discussion itself will give the teacher information about the strengths and weaknesses of various student's thinking processes as well as the group's ability to engage in purposeful dialogue. Future lessons can then be planned to strengthen areas targeted for improvement.

GRADING

Grading classroom discussion poses a perplexing problem for most teachers. On the one hand, if participation is not graded students may view this part of their work as less important than work for which a grade is given. Remember the work-for-grade exchange concept described in Chapters 4 and 7. On the other hand, it is practically impossible to quantify participation in any satisfactory way. In order to grade discussions teachers need to ask themselves these questions: Do I reward quantity or quality? What constitutes a quality contribution? What about the student who talks all the time, but says nothing? What about the student who is naturally shy, but has good ideas?

There are two ways experienced teachers have confronted the grading dilemma. One is to give bonus points to students who consistently appear to be prepared for discussions and who make significant contributions. If this method is used it needs to be discussed thoroughly with the class and opportunities provided that allow each student equal access to the bonus points available.

A second way to grade discussions is to use the discussion as a springboard for a reflective writing assignment. The grade in this instance is given not for participation but for the student's ability to reflect on the discussion and put in words what the discussion meant to him or her. Properly conceived and managed, postdiscussion essays can heighten student attention during the discussion and have

Figure 13-2   Cues for using think-pair-share

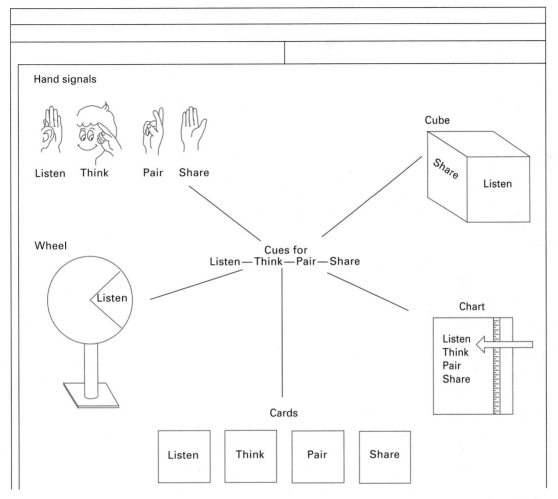

SOURCE: From F. Lyman, (1985), *Think-pair-share*. (Mimeographed.) College Park, Maryland: University of Maryland.

tice the skill and receive feedback on how they are doing. In general, this is the model that teachers should use when teaching important discourse skills.

LEARN TO TEACH TOWARD MULTIPLE OBJECTIVES

Until very recently, beginning teachers were admonished to teach toward a single objective. This idea should be rejected by beginning teachers. It would be similar to telling a doctor to pay attention only to the way incisions are made during an operation or an NFL quarterback to pay attention only to the behavior of the linebackers. Experts in any profession must learn how to "read" complex environmental cues and respond appropriately so that a number of objectives can be accomplished simultaneously. Many thinking and discourse skills can be taught by skillful teachers right along with academic content with little additional time required. Here are several examples:

- A high school literature teacher who is discussing how the short stories of Ernest Hemingway reflect his life and his times can use think-pair-share strategies to encourage broader participa-

Figure 13-3 Teaching thinking skills with question-response cues

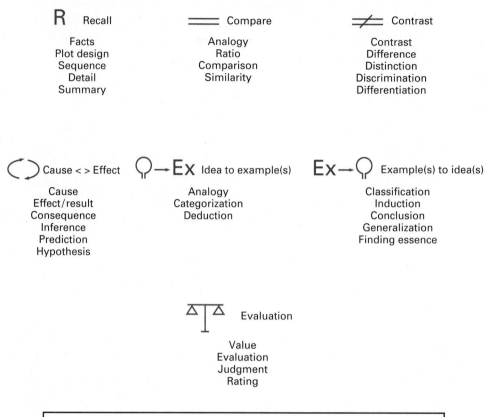

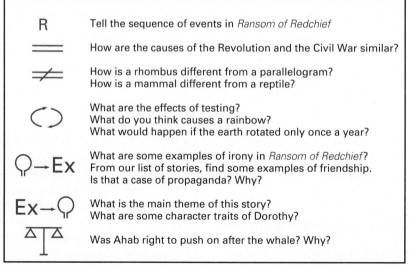

SOURCE: From F. Lyman, (1986), *Procedures for using the question/response cues.* (Mimeographed.) College Park, Maryland: University of Maryland and the Howard County Public Schools.

Figure 13-4   The fishbowl arrangement.

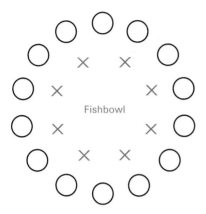

Fishbowl

tion by students. Also by taking a few moments at the end of the lesson to answer the question, "How did our discussion go today?" she can focus student attention on important classroom discussion and discourse skills.

- A teacher who is helping elementary students plan an important field trip to the airport as part of their economic unit on transportation systems can form the class into two groups and arrange them in the fishbowl seating pattern displayed in Figure 13-4. The group in the inner circle will do the planning for 20 minutes and the other group will act as observers. Observers will be assigned to watch the specific behaviors associated with the planning task. After 20 minutes they will give a short report on what they saw and then exchange roles. The original observers become the planners and original planners the observers.
- A junior high teacher who is giving a lecture on reproduction can instruct students prior to the lecture about how buzz groups work; then he can stop two or three times during the lecture and ask students to discuss what he has been talking about.
- A high school Spanish teacher who wants students to work on their conversation skills and also on the interpersonal communication skill of paraphrasing can conduct a discussion on Spanish culture and ask each discussant to paraphrase what the prior student said before making a new contribution. She provides feedback

to students on the content of their discussion (Spanish culture), their use of vocabulary, and their use of the paraphrase.

SUMMARY

- Discourse and discussion are key ingredients for enhancing student thinking and for uniting the cognitive and social aspects of learning.
- Discourse can be thought of as externalization of thinking and has both cognitive and social importance.
- Studies for a good many years have described how discourse patterns in most classrooms do not afford effective dialogue among students or promote much discovery or higher-level thinking.
- A substantial knowledge base exists that informs teachers on how to create positive discourse systems and hold productive discussions. Studies also provide guidelines about the types of questions to ask and how to provide appropriate pacing for students to think and respond.
- Most classroom discourse proceeds at too rapid a pace. Teachers can obtain better classroom discourse by slowing down the pace and giving themselves and their students opportunities to think before they respond.
- When experienced teachers refer to classroom discourse they often use the label *discussion* to describe what they are doing.
- Classroom discussions are characterized by students, as well as teachers, talking about academic materials and by students willingly displaying their thinking processes publicly.
- The primary instructional effects of a discussion lesson are to improve student thinking, promote involvement and engagement around academic materials, and learn important communication and thinking skills.
- There are many variations to discussions. Four of the major approaches include using discussion in conjunction with other teaching models, recitation discussions, discovery or inquiry discussions, and discussions to clarify values and share personal experiences.

- Regardless of the approach, the general flow or syntax for a discussion lesson consists of five major phases: providing objectives and set, focusing the discussion, holding the discussion, ending the discussion, and debriefing the discussion.
- The structure of the learning environment for discussion lessons is characterized by open processes and active student roles.
- Important preinstructional tasks for teachers to consider include determining the purposes of the discussion, being aware of students' prior knowledge and discourse skills, making plans for how to approach the discussion, and determining the type of questions to ask.
- Placing students in circles or using U-shape seating arrangements facilitates classroom discussions.
- Primary tasks for teachers as they conduct the discussion consist of focusing the discussion, keeping the discussion on track, keeping a record of the discussion, making sure students' ideas are listened to, and providing appropriate wait-time.
- Students' ideas should be responded to with dignity, and teachers should help students extend their ideas by seeking clarification, by getting students to consider alternative ideas, and by labeling thinking processes students are displaying.
- In general, discussion and classroom discourse patterns can be improved if teachers slow the pace and use methods to broaden participation and if they teach students to try to understand one another and have high interpersonal regard for each other's ideas.
- Teaching students four specific interpersonal communication skills (paraphrasing, behavior description, feeling description, and impression checking) can enhance the quality of classroom discourse and the interpersonal regard students hold for each other.
- Specific visual tools such as the think-pair-share cueing device and the thinking matrix can help students learn discourse and thinking skills.
- For students to become effective in the discourse

system and during specific discussion and discovery lessons requires teaching student discourse skills just as directly as academic content and other academic skills are taught.

KEY TERMS

classroom discourse
externalization of thinking
cognitive-social connection
recitation teaching
level of questions
wait-time
wait-time 1
wait-time 2
discussion focus
dignifying student errors
debriefing
think-pair-share
buzz groups
interpersonal communication skills
visual cues
thinking matrix

BOOKS FOR THE PROFESSIONAL

Cazden, C. B. (1988). *Classroom discourse*. Portsmouth, N.H.: Heinemann. This excellent book reviews the research on classroom discourse and describes implications for teaching. It contains extended actual transcripts of teacher and student classroom talk.

Garner, R. (1987). *Metacognition and reading comprehension*. Norwood, N.J.: Ablex. Although the focus is on reading, this book contains a good review of the research on metacognition and many ideas about how teachers can promote better student thinking and learning through direct instructional strategies.

Morine-Dershimer, G. (1985). *Talking, listening, and learning in elementary classrooms*. New York: Longman. This book describes students' perception of classroom discourse as well as effects of various types of classroom discourse and interaction patterns.

Resnick, L. B. (1987). *Education and learning to think*. Washington, D.C.: National Academy Press. This book provides a review of cognitive research along with justification and means for helping students develop dispositions and skills for higher-level thinking.

Resnick, L. B., and Kloper, L. E. (eds.). (1989). *Toward the thinking curriculum: Current cognitive research*. Alexandria, Va.: Association for Supervision and Curriculum Development. The yearbook of ASCD provides an excellent review of the research in the cognitive sciences that has implications for curriculum development in the various subject areas and for teaching students how to think.

LEARNING AIDS FOR PLANNING, OBSERVATION, AND REFLECTION

- Assessing My Discussion and Discourse Skills
- Observing Student Participation in Discussion
- Observing Teacher Use of Questions and Wait-Time
- Reflecting on Teaching toward Multiple Objectives

ASSESSING MY DISCUSSION AND DISCOURSE SKILLS

PURPOSE: Use the chart below to assess your level of skill in building productive discourse systems and conducting effective discussions.

DIRECTIONS: Check the level of skill you think you have for the areas listed below.

SKILL OR COMPETENCY	LEVEL OF EFFECTIVENESS		
	HIGH	MEDIUM	LOW
Preinstructional tasks			
Considering purposes for discussions	———	———	———
Considering student skill prior to discussions	———	———	———
Making plans for discussions	———	———	———
Instructional tasks			
Focusing discussions	———	———	———
Keeping discussions focused	———	———	———
Keeping records of discussions	———	———	———
Listening to student ideas	———	———	———
Using wait-time	———	———	———
Responding to students' answers	———	———	———
Responding to students' ideas	———	———	———
Closing and debriefing discussions	———	———	———
Postinstructional tasks			
Making plans for follow-up	———	———	———
Grading	———	———	———
Helping students become more effective in discourse systems			
Slowing down the pace	———	———	———
Broadening participation	———	———	———
Increasing interpersonal regard	———	———	———
Using tools to help students learn discourse skills	———	———	———

OBSERVING STUDENT PARTICIPATION IN DISCUSSION

PURPOSE: Broad student participation is an important goal in classroom discussions. This aid can be used to gather information about patterns of student participation in class discussions.

DIRECTIONS: Obtain a copy of the class seating chart, or, if observing a small group, note everyone's name and location on your paper. You can use a format like the one pictured below. Whenever a student contributes to the discussion, make a "tick" on your chart by that student's name.

Front

☐ —————————   ☐ —————————   ☐ —————————   ☐ —————————
☐ —————————   ☐ —————————   ☐ —————————   ☐ —————————
☐ —————————   ☐ —————————   ☐ —————————   ☐ —————————
☐ —————————   ☐ —————————   ☐ —————————   ☐ —————————

Analysis and Reflection: Who talks the most? The least? Is there an action zone, that is, an area of the room that the teacher seems to favor during whole-class discussions? Are there any sex differences in participation? Racial differences? Any other patterns observed? How might the quieter students be encouraged to participate?

22,   shyness, some ask "no ? s please

18.   8/18   12/30

OBSERVING TEACHER USE OF QUESTIONS AND WAIT-TIME

PURPOSE: In order to extend and strengthen student thinking, teachers need to have good questioning skills. This aid is to help you analyze teachers' use of questions, such as number of questions asked, cognitive level of questions, and wait-time.

DIRECTIONS: There is a column labeled *Code,* another labeled *Question No.,* and other columns labeled *A, B, C,* and *D.* The *Code* column is your key for determining what code goes in each column. For the first question the teacher asks, go to the *Question No.* column and find *1.* Then read across to column *A* and code in that column the level of question that the teacher asked—a knowledge question would be coded *1,* an application question *3,* and so on. Then code in column *B* for question *1* the appropriate wait-time code. Follow the same procedure for columns *C* and *D,* and repeat the procedure for each question the teacher asks.

CODE	QUESTION NO.	A	B	C	D
A. Level of question					
1. Knowledge	1.	——	——	——	——
Can the students recall what they have seen, heard, or read? For example, What is the meaning of *longitude?*	2.	——	——	——	——
	3.	——	——	——	——
2. Comprehension	4.	——	——	——	——
Can the student organize facts in various ways? For example, What is the main idea in this paragraph?	5.	——	——	——	——
3. Application	6.	——	——	——	——
Can the student apply techniques and rules to solve problems that have single correct answers? For example, if Bill has 49 cents, how many 8-cent balloons can he buy?	7.	——	——	——	——
	8.	——	——	——	——
	9.	——	——	——	——
4. Analysis	10.	——	——	——	——
Can the student explain relationships, make inferences, and find examples to support generalizations? For example, Religion was the focal point of life in the Middle Ages. What have you read that supports this idea?	11.	——	——	——	——
	12.	——	——	——	——
	13.	——	——	——	——
5. Synthesis	14.	——	——	——	——
Can the student make predictions, solve problems, or produce original communications? For example, If school were not required, what would happen?	15.	——	——	——	——
	16.	——	——	——	——

CODE	QUESTION NO.	A	B	C	D
6. Evaluation Can the student give opinions about issues, and judge the merit of ideas, problem solutions, art, and other products? For example, Do you agree that honesty is always the best policy?	17. 18. 19. 20.	—— —— —— ——	—— —— —— ——	—— —— —— ——	—— —— —— ——

    7. Rephrasing the previous question, cueing.

B. Wait-time
1. Teacher paused a few seconds *before* calling on student.
2. Teacher paused a few seconds *after* calling on student.
3. Teacher did not pause.
4. Not applicable; student answered readily.

C. Level of difficulty
1. Student response was accepted by teacher.
2. Response was not accepted by teacher.

D. Teacher response to student answers
1. Teacher gave a brief acknowledgment of correct answer.
2. Teacher gave gushy praise.
3. Student error was "dignified."
4. Student error was handled inappropriately.

Comments:

_____

_____

_____

_____

REFLECTING ON TEACHING TOWARD MULTIPLE OBJECTIVES

PURPOSE: It is important to teach toward multiple objectives. This aid will help you analyze your own or another teacher's current level of skill in this area.

DIRECTIONS: If you are teaching, at the end of a week spend some time reviewing your plan book and that week's lessons. Make a "tick" on the chart any time one of the lesson's objectives fits one of the categories provided. Add new categories as you learn more about the kinds of objectives you wish to achieve. If you are a student, observe one of your own teachers and categorize the goals you note the same way. Keep track this way for two or three weeks.

Goals that relate to

Content	_____
Learning strategies	_____
Classroom discourse	_____
Group development	_____
Motivation	_____

Analysis and Reflection: Examine the pattern of goals you have uncovered. Is the distribution of goals between the various categories appropriate? Compare this week's pattern with previous weeks. Are some categories underused? Are some overused? If you are a student teacher, use this information in planning for the upcoming week.

THE ORGANIZATIONAL FUNCTIONS OF TEACHING

INTRODUCTION

Part 3 of *Learning to Teach* is devoted to the organizational functions of teaching. Teachers, like other professionals, are expected not only to perform their primary function (in this case providing instruction to students) but also to provide leadership to the organization as a whole. For teachers this means working alongside others in the school —colleagues, administrators, parents, and students themselves—to help set schoolwide expectations and gain clarity of purposes and actions.

The two chapters that follow focus on three specific organizational functions that are important for beginning teachers: working with other members of the school community, helping schools improve, and surviving and flourishing as a professional. To perform these functions effectively, we must understand the nature of the school not only as a place where children come to learn but also as a place where adults work. We also need specific organizational skills aimed at making work with others in the school productive.

As you read and study these topics, you will discover two reasons why they are so important. One, there appears to be a certain synergy at work in schools in which teachers and others have come together and made agreements about what is going to be taught and how that makes a difference in how much students learn. Two, your ability to relate to and work with others within the school and larger professional community will have a significant impact on your career.

It is in this arena (not inside the classroom) that you will become known to others and where you will build your professional reputation. Teachers who grow and progress in their careers are those who can enter into schoolwide dialogue about educational and professional issues.

Chapter Outline

PERSPECTIVE AND RATIONALE
* Schools Are Social Systems * Schools Have Histories and Cultures * Schools Have Common Features with Other Organizations * Schools Have Special Features * Norms, Roles, and the Culture of Teaching

SAMPLING THE KNOWLEDGE BASE
* The Nature of Teachers' Work * Effective Schools Research * Attributes of Effective Schools

USING THE EFFECTIVE SCHOOLS RESEARCH
* Working with Colleagues * Working with Administrators and Leadership Personnel * Working with Parents

CHAPTER 14

The School as Workplace

Previous chapters described what teachers do as they plan for and deliver instruction and manage complex classroom settings. Providing leadership and teaching students in classrooms, however, are not the only aspects of a teacher's job. Teachers are also members of an organization called "school" and as such are asked to perform important leadership and organizational functions, including working with colleagues, serving on committees, and working with administrators and parents. The way these organizational functions are performed by teachers makes a significant difference in how students behave and what they learn. The way particular teachers carry out these functions also makes a significant difference in their own professional careers.

The aim of this chapter is to describe the work environment of schools and the corresponding culture of teaching. Emphasis is placed on the idea that schools are not only places where students come to learn; they are also places where adults work. After providing a conceptual framework for viewing schools as workplaces, we will summarize the emerging knowledge base on the nature of teachers' work behavior and what makes some schools more effective than others. We conclude with a discussion of several important organizational skills that be-

ginning teachers need as they become fully involved in their first school and community. Learning aids at the end of the chapter have been designed to assist you with study and reflection about some aspects of the school that you may not have considered before.

PERSPECTIVE AND RATIONALE

At this point in your career it is likely that your view of schools stems mainly from many years of being a learner in classrooms. You are familiar with the classroom portion of the teacher's role, with the role of student, and with the way that students and teachers interact around academic tasks. However, you may not have had much chance to observe or reflect about schools as social organizations or about the various nonteaching functions performed by teachers. In fact, many people (including those in the media) rarely view schools from the perspective of the complex social organizations they are. This is unfortunate because views of schools, stemming only from experiences as students, have caused misunderstanding on the part of many (teachers, parents, and policymakers) regarding school improvement efforts. Unrealistic views also have led to disillusionment on the part of many beginning teachers. The section that follows provides a view of schools from behind, instead of in front of, the teacher's desk.

Schools Are Social Systems

In discussing schools, we will rely on both the research literature and the wisdom of experienced educators. The set of understandings described here can best be labeled a **social-systems perspective**. This perspective looks at the complex structure of the school and how its various interactions (including those within the classroom) are shaped by the larger social context.

When schools are called social systems this means that they are not simply places where individuals act in totally free and disconnected ways but, instead, in more or less interdependent and predictable ways. Although individuals come together in schools to promote purposeful learning, each person does not chart his or her own course alone, nor do the actions of each have consequences only for that person. Also, as will be described later, the synergy developed by teachers acting in concert can have important consequences for student learning. To understand the social system view of schools, think for a moment about the number of interdependent actions required to bring about a day's worth of instruction for students:

Paper, pencils, and chalk have been ordered.

Rooms have been cleaned.

Curriculum guides have been prepared and textbooks ordered.

Parents have chosen to send their children to school.

Teachers have chosen to be professionally trained.

Buses have been driven and breakfasts and lunches prepared.

Schedules have been determined and children assigned to classes.

Health services for students have been planned and managed.

This list could go on and on. The point, however, is that the contemporary school is a complex social system requiring its members to perform important functions in interdependent ways.

Schools Have Histories and Cultures

Schools, like other organizations, have histories and cultures consisting of values, beliefs, and expectations that have developed and grown over time. The history of a school provides traditions and a multitude of routines (some good and some not so good) that are taken for granted by organizational members. The **culture of a school** provides the organizational arrangements that hold it together and give it power as a social entity. Lortie (1975) has referred to culture as the "way members of a group think about social action; culture encompasses alternatives for resolving problems in collective life" (p. 216). Others have provided similar definitions, although they sometimes use different labels. Rutter et al. (1979), for example, refer to the common set of values, beliefs, and ways of doing things as the school's **ethos;** Glass (1981) has called it tone; Joyce and his colleagues (1983) prefer the word *community*. Regardless of how it is labeled, culture greatly influences what goes on in schools and determines expectations and roles for beginning teachers.

Schools Have Common Features with Other Organizations

In some ways schools are similar to other organizations in society. For example, as in other organizations, members are directed toward the accomplishment of some goal. In a textile plant, the goal may be the production of men's shirts; IBM says information is its business. The overriding goal for schools is to provide *purposeful learning experiences* for students. Members of schools—principals, teachers, and students—are rewarded, as are members in other organizations, when they strive for and accomplish common organizational goals. Similarly, they are punished when they fail. An example of reward would be experiments in some states in which teaching faculties are given merit increases if, as a group, they can lift achievement in their school above a set criterion. An example of punishment would be instances in which beginning teachers are dismissed if they cannot provide purposeful learning activities.

Another organizational feature of schools is their division of labor and the resulting coordination efforts that are needed. Some teachers specialize according to subjects taught, whereas others specialize by grade level. In addition to teachers, school staffs include curriculum coordinators, administrators, nurses, counselors, janitors, and other support personnel. Most of the people in schools, however, are students, and they too must be considered organizational members. Because school roles are specialized, normative routines and structures are created to help members carry out their special tasks in ways that will more or less facilitate what others are doing. The reason why coordination of effort is not easy to accomplish in schools is described later.

Finally, the people in schools are pretty much like people in other organizations. They not only have jobs to perform, they also have psychological needs and motives to satisfy. In Chapter 4 a particular view of motivation was described in relation to students. This same perspective can help you understand adults in schools. This perspective, you remember, says that people are motivated to invest energy in three domains: achievement, affiliation, and influence. Achievement manifests itself in teachers and other adults in schools as they strive to provide good instruction and act as competent professionals. Affiliative motives become important when teachers come to value their peers for support, friendship, and collegiality. Influence motives are evident in schools as teachers strive to have a larger say in the way schools are run. Organizational members' feelings of self-esteem are related to the feelings they have about their competence, affiliation, and influence. Students whose self-esteem is frustrated by the school may become less involved in the school. Similarly, when these states are frustrated for teachers, or other adult workers, they are likely to feel incompetent, lonely, and powerless.

These three motivational domains (achievement, affiliation, and influence), while central to each individual in the school, are also central to the school as an organization. A school's ability to provide targeted learning cannot be accomplished without strong achievement motivation on the part of teachers and students. Likewise, affiliation and influence are directly needed to coordinate and manage the academic activities of schools and to make the schools a pleasant place to be. Learning aids at the end of this chapter have been designed to help you study a particular school to see what it is doing to help satisfy both student and adult psychological needs.

Schools Have Special Features

Just as schools have features in common with other organizations, so too they have features that are special. In some ways it is the special features of schools that are most significant for beginning teachers to understand.

AMBIGUOUS AND CONFLICTING GOALS

It has been stated several times in this book that the overriding goal of schools is to facilitate purposive learning for students. Stated at this level of abstraction, most people would readily agree with this goal. However, when people in schools speak more precisely about what purposive learning means, many of their statements may seem ambiguous and may conflict with the aims of one group or another in the community.

Goal ambiguity can be illustrated with reference to citizenship education. Most people in western societies believe that the schools should socialize students as good citizens who accept the values of democratic political systems and who embrace some degree of freedom in their own economic activities. However, how do school people, parents, and others know whether or not this goal is being accomplished? Parents, for example, are never sure their sons or daughters are embracing the values parents desire for them. Teachers seldom know how their former students behave as adult citizens. Do they vote, and are they participating community members?

As for goal conflict, do citizenship goals compete with academic learning goals? Which are most important and how should time be allocated between the two? What constitutes good citizenship? Some argue that the most important aspect of citizenship education is the socialization of students into traditional values and beliefs. Some church-related and private schools are inclined toward this position. On the other hand, others argue that this approach to citizenship education is simply indoctrination and leads to narrowness and conformity. The good citizen, from this point of view, might be the critical thinker who questions existing values and structures and attempts to modify them.

COMPULSORY ATTENDANCE

A second special feature of schools is that their clients are required to be there. All states have compulsory attendance laws that require parents to send their children to school, normally until age 16. Although most people support these laws because they guarantee a minimum education for all children and help prevent forced child labor, they do create the problem of keeping unmotivated students involved in school life. Schools with large numbers of academically unmotivated students are normally schools where teachers choose not to work. Recent innovations in some school systems, such as the creation of alternative and magnet schools, have attempted to combat the compulsory nature of schooling by giving students and their parents more choices as to the type of school the students attend. The fact still remains, however, that students *must* go to school.

POLITICAL VISIBILITY AND LIMITED RESOURCES

Finally, schools are highly visible and political in most communities but have very few extra resources for taking the initiative or answering their critics. Many people take an active interest in their schools and, given local control, schools offer one of the few opportunities where people in complex societies feel their voices can be heard. For example, it is quite easy in many communities to stay informed about school events since large portions of the daily newspapers are devoted to school news, including the school's budget. It is also easy to attend local school board or council meetings and voice opinions, just as it is easy to walk directly into most principals' offices without an appointment. The whole system is open and permeable. Some aspects of this situation are positive. Local control and the openness of the educational system have helped maintain strong support for education over the past century. At the same time, this situation leaves the school and those who work there vulnerable to political whims and sometimes unfair attacks. And, as with most nonprofit, public service agencies, local political control tends to leave schools underfunded and always striving to satisfy demands for services without sufficient resources to provide them.

Norms, Roles, and the Culture of Teaching

Another way to think about schools is to think about the norms, roles, and organizational arrangements that exist for the purpose of getting work accomplished. These will have strong influences on the experiences that beginning teachers have during both internships and their first year.

NORMS

Norms are the expectations that people have for one another in particular social settings. They define the range of social behaviors that are allowed in given situations. Some norms are informal, such as the norm that prescribes a swimsuit rather than a cocktail dress on the beach. Some norms, however, are formal. For example, a person might not be arrested if he wore a tuxedo to the beach, but he would be if he broke the local ordinance that restricts bathing in the nude.

In schools many formal and informal norms exist that affect organizational members, including new teachers. For example, in some schools new teachers will find norms supporting friendliness and openness which will make them feel welcome. In other schools people may act toward one another in more reserved and formal ways. In some schools norms to encourage experimentation may make beginning teachers feel comfortable in trying out new ideas, whereas in other schools few risks will be encouraged. Two important norms associated with schools and the culture of teaching need highlighting because they affect the lives of beginning teachers most directly.

Autonomy Norm. In some ways teachers have relatively little power and influence in the larger school system. They do, however, have a great deal of influence in their own classrooms, supported by what has been labeled the **autonomy norm.** Teachers, including beginning teachers, do pretty much what they want to once they are in their classrooms and their doors are closed. They alone are responsible for the day-to-day curricula and make almost all instructional decisions for themselves.

The Hands-Off Norm. Closely paralleling the autonomy norm is a norm labeled by Lortie (1975), Sarason (1982), and Joyce, Hersh, and McKibbin (1983) as the **hands-off norm.** Not only are teachers given autonomy in their classrooms, but strong sanctions exist against interfering with other teachers in any but the most superficial ways. It is not appropriate, according to Lortie (1975), for teachers to ask for help, for example. Such a request would suggest that the teacher is failing. Similarly, according to Feiman-Nemser and Floden (1986), it is not permissible for teachers to tell a peer what to do or to suggest that he or she teach something differently.

This is not to suggest to beginning teachers that colleagues within a particular school will be unfriendly or unsupportive. Teachers socialize a great deal with one another and on an emotional level are concerned and supportive of one another. Even so, according to Feiman-Nemser and Floden (1986), teachers will "avoid talking about instructional practices." Talk will deal instead with "politics, gripes, home life, and the personalities and family background of students rather than curriculum, instructional content, or teaching methods" (p. 509). Many contemporary school reform projects aim at breaking down the hands-off norm by encouraging and helping teachers work together.

ROLES AND ROLE SYSTEMS

A cluster of norms detailing the way a particular job should be performed is called a **role.** The teacher's role, for example, includes norms about (1) how teachers should behave toward students and students toward them, (2) how teachers should interact with each other and with the principal, and (3) how much teachers should participate in school-level problem solving and decision making. The way various roles are interconnected within a particular setting is called a **role system.** People in schools learn roles and role systems from interaction with each other.

Many aspects of the teacher's role are clear and straightforward. For example, it is clear that teachers should teach academic content to students and evaluate their students' progress. Some aspects of the teacher's role, however, are not so clear and sometimes provide contradictory expectations. Contradictions in role expectations cause anxiety and trouble for beginning teachers.

One of the most basic contradictions in the teacher's role stems from strong expectations that teachers should treat each child as an individual even though schools are organized so that teachers must deal with students in groups. This conflict is particularly acute with secondary teachers who face as many as 150 to 180 students a day for rather brief periods of time. This role conflict, according to Lieberman and Miller (1984), is what makes teaching so personal because to deal with the contradictory demands of individualization and group instruction requires the development of a teaching style that is "individual and personal."

A second basic contradiction in the teacher's role involves the degree of distance between teacher and students. On the one hand, teachers are expected to maintain a certain social distance from students so authority and discipline can be maintained. In fact, as described in Chapters 4 and 6, control is an overriding concern for beginning teachers, since they know they are being heavily judged on this score. On the other hand, most teachers know that they must form some type of bond with students in order to motivate them and help them to learn. Beginning teachers manifest the tensions of this role contradiction in a number of ways. They worry whether or not they should allow students to call them by their first name or how friendly they should become with a particular student they really like and so on. Such tensions are quite normal and only experience, it seems, provides the means for dealing with the many contradictions built into the teacher's role.

ORGANIZATIONAL ARRANGEMENTS

Compared to most other organizations, schools are rather flat organizations. In elementary schools there are mainly teachers and a principal, and in most secondary schools one additional role, the department chair, is added. Lortie (1975) described the school's organizational structure as "cellular," that is, each classroom can be regarded as a cell within which the teacher is responsible for organizing the students, managing discipline, and teaching academic content. This organizational scheme, coupled with the hands-off norm, all too often creates an isolated work situation for teachers. They make independent decisions about when and how to teach each subject and they do not ask other teachers for help. Joyce et al. (1983) have observed that this situation has made it customary for principals to relate to the teachers on a diadic basis, that is, in a one-to-one relationship rather than as an organized faculty prepared to take collective responsibility. This professional isolation has led some observers, such as Lortie, to refer to teaching as a "lonely profession." With the addition of many new roles in schools over the past few years, such as special teachers and lead teachers of one kind or another, and new approaches for organizing curricula, it may be that the cellular structure of schools is changing. Currently, it remains the most common arrangement.

LOOSELY COUPLED STRUCTURE

The school's cellular structure also causes an organizational arrangement that Weick (1976) has labeled **loosely coupled.** This means that what goes on in classrooms is not very tightly connected to what goes on in other parts of the school. Teachers can and do carry out their own instructional activities independent of administrators and others. The central office may initiate new curricula or new teaching procedures, but if teachers choose to ignore these initiatives, they can. On the positive side, loose coupling allows considerable room for individual teacher decision making in situations where a substantial knowledge about "best" teaching practice is lacking. Conversely, loose coupling can stymie efforts to establish common goals and coordinated activities, something that is important for effective schooling, as you will see later.

SMALL GROUPS AND SUBSYSTEMS

A final observation regarding the social arrangements of schools is that some of the work is carried out in small groups or **subsystems.** Examples of subsystems in schools would be a team of first- and second-grade teachers in an elementary school, an academic department in a secondary school, the principal's administrative team, or all the social studies teachers in a school district. Special task forces or committees to improve the science curriculum, to select a new basal reading series, or to develop schoolwide guidelines for student conduct would be other examples, as would student councils, the football team, and the school band.

Important organizational goals are accomplished through these subsystems, and their effective functioning is crucial for effective schooling. But what makes for effective functioning of small groups and subsystems? Effective subsystems are those whose members have good interpersonal and group skills that enable them to communicate with one another, establish goals, uncover conflict and work with it, hold effective meetings, solve problems, make decisions, and assess progress toward goals. This topic will be discussed in more detail in the next chapter when ways beginning teachers can improve schools by helping small groups become more effective are described.

SAMPLING THE KNOWLEDGE BASE

Educators have for many years thought about the school as a formal organization. In fact, a very important book written by Waller in 1932 on the sociology of teaching provided many important insights into the nature of schools and of teaching. However, it is only in the last two decades that educators and educational researchers have started to highlight the importance of schools as workplaces and the importance of the organizational functions of teaching. This section provides examples from fairly recent research about the nature of the work teachers do in schools and about why some schools seem to be more effective than others.

The Nature of Teachers' Work

Many people think teaching is an easy job, with short work days and long summer vacations. They also think that it consists mainly of working with students during the time they are in school from

Table 14-1   Time Spent for Each Activity and Percentage of Total Time
per Teacher per Day

ACTIVITY	TOTAL TIME IN MINUTES	% TOTAL TIME	RANGE
Instruction-centered			
Direct instruction	95.40	20.6%	12.8–37.6
Organizing	15.85	3.4	2.7– 4.2
Reviewing	21.00	4.5	0 –13.7
Testing	22.96	5.0	0.1–11.9
Monitoring	23.60	5.1	0.1– 7.7
Scheduled meetings	2.68	0.6	0 – 0.9
Unscheduled meetings	46.52	10.0	5.3–17.8
Exchanges (out of class)	67.52	14.6	11.8–17.8
Study hall supervisor	17.40	3.8	0 – 6.4
Monitoring assemblies, clubs	5.88	1.3	0.9– 4.3
Control and supervision	12.68	2.7	0.2– 9.3
Desk work	57.24	12.3	7.9–19.9
Routine tasks	34.60	7.5	3.7–14.2
Travel time	24.60	5.3	3.2–10.7
Private time	16.16	3.5	0.8– 5.3

SOURCE: Adapted from T. Cypher and D. J. Willower, The work behavior of secondary school teachers, *Journal of Research and Development*, 18 (1984), pp. 19–20.

9:00 A.M. to 3:00 P.M. Experienced teachers do not agree with this perception. They know that teachers do many other things in addition to directly working with students. They also know that the time demands of teaching are very great. Until recently, the exact nature of the work behavior of teachers and the time they spend on various aspects of their work was not fully known. However, recently two researchers tackled this lack of information head-on when they went to a high school and actually observed the work behavior of teachers.

Cypher and Willower (1984) sought answers to two important questions: How can we determine how much time a teacher spends working? How is that time spent? Five secondary school teachers were randomly selected from a list of teachers representing schools of different socioeconomic and geographical distribution. Two teachers taught English, one math, one social studies, and one biology. Each teacher was observed for 5 full days. In addition, work done after school was recorded by each teacher in diary form.

Table 14-1 indicates the different types of in-school activities with the mean number of minutes and the percentage of total time on each activity per day. Also included is the range of total percentages, to indicate that teachers differed quite considerably in their use of time.

Cypher and Willower's research showed that teachers averaged 38 hours per week in in-school activities, and an additional 10.5 hours in after-school work. They spent 38.6 percent of their time on instruction-centered activities. Noninstructional time, as you can observe, took a considerable amount of time. From a different perspective, the researchers concluded that instructional time took 34.4 percent of the time; classroom support, 27.8 percent; pupil control, 19.3 percent; private-personal (including talking to other teachers on non-school-related topics at lunch), 11.6 percent; travel (time from class to class), 5.3 percent; and extracurricular, 1.8 percent. What this study indicated is that teaching is extremely active and it involves many interactions with many students and other adults in the school.

The study of Cypher and Willower provides rather a detailed account of teachers' work behavior as a whole. The following examples are intended to give you a more up-close view of a day in the lives of three beginning teachers. These examples are hypothetical; however, they have been constructed to be consistent with the Cypher and Willower data.

Neil is a third-grade teacher at Holbrook Elementary School. He usually arrives at school about 7:30 A.M. This particular morning Neil opens his room, then joins other third- and fourth-grade teachers who are planning a field trip to the local airport for their students. Back in his room in time to start class at 8:35 A.M., Neil spends the rest of the morning with his third-graders. However, he is joined at several points by other adults. The principal drops in for a few minutes to observe and see if Neil needs any help; two mothers join the class at 9:30 A.M. to assist Neil with his reading groups, and they stay through morning recess. The reading specialist in the school comes by and tests a student who Neil thinks is having a severe word recognition problem; the special education resource teacher joins Neil's classroom to work for 30 minutes with two mildly handicapped students mainstreamed in Neil's room.

Over lunch, Neil talks with two second-grade teachers, and they exchange ideas with Neil about students who were in their classrooms last year. Neil drops by the library on his way back to his classroom to pick up a film he plans to show as part of his social studies class and to remind the librarian that he will be bringing a small group of students to the library next Tuesday.

School is out at 2:45 P.M.; Neil drops by the reading specialist's office to discuss the results of her testing before heading to a meeting at the central office to participate on a science textbook selection committee. Neil was appointed to this committee by his principal because the principal knew that he had a very strong background in science and had worked at the Marine Biology Research Center for the past two summers.

Helen, another new teacher, teaches tenth-grade English at Cordoza High School. She, too, arrives at school about 7:30 A.M., and she meets with another new teacher to have a cup of coffee and discuss an exchange of teaching materials. Helen teaches three classes of sophomore English in the morning. Just before lunch she is visited by her department chairperson, who is conducting one of his required formal observations of new teachers.

During her afternoon planning period, Helen and the department chair meet, and he gives her feedback on her lesson, pointing out that her lecture was brilliant, but that her students took a long time getting to work in the small-group exercise she had planned.

After school Helen meets for a few minutes with members of the school's debate team for whom she serves as advisor, then dashes home to have a quick dinner. This particular night is the school's open house, and Helen has scheduled meetings with several parents to discuss their children's work.

José is a new teacher at Pulaski Middle School. His day begins with a meeting of his "house" (a group of students assigned to José for advising and counseling). These students will stay in José's house throughout their middle school careers. On this particular morning, José spends 20 minutes going over the students' schedules for next semester and talking to one student who has missed school regularly over the past month.

José does not teach his regular classes on this particular day. Instead, a substitute has been provided so he can attend a full-day seminar for new teachers. At the seminar, José learns some new classroom management strategies, and he gets a chance to discuss mutual concerns with other new teachers in the district.

José enjoys the new-teacher seminars, although he always worries about whether or not the substitute will be able to follow his lesson plans and whether or not his students will behave themselves and not cause him any embarrassment. On this day, José leaves the seminar a bit early because he wants to participate in the discussion on student advising planned for this week's faculty meeting.

After the faculty meeting, José finds a note from the substitute teacher telling him that two of his third-period students were acting up and she referred them to the vice principal. José drops by the vice principal's office and talks with her about the problem. They plan steps to get the two students more involved and motivated in learning.

Analyzing these typical days in the lives of three beginning teachers illustrates that they do many things in addition to interacting with students in classrooms. They meet with students about non-academic tasks; they meet with fellow teachers and specialists within the school; they go to meetings; they work with parents; and they attend to their own learning. These are what are called the organizational functions of teaching.

Effective Schools Research

Most beginning teachers are primarily concerned about what goes on in their own classrooms and with their own students. Although this is natural and healthy, you should be aware that it is the overall culture or ethos of the school that contributes a great deal to student learning and not only one's individual teaching performance. It is only in the last two decades that educators and educational researchers have started to discover this important principle. This section provides an example of what has come to be called **school effectiveness research.** Most of this research has been done over the past 15 or 20 years and is in response to earlier studies, such as Coleman et al. (1966) and Jencks et al. (1972), which argued that schools did not make much difference. This is a rather new field of study and some of the results remain controversial. Nonetheless it points toward the importance of the organizational functions of teaching. As you will see, this research suggests that the behavior of teachers, administrators, students, and parents within the school setting (not just the classroom setting) can make a difference in how much students learn.

This research also points to the importance of participants coming together and making schoolwide agreements about what is taught and how it is taught. It seems that there is a certain synergy working in schools that produces results that cannot be achieved when each teacher works alone on particularistic goals. Finally, this research emphasizes the people aspect of schooling. The quality of teaching and the climate of the school have been found to be much more important than the amount of money spent on concrete, books, or paper. School effectiveness research does not say that resources are not important; it does say that the amount of money spent on the school library collection or on the physical plant takes a back seat to other conditions that people within school can create.

To illustrate these principles, we will discuss a study conducted in Great Britain in the late 1970s (see Research Summary 14-1). It is important because it was one of the first to provide data supporting the importance of whole-school environments and it provided a model for other researchers to follow.

Attributes of Effective Schools

Since Rutter's ground-breaking study, several other researchers have conducted similar studies (Brookover et al., 1979, for example) with schools in the United States and with elementary and secondary schools. Several of these studies have produced similar results and conclusions, namely, that some schools develop norms and expectations that support student learning whereas other schools do not. More specifically, some norms and expectations appear to make some schools more effective than others.

Joyce, McKibbin, and Hersh (1983) reviewed the school effectiveness literature and provided a helpful list of the features that characterize effective schools. These are described here and they will serve as a springboard for considering the organizational skills needed by beginning teachers. Joyce and his colleagues say that attributes of **effective schools** can be divided into two categories—those having to do with the school's social organization and those having to do with the school's instructional and curriculum patterns. These attributes are listed in Table 14-3 and described below.

SOCIAL ORGANIZATION

Definitions of the social organizational attributes are:

Clear academic and social behavior goals: Academic achievement is constantly emphasized, and teachers, parents, and students share common values and understandings about the school's achievement goals.

Order and discipline: Basic rules of conduct have been agreed upon throughout the school, and teachers feel responsibility for enforcing be-

RESEARCH SUMMARY   14-1

Rutter, M., Maughan, B., Mortimore, P., Ouston, J., and Smith, A.   (1979).
Fifteen thousand hours: Secondary schools and their effects on children. Cambridge,
Mass.: Harvard University Press.

PROBLEM: During the late 1960s and early 1970s several influential books, such as
James Coleman's (1966) *Equality of Educational Opportunity* and Christopher Jencks's
(1972) *Inequality: A Reassessment of the Effect of Family and Schooling in America,*
presented information that led many to believe that schools made little difference in the
education of children. One accepted hypothesis, at that time, was that most student
achievement could be attributed to factors outside the school, such as family background,
heredity, and just plain luck. Michael Rutter, an English child psychiatrist, set out to investigate if schools did make a difference in student behavior and in educational attainment.

SAMPLE AND SETTING: Rutter chose to study 12 secondary schools in inner-city London, England. Schools participating in the study, according to Rutter, (1) were in neighborhoods that were a bit "rundown or drab," (2) had a predominance of families from working-class backgrounds, (3) had a substantial number of families from immigrant
backgrounds, and (4) included boys' schools, girls' schools, and coeducational schools.
These schools had similar and varied external characteristics in terms of size, space, resources, experience of the teachers, and educational aims as expressed by teaching staff.

PROCEDURES: Rutter and his colleagues systematically collected information about a
group of students who were to enter the 12 schools while they were still in primary schools.
This information included:

- Ability and achievement data in math, English, and verbal reasoning
- Parental occupations
- Emotional and behavioral difficulties

The researchers then followed the students during secondary school and collected outcome
measures on four variables:

- Behavior in school
- Achievement
- Attendance
- Delinquency

---

havioral norms both in their own particular
classes and across the school.

High expectations: Teachers and other staff
hold high standards for students. They convey to
students an "I care" and "can do" attitude and
demand that each student aspire to excellence.

Teacher efficacy: Teachers also have high expectations for themselves and a strong belief that
they can teach every child.

Pervasive caring: Teachers and other adults in
the school develop a caring atmosphere. Their
demands on students are not viewed as cruel and

The researchers also gathered data on what they called physical and administrative features of the schools and on "school processes." Measures of administrative features included:

- Status and sex of staff
- Age of building and number of sites
- Internal organization of staff
- Size and space of building
- Staff provision and class size

School process variables included:

- Academic emphasis
- Rewards, punishments, and praise
- Responsibility and participation
- Stability of teaching and friendship groups
- Teacher's actions in lessons
- Pupil conditions
- Skills of teachers

POINTERS FOR READING RESEARCH: In the preceding chapters, particularly those in Part 2, the research summaries focused mainly on relationships among particular models or procedures of teaching and student achievement. This study focuses on school effects. Good school effects studies are large and complex, and it is difficult to describe every detail of the researchers' methods. It is also impossible to summarize all the results of these large studies. It is important to point out, however, that the collection of data in Rutter's study was very carefully done and included such features as: (1) a researcher who worked in each school, (2) observations in schools done in pairs to ensure reliable data, (3) observations conducted both in schools and in classrooms, (4) in-depth interviews with staff, administrators, and students, (5) a wide range of information collected over an extended period of time.

RESULTS: Two aspects of Rutter's study are highlighted here. Table 14-2 compares the 12 schools on three of the four important outcome measures in the study: student attendance, student behavior, and academic attainment. The important thing to observe in these data is that, on the whole, schools that have high levels on one measure also have high levels on the others, and vice versa.

Remember that Rutter chose to collect information on a variety of schools, information about their physical and administrative arrangements and their social processes. On such things as size and space of school, age of building, class size, and administrative organization, Rutter found no relationship between these variables and his outcome measures.

However, when he collected information about the school's academic emphasis, such as high expectations, homework, library use, teacher reporting on progress, teacher actions in class, use of time, rewards and punishments, display of students' work, opportunities for student responsibility and participation, he found the relationships described in Figure 14-1. Note the high correlations between school processes and academic attainment.

(Continued on page 432)

TABLE 14-2 Attendance, Behavior, and Academic Attainment in 12 Schools

ATTENDANCE	ACADEMIC	BEHAVIOR
1	1	1
2	2	4
3	6	3
4	5	5
5	8	10
6	4	6
7	10	11
8	9	9
9	3	8
10	7	7
11	12	12
12	11	2

NOTE: Rank: 1 = best school; 12 = worst school.
SOURCE: Adapted from M. Rutter et al. (1979), p. 93.

Figure 14-1 Relationships between combined process measures and student academic outcome

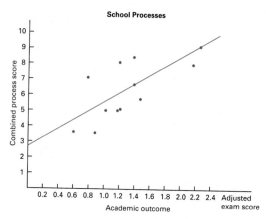

SOURCE: Adapted from M. Rutter et al. (1979), p. 143.

DISCUSSION AND IMPLICATIONS: The Rutter study was large and complex and the details of all results cannot be summarized here. The main conclusions, however, are as follows:

- The behavior and achievement of students in London secondary schools varied markedly from school to school.
- Students were more likely to show good behavior and higher achievement in some schools than others.
- Differences in outcomes produced by schools remained stable over time.
- Schools performed similarly on all outcome measures. That is, schools which produced good behavior also produced higher achievement and vice versa.
- Outcomes were not related to physical factors (size, building, library) but instead related to characteristics of the school as a social organization.

The important implication for teachers was that individual actions of teachers and others combine to create a particular ethos—a set of values, attitudes, and behaviors—that becomes characteristic of the school as a whole, and it is this total pattern that makes some schools more effective than others.

Table 14-3   **Attributes of Effective Schools**

SOCIAL ORGANIZATION	INSTRUCTION AND CURRICULUM
Clear academic and social behavior goals	High academic learning time
Order and discipline	Frequent and monitored homework
High expectations	Frequent monitoring of student progress
Teacher efficacy	Coherently organized curriculum
Pervasive caring	Variety of teaching strategies
Public rewards and incentives	Opportunities for student responsibility
Administrative leadership	
Community support	

SOURCE: B. Joyce, R. Hersh, and M. McKibbin, *The structure of school improvement,* New York: Longman, 1983, p. 25. Copyright © 1983 by Longman, Inc. All rights reserved.

judgmental but as fair and caring. They communicate and celebrate student achievement.

Public rewards and incentives: Effective schools have devised ways to publicly reward student successes and achievements. Student work is displayed, honor rolls are published, and active communication exists between the school and parents.

Administrative leadership: Principals in effective schools care deeply about the school's academic programs. They support teacher and student efforts and they help set the tone for high expectations and pervasive caring.

Community support: Staff in effective schools find ways to involve parents and community in the school's programs. This involvement goes beyond open houses to include such activities as school beautification, tutoring, and active fundraising for the school.

INSTRUCTION AND CURRICULUM

The description of attributes associated with the instructional curriculum of effective schools includes:

High academic learning time: Teachers in effective schools have found ways to maximize the time devoted to academic learning. They waste little time getting classes started and move smoothly from one activity to another with minimum disruption. Schoolwide, they have found ways to keep administrative disruptions to a minimum.

Frequent and monitored homework: Homework is required and is checked by the teachers in effective schools. Checking and giving feedback to students is one way for teachers and other adults in the school to tell students they have high expectations and that they care.

Frequent monitoring of student progress: Through tests, quizzes, and informal devices, teachers keep track of student progress and give students and parents helpful feedback on this progress.

Coherently organized curriculum: The curriculum in effective schools is closely connected to the goals and objectives of the schools and is linked to the major evaluation and testing procedures. Teachers know what teachers at other levels or in other subjects are teaching and match their own instruction accordingly.

Variety of teaching strategies: Teachers in effective schools have broad repertoires of teaching strategies and employ these to help meet the school's instructional goals.

Opportunities for student responsibility: The adults in effective schools find ways to engage students in running their school through devices such as student government, and they encourage peer tutoring, hall monitoring, and other opportunities for students to engage in leadership behaviors.

USING THE EFFECTIVE SCHOOLS RESEARCH

The effective schools research can be helpful to beginning teachers in two ways. First, it can help round out your understanding of schools as social organizations, and second, it can serve as a reminder that your own classroom will be but part of a larger school effort. This research also draws attention to several contradictions that stem from the way schools have been organized. On the one hand, it appears that effective schools are places where people have common goals, where teachers have organized their curriculum coherently, and where common rules and norms guide teachers' expectations for students, homework policies, and discipline. On the other hand, the cellular structure of schools and traditional norms that support teacher autonomy make it difficult for people in a school to create the conditions that will make their school effective. This dilemma is treated more fully in Chapter 15, where actions teachers can take to improve classrooms and schools are described. Learning aids at the end of this chapter have been designed to help you explore the concept of effective schools in more detail.

The remainder of this chapter looks at specific organizational skills which will be of concern to the beginning teacher. These are organized according to the other major role holders in schools with whom teachers are expected to work. As you read about these organizational skills keep in mind the main idea from the effective schools research, namely, coordinated effort schoolwide can produce important conditions for student learning.

Working with Colleagues

Establishing good working relationships with colleagues is an important challenge for the beginning teacher. To be successful in this endeavor requires an understanding of important norms governing collegiality and specific actions that can be taken.

NORMS

When beginning teachers enter their first school they should be aware of the norms that will govern many of the relationships between themselves and their colleagues. The hands-off norm, which allows colleagues within the school to be friendly and supportive but discourages specific suggestions about instructional practices, has already been described. The beginning teacher is likely to be included in lunchroom talk about school politics and the personalities of individual students but will not find much talk about curriculum or teaching methods. Beginning teachers will find they can ask colleagues to provide assistance in finding a place to live or locating a good doctor; they will not, however, be able to ask for help (at least very directly) if they are having a classroom management problem.

The cellular structure of most schools means that beginning teachers may be expected to work alone. They will not be observed by other teachers, nor will they be invited to observe their peers. Teaching success will be known only to students, spouses, or close friends; failures will be kept secret.

POSSIBLE ACTIONS

All schools will not reflect the norms described above in exactly the same way. Some schools, in fact, may have norms that support professional collegiality. Regardless of the situation, beginning teachers do have some latitude for working with colleagues in open and constructive ways. However, it may require well-planned initiatives on their part. The following activities are usually possible:

Observing Other Teachers This book has stressed the importance of focused observation and reflection in the process of learning to teach. This process should continue for first-year teachers. In fact, many of the observation schedules provided can be used again and again—during early field experiences, during student teaching, and in the beginning years.

Beginning teachers who want to observe other teachers should inquire early about whether or not classroom visits and observations are acceptable practice in their schools. If they are, principals, department chairs, or lead teachers can facilitate observation opportunities. If norms prevent collegial observations, it is still likely that these can be done in other schools where the beginning teacher is not known. These visits will have to be arranged by principals or by system-level curriculum specialists because they will require substitute teachers. Procedures to follow and courtesies to extend when visiting teachers' classrooms in other schools are described in a special section at the end of this book.

Discussing Educational Issues with Colleagues. Even if school norms prevent widespread collegial interaction concerning the problems of teaching, most schools have at least a handful of teachers who would like more discussion and collegiality. The beginning teacher can take the initiative in seeking out these teachers and promoting this type of exchange. Initial discussions may eventually lead to exchanges of materials and perhaps exchanges of classroom visits and observations.

Finally, beginning teachers can seek out other beginning teachers who have not yet been socialized into the hands-off norm and who are probably suffering from many of the same problems and concerns. Instances have been reported where beginner teachers have established their own weekly study and support group where mutual concerns and teaching strategies are shared.

Working in Small Groups and at Meetings. It will be a rare school where the beginning teacher will not find at least a few meetings at which teachers come together for the purpose of mutual planning. Some beginning teachers may not feel comfortable speaking up at faculty assemblies, but they can seek out membership within numerous small groups in the school. In these small group settings, they can promote collegial norms through modeling good group behavior such as open communication and effective problem solving and decision making.

Working with Administrators and Leadership Personnel

A second group of people beginning teachers need to relate to is the leadership personnel within the school. School norms govern these relationships also, and specific actions are required.

NORMS

Most careful observers of teachers' relationships with principals and other school leaders (Feiman-Nemser and Floden, 1986; Walcott, 1973) have pointed out that norms governing these relationships are somewhat ambiguous. On the one hand, the school's professional ethos supports the concept of the principal's serving as the school's instructional leader and as a role model for teachers. On the other hand, the hands-off norm applies to principals and other leadership personnel as well as to other teachers. Often this norm inhibits direct participation by principals in matters of curriculum or teaching strategies. Teachers, according to Feiman-Nemser and Floden (1986), want the principal to act as a "buffer between themselves and outside pressures from district administrators, parents, and other community members. . . . In addition, they want the principal to be a strong force in maintaining student discipline—backing the teachers in their classroom discipline policies and maintaining consistent school-wide policies. In return for these services, the teachers are willing to cooperate with the principal's initiatives" (p. 509). In many schools norms do not support the direct involvement and participation of the principal in instructional activities, although this may be changing.

POSSIBLE ACTIONS

Obviously, principals vary greatly in their educational beliefs and management styles. Some will be very supportive, and some will not. Some will have excellent organizational and interpersonal skills, and some will not. One principal's priorities and values will be different from another's. In some instances these values and priorities will be consistent with the values and beliefs of the beginning teacher; in other cases they will be diametrically opposed.

Several specific actions can be taken by beginning teachers to gain the support of principals and to establish positive working relationships, regardless of the type of person he or she turns out to be. These include:

1. Initiate regular weekly meetings with the principal during the first few weeks to discuss expectations for teacher and student behavior, academic goals, and other features of the school. Find out the principal's thoughts on the attributes of effective schools and effective teaching.
2. Keep the principal informed in writing about what you are doing in your classroom, particu-

larly on such topics as special successes you have had, such as a good lesson; a complimentary note from a parent; any conflicts that arise with students or parents; special events such as guest speakers, field trips, or parties you are planning.

3. Invite the principal to your classroom, particularly for a lesson that is unique or special, and for parties in elementary schools or special celebrations in secondary schools.

4. Write complimentary notes to the principal when he or she has done something that you liked or something that was particularly helpful to you or one of your students.

All of these suggestions fall under the category of building positive communication channels between the beginning teacher and the principal. They are efforts by beginning teachers to get clear about the principal's expectations on the one hand, and on the other, to make sure the principal understands your instructional program and activities.

OTHER SCHOOL LEADERS

In many schools beginning teachers will work with other school leaders besides the principal, including counselors, reading specialists, special education resource teachers, librarians, media specialists, and curriculum specialists. The beginning teacher should remember that roles within organizations are governed by norms that role holders shape as they interact with each other. This means that beginning teachers will have some latitude in their interactions with leadership personnel. These interactions could range from ignoring them completely to actively seeking out their support and assistance. The latter is recommended in most instances.

Beginning teachers should strive, in the very early weeks of school, to build positive working relationships with school leaders and specialists for several reasons. First, unlike teacher colleagues, leadership personnel often are expected to help beginning teachers and to provide help in confidential ways free of evaluation. Second, most counselors and resource teachers got to their current positions because they were effective classroom teachers who received advanced training. This means they probably possess important knowledge that can be passed along to beginning teachers if appropriate relationships are established. Finally, resource personnel have more time to provide assistance and support than do principals or other teachers in the school. Beginning teachers should set up regular meetings with resource personnel to discuss roles and expectations, and they should try to keep these persons informed of their classroom programs and activities.

Working with Parents

Other important organizational members with whom beginning teachers will want to establish positive relationships are parents.

NORMS

Teachers want the norms governing their relationships with parents to include both concern for the child and support for their instructional program. At the same time, many teachers do not want parents to interfere with their classrooms (see Feiman-Nemser and Floden, 1986). On the whole, teachers tend to keep a good distance between themselves and parents and, in fact, have little interaction with them. This is particularly true of teachers in middle and secondary schools.

Working with and for parents is an important organizational function of teaching and, when done properly, can create a strong support system for beginning teachers and their students. It can also be a very rewarding aspect of the teacher's work. Following are several ways beginning teachers can build positive, supporting relationships with parents or other significant adults in students' lives. It should be remembered that, as with other aspects of teaching, guidelines for working with parents will vary from one context to another. You need to remain sensitive to the fact that in many communities the two-parent home may no longer be the norm. You also need to recognize that even when two parents or adults live in the same home, it is likely that both are working.

POSSIBLE ACTIONS

Teacher-parent interactions can take several forms, including reporting to parents, holding conferences with parents, and enlisting parents' help in school and at home.

Reporting to Parents. Remember the idea described in Chapter 7 that parents of children at any age want to know how their children are doing in school. The traditional report card is one means of giving parents this information. Experienced teachers, however, often use additional means to keep parents informed because the formal report card is only issued on a quarterly basis and only summarizes progress in general terms.

Some teachers, particularly of younger children, try to make weekly or biweekly contacts with parents through notes or telephone calls. Such contacts allow teachers to explain what is going on in their classrooms and how the parent's child is doing on specific lessons. Such frequent and regular contact provides the teacher with a natural means for communicating children's successes, not just their deficiencies, which often dominate more formal reports.

Another means of parent communication—one that works well for middle and high school teachers who have many students—is the use of a weekly or monthly newsletter. The use of newsletters was described in the chapter on cooperative learning and here additional guidelines are offered. Jane Bluestein (1982) has suggested the following guides to the production and circulation of classroom newsletters:

- Newsletters can be either formal or informal. They can be in handwritten letter format, on a ditto sheet, or typed with headings in a newspaper format.
- Newsletters should be sent home consistently, at least once every four to six weeks.
- Newsletters should give the parents information such as: what the class is studying this week or month, changes in formats, grouping, environment, new goals and directions, special events or projects, special contributions of students, upcoming programs, projects, or events.
- The content and language of the newsletters should "fit" the community and be written with the parent's interest in mind.
- Newsletters can directly involve parents by inviting them to participate in activities, attend programs or presentations, contribute materials for school activities, or remind students to do certain things or bring in certain items.
- Newsletters may contain samples of students' work, such as poems or writings that illustrate

current topics and concepts. If student work is included, be sure each child is featured eventually.
- Share newsletters with students and make sure the principal gets a copy. (pp. 183–184)

Holding Conferences with Parents. Most beginning teachers will be involved with parent conferences. Teachers of younger children are sometimes required to make a home visit early in the school year and to hold quarterly in-school meetings with parents. Teachers of older students are normally given more latitude to initiate conferences as needed or when parents request them. In either event, holding parent conferences is an important organizational function of teaching and can provide valuable experiences for the teacher and the parents if done properly. This is also a function that some beginning teachers feel somewhat nervous about.

Using information from the New Mexico Institute for Parent Involvement, Jane Bluestein (1982) suggested the following strategies for teachers to use for parent conferences:

Preconference preparations include the following:

1. Notify: Purpose, place, time, length of time allotted. Consider the parent's schedule and availability; offer choices of time whenever possible.
2. Prepare: Review child's folder, gather examples of work, and prepare materials. Be very familiar with the student's performance and progress before the parent arrives.
3. Plan agenda: List items for discussion and/or presentation.
4. Arrange environment: Comfortable seating, eliminate distractions. The parent is at an immediate disadvantage by being on your "turf." To help avoid power implications, arrange the environment so that you and the parent are on equal planes (same-sized chairs), sitting side-by-side at a table, as opposed to face-to-face across your desk.

The actual conference includes the following:

1. Welcome: Establish rapport.
2. State: Purpose, time limitation, note taking, options for follow-up. This is where you share information and present data. You may find note taking during the conference useful in recording your interactions—particularly the parent's

feedback and responses. In addition, discuss various avenues you (each) may follow in future dealings with the student, including directions for your instruction and expectations.

3. Encourage: Information sharing, comments, questions.
4. Listen: Pause once in a while. Look for verbal and nonverbal cues. The above two recommendations support the concept of a conference being an *exchange* between the teacher and the parent.
5. Summarize.
6. End on a positive note.

Postconference steps and recommendations include the following:

1. Review conference with child, if appropriate.
2. Share information with other school personnel, if needed.
3. Mark calendar for planned follow-up. (pp. 385–386)

Enlisting Parents' Help in School and at Home. A final way that beginning teachers can work with parents is by involving them as teachers and assistants, both in school and at home. This practice is more common in elementary and middle schools than in high schools. It is also easier in communities where *not all* the parents hold jobs. Regardless of the situation, beginning teachers will always find some parents or parent surrogates willing to help if proper encouragement is given. Some guidelines for involving parents include:

- **To assist with small groups:** Conducting small-group activities is difficult for teachers because there are so many simultaneous demands in the classroom. Effective teachers sometimes find parents who will come to the school and help on a regular basis. If beginning teachers choose to use parents in this way, they should consider the parents' schedules and plan some training so that parents know what is expected of them.
- **To assist with field trips and other special events:** Field trips and many other special events such as parties or celebrations take an extra set of hands. Again, with proper encouragement and training, parents can be most useful during these times.

- **As teacher aides:** Some teachers have found ways to use parents as aides in their classrooms, thus getting valuable assistance in correcting papers, writing and publishing class newsletters, organizing parties, and the like.
- **To help with homework:** Most parents feel a responsibility for helping their children with homework. Unfortunately, many do not know how to be helpful. Effective teachers teach parents how to teach their own children (This can be done on a schoolwide basis.) This normally requires holding special evening sessions where the teacher explains to parents what the homework is trying to accomplish, shows them how to help students practice, and provides them with guidelines for giving students feedback. Many of the skills described in Chapters 8 to 13 can be taught to parents. Teaching parents teaching skills may be time-consuming, but it can extend the teacher's influence over student learning, perhaps more than any other single action.

SUMMARY

- Schools are social organizations and, as such, are adult workplaces as well as places where students come to learn.
- People in schools act not in totally free and disconnected ways but in more or less interdependent and predictable ways.
- Schools have individual histories and cultures (tone, ethos) whose norms and roles influence school goals and processes and the way people work to achieve them.
- Although schools, like other organizations, are characterized by goals and control structures, they also have special features, such as goal ambiguity, compulsory attendance, political visibility, and limited resources.
- Two important norms that regulate the culture of teaching and behavior in schools are the autonomy norm and the hands-off norm. The autonomy norm allows teachers to do pretty much what they want inside their classrooms. The hands-off norm sanctions teachers who try to interfere with other teachers' teaching methods or processes.

- Roles also define how teachers do their work. Some aspects of a teacher's role are contradictory: for example, the need to provide individual attention to students in group settings and the need to maintain a certain amount of social distance from students.

- Some of the work of schools is carried out through small groups or subsystems (departments and teams) whose combined efforts are needed to make schools effective as a whole.

- A moderately strong knowledge base exists that helps explain why some schools are more effective than others. Some aspects of this research are still controversial.

- Effective school research illustrates that while teaching performance in individual classrooms is very important, the way that principals, teachers, parents, and students all come together to define common goals, expectations, and procedures makes the most difference in what students learn.

- In general, school effectiveness research takes the perspective that more effective schools have processes and procedures characterized by clear goals, high expectations, pervasive caring, strong leadership, community support, high academic learning time, frequent monitoring of student progress, coherent curricula, and variety in the methods used by teachers.

- Teachers contribute to effective schools by successfully carrying out three important organizational functions: working with colleagues; working with school leaders, such as the principal; and working with parents.

KEY TERMS

social-systems perspective
school culture
ethos
norms
autonomy norm
hands-off norm
role
role system
loosely coupled
subsystems
school effectiveness research
effective schools
high expectations
teacher efficacy
coherent curriculum

BOOKS FOR THE PROFESSIONAL

Boyer, E. L. (1983). *High school: A report on secondary education in America.* New York: Harper & Row. This book reports the results of a major study of the American high school sponsored by the Carnegie Foundation for the Advancement of Teaching. It is a thorough look at the people who participate in schools (students, teachers, and principals) and what happens in secondary school classrooms.

Goodlad, J. I. (1984). *A place called school: Prospects for the future.* New York: McGraw-Hill. This book reports a comprehensive study of the American school. It looks inside classrooms and schools with insightful detail and proposes ways effective schools can be achieved.

Jackson, P. W. (1968). *Life in classrooms.* New York: Holt, Rinehart & Winston. *Life in Classrooms* is just what its name implies: a very careful description of what happens in elementary classrooms. This text is scholarly yet easy to read for beginning teachers.

Lieberman, A. (ed.). (1988). *Building a professional culture in schools.* New York: Teachers College Press. This excellent collection of readings describes how schools should be restructured for the purpose of enhancing student learning and for building a new professional culture for teachers.

Lieberman, A., and Miller, L. (1992). *Teachers—Their world and their work: Implications for school improvement.* New York: City College Press. This is an excellent and very readable book on the social work of teaching, told from the perspective of the teachers.

Lortie, D. C. (1975). *School-teacher: A sociological study.* Chicago: University of Chicago Press. This book is now considered a classic work on the nature and ethos of the teaching profession. Lortie defined many of the concepts that now have become commonplace in educational discussions.

LEARNING AIDS FOR PLANNING, OBSERVATION, AND REFLECTION

- Assessing My Workplace Skills
- Diagnosing the School's Ability to Meet Personal Needs
- Interviewing Teachers about Resolving Role Conflict
- Observing Attributes of Effective Schools
- Interviewing Teachers about Using Parents as Helpers

ASSESSING MY WORKPLACE SKILLS

PURPOSE: Norms in schools, as in any organization, are powerful forces that shape teacher, administrator, student, and even parent behavior. It is possible for teachers to influence these norms in a positive way. In this aid, you have the opportunity to assess what you consider your level of effectiveness might be in helping develop positive norms of collegiality.

DIRECTIONS: Mark the response that you think reflects what your level of skill or understanding would be in each area. If you discover that you feel a weakness in any, discuss with other students or practicing teachers how it might be overcome.

UNDERSTANDING OR SKILL	LEVEL OF UNDERSTANDING OR SKILL		
	HIGH	MEDIUM	LOW
Developing collegiality in my work with colleagues			
Observing teachers	_____	_____	_____
Discussing educational issues	_____	_____	_____
Working in small groups	_____	_____	_____
Developing collegiality in my work with administrators			
Meeting with principal	_____	_____	_____
Informing principal of classroom activities	_____	_____	_____
Inviting principal to observe my class	_____	_____	_____
Writing complimentary notes to principal	_____	_____	_____
Seeking out support from other school and district leaders	_____	_____	_____
Developing collegiality in my work with parents			
Reporting classroom activities to them	_____	_____	_____
Holding conferences	_____	_____	_____
Using parents as helpers	_____	_____	_____

DIAGNOSING THE SCHOOL'S ABILITY TO MEET PERSONAL NEEDS

PURPOSE: The purpose of this aid is organizational understanding. It is intended to increase your ability to see the ways schools can operate to help or hinder their members in meeting their needs for achievement, affiliation, and influence.

DIRECTIONS: Use the questions below to interview teachers or administrators about their schools. Be sure to probe for specific examples.

School Interview Schedule

Our _____ class has been studying some aspects of organization psychology. We have been learning about how organizations can serve as vehicles to satisfy such basic human needs as:

1. *Affiliation:* The need for friendship, for working with others, for warmth and caring
2. *Influence:* The need for power, for having control over one's life and one's destiny
3. *Achievement:* The need to experience success, to do well in work, to find new and better ways of doing things

We are trying to find out how this school provides opportunities to experience friendship, influence, and success to the people who come here every day to work and learn. We appreciate your willingness to give us your views on this topic.

Let's start with some questions regarding you and the way you experience the school as a (principal, vice principal, teacher).

1. Over what aspects of your work do you feel most influential? *(Probe to get the person to list specific tasks such as, "I feel I have a great deal of influence when I make out the daily schedule or when I determine which textbook to use in my class.")*

   a. _____

   b. _____

   c. _____

   d. _____

2. Over what aspects do you feel least influential?

   a. _____

   b. _____

   c. _____

   d. _____

3. Can you name two or three things (pertaining to work here at school) that you have done in the past year that gave you a real sense of accomplishment?

   a. _____

   b. _____

   c. _____

   d. _____

4. What happens here at school that makes you feel close and warm toward others or that enables you to experience feelings of closeness and warmth from others? _____

   _____

   _____

   _____

   Now let's turn to the school in relation to experiences provided for students.

5. From your viewpoint, which experiences provided here at _____ give students the best chance to feel influential?

   a. _____

   b. _____

   c. _____

   d. _____

6. From your viewpoint, is _____ a place where students have a lot of friends and like being involved with others? *(If yes, ask for examples; if no, probe for*

   reasons.) _____

   _____

   _____

   _____

7. From your viewpoint, is _____ a place where most students take pride in their work and strive to do well? *(If yes, ask for examples; if no, probe for reasons.)*

   _____

   _____

   _____

   _____

8. What ideas or suggestions do you have that could make _____ a place where students would experience more friendship, greater influence, and more success? _____

_____

_____

_____

Analysis and Reflection: Write a paragraph responding to the following questions: What are your reactions to the activities teachers mentioned as contributing to their influence, achievement, and affiliation needs? Would these kinds of activities satisfy you? Why or why not?

INTERVIEWING TEACHERS ABOUT RESOLVING ROLE CONFLICT

PURPOSE: Teachers work with many role expectations, some of which are clear and straightforward, and some of which conflict with each other. Teachers wrestle with how to resolve conflicting role expectations and arrive at different strategies for accomplishing it. This aid is to give you some ideas about how you might achieve your own resolution of role conflict by discovering how other teachers have achieved it.

DIRECTIONS: Use the following questions to guide you in interviewing one or two teachers about role conflict.

1. Do you value treating students as individuals?
2. What do you do to show students that you value them as individuals and are attempting to tailor instruction to their needs?
3. How many students do you teach every day? Do you teach mostly to groups of students or individuals?
4. How do you resolve the dilemma between treating students as individuals and teaching that many students every day?
5. Do you think it is important to be on close terms with students in order to better teach them?
6. Do you think it is important to maintain some social distance from students in order to maintain discipline?
7. How do you resolve the dilemma between fostering closeness with students for teaching purposes and yet maintaining distance for discipline purposes?

Analysis and Reflection: Using these teachers' responses as a jumping-off place, write a paragraph about how you might initially try to deal with resolving these conflicting role expectations for yourself.

OBSERVING ATTRIBUTES OF EFFECTIVE SCHOOLS

PURPOSE: Listed in Table 14–3 in the chapter are the social and instructional attributes of effective schools. The purpose of this aid is to help you recognize these attributes in practice. Refer to the chapter for definitions of these attributes.

DIRECTIONS: Spend a half day visiting a school. Observe in several classrooms, the library, cafeteria, outdoor activity areas, and so forth. Read fliers and newsletters sent home. Make a checkmark in the "Yes" column if you observe one of the following effective school attributes. Next, write under "Evidence" what you observed that led you to conclude that the attribute was present. Conversely, check the "No" column if you observed something that led you to conclude that the attribute was absent. For example, if you see student work prominently displayed in hallways, then you would check "Yes" for "Public rewards and incentives," and write under "Evidence" that "student work was displayed."

ATTRIBUTES	YES	NO	EVIDENCE
Social organization			
Clear academic and social behavior goals			
Order and discipline			
High expectations			
Teacher efficacy			
Pervasive caring			
Public rewards and incentives			
Administrative leadership			
Community support			
Instruction and curriculum			
High academic learning time			
Frequent and monitored homework			
Frequent monitoring of student progress			
Coherently organized curriculum			
Variety of teaching strategies			
Opportunities for student responsibility			

Analysis and Reflection: While research shows the above attributes to be associated with effective schools, there is still some controversy around it. What is your impression of the validity of these attributes? Did you think that the attributes you observed during your visit were contributing to student achievement in the school? Think back to your own schooling —to what extent were these attributes present, and were they contributing to student achievement in your school? Write a paragraph in response to these questions.

INTERVIEWING TEACHERS ABOUT USING PARENTS AS HELPERS

PURPOSE: Establishing good working partnerships with parents is very important. One way this can be done is by using parents as helpers in the classroom. The purpose of this aid is twofold: to help you develop an awareness of the things parents can do and to alert you to how you can plan to make parent helping go smoothly.

DIRECTIONS: Use these questions as a guide in talking with teachers about using parents as helpers.

1. In what ways do you use parents as helpers?

   _____ In class, conducting small groups

   _____ As assistants for field trips

   _____ As assistants for special events in school

   _____ As teacher aides (correcting papers, putting out newsletter, and so on)

   _____ At home, helping with homework

   _____ Other (Specify)

   _____

   _____

   _____

2. How did you locate parents for these tasks? _____

   _____

   _____

   _____

   _____

3. Was it necessary to train parents for these tasks? If so, what did the training consist of? Who conducted the training? How long did it last? _____

   _____

   _____

4. What sorts of problems have you run into in using parents? How have you solved these problems? _____

   _____

   _____

5. How have you provided recognition to parents for their efforts? _____

_____

_____

_____

6. What benefits have accrued to you, to parents, and to students as a result of using parents as helpers?

Benefits for teacher: _____

_____

_____

Benefits for parents: _____

_____

_____

Benefits for students: _____

_____

_____

_____

Analysis and Reflection: Consider your own subject area or grade level. In light of what this teacher has told you about using parents for helpers, how might you utilize parent help? What kind of training will parents need? How will you arrange for parent training? How will you arrange for parent recognition? Write a paragraph in response to these questions.

Chapter Outline

PERSPECTIVE AND RATIONALE

• Concerns and Problems of Beginning Teachers •

• Organizational Socialization • The Socialization of Teachers

SAMPLING THE KNOWLEDGE BASE

• The First Year and Reality Shock • Beginning the School Year

MAKING THE FIRST YEAR PRODUCTIVE

• Getting Off to a Good Start in the Community • Getting Off to a Good Start with Students • Exhibiting Leadership and Establishing Professional Networks • Working toward School Improvement • Staying Alive and Flourishing the First Year

CHAPTER 15

The First Year of Teaching: Career Development and School Improvement

S tarting any new endeavor, particularly one's first professional job, is as difficult and anxiety producing as it is stimulating. In some ways what beginning teachers face as they meet their first classes is not much different from what other professionals face in new jobs. After a long period of education, professionals are eager to meet challenges and rewards associated with their chosen careers. At the same time they are worried about how well they are going to do. Trial attorneys, for example, worry about presenting their first case; nurses experience anxiety as they work their first night shifts alone; and business school graduates feel nervous as they apply their newly acquired skills for the first time in large corporations. Regardless of how well individuals are prepared technically, anxiety and difficulties inevitably attend initial practice in real-life settings. As beginners pass from the status of novice to that of fully socialized member of a profession, these difficulties and anxieties gradually disappear.

Surviving and flourishing is not the only challenge considered by beginning teachers during the first year of teaching. Many beginning teachers come out of their teacher preparation programs and enter their new careers with strong idealistic tendencies. They want to make schools and classrooms better places for students to learn and for teachers to

work. They believe that they can be agents for reform. However, these tendencies and beliefs will not make much difference unless they are supported with a set of understandings and skills that will help make school improvement efforts successful.

Fortunately, a great deal is known about the problems faced by beginning teachers as well as what successful beginners do to make their first teaching experiences satisfying and growth-producing. This chapter shows how you can survive and flourish during your first years of teaching and how you can go about making the business of improving classrooms and schools an integral and satisfying part of your professional life.

PERSPECTIVE AND RATIONALE

Succeeding in one's first teaching job seems crucial to someone who has prepared long and hard for teaching. Although the first year is always difficult, it can also be rewarding, particularly for those who are prepared for the professional and technical demands of teaching and for the psychological stress of the induction period. No amount of preparation, however, will eliminate completely the problems faced by beginning teachers. An understanding of several important ideas associated with initial teaching and professional socialization can provide a needed perspective on what happens during the first year.

Concerns and Problems of Beginning Teachers

Studies such as those conducted by Tisher (1980) in Australia, by Lacey (1977) in Great Britain, and by Ryan et al. (1980), McDonald and Elias (1980), and Veenman (1984) in the United States found that beginning teachers reported a common set of concerns. Those mentioned most often included: (1) classroom management and discipline, (2) inability to find needed materials, (3) evaluation of student work, (4) interacting with parents, and (5) feelings of isolation.

Organizational Socialization

Sociologists view entry into the world of work as a universal process involving the young adult's transition from the family and educational institutions to the work institution. Each society has social arrangements that facilitate or hinder this transition. In agricultural communities, for example, the transition process usually moves quite smoothly. Youths learn adult roles directly from their parents and other adults by performing work-related tasks from a very young age. Similarly, the apprenticeship system used in some occupations helps complete the transition to work through carefully supervised, on-the-job training over a long period of time. As societies become more complex, this transition process is less smooth and informal, particularly for complex jobs. Families cannot begin to provide the necessary training, and the natural alternative, formal schooling, gives only general and incomplete preparation, particularly for such complicated jobs as teaching.

In Chapter 14, the concepts role and role systems were introduced. You will remember that *role* was defined as a set of behavioral expectations associated with a particular position, such as teaching. **Role system** expresses the interconnections of various roles within a particular organizational setting. In schools the role system includes such major roles as teacher, student, administrator, various

specialists, and parents. Sociologists use the term **organizational socialization** to describe the process of learning a role and a role system. Through this process individuals come to appreciate the values, knowledge, and behavior associated with a particular profession and organization. For teachers, this process proceeds through certain stages.

ANTICIPATORY SOCIALIZATION

Anticipatory socialization is the period of formal training, including student teaching, during which many aspects of the teacher's work are learned and during which certain expectations are developed. During this period positive rather than negative aspects of the role are usually emphasized, and ideal rather than realistic teaching practices are generally taught.

INITIAL CONTACT

This is the contact usually made during the job interview or initial visit to a school system. Employers generally put their best face forward during the interview by emphasizing the positive characteristics of the teaching position.

REALITY SHOCK

When teachers actually begin their first jobs, many of them experience numerous surprises, or what some have labeled **reality shock.** Drawing on the work of Louis (1980), Isaacson (1981) described the following surprises typically experienced by first-job holders:

1. The first form of surprise occurs when *conscious expectations about the job* are not fulfilled in the newcomer's early job experience.
2. A second form of surprise arises when *expectations (both conscious and unconscious) about oneself* are not met. Choice of occupation and the new organization are often based on assumptions about one's own skills, values, etc. During the encounter phase, errors in assumptions sometimes emerge, and the newcomer must cope with the recognition that s/he is different from her/his previous perceptions.
3. A third form of surprise arises when *unconscious job expectations* are unmet or when features of the job are unanticipated. Job aspects not previously considered become significant because

their presence or absence is undesirable once encountered.

4. A fourth form of surprise arises from difficulties in *accurately forecasting internal reactions* to a particular new experience. How new experiences feel, as opposed to how the person expected them to feel, is difficult to anticipate and often surprising.

5. A final form of surprise comes from *cultural assumptions* brought by the newcomer from previous settings as operating guides in the new setting, and they fail. (pp. 2.11–2.12)

The Socialization of Teachers

The socialization process is difficult in any profession, and novices always experience some degree of reality shock. Beginning teachers have special challenges not faced by new role occupants in other professions because of the way education and schools are organized. For example, beginning teachers normally are given the same leadership responsibilities as the more experienced teachers on the faculty. Full leadership responsibility is something other professionals do not have to worry about until they have learned their jobs more fully. Also, socialization and induction in other professions are the responsibility of experienced peers. Because of the ways schools are organized, beginning teachers are in many instances left alone with little direct help from colleagues. Even though this organizational neglect presents special problems for beginning teachers, there is a bright side. One, it gives beginning teachers considerable leeway to chart their own course; and two, the knowledge base regarding initial teaching is rather well developed and can provide valuable insights for making the first year successful. A sample of that research is described in the next section.

SAMPLING THE KNOWLEDGE BASE

Many aspects of the experiences of teachers during their first year on the job have been studied. Three specific lines of inquiry have yielded information about what beginning teachers can do to make their first year successful: (1) studies about the nature of the first-year experience, (2) studies about how successful teachers start the school year, and (3) studies

about how successful teachers continue to grow and learn during their early years of teaching.

The First Year and Reality Shock

For over three decades researchers have studied the experiences of beginning teachers. A common theme running through all of this research is that the reality shock for teachers is more severe than it is for novices in other professions. McDonald and Elias (1980), who conducted comprehensive research on the problems of beginning teachers, attribute much of the difficulty to the feeling of being a "stranger in a new land":

> The beginning teacher is a stranger in a new land, the territory of which and whose rules and customs and culture are unknown, but who has to assume a significant role in that society. If the problem is put in this manner, it is easy to see that we are studying a general problem in human experience as well as a particular problem in adaptation to a specific institution and to a specific social role. (p. 200)

Kevin Ryan (1980), who has studied beginning teachers for almost three decades, explained why the reality shock for new teachers is so overwhelming. He argued that the beginning teacher's familiarity (not strangeness) with the classroom environment leads to much of the problem.

> [The beginning teacher] thinks he knows what he's getting into. The daily life of a teacher holds few secrets for him; he is no stranger to the school. He has been there before. The shock comes when the beginner changes from audience to actor. The role which he had seen played out thousands of times is now his. The familiar scene of the classroom is reversed, and he encounters a startling new situation. (p. 171)

Nancy Isaacson (1981) was part of a team of researchers at the University of Oregon who studied beginning teachers in that state for a number of years in the late 1970s. She expanded on the analyses of Ryan and of McDonald and Elias:

> The reasons for the reality/culture shock are many and varied. . . . Surprise about how difficult it is to reach secondary students, underestimation of the difficulties in motivating them; overestimation of their own skills as

disciplinarians; failure to anticipate the amount of time and work necessary to keep up with daily paperwork; surprise at the volume of administrative tasks; emotional and physical drain which leaves little energy for anything else in their lives; pain from the unprovoked hostility from their students and the students' disdain for the subject the teacher cherishes. . . . [For] many new teachers, the role of teacher is not the only adjustment they are making in their lives. Many are first encountering adjustments from living alone, a new marriage, adjusting to a new community, financial independence, and the complexities of social interaction with members of the opposite sex. Perhaps the most surprising thing of all . . . is that the newcomer learns that the teacher's official role in the classroom does not permit her/him the luxury of being oneself. (p. 217)

Beginning the School Year

Some observer has written that "discipline problems seem to belong to the beginning teacher in the way that pimples belong to the teenager." Studies in classroom management, particularly as it is influenced by teacher behaviors during the opening of school, represent a second line of inquiry important for beginning teachers.

Common sense and personal experience suggest that what happens during the first few moments in any relationship shapes future interactions. This is certainly true in classrooms. As teachers meet their classes for the first time, they are sized up by their students. Initial lessons are perceived as potentially interesting or boring; management procedures are judged as tight or loose; and teachers themselves are judged as good, bad, nice, or cranky. Once relationships are fixed, they seem to stay that way. Particularly in the area of classroom management, patterns established at the beginning of the year are difficult to change later. If students get out of control early, it becomes difficult to get them back; if initial lessons are disjointed, it becomes difficult for later learning activities to proceed smoothly.

But what should beginning teachers do to start the school year successfully? During the late 1970s and early 1980s, a comprehensive research effort was launched at the University of Texas to find answers to this question. You are already familiar with some of this research. It was introduced in the chapter on classroom management and served as the

basis for many of the recommendations made there. Research Summary 15-1 summarizes another study that focuses directly on effective classroom management at the beginning of the school year.

MAKING THE FIRST YEAR PRODUCTIVE

Previous sections of this chapter have emphasized the difficulties faced by beginning teachers and the problems they encounter as they begin their teaching careers. Beginning teachers should not leave this discussion with the feeling that these problems and difficulties are insurmountable. They are not. As Kevin Ryan and his colleagues (1980) observed, "Three million people have gone through the first year of teaching" (p. 3), and they have survived. In fact, many look back upon the first year of teaching and remember it as incredibly stimulating and growth-producing. This section provides specific actions that will help beginning teachers as they get started with a new community, new students, and a new career.

Getting Off to a Good Start in the Community

Earlier it was noted that one of the reasons the first year is so difficult is because many life adjustments are forced upon a beginning teacher at one time: getting settled in a strange community, setting up housekeeping, getting married or choosing not to marry, learning how to cook, handling a budget, and so on. With appropriate planning, many of these nonteaching adjustments can be handled prior to the arrival of students. Here are several suggestions that can help:

- Plan to relocate in the community well before the first week of school to allow uninterrupted time for handling of relocation problems. This is a time to get a phone installed, to find a doctor, and to seek out favorite places to shop, eat, and entertain.
- Get to know the community, particularly if it is different from the one you grew up in. Walking through the neighborhoods that comprise the attendance boundaries of the school will provide insights into the backgrounds and the

values of students. Reading a little about the history of the community also helps. A learning aid has been designed at the end of this chapter to assist with this task.

- Get to know the school. Several visits to the school prior to opening day will provide a working knowledge of important places in the school and make the place feel less strange and foreboding. Visiting the school at this time is also an excellent way to meet new colleagues before they are faced with their own day-to-day teaching demands.

Accomplishing these activities before the school year begins will permit you to concentrate your energy on students and instructional tasks.

Getting Off to a Good Start with Students

Research Summary 15-1 provides information indicating how important the first few days of school can be in determining later success for teachers. The recommendations of the investigators who conducted that research are summarized here and organized into specific procedures beginning teachers can follow as they strive to get off to a good start with their students.

ESTABLISHING RAPPORT

Knowing that first impressions are important, a beginning teacher should be ready to make a good impression when students arrive the first morning. Students should be greeted at the door in a friendly and pleasant manner and encouraged to enter the room and find a seat. On the first day, most students will be on their good behavior because they are also trying to make good impressions. However, if inappropriate behavior is observed a beginning teacher must correct it immediately.

It is likely that beginning teachers will focus on their own discomfort and uncertainties during these first few minutes. Since many students will be experiencing these same feelings, teachers should be prepared to deal with students' anxieties along with their own.

Remain Visible.   A beginning teacher should expect to be nervous during the first few minutes of student contact. Teachers with 25 years of teaching experience still get nervous as students enter the room for the first time. For some, a natural response to this anxiety is to hide in the crowd or to find something to do such as stacking books, sharpening pencils, or sorting papers. A beginning teacher must guard against such behavior and remain visible to students regardless of personal discomfort.

Extend a Warm Welcome.   As the bell rings, the teacher should be ready to start immediately. Introduce yourself to the class in a firm voice and extend a formal welcome to students. Again, this is likely to be a scary moment. If introductions and welcoming remarks do not come naturally to you, it would be a good idea to spend considerable time rehearsing them the night before.

Getting Acquainted.   In most classrooms, some students will know each other but others will be strangers. Teacher should start acquainting students with each other on the first day of school. One approach used by many experienced teachers is to have students write their names on five-by-eight cards that can be placed on their desks. This will also help the teacher learn the students' names. Some teachers also ask students who have not been in the school before to raise their hands and then extend a special welcome to them and spend a few minutes talking about where they went to school last year. Too much time should not be spent getting acquainted at this point because it is also important to teach a "real" lesson on the first day.

THE FIRST LESSON

It is always difficult for teachers to decide whether course content or class rules and procedures should receive primary emphasis during their first class meeting. *Both must be done on the first day.* With older students, some teachers prefer to focus on the content of the course first, then follow with information about rules and procedures. With younger students, this order is often reversed. Regardless, the first learning activities should be selected to ensure high motivation and a high degree of student success. This can be accomplished by selecting a very interesting topic and by planning the lesson based on information about students' prior knowledge. Ex-

RESEARCH SUMMARY 15-1

Emmer, E. T., Evertson, C., and Anderson, L. M. (1980). Effective classroom management at the beginning of the school year. *The Elementary School Journal, 80,* 219–231.

PROBLEM: The researchers were interested in finding out how effective teachers begin the school year, specifically, what basic principles of classroom organization and management they use.

SAMPLE AND SETTING: The sample in this study was composed of 27 third-grade teachers and their students in eight elementary schools. The schools served populations of students from upper-lower and lower-middle-class backgrounds. In one school most children were black, in two schools most were Mexican American, and five schools had a mix of students. Six of the teachers were first-year teachers.

PROCEDURES: Trained observers gathered information about each teacher's organization and management practices by visiting classrooms. Twelve classrooms were visited during the first morning of school; all 27 classrooms were observed at least once during the first two days. Each teacher in the study was observed at least eight times during the first three weeks. Teachers were also observed later in the year and were interviewed twice. Data collected included:

- Organization and management practices using a Classroom Narrative Record
- Student on-task behavior using a Student Engagement Rating Form
- Ratings of teacher organization and management behaviors

Using a variety of ratings, and controlling for the achievement of students in the classrooms, the researchers were able to identify seven teachers who were very effective managers and seven who were clearly less effective on student engagement compared to off-task behaviors.

POINTERS FOR READING RESEARCH: There are no new research concepts introduced in this study. The researchers did, however, include considerable information in their data table, and readers will have to study it very carefully.

RESULTS: This is a two-part study. First the researchers studied the differences between more effective and less effective managers during the first 3 weeks of school. They found considerable and significant differences as can be observed in Table 15-1. Several of the variables included in the study have been excluded because they are similar to those you already studied in Chapter 6. As can be observed in Table 15-1, there are considerable and significant differences between more and less effective managers. The important part of this study, however, is the researchers' finding that there is considerable stability between beginning-of-the-year management effectiveness and later-in-the-year behaviors.

TABLE 15-1 Component Ratings and Student Engagement Rates for Seven More Effective and for Seven Less Effective Managers During the First Three Weeks of School

VARIABLE	MORE EFFECTIVE MANAGERS' MEAN	LESS EFFECTIVE MANAGERS' MEAN	$p<$
Behavior management			
Variety of rewards	4.3	3.1	.05
Signals appropriate behavior	5.4	3.8	.01
Eye contact	6.1	4.9	.01
States desired attitude	5.5	3.9	.01
Reinforces inattentive behavior	2.7	3.6	.ns
Disruptive pupil behavior	3.0	4.8	.05
Meeting student's concerns			
Attention spans considered in lesson design	5.2	2.8	.01
High degree of student success	5.5	3.9	.01
Content related to student interest	5.2	3.6	.01
Reasonable work standards	5.8	4.6	.05
Student engagement rates			
On-task, all activities	.86	.75	.05
On-task, in content	.65	.59	.10
Off-task, unsanctioned	.07	.16	.05

SOURCE: Adapted from E. T. Emmer, C. M. Evertson, and L. M. Anderson (1980), p. 224.

DISCUSSION AND IMPLICATIONS: As can be observed from Table 15-1, there were considerable and significant differences between the more effective managers and the less effective managers in two important areas: behavior management and meeting student concerns. The researchers reached the following conclusions about differences between more and less effective managers:

1. More effective managers had more contact with students during the first few days and spent considerable time explaining rules and procedures.
2. More effective managers had better instructional procedures and made the "first" academic activities enjoyable.
3. More effective managers were sensitive to student needs and concerns during the first few days of school, specifically in gauging attention span, level of difficulty of lessons, and overall judgment about what to do.
4. More effective managers exhibited better listening and affective skills.

able resource for getting ideas for the first few lessons. They know about the interests of students in the school, and they also have a good understanding of students' prior knowledge.

Lessons during the first day and the first week should be uncomplicated, and they should focus on the whole class. A whole-class focus is recommended for two reasons. One, most students know how to behave in this learning setting, and two, a whole-group focus enables the teacher to be visible and in charge. Small-group work, cooperative learning, and many other approaches that require student movement should be avoided until the beginning teacher feels confident with the class and students have learned the rules and expectations needed to make such learning activities successful.

INTRODUCING RULES AND PROCEDURES

Chapter 6 described the importance of clear rules and procedures for effective classroom management. The first day and week of school are the times when these rules and procedures must be introduced and taught to students. Experienced teachers post important rules and procedures and go over these with students on the first day. They keep their list of rules short, they explain the logic behind the rules, and they teach them with the same care as any other skill.

Getting off to a good start with students is crucial because it influences the rest of the school year. Many aspects of the first week can be greatly enhanced by good planning and attention to detail. Table 15-2 shows some important tasks for the first week of school and provides the recommendations made by the University of Texas researchers on how to "plan for a good beginning."

Exhibiting Leadership and Establishing Professional Networks

It is natural for beginning teachers to spend most of their energy on planning and delivering instruction. There are, however, other important functions that need attention. Launching one's career is just as important as launching one's first class.

EXHIBITING LEADERSHIP

The previous sections emphasized the importance that first impressions have on students. First impressions also affect the way beginning teachers are received by professional colleagues both inside and outside school.

One way that beginning teachers can become known among colleagues and win their regard is to exhibit leadership potential within the school or school system. Below are some examples, reported by principals and colleagues, of what several successful beginning teachers did to exhibit leadership during their first year (see Arends, 1979).

- Elaine taught on a fifth-and-sixth-grade teaching team that had a weak science curriculum. Elaine had majored in biology in college and had more science background than other more experienced teachers on the team. She volunteered to revise the science curriculum for the team and found suitable materials for teachers to use. This leadership was applauded by team members and made Elaine a highly valued and respected team member.
- George was hired as a social studies teacher in a middle school. In discussions with students and colleagues, he found that for the past 3 years no one had paid any attention to the school's drama program. George had been in numerous college plays and volunteered to head up the drama club and to sponsor a spring play. The play was a huge success, and George won respect for his willingness to take on this schoolwide job.
- Valerie, a high school English teacher, was upset about the hall behavior of the students in the building wing where she had been assigned. After getting things off to a good start in her own class, she began discussing the hall problem with other teachers in the wing. Under her leadership they established a set of rules for hall behavior and together agreed on ways to monitor student behavior between classes.

Obviously, beginning teachers should not overextend themselves by assuming too many leadership responsibilities. However, it is important to pick at least one project that has the potential for schoolwide attention and devote energy toward getting successful results.

Table 15-2   Planning for a Good Start

TASK	RECOMMENDATION
Obtaining books and checking them out to students	Know school procedures for keeping track of books. Be prepared to record book numbers for each student on forms or in the grade book. Some teachers wait until the second day and check out textbooks during a seatwork assignment.
Required paperwork	Make sure all required forms, reports, etc. are on hand and organized for appropriate use. Required paperwork will vary from school to school.
Class rosters	Have class rosters organized (by period in high school) and pay attention to students with any special needs. Class rosters will change over the first days of school as new students arrive and as class sizes are leveled out across the school.
Seating assignments	Wait until class rosters have stabilized before assigning seats (normally the third or fourth day of school). Some teachers seat students alphabetically; others let students choose their own seat. Seating assignments, regardless of the method used, help the beginning teacher learn students' names and control student movement. Most teachers change the seating arrangement periodically.
First-week schedules	Know in detail the schedules for the first week. In secondary schools, classes are often shortened for one reason or another during this time. In elementary schools, planned assemblies are common.
Tardiness	Many students will be tardy during the first days of school. They, too, are struggling to find the right room and so on. Start enforcing tardiness policies during the third or fourth day. Warn students of this policy the previous day.
Administrative tasks	Be prepared to accomplish administrative tasks efficiently. These tasks will vary, but in most schools will include attendance checking, hall procedures, use of school equipment, various signups for special school events, and reporting requirements.
Rules and procedures	Explain rules on the first day. Teach procedures during the first week. Come back to both as needed and try to remain consistent in their use.
Course requirements	Course or class requirements should be explained to students during the first week. For older students these requirements (tests, major papers, projects, etc.) should be given to students in writing. Teachers should emphasize that major requirements are not just tasks to be accomplished for a grade, but major challenges for students to enhance their education.
Beginning-class routine	Be prepared to start class smoothly. Whatever routine is chosen, it should be efficient and one where students remain in their seats without talking while waiting for instruction to begin.
Time fillers	Be prepared with special work sheets, puzzles, or special reading materials which can be used in case a lesson runs short or periods or the school day are extended.
Closing-class routine	Be prepared for closing class smoothly. Plans should include ways to collect student work and materials. In secondary schools, teachers must insist that dismissal is when they "say" and not the school's bell or buzzer system.

SOURCE: Adapted from E. T. Emmer, C. Evertson, J. Sanford, B. S. Clements, and W. E. Worsham, *Classroom management for secondary teachers* (2nd ed.), Englewood, N.J.; Prentice-Hall, 1989, pp. 73–76. Copyright © 1989 by Prentice-Hall. Used by permission.

ATTENDING TO PROFESSIONAL GROWTH

Throughout this book the idea that learning to teach is a lifelong process has been emphasized. The learning process for teachers includes developing habits of reflection, finding ways to keep abreast of current research on teaching and learning, and keeping up-to-date in one's subject. It is easy for beginning teachers to fall into the trap of having their first class and their first school become all-consuming and to forget about their own needs as learners. From the very first week, time should be set aside for the teacher's own professional development and for establishing professional networks beyond the environs of a particular school. This can be accomplished in a variety of ways.

Attend Beginning Teacher Workshops and Seminars. Many school systems sponsor workshops and seminars for beginning teachers. Sometimes these are required; most often participation is voluntary. Beginning teachers should take advantage of these opportunities. Useful ideas about classroom management and teaching strategies can be found in these workshops and seminars. They also provide opportunities for the beginning teacher to meet other beginning teachers in the school system as well as more experienced teachers who often have been selected to lead these events.

Attend Regional and National Conferences. One important way for beginning teachers to keep abreast of their subject fields and the latest instructional research is by attending regional and national conferences. In some school systems conference attendance will be encouraged through financial incentives. In other systems, beginning teachers will have to use their own funds. Either way, it is important for beginning teachers to set goals for themselves that will ensure professional growth and professional networking through conference attendance. The resource handbook at the end of this book lists the names and addresses of professional organizations that sponsor local and national meetings organized around research or topics of interest to classroom teachers.

Working toward School Improvement

"The more things change the more they stay the same," quoted Seymour Sarason (1971) after 10 years of observing reform in American education. In this one sentence, Sarason captured both the hope and the frustration many have with school reform. On the one hand, numerous lay and professional groups have worked hard over the years and have spent enormous resources to make schools and classrooms better. On the other hand, many of these change initiatives have not met the expectations of reformers, and consequently, many people feel today's schools are about the same as they have always been, perhaps worse.

This final section of *Learning to Teach* is not based on the belief that improving schools will be the major concern of beginning teachers. It is, however, based on the belief that it is the teacher's responsibility to help make classrooms and schools better and that involvement in improvement processes, if only in a very small way, should start early in one's career. Thoughtful beginning teachers will want to consider three important questions about education improvement and change: Why is educational change needed? What are the emerging problems requiring reform? Why have many past attempts at reform failed?

WHY IS EDUCATIONAL CHANGE NEEDED?

Per Dalin (1978), a Norwegian researcher, wrote that from a historical perspective "dissatisfaction with schools is not a new phenomenon. Schools have been the focus of public concern for nearly as long as they have existed" (p. 1). Michael Fullan (1982), a Canadian educational sociologist and perhaps the foremost expert on the processes of educational change, made the same observation, noting that desire for change is neither new nor localized. In fact, "Dissatisfaction with and interest in improving current efforts at bringing about educational change is a worldwide phenomenon" (p. xi).

Schools as they exist today assumed their basic design in the early 1800s. Curiously, people in most developed countries are ambivalent about this design. Although most citizens are comfortable with the familiar patterns of the schools they experienced as children and get upset with changes that challenge these patterns, they are quick to find fault with the schools when they fail to live up to contemporary expectations. Bruce Joyce and his colleagues (1983) caught the essence of this paradox when they wrote:

> Throughout history . . . [critics] . . . have found [the school] both too backward and too advanced. It falls behind the times and fails to keep us in simultaneous cadence. . . . Most citizens are cautious about educational innovation. People like the familiar old schoolhouse as much as they criticize it. They tend to believe that current problems in education are caused by changes (perceived as "lowering of standards") rather than because the old comfortable model of the school may be a little rusty and out-of-date. In fact, our society has changed a great deal since the days when the familiar and comfortable patterns of education were established, and many schools have become badly out of phase with the needs of children in today's world. (pp. 3–4)

Joyce and his colleagues are right. The world has changed considerably since the idea of formal schooling was first conceived. During the past two decades, for example, many aspects of peoples' lives and of their social institutions have been drastically transformed. A shrinking world produced by new communication and transportation technologies has replaced older parochial views with more cosmopolitan outlooks and interests. Shifting population patterns have made diverse, multicultural communities the norm and have greatly increased social sensitivity. Diminishing natural resources have also impacted significantly on people's values and lifestyles.

Similarly, information technologies that include telecommunication satellites, word processors, microcomputers, and information retrieval systems have substantially changed the way information can be thought about and used. The printing technologies that only came into being during the last 200 years, making possible the current system of schools and libraries, must now compete with electronic communications. It is possible right now, and affordable in the near future, for every classroom and home to have electronic access to the information and wisdom stored in the major libraries of the world.

It is important to keep these changing conditions in mind when discussing educational change because they provide the context in which education and schools must operate. They also influence the values and interests of the youth found in classrooms, including the values and beliefs you have about teaching and about schools.

WHAT EMERGING PROBLEMS REQUIRE REFORM?

Schools in most developed countries provide educational opportunities far surpassing those provided in earlier eras. Perhaps schools have not failed in some absolute sense so much as they have failed to live up to the rising expectations people have for them. Some of these unrealized educational goals exist because educational procedures have become antiquated, and others exist because of emerging problems. These problems can be divided into three general areas: the inability to achieve equal educational opportunity, the inability to develop each person's unique talents to their fullest, and outdated curricula that fail to provide relevant experiences for a large portion of students. This list of challenges is not altogether new; nor is it unique to a single educational system. It represents a challenge faced in North America, Europe, and the developed countries on the Pacific rim.

Unequal Educational Opportunities. Per Dalin (1978) wrote, "After World War II, education was looked upon as the main instrument for individual and economic development as well as the major social force for equalization of opportunity . . . and most educational systems were quite successful in 'expanding,' that is, in making the same opportunities available for more individuals" (pp. 2–3). He also wrote, "In most countries, particularly in America, Canada, the Scandinavian countries and the United Kingdom, we experienced two decades (1950–1970) of active, innovative activities" (p. 3). This growth and the educational innovations of those two decades, however, failed to live up to some of the hopes held for them regarding "equal opportunities," and most countries were left after two decades of experimentation with conditions about the same as when they started. In other words, even though educational opportunities were expanded quite extensively, the promise of equal education for all remains elusive.

Failure to Develop Each Person's Talents. Even though this educational goal has been around for some time, it still has not been fully achieved. School organization that is keyed to academic disciplines and divided into brief class periods makes it difficult for teachers to develop a sense of personal responsibility for students' total development. Instead, it has been the norm to stick with a common curriculum and traditional strategies regardless of developmental levels, motivation, and unique learning styles of particular groups of students. The number of students staying in school to finish rather than dropping out has not increased over the past three decades. In fact, fewer students are staying in school today to develop their talents than 10 years ago. Many believe this is unfortunate because today it is more important than ever for each person to use every ounce of potential that he or she possesses.

Outdated Curricula. A third challenge is the inability to keep school curricula up-to-date and relevant. In 1939, J. A. Peddiwill (a pen name for Harold Benjamin) wrote a little book titled *The Saber-Tooth Curriculum*. In it he described a mythical society whose educational system prepared its young to fight off saber-toothed tigers with fire clubs, catch fish with their bare hands, and club horses with large sticks. Then, as a result of an ice age, the society changed; the saber-toothed tigers and horses became extinct and were replaced in nature's scheme by antelope. The fish disappeared into the muddy waters of glacial pools. The traditional skills of the old educational program were no longer needed, and soon students started to complain that they could not see the relevance of learning tiger scaring, horse clubbing, and fish catching. After ample debate and discussion, the elder members of the society, who were responsible for the educational program, declared:

> We don't teach fish-grabbing to grab fish; we teach it to develop generalized agility which can never be developed by mere training. We don't teach horse-clubbing to club horses; we teach it to develop a generalized strength in the learner which he can never get from

so prosaic and specialized things as antelope-snare-setting. We don't teach tiger-scaring to scare tigers; we teach it for the purpose of giving noble courage which carries over into all the affairs of life. (pp. 42–43)

Peddiwell was poking fun at the school curriculum of 50 years ago. His point about relevancy, however, has a timeless quality. The curriculum in schools is too often organized around obsolete concepts that fail to meet the needs and demands of youth. This will be a continuing problem for educators living in a society where knowledge and institutions are constantly expanding and changing. It is exceedingly difficult to keep up in any field today, and the answer to the question about how best to prepare youth for a world that will certainly be different from the one they now experience will remain elusive, particularly when no one can predict future changes with certainty.

Social changes are also accompanied by changes in childhood and adolescence. Youth mature sooner than in earlier times, and each generation is confronted with a different set of questions and priorities that must be addressed. Some years ago, James Coleman (1972), an American sociologist, illustrated this problem in an article entitled "The Children Have Outgrown the Schools." In this article, he put forth the argument that schools fail students because they are pursuing the wrong goals with inappropriate experiences. Schools were created at a time in history when the society, according to Coleman, was "information poor and action rich." This meant that people, including youth, had plenty of things to do but little information to assist them. Over time, however, society has become "information rich but action poor"—people now have access to all kinds of information, but fewer opportunities exist for applying and taking action on the information. Coleman suggested that modern curricula should require more opportunities for active learning and involvement rather than merely providing exposure to more and more information. He argued that it is no longer sufficient to view the transmitting of information as the only purpose of schooling. Programs are needed that provide youth with realistic links between education and daily living. How to do this, however, is a difficult and perplexing problem.

WHY HAVE PREVIOUS EFFORTS FAILED?

Certainly no one will deny that schools have changed. If, for instance, you returned to your high school, you would likely find noticeable changes in school policies, educational programs, and student conversations. Similarly, you can pick up almost any newspaper and find an account of a new educational program in one of the local schools. If you chose to study educational change more systematically, you would find many innovations. Over 1,000 reform reports have been written about schools between 1983 and 1990, for instance.

But have schools really changed? Some would argue that most changes have been only on the surface. Earlier you read Sarason's observation that in education "the more things change, the more they stay the same." Others who have looked for new and potentially exciting practices in schools have come away equally disappointed (see Goodlad, 1975, 1984; Goodlad and Klein, 1970; Silberman, 1970; Sizer, 1984). All concluded that schools do appear to change over time, but the amount of change is modest, given the time and energy required.

Perhaps part of the reason for the lack of significant change and improvement can be attributed to inadequate conceptualizations about the nature of schools and the role of teachers in the process of educational change. (See Berman and McLaughlin, 1975.) Often it has been assumed that externally imposed change could be accomplished if careful plans were devised and adequate resources provided. Also, reformers have frequently based change efforts on short-term strategies that bypassed teachers in favor of "teacher-proof" strategies and curricula. This is not to imply that changes imposed from outside the school will not help with school reform. It just means that external rules and regulations alone will not get the job done. Perhaps reformers have also underestimated the complexities of the school as a social organization and have failed to realize the time span needed for successful change to occur.

PERSPECTIVES ABOUT SCHOOL IMPROVEMENT

As you think about educational change and how you might make working toward school improvement an integral part of your career, two big ideas are important to consider. The first is a theoretical orientation that stems from psychology and focuses on how individuals react to change in their lives. The second is based on systems theory applied to organizations and focuses on the nature of the school as a social system and how organizational norms, roles, and culture restrain educational change.

The Process of Change for Individuals. Michael Fullan (1982) wrote, "We have become so accustomed to the presence of change that we rarely stop and think what change means as we are experiencing it at the personal level . . . [and] more important, we almost never stop to think what it means for those others around us who might be in change situations" (p. 82). Fullan pointed out that the "crux of change" in education is how individuals within schools come to grips with new realities, expectations, and behaviors.

If you stop and think for a moment, your own experiences will probably confirm Fullan's ideas. Many of you have experienced the changes associated with leaving home and going away to college; others have experienced the death of a loved one or a happier experience such as marriage or having a first child. Some of you have experienced jobs where duties and responsibilities were suddenly and radically restructured. All of these changes probably caused anxiety, a sense of loss, and a struggle to adapt and find meaning in the new set of circumstances.

Drawing on the work of others, Fullan (1982) also explained more fully why and how individuals react to new situations. He said, "New experiences are always initially reacted to in the context of some 'familiar, reliable construction of reality' in which people must be able to attach personal meaning to the experiences regardless of how meaningful they might be to others" (p. 25). Combs (1965), writing several years earlier, presented a similar point of view. He said that people's behaviors are a result of the worldview they hold. This worldview evolves over a very long period of time as each person strives to make meaning out of experience. As people grow older, their worldview becomes more and more consistent and their behavior more patterned. Therefore, according to Combs (1965), when one thinks about teachers or students changing their behavior the importance of their current beliefs and patterns must be recognized, and the importance of involving them in the change process must be considered:

> [Changing] must concern itself with the inner life. Simple exposure to subject matter (or new information or ways of doing things) is not enough. The maturation of an effective professional worker requires changes . . . in perceptions—his feelings, attitudes, and beliefs and his understanding of himself and his world. This is no easy matter, for what lies inside the individual is not open to direct manipulation and control. It is unlikely to change except with the active involvement of the . . . [person] in the process. (p. 14)

These concepts allow three predictions about the process of change within schools. First, change will be slow because it will come about only as individuals change their perceptions about new experiences and their relationships to self. Take for instance the beginning teacher who chooses to use the cooperative learning model described in Chapter 11. If this model has not been used in the school before, it is likely that students will at first resist key features of the model, such as working in groups and sharing rewards with other students. It will take time for students to adjust to the new realities and to find personal meaning in this novel educational experience.

Second, adjustments are most likely to occur in areas that are personally meaningful and least likely to occur in unfamiliar areas. Again, using cooperative learning as an example, its introduction into the classroom will probably necessitate the spending of a considerable amount of time explaining its rationale and advantages to students and other school staff.

Finally, individuals in schools will change only as a result of experiences that help them perceive themselves in new or different ways or help them see events from a new perspective. Change in self follows changed perceptions of others. In practice this means that most people cannot change simply as a result of new information or admonitions about the value of some new thing. It is only through first-hand experience that they are able to replace old realities with new ones.

Schools as Social Systems.   The impact of change rests mainly on the individuals who work in schools, and their responses will ultimately determine the success or failure of nearly all educational innovations. However, unless a climate that is conducive to change and innovation exists within the school and its surrounding environment, few **innovations** that are programmatic or organizational in nature will succeed. Despite the fact that individual teachers or students are taught new skills and new ways of perceiving their world, these new behaviors are often not observed in the school setting because the school as an organization has failed to change its norms, routines, and **culture** in ways that support the new behaviors. Examples of past educational innovations that have failed on occasion for this reason include:

- **Team teaching:**   The program flexibility and the time needed for planning were never provided to teachers, and students were not taught how to learn from a teaching team in contrast to a single teacher.
- **Open-space schools:**   New routines and structures to account for student control and movement were not developed. The hands-off norm was not changed.
- **Complex curriculum:**   Teachers were not given the facilities and assistance needed to store, purchase, and use the materials required in these curricula.

A view of schools as complex **social systems** helps us understand these phenomena. Theorists and researchers in this tradition (Lortie, 1975; Miles, 1964; Rutter et al., 1979; Sarason, 1971; Schmuck and Runkel, 1985; Schmuck, Runkel, Arends, and Arends, 1977) view school life as a process of individuals interacting in predictable patterns within a group setting. This view of patterned interaction provides a means of understanding the stability of schools over time and their resistance to change. It also provides a set of concepts for thinking about the school as a complex social system that in many ways resembles a spider's web or a geodesic dome in which each strand or part is related to all the others. When one strand is affected or changed all other parts must also be changed. Organizational development as a strategy for helping schools change has been based on this set of principles.

Research in this tradition looks at school innovation from the standpoint of how the school's overall social system responds to change, as opposed to how individuals within the school respond.

SCHOOL IMPROVEMENT SKILLS FOR BEGINNING TEACHERS

As a beginning teacher encountering your first classroom, it is likely that you will be faced with many dilemmas and unanswered questions. It is also likely that some of the discrepancies between professional ideals and the realities you find may be troublesome. Some beginning teachers have been known to accept these realities with a sense of resignation or defeat. Others have faced the complexities of teaching with a desire for improvement. There are some concrete things teachers can do, even in their beginning years, that will establish healthy patterns and contribute to school improvement.

Becoming a Student of One's Own Teaching. The point has repeatedly been made that when the "classroom doors" are closed, teachers are pretty much in charge of what goes on. Teachers report that they set their own objectives, procedures, and approaches to instruction, and most observers (Goodlad and Klein, 1970; Goodlad, 1984; Lortie, 1975) concur with the accuracy of these reports. Although this situation has its drawbacks, it does provide freedom for beginning teachers to work toward change and improvement in their own classrooms.

One means to improve classrooms is to become a student of one's own teaching. This type of activity is sometimes called **action research**, and it serves as a means for teachers to engage in critical inquiry and reflection into the processes of teaching. The specifics of how to carry out action research projects is described in the Resource Handbook at the end of *Learning to Teach*.

Working at the School Level. Most beginning teachers will be mainly interested in how they can improve their own classrooms. However, opportunities for taking action at the school level will also occur as they work with others in the school.

A beginning teacher's role in schoolwide improvement efforts at first involves being a thoughtful participant in proposals that come from others. Such proposals may involve policies for beginning teacher evaluation created by the state legislature, a new science curriculum adopted by the school district, or perhaps new approaches for classroom management offered by the principal. In all of these instances beginning teachers will be primarily on the receiving end. According to Fullan (1982), when teachers are faced with new proposals they should ask three questions before commiting themselves or deciding to throw their energies into a new approach:*

1. **Is the change needed?** "Does it address an important educational goal which is currently not being achieved adequately, and does the particular change offer some potential for accomplishing the goal more effectively? . . . Being self-critical (analytic) is necessary in order to avoid the problem of false clarity, when a teacher superficially assumes that the goal is already being addressed but in reality is not employing teacher resources and behaviors which would maximize attainment. Related to this issue is the current tendency for many teachers to reject all external changes (particularly if they come from certain sources, such as governments). Rejecting all proposed changes out of hand may be just as regressive as accepting them all. However, even if the change is desired and needed, it will also be necessary to determine its priority. Since teachers are often faced with too many changes at once, they individually or jointly must choose where to put their efforts. If everything is attempted (or rejected), nothing will succeed. In one sense, the best a teacher can do is work hard on one or two of the most important priorities at one time, and cope with the others as well as possible" (pp. 123–124).

2. **Is the administration endorsing the change and why?** "Some form of active commitment by administrators will be necessary for freeing up necessary resources (reducing the cost) for the innovation to succeed. It may still be possible to go it alone, if the specific change is highly valued by the teacher, but it will be difficult unless there is some support from the administration. It is also important that teachers should not automatically accept apparent lack of interest on the part of an administrator at face value. Administrators have their own worlds of pressure, which they frequently keep private. . . . It

---

* Quotations from M. Fullan, *The meaning of educational change* (1982), beginning on this page and on page 466, are used with permission of Teachers College Press, New York.

may be that individual or group-based teacher initiative and negotiation with the administration could lead to significant changes in support in some cases. Untested assumptions are fertile ground for false attribution of motives and intentions. Apparent lack of attention by the administrator may or may not mean lack of interest" (p. 124).

3. **Do fellow teachers show an interest in the change?** "If collegiality among teachers in a school is already strong, the degree of teacher interest can usually be found out quite quickly. As before, one should not assume lack of interest. Because of the isolation of teachers from each other, there may be a lot of 'pluralistic ignorance'—that is, each one assumes that no one else is interested, everyone is making the same assumption, but no one bothers to test it out. In any case, if peer interest exists or can be stimulated, it can represent one of the most satisfying (and necessary) aspects of the change process" (p. 124).

Staying Alive and Flourishing the First Year

The final topic for this chapter is one that is extremely important for the beginning teacher: how to stay alive mentally and emotionally during the first year and how to flourish regardless of the circumstances.

KEEPING THINGS IN PERSPECTIVE

A description of role taking and organizational socialization was provided in the beginning section of this chapter. It is important for beginning teachers to understand this perspective. Regardless of a beginning teacher's readiness to perform the technical aspects of teaching, there will be difficulties to face because many of the problems of teacher induction are associated with the way schools are structured and the complexity of the teacher's role in our society. If this is kept in mind, beginning teachers will not assume total blame for difficulties they experience.

FINDING TIME

A common complaint of beginning teachers is that they simply cannot find the time to perform all the important tasks and functions associated with teaching. This is a common complaint of educators in general. Experienced teachers, principals, counselors, and the author of this book also express frustration in handling the multiple roles and task demands of their jobs. This lack of time is tightly connected with role overload and role complexity in education jobs. It also reflects many educators' inability to **manage time** effectively and to develop the determination and discipline to keep work demands realistic.

SOME COMMON TIME TRAPS FOR BEGINNING TEACHERS

Planning for more effective use of time can also be enhanced by avoiding some common **time traps**. Following are examples reported by beginning teachers.

Every Piece of Curriculum and All Materials Must Be Original. Most college methods instructors place a premium on the creation of original materials. In many instances this practice is carried over into student teaching. It is important for teachers to be able to design materials for their students' use; consequently, the aim in methods courses and student teaching is to teach this skill. The time demands of full-time teaching, however, require beginning teachers (and experienced teachers for that matter) to use materials created by others. It is not plagiarism to use materials found in curriculum guides, workbooks, or materials given to you by other teachers in the school. In fact, one mark of a good teacher is knowing how to keep his or her eyes open for good ideas and how to borrow and to adapt freely for specific purposes.

Every Paper Must Be Read and Graded. Several sections of this book have emphasized the importance of giving students good feedback about their work. The principle that good feedback promotes student growth is true. A beginning teacher, however, must guard against applying the principle in unrealistic ways. For example, a high school teacher who has 150 students might assign one paper a week and have students write one essay exam a week. If 10 minutes were spent reading each paper and 10 minutes correcting each exam, that would total 50 grading hours a week. Obviously, spending 50 hours beyond the school day would be unrealistic. Cutting it in half would be equally unrealistic, given all the other things teachers must do. The demands of the teacher's job require teachers to find ways to give feedback to students informally and to limit assignments that take a great deal of grading time. Beginning teachers should not feel guilty about this situation.

The Teacher Should Do It All.   Many beginning teachers, as a result of being in a leadership role for the first time, assume they must do everything themselves. However, they should not be reluctant to delegate responsibilities and tasks to others. Following are some tactics used by many experienced teachers:

- Delegate many classroom administrative and paperwork tasks to students. Students see this as a privilege and it can save teachers time.
- Delegate grading of objective tests to students. If done appropriately, this approach can be a valuable learning experience.
- Delegate typing and duplication tasks to the school secretary and teacher aides. This requires some planning, but pays off in the long run.
- Delegate collecting materials for important units and lessons to the school librarian. They normally are delighted to provide assistance to beginning teachers.
- Delegate all of the above to parent helpers. Particularly in the elementary school, there are parents who want to help. This requires some planning and organization, but again it will be a timesaver in the long run.

Every Request Must Be Responded To with "Yes."   The complexity of the school as a social organization means that many requests and demands are made on people's time. Most of these are legitimate and important in their own right. Beginning teachers, however, have to be careful that they do not become involved with too many tasks and experience extreme role overload during the first year. Most colleagues will understand when a beginning teacher says, "I would love to work with you on that project, but right now I don't have a minute to spare." The principal and others in authority positions will also understand when a beginning teacher gives a polite but firm *no* to a request to take on a special assignment.

FINDING A MENTOR

In several places in this book, the loneliness and helplessness are described that sometimes characterize the teacher's role. These psychological conditions are experienced most acutely by beginning teachers. Trapped in their room all day with little adult interaction, beginning teachers may start to feel they are the only ones who care and may not know how to ask for assistance in a system poorly organized for providing help. In teaching, as with most other adult roles, a mentor can be quite useful for learning complex roles.

In some schools, formal structures exist to help beginning teachers find and work with an experienced teacher who cares about how the beginner is doing and who is willing to take a special interest in his or her career development. In other schools, more informal means will have to be used to make this important connection. Regardless of whether the mentoring structure is formal or informal, the beginning teacher will need to make special efforts to make it work.

A mentor is not obtained by wearing a sign that says "I'm looking for a mentor." Instead, it comes by showing interest in a particular colleague's work, giving support to a colleague, and asking for help. The beginning teacher's initiation of this process with one or two likely candidates will in most instances bring results. From limited initial exchanges, the relationship may flourish until the beginning teacher can ask for daily feedback regarding ongoing teaching problems as well as larger professional and career development issues.

SUMMARY

- Entry into the world of work is an event that is experienced universally by people in all walks of life. Sometimes the process is easy; often it is difficult. Sociologists refer to the transitions from the family and educational institutions to the work institution as organizational socialization.
- There is a well-established knowledge base on the socialization of beginning teachers, including studies of what happens to beginning teachers, how successful beginning teachers start school their first year, and how successful beginning teachers launch their careers. For many

beginning teachers, the first year of teaching is characterized by reality shock. Regardless of initial preparation, many of the subtle and contextual aspects of teaching take time to learn. This process can be both painful and rewarding.

- Successful beginning teachers are those who get settled into their communities well ahead of the opening of school and who prepare carefully for the many new things happening to them at once.
- Doing the "right things" early in regard to classroom management and student motivation can get beginning teachers off to a good start with students and make the rest of the year productive.
- Effective beginning teachers are prepared to use the following procedures in their classrooms: make a lot of personal contact with students during the first few days, explain rules and procedures carefully, make initial learning experiences enjoyable, be sensitive to student needs, and exhibit effective listening and affective skills.
- Finding time to build positive relationships with colleagues and school leaders will get beginning teachers off to a good start in their careers, as will establishing goals for personal development.
- Helping to improve classrooms and schools is as much a part of the teacher's job as planning and delivering instruction directly to students.
- Educational change is needed because schools, in many instances, are out of phase with the needs of today's youth and do not live up to rising expectations people have for education.
- The most pressing problems include the school's inability to provide equal educational opportunities to all youth, the need to develop each person to his or her full potential, and the need to keep curricula and methods up-to-date in light of contemporary research.
- Many previous reform efforts have failed because reformers had inadequate conceptualizations about schools and the processes of educational change. Change efforts have also failed in the past because reformers too often underestimated the complexities of schools and the time span required to change things.
- The knowledge base on educational change es-

tablishes how change is experienced by individuals who work in schools and how schools change as social systems. The change process for individuals involves being connected to innovations which are personally meaningful, developing new understandings about particular innovations, and having opportunities to experience and practice new behaviors. Changes made by teachers will not have any lasting impact unless the school as an organization also changes to accommodate new teacher behaviors.

- Teachers who choose to work toward school improvement can do so by becoming thoughtful and informed about change initiatives proposed by others and by helping to create conditions for change.
- Time is a very scarce commodity for beginning teachers. Time can be freed up for most pressing concerns when teachers learn to avoid certain time traps. Every piece of material does not have to be original, every paper does not have to be graded, the teacher does not need to do it all, and you don't have to respond to every request with *yes*.

KEY TERMS

role system
organizational socialization
anticipatory socialization
reality shock
teacher socialization
professional networks
innovation
school culture
social system
time management
time traps
mentor

BOOKS FOR THE PROFESSIONAL

Fuchs, E. (1969). *Teachers talk: View from inside city schools.* New York: Doubleday. This book gives an anthropologist's description of the experience of beginning teachers in inner-city schools during the sixties. It is still relevant today.

Fullan, M. (1992). *The new meaning of educational change.* (2d ed.). New York: Teachers College Press. This is an excellent book on educational change. It reviews the research on this topic and in addition provides concrete actions educators can take to get new educational programs to work.

Joyce, B., Hersh, R., and McKibbin, M. (1983). *The structure of school improvement.* New York: Longman. Based on the effective schools reserach, this book provides an insightful analysis of the change process and step-by-step directions for educators interested in improving schools from the inside.

Lieberman, A. (ed.). (1988). *Building a professional culture in schools.* New York: Teachers College Press. This excellent selection of essays considers school culture and what teachers can do to help change that culture for the purpose of improving schools.

Loucks-Horsely, S., and Hergert, L. F. (1985). *An action guide to school improvement.* Alexandria, Va.: The Network and Association for Supervision and Curriculum Development. Based on over a decade of research on school improvement and effective schooling, this book provides practical, concrete suggestions for embarking on and completing school improvement projects.

Ryan, K., et al. (1980). *Biting the apple: Accounts of first year teachers.* New York: Longman. This book contains detailed accounts of the personal and professional experiences of 13 first-year teachers.

Schmuck, R. A., and Runkel, P. J. (1985). *The handbook of organization development in schools* (3d ed.). Prospect Heights, Ill.: Waveland Press. Based on 20 years of research on school improvement at the University of Oregon, the handbook describes the theory and technology that guide organization development in educational settings and provides hundreds of concrete suggestions for educators who want to improve small-group and organizational functioning.

LEARNING AIDS FOR PLANNING, OBSERVATION, AND REFLECTION

- Observing the Opening of School
- Charting the Characteristics of a School's Attendance Boundaries
- Interviewing Teachers about Their First Year
- Change Process Interview

OBSERVING THE OPENING OF SCHOOL

PURPOSE: There are many beginning-of-the-year tasks that need to be accomplished to ensure that the school year starts smoothly and continues smoothly. Observing an experienced teacher open school will help you understand how these tasks can be efficiently carried out.

DIRECTIONS: Observe a teacher in your subject area or grade level over the first few days of the school year. For each task listed, write under Comments what the teacher does or says that accomplishes that task.

TASK	COMMENTS
Obtaining books and checking them out to students	
Required paperwork on hand and organized	
Class roster organized	
Making seat assignments	
First-week schedule known	
Enforcing tardy policy	
Doing administrative tasks efficiently	

TASK	COMMENTS
Explaining rules	
Teaching procedures	
Explaining course requirements	
Beginning class routine	
Time fillers on hand	
Closing class routine	
Other (specify)	

Analysis and Reflection: Did the teacher you observed accomplish all of the listed tasks? Did he or she accomplish other tasks that you think facilitated beginning school? Write a paragraph about how you might accomplish these tasks when you begin your first job.

CHARTING THE CHARACTERISTICS OF A SCHOOL'S ATTENDANCE BOUNDARIES

PURPOSE: One very important beginning task is to get to know the community you will be teaching in. The purpose of this aid is to give a systematic means of doing so. Use it during student teaching to gain familiarity with the process and with your students' community, and again before you begin teaching.

DIRECTIONS: Go to the central office of your school district and obtain an attendance boundary map for the school you will be charting. Spend an afternoon walking and/or driving around the area and make note of the characteristics listed below. Walking is best.

1. Make a rough sketch of the area, noting major streets and landmarks.

2. What is the predominant socioeconomic status (SES) of the neighborhood?

   _____

   _____

3. Is this neighborhood's SES homogeneous, or are there pockets of differing SES? What are these? Where are they? _____

   _____

   _____

4. What conditions are homes in around the neighborhood? Are they mostly apartments, single family homes, or a mix? _____

   _____

   _____

5. What ethnic or racial groups are represented in the neighborhood? Which one is the majority group? _____

   _____

   _____

6. What age groups are represented in the neighborhood? Which is the majority? ____

_____

_____

_____

7. Count the number of churches. What religions do they represent? Where are they concentrated? _____

_____

_____

_____

8. What is the economic base of the community? What industries are here? What commercial enterprises? What is the community's level of economic health? _____

_____

_____

9. Does the community contain any centers for the arts or other cultural centers? What is their focus? Where are they located? _____

_____

_____

10. Where are the public libraries located? Stop in the library and skim the local newspaper. Find out if there is a local newspaper. Find out if there is a local history you might read. _____

_____

_____

11. What services does the community provide for children? _____

_____

_____

12. Describe the parks and other recreation facilities. _____

_____

_____

13. Where are the "hangouts"? _____

_____

_____

14. How would you characterize the "tone" of the community? Optimistic? Busy? Depressed? Orderly? Unruly? Quiet? _____

_____

_____

15. What other characteristics of this community stand out for you? _____

_____

_____

Analysis and Reflection: Write a paragraph about how you might incorporate the knowledge you've obtained about the community into your teaching. How will it help you establish rapport with students? How will it help you develop good working relationships with parents? How can you use the information in your lessons?

INTERVIEWING TEACHERS ABOUT THEIR FIRST YEAR

PURPOSE: When faced with difficulties, it's often helpful to find out how others have coped with similar difficulties. As discussed in the chapter, the first teaching year can be a stressful time, a time of reality shock. The purpose of this aid is to give you some ideas about how you might better deal with this stress by talking with other teachers about their first-year experiences.

DIRECTIONS: Use the following questions as a guide in interviewing one to three teachers about their first teaching year.

1. What expectations did you hold about teaching prior to your first job?
2. What surprises occurred during your first year relative to those expectations?
3. What expectations did you have about your own skills for teaching prior to your first job?
4. What surprises occurred during your first year relative to those expectations?
5. During your first year of teaching what did you find most difficult?
   a. About students
   b. About colleagues
   c. About the principal
   d. About the school in general
6. What did you do to alleviate those difficulties?
7. During your first year what did you find most rewarding and stimulating?
8. What advice would you give to a beginning teacher about how to survive and flourish during the first year of teaching?

Analysis and Reflection: What expectations do you have about teaching? How have they been influenced by your talks with teachers about their first year? Write a few paragraphs about your expectations of teaching and how you might cope if these expectations are not met.

CHANGE PROCESS INTERVIEW

PURPOSE: School change is a very complex process involving individual change as well as organizational change. This aid will give you the opportunity to investigate change from the perspective of people who have experienced it. This in turn may help you cope with change in your own career.

DIRECTIONS: Use the questions below as a guide in interviewing teachers or principals about change projects with which they are familiar.

1. Have you ever been involved with a school change or improvement project?
2. Can you describe the nature of the change or improvement?
3. Where did the idea for the change come from? The central office? The principal? Teachers? Parents?
4. How did you react at first to the change? Were you all for it, or did you have reservations? What kinds of reservations did you have?
5. How did others react to the change at first? What were their reservations?
6. What was your role in implementing the change? How did you react?
7. How did the change project turn out? Successfully? Unsuccessfully?

CONTENTS

UNIT 1
READING AND USING RESEARCH

Chapter 1 of *Learning to Teach* describes the importance of the knowledge base on teaching and learning for beginning teachers and how educational research supports the practice of teaching and frees teachers from an overreliance on the commonsense and rule-of-thumb approaches of earlier eras. Like other complex human activities, research has its own set of rules and a specialized language that can be very confusing to the novice. Learning to learn from research requires some understanding of the methods and language used by researchers and an awareness of where to go for research information. Whereas a broad understanding of educational research is obviously beyond the scope of this book, certain key concepts that are important for reading and understanding research are presented in this special resource section. The aim of this section is to help beginning teachers to use research, read research reports with a critical eye, and find research that may be needed during a career in teaching.

KEY RESEARCH CONCEPTS

Researchers strive to find answers to **research problems** by posing particular **research questions**. The perspective taken by researchers, however, sometimes differs from the perspective of teachers and their definition of problems differs from the common usage of that term. A problem, from the researcher's perspective, normally has three ingredients. It is clearly stated in question form, it focuses on relationships (particularly causal relationships) between two or more variables, and it implies the possibility of testing from a scientific perspective. Practical problems, on the other hand, although sometimes stated in question form, rarely focus on relationships that can be tested. Instead, they normally strive to state a discrepancy between the "way things are" and the way the problem solver

would like them to be. To show the difference between a practical problem faced by teachers and a researchable problem posed by researchers, consider two types of questions that might be asked about student motivation. A teacher might ask a practical question, such as "How can I get my unmotivated students to do their homework each night?" A researcher might ask a researchable question, such as "What are the effects of two different reward systems (free time in school versus parental praise) on time devoted to homework by unmotivated students?" Both problems are clearly stated in question form, but only the latter focuses on relationships among variables and has a built-in procedure for empirical testing.

Research Variables

When educational researchers study problems they normally do so by thinking about variables within a particular situation that can help explain relationships and causation. A research **variable** is a characteristic of a person (teacher, student, parent) or of some aspect of the environment (classroom, home, school) that can vary. Essentially, researchers try to sort out what goes with and influences what in the very complex environment of teaching and learning. They are also interested in arranging these variables into models that can explain teaching more fully. Much of the research during the last few decades has come from researchers who think about variables in a way similar to that shown in the model provided by Dunkin and Biddle (1974), displayed in Figure R1-1.

As can be observed, this model organizes 12 sets of variables into four larger classes that were first named by Mitzel (1960):

1. **Presage variables:** These variables refer to the characteristics of teachers, namely their experiences, their training, and special properties they have such as skills and motivations.
2. **Context variables:** These variables refer to the environment to which teachers must adjust, such as students' formative experiences, prior

Figure R1-1   Dunkin and Biddle model for the study of classroom teaching

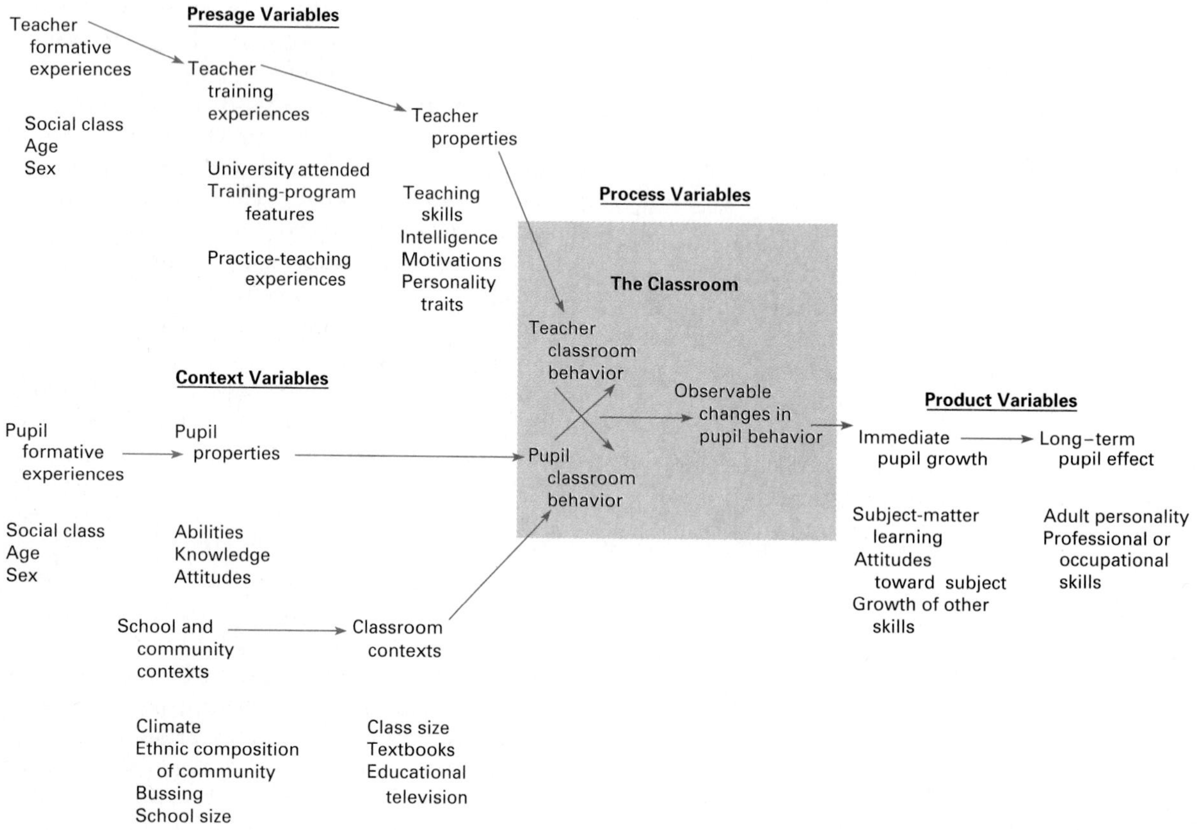

SOURCE: From M. J. Dunkin and B. J. Biddle (1974), *The study of teaching*. New York: Holt, Rinehart and Winston, p. 38. Used with permission of the publisher.

knowledge, students' abilities, and school, community, and classroom characteristics.

3. **Process variables:**   These variables refer to the activities and procedures that occur in classrooms. They are variables associated with what teachers and students do. Process variables are those of most concern in this book.

4. **Product variables:**   These variables refer to the outcomes of teaching and classroom interaction. They have been divided into two subsets by Dunkin and Biddle—immediate pupil growth and long-term effects. Two very important outcomes most teachers are concerned with are academic achievement and self-esteem.

Other researchers have developed models that differ from Dunkin and Biddle's, but the essential variables and their arrangement are the same. No-

tice the arrows in the model. These are provided to show the presumed causative relationships among the variables. It is important to point out, however, as do Dunkin and Biddle (1974), that "each arrow is but a source of hypotheses and not a symbol of invariant truth." As they explain:

For example, let us assume that teachers who come from middle-class backgrounds are known to approach pupils somewhat differently than those with lower-class backgrounds. Does this mean that social class "causes" differential classroom behavior? Indeed this interpretation might be correct. But it might also be true that teachers who come from middle and lower-class backgrounds are more likely to attend different colleges and thus to have had different experiences in teacher training; this latter factor, then, would be the actual cause of their different behaviors in the classroom. (p. 37)

Independent and Dependent Variables

When you read the research on teaching summarized in this book and elsewhere, you will often come across words such as "independent" and "dependent variable." These are words used by researchers to describe a particular aspect of the variables they are studying. Strictly speaking, **independent variable** refers to a property that is the presumed *cause* of something, whereas **dependent variable** is the *consequence*. In the study of teaching, variables associated with teacher behavior (causes) are normally important independent variables, and student self-esteem or achievement (consequences) are important dependent variables.

Knowledge about teaching is really knowledge about the relationships between the many independent and dependent variables in the model displayed in Figure R1-1. Many of the relationships that appear to exist are only tentative and are always open to alternative interpretations. It is important to remember that an enterprise as complex as teaching does not always fall neatly into the models devised by researchers.

APPROACHES TO EDUCATIONAL RESEARCH

Educational researchers use several methods to study problems related to teaching and learning. The critical differences between the various approaches include: (1) the ways researchers design their studies, (2) the ways they collect information, and (3) the means they use to interpret their results. Four of the most common approaches are described briefly in the following section.

Descriptive Research

Most of you can readily cite examples of **descriptive research**, not only in the field of education but also in noneducational fields. On any given day you can pick up a newspaper and read the results of a survey someone has done. A survey is one type of descriptive research. Researchers adopting this approach commonly use questionnaires or interviews to gather information about the characteristics of some phenomenon or measure people's opinions or attitudes on some subject.

Although it is difficult to do "good" survey research, the results of such research are easily understood. In most cases the results are presented numerically and describe the number and percentage of people who have a specific characteristic or who believe in a particular way. The part of Lortie's study summarized in Chapter 1 is an example of one type of survey research. In this instance, information was collected by interview on why people chose to go into teaching. The well-known yearly survey conducted by Gallup to get citizens' opinions about the schools is another example of survey research.

Sometimes researchers using the descriptive approach are interested in a type of problem that can best be studied through direct observation of a single case or a small number of cases. These approaches take the form of case studies or, in some instances, ethnographies. **Ethnography** is a word that comes from the field of anthropology and means an extensive study of an intact group of people, such as a culture, a society, or a particular role group. Normally what the researcher does when conducting this type of research is to select from many possibilities what might be called a typical case, and then to conduct in-depth observations of that single case. The aim of a case study, or an ethnography, is to collect extensive information so that a rich description and an in-depth understanding of the research problem will result. Examples of this type of research would include the work of anthropologists such as Margaret Mead, who lived with and studied the people in Samoa to discover some of the important underlying patterns of that culture; or the work of Jean Piaget, who conducted in-depth case studies of children to discover how a young child's mind develops and grows.

As a rule, researchers using observational techniques must get quite close to the subjects they are studying. In fact, some become participants themselves and try to influence the problems they are studying.

As contrasted to collecting information using questionnaires or interviews, observation allows the researcher to study the point of view of a group or person and, in turn, construct a more complete picture of the situation. A weakness of this type of research, however, is that the researcher is only studying a single or small number of cases. Readers or users of this research must always ask how typical or representative the researcher's case was and whether the researcher's conclusions would hold up in other cases or other settings.

Experimental Research

A second approach to research in education is the experiment. Most readers are already familiar with the basic logic and procedures of this approach through their high school and college science and social science classes. The results of this type of research are also frequently reported in the mass media.

The experimental study of teaching involves procedures in which the researcher, instead of describing or studying variables as they exist naturally in the world, sets up conditions so specified variables can be manipulated. Although there are over a dozen variations of educational experiments, the classical approach is for the researcher to perform three important acts: (1) to establish two groups believed to be the same, (2) to give one group (the experimental group) a special treatment and withhold the treatment from the other (the control group), and (3) to compare some measurable feature of the two groups to see if the treatment made any difference.

True experiments are difficult to do in education because many of the problems teachers and researchers are interested in are not amenable to experiments for either logistical or ethical reasons. When they can be done, however, experiments produce powerful results because they allow the researcher to draw conclusions about cause-and-effect relationships among variables. The educational problems most amenable to experimental manipulations are those associated with particular models and methods of teaching.

Correlational Research

Because so many aspects of teaching and learning cannot be studied experimentally, a third major research approach is often employed. Correlational research is used when the researcher explores the relationships between two or more variables that exist naturally and tries to sort out what goes with what. This approach is also familiar to most of you. Take, for example, the now well-known correlational studies showing strong relationships between cigarette smoking and certain diseases. Over many years, medical researchers have shown that people who smoke have a higher incidence of lung cancer and heart attacks than nonsmokers have. Nonetheless, the cause-and-effect relationship remains experimentally unproven because of the ethics of setting up a true experiment in which members of one group would be given a treatment that might lead to their deaths. Much of the research on effective teaching is also correlational research. For example, the many studies that show strong relationships between certain features of classroom management and student learning are nearly all correlational.

In the study of teaching, the researcher is normally interested in finding relationships between some type of teacher behavior and student learning. Although very useful in education, it is important to keep in mind that correlational research does not establish cause and effect among variables, only relationships. More will be said about this later.

Causal-Comparative Research

Many times in education variables of interest to the researcher cannot be manipulated and data must be used from already defined groups. A method used to explore causal relationships in this situation is the causal-comparative method. In this type of research, unlike experimental research, the independent variable is not manipulated by the researcher because it already exists. Researchers compare two groups: subjects (normally in already existing groups) for whom a particular trait or pattern exists and similar subjects for whom it is absent. Two examples are given below.

In both examples the researcher has studied variables that already exist and has studied groups (classrooms) that have already been defined.

- A researcher believes teachers are more critical toward Hispanic students than toward Anglo students. They record teacher behaviors and then compare the teachers' interactions with the two groups. The independent variable in this case is ethnic origin—a trait in students that obviously already exists and is not manipulated.
- A researcher is interested in the attitudes of students toward school in two classrooms—one where the teacher is using cooperative learning

strategies, the other where the teacher relies mainly on direct instruction. Attitudes are measured in the two classrooms and compared. Again, the independent variable (cooperative learning versus direct instruction) is a condition that already exists in the classroom and is not one the researcher has manipulated.

In causal-comparative studies, differences between means are observed. The statistical tests employed are similar to those used in experimental research. This differs from correlational studies, in which the correlation coefficient is observed. Like correlational research, the results from causal-comparative studies are limited and must be interpreted with care because it is not clear whether the variables observed are a cause or a result or whether some third factor is present that may be influencing both the independent and dependent variables.

STATISTICAL CONCEPTS AND RESEARCH CONVENTIONS

The vast majority of educational research involves measuring individual or group traits that produce quantitative data. Over the years researchers have developed statistical procedures to help organize, analyze, and interpret their data. To read and to use research requires an understanding of some of the basic procedures and agreed-upon conventions used by researchers. There is nothing magic about statistics or about symbols used by researchers. They are merely a means to communicate clearly and objectively. They may, however, appear mysterious to the novice. Brief descriptions of several key ideas can help beginning teachers understand research and perhaps motivate further study.

Sampling

Since it is obviously impossible to study all teachers or all students, educational researchers must, out of necessity, confine their studies to a small portion, or **sample**, of a total population. An example of this technique is the **sampling** done by Nielsen to find out which TV shows people watch. From the millions of viewers at a given programming hour, Nielsen polls 1,500 to 2,000 persons selected from known segments of the viewing population. Users of the Nielsen ratings accept the results because they know that what the sample is watching represents (more or less) the habits of the total viewing audience.

The way a sample is selected is very important because, if it does not accurately represent the intended larger population, the results will obviously be biased. A famous mistake in sampling occurred in the 1948 presidential election when a sample of citizens drawn from telephone directories across the country the night before the election indicated that Thomas Dewey, the Republican candidate, would be elected. The next day, however, Harry Truman, the Democratic candidate, was elected. Upon analysis the polling firm discovered that in 1948 many voters still did not have telephones and those without phones, who could not be included in the sample, were more prone to vote Democratic. Drawing a sample from the telephone directory was not appropriate if the pollsters wanted to know what the total population of voters was going to do. When reading reports of educational research, it is important to study carefully the sampling techniques used by the researcher.

Randomness

The concept of **randomness** is also very important in educational research. Normally random sampling or random assignment to groups means that individuals in any population have an equal chance of being selected for study. In survey research, this means that the researcher strives to define the total population of people he or she is going to study and then decides by chance which ones will be chosen for study. In experiments where one group is to receive a special treatment and the other to serve as a control, the researcher is careful that subjects are assigned to one of the two groups on a random basis. The logic behind random sampling or random assignment to groups is that by using this procedure the sample or the groups under investigation will have the same characteristics. This, however, is not always the case. For example, just as there is a chance, although very small, of flipping heads in a coin toss 100 times in a row, there is also always a chance that a random sample will indeed not represent the total population or that two groups assigned at random will differ from one another in important ways.

Numbers and Conventions

Researchers also use certain conventions to organize and report the results of their work to others.

MEAN SCORES

In many of the research studies summarized in this book as well as elsewhere, researchers report mean scores that allow comparison of one group with another. A **mean score** is nothing more than an average score and is calculated by adding all scores and dividing by the number of cases. The reporting convention of researchers is to use the symbol $\overline{X}$ or M to designate the mean score and the symbol N to communicate to readers the number of cases used to compute a particular mean. Mean scores are used to perform many of the statistical tests employed in educational research.

STANDARD DEVIATION

Standard deviation is another statistic that provides information about a set of scores. This statistic, found in many data tables, indicates the spread of a particular set of scores from the mean. Differences in means as well as differences in standard deviation are used to compute tests of statistical significance.

CORRELATION AND CORRELATION COEFFICIENTS

Correlation expresses the degree to which a relationship exists between two or more variables. Familiar examples would be the relationship between student IQ and student achievement, or the relationship between particular teaching behaviors (keeping students on task) and student achievement. Another might be the relationship between a person's height and his or her performance on the basketball court.

To express these relationships in mathematical terms, researchers use a statistic called the **correlation coefficient**. A correlation coefficient can range from +1.00 through .00 to −1.00. The sign does not have the traditional mathematical meaning. Instead, a plus sign represents a positive relationship, a minus sign a negative relationship. Thus, .00 means no relationship exists, +1.00 means a perfect relationship exists, and −1.00 means a perfect reverse relationship exists. As observed in many of the studies summarized in this book, few instances are found in education (or any other aspect of human behavior) where perfect positive or negative relationships exist.

As described earlier, an important thing to remember about correlational studies and correlational coefficients is that even though they may show relationships among variables, they do not explain cause and effect. As an example, many studies show a positive relationship between students' time on task and academic achievement. Consequently, it is assumed that teachers who can keep students on task more will produce superior scores on achievement tests. Although this may be true, the time-on-task principle could be turned around. It could be logically argued that it is not time on task that produces achievement, but instead it is high-achieving students who produce high time-on-task ratios.

TESTS OF SIGNIFICANCE

In any research on human behavior there is always the possibility that a specific outcome is the result of chance instead of some presumed relationship that is being studied. Researchers have developed a procedure called the *test of statistical significance* to help decide whether research results are indeed true or perhaps a matter of chance. Several different tests of significance occur in the research reports found in subsequent chapters. The main idea to remember is that when researchers use the word "significance" they are using it differently than in common usage, where it normally means "important." In the language of researchers, **significance** means the degree of truth rather than chance that they assign to their results. In general, researchers agree that differences between two sets of scores are statistically significant if they could occur by chance only 1 to 5 times out of 100. When you read the research reports in this text you will often see the notation $p <$

.01 or $p < .05$. This means that the probability (p) of such results could occur by chance less than ($<$) 1 time out of 100 (.01) or 5 times out of 100 (.05).

READING AND KEEPING ABREAST OF RESEARCH

Reading Research with a Critical Eye

Most research in education today is subjected to a review process before it is published. Nonetheless, the teacher who is reading and using the results of research should learn to approach studies with a critical eye. Borg and Gall (1983) have listed a number of weaknesses that occur in research studies and reports. Part of their list is summarized briefly here.

- **Deliberate bias:** Although the goal of research is to discover truth, sometimes research is done to convince others of a point of view or of the effectiveness of a particular educational program.
  Example: Readers of research look to see if the researcher has anything to gain if the results turn out in a particular way. If so, the possibility of bias is greatly increased and the study has to be examined very carefully. This does not mean, however, that all inventors of new programs or approaches who also conduct research on their inventions will deliberately bias the results. In most instances, they do not.
- **Nondeliberate bias:** Sometimes bias enters into research without the researchers' being aware of it. As with many other aspects of life, distortion can exist and influence us without our knowing it.
  Example: Look for emotional language and imbalanced presentation of research studies.
- **Sampling bias:** Sampling bias is something that plagues educational research, because it is so difficult to get random samples from total populations. However, as you learned in a previous section, if a sample contains bias, results can be spurious.
  Example: Studies where volunteers have been used, where many subjects have been lost from the sample, or where intact groups have been

used for convenience purposes should raise red flags for readers and users of research.
- **Observer and measurement bias:** Borg and Gall (1983) write that "human beings have a disturbing tendency to see what they want to see, hear what they want to hear, and remember what they want to remember" (p. 211). Even though researchers go to great lengths to guard against observer bias, they are always open to subtle error.
  Example: Looking at observation instruments or protocols to see if the researcher has included features to ensure objectivity or looking at interview questions for leading or threatening questions are means to check if observer bias has influenced the results of a study.

Reading a Research Report: An Example

It is time now to see if you can apply these research concepts to an actual research report. The following pages summarize research done by Wayne Hoy. Hoy was studying the general problem of how people learn to be teachers and what influence prior experience has on that learning. Read the summary of Hoy's study (Research Summary R1-1) carefully and see if you can answer the following questions:

1. Is Hoy's study an example of descriptive, experimental, correlational, or causal-comparative research?
2. What two variables were studied? Which variable is the independent variable? Which is the dependent variable?
3. Where would Hoy's variables fit in the Dunkin and Biddle research model?
4. How did Hoy use the mean statistic? From studying the mean scores and tests of significance, what conclusions would you draw?
5. Based on your conclusion, what might you say about the impact of experience on teaching and how might this influence your own experiences?
6. Which forms of bias do you find in the Hoy study? Deliberate bias? Nondeliberate bias? Observer bias? What about the sample? Is it biased?

RESEARCH SUMMARY R1-1

Hoy, W. K. (1968). The influence of experience on the beginning teacher. *School Review, 76*, 312–323.

PROBLEM: Hoy was interested in the degree to which teaching experience influenced beginning teachers, particularly the way beginners control students. The specific question he posed for his research was: What is the relationship between teaching experience and the pupil control ideology (PCI) of beginning teachers?

SAMPLE AND SETTING: Hoy studied 82 elementary and 93 secondary student teachers at Oklahoma State University. This sample was essentially all the student teachers at the university during the term in which Hoy started his study.

PROCEDURES: Hoy developed a 20-item instrument to measure how humanitarian versus custodial (authoritarian) beginning teachers were in their pupil control ideology. Examples of items included: "A few pupils are just young hoodlums and should be treated accordingly"; "It is often necessary to remind pupils that their status in schools differs from that of the teachers"; and "Pupils can be trusted to work together without supervision." This instrument produced a mean score. High mean scores meant the teacher was more custodial or authoritarian; more humanitarian teachers had lower mean scores. All subjects completed Hoy's questionnaire three times—just prior to student teaching, again after the completion of student teaching, and 1 year later. One year later found some subjects teaching in public schools, some in graduate school serving as graduate teaching assistants, and others who had decided not to go into teaching.

RESULTS: Table 1 shows the results of Hoy's study. Note that Hoy reports his results using mean scores. The symbol *t* and the numbers found in the last column stand for the test of significance used by Hoy.

DISCUSSION AND IMPLICATIONS

1. Hoy's study is an example of causal-comparative research. Even though he measures attitudes at three points in time, he does not manipulate the independent variables (experimental research) nor does he use correlation coefficients to look at the relationships under investigation.
2. The independent variable in Hoy's study was experience; the dependent variable was attitude toward pupil control.
3. Hoy was studying the relationships between a particular presage variable (teacher experience) and a process variable (teacher classroom behavior).
4. Hoy's sample was confined to the total population of student teachers at one university at one point in time.
5. A study of the mean scores of the beginning teachers at three points in time provides a fairly convincing argument that experience does influence beginning teachers' attitudes toward student control and in a significant way. However, experience does not

TABLE 1   A Comparison of the Pupil Control Ideology of Teachers Before and After Student Teaching and After the First Year of Teaching

Position	N	Experience	PCI Mean SCORE	t
Public school teachers	116	Before student teaching	44.56	—
		After student teaching	48.93	6.569*
		After first year teaching	51.48	3.783*
Graduate assistants	7	Before student teaching	43.86	—
		After student teaching	48.00	2.008
		After first year teaching	43.14	2.303
Not teaching	39	Before student teaching	44.80	—
		After student teaching	47.31	2.404*
		One year later	47.05	.270

* Significant at the .01 level of confidence ($p < .01$).
SOURCE: W. K. Hoy (1968), p. 317.

always teach what is desired. For example, beginning teachers in Hoy's study became more custodial (authoritarian) toward their students as they gained more experience and lost some of the humanistic qualities and idealism that most people would desire in teachers.

6. For the people who did not go into teaching, their PCI stayed the same after student teaching. The lesson from this research drawn by Hoy is that the culture of schools is very powerful and moves beginning teachers toward more custodial and authoritarian attitudes. If a beginning teacher wants to embrace humanistic norms regarding pupil control, it is probably important that during student teaching and the first year beginners seek out experienced teachers who value and demonstrate these qualities.

7. One has to be careful about the results of Hoy's study. Hoy himself stated in his report that the results of this study should be interpreted with some care because the sample came from only one university and had a high proportion of female teachers in the group of teachers completing their first year of teaching. In other words, Hoy is warning readers that what he found may be true for female teachers in Oklahoma and not for other teachers or in other places.

You may be interested to know that since this study Hoy and others have found similar results in other parts of the country and with different samples.

7. What are the strengths of the Hoy study? What are the limitations?

Keeping Abreast of Research

Once one starts teaching full time, it is sometimes difficult to keep up with research. There are just so many other things to do. Fortunately, there are special services available to teachers which can cut down the time needed to keep abreast of the research on teaching and learning. Beginning in the mid-1960s, the federal government became more interested in educational research and created several services to encourage the dissemination of educational research to classroom teachers. Three of these services can be useful to the beginning teacher.

REGIONAL EDUCATIONAL LABORATORIES

Knowing that most research and research centers were not directly applicable to classroom teachers, regional educational laboratories were created in 1964 to translate research into classroom materials and strategies and to disseminate the results to teachers. Even though their budgets do not allow direct assistance in every classroom in their region, laboratory staffs hold many useful workshops and are eager to have classroom teachers visit their labs and learn about the work they are doing. These laboratories also provide opportunities for the more energetic teachers to participate in ongoing research and development projects. A complete list of centers and regional laboratories appears at the end of the Resource Handbook Section.

EDUCATIONAL RESEARCH INFORMATION CENTERS

Also in the mid-1960s, the federal government started to put together a network of educational research information centers called ERIC. Today there are 16 of these centers. ERIC centers are charged with three major tasks: (1) collecting the available knowledge on topics associated with various specialized areas of education, (2) organizing this information so it can be retrieved via computers from any place in the United States, and (3) summarizing these data in short bulletins and papers on topics of particular interest to teachers and other educators.

Today, all libraries in major universities and many large school districts or intermediate educational agencies have direct computer connections to the ERIC centers. To access these centers you need only contact the person in charge of ERIC searches in your library or school. That person will set up an appointment and discuss the type of problem about which you would like research information. The contact person can then perform on-line searches to give you an example of the types of articles and reports that are available. You can then order abstracts of the most relevant articles. These come to you on computer printouts and are useful for making decisions about the complete reports you may want to read. Since most university libraries and major school districts have the complete ERIC collection on microfiche, all of this can be done with minimal charge, and in many instances, for free. Additional information is provided about the ERIC system at the end of the Resource Handbook Section.

THE NATIONAL DIFFUSION NETWORK

A third service available to teachers is the National Diffusion Network (NDN). Created in 1974, NDN now exists in every state for the purpose of disseminating information on classroom practices and curriculum materials that have been shown through research to work. Akin to the farm extension system that takes the results of research to farmers, NDN works through the following two procedures:

1. **Programs that work:** Each year many educational programs are developed by educational researchers and by practicing classroom teachers. If they wish, and if they have evidence that their program produces the results they claim for it, they can submit it to a national review board for consideration. If approved by the national review board, the program is then described and appears in a yearly publication called *Programs That Work*. This publication is readily available to classroom teachers and other interested educators.
2. **State facilitators:** More important for the classroom teacher, however, is the availability of a person or team in each state who will respond to requests by teachers for information

about various programs that might be available to assist with a particular classroom or school problem. For example, suppose you are in your first year of teaching and you discover during your first open house that few parents show up. This confirms your previous hunch that your students are receiving little support and encouragement from home. Consequently, you call the NDN state facilitator and find that indeed there are programs that have been shown to be successful in increasing parental involvement. The facilitator may come to your school or invite you to his or her office and go over the programs that have received national endorsement. You can then order these programs and obtain materials explaining their use. You may also decide to involve other teachers in the school and together establish a schoolwide program to increase parental support. When this happens, the state facilitator can often provide assistance to get you and the faculty started, sometimes even to the point of bringing the original developer of the program to your school.

UNIT 2
ACTION RESEARCH FOR CLASSROOM TEACHERS

Throughout *Learning to Teach* the point of view has been taken that it is important for teachers to have a command of the knowledge base on teaching and that research is a valuable resource to guide teaching practices. In addition, Chapter 15 described the importance for teachers to assume responsibility and take individual initiative for improving the classrooms and schools in which they work. A logical extension of these admonitions is the idea that teachers can become researchers for the purposes of improving their teaching and the learning environments in their classrooms. This resource unit provides the rationale for classroom research and describes how you can use action research for the purpose of improving your teaching.

PERSPECTIVE AND RATIONALE

When teachers engage in classroom research, it is commonly called **action research.** In many ways action research is like any other research. It is the process of asking questions, seeking valid and objective answers, and interpreting and using the results. But it differs from some other kinds of research in that its goal is to produce valid information and knowledge that has immediate application—in this instance for teachers or their students. And unlike some researchers, teacher researchers are more interested in knowledge about a specific situation (their own classroom) than about more general applications. In other words, action research is guided by the processes and standards of scientific inquiry, but it is not intended to inform the larger research or educational community. Instead it is a process of acquiring information and seeking knowledge which will serve your own actions.

A Short History

Action research as conceptualized and practiced today is the outgrowth of over a half century of thought that has been most influenced by the early traditions of John Dewey, Kurt Lewin, and Les

Corey and his associates at Teachers College. More recently the field has been influenced by Donald Schön and Chris Argyris. Schön's ideas about reflective practice were introduced in Chapter 1. Argyris and colleagues (1985), who studied the traditions of action research, pointed out the importance of Dewey's contributions:

> Dewey (1929, 1933) was eloquent in his criticism of the traditional separation of knowledge and action, and he articulated a theory of inquiry that was a model both for scientific method and for social practice. He hoped that the extension of experimental inquiry to social practice would lead to an integration of science and practice. He based his hope on the observation that "science in becoming experimental has itself become a mode of directed practical doing" (1929, p. 24). This observation that experimentation in science is but a special case of human beings testing their conceptions in action, is at the core of the pragmatist epistemology. For the most part, however, the modern social sciences have appropriated the model of the natural sciences in ways that have maintained the separation of science and practice that Dewey deplored. Mainstream social science is related to social practice in much the same way that the natural sciences are related to engineering. This contrasts sharply with Dewey's vision of using scientific methods in social practice. (pp. 6–7)

Why Action Research?

Today the notion of teacher as researcher has gained widespread popularity in the United States, Great Britain, Canada, and Australia. In Great Britain much of the interest has stemmed from the work of such people as Lawrence Stenhouse (1975, 1983, 1984), who has written widely about why action research is important, and David Hopkins (1985), who has provided concrete advice to teachers about how to conduct classroom research and use the results for school improvement. In the United States many individuals, such as Oja and Smulyan (1989), have written about action research. In addition, the use of research and classroom teachers as action researchers has been high on the agenda of both major teacher associations, the American Federation of Teachers (AFT) and the National Education Association (NEA). (See Livingston and Castle, 1989.) The individuals and organizations advancing action research worldwide base their argument on two common premises about the role of the teacher and the processes of improving classroom teaching.

THE AUTONOMOUS PROFESSIONAL

Many thoughtful observers believe that the time has come for teachers to become autonomous professionals. By this they mean that instead of teachers relying on principals, central office supervisors, or college professors to tell them what to do, they should instead have command of their own knowledge and information to support decisions they make about teaching practices. Stenhouse (1984) has strongly supported this point of view.

> Good teachers are necessarily autonomous in professional judgement. They do not need to be told what to do. They are not professionally the dependents of researchers or superintendents, or innovators or supervisors. This does not mean that they do not welcome access to ideas created by other people at other places or in other times. Nor do they reject advice, consultancy or support. But they do know that ideas and people are not of much real use until they are digested to the point where they are subject of teachers' own judgement . . . .

For Stenhouse and others, the key to becoming an autonomous professional rests on teachers' disposition and ability to engage in self-study of their teaching and testing their classroom practices to see if they work. Obviously, this is a revolutionary view of teaching and one that departs dramatically from more traditional conceptions.

INFORMATION IS POWER

In addition to the point of view that teachers should be autonomous professionals, action research is also based on several premises about the processes of school improvement and the power of valid information to bring about improvement. Chapter 15 described how change and improvement for individuals or organizations comes about only as people construct new realities to replace existing ones and thereby make proposed improvements meaningful to themselves. New realities are constructed from new information and knowledge that challenges current ways of thinking. Thus, one can think of action research as a way to help construct new realities about one's teaching. It is a way for teachers to

- Collect *valid information* about their classrooms
- Use this information to make *informed choices* about teaching strategies and learning activities
- Share the information with students in order to gain their ideas and *internal commitment* to specified learning activities and procedures.*

DOING ACTION RESEARCH

To do action research successfully requires careful attention to several aspects of the process. In general, there is a flow or set of steps for initiating and completing an action research project. The three important parts of the process include (1) deciding on problems to study and framing questions, (2) collecting valid information, and (3) interpreting and using this information for the purpose of improving one's teaching.

Steps in Action Research

Action research starts with classroom situations which teachers find unsatisfactory and in need of improvement. The process consists of isolating a problem for inquiry, taking action, collecting data, observing what happens, and then reflecting on the whole process before recycling into further study. Australia's Kemmis and McTaggart (1981) have illustrated their view of the action research process in Figure R2-1.

Frank Lyman (1984), who has helped many teacher candidates and beginning teachers launch and successfully complete action research projects, prefers a more step-by-step approach. The seven steps recommended by Lyman are summarized in Figure R2-2.

Problem and Question Formulation
OVERALL CONSIDERATIONS

The beginning teacher is confronted with literally hundreds of problems or questions that could be

---

* The concepts of valid information, informed choice, and internal commitment come from Argyris 1970.

Figure R2-1   Kemmis's conception of the action research process

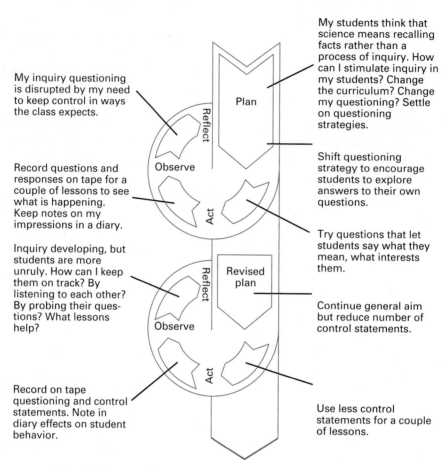

My students think that science means recalling facts rather than a process of inquiry. How can I stimulate inquiry in my students? Change the curriculum? Change my questioning? Settle on questioning strategies.

My inquiry questioning is disrupted by my need to keep control in ways the class expects.

Plan

Reflect

Observe

Act

Shift questioning strategy to encourage students to explore answers to their own questions.

Record questions and responses on tape for a couple of lessons to see what is happening. Keep notes on my impressions in a diary.

Try questions that let students say what they mean, what interests them.

Inquiry developing, but students are more unruly. How can I keep them on track? By listening to each other? By probing their questions? What lessons help?

Revised plan

Reflect

Observe

Act

Continue general aim but reduce number of control statements.

Record on tape questioning and control statements. Note in diary effects on student behavior.

Use less control statements for a couple of lessons.

SOURCE: From S. Kemmis and R. McTaggart, *The action research planner,* Victoria, Australia, Deakin University Press, 1981.

topics for action research. The most difficult part of an action research project, however, is identifying a specific problem for study and defining carefully the variables involved. David Hopkins (1985) has identified five principles to use in deciding on a problem for study.

1. **The project should not interfere with the teacher's first job, which is teaching.**   Obviously, there is no easy way to say whether an action research project will disrupt teaching. Hopkins is just reminding us that action research is used for the purpose of understanding and improving our teaching, and not for the pleasure of doing research for its own sake.

2. **Methods of collecting data should not be too demanding of the teacher's time.**   This too is a reminder to keep projects, particularly first efforts, rather simple so that the action research does not make undue demands on already busy schedules.

3. **The methods used should produce reliable and valid information.**   Even though information generated from action research is to improve a particular teacher's practice rather than more generalizable results, the validity and reliability of the information are still important. If the methods are not rigorous and if the information is not reliable and valid, it will be of little value to anyone.

Figure R2-2   Lyman's steps for action research

Step 1: Consider your present classroom, and isolate a problem you think would be improved by a different approach or teaching strategy.

Step 2: Frame a question that includes the independent variable and dependent variable(s).

Step 3: Note that the difference or differences you are looking for are the dependent variable(s).

Step 4: Decide what the indicators of the dependent variables are. (For example, accuracy could be indicated by the number of words written and by the correctness of their spelling. Number of student questions could be tabulated in a discussion).

Step 5: Design your experiment to keep constant as many variables as possible (for example, the same group of children, at the same time of day).

Step 6: Arrange for someone to help with the data collection (for example, a cooperating teacher or a teacher next door to count the number of questions asked by students).

Step 7: Organize and write up the results to share with others, particularly with colleagues and students.

SOURCE: Adapted from F. Lyman et al. (1984), *Action research by student teachers and beginning teachers: An approach to developing problem solving in classrooms.* (Mimeographed.) College Park, Maryland: University of Maryland, p. 42.

4. **The problem studied should be one to which the teacher is committed and one which is capable of solution.**   This is a reminder that if the problem is too complex or if it is influenced by factors for which the teacher has little control, then information collected, regardless of how valid or reliable, will make little difference.

5. **Ethical standards for research governs teachers' research, just as it does any other research.**   Standards such as keeping people informed about purposes of the project, obtaining authorization before collecting sensitive information, maintaining confidentiality, and respecting the rights of subjects are just as important for teacher researchers to maintain as they are for other researchers.

GETTING TO SPECIFICS ABOUT PROBLEMS AND QUESTIONS

As with any research, a good problem for action research is one that (1) can be stated in a question form, (2) focuses on the relationships among variables, and (3) has the possibility of empirical testing

Remember from the previous resource unit the distinctions made between independent and dependent variables. An independent variable refers to some aspect or property of the problem that is the presumed cause (teacher behavior, for instance); a dependent variable is a consequence (student engagement or learning).

Sometimes problems or questions cannot be stated very clearly in the beginning. The problem is likely to consist of a general uneasiness a teacher has about a classroom situation. Things are just not working quite the way one desires. Sometimes this general uneasiness about a problem or question can be transformed into something more specific by thinking about discrepancies or gaps that exist between the "way things are" and the "way you would like them to be." For instance, a teacher may have a situation where only 4 or 5 students out of a class of 25 participate in discussions (the way things are). The desired state may be to have all students participate fully. The question for study thus becomes, "How can I increase participation in my classroom during discussion periods?"

Sometimes discrepancies exist between what

we think we are doing and what we are actually doing. These too can become the focus for inquiry. As you will see in an example provided later, teachers may think they are interacting with all students in an equitable fashion, but upon careful study find that they indeed interact differentially toward different types or groups of students. The first question that stems from this type of problem situation is, "Do I interact differentially with different types of students?" If so, a second question for study becomes evident: "How can I change my behavior?"

In general, the recommendation for beginning teachers is to tackle problems from their own immediate experiences and concerns and ask questions that can be tested with rather straightforward plans and data collection efforts. Some of these questions will be amenable to informal data collection and testing procedures; others will require more formal methods. Below are several categories of questions that have been posed by teacher researchers during student teaching or early in their careers.

1. **Questions associated with student opinions:** Sometimes teachers are not sure what their students think about their teaching or about life in their classrooms. Questions might include the following: "Do students have high opinions of my instruction?" "Do my students find the learning environment pleasant?" "Do my students find the learning environment challenging?" "Do my students have the perception that I am treating them fairly?"

2. **Questions associated with particular teaching strategies or procedures:** Another set of questions which are amenable to action research are those that provide descriptive information about what a teacher is doing, for example, "What type of questions do I use during a discussion?" "Who talks most in my classes?" "Do I question and respond to all students in an equitable fashion?" "Do I give all students fair access to public time?" "How long do I wait for students to respond after asking a question?" "What proportion of the day is devoted to my own talking? To student talking? To seatwork?" "When I give an assignment to be completed in class, what proportion of the students are on task?"

3. **Questions comparing different approaches or variations of the same approach over time or with different groups:** Good teachers have a variety of teaching strategies and procedures at their command. As emphasized many times in this book, they match appropriate strategies to particular learning situations or groups of students. Here are some obvious questions about this matching process. What is most appropriate? What produces the best results? Here are some examples of action research questions which aim at comparing different strategies or procedures. "If I use think-pair-share (described in Chapter 13) after a lecture or after showing a film in my social studies class, will it result in more student participation and learning as compared to holding a whole-class discussion?" "If I make a contract (with a reward system built in) for my noninvolved students, will this increase their engagement in learning activities as compared to not having a contract system?" "If I use manipulatives and visual graphics when teaching a particular math concept, will students' test results be better as compared to just a straight verbal presentation?" "If I use direct instruction to teach a particular skill, will five independent practices be as effective as ten in helping students acquire proficiency?" "If I increase my wait-time to 5 seconds, will this change the nature of the discourse patterns in my classrooms as compared to a 2-second wait-time?"

Gathering Information

Once a problem or question has been identified for inquiry the next issue to be resolved by the teacher researcher is how to gather information. There are many techniques for doing this, some quite simple and others more complex. Four specific approaches to data collection are described below. The choice of which approach to use depends on the question being asked and the time teachers have to gather and analyze the information.

QUESTIONNAIRES

When teachers want information about the attitudes or opinions of their students toward some aspect of their teaching or classroom, the easiest and most

Figure R2-3 Happy, neutral, and sad face responses

economical way to gather this type of information is by giving students a questionnaire to fill out. Most of you are familiar with questionnaires about teaching because you have been asked many times to fill out course evaluations in your college classes. Many examples of this type of questionnaire can be found in the learning aids section of *Learning to Teach*. For example, Chapter 4 has a questionnaire to get information about how students feel about life in their classrooms. Chapter 5 has an example of a questionnaire to get perceptions students have about how fairly their teacher is treating them.

Questionnaire format normally poses a question or makes a statement with which respondents can agree or disagree. For example:

My teacher treats all students the same.

| Agree strongly | Agree | Neither agree nor disagree | Disagree | Disagree strongly |

or

Does the teacher help you when you are stuck?

| All the time | Most of the time | Sometimes/ sometimes not | Hardly ever | Never |

Many of the same rules apply for constructing questionnaire items as those described in Chapter 7 for constructing multiple-choice test questions. Remember to write questions which are simple and straightforward and make sure the response categories are consistent. When constructing a questionnaire for younger children, it is normal practice to use three rather than five response categories. For very young children the happy, neutral, or sad face response categories illustrated in Figure R2-3 can be used.

Sometimes teachers prefer more open-ended responses. In this case asking questions such as "What did you like best about the lesson? or "What did you like least?" provides valuable information. This type of item will provide more in-depth information and will not be biased by the response categories. However, it can be a bit more difficult to organize and interpret the responses from this type of question as compared to questions with definite response categories.

INTERVIEWS

Whereas questionnaires have the advantage of being easier to construct and score, they also have their disadvantages. One is never sure what students are actually thinking when they check one of the response categories. It is also difficult to write good questionnaire items that explore issues in any depth. An alternative way to collect information about student attitudes and opinions is to interview them.

Information can be obtained from students either individually or in small groups through an interview. As with questionnaires, it is important to write interview questions ahead of time and keep them straightforward and directed toward the question for which answers are sought. During the interview process itself, it is important to reassure students that they will not be punished for being candid, to employ good listening skills, and to emphasize how important their ideas are to you. The disadvantages of using interviews are that they are time-consuming (although the time factor can be reduced if students are interviewed in small groups), and it is frequently difficult to get students to express their true feelings and opinions candidly.

OBSERVATIONS

Many questions require some type of direct observation of teaching and student behavior. The procedures for observation and the recording devices can vary according to the type of question being asked. Normally, better information is acquired if a specific observation instrument is designed and used. Many specific observation instruments are provided in the learning aids sections of this book. Their use (with adaptation) will help collect needed information for many of the questions posed by beginning teachers.

There are essentially three ways to collect information through observation. The choice again depends upon the situation. One, the teacher may ask a colleague to observe classroom interactions and collect needed information. If this approach is used, the teacher researcher needs to make sure the colleague understands the observation instrument and can use it effectively.

Many times, it is better (and less threatening) to make audio or video recordings of a lesson and then observe and code specific behaviors from the videotapes or audiotapes. When verbal behavior of students or teachers is the subject of inquiry, audiotapes work fine. However, subtler nonverbal behaviors require video recordings. How one teacher used both audio and video recording to study his interactions with second-grade students will be described later.

NOTES, DIARIES, AND JOURNALS

Taking careful notes or keeping a diary or journal is a fourth means for collecting information about classroom events, your teaching, or your students' behavior. In general, observations must be committed to paper as soon as possible after an event, and they are more helpful if they are guided by a specific set of questions posed ahead of time as compared to more general observations which may come to mind. Notes and journals are particularly helpful for collecting information when the focus of inquiry is a particular student. They are also a good way to systematically study aspects of teaching which are not amenable to observation, such as your own thinking processes.

Interpreting and Using Information from Action Research

The final step in the action research process described in Figure R2-2 is to organize the results from a project and share it with others. Some teachers share the results with colleagues and use the data they have collected as a springboard for discussions about different approaches to teaching. Other teachers choose to share the results of an action research project with their students. The information collected in many projects can provide students with insights about their classroom and the teaching approaches being used by the teacher. This type of information can also help students gain commitment to learning activities found effective and provide a vehicle for them to think about and help plan classroom activities.

ACTION RESEARCH: AN EXAMPLE

This example is of an actual action research project done by a beginning teacher, David Weisz of Silver Spring, Maryland, while he was a student teacher in a second-grade classroom (see Weisz, 1989).

David's Questions

David was a very sensitive person and held strong beliefs about the importance of social justice in our society. He thought a lot about what teachers could do to promote justice and equality in their classrooms and was specifically concerned about his own treatment of students. His intentions were to treat all students equally and to communicate the same expectations to all students regardless of their abilities. He decided to study his use of questions and feedback in math groups from an equity perspective. He determined that the following questions would guide his action research project:

1. Do I favor students I perceive to be high achievers by directing more questions to them and by focusing high-level questions at them rather than at perceived low achievers and/or by giving them qualitatively or quantitatively better feedback?
2. Do I favor boys or girls in these same regards? (p. 2)

David explained that two things prompted his interest in this project. First, he had noticed during his student teaching the "relative ease with which a lesson can proceed if I focus exclusively or primarily on those students who appear to listen well, who have studied the materials, and who can be relied on to respond correctly or, at least, intelligently" (p. 2). He wondered if in his desire to have a smooth lesson he was favoring those he perceived as good students by asking them more questions and giving them more feedback and at the same time ignoring those students who he perceived as not so good. He

Figure R2-4   David's data sheet for coding particular types of teacher-student interaction

STUDENT'S NAME	RESPONSE OPPORTUNITIES	TYPE OF QUESTIONS		TYPE OF FEEDBACK
		High	Low	None ++ −+ −− +−

Coding schemes:	Response opportunity:	Student was called on by teacher
	High questions:	Questions that required students to think
	Low questions:	Questions that required recall of information
	None:	Teacher moved on with no response
	++	Teacher praised a correct student response
	−+	Teacher identified an incorrect response but dignified the error
	−−	Teacher identified an incorrect response and was critical of the error
	+	Teacher was positive but with no affect
	−	Teacher was negative but with no affect

believed that teachers could be easily tempted into doing this as the pressures of teaching increase and wrote that "he wanted to avoid falling into this trap —or to get out of the trap if I've already fallen in it" (p. 2).

Second, David had studied gender differences in mathematics participation and written a paper on that topic for one of his college classes. He knew that some teachers show differential treatment to boys as compared to girls. He also had observed in a journal he kept that he was able to learn the names of the boys in his classes more readily than the names of the girls. So he wondered, "Will I be surprised to find that I differentiate between boys and girls in the questions I ask and the feedback I provide?" (p. 3).

David's Data Collection Methods

To carry out his study, David made five audiotapes and one videotape of lessons he identified in advance as those where he planned to have considerable teacher-student interaction. In addition, a week prior to taping, David identified the names of five students in the class whom he perceived to be high achievers and five whom he perceived to be low achievers. These perceptions were based on 4 weeks

of experience with his students and knowing how well they did in mathematics. He reported, however, that he "quickly put this list away and tried not to think about it anymore until the taping was finished" (p. 4). David knew if the names became too embedded in his mind it could bias his interactions and diminish the value of the information he was about to collect.

Once he had his videotapes and audiotapes, David constructed and used a data sheet as shown in Figure R2-4 to analyze his interaction with students.

David's Results and Interpretations

After organizing his data and putting them in table format, David found that indeed he was showing slight differential treatment for high achievers as contrasted to low achievers and to boys as contrasted to girls. What is most interesting about David's action research project, however, is his careful and thoughtful interpretation of these data. His own words says it better than any summary: "There were certain areas where my treatment was not equitable (high- and low-order questions and the no-response, praise, and incorrect/dignified types of feedback)" (p. 7). David did not conclude from this information, however, that his differential treatment of students was necessarily bad teaching or unfair. Instead, he thought about what it meant and posed a question that even many professional researchers have ignored: "Is differential treatment always undesirable?"

> One important question which must be dealt with at the outset is whether an equal distribution of response opportunities, types of questions, and feedback is indeed desirable when comparing my treatment of perceived high achievers and perceived low achievers. Low achievers, high achievers and midrange achievers have different needs and may therefore require some kind of differential treatment: for example, low achievers may need more response opportunities, a more judicious blend of high-order and low-order questions, more praise—as long as it is measured and sincere—and more "dignifying" follow-up to incorrect responses. If I perceive certain students to be low achievers, would I be aiming at equal treatment of them vis-à-vis those I perceive to be high achievers, or *should I develop a more sophisticated approach to both the low achievers and the high achievers?*
>
> A case then can be made for differential treatment of high and low achievers. The problem is, however, that when educational researchers find such differential treatment it often goes in the wrong direction—that is, it is often biased against low achievers. I refer, for example, to the work of Good and Brophy (1987). While equal treatment may not be ideal, it is nevertheless better than differential treatment that works against those who are perceived to be most in need of help. (p. 11)

So, David has concluded that differential treatment may be desired as long as it is meeting individual needs and not always going against those of low ability. He turns next to his differential treatment of boys and girls and in this instance reaches a different conclusion.

> Differential treatment on the basis of sex would seem to be much less defensible than differential treatment for perceived high and low achievers. What is significant in my results is that even though not great, it is the fact that in each case the imbalance in my treatment favored the boys: proportionately more of the total response opportunities went to boys, proportionately more high-order questions went to boys and substantially more low-order questions went to the girls. Again, while the differential is not large, the imbalance in all three instances works to the detriment of girls. Given the generally lower participation and achievement of girls in mathematics at higher levels, *I would have felt better had the imbalance gone the other way* (p. 13).

Finally, David concludes his thoughts about his action research project and sets some goals for his teaching behavior in the future.

> As I teach, I do not consciously think in terms of categories such as perceived high and low achievers and boys and girls. Nevertheless, the patterns found in the types of teacher-student interaction I studied in my action research indicated that, in some cases, I am interacting with students on the basis of these categorizations rather than on the basis of the individual student and thus may be communicating to them certain expectations for their performance based on these categorizations.
>
> I am, now, as a result of this action research, more sensitive to the many ways that this can be done. I now must work to keep this sensitivity alive and ensure that I apply it in my teaching in the years ahead. (p. 13)

For those who choose to become students of their own teaching, David's action research project can be a model to follow. He chose to study a problem—differential treatment of students—which has been of concern to professional researchers for over two decades. It is also a problem for which teachers, regardless of their good intentions, find discrepancies between what they believe and what they actually do. David's use of audio and video recordings, along with the rather simple but effective coding scheme, produced objective information about his teaching behavior. The limited scope of the study and its overall design conform to the principles for action research described by Hopkins (1985). Most important, David's thoughtful interpretation of his results shows the significant progress he has made in his young career toward becoming a reflective, autonomous professional.

UNIT 3
OBSERVATION, REFLECTION, AND MICROTEACHING

There are some aspects of teaching that can be learned in a college classroom; others can be learned by studying what researchers and experienced teachers have to say about the topic. However, many of the most important features of the art of professional practice can be learned only through experience. This resource unit describes how you can learn from your experiences while you are still in your teacher preparation program and beginning years of your career. It reinforces a point of view described in Chapter 1: learning to teach is a lifelong process and effective teachers become that way by having a learning agenda for lifelong growth coupled with careful analysis and reflection that produces this growth. Three facets of learning from experience are described here: (1) the nature of experiential learning, (2) developing the receptive skills—listening and observing—that promote learning from experience, and (3) critical review and reflection.

NATURE OF EXPERIENTIAL LEARNING

Everyone learns from experience and knows that experience is a basis for new ideas and behavior. For example, you probably learned to ride your first bicycle by riding one, and you learned about being a sister or brother by being one. Similarly, most people have learned a great deal about teaching by the informal teaching they have done in their day-to-day lives. Conversely, even though everyone can read books about marriage and child rearing, those who have married and raised children know that it is never the same as described in the books. Experience provides insights, understandings, and techniques that are difficult to describe to anyone who has not had similar experiences. The same is true for teaching.

Experiential learning differs from much of the learning people are exposed to as students. Instead of starting with a set of academic principles or rules, in experiential learning learners start with concrete experiences, or activities, and then, by observing

their own behavior and that of others, formulate concepts and principles that can be applied to new situations. This perspective is illustrated in Figure R3-1.

Dewey (1938) suggested that to learn from experience is to make a backward-forward connection between what we do to things and what we learn from these things and experiences. Johnson and Johnson (1975) have provided a more detailed explanation:

> Experiential learning is based upon three assumptions: that you learn best when you are personally involved in the learning experience, that knowledge has to be discovered by yourself if it is to mean anything to you or make a difference in your behavior, and that a commitment to learning is highest when you are free to set your own learning goals and actively pursue them within a given framework. Experiential learning is a process of making generalizations and conclusions about your own direct experiences. It emphasizes directly experiencing what you are studying, building your own commitment to learn, and your being partly responsible for organizing the conclusions drawn from your experiences. (p. 7)

Experiential learning is especially useful in complex learning situations such as teaching, which can never be completely described to the beginner. It is also useful for applying many of the skills and guidelines described in this book.

Experience alone, however, is not sufficient. For best results, the learner must be willing to depend less upon the teacher than in other types of learning. The learner must have a set of "learning skills," that is, must be able to observe and reflect on experiences in order to conceptualize from them. The following sections describe some of these skills in more detail.

TRAINING THE SENSES FOR EXPERIENTIAL LEARNING

People learn from experience primarily through their senses. Two are of particular importance for learning to teach—listening critically and observing keenly. These come together through reflective thinking and analysis.

Figure R3-1   Cyclical nature of experiential learning

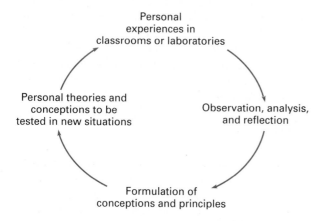

Listening

Learning to listen carefully and pick up subtle cues from experienced, expert teachers is one important skill for those learning to teach. On the surface, listening appears simple but, in fact, it is a rather complex, sophisticated process. Jung (1972) has written that most people strike one of three listening postures when they hear new information or are experiencing a new environment for the first time:

LISTENING TO CONFIRM

The first listening posture, and by far the most common, is to listen for information that confirms what you already know. Although such information can be important, such a posture is obviously limiting. You may think that a person who says things you already believe is pretty smart, but you don't really learn much from what you hear. If your posture is only to listen for supporting comments, you may actively distort the meanings of what others say.

LISTENING TO ANSWER QUESTIONS

The second listening posture, one which seems fairly rare, is to seek answers to honest questions. When you recognize a discrepancy or dilemma for which you personally need an answer, you can formulate honest questions about it. Often the need for certainty in our lives makes us uncomfortable with honest questions, so we either discredit the questions or seek only superficial answers. If, however,

you seek answers to honest questions, you are likely to hear more and differently than those who do not. Honest questions that are not simply critical doubting give direction to listening and new meanings to information. However, questions also have a limiting effect. They tend to limit your attention to information that seems relevant to your questions, a process referred to as selective perception. Also questions invite certain interpretations of information to the exclusion of other possibilities. They tend to create a "set" for understanding.

LISTENING TO CONFRONT

The third listening posture, which is very rare, involves being open to information as a means of creating new insights and perspectives. How many people saw apples fall before Newton conceived the laws of gravity? In a world of continuous, accelerating change and awesome technologies, it is essential that we listen for new understandings and new ways to comprehend our experience. Paradoxically, we simultaneously sense that our ways of experiencing are limited yet believe that the basis for all human understanding already lies within our experiences.

Observing

Although classroom observation is one of the most frequently used ways to learn about teaching, observation alone is insufficient and can, in fact, lead to incorrect conclusions. This is true for several reasons, two of which are most important. First, when you go into a classroom to observe you take with you a whole set of anxieties and biases from past experiences, and, second, life in classrooms is a series of rapidly moving, complex events. Each of these problems is described in more detail in the sections that follow.

BIAS AND ANXIETY

You are all aware of many instances in everyday life in which bias and anxiety distort people's perceptions. Note the number of times that victims or eyewitnesses of criminal acts are unable to give investigators a detailed or complete description of the event, even moments after it occurred. Or think of the times that the wrong person is picked out of a police lineup. Think also of the times that you have heard two friends tell you about what they saw on their vacation, and the wide discrepancies in their reports.

Being an eyewitness of classroom events is no different from witnessing other events, except it may be a bit more complicated. Every person in the process of learning to teach has biases that influence what he or she attends to while observing classrooms. These may concern concepts of good teaching or, perhaps, values about what is appropriate behavior for children and young adults. They may be attitudes about classroom life carried over from early experiences as a student—a sense of boredom and withdrawal associated with a grammar lesson or antipathy to a teacher with a gruff voice. The important point is that these concepts, values, attitudes, and past experiences inevitably influence what an observer perceives and learns from classroom observation.

Anxiety is another important influence, particularly for beginning teachers. When people are nervous and anxious in a situation, their vision and perceptual fields tend to narrow, and they miss much that they normally would attend to. When beginning teachers are observers in someone else's classroom, it is natural for them to be unsure and to worry, "Are we intruding on the teacher's lesson? Why are the children looking at us?" Similarly, initial teaching situations are stressful, anxiety producing, uncomfortable. A normal reaction is to distort what is observed and, many times, to ignore threatening information.

CLASSROOM COMPLEXITY

Finally, it is difficult to observe accurately in classrooms because events move rapidly and the total classroom environment is complex. Philip Jackson (1968) has observed that teachers have literally thousands of independent interactions daily with students—more interactions with clients than occur in any other occupation except perhaps air traffic controlling. Classrooms with teacher aides and ones where teachers have several small groups working simultaneously present even more rapid movement and complexity.

GUIDELINES FOR OBSERVING IN CLASSROOMS

Several things can be done to overcome bias in observation and to reduce the complexity of classroom life. If followed, they can make observations more accurate and more valuable as learning experiences. Several guidelines are offered below that have been found useful by beginning teachers as well as researchers (see, for example, Good and Brophy, 1987).

Become Aware of One's Own Values, Attitudes, and Conceptual Blinders. People never become completely aware of the attitudes and prejudices they hold, just as they are never completely aware of the sources of daily fears and anxieties. However, setting aside time now and then for self-reflection and introspection heightens awareness.

Make Careful Arrangements with Teachers Prior to Observations. Careful arrangements prior to a visit will relieve some of the anxiety associated with observations in a strange classroom. A talk with the teacher, either in person or over the phone, a few days prior to a visit will help clarify expectations about what you want to accomplish as an observer and about how the teacher wants you to behave during the visit. Arrangements can be made about where you should sit, how you are to be introduced to the class, and so on.

Reduce Complexity by Focusing Observations. Even the most experienced observers cannot see everything going on in a classroom, so they focus on particular events or behaviors. This is particularly important for the beginner. One does this either by observing a *few of the actors* in the classroom—four or five students rather than the whole class—or watching for a *few behaviors* at a time, such as the way students respond to a teacher's questions or praise. In the learning aid sections of this book several recommendations are provided for focusing classroom observations by reducing complexity.

Attend Only to Observable Behaviors. A very common cause of distortion in what a person sees is that too often the observer tries to interpret motives from behavior instead of just observing it. Take, for example, the following written notes from an observation.

The teacher spoke in a loud voice and frowned.
The teacher was angry with the children.

The first is an example of what the observer actually saw. The second is an interpretation of the teacher's feelings. Observers should concentrate on observable behavior, as in the first example.

Remain Unobtrusive during Observations. Harry Walcott, a noted educational anthropologist, says that when he is observing people in any social setting he keeps his eyes on his paper and his pencil going all the time. This is important advice for classroom observers. A note taken once in a while cues teachers and students about what the observer is looking for. Making eye contact with students in class increases the chances of their wanting to interact with the observer, thus interrupting the observer's concentration and perhaps the teacher's lesson.

Extend a Thank You to the Teacher and to the Students (If Appropriate) after Your Observation. Observers are guests in classrooms. A thank you is required just as it would be to a friend at whose home you spent a weekend.

Figure R3-2 provides a checklist for you to follow when arranging for a classroom observation.

MICROTEACHING

Listening and observing in classrooms is one form of experience. Another is actual practice in scaled-down situations called microteaching. In **microteaching** you arrange to teach a brief lesson to a small group of students in an actual classroom or you teach a short lesson to your peers. Microteaching is an invaluable experiential process for learning to teach and for helping you begin to consolidate your teaching knowledge and skill. It is an effective means of offering practice and feedback and an activity that is valued very highly by beginning teachers who participate in it. As in anything else, micro-

teaching requires planning and organizing to ensure its success. The following guidelines are offered to assist you in your planning for microteaching whether as a part of your teacher education program or something you decide to arrange on your own.

1. **Microteaching requires a small-group setup:** Microteaching is best accomplished with groups of six to eight students or peers. If using peers, each group needs a facilitator. This can be one of your peers, a professor, or a clinical teacher. The role of the facilitator is to ensure that all microteachers have adequate time to give their lesson and to receive feedback.
2. **Microteaching with peers requires a large chunk of time:** Each microteacher needs enough time to adequately present a brief lesson and receive feedback on it. Generally, lesson presentations run about 10 to 12 minutes, followed by 5 to 10 minutes of feedback from peers or students and the facilitator. This means that $2\frac{1}{2}$ to 3 hours must be set aside for each microteaching if six to ten persons are involved. In actual classrooms, with just one person microteaching, less time is required.
3. **Special equipment is needed:** Ideally a microteaching lab should be available and many colleges and universities have this type of facility. The lab should be outfitted with a video camera and recording equipment and should contain the audiovisual supplies usually found in classrooms (for example, overhead projector and screen, chalkboard, chalk, and erasers) for use by students in their presentations. Microteachers need to bring a blank tape with them so their lessons can be recorded for later use. In a laboratory where microteaching is being done with peers, the job of recording each lesson can be rotated. In a real classroom, the teacher or one of the students can be asked to assist with recording the lesson.

   If a special room set aside for microteaching cannot be arranged, a roll-around video recording system or camcorder can be arranged. With a roll-around, the camera and recorder system are lodged on a cart and wheeled to rooms where microteaching sections are to be held. If

Figure R3-2 Checklist for arranging and observing in classrooms

---

Arranging for Classroom Visit

_____ Called teacher or appropriate person prior to visit

_____ Checked map to ensure timely arrival

_____ Found out time class begins and topic of lesson to view

_____ Decided on classroom actors to observe (teacher, students, few students, aides, etc.)

_____ Decided on behaviors to observe

_____ Collected observational schedule if appropriate

_____ Planned strategy to remain unobtrusive (note taking, seating, avoiding eye contact with students)

_____ Prepared a note to the teacher and class thanking them for the visit

---

video is not at all feasible, audio recording can be used as a last resort.

4. **Feedback is a vital element of microteaching:** Whether you are microteaching with real students or peers, feedback on the lesson is critical. Feedback should be specific and should include both recognition for good performance and constructive criticism. Comments such as "I liked how you projected enthusiasm with all your gesturing," or "It would have been easier to understand your advance organizer if you had provided a visual aid" are much more useful than a general "I enjoyed your lesson." If real students are being asked to provide feedback, they will need to be given explicit directions on how to provide feedback. Chapter 10 contains information on how to give feedback.

   If you are using microteaching to practice one of the models described in Chapters 8 to 13 in *Learning to Teach*, it will be helpful to use the appropriate observation instruments provided at the end of each chapter as a guide. Students or your peers can fill out the instrument as they follow the lesson and recall the particulars during the feedback phase, and you will have something concrete to take away and reflect upon.

5. **Don't forget analysis and reflection:** A microteaching practice session will be of most value if you watch the videotape of your lesson and reflect on the feedback you received. Some-

times a short written critique about how the lesson went, incorporating the feedback you received, is a good learning device.

REFLECTION AND JOURNALING

Through reflection, experiences become more valuable. It is when teachers start to conceptualize and formulate their own rules and principles that they start to build personal theories that can guide teaching practice and serve as springboards for new discoveries. But how does one begin reflecting? Although reflective thinking is not a haphazard trial-and-error process, neither can it be scheduled to happen every morning at 9:15 A.M., as jogging can be.

One of the most productive ways to foster reflective thinking is by using a journal. Here is advice to beginning teachers provided by Frank Lyman (1983), a teacher educator at the University of Maryland, about how to approach the process of reflection:

A person learns by experience. However, for the fastest, most advanced learning to take place, disciplined reflection is necessary. Experience is not the best teacher; reflection, or analysis, is. There are many ways to reflect on experience and it is helpful to try out several. During student teaching, you will master one way and be invited to invent others. The journaling strategy is the prescribed way. Use it four times a week. For the fifth entry use any format to probe an issue re-

Figure R3-3   Guidelines for journaling

A person learns by experience. However, for the fastest, most advanced learning to take place, disciplined reflection is necessary. Experience is not the best teacher; reflection or analysis is. There are many ways to reflect on experience. It is helpful to try out several. Start with the following strategy and use it for one week. When you make a journal entry, try to include content from each category.

Model for Journal Strategy

Content	Example
Brief description of teaching/learning event	A small group discussion on . . . in which I . . . the children . . . connected to literature.
Some consequences (effects, outcomes) of the event	Very few listened to directions . . . Most were on task in the pair talk . . . About 60% got the concept.
Value (worthiness of outcomes and projected outcomes)	It is important for children to consider connections between themselves and book characters, because . . .
Some causes of success and/or failure	Interaction pattern Relevance (stories they like) Zoning (seating arrangements) Social considerations (pairing) Abstract/concrete
Some next steps	Allow free pattern of talk Maintain relevant examples Change seating Reduce potential friction in pairing Connect examples to ideas
Some hypothetical principles	If pairs are allowed to speak freely, both individuals will talk more in pairs. People learn those things they can connect to their own experience. Extreme extroverts will show off less when seated in less central positions. The more that pairing in a group is made of friends, the easier it is to manage the pair mode. Learning of concepts proceeds best when sufficient concrete examples are connected to an abstract idea.
Analogs, if any	This event reminds me of what happened in a Sunday School class . . .
Questions for inquiry	What is the difference in involvement when pairs talk freely as opposed to when they follow a certain interaction pattern? What happens during directions when children have eye contact with each other?

SOURCE: Adapted from F. Lyman (1983), *Journaling procedures.* (Mimeographed.) College Park, Maryland: University of Maryland.

lated to curriculum/instruction/school climate. (If you can invent an effective strategy for analyzing a teaching/learning event, show me.) (p. 1)

More information about Lyman's reflective journaling strategy is provided in Figure R3-3.

LEARNING FROM COLLEAGUES

A final source of experiential learning for beginning teachers is the learning that comes from interaction with colleagues and at professional meetings. Unfortunately, many beginning teachers do not seem to have good professional networks and do not regularly attend professional meetings. It is important for beginning teachers to set goals for themselves early in their careers which will help guide professional experiences and growth. At the end of this resource unit is a list of the names and addresses of several professional organizations that have meetings nationally and locally where teachers can learn about research and interact with colleagues. An example of such a professional organization is the Association for Supervision and Curriculum Development (ASCD). This organization publishes a monthly journal, *Educational Leadership*, that contains many interpretive articles on research. The organization also has local units in every state that produce newsletters and hold regular meetings of interest to teachers. Phi Delta Kappa also provides similar services to teachers, as do the National Education Association, the American Federation of Teachers, and many subject-specialty associations. The beginning teacher who wants to grow will become a member of some of these associations and will build a network of colleagues interested in improving their teaching by keeping abreast of the latest research and practices.

PROFESSIONAL ASSOCIATIONS FOR TEACHERS

There are hundreds of associations whose purpose it is to help teachers and to improve education. This is a list of the names and addresses of several major associations. Although most of these are supported by membership dues, students and nonmembers can obtain information upon request. Many have reduced membership fees for university students who are in the process of learning to teach.

American Council on the Teaching of Foreign Languages (ACTFL)
579 Broadway
Hastings-on-Hudson, NY 10706
(914) 478-2011

Teachers, program directors, and organizations involved in classical and modern foreign language instruction at all levels of education.

Association for Education Communications and Technology (AECT)
1126 16th Street NW
Washington, DC 20036
(202) 466-4780

Professional organization for persons interested in instructional technology; contains nine specific area divisions. Educational affiliates: Association for Special Education Technology, Community College Association for Instruction and Technology, Health Education Media Association, International Visual Literacy Association, Women in Instructional Technology, Minorities in Media, and Consortium of University Film Centers.

American Educational Research Association (AERA)
1230 17th Street NW
Washington, DC 20036
(202) 223-9485

Professional organization for education researchers; membership is divided among 11 divisions, each specific to a field of education research.

American Federation of Teachers (AFT)
555 New Jersey Avenue NW
Washington, DC 20001
(202) 879-4400

Professional union comprising teachers and nonsupervisory school personnel. AFT supports a wide variety of research and development projects on in-service teacher training for professional development and instructional improvement.

American Home Economics Association (AHEA)
2010 Massachusetts Avenue NW
Washington, DC 20036
(218) 862-8300

Professional organization for all persons involved in home economics and home economics education.

Association for Supervision and Curriculum Development (ASCD)

225 N. Washington Street
Alexandria, VA 22039
(703) 549-9110

Professional organization of school principals, curriculum directors, administrators, and teachers at the elementary, secondary, and university levels involved in curriculum development, supervision, and instruction, and interested in leadership development.

International Reading Association (IRA)

P.O. Box 8139
800 Barksdale Road
Newark, DE 19714-8139
(302) 731-1600

Professional organization for teachers and administrators of reading programs at all educational levels and for teacher educators.

Journalism Education Association (JEA)

Box 99
Blue Springs, MO 64015
(816) 229-1666

Professional organization for secondary school journalism teachers and publications directors and for educators of journalism teachers.

Music Teachers National Association (MTNA)

441 Vine St., Suite 2113
Cincinnati, OH 45202
(513) 421-1420

Professional society of music teachers in elementary, secondary, and university public and private schools and studios.

National Art Education Association (NAEA)

1916 Association Drive
Reston, VA 22091
(703) 860-8000

Professional organization for teachers of art at all school levels; also member institutions: museums, libraries, and colleges.

National Council for the Social Studies (NCSS)

3501 Newark Street NW
Washington, DC 20016
(202) 966-7840

Professional organization for teachers of social studies: anthro-

pology, civics, economics, geography, history, political science, psychology, and sociology.

National Council of Teachers of English (NCTE)

1111 Kenyon Road
Urbana, IL 61801
(217) 328-3870

Professional organization for teachers of English at all educational levels and for professors of English education and administrators of language arts programs. Affiliated organizations: Conference on College Composition and Communication, Conference on Secondary School English Education, Conference for Secondary School English Department Chairs.

National Council of Teachers of Mathematics (NCTM)

1906 Association Drive
Reston, VA 22091
(703) 620-9840

Professional organization for teachers of mathematics K-12 and in two-year colleges and for educators of mathematics teachers.

National Education Association, Division of Instruction and Professional Development (NEA/IPD)

1201 16th Street NW
Washington, DC 20036
(202) 833-4000

NEA is a 1.7 million member teachers' union. Many special interest divisions conduct programs in teacher education; however the IPD division is most strongly dedicated to that area.

National Science Teachers Association (NSTA)

1742 Connecticut Avenue NW
Washington, DC 20009
(202) 328-5800

Professional organization for science educators at all educational levels.

National Vocational Agricultural Teachers' Association (NVATA)

P.O. Box 15051
Alexandria, VA 22309
(703) 780-1862

Professional organization for secondary, postsecondary, and adult education teachers of vocational agriculture and teacher education personnel.

Phi Delta Kappa (PDK)
Eighth and Union
P.O. Box 789
Bloomington, IN 47401
(812) 339-1156

Professional organization expanded from an honorary fraternity for educators at all levels.

Teachers of English to Speakers of Other Languages (TESOL)
1118 22nd St NW
Washington, DC 20057
(202) 872-1271

Professional organization for teachers of English as a second language at all levels. Organization has developed teacher certification standards adopted by state education agencies.

SOURCE: From the *Directory of Organizations Related to Teacher Education* (1986), Washington, DC: ERIC Clearinghouse on Teacher Education. Updated 1990.

UNIT 4
EDUCATIONAL LABORATORIES, RESEARCH CENTERS, AND CLEARINGHOUSES

EDUCATIONAL LABORATORIES AND RESEARCH CENTERS FUNDED BY THE UNITED STATES OFFICE OF EDUCATIONAL RESEARCH AND IMPROVEMENT

Regional Educational Laboratories

OERI helps educators and policymakers solve pressing education problems in their schools through a network of 10 regional educational laboratories. Using the best available information and the experience and expertise of professionals, the laboratories identify solutions to education problems, try new approaches, furnish research results and publications, and provide training to teachers and administrators. As part of their individual regional programs, all laboratories pay particular attention to the needs of at risk students and small rural schools. The 10 laboratories are:

Appalachia Educational Laboratory, Inc. (AEL)
Region Served: Kentucky, Tennessee, Virginia, and West Virginia
Executive Director: Terry L. Eidell
1031 Quarrier Street
P. O. Box 1348
Charleston, WV 25325
800-624-9120 (outside West Virginia)
800-344-6646 (in West Virginia)
304-347-0400, Fax 304-347-0487

Far West Laboratory for Educational Research and Development (FWL)
Region Served: Arizona, California, Nevada, and Utah
Executive Director: Dean H. Nafziger
730 Harrison Street
San Francisco, CA 94107-1242
415-565-3000, Fax 415-565-3012

Mid-continent Regional Educational Laboratory (McREL)
Region Served: Colorado, Kansas, Nebraska, Missouri, Wyoming, North Dakota, and South Dakota

Executive Director: C. L. Hutchins
Colorado Office:
2550 S. Parker Rd., Suite 500
Aurora, CO 80014
303-337-0990, Fax 303-337-3005
Missouri Office:
3100 Broadway, S. 209
Kansas City, MO 64111
816-756-2401, Fax 816-753-4565

North Central Regional Educational Laboratory (NCREL)
Region Served: Minnesota, Wisconsin, Iowa, Illinois, Michigan, Indiana, and Ohio
Executive Director: Jeri Nowakowski
1900 Spring Rd., Suite 300
Oak Brook, IL 60521
708-571-4700, Fax 708-571-4716

Northwest Regional Educational Laboratory (NWREL)
Region Served: Alaska, Idaho, Oregon, Montana, and Washington
Executive Director: Robert R. Rath
101 SW Main Street, Suite 500
Portland, OR 97204-3212
503-275-9500, Fax 503-275-9489

Pacific Region Educational Laboratory (PREL)
Region Served: American Samoa, Commonwealth of the Northern Mariana Islands, Federated States of Micronesia, Guam, Hawaii, Republic of the Marshall Islands, and Republic of Palau
Executive Director: John W. Kofel
1164 Bishop Street, Suite 1409
Honolulu, HI 96813
808-532-1900, Fax 808-532-1922

Regional Laboratory for Educational Improvement of the Northeast and Islands
Region Served: Connecticut, Maine, Massachusetts, New Hampshire, New York, Rhode Island, Vermont, Puerto Rico, and the Virgin Islands
Executive Director: David P. Crandall

300 Brickstone Square, Suite 900
Andover, MA 01810
508-470-0098, Fax 508-475-9220

Research for Better Schools, Inc. (RBS)
Region Served: Delaware, Maryland, New Jersey, Pennsylvania, and the District of Columbia
Executive Director: John E. Hopkins
444 North Third Street
Philadelphia, PA 19123-4107
215-574-9300, Fax 215-574-0133

SouthEastern Regional Vision for Education (SERVE)
Region Served: Alabama, Florida, Georgia, Mississippi, North Carolina, and South Carolina
Executive Director: Roy H. Forbes
Headquarters:
UNC at Greensboro
PO Box 5367
Greensboro, NC 27435
919-334-3211 or 800-755-3277
Fax 919-334-3268
Field Offices:
SERVE, Florida
345 S. Magnolia Dr., S. D-23
Tallahassee, FL 32301-2950
904-922-2300; 800-352-6001
Fax 904-922-2286
SERVE, Georgia
41 Marietta St. NW, S. 1000
Atlanta, GA 30303
404-577-7737; 800-659-3204
Fax 404-577-7812
SERVE, Mississippi
Delta State University, Box 3121
Cleveland, MS 38733
601-846-4400; 800-326-4548
Fax 601-846-4016

Southwest Educational Development Laboratory (SEDL)
Region Served: Arkansas, Louisiana, New Mexico, Oklahoma, and Texas
Executive Director: Preston C. Kronkosky
211 East Seventh Street
Austin, TX 78701
512-476-6861, Fax 512-476-2286

National Educational Research and Development Centers

To help strengthen student learning in the United States, OERI supports 25 university-based national educational research and development centers. The centers are conducting research on topics that will help policymakers, practitioners, and parents meet the national education goals by the year 2000. In addition to addressing specific topics, most also will focus on children at risk. Many are collaborating with other universities, and many work with elementary and secondary schools. All have been encouraged by OERI to make sure the information they produce reaches parents, teachers, and others who can use it to make meaningful changes in America's schools. The 25 centers and their collaborating partners are:

Center on Families, Communities, Schools, and Children's Learning
Boston University
605 Commonwealth Avenue
Boston, MA 02215
617-353-3309
Co-directors: Dr. Don Davies and Dr. Joyce Epstein
Affiliated Organizations: Institute for Responsive Education, Boston; Johns Hopkins University; University of Illinois at Urbana-Champaign; Wheelock College, Boston; and Yale University

National Research Center on Education in the Inner Cities
Temple University
933 Ritter Hall Annex
13th Street and Cecil B. Moore Avenue
Philadelphia, PA 19122
215-787-3001
Director: Dr. Margaret C. Wang
Affiliated Organizations: University of Illinois at Chicago and University of Houston

Center for Research on Effective Schooling for Disadvantaged Students
Johns Hopkins University
3505 North Charles Street
Baltimore, MD 21218
410-516-0370
Director: Dr. Jomills H. Braddock II

Affiliated Organizations: University of California at Santa Barbara; Northern Arizona University; Teachers College, Columbia University; and Council of Chief State School Officers, Washington, DC

**National Research Center on
the Gifted and Talented
University of Connecticut at Storrs
Department of Educational Psychology**
Storrs, CT 06269
203-486-5279
Director: Dr. Joseph Renzulli
Affiliated Organizations: University of Georgia, University of Virginia, and Yale University

**National Research Center on
Cultural Diversity and Second
Language Learning**
University of California at Santa Cruz
Kerr Hall
Santa Cruz, CA 95064
408-459-3501
Co-directors: Dr. Eugene Garcia and
  Dr. Barry McLaughlin
Affiliated Organizations: Linguistic Minority Research Project of the University of California and Center for Applied Linguistics, Washington, DC

**National Center for Research
on Educational Accountability
and Teacher Evaluation**
Western Michigan University
401 B. Ellsworth Hall
Kalamazoo, MI 49008
616-387-5895
Director: Dr. Daniel Stufflebeam
Affiliated Organizations: University of Alabama at Tuscaloosa, College of William and Mary, and University of South Florida

**National Center for Research
on Teacher Learning**
Michigan State University
College of Education
116 Erikson Hall
East Lansing, MI 48824-1034
517-355-9302
Director: Dr. Mary Kennedy
Affiliated Organizations: University of Wisconsin at Madison and Education Matters, Inc., Boston

**National Center on
Postsecondary Teaching,
Learning, and Assessment**
Pennsylvania State University
Center for the Study of Higher Education
403 S. Allen Street, Suite 104
University Park, PA 16801-5202
814-865-5917
Co-Directors: Dr. James L. Ratcliff and
  Dr. Patrick T. Terenzini
Affiliated Organizations: University of Illinois at Chicago, Syracuse University, Northwestern University, University of Tennessee at Knoxville, and Arizona State University

**Center for Research on the
Context of Secondary School
Teaching**
Stanford University
School of Education
CERAS
Stanford, CA 94305-3084
415-723-4972
Director: Dr. Milbrey W. McLaughlin
Affiliated Organization: Michigan State University

**Center for Research on
Evaluation, Standards, and
Student Testing (CRESST)**
University of California at Los Angeles
Center for the Study of Evaluation
145 Moore Hall
Los Angeles, CA 90024-1522
213-206-1530
Co-directors: Dr. Eva Baker and
  Dr. Robert L. Linn
Affiliated Organizations: University of Colorado; RAND Corporation, Washington, DC; National Opinion Research Center, University of Chicago; and Learning Resource Development Center, University of Pittsburgh

**National Research Center on
Student Learning**
University of Pittsburgh
Learning Research and Development
  Center
3939 O'Hara Street
Pittsburgh, PA 15260
412-624-7450
Co-directors: Dr. Robert Glaser, Dr. Lauren Resnick, and
  Dr. James Voss
Affiliated Organizations: None

**Center for the Learning and
Teaching of Elementary
Subjects**
Michigan State University
College of Education
East Lansing, MI 48824
517-353-6470
Co-directors: Dr. Jere Brophy and
   Dr. Penelope L. Peterson
Affiliated Organizations: None

**National Center for Science
Teaching and Learning**
Ohio State University
Room 104, Research Center
1314 Kinnear Road
Columbus, OH 43212-1194
614-292-3339
Co-directors: Dr. Arthur L. White and
   Dr. Michael H. Klapper
Affiliated Organizations: None

**National Center for Research
in Mathematical Sciences
Education**
University of Wisconsin at Madison
Wisconsin Center for Education
   Research
1025 West Johnson Street
Madison, WI 53706
608-263-4285
Director: Dr. Thomas Romberg
Affiliated Organizations: Harvard University and San
Diego State University

**Center for Technology in
Education**
Bank Street College of Education
610 West 112th Street
New York, NY 10025
212-222-6700
Director: Dr. Jan Hawkins
Affiliated Organizations: Bolt, Beranek, & Newman, Inc.,
Cambridge, MA; Brown University; and Harvard
University

**National Center on Adult
Literacy**
University of Pennsylvania
Graduate School of Education
3700 Walnut Street
Philadelphia, PA 19104-6216

215-898-2100
Director: Dr. Daniel Wagner
Affiliated Organizations: Center for Applied Linguistics,
Washington, DC; City University of New York;
Educational Testing Service, Princeton, NJ; Indiana
University; Johns Hopkins University; National Center
for Family Literacy, Louisville, KY; Northwest Regional
Laboratory, Portland, OR; University of California at
Santa Barbara; and University of Delaware

**National Center on the
Educational Quality of the
Workforce**
University of Pennsylvania
Institute for Research on Higher
   Education
4200 Pine Street
Philadelphia, PA 19104-4090
215-898-4585
Co-directors: Dr. Robert M. Zemsky and
   Dr. Peter Cappelli
Affiliated Organizations: Wharton School, University of
Pennsylvania and Cornell University

**National Center for the Study
of Writing and Literacy**
University of California at Berkeley
School of Education
5513 Tolman Hall
Berkeley, CA 94720
415-643-7022
Director: Dr. Sarah W. Freedman
Affiliated Organization: Carnegie Mellon University,
National Writing Project

**National Research Center on
Literature Teaching and
Learning**
State University of New York at Albany
School of Education
1400 Washington Avenue
Albany, NY 12222
518-442-5026
Director: Dr. Arthur N. Applebee
Affiliated Organizations: None

National Reading Research Center
University of Georgia
Graduate Studies Research Center
Rm. 621
Athens, GA 30602
404-542-2718

Co-Directors: Dr. Donna E. Alvermann
and Dr. John T. Guthrie
Affiliated Organization: University of Maryland at College Park

**The Finance Center of the
Consortium for Policy
Research in Education**
University of Southern California
School of Education
Waite Phillips Hall 901
Los Angeles, CA 90089-0031
213-740-3299
Co-directors: Dr. Allan Odden and
Dr. Susan Fuhrman
Affiliated Organizations: Rutgers University; Michigan State University; Stanford University; University of Wisconsin at Madison; Harvard University; Cornell University; SMB Economics, Washington, DC; and Educational Testing Service, Princeton, NJ

**National Center for Education
Leadership**
Harvard University
Gutman Library
6 Appian Way
Cambridge, MA 02138-3704
617-495-3575
Co-directors: Dr. Lee G. Bolman and
Dr. Terrence E. Deal
Affiliated Organizations: Vanderbilt University and University of Chicago

**Center on Organization and
Restructuring of Schools**
University of Wisconsin at Madison
Wisconsin Center for Education
Research
1025 West Johnson Street
Madison, WI 53706
608-263-7575
Director: Dr. Fred M. Newmann
Affiliated Organizations: University of Minnesota, Harvard University, University of Pennsylvania, Stanford University, and University of Chicago

**The Policy Center of the
Consortium for Policy
Research in Education**
Eagleton Institute of Politics
Rutgers University
90 Clifton Avenue
New Brunswick, NJ 08901-1568

908-828-3872
Director: Dr. Susan Fuhrman
Affiliated Organizations: Harvard University, Michigan State University, Stanford University, and University of Wisconsin at Madison

**National Center for School
Leadership**
University of Illinois at
Urbana-Champaign
College of Education
1208 West Springfield Avenue
Urbana, IL 61801
217-244-1122 or 800-356-0069
Director: Dr. Paul W. Thurston
Affiliated Organizations: University of Michigan; Metritech, Inc. at Urbana, IL; and Illinois State Board of Education

EDUCATIONAL RESEARCH INFORMATION CLEARINGHOUSES

The ERIC Clearinghouses have responsibility within the network for acquiring the significant educational literature within their particular areas, selecting the highest quality and most relevant material, processing (i.e., cataloging, indexing, abstracting) the selected items for input to the database, and also for providing information analysis products and various user services based on the database.

The exact number of Clearinghouses has fluctuated over time in response to the shifting needs of the educational community. There are currently 16 Clearinghouses. These are listed below, together with full addresses, telephone numbers, and brief scope notes describing the areas they cover.

**Educational Resources Information Center
(Central ERIC)**
U.S. Department of Education
Office of Educational Research and Improvement (OERI)
555 New Jersey Avenue, N.W.
Washington, DC 20208-5720
202-219-2289, Fax 202-219-1817

ERIC Clearinghouse on *Adult, Career, and Vocational Education* (CE)
Ohio State University
Center on Education and Training for Employment

1900 Kenny Road
Columbus, OH 43210-1090
614-292-4353, 800-848-4815; Fax 614-292-1260

All levels of adult and continuing education from basic literacy training through professional skill upgrading. The focus is upon factors contributing to the purposeful learning of adults in a variety of life situations usually related to adult roles (e.g., occupation, family, leisure time, citizenship, organizational relationships, retirement).

ERIC Clearinghouse on *Counseling and Personnel Services* (CG)
University of Michigan
School of Education, Room 2108
610 East University Street
Ann Arbor, MI 48109-1259
313-764-9492, Fax 313-747-2425

Preparation, practice, and supervision of counselors at all educational levels and in all settings. Theoretical development of counseling and guidance, including the nature of relevant human characteristics. Use and results of personnel practices and procedures. Group process (counseling, therapy, dynamics) and case work.

ERIC Clearinghouse on *Educational Management* (EA)
University of Oregon
1787 Agate Street
Eugene, OR 97403-5207
503-346-5043, Fax 503-346-2334

All aspects of the governance, leadership, administration, and structure of public and private educational organizations at the elementary and secondary levels, including the provision of physical facilities for their operation.

ERIC Clearinghouse on *Elementary and Early Childhood Education* (PS)
University of Illinois
805 W. Pennsylvania Avenue
Urbana, IL 61801-4897
217-333-1386, Fax 217-333-3767

All aspects of the physical, cognitive, social, emotional, educational, and cultural development of children, from birth through early adolescence. Among the topics covered are: prenatal and infant development and care, parent education, home and school relationships, learning theory research and practice related to children's development, preparation of early childhood teachers and caregivers, and educational programs and community services for children.

ERIC Clearinghouse on *Handicapped and Gifted Children* (EC)
Council for Exceptional Children

1920 Association Drive
Reston, VA 22091-1589
703-264-9474, Fax 703-264-9494

All aspects of the education and development of persons (of all ages) who have disabilities or who are gifted, including the delivery of all types of education-related services to these groups. Includes prevention, identification and assessment, intervention, and enrichment for these groups, in both regular and special education settings.

ERIC Clearinghouse on *Higher Education* (HE)
George Washington University
One Dupont Circle, N.W., Suite 630
Washington, DC 20036-1183
202-296-2597, Fax 202-296-8379

All aspects of the conditions, programs, and problems at colleges and universities providing higher education (i.e., four-year degrees and beyond). This includes: governance and management, planning, finance, interinstitutional arrangements, business or industry programs leading to a degree, institutional research at the college/university level, federal programs, legal issues and legislation, professional education (e.g., medicine, law), and professional continuing education.

ERIC Clearinghouse on *Information Resources* (IR)
Syracuse University
Huntington Hall, Room 030
800 University Avenue
Syracuse, NY 13244-2340
315-443-3640, Fax 315-443-5448

Educational technology and library/information science at all academic levels and with all populations, including the preparation of professionals. The media and devices of educational communication, as they pertain to teaching and learning (in both conventional and distance education settings). The operation and management of libraries and information services. All aspects of information management and information technology related to education.

ERIC Clearinghouse for *Junior Colleges* (JC)
University of California at Los Angeles (UCLA)
Math-Sciences Building, Room 8118
405 Hilgard Avenue
Los Angeles, CA 90024-1564
310-825-3931, Fax 310-206-8095

Development, administration, and evaluation of two-year public and private community and junior colleges, technical institutes, and two-year branch university campuses. Two-year college students, faculty, staff, curricula, programs, support services, libraries, and community services. Linkages between two-year colleges and business/industrial/community organi-

zations. Articulation of two-year colleges with secondary and four-year postsecondary institutions.

ERIC Clearinghouse on *Languages and Linguistics* (FL)

Center for Applied Linguistics
1118 22nd Street, N.W.
Washington, DC 20037-0037
202-429-9292, Fax 202-659-5641

Languages and language sciences. All aspects of second language instruction and learning in all commonly and uncommonly taught languages, including English as a second language. Bilingualism and bilingual education. Cultural education in the context of second language learning, including intercultural communication, study abroad, and international educational exchange. All areas of linguistics, including theoretical and applied linguistics, sociolinguistics, and psycholinguistics.

ERIC Clearinghouse on *Reading and Communication Skills* (CS)

Indiana University, Smith Research Center
2805 East 10th Street, Suite 150
Bloomington, IN 47408-2698
812-855-5847, Fax 821-855-4220

Reading and writing, English (as a first language), and communications skills (verbal and nonverbal), kindergarten through college. Includes family or intergenerational literacy. Research and instructional development in reading, writing, speaking, and listening. Identification, diagnosis, and remediation of reading problems. Speech communication (including forensics), mass communication (including journalism), interpersonal and small group interaction, oral interpretation, rhetorical and communication theory, and theater/drama. Preparation of instructional staff and related personnel in all the above areas.

ERIC Clearinghouse on *Rural Education and Small Schools* (RC)

Appalachia Educational Laboratory
1031 Quarrier Street
P.O. Box 1348
Charleston, WV 25325-1348
800-624-9120 (Outside WV),
800-344-6646 (In WV); Fax 304-347-0487

Curriculum and instructional programs and research/evaluation efforts that address the education of students in rural schools or districts, small schools wherever located, and schools or districts wherever located that serve American Indian and Alaskan natives, Mexican Americans, and migrants, or that have programs related to outdoor education. Includes the cultural, ethnic, linguistic, economic, and social conditions that affect these educational institutions and groups. Preparation

programs, including related services, that train education professionals to work in such contexts.

ERIC Clearinghouse for *Science, Mathematics, and Environmental Education* (SE)

Ohio State University
1200 Chambers Road, Room 310
Columbus, OH 43212-1792
614-292-6717, Fax 614-292-0263

Science, mathematics, engineering/technology, and environmental education at all levels. The following topics when focused on any of the above broad scope areas: applications of learning theory, curriculum and instructional materials, teachers and teacher education, educational programs and projects, research and evaluative studies, applications of educational technology and media.

ERIC Clearinghouse for *Social Studies/Social Science Education* (SO)

Indiana University
Social Studies Development Center
2805 East 10th Street, Suite 120
Bloomington, IN 47408-2698
812-855-3838, Fax 812-855-0455

All aspects of social studies and social science education, including values education (and the social aspects of environmental education and sex education), international education, comparative education, and cross-cultural studies in all subject areas (K–12). Ethnic heritage, gender equity, aging, and social bias/discrimination topics. Also covered are music, art, and architecture as related to the fine arts.

ERIC Clearinghouse on *Teacher Education* (SP)

American Association of Colleges for Teacher Education (AACTE)
One Dupont Circle, N.W., Suite 610
Washington, DC 20036-1186
202-293-2450, Fax 202-457-8095

School personnel at all levels. Teacher recruitment, selection, licensing, certification, training, preservice and inservice preparation, evaluation, retention, and retirement. The theory, philosophy, and practice of teaching. Organization, administration, finance, and legal issues relating to teacher education programs and institutions. All aspects of health, physical, recreation, and dance education.

ERIC Clearinghouse on *Tests, Measurement, and Evaluation* (TM)

American Institutes for Research (AIR)
Washington Research Center
3333 K Street, N.W.
Washington, DC 20007-3541
202-342-5060, Fax 202-342-5033

All aspects of tests and other measurement devices. The design and methodology of research, measurement, and evaluation. The evaluation of programs and projects. The application of tests, measurement, and evaluation devices/instrumentation in educational projects and programs.

ERIC Clearinghouse on *Urban Education* (UD)
Teachers College, Columbia University
Institute for Urban and Minority Education
Main Hall, Room 300, Box 40
525 W. 120th Street
New York, NY 10027-9998

212-678-3433, Fax 212-678-4048

The educational characteristics and experiences of the diverse racial, ethnic, social class, and linguistic populations in urban (and suburban) schools. Curriculum and instruction of students from these populations and the organization of their schools. The relationship of urban schools to their communities. The social and economic conditions that affect the education of urban populations, with particular attention to factors that place urban students at risk educationally, and ways that public and private sector policies can improve these conditions.

References

Abi-Nader, J. (1991). Creating a vision of the future: Strategies for motivating minority students. *Phi Delta Kappan, 72,* 546–549.

Adams, R. S., and Biddle, B. J. (1970). *Realities of teaching: Exploration with videotape.* New York: Holt, Rinehart & Winston.

Air force's B-1 bomber. *Washington Post,* August 18, 1985.

Airasian, P. (1991). *Classroom assessment.* New York: McGraw-Hill.

Allen, V. (1991). Teaching bilingual and ESL children. In J. Flood, J. M. Jensen, D. Lapp, and J. R. Squire (eds.), *Handbook of research on teaching the English language arts.*

Allport, F. (1924). *Social psychology.* Boston: Houghton Mifflin.

Allport, G. (1954). *The nature of prejudice.* Cambridge, Mass.: Addison-Wesley.

Alschuler, A. S., Tabor, D., and McIntyre, J. (1970). *Teaching achievement motivation: Theory and practice in psychological education.* Middletown, Conn.: Education Ventures.

American Association of School Administrators. (1982). *Time on task.* Alexandria, Va.: Author.

American Educational Research Association, American Psychological Association, and National Council on Measurement in Education. (1985). *Standards for educational and psychological testing.* Washington, D.C.: American Psychological Association.

Anderson, C. W., and Smith, E. L. (1983). *Children's conceptions of light and color:* *Developing the concept of unseen rays.* Paper presented at the annual meeting of the American Educational Research Association, Montreal, Canada.

Anderson, R. C., Spiro, R., and Montague, W. (eds.). (1977). *Schooling and the acquisition of knowledge.* Hillsdale, N.J.: Erlbaum.

Anyon, J. (1980). Social class and the hidden curriculum of work. *Journal of Education, 162,* 67–69.

Arends, R. I. (1979). Evaluation of secondary teacher education graduates. (Mimeographed.) Eugene, Ore.: University of Oregon.

Argyris, C. (1970). *Intervention theory and method.* Reading, Mass.: Addison-Wesley.

Argyris, C., Putnam, R., and Smith, D. M. (1985). *Action science.* San Francisco: Jossey-Bass.

Aronson, E., Blaney, S. C., Sikes, J., and Snapp, M. (1978). *The Jigsaw classroom.* Beverly Hills, Calif.: Sage Publications.

Atkinson, J. W. (ed.). (1958). *Motives in fantasy, action and society.* New York: Van Nostrand.

Atkinson, J., and Feather, N. (1966). *A theory of achievement motivation.* New York: Wiley.

Ausubel, D. P. (1960). The use of advance organizers in the learning and retention of meaningful verbal material. *Journal of Educational Psychology, 51,* 267–272.

Ausubel, D. P. (1963). *The psychology of meaningful verbal learning.* New York: Grune & Stratton.

Bandura, A. (1977). *Social learning theory.* Englewood Cliffs, N.J.: Prentice-Hall.

Barker, R. G. (1968). *Ecological psychology.* Stanford, Calif.: Stanford University Press.

Barzun, J. (1991). *Begin here: The forgotten conditions of teaching and learning.* Chicago: University of Chicago Press.

Beane, J. A., Toepfer, C. F., and Alesi, S. J. (1986). *Curriculum planning and Development.* Newton, Mass.: Allyn and Bacon.

Berliner, D. C. (1982a). Recognizing instructional variables. In D. E. Orlosky (ed.), *Introduction to education.* Columbus: Charles E. Merrill.

Berliner, D. C. (1982b). *The executive functions of teaching.* Paper presented at Wingspread Conference on Relating Reading Research to Classroom Instruction, Racine, Wisc.

Berman, P., and McLaughlin, M. W. (1975). *Federal programs supporting education change. Vol. 4: The findings in review.* Santa Monica, Calif.: Rand Corporation.

Bettencourt, E. M. (1979). *Effects of training teachers in enthusiasm on student achievement and attitudes.* (Doctoral dissertation.) Eugene, Ore.: University of Oregon.

Biklen, D. (1985). *Achieving the complete school.* New York: Teachers College Press.

Bloom, B. S. (1976). *Human characteristics and school learning:* New York: McGraw-Hill.

Bloom, B. S. (ed.). (1956). *Taxonomy of edu-*

cational objectives. *Handbook 1: Cognitive domain.* New York: David McKay.

Bloom, B. S., Hastings, T. J., and Madaus, G. F. (1971). *Handbook on formative and summative evaluation of student learning.* New York: McGraw-Hill.

Bluestein, J. (1982). *The beginning teacher's resource handbook.* Albuquerque, N. M.: Instructional Support Services.

Borg, W. R., and Gall, M. D. (1983). *Educational research: An introduction* (4th ed.). New York: Longman.

Borko, H., and Niles, J. A. (1987). Descriptions of teacher planning: Ideas for teachers and researchers. In V. Richardson-Koehler (ed.), *Educators' handbook: A research perspective.* New York: Longman.

Bossert, S. T. (1985). Effective secondary schools. In R. Kyle (ed.), *Reaching for excellence: An effective schools sourcebook.* Washington, D.C.: U.S. Department of Education.

Boyer, E. L. (1983). *High school: A report on secondary education in America.* New York: Harper & Row.

Bozeman, M. (1985). *Signaling in the classroom.* (Mimeographed.) Salisbury, Md.: Salisbury State College.

Bramson, R. M. (1981). *Coping with difficult people.* New York: Random House.

Brenton, Myron (1970). *What's happened to teacher?* New York: Coward-McCann.

Brislin, R. W., Cushner, K., Cherrie, C., and Yong, M. (1986). *Intercultural interaction: A practical guide.* Beverly Hills, Calif.: Sage.

Brookover, W., Beady, C., Flood, P., Schweitzer, J., and Wisenbaker, J. (1979). *School social systems and student achievement: Schools can make a difference.* New York: Praeger.

Brophy, J. E. (1980). *Recent research on teaching.* East Lansing, Mich.: Institute for Research on Teaching, Michigan State University.

Brophy, J. E. (1981). Teacher praise: A functional analysis. *Review of Educational Research,* Spring, 5–32.

Brophy, J. E. (1983). Classroom organization and management. *The Elementary School Journal, 83,* 265–286.

Brophy, J. E., and Good, T. L. (1974). *Teacher-student relationships: Causes and consequences.* New York: Holt, Rinehart & Winston.

Brophy, J. E., and Good, T. L. (1986). Teacher behavior and student achieve-ment. In M. C. Wittrock (ed.), *Handbook of research on teaching* (3d ed.). New York: Macmillan.

Brophy, J. E., and Putnam, J. (1979). Classroom management in the early grades. In D. L. Duke (ed.), *Classroom management.* Chicago: University of Chicago Press.

Bruner, J. (1960). *The process of education.* Cambridge, Mass.: Harvard University Press.

Bruner, J. (1962). *On knowing: Essays for the left hand.* Cambridge, Mass.: Harvard University Press.

Bruner, J. (1966). *Toward a theory of instruction.* Cambridge, Mass.: Harvard University Press.

Bruner, J., Goodnow, J., and Austin, G. (1956). *A study of thinking.* New York: Wiley.

Bulletin of information. (1989). Princeton, N.J.: Educational Testing Service.

Burgess, D. M., and Streissguth, A. P. (1992). Fetal alcohol syndrome and fetal alcohol effects: Principles for educators. *Phi Delta Kappan, 74,* 24–30.

Calderhead, J. (1988). The development of knowledge structures in learning to teach. In J. Calderhead (ed.), *Teachers' professional learning.* London: Falmer Press.

Cangelosi, J. S. (1988). *Classroom management strategies: Gaining and maintaining students' cooperation.* New York: Longman.

Canter, L., and Canter, D. M. (1976). *Assertive discipline.* Los Angeles: Canter and Associates.

Carnegie Corporation. (1986). *A nation prepared: Teachers for the twenty-first century.* (1986). New York: Author.

Carroll, J. B. (1963). A model of school learning. *Teachers College Record, 64,* 723–733.

Cazden, C. B. (1972). *Child language and education.* New York: Holt, Rinehart & Winston.

Cazden, C. B. (1986). Classroom discourse. In M. C. Wittrock (ed.), *Handbook of research on teaching* (3d ed.). New York: Macmillan.

Cazden, C. B. (1988). *Classroom discourse.* Portsmouth, N.H.: Heinemann.

Cazden, C. B., and Mehan, H. (1989). Principles from sociology and anthropology: Context, code, classroom, and culture.In M. C. Reynolds (ed.), *Knowledge base for the beginning teacher.* New York: Pergamon Press.

Claiborn, W. L. (1969). Expectancy effects in the classroom: A failure to replicate. *Journal of Educational Psychology, 60,* 377–383.

Clark, C. M., and Lampert, M. (1986). The study of teacher thinking: Implications for teacher education. *Journal of Teacher Education, 37,* 27–31.

Clark, C. M., and Yinger, R. J. (1979). *Three studies of teacher planning.* East Lansing, Mich.: Institute for Research on Teaching, Michigan State University.

Clark, D. L., McKibbin, S., and Malkas, M. (1980). *New perspectives on planning in educational organizations.* San Francisco: Far West Laboratory for Educational Research and Development.

Clark, D. L., McKibbin, S., and Malkas, M. (1981). *Alternative perspectives for viewing educational organizations.* San Francisco: Far West Laboratory for Educational Research and Development.

Coats, E., and Smidchens, V. (1966). Audience recall as a function of speaker dynamism. *Journal of Education Psychology, 57,* 189–191.

Coleman, J. (1961). *The adolescent society.* New York: Free Press.

Coleman, J. (1972). The children have outgrown the schools. *Psychology Today,* February, 72–82.

Coleman, J., Campbell, E., Hobson, C., McPartland, J., Mood, A., Weinfield, F., and York, R. (1966). *Equality of educational opportunity.* Washington, D.C.: U.S. Government Printing Office.

College Entrance Examination Board (1985). *Equality and excellence: The educational status of black Americans.* New York: Author.

Collins, A. (1977). Processes in acquiring knowledge. In R. C. Anderson, R. J. Spiro, and W. E. Montague (eds.), *Schooling and the acquisition of knowledge.* Hillsdale, N.J.: Erlbaum.

Collins, A. M., and Quillan, M. R. (1969). Retrieval time from semantic memory. *Journal of Verbal Learning and Verbal Behavior. 8,* 124.

Collins, M. L. (1978). Effects of enthusiasm training on preservice elementary teachers. *Journal of Teacher Education, 29,* 53–57.

Combs, A. W. (1965). *The professional education of teachers.* Boston: Allyn & Bacon.

Comer, J. P. (1988). Educating poor minority children. *Scientific American, 259* (5), 42–48.

Concept to guide multicultural education. Charles County, Md., Teacher Corp Project, no date.

Cooper, H. (1989). *Homework*. New York: Longman.

Cooper, H. M., and Good, T. (1983). *Pygmalion grows up: Studies in the expectation communication process*. New York: Longman.

Copeland, W. D. (1980). Teaching-learning behaviors and the demands of the classroom environment. *Elementary School Journal, 80,* 163–177.

Costa, A. L. (1985). *Developing minds: A resource book for teaching thinking*. Alexandria, Va.: Association for Supervision and Curriculum Development.

Csikszentmihalyi, M. (1990). *Flow: The psychology of optimal experience*. New York: Harper and Row.

Cuban, L. (1982). Persistent instruction: The high school classroom, 1900–1980. *Phi Delta Kappan, 64,* 113–118.

Cuban, L. (1984). *How teachers taught: Constancy and change in American classrooms, 1900–1980*. New York: Longman.

Cullen, F. T., Cullen, J. B., Hayhow, V. L., and Plouffe, J. T. (1975). The effects of the use of grades as an incentive. *Journal of Educational Research, 68,* 277–279.

Cummins, J. (1981). The role of primary language development in promoting educational success for language minority students. In California State Department of Education, *Schooling and language minority students: A theoretical framework*. Los Angeles: National Evaluation, Disseminations, and Assessment Center, California State University.

Curtis, C. K., and Shaver, J. P. (1980). Slow learners and the study of contemporary problems. *Social Education, 44,* 302–309.

Cushner, K., McClelland, A., and Safford, P. (1992). *Human diversity in education: An integrative approach*. New York: McGraw-Hill.

Cypher, T., and Willower, D. J. (1984). The work behavior of secondary school teachers. *Journal of Research and Development, 18,* 17–24.

Dalin, P. (1978). *Limits to educational change*. London: Macmillan.

Dashiell, F. F. (1935). Experimental studies of the influence of social situations on the behavior of individual adults. In C. Murchison (ed.), *A handbook of social psychology*. Worcester, Mass.: Clark University Press.

Davidson, N. (ed.). (1989). *Cooperative learning in mathematics: A handbook for teachers*. Reading, Mass.: Addison-Wesley.

Denham, C., and Lieberman, A. (eds.). (1980). *Time to learn*. Washington, D.C.: U.S. Department of Education.

Dewey, J. (1916). *Democracy and education*. New York: Macmillan.

Dewey, J. (1929). *The quest for certainty*. New York: Minton, Balch.

Dewey, J. (1933). *How we think* (rev. ed.). Lexington, Mass.: D. C. Heath.

Dewey, J. (1938). *Experience and education*. New York: Macmillan.

Dilworth, M. E. (ed.). (1992). *Diversity in teacher education: New expectations*. San Francisco: Jossey-Bass.

Doyle, W. (1979). Classroom tasks and students' abilities. In P. L. Peterson and H. J. Walberg (eds.), *Research on teaching: Concepts, findings and implications*. Berkeley, Calif.: McCutchan.

Doyle, W. (1980). *Classroom management*. West Lafayette, Ind.: Kappa Delta Pi.

Doyle, W. (1986). Classroom organization and management. In M. C. Wittrock (ed.), *Handbook of research on teaching* (3d ed.). New York: Macmillan.

Doyle, W. (1990) Themes in teacher education research. In Houston, W. R. (ed.). *Handbook of Research on Teacher Education*. New York: Macmillan.

Doyle, W., and Carter, K. (1984). Academic tasks in classrooms. *Curriculum Inquiry, 14,* 129–149.

Dreikurs, R. (1968). *Psychology in the classroom: A manual for teachers* (2d ed.). New York: Harper & Row.

Dreikurs, R., and Grey, L. (1968). *A new approach to discipline: Logical consequences*. New York: Hawthorne Books.

Duchastel, P. C., and Brown, B. R. (1974). Incidental and relevant learning with instructional objectives. *Journal of Educational Psychology, 66,* 481–485.

Duckworth, E. (1987). *The having of wonderful ideas and other essays on teaching and learning*. New York: Teachers College Press.

Duckworth, E. (1991). Twenty-four, forty-two, and I love you: Keeping it complex. In K. Jervis, and C. Montag, (eds.), *Progressive education for the 1990s: Transforming practice*. New York: Teachers College Press.

Dunkin, M. J., and Biddle, B. J. (1974). *The study of teaching*. New York: Holt, Rinehart & Winston.

Edwards, D., and Mercer, N. (1987). *Common knowledge: The development of understanding in the classroom*. London: Methuen.

Egan, G. (1974). *The skilled helper: A model for systematic helping and interpersonal relationships*. Monterey, Calif.: Brooks/Cole.

Emmer, E. T., Evertson, C., and Anderson, L. M. (1980). Effective classroom management at the beginning of the school year. *The Elementary School Journal, 80,* 219–231.

Emmer, E. T., Evertson, C., Sanford, J., and Clements, B. S. (1982). *Improving classroom management: An experimental study in junior high school classrooms*. Austin, Tex.: Research and Development Center for Teacher Education, University of Texas.

Emmer, E. T., Evertson, C., Sanford, J., Clements, B. S., and Worsham, W. E. (1989). *Classroom management for secondary teachers*. (2d ed.). Englewood Cliffs, N.J.: Prentice-Hall.

Epstein, J. L. (1991). Paths to partnership: What we can learn from federal, state, district, and school initiatives. *Phi Delta Kappan, 72,* 344–349.

Evertson, C. M., and Emmer, E. T. (1982). Preventive classroom management. In D. Duke, (ed.). *Helping teachers manage classrooms*. Alexandria, Va.: Association for Supervision and Curriculum Development.

Evertson, E., Emmer, E., Clements, B., Sanford, J., and Worsham, M. (1989). *Classroom management for elementary teachers*. (2d ed.). Englewood Cliffs, N.J.: Prentice-Hall.

Evertson, C. M., Emmer, E. T., Sanford, J. P., and Clements, B. S. (1983). Improving classroom management: An experiment in elementary classrooms. *Elementary School Journal, 84,* 173–188.

Feiman-Nemser, S. (1983). Learning to teach. In L. S. Shulman and G. Sykes (eds.), *Handbook of teaching and policy*. New York: Longman.

Feiman-Nemser, S., and Floden, R. E. (1986). In M. C. Wittrock (ed.), *Handbook of research on teaching* (3d ed.). New York: Macmillan.

Feitler, F., Weiner, W., and Blumberg, A. (1970). *The relationship between interpersonal relations orientations and preferred classroom physical settings.* Paper presented at the annual meeting of the American Educational Research Association, Minneapolis. (ERIC No. ED 039.)

Fenstermacher, G. D. (1986). Philosophy of research on teaching: Three aspects. In. M. C. Wittrock (ed.), *Handbook of research on teaching* (3d ed.). New York: Macmillan.

Fenstermacher, G. D., and Soltis, J. F. (1986). *Approaches to teaching.* New York: Teachers College Press.

Fenton, E. (1966). *Teaching the new social studies in secondary schools: An inductive approach.* New York: Holt, Rinehart & Winston.

Fisher, C. W., and Berliner, D. (eds.). (1985). *Perspectives on instructional time.* New York: Longman.

Fisher, C. W., Berliner, D., Filby, N., Marliave, R., Cahen, L., and Dishaw, M. (1980). Teaching behavior, academic learning time, and student achievement: An overview. In C. Denham and A. Lieberman (eds.), *Time to learn.* Washington, D.C.: National Institute of Education, Department of Education.

Flanders, N. A. (1970). *Analyzing teaching behavior.* Reading, Mass.: Addison-Wesley.

Fleener, Ann (1989). *Sample lesson plan format.* (Mimeographed). Minneapolis, Minn.: Augsburg College.

Floyd, W. D. (1960). *An analysis of the oral questioning activity in selected Colorado primary classrooms.* (Doctoral dissertation.) Colorado State College.

Ford, G. W., and Pugno, L. (eds.). (1964). *The structure of knowledge and the curriculum.* Chicago: Rand McNally.

Fosmire, F., and Wallen, R. (1971). *STP problem solving.* (Mimeographed.) Eugene, Ore.: University of Oregon.

Fosnot, C. T. (1989). *Enquiring teachers, enquiring learners.* New York: Teachers College Press.

Fox, R., Luszki, M., and Schmuck, R. (1966). *Diagnosing classroom learning environments.* Chicago: Science Research Associates.

Freeman, D., Kuhs, T., Porter, A., Knappen, L., Floden, R., Schmidt, W., Schwille, J. (1980). *The fourth grade mathematics curriculum as inferred from textbooks and tests.* East Lansing, Mich.: Institute for Research on Teaching, Michigan State University. Research Series #82.

Freiberg, H. J., Cooper, J. M., and Ryan, K. (1980). *Those who can, teach: Learning guide.* Boston: Houghton Mifflin.

French, J. R. P., and Raven, B. H. (1959). The bases of social power. In D. Cartwright (ed.), *Studies in social power.* Ann Arbor: University of Michigan Press.

Friedman, W. J. (1980). *The development of relational understanding of temporal and spatial terms.* (ERIC No. ED 178 176: Resources in Education.)

Fuchs, E. (1969). *Teachers talk: View from inside city schools.* New York: Doubleday.

Fullan, M. (1982). *The meaning of educational change.* New York: Teachers College Press.

Fullan, M. (1992). *The new meaning of educational change* (2d ed.). New York: Teachers College Press.

Fuller, F. (1969). Concerns of teachers: A developmental conceptualization. *American Educational Research Journal, 6,* 207–226.

Gage, N. L. (1978). *The scientific basis of the art of teaching.* New York: Teachers College Press.

Gage, N. L. (1984). *An update of the scientific basis of the art of teaching.* (Mimeographed.) Palo Alto, Calif.: Stanford University.

Gagné, E. D. (1985). *The cognitive psychology of school learning.* Boston: Little, Brown.

Gagné, R. M. (1977). *The conditions of learning and theory of instruction* (3d ed.). New York: Holt, Rinehart & Winston.

Gagné, R. M. (1985). *The conditions of learning and theory of instruction* (4th ed.). New York: Holt, Rinehart & Winston.

Gagné, R. M., and Briggs, L. J. (1979). *Principles of instructional design.* New York: Holt, Rinehart & Winston.

Gagné, R. M., and White, R. (1978). Memory structures and learning outcomes. *Review of Educational Research, 48*(2), 187–222.

Gall, M. (1984). Synthesis of research on teachers' questioning. *Educational Leadership, 42,* 40–47.

Gall, M. D. (1970). The use of questions in teaching. *Review of Educational Research, 40,* 707–721.

Gall, M. D., Dunning, B., and Weathersby, R. (1971). *Higher cognitive questioning: Teachers handbook.* Beverly Hills, Calif.: Macmillan Educational Services.

Gardner, H. (1983). *Frames of mind.* New York: Basic Books.

Gardner, H. (1985). *The mind's new science.* New York: Basic Books.

Gardner, H. (1991). *The unschooled mind: How children think and how schools should teach.* New York: Basic Books.

Garner, R. (1987). *Metacognition and reading comprehension.* Norwood, N.J.: Ablex.

Gay, G. (1974). *Differential dyadic interactions of black and white teachers with black and white pupils in recently desegregated social studies classrooms: A function of teacher and pupil ethnicity.* Washington, D.C.: Office of Education, National Institute of Education.

Getzels, J. W., and Thelen, H. A. (1960). The classroom group as a unique social system. In N. Henry (ed.), *The dynamics of instructional groups.* Chicago: National Society for the Study of Education, 59th Yearbook, Part 2.

Glass, G. (1981). *Effectiveness of special education.* Paper presented at Wingspread Conference, Racine, Wis.

Glass, G., Cahen, L., Smith, M. L., and Filby, N. (1982). *School class size: Research and policy.* Beverly Hills, Calif.: Sage.

Glasser, W. (1969). *Schools without failure.* New York: Harper & Row.

Glasser, W. (1986). *Control theory in the classroom.* New York: Harper & Row.

Gold, R. M., Reilly, A., Silberman, R., and Lehr, R. (1971). Academic achievement declines under pass-fail grading, *Journal of Experimental Education, 39,* 17–21.

Good, T. L., and Brophy, J. E. (1987). *Looking in classrooms* (4th ed.). New York: Harper & Row.

Good, T. L., and Grouws, D. A. (1979). The Missouri mathematics effectiveness project: An experimental study in fourth-grade classrooms. *Journal of Educational Psychology, 71,* 355–362.

Good, T. L., Grouws, D. A., and Ebmeier, H. (1983). *Active mathematics teaching.* New York: Longman.

Goodlad, J. (1975). *The dynamics of educational change.* New York: McGraw-Hill.

Goodlad, J. (1984). *A place called school: Prospects for the future.* New York: McGraw-Hill.

Goodlad, J., and Klein, M. (1970). *Behind the classroom door.* Worthington, Ohio: Charles A. Jones.

Griffin, G. (1986). Clinical teacher education. In J. V. Hoffman and S. A. Edwards (eds.), *Reality and reform in clinical teacher education.* New York: Random House.

Griffith, D. P. (1992). Prenatal exposure to cocaine and other drugs: Developmental and educational prognoses. *Phi Delta Kappan, 74,* 30–34.

Gronlund, N. E. (1978). *Stating objectives for classroom instruction.* New York: Macmillan.

Gronlund, N. E. (1982). *Constructing achievement tests.* Englewood Cliffs, N.J.: Prentice-Hall.

Gronlund, N. E., and Linn, M. (1990). *Measurement and evaluation in teaching* (6th ed.). New York: Macmillan.

Gump, P. V. (1967). *The classroom behavior setting: Its nature and relation to student behavior.* Washington, D.C.: U.S. Office of Education.

Gump, P. V. (1982). School settings and their keeping. In D. L. Duke (ed.), *Helping teachers manage classrooms.* Alexandria, Va.: Association for Supervision and Curriculum Development.

Guskey, T. R., and Gates, S. L. (1986). Synthesis of research on mastery learning. *Educational Leadership, 43,* 73–81.

Guthrie, G. P., and Guthrie, L. F. (1991). Streamlining interagency collaboration for youth at risk. *Educational Leadership, 49*(1), 17–22.

Haberman, M. (1991). The pedagogy of poverty versus good teaching. *Phi Delta Kappan, 72,* 290–294.

Hallinan, M. T., and Sorensen, A. B. (1983). The formation and stability of instructional groups. *American Sociological Review, 48,* 838–851.

Hardman, M. L., Drew, C. J., and Egan, M. W. (1984). *Human exceptionality.* Boston, Mass.: Allyn & Bacon.

Harnischseger, A., and Willey, D. (1978). Model of school learning. *Journal of Curriculum Studies, 10,* 214–220.

Hawk, P. (1986). Using graphic organizers to increase achievement in middle school life science. *Science Education, 70,* 81–87.

Heath, S. B. (1983). *Ways with words: Language, life and work in communities and classrooms.* Cambridge, England: Cambridge University Press.

Hebert, E. A. (1992). Portfolios invite reflection — from student and staff. *Educational Leadership 49,* 8:59–62.

Heider, E. R., Cazden, C. B., and Brown, R. (1968). *Social class differences in the effectiveness and style of children's coding ability.* (Project Literacy Reports, No. 9.) Ithaca, N.Y.: Cornell University.

Hiller, J. H., Gisher, G. A., and Kaess, W. (1969). A computer investigation of verbal characteristics of effective classroom lecturing. *American Educational Research Journal, 6,* 661–675.

Hodgkinson, H. L. (1983). Guess who's coming to college? *Higher Education, 17,* 281–287.

Hopkins, D. (1985). *A teacher's guide to classroom research.* Philadelphia: Open University Press.

Horowitz, P., and Otto, D. (1973). *The teaching effectiveness of an alternative teaching facility.* Alberta, Canada. (ERIC No. ED 083 242.)

Housner, L. D., and Griffey, D. C. (1985). Teacher cognition: Differences in planning and interactive decision making between experienced and inexperienced teachers. *Research Quarterly for Exercise and Sport, 56,* 45–53.

Hoy, Wayne K. (1968). The influence of experience on the beginning teacher. *School Review, 76,* 312–323.

Hunt, D. (1970). A conceptual level matching model for coordinating learner characteristics with educational approaches. *Interchange: A Journal of Educational Studies, 1,* 2–16.

Hunt, D. (1974). *Matching models in education.* Toronto: Ontario Institute for Studies in Education.

Hunter, M. C. (1976). *Improved instruction.* El Segundo, Calif.: TIP Publications.

Hunter, M. C. (1982). *Mastery teaching.* El Segundo, Calif.: TIP Publications.

Hunter, M. C. (1987). Beyond rereading Dewey: What's next? A response to Gibboney. *Educational Leadership, 44,* 51–53.

Hvitfeldt, C. (1986). Traditional culture, perceptual style, and learning: The classroom behavior of Hmong adults. *Adult Education Quarterly, 36,* 65–77.

Hyde, A. A., and Bizar, M. (1989). *Thinking in context: Teaching cognitive processes across the elementary school curriculum.* New York: Longman.

Isaacson, N. S. (1981). *Secondary teachers' perceptions of personal and organizational support during induction to teaching.* (Doctoral dissertation.) Eugene, Ore.: University of Oregon.

Jackson, P. W. (1968). *Life in classrooms.* New York: Holt, Rinehart & Winston.

Jackson, P. W. (1986). *The practice of teaching.* New York: Teachers College Press.

Jacobs, H. R. (1970). *Mathematics: A human endeavor.* San Francisco: W. H. Freeman and Company.

Jencks, C., Smith, M., Ackland, H., Bane, M., Cohen, D., Gintis, H., Heyns, B., and Michelson, S. (1972). *Inequality: A reassessment of the effect of family and schooling in America.* New York: Basic Books.

Jervis, K., and Montag, C. (eds.). (1991). *Progressive education for the 1990s: Transforming practice.* New York: Teachers College Press

Johnson, D. W., and Johnson, F. P. (1975). *Joining together: Group theory and group skills.* Englewood Cliffs, N.J.: Prentice-Hall.

Johnson, D. W., and Johnson, F. P. (1987). *Joining together: Group theory and group skills* (3d ed.). Englewood Cliffs, N.J.: Prentice-Hall.

Johnson, D. W., and Johnson, R. T. (1986). *Learning together and alone. Cooperation, competition, and individualization* (2d ed.). Englewood Cliffs, N.J.: Prentice-Hall.

Johnson, R., Rynders, J., Johnson, D. W., Schmidt, B., and Haider, S. (1979). Interaction between handicapped and nonhandicapped teenagers as a function of situational goal structuring: Implications for mainstreaming. *American Educational Research Journal, 16,* 161–167.

Johnston, J. H., and dePerez, R. J. M. (1985). Four climates of effective middle level schools. In National Association of Secondary School Principals, *Schools in the middle: A report on trends and practices,* Reston, Va.: Author.

Jordan, J. (1988). Nobody mean more to me than you and the future life of Willie Jordan. *Harvard Educational Review, 58,* 363–374.

Joyce, B., and Hartoonian, B. (1964). Teaching as problem solving. *Journal of Teacher Education, 15,* 420–427.

Joyce, B., Hersh, R., and McKibbin, M. (1983). *The structure of school improvement.* New York: Longman.

Joyce, B., and Weil, M. (1972). *Models of teaching.* Englewood Cliffs, N.J.: Prentice-Hall.

Joyce, B., and Weil, M. (with Beverly Showers) (1992). *Models of teaching* (4th ed.). Englewood Cliffs, N.J.: Prentice-Hall.

Jung, C. (1972). Listening effectively. (Mimeographed.) Portland, Ore.: Northwest Regional Educational Laboratory.

Kagan, S. (1992). *Cooperative learning.* San Juan Capistrano, Calif.: Resources for Teachers.

Kallen, H. M. (1924). *Culture and democracy in the United States.* New York: Boni & Liveright.

Kaplan, M. (1992). *Thinking in education.* Cambridge: Cambridge University Press.

Kay, H. (1991). Jason and Matt. In K. Jervis and C. Montag (eds.), *Progressive education for the 1990s: Transforming practice.* New York: Teacher College Press.

Keller, F. S. (1966). A personal course in psychology. In T. Urlich, R. Stachnik, and T. Mabry (eds.), *Control of human behavior.* Glenview, Ill.: Scott, Foresman.

Kemmis, S., and McTaggart, R. (1981). *The action research planner.* Victoria, Australia: Deakin University Press.

Kennedy, J. J., Bush, A. J., Cruickshank, D. R., and Haefele, D. (1978). *Additional investigations into the nature of teacher clarity.* Paper presented at annual meeting of American Educational Research Association, Toronto.

Klausmeier, H. (1980). *Learning and teaching concepts.* New York: Academic Press.

Kounin, J. S. (1970). *Discipline and group management in classrooms.* New York: Holt, Rinehart & Winston.

Krantz, P., and Risley, T. (1972). *The organization of group care environments: Behavioral ecology in the classroom.* Lawrence, Kan.: Kansas University. (ERIC No. ED 078 915.)

Krug, M. (1976). *The melting of the ethnics.* Bloomington, Ill.: Phi Delta Kappa.

Kyzar, B. L. (1977). Noise pollution and schools: How much is too much? *CEFP Journal, 4,* 10–11.

Lacey, C. (1977). *The socialization of teachers.* London: Methuen.

Lard, M., and Smith, L. (1979). *Low inference teacher clarity variables: Effects on student achievement.* Paper presented at the annual meeting of American Educational Research Association, San Francisco.

Lawler-Prince, D., and Holloway, D. (1992–93). The family dynamics and characteristics of homeless children: Barriers to education. *National Forum of Teacher Education Journal, 2,* 49–53.

Leinhardt, G. (1989). Math lessons: A contrast of novice and expert competence. *Journal for Research in Mathematics Education, 20,* 52–75.

Leinhardt, G., and Greeno, J. (1986). The cognitive skill of teaching. *Journal of Educational Psychology, 78,* 75–95.

Lepper, M. R., Greene, D., and Nisbett, R. (1973). Undermining children's intrinsic interest with extrinsic reward: A test of the "overjustification" hypothesis. *Journal of Personality and Social Psychology, 28,* 129–137.

Lerup, L. (1977). *Building the unfinished: Architecture and human action.* Beverly Hills, Calif.: Sage Publications.

Levin, H. M. (1987). Accelerated schools for disadvantaged students. *Educational Leadership, 44,* 19–21.

Lewin, K., Lippitt, R., and White, R. (1939). Patterns of aggressive behavior in experimentally created social climates. *Journal of Social Psychology, 10,* 271–299.

Lieberman, A. (ed.). (1988). *Building a professional culture in schools.* New York: Teachers College Press.

Lieberman, A., and Miller, L. (1984). *Teachers, their world, and their work.* Alexandria, Va.: Association of Supervision and Curriculum Development.

Lieberman, A., and Miller, L. (1992). *Teachers—Their world and their work: Implications for school improvement.* New York: City College Press.

Linehan, M. F. (1992). Children who are homeless: Educational strategies for school personnel. *Phi Delta Kappan, 74,* 61–66.

Linn, M. C., and Hyde, J. S. (1989). Gender, mathematics, and science. *Educational Researcher, 18*(8), 17–27.

Lippitt, R., and White, R. (1958). An experimental study of leadership and group life. In E. E. Macoby, T. M. Newcomb, and F. L. Hartley (eds.). *Readings in social psychology.* New York: Holt, Rinehart & Winston.

Livingston, C., and Castle, S. (eds.). (1989). *Teachers and research in action.* Washington, D.C.: National Education Association.

Lortie, D. C. (1975). *School-teacher: A sociological study.* Chicago: University of Chicago Press.

Lotan, R. A., and Benton, J. (1990). Finding out about complex instruction: Teaching math and science in heterogeneous classrooms. In N. Davidson (ed.), *Cooperative learning in mathematics: A handbook for teachers.* Menlo Park, Calif.: Addison-Wesley.

Loucks-Horsley, S., and Hergert, L. F. (1985). *An action guide to school improvement.* Alexandria, Va.: The Network and Association for Supervision and Curriculum Development.

Louis, M. (1980). Surprise and sense-making: What newcomers experience in entering unfamiliar organizational settings. *Administrative Science Quarterly, 25,* 226–251.

Luft, J. (1970). *Group processes: An introduction to group dynamics.* Palo Alto, Calif.: National Press Books.

Luiten, J., Ames, W., and Aerson, G. (1980). A meta-analysis of advance organizers on learning and retention. *American Educational Research Journal, 17,* 211–218.

Lyman, F. (1983). *Journaling procedures.* (Mimeographed.) College Park, Md.: University of Maryland.

Lyman, F. (1985). *Think-pair-share.* (Mimeographed.) College Park, Md.: University of Maryland.

Lyman, F. (1986). *Procedures for using the question/response cues.* (Mimeographed.) College Park, Md.: University of Maryland and the Howard County Public Schools.

Lyman, F., Davie, A. R., and Eley, G. (1984). *Action research by student teachers and beginning teachers: An approach to developing problem solving in the classroom.* (Mimeographed.) College Park, Md.: University of Maryland.

Maccoby, E., Newcomb, T., and Hartley, E. (eds.). (1958). *Readings in social psychology* (3d ed.). New York: Holt, Rinehart & Winston.

Macias, J. (1990). Scholastic antecedents of immigrant students: Schooling in a Mexican immigrant-sending community. *Anthropology and Education Quarterly, 21,* 291–318.

Madden, N. A., Slavin, R. E., Karweit, N. L., Dolan, L., and Wasik, B. A. (1992, April). *Success for all: Longitudinal effects of a restructuring program for inner-city elementary schools.* Paper presented at the annual meeting of the American Educational Research Association, San Francisco.

Mager, R. F. (1962). *Preparing instructional objectives.* Palo Alto, Calif.: Fearon Publishers.

Mager, R. F. (1984). *Preparing instructional objectives* (2d rev. ed.). Palo Alto, Calif.: D. S. Lake.

Mann, D. (1981). *Education policy analysis and the rent-a-troika business.* Paper presented at annual meeting of the American Educational Research Association, Los Angeles.

Markle, S. (1975). They teach concepts, don't they? *Educational Researcher, 4,* 3–9.

Martorella, P. H. (1982). Cognition research: Some implications for the design of social studies instructional materials. *Theory and Research in Social Education, 19,* 1–16.

Marzano, R. J. (1992). *A different kind of classroom: Teaching with dimensions of learning.* Alexandria, Va.: Association for Supervision and Curriculum Development

McClelland, D. C. (1958). Methods of measuring human motivation. In J. W. Atkinson (ed.), *Motives in fantasy, action and society.* New York: Van Nostrand.

McClelland, D. C. (1961). *The achieving society.* New York: Van Nostrand.

McClelland, D. C. (1965). Toward a theory of motive acquisition. *American Psychologist, 20,* 321–333.

McCown, R. R., and Roop, P. (1992). *Educational psychology and classroom practice: A partnership.* Needham Heights, Mass.: Allyn & Bacon.

McDonald, F., and Elias, P. (1980). *Study of induction programs for beginning teachers.* Princeton, N.J.: Educational Testing Services.

McLaughlin, D. (in press). Personal narratives for school change in Navajo settings. In D. McLaughlin and W. Tierney (eds.), *Naming silenced lives: Personal narratives and processes of school change.* London: Routledge Press.

McTighe, J., and Lyman, F. T. (1988). Cueing thinking in the classroom: The promise of theory-embedded tools. *Educational Leadership, 45,* 18–24.

Means, B., Chelemer, C., and Knapp, M. S. (1991). *Teaching advanced skills to at-risk students: Views from research and practice.* San Francisco: Jossey-Bass.

Mehrens, W. A., and Lehmann, I. J. (1984). *Measurement in education and psychology.* New York: Holt, Rinehart & Winston.

Merrill, M. D., and Tennyson, R. D. (1977). *Teaching concepts: An instructional design approach.* Englewood Cliffs, N.J.: Educational Technology.

Mid-Atlantic Association for Cooperation in Education (MAACIE) Cooperative News. (1990). ''Swing from Wings.'' Vol. 3, no. 3, February, p. 5. Columbia, Md.: Author.

Miles, M. B. (ed.). (1964). *Innovations in education.* New York: Teachers College Press.

Mitchell, R. (1992). *Testing for learning: How new approaches to evaluation can improve American schools.* New York: The Free Press.

Mitzel, H. (1960). Teacher effectiveness. In C. W. Harris (ed.), *Encyclopedia of educational research* (3d ed.). New York: Macmillan.

Morine-Dershimer, G. (1985). *Talking, listening, and learning in elementary classrooms.* New York: Longman.

Mosenthal, P. B., Conley, M. W., Colella, A., and Davidson, R. (1985). The influence of prior knowledge and teacher lesson structure on children's production of narratives. *The Elementary School Journal, 85,* 621–633.

Moyer, J. R. (1966). *An exploratory study of questioning in the instructional processes in selected elementary schools.* (Doctoral dissertation.) Columbia University.

Muir, R. (1980). A teacher implements instructional changes using the BTES framework. In C. Denham and A. Lieberman (eds.), *Time to learn.* Washington, D.C.: National Institute of Education, Department of Education, 197–209.

Naftulin, D., Ware, J., and Donnelly, F. (1973). The doctor fox lecture: A paradigm of educational seduction. *Journal of Medical Education, 48,* 630–635.

Needleman, H. L. (1992). Childhood exposure to lead: A common cause of school failure. *Phi Delta Kappan, 74,* 35–37.

Nettles, S. M. (1991). Community involvement and disadvantaged students: A review. *Review of Educational Research, 61,* 379–406.

Newcomb, T. M. (1961). *The acquaintance process.* New York: Holt, Rinehart & Winston.

Newton, F. (1972). *Facilitating inquiry in the classroom.* Portland, Ore.: Northwest Regional Education Laboratory.

Oakes, J. (1985). *Keeping track: How schools structure inequality.* New Haven, Conn.: Yale University Press.

Oakes, J. (1992). Can tracking research inform practice? Technical, normative, and political considerations. *Educational Researcher, 21*(4), 12–21.

Oja, S. N., and Smulyan, L. (1989). *Collaborative action research: A developmental approach.* New York: Falmer Press.

Orlosky, D. E. (ed.). (1982). *Introduction to education.* Columbus, Ohio: Charles E. Merrill.

Palinscar, A. S., and Brown, A. L. (1984). Reciprocal teaching of comprehension-fostering and comprehension-monitoring activities. *Cognition and Instruction, 1*(2), 117–175.

Palincsar, A., and Brown, A. (1989). Instruction for self-regulated reading. In L. Resnick and L. Kloper (eds.), *Toward the thinking curriculum: Current cognitive research.* Alexandria, Va.: Association for Supervision and Curriculum Development.

Palincsar, A. S., and Klenk, L. J. (1991). Dialogues promoting reading comprehension. In B. Means, C. Chelemer, and M. S. Knapp (eds.), *Teaching advanced skills to at-risk students: Views from research and practice.* San Francisco: Jossey-Bass Publishers.

Pallas, A., Natriello, G., and McDill, E. (1989). The changing nature of the disadvantaged population: Current dimensions and future trends. *Educational Researcher, 18,* 16–22.

Peddiwell, J. A. (1939). *The saber-tooth curriculum.* New York: McGraw-Hill.

Perrone, V. (1991). *Expanding student assessment.* Alexandria, Va.: Association for Supervision and Curriculum Development.

Perry, W. (1969). *Forms of intellectual and ethical development during the college years.* New York: Holt, Rinehart & Winston.

Persell, C. H. (1977). *Education and inequality.* New York: Free Press.

Peterson, P. L., Marx, R. W., and Clark, C. (1978). Teacher planning, teacher behavior and student achievement. *American Educational Research Journal, 15,* 417–432.

Petty, O., and Jannson, L. (1987). Sequencing examples and nonexamples to facilitate concept attainment. *Journal for Research in Mathematics Education 18,* 112–125.

Phillips, S. (1972). Participant structures and communicative competence: Warm Springs children in community and classroom. In C. Cazden and D. Hymes (eds.), *Functions of language in the classroom.* New York: Teachers College Press.

Piaget, J. (1963). *Psychology of intelligence.* Paterson, N.J.: Littlefield Adams.

Pogrow, S. (1990). Challenging at-risk students: Findings from the HOTS program. *Phi Delta Kappan, 71,* 389–397.

Popham, W. J., and Baker, E. I. (1970). *Systematic instruction.* Englewood Cliffs, N.J.: Prentice-Hall.

Posner, G. J., and Rudnitsky, A. N. (1986). *Course design: A guide to curriculum development for teachers* (3d ed.). New York: Longman.

Prescott, E., Jones, E., and Kritchevsky, S. (1967). *Group day care as a child rearing environment: An observational study of day care programs.* (ERIC No. ED 024 453.)

Project 2000 with Stephen Goldsmith. (1989). *Community problem solving.* Unpublished manuscript.

Redfield, D., and Rousseau, E. (1981). A meta-analysis of experimental research on teacher questioning behavior. *Review of Educational Research, 51,* 237–245.

Reed, S., and Sautter, R. C. (1990). Children of poverty: The status of 12 million young Americans. *Phi Delta Kappan, 71,* K1–K12.

Resnick, L. B. (1987). *Education and learning to think.* Washington, D.C.: National Academy Press.

Resnick, L. B., and Kloper, L. E. (eds.). (1989). *Toward the thinking curriculum: Current cognitive research.* Alexandria, Va.: Association for Supervision and Curriculum Development.

Reynolds, M. C. (ed.). (1989). *Knowledge base for the beginning teacher.* New York: Pergamon Press.

Reynolds, M. C., Wang, M. C., and Walberg, H. J. (1987). The necessary restructuring of special and regular education. *Exceptional Children, 53,* 391–398.

Richardson-Koehler, V. (ed.). (1987). *Educators' handbook: A research perspective.* New York: Longman.

Rist, R. C. (1970). Student social class and teacher expectations: The self-fulfilling prophecy in ghetto education. *Harvard Education Review, 40,* 411–451.

Rosenbaum, J. E. (1976). *Making equality: The hidden curriculum in high school tracking.* New York: Wiley.

Rosenfield, P., Lambert, N., and Black, A. (1985). Desk arrangement effects on pupil classroom behavior. *Journal of Educational Psychology, 77,* 101–108.

Rosenshine, B. (1970). Enthusiastic teaching: A research review. *School Review, 78,* 499–514.

Rosenshine, B. (1971a). Objectively measured behavioral predictors of effectiveness in explaining. In I. D. Westbury and A. A. Bellack (eds.), *Research into classroom processes.* New York: Teachers College Press.

Rosenshine, B. (1971b). *Teaching behaviors and student achievement.* London: National Foundation for Educational Research.

Rosenshine, B. (1979). Content, time and direct instruction. In P. L. Peterson and H. J. Walberg (eds.), *Research on teaching.* Berkeley, Calif.: McCutchan.

Rosenshine, B. (1980). How time is spent in elementary classrooms. In C. Denham and A. Lieberman (eds.). *Time to learn.* Washington, D.C.: U.S. Department of Education.

Rosenshine, B., and Furst, N. (1973). The use of direct observation to study teaching. In R. M. W. Travers (ed.), *Second handbook of research on teaching.* Chicago: Rand McNally.

Rosenshine, B., and Stephens, R. (1986). Teaching functions. In M. C. Wittrock

(ed.), *Handbook of research on teaching* (3d ed.). New York: Macmillan.

Rosenthal, R., and Jacobson, L. (1968). *Pygmalion in the classroom.* New York: Holt, Rinehart & Winston.

Rowe, M. B. (1974a). Wait-time and rewards as instructional variables, their influence on language, logic, and fate control. Part One: Wait-time. *Journal of Research in Science Teaching, 11,* 81–94.

Rowe, M. B. (1974b). Relation of wait-time and rewards to the development of language, logic, and fate control: Part II: Rewards. *Journal of Research in Science Teaching, 11,* 291–308.

Rowe, M. B. (1986). Wait time: Slowing down may be a way of speeding up. *Journal of Teacher Education, 37,* 43–50.

Russell, T., and Munby, H. (eds.). (1992). *Teachers and teaching: From classroom to reflection.* New York: The Falmer Press.

Rutter, M., Maughan, B., Mortimore, P., Ouston, J., and Smith, A. (1979). *Fifteen thousand hours: Secondary schools and their effects on children.* Cambridge, Mass.: Harvard University Press.

Ryan, K., and Cooper, J. M. (1980). *Those who can, teach* (3d ed.). Boston: Houghton Mifflin.

Ryan, K., Newman, K., Mager, G., Applegate, J., Lasley, T., Flora, R., and Johnston, J. (1980). *Biting the apple: Accounts of first year teachers.* New York: Longman.

Ryle, G. (1949). *The concept of mind.* London: Hutchinson's University Library.

Sadker, M. (1985). *Women in educational administration.* Washington, D.C.: Mid-Atlantic Center for Sex Equity.

Sadker, M., and Sadker, D. (1990). *Sex equity handbook for schools* (2d ed.). New York: Longman.

Santrock, J. W. (1976). Affect and facilitative self-control. Influence of ecological setting, cognition, and social agent. *Journal of Educational Psychology, 68*(5), 529–535.

Sarason, S. (1971). *The culture of school and the problem of change.* Boston: Allyn & Bacon.

Sarason, S. (1982). *The culture of school and the problem of change* (2d ed.). Boston: Allyn & Bacon.

Schlosser, L. K. (1992). Teacher distance and student disengagement: School lives on the margin. *Journal of Teacher Education, 43,* 128–140.

Schmuck, R. A. (1963). Some relationships of peer liking patterns in the classroom to pupil attitudes and achievement. *School Review, 71*, 337–339.

Schmuck, R. A., and Runkel, P. (1985). *The handbook of organization development in schools* (3d ed.). Prosper Heights, Ill.: Waveland Press.

Schmuck, R. A., Runkel, P., Arends, J., and Arends, R. (1977). *The second handbook of organization development in schools.* Palo Alto, Calif.: Mayfield.

Schmuck, R. A., and Schmuck, P. (1975). *A humanistic psychology of education: Making the school everybody's house.* Palo Alto, Calif.: Mayfield.

Schmuck, R. A., and Schmuck, P. (1975). *Group processes in the classroom* (2nd ed.). Dubuque, Iowa: W. C. Brown.

Schmuck, R. A. and Schmuck, P. (1988). *Group processes in the classroom* (5th ed.). Dubuque, Iowa: W. C. Brown.

Schuck, R. (1981). The impact of set induction on student achievement and retention. *Journal of Educational Research, 74*, 227–232.

Schön, D. A. (1983). *The reflective practitioner.* San Francisco: Jossey-Bass.

Schreiber, J. E. (1967). *Teachers' question-asking techniques in social studies.* (Doctoral dissertation.) University of Iowa.

Schulman, L. S. (1987). Knowledge and teaching: Foundations of the new reform. *Harvard Education Review, 57*, 1–22.

Schwab, J. J. (coordinator). (1965). *Biological sciences curriculum study, Biology teachers' handbook.* New York: Wiley.

Schwebel, A., and Cherlin, D. (1972). Physical and social distancing in teacher-pupil relationships. *Journal of Educational Psychology, 63*, 543–550.

Scott, K. (1986). Effects of sex-fair reading materials on pupils' attitudes, comprehension, and interest. *American Educational Research Journal, 23*, 105–116.

Scott, Foresman. (1979). *Third grade social studies.* Glenville, Ill.: Author.

Shaefer, W., and Lissitz, R. (1987). Measurement training for school personnel: Recommendations and reality. *Journal of Teacher Education, 38*, 57–63.

Sharan, S., Kussell, P., Hertz-Lazarowitz, R., Bejarano, Y., Raviv, S., and Sharan, Y. (1984). *Cooperative learning in the classroom: Research in desegregated schools.* Hillsdale, N.J.: Erlbaum.

Sharan, S., and Sharan, Y. (1976). *Small group teaching.* Englewood Cliffs, N.J.: Education Technology.

Shavelson, R. (1976). Teacher decision making. In N. L. Gage (ed.), *The psychology of teaching method.* Chicago: University of Chicago Press.

Shavelson, R., and Baxter, G. (1992). What we've learned about assessing hands-on science. *Educational Leadership, 49*, 20–25.

Silberman, C. (1970). *Crisis in the classroom.* New York: Vintage Books.

Sizer, T. (1984). *Horace's compromise: The dilemma of the American high school.* Boston: Houghton-Mifflin.

Slavin, R. (1980). Effects of individual learning expectations on student achievement. *Journal of Educational Psychology, 72*, 520–524.

Slavin, R. (1983). *Cooperative learning.* New York: Longman.

Slavin, R. (1984). Students motivating students to excel: Incentives, cooperative tasks and student achievement. *The Elementary School Journal, 85*, 53–62.

Slavin, R. (1986). *Student team learning* (3d ed.). Baltimore, Md.: Center for Research on Elementary and Middle Schools, Johns Hopkins University.

Slavin, R., Sharan, S., Kagan, S., Hertz-Lazarowitz, R., Webb, C., and Schmuck, R. (eds.). (1985). *Learning to cooperate, cooperating to learn.* New York: Plenum Press.

Sleeter, C. E., and Grant, C. A. (1988). *Making choices for multicultural education: Five approaches to race, class, and gender.* Columbus, Ohio: Charles M. Merrill.

Sorensen, A. B., and Hallinan, M. T. (1986). Effects of ability grouping on growth in academic achievement. *American Educational Research Journal, 23*, 519–542.

Sprinthall, N., and Thies-Sprinthall, L. (1983). The teacher as an adult learner: A cognitive-developmental view. In G. Griffin (ed.), *Staff development.* Chicago: University of Chicago Press.

Stallings, J. (1985). Instructional time and staff development: How useful is the research on time to teachers? In C. Fisher and D. Berliner (eds.), *Perspectives on instructional time.* New York: Longman.

Stallings, J., and Kaskowitz, D. (1974). *Follow-through classroom observation evaluation 1972–1974.* (SRI project URU-7370.) Stanford, Calif.: Stanford Research Institute.

Stallings, J., and Robertson, A. (1979). *Fac-tors affecting women's decision to enroll in elective mathematics classes in high school.* Final report to the National Institute of Education. Menlo Park, Calif.: SRI International.

Starch, D., and Elliot, E. C. (1912). Reliability of grading high school work in English. *Scholastic Review, 20*, 442–456.

Starch, D., and Elliot, E. C. (1913). Reliability of grading high school work in history. *Scholastic Review, 22*, 676–681.

Starkey, D. (1980). *The origins of concept formation: Object sorting and object preference in early infancy.* (ERIC No. ED 175555: Resources in Education.)

Steele, C. M. (1992, April). Race and the schooling of Black Americans. *The Atlantic, 68*–78.

Stenhouse, L. (1975). *An introduction to curriculum research and development.* London: Heinemann.

Stenhouse, L. (1983). *Authority, education and emancipation.* London: Heinemann.

Stenhouse, L. (1984). Artistry and teaching: The teacher as focus of research and development. In D. Hopkins and M. Wideen (eds.), *Alternative perspectives on school improvement.* New York: The Falmer Press.

Stevens, R. (1912). The question as a measure of efficiency in instruction: A critical study of classroom practice. *Teachers College Contributions to Education*, no. 48. New York: Teachers College Press.

Stiggins, R. J. (1987). *Profiling classroom assessment environments.* Paper presented at the annual meeting of the National Council on Measurement in Education, San Francisco.

Stipek, D. J. (1988). *Motivation to learn: From theory to practice.* Englewood Cliffs, N.J.: Prentice-Hall.

Suchman, R. (1962). *The elementary school training program in scientific inquiry.* Report to the U.S. Office of Education. Urbana, Ill.: University of Illinois.

Tennyson, R. (1978). Pictorial support and specific instructions as design variables for children's concept and rule learning. *Educational Communication and Technology: A Journal of Research and Development, 26*, 291–299.

Tennyson, R., and Cocchiarella, M. (1986). An empirically based instructional design theory for teaching concepts. *Review of Educational Research, 56*, 40–71.

Tennyson, R., Youngers J., and Suebsonthi, P. (1983). Concept learning by children using instructional presentation forms for prototype formation and classification-skill development. *Journal of Educational Psychology, 75,* 280–290.

Thelen, H. A. (1954). *Dynamics of groups at work.* Chicago: University of Chicago Press.

Thelen, H. A. (1960). *Education and the human quest.* New York: Harper & Row.

Timpson, W. M., and Tobin, D. N. (1982). *Teaching as performing.* Englewood Cliffs, N.J.: Prentice-Hall.

Tisher, R. (1980). The induction of beginning teachers. In E. Hoyle and J. Megarry (eds.), *The professional development of teachers.* London: Kogan Page.

Tobin, K. (1990) Teacher mind frames and science learning: Beliefs about teaching and learning. In Tobin, K., Kahle, J. B., and Fraser, B. J. (eds.). *Windows into science classrooms: Problems associated with higher-level cognitive learning.* New York: The Falmer Press.

Tobin, K., Kahle, J. B., and Fraser, B. J. (eds.). (1990). *Windows into science classrooms: Problems associated with higher-level cognitive learning.* New York: Falmer Press.

Tyler, R. W. (1950). *Basic principles of curriculum and instruction.* Chicago: University of Chicago Press.

Veenman, S. (1984). Perceived problems of beginning teachers. *Review of Educational Research, 54,* 143–178.

Villegas, A. M. (1991). *Culturally responsive teaching.* Princeton, NJ: Educational Testing Service.

Walberg, H. J. (1986). Syntheses of research on teaching. In M. C. Wittrock (ed.), *Handbook of research on teaching* (3d ed.). New York: Macmillan.

Walberg, H. J., Schiller, D., and Haertel, G. D. (1979). The quiet revolution in educational research. *Phi Delta Kappan, 61,* 179–182.

Walcott, H. (1973). *The man in the principal's office: An ethnography.* New York: Holt, Rinehart & Winston.

Waller, W. (1932). *The sociology of teaching.* New York: Russell & Russell.

War Manpower Commission (1945). *The training within industry report.* Washington, D.C.: Bureau of Training.

Warren, D. (ed.). (1989). *American teachers: Histories of a profession at work.* New York: Macmillan.

Weick, K. E. (1976). Educational organizations as loosely coupled systems. *Administrative Science Quarterly, 21,* 1–19.

Weick, K. E. (1979). *The social psychology of organizing* (2d ed.). Reading, Mass.: Addison-Wesley.

Weiner, B. (ed.). (1974). *Achievement motivation and attribution theory.* Morristown, N.J.: General Learning Corporation.

Weiner, B. (1979). A theory of motivation for some classroom experiences. *Journal of Educational Psychology, 71,* 3–25.

Weinstein, C. S. (1977). Modifying student behavior in an open classroom through changes in the physical design. *American Educational Research Journal, 14,* 249–262.

Weinstein, C. S., and Mignano, A. J., Jr. (1992). *Elementary classroom management: Lessons from research and practice.* New York: McGraw-Hill.

Weisz, D. (1989). *Action research project: Equitable distribution of questioning and feedback in the classroom.* (Mimeographed.) College Park, MD.: University of Maryland.

Welch, L., and Long, L. (1940). The higher structural phases of concept formation. *Journal of Psychology, 9,* 59–95.

Winne, P. H., and Marx, R. W. (1982). Students' and teachers' views of thinking processes for classroom learning. *Elementary School Journal, 82,* 499.

Wittrock, M. C. (ed.). (1986). *Handbook of research on teaching* (3d ed.). New York: Macmillan.

Wong Fillmore, L. (1976). *The second time around: Cognitive and social strategies in second language acquisition.* (Unpublished doctoral dissertation.) Stanford, Calif.: Stanford University.

Wong Fillmore, L. (1982). Instructional language as linguistic input: Second language learning in classrooms. In L. C. Wilkinson (ed.), *Communicating in the classroom.* New York: Academic Press.

Yinger, R. (1980). A study of teacher planning. *The Elementary School Journal, 80,* 107–127.

Zahorik, J. (1970). The effects of planning on teaching. *The Elementary School Journal, 71,* 143–151.

Glossary

academic learning time: The amount of time a student is engaged in a particular subject or learning task at which he or she is successful.

accountability: The idea that teachers should be held responsible for their teaching practices and for what their students learn.

achievement motivation: The desire to take action and to excel for the purpose of experiencing success and feeling competent.

action research: Research conducted by teachers for the purpose of improving their own teaching or schools.

action zone: The section of the classroom (normally the front rows and center columns) where students tend to be called on most often and where most verbal interaction occurs.

active teaching: Term used by Good, Grouws, and Ebmeier to describe their approach to direct instruction.

activity structures: Patterns of behavior that characterize what teachers do as they teach and what students do as they engage in learning tasks. Activity structures can be viewed as the basic unit for planning.

advance organizer: A statement made by teachers, before presenting new information, for the purposes of providing a structure for the new information and linking it to students' prior knowledge.

affective domain: The domain classifying emotional responses in Bloom's taxonomy.

affiliation motivation: The desire to take action for the purpose of experiencing friendship and close relationships with others.

allocated time: The amount of time teachers actually spend on a particular subject or learning activity.

Americanization: The idea that one goal for education is to get minority groups to forsake their own cultures and assimilate into the dominant culture.

anticipatory set: Technique used by teachers at the beginning of a lesson to prepare students to learn and to establish a communicative link between the learner's prior knowledge and the new information to be presented. Same as *set induction* and *establishing set*.

anticipatory socialization: Occurs when people learn how to perform a role before assuming it.

art of teaching: Teaching in which complex decisions are based more on the teacher's experience than on research and scientific evidence.

attraction: The degree to which classroom participants respect and like one another.

assertive discipline: An approach to classroom management that emphasizes teachers asserting their right to teach by insisting on appropriate student behavior and by responding assertively to student infractions.

assessment: Process of collecting a full range of information about students and classrooms for the purpose of making instructional decisions.

attribution theories: View of motivation that emphasizes the way persons come to perceive and interpret the causes of their successes and failures.

authentic assessment: Assessment procedures which have students demonstrate their abilities to perform particular tasks in real-life settings.

autonomy norm: Set of expectations in many schools that teachers can do pretty much what they want within the confines of their classroom.

behavioral objective: A form for writing an instructional objective that emphasizes precision and careful delineation of expected student behaviors, the testing situation, and a performance criterion.

behavior-content matrix: A planning tool that helps integrate instructional objectives, student behaviors, and course content.

behavior modeling: Term used in social-learning theory to describe how people learn as a result of observing others.

best practice: Teaching methods, processes, and procedures that have been shown to be effective for helping students learn.

causal-comparative research: Research that explores causal relationships when the independent variable cannot be manipulated.

checking for understanding: Technique used by teachers to see if students have grasped new information or skills that have been presented.

classroom climate: The overall atmosphere or ethos of a classroom; results from an interaction of individual needs and institutional norms and roles.

classroom discussion: Term often used by teachers to describe teaching methods that rely on verbal exchange of ideas and on discovery and inquiry.

classroom management: The ways teachers organize and structure their classrooms for the purposes of maximizing student cooperation and engagement and minimizing disruptive behavior.

classroom meetings: An approach to classroom management in which the teacher holds regular meetings for the purpose of helping students identify and resolve problem situations.

classroom processes: Interpersonal and group processes that help classroom participants deal with issues of expectations, leadership, attraction, norms, communication, and cohesiveness.

classroom properties: Distinctive features of classrooms, such as multidimensionality, simultaneity, immediacy, unpredictability, publicness, and history, which shape behavior of participants.

classroom routines: Procedures for efficiently performing certain classroom housekeeping tasks such as taking attendance, collecting papers, or distributing books.

classroom structures: The ways classrooms are organized around learning tasks and participation and the ways goals and rewards are defined.

classroom tasks: The work students are expected to do in classrooms and the cognitive and social demands placed on students as they perform particular lessons. See also *task structures*.

cognitive domain: The domain describing the thinking and reasoning processes in Bloom's taxonomy.

cognitive processes: The thinking engaged in by teachers and students.

cognitive psychology: Psychology of learning that focuses mainly on mental processes.

cognitive strategies: Complex thinking strategies associated with receiving, storing, and retrieving information.

cognitive structures: The way knowledge is organized and stored in the mind.

cohesiveness: The feelings and commitments classroom participants have to the classroom group as a whole.

communication: Verbal and nonverbal exchange within the classroom.

competitive goal structure: Occurs when students perceive that they can obtain their goal if, and only if, the other students with whom they work fail to obtain their goals.

concept attainment: An inductive approach to teaching concepts by which students derive the meaning and attributes of a concept from examples and nonexamples of the concept given by the teacher.

concepts: Ways of organizing knowledge and experiences in categories whose members have common attributes.

concept teaching: Approaches to teaching in which the emphasis is on helping students learn how to make and label categories of ideas, objects, and experiences.

conceptual approach: An approach to multicultural education in which teachers incorporate a series of concepts associated with cultural pluralism into ongoing lessons.

conceptual mapping: A technique of visually organizing and diagraming a set of ideas or concepts in a logical pattern so relationships can be readily observed.

conjunctive concept: A concept that has a constant rule structure.

constructivist perspective: A view that knowledge is oftentimes personal and that humans construct knowledge and meaning through experience.

control group: Group of subjects that receives no special treatment during experimental research.

cooperative goal or task structures: Occur when students perceive they can obtain their goal if, and only if, the other students with whom they work can obtain their goals, also.

cooperative incentive structures: Occur when students are interdependent for a reward they will share if they are successful as a group.

cooperative learning model: An approach to teaching where students work in mixed-ability groups and are partially rewarded for group, rather than individual, effort and success.

corrective feedback: Information given to students about how well they are doing.

correlation: A term used to express how two or more variables are related.

correlation coefficient: Numbers ranging from +1.00 to −1.00 that describe the numerical relationship between variables.

correlational research: A type of research that investigates relationships between variables that exist naturally.

criterion-referenced grading: A practice where criteria for success are defined in advance and all students have an opportunity to earn any possible grade.

criterion-referenced test: A test that evaluates a particular student's performance against a preestablished standard or criterion.

critical attribute: Feature of a concept that distinguishes it from all other concepts.

cueing: A situation where teachers alert or set up situations for students to help them get ready to make an appropriate response.

cultural deficit theory: The now-discredited theory that accounts for the low achievement of minorities by postulating some defect in their culture or race.

cultural difference theory: The currently accepted theory that accounts for the low achievement of minorities by postulating that the discontinuity between home culture and school culture interferes with learning.

cultural pluralism: An ideology encouraging minority cultures to maintain their distinctive identities within the larger culture and to value cultural diversity within societies.

culture shock: The anxious emotional response to the ambiguity and disconfirmed expectations that come from dealing with unfamiliar cultures.

dangle: When a teacher starts an activity and then leaves it in midair.

declarative knowledge: Knowledge about something or that something is the case. Knowledge of facts, concepts, or principles.

demography: Study of population patterns. In education this study is most concerned with size and distribution of school-aged children and youth.

dependent variable: In research the variable that may change as a result of the independent variable; the consequences of the independent variable.

descriptive research: Research aimed at gathering detailed information about some phenonemon.

desist: A teaching behavior aimed at stopping disruptive student behavior.

desist incidence: A classroom incident serious enough that if not dealt with will lead to widening management problems.

diagnostic test: Test used by teachers to determine students' prior knowledge and level of skill development. Information used to assist in planning.

differential treatment: The difference in the educational experiences of the majority race, class, culture, or gender versus those of minorities, referring to differences in quality of curriculum, instruction, classroom interaction, funding, enrollment, etc.

dignifying errors: Technique used by teachers when responding to student answers that are wrong.

direct instruction model: An approach to teaching basic skills and sequential material, in which lessons are highly goal directed and learning environments are tightly structured by the teacher.

discourse: The larger patterns of verbal exchange and communication that occur in classrooms.

discovery teaching or learning: An approach to teaching that emphasizes encouraging students to learn concepts and principles through their own explorations and to solve problems on their own.

disjunctive concept: A concept that contains alternative sets of attributes.

distracters: Plausible but wrong answers in a multiple-choice test question.

distributed practice: Practice assigned to students to be done for brief periods spread over several sessions or periods of time.

downtime: Times in classrooms when lessons are completed early or when students are waiting for upcoming events such as moving to another class or going home.

ecological system: A view of classrooms in which inhabitants (teachers, students, and others) interact within a highly interdependent environment.

engaged time: The amount of time students actually spend on a particular subject or learning activity.

ESL: Acronym for "English as a Second Language."

establishing set: Same as *anticipatory set* and *set induction*.

ethnography: Term from the field of anthropology to describe an extensive descriptive study of a single culture, society, or particular phenonemon.

ethos: Common set of values, beliefs, and ways of doing things found in particular classrooms or schools. See also *school culture*.

evaluation: Process of making judgment, assigning value, or deciding on the worth of a particular program or approach or of a student's work.

example-to-rule: Technique of giving examples to students, helping them to come up with the rule or principle.

exceptionality: Term used to define students who have special social, mental, emotional, or physical needs.

executive functions of teaching: See *leadership functions of teaching*.

expectations: The amount and quality of work and behavior expected of students in classrooms and schools.

experiential learning: Theory of learning that explains how people learn from their experiences and subsequent reflections about their experiences.

experiment: A type of research in which the researcher manipulates one or more variables so cause-and-effect relationships can be examined.

experimental group: A group of subjects that receives a special treatment in experimental research.

explaining links: Prepositions or conjunctions used in a presentation that indicate the cause, result, means, or purpose of an event or idea.

explicit instruction: Term used by Rosenshine and Stephens to describe direct instruction.

extending student thinking: Techniques used by teachers following a presentation to help students strengthen their understanding of the new material and to expand their cognitive structures.

extrinsic reward: A reward that is external to the activity itself, such as points, grades, or stars.

feedback: Information given to students about their performance. Same as *knowledge of results.*

feeling tone: The degree to which a learning environment or a particular learning task is perceived as pleasant or unpleasant.

flip-flop: A situation where a teacher starts an activity, then stops and starts another one, and finally returns to the original activity.

flow experience: State when individuals feel total involvement and concentration and strong feelings of enjoyment as a result of a particular experience.

formative evaluation: Evaluation that occurs prior to or during instruction and is used to assist with planning or making adaptations.

fragmentation: A situation in which a teacher breaks a learning activity into overly small units.

full bilingual program: A program in which instruction is carried out equally in two languages and in which the goals are full oral proficiency and literacy in both.

goal structures: The way that goals specify the degree of interdependence sought among students. There are three different types of goal structures: individualistic, competitive, and cooperative.

grading on the curve: A practice of assigning grades so they will follow a normal curve.

graphic organizers: Visual images presented to students to provide structures for new information about to be presented. Similar to an *advance organizer.*

group development: Stages classroom groups go through in the process of developing into a cohesive and effective group.

group investigation: An approach to cooperative learning in which students help define topics for study and then work together to complete their investigations.

group processes: See *classroom processes.*

guided practice: Practice assigned to students to be completed under the guidance or watchful eye of the teacher.

hands-off norm: Expectations in many schools that teachers will not interfere in other teachers' work.

higher-order thinking: Thinking that goes beyond simple recall of facts and considers cause-and-effect relationships and making nuanced judgments about complex situations.

holistic scoring: Technique for scoring essay questions or other written work which emphasizes looking at the work as a whole rather than at its individual parts.

homework: Assignments that students are expected to complete outside of class.

independent practice: Practice given to students to accomplish on their own without the teacher's guidance.

independent variable: In research, the variable that is treated and presumed to cause some change in the dependent variable.

individualistic goal structure: When achievement of the goal by one student is unrelated to the achievement of the goal by other students.

individualized education plan (IEP): A learning plan specifying long- and short-term educational goals for handicapped students and agreed upon by teachers, parents, and special educators.

inductive reasoning: Process of coming up with general rules or principles based on information from specific examples or data.

influence motivation: The desire to take action for the purposes of having control and having a say in what's going on.

information processing: The process used by the mind to take in, store, and retrieve information for use.

inquiry teaching or training: An approach to teaching in which the emphasis is on helping students inquire on their own and to develop such skills as asking questions and drawing conclusions from data.

instructional effects: The learning goals a particular teaching model has been designed to achieve.

instructional objectives: Statements which describe the teacher's instructional intents.

interactive functions of teaching: Those aspects of teachers' work during which they are providing face-to-face instruction to students in classrooms.

interactive planning and decision making: Planning and decision making that occurs "in-flight" or during a particular lesson.

interest level: The degree to which students are attracted to various learning tasks because of intrinsic interest in the tasks.

interpersonal communication skills: Skills that promote honest communication and positive regard among students.

interpersonal influence: Processes people use to effect outcomes in social settings.

intrinsic motivation: Occurs when people behave because the act brings personal satisfaction or enjoyment.

Jigsaw: An approach to cooperative learning in which students work in mixed ability groups and each student is responsible for a portion of the material.

journaling: A technique of writing on a regular basis one's thoughts and reflections about teaching experiences.

knowledge acquisition: The process in which students acquire and assimilate new information and knowledge.

knowledge base: Information, accumulated over time from research and from the wisdom of experienced teachers, which informs teaching practices.

knowledge of results: Feedback given to students about their performance.

leadership: How power and influence are exerted within the classroom and their impact on group interaction.

leadership functions of teaching: The leadership aspects of teachers' work, such as providing motivation and coordinating and controlling learning environments and activities.

learning environment: The overall climate and structures of the classroom which influence how students respond to and remain engaged in learning tasks. The context in which teaching acts are carried out.

least restrictive environment: The placement situation for handicapped students which is the most normal and least confining based on the student's particular needs and problems.

LEP: Acronym for "limited English proficiency."

lesson structures: The way learning activities and series of lessons are woven together.

level of concern: The amount of stress and concern students have toward a particular learning task.

logical consequences: Punishments administered for misbehavior which are directly related to the infraction.

long-term memory: Place in the mind where information is stored, ready for retrieval when needed.

loosely coupled systems: An organizational arrangement in which what goes on in one part of an organization is not very connected to what goes on in other parts of the organization.

mainstreaming: Placing handicapped children in regular classes for full time or part-time.

massed practice: Practice assigned to students to be done during a single, extended period of time.

mastery teaching: Term used by Madeline Hunter to describe her approach to direct instruction.

mean score: The arithmetic average of a group of scores.

meaningful verbal learning: Information and ideas and the relationships among them.

melting pot: Ideology of education that believes the strengths of minority cultures should be blended into a new, single, superior culture.

metacognition: Process of knowing and monitoring one's own thinking or cognitive processes.

metacognitive strategies: Strategies used to recognize one's cognitive processes and ways to think about how information is being processed.

motivation: The process by which behavior is directed toward important human goals or toward satisfying needs and motives.

multicultural education: An approach to teaching aimed at helping students recognize and value cultural diversity.

needs disposition theory: Theory of motivation positing that people are motivated to take action to satisfy basic and higher-level needs.

noncritical attributes: Features found in some members of a category but not in all members.

nonlinear planning: An approach to planning in which planners start with actions or activities deemed important and later attach goals to the action to help explain what happened.

norm-referenced grading: A grading practice whereby students' grades are determined by comparison to others in the class.

norm-referenced test: A standardized test that evaluates a particular student's performance by comparing it to the performance of some other well-defined group of students.

norms: The shared expectations students and teachers have for classroom behavior.

objective tests: Tests with items that produce answers that can be scored relatively free from bias.

objectivist perspective: A view that knowledge consists of "truths" and an objective reality that humans have access to and can learn through discovery and inquiry.

observation: A research procedure in which the researcher watches and records behaviors; a procedure for learning to teach by watching, recording, and reflecting about teacher and student behavior in classrooms.

opportunity to learn: Same as *allocated time.*

organizational functions of teaching: Those aspects of teachers' work involving interactions with other adults in the school setting for the purpose of schoolwide planning and coordination.

organizational development: A systematic effort to help people in schools improve their organizational functioning and performance.

organizational socialization: The process of learning a role and a role system.

overdwelling: Occurs when a teacher goes on and on after a subject or a set of instructions is clear to students.

overlappingness: The ability of teachers to spot disruptive behavior and to deal with it without interrupting the flow of the lesson.

overlearning: Working or practicing a task or skill until it is learned completely and until it can be performed automatically.

participation structures: The established rules and processes that determine who can say what, when, and to whom during classroom discourse.

pedagogy: The study of the art and science of teaching; also refers to the methods and approaches to instruction.

performance assessment: Assessment procedures which have students demonstrate their abilities to perform particular tasks in testing situations.

planned time: The amount of time that teachers set aside for different subjects and activities.

planning cycles: The spans of time considered for various aspects of planning: daily, weekly, unit, term, and yearly.

portfolio: A collection of a student's work which demonstrates the student's ability to perform particular tasks.

postinstructional planning: Teacher planning whereby decisions are made about how to provide feedback to students and how to assess and evaluate student learning.

practical arguments: Reasoning, based on knowledge and beliefs, which is used by teachers as they make pedagogical decisions.

praise: Positive verbal and nonverbal statements offered by teachers as reinforcers to encourage and strengthen desirable student behaviors.

preinstructional planning: Teacher planning conducted prior to instruction, during which goals, content, and approaches are decided.

presentation teaching model: An approach to teaching wherein the primary emphasis is on explaining new information and ideas to students.

principle: A cause-and-effect relationship between variables that has been established from results of several studies or experiments conducted over time.

prior knowledge: Information and knowledge held by students before they receive instruction.

privileges: Special activities and extra time bestowed by teachers to encourage desirable pupil behavior.

problem solving: Finding ways to apply new solutions to complex problem situations rather than relying on fixed rules or recipes.

procedural knowledge: Knowledge about how to do something. Can pertain to specific behavioral skills or to complex cognitive strategies.

procedures: Systems established by teachers for dealing with routine tasks and for coordinating student talk and movement.

propositional network: Units or sets of interconnected knowledge. A proposition is the basic unit in a person's cognitive structure.

psychomotor domain: The domain which classifies objectives dealing with physical movement and coordination in Bloom's taxonomy.

punishments: Penalties imposed by teachers to discourage undesirable behaviors.

randomness: Without a definite or biased pattern. By chance.

rational-linear planning: An approach to planning that puts the focus on setting goals and objectives first and then selecting particular strategies or activities to accomplish these predetermined goals.

reality shock: Term used to describe the surprises and frustrations experienced by beginning teachers during their first years of teaching.

reciprocal teaching: An approach to teaching reading in which peer teaching is used to help students master comprehension skills.

recitation: An approach to teaching characterized by the teacher providing bits of information, asking questions, getting students to respond, and then providing feedback by praising or correcting.

reflection: Careful and analytical thought by teachers about what they are doing and the effects of their behavior on their instruction and on student learning.

reinforcement: Consequences administered by teachers to encourage and strengthen certain desirable behaviors.

relational concept: A concept whose rule structure depends on its relationship to other concepts.

reliability: The degree to which a test produces consistent results over several administrations.

repertoire: The number of teaching approaches and strategies that teachers are able to use to help students learn.

rewards: Reinforcers, such as points, grades, symbols, given to students to encourage and strengthen desirable behaviors.

reward structures: The ways in which rewards can be distributed within a classroom. There are three types: individualistic, competitive, and cooperative.

role: Term used to describe a set of norms that details how various aspects of a particular job should be carried out.

role system: Term used to describe how various roles within a particular setting or organization are interconnected.

rule-example-rule technique: A technique used when explaining something whereby the general principle or rule is given first, then elaborated with specific examples, and finally summarized by a restatement of the rule.

rules for behavior: Statements that specify expected classroom behaviors and define behaviors that are forbidden.

sample: A group of subjects drawn from a larger population for the purpose of research.

schemata: An individual's (teacher or student) knowledge structure or the way information has been organized and stored in memory.

school culture: The ways members of a school think about social action; the embedded beliefs, values, and attitudes of members of a school. *Ethos, tone,* and community are often used to describe the same phenomenon.

school effectiveness research: Research that tries to uncover features that make some schools more effective than others.

school improvement: The process of helping schools change and adopt innovative practices.

scientific basis of teaching: Teaching in which decisions are based on research and scientific evidence.

seatwork: Independent work done by students, such as reading, answering questions, or completing worksheets.

self-fulfilling prophecy: A situation where teachers' expectations and predictions about student behavior or learning cause it to happen.

self-management: An approach to classroom management in which teachers help students define problems, set their own goals, and monitor progress toward goal accomplishment.

set induction: A technique used by teachers at the beginning of a lesson to prepare students to learn and to establish a communicative link between the learner's prior knowledge and the new information to be presented. Same as *anticipatory set* and *establishing set*.

short-term memory: Same as *working memory*.

single-group curriculum: An approach to multicultural education in which special units or courses are devoted to a particular group or culture.

social-system perspective: A way of viewing classrooms, schools, and other human organizations by considering how the various parts of the organization are interrelated and interdependent.

socioeconomic status (SES): Variations among peoples based on income, family background, and relative prestige within the society.

stages of teacher concerns: A theory, attributed to Francis Fuller, explaining how teachers are concerned about different things as they learn to teach. First the focus of concern is on survival; later concerns are expressed about the teaching situation and finally about pupil growth.

stages of teacher development: A theory explaining how growth in teaching occurs over time and occurs first within a particular stage and then progresses to the next stage in sequence.

standard deviation: A measure that shows the spread of a set of scores from the mean.

standardized tests: Tests that are normally designed by professional testmakers for nationwide use and are commercially distributed.

statistical test and significance: Procedures used to determine whether results from research are indeed true or a result of chance.

stem: A statement that poses a problem or asks a question in a multiple-choice test question.

structures of knowledge: The way particular subject matters or disciplines are organized; the major concepts, ideas, and relationships that define a particular field.

student accountability: Holding students responsible for their learning and for their behavior.

Student Teams Achievement Divisions (STAD): An approach to cooperative learning in which students work in mixed-ability groups and where rewards are administered and recognized for both individual and group effort.

submersion approach: The now-illegal practice of simply placing LEP (limited English proficiency) students in the classroom and expecting them to pick up English on their own without any formal teaching or other support from the school.

subsystem: A subpart of an organization where work is carried out. Examples in schools include teams, departments, and management units.

success level: The level at which students succeed in academic tasks.

summative evaluation: Evaluation done after instruction to determine program effectiveness or the worth of students' work.

sustaining expectation effect: Occurs when teachers do not change their previous expectations about a student, even after the student's performance has improved or regressed.

syntax: The overall flow, sequence, or major steps of a particular lesson.

systems analysis: Study and way of thinking about the relationships that exist between the interdependent parts of some whole.

table of specifications: A tool for constructing tests that have a balance of questions, representing an array of instructional objectives and levels of student understandings.

task analysis: A process for breaking down complex learning tasks into fundamental parts or subdividing complex skills into specific subskills so they can be mastered one at a time.

task structures: The way lessons are arranged and the learning demands that lessons place on students.

taxonomy: A classification system or device that helps classify and show relationships among objects and ideas.

taxonomy of educational objectives: A system developed by Bloom for classifying objectives into three domains: cognitive, affective, and psychomotor.

teacher enthusiasm: A set of behaviors used by teachers, such as using uplifting language and dramatic body movements, to make students interested in learning materials.

teaching model: A term used by Bruce Joyce to describe an overall approach or plan toward instruction. The attributes of teaching models are a coherent theoretical framework, an orientation toward what students should learn, and specific teaching procedures and structures.

test anxiety: Phenomenon that occurs when students experience undue stress when taking a test and do poorly as a result.

thinking matrix: A visual device to help students think about the types of questions and answers they provide during a discussion. Used to teach thinking skills.

think-pair-share: A technique used by teachers to slow down the pace of discourse and to increase student participation.

time needed: The time an individual student actually needs to master a particular subject or task. Usually determined by ability and aptitude.

time on task: Same as *engaged time.*

timetabling techniques: Planning tools that consist of making chronological maps to show time relationships among various instructional activities.

tone: See *ethos* and *school culture.*

topical approach: An approach to multicultural education in which special lessons are devoted to studying heroes, holidays, art, literature, or the cuisine of a particular culture.

transfer of learning: The process of applying knowledge or skills learned in one situation to new situations.

transitional bilingual programs: Programs in which LEP (limited English proficiency) students are initially provided instruction in their native language, with gradual increases in English until proficiency is achieved.

transitions: The times during a lesson when the teacher is moving from one type of learning activity to another.

unit: An integrated plan for instruction covering several days and including several lessons aimed at a common set of goals and objectives.

validity: The degree to which a test measures what it claims to measure.

variable: A characteristic of a person or a physical or social situation that can change or vary from one instance to the next.

verbal signposts: Statements made by teachers when explaining something that tells the student what is important or alerts them to important points coming up.

wait-time: The time a teacher waits for a student to respond to a question and the time a teacher waits before responding back.

web: See *conceptual mapping.*

with-itness: The ability of teachers to spot disruptive student behavior quickly and accurately.

working memory: The place in the mind where conscious mental work is done.

Acknowledgments

Name Index

Abi-Nader, J., 157
Adams, R. S., 81
Aerson, G., 256
Alesi, S. J., 61
Allen, V., 138, 139
Allport, G., 340, 346
Alschuler, A. S., 115
Ames, W., 256
Anderson, C. W., 286
Anderson, L. M., 454, 455
Anderson, R. C., 261
Anyon, J., 141
Arends, J. H., 464
Arends, R. I., 464
Argyris, C., 490, 491
Aronson, E., 346, 356
Atkinson, J., 115
Austin, G., 300
Ausubel, D., 250, 252, 255–257, 284

Baker, E. I., 40
Bandura, A., 313
Barker, R. G., 174
Barzun, J., 24
Baxter, G. P., 232
Beane, J., 61
Benjamin, H., 462
Benton, J., 155, 156
Berliner, D. C., 13, 58, 59, 90
Berman, P., 463
Bettencourt, E. M., 258
Biddle, B. J., 81, 174, 249, 390, 479, 480
Biklen, D., 163
Bizar, M., 300, 369, 370
Black, A., 82, 83
Blaney, S. C., 356
Bloom, B. S., 51, 52, 220, 223, 229, 235, 398
Bluestein, J., 437, 438
Blumberg, A., 81
Borg, W. R., 219, 258, 485
Borko, H., 23

Bossert, S. T., 84
Boyer, E. L., 439
Bozman, M., 184
Bramson, R. M., 197
Brenton, M., 2
Briggs, L. J., 40, 298, 312, 320, 327
Brislin, R. W., 148
Brookover, W., 434
Brophy, J. E., 149, 151, 174, 189, 190, 266, 362, 390, 501
Brown, A., 368
Brown, B. R., 41, 42
Brown, R., 140
Bruner, J., 250, 260, 271, 284, 285, 290, 300, 367
Burgess, D. M., 144
Bush, A. J., 266

Cahen, l., 83
Calderhead, J., 23
Cangelosi, J. S., 192, 197
Canter, L., 174, 191, 192
Canter, M., 174, 191, 192
Carroll, J. B., 74, 75
Carter, K., 106, 175, 181, 188
Castle, S., 490
Cazden, C., 108, 140, 388, 390, 410
Chelemer, C., 163
Cherlin, D., 81
Cherrie, C., 148
Claiborn, W. L., 149
Clark, C. M., 23, 40, 43, 44
Clark, D., 40
Clements, B. S., 193, 197, 459
Coats, E., 259
Coleman, J., 112, 345, 429, 431, 462
Collins, A. M., 261
Collins, M. L., 250, 258, 279
Combs, A. W., 463
Comer, J. P., 162
Cooper, H., 80, 90, 217
Cooper, J. M., 29
Copeland, W. D., 113, 114

Subject Index